Fodor's

NEW MEXICO

8th Edition

Where to Stay and Eat
for All Budgets

Must-See Sights
and Local Secrets

Ratings You Can Trust

Fodor's Travel Publications   New York, Toronto, London, Sydney, Auckland
www.fodors.com

FODOR'S NEW MEXICO

Editors: Eric B. Wechter, Andrew Collins

Editorial Contributors: Lynne Arany, Andrew Collins, Francesca Drago, Barbara Floria, Georgia de Katona

Production Editor: Evangelos Vasilakis
Maps & Illustrations: David Lindroth, *cartographers;* Bob Blake, Rebecca Baer, *map editors;* William Wu, *information graphics*
Design: Fabrizio La Rocca, *creative director;* Guido Caroti, Siobhan O'Hare, *art directors;* Tina Malaney, Chie Ushio, Ann McBride, Jessica Walsh, Nora Rosansky, *designers;* Melanie Marin, *senior picture editor*
Cover Photo: (Santa Fe): Pete Foley, Fodors.com member
Production Manager: Angela L. McLean

8th Edition

ISBN 978-1-4000-0530-7

ISSN 1526-4734

SPECIAL SALES

This book is available at special discounts for bulk purchases for sales promotions or premiums. Special editions, including personalized covers, excerpts of existing books, and corporate imprints, can be created in large quantities for special needs. For more information, write to Special Markets/Premium Sales, 1745 Broadway, MD 6-2, New York, NY 10019, or e-mail specialmarkets@randomhouse.com.

AN IMPORTANT TIP & AN INVITATION

Although all prices, opening times, and other details in this book are based on information supplied to us at press time, changes occur all the time in the travel world, and Fodor's cannot accept responsibility for facts that become outdated or for inadvertent errors or omissions. So **always confirm information when it matters**, especially if you're making a detour to visit a specific place. Your experiences—positive and negative—matter to us. If we have missed or misstated something, **please write to us.** Share your opinion instantly through our online feedback center at fodors.com/contact-us.

PRINTED IN THE UNITED STATES OF AMERICA

10 9 8 7 6 5 4 3 2 1

Eugene Fodor:
The Spy Who Loved Travel

As Fodor's celebrates our 75th anniversary, we are honoring the colorful and adventurous life of Eugene Fodor, who revolutionized guidebook publishing in 1936 with his first book, *On the Continent, the Entertaining Travel Annual.*

Eugene Fodor's life seemed to leap off the pages of a great spy novel. Born in Hungary, he spoke six languages and graduated from the Sorbonne and the London School of Economics. During World War II he joined the Office of Strategic Services, the budding spy agency for the United States. He commanded the team that went behind enemy lines to liberate Prague, and recommended to Generals Eisenhower, Bradley, and Patton that Allied troops move to the capital city. After the war, Fodor worked as a spy in Austria, posing as a U.S. diplomat.

In 1949 Eugene Fodor—with the help of the CIA—established Fodor's Modern Guides. He was passionate about travel and wanted to bring his insider's knowledge of Europe to a new generation of sophisticated Americans who wanted to explore and seek out experiences beyond their borders. Among his innovations were annual updates, consulting local experts, and including cultural and historical perspectives and an emphasis on people—not just sites. As Fodor described it, "The main interest and enjoyment of foreign travel lies not only in 'the sites,' . . . but in contact with people whose customs, habits, and general outlook are different from your own."

Eugene Fodor died in 1991, but his legacy, Fodor's Travel, continues. It is now one of the world's largest and most trusted brands in travel information, covering more than 600 destinations worldwide in guidebooks, on Fodors.com, and in ebooks and iPhone apps. Technology and the accessibility of travel may be changing, but Eugene Fodor's unique storytelling skills and reporting style are behind every word of today's Fodor's guides.

Our editors and writers continue to embrace Eugene Fodor's vision of building personal relationships through travel. We invite you to join the Fodor's community at fodors.com/community and share your experiences with like-minded travelers. Tell us when we're right. Tell us when we're wrong. And share fantastic travel secrets that aren't yet in Fodor's. Together, we will continue to deepen our understanding of our world.

Happy 75th Anniversary, Fodor's! Here's to many more.

Tim Jarrell, Publisher

CONTENTS

MAPS

ABOUT
THIS BOOK

Our Ratings

Sometimes you find terrific travel experiences, and sometimes they just find you. But usually the burden is on you to select the right combination of experiences. That's where our ratings come in.

As travelers we've all discovered a place so wonderful that its worthiness is obvious, a place is so unique that superlatives don't do it justice. These sights, properties, and experiences get our highest rating, **Fodor's Choice**, indicated by orange stars.

Black stars highlight sights and properties we deem **Highly Recommended**, places that our writers, editors, and readers praise for consistency and excellence.

By default, there's another category: any place we include in this book is by definition worth your time, unless we say otherwise. And we will.

Disagree with any of our choices? Care to nominate a place or suggest that we rate one more highly? Visit our feedback center at www.fodors.com/feedback.

Budget Well

Hotel and restaurant price categories from ¢ to $$$$ are defined in the opening pages of each chapter. For attractions, we always give standard adult admission fees; reductions are usually available for children, students, and senior citizens. Want to pay with plastic? **AE, D, DC, MC, V** following restaurant and hotel listings indicate whether American Express, Discover, Diners Club, MasterCard, and Visa are accepted.

Restaurants

Unless we state otherwise, restaurants are open for lunch and dinner daily. We mention dress only when there's a specific requirement and reservations only when they're essential or not accepted—it's always best to book ahead.

Hotels

Hotels have private bath, phone, TV, and air-conditioning and operate on the European Plan (EP, meaning without meals), unless we specify that they use the Continental Plan (CP, with a Continental breakfast), Breakfast Plan (BP, with a full breakfast), or Modified American Plan (MAP, with breakfast and dinner) or are all-inclusive (including all meals and most activities).

We always list facilities but not whether you'll be charged an extra fee to use them.

Many Listings	
★	Fodor's Choice
★	Highly recommended
⊠	Physical address
✣	Directions or Map coordinates
⏍	Mailing address
☎	Telephone
🖶	Fax
⊕	On the Web
✍	E-mail
⊡	Admission fee
⊙	Open/closed times
Ⓜ	Metro stations
▱	Credit cards
Hotels & Restaurants	
▦	Hotel
⊷	Number of rooms
⟁	Facilities
⑂⊙⑂	Meal plans
✕	Restaurant
⟁	Reservations
⋔	Dress code
↘	Smoking
⑂⑂	BYOB
Outdoors	
⤳	Golf
⚭	Camping
Other	
ℂ	Family-friendly
⇨	See also
⊠	Branch address
☞	Take note

Experience
New Mexico

WORD OF MOUTH

"Saturday spent a great day in Santa Fe starting with the amazing farmers' market. Being a foodie, I just love to see/sample foods from the local area, and this market was huge. Still haven't figured out all the differences in the chiles and how they're used, but I tried. Bought some posole there, too."
—Clousie

WHAT'S WHERE

The following numbers refer to chapters.

2 Albuquerque. Albuquerque is the gateway to New Mexico, by far the state's largest city, and its business and education capital. Its residents—like its architecture, food, and art—reflect a confluence of Native American, Hispanic, and Anglo culture.

3 Santa Fe. On a 7,000-foot-high plateau at the base of the Sangre de Cristo Mountains, Santa Fe is one of the most visited small cities in the United States, with an abundance of museums, one-of-a-kind cultural events, art galleries, and distinctive restaurants and shops.

4 Taos. World-famous museums and galleries, stunning views of the desert and Sangre de Cristo Mountains, and charming, cottonwood-shaded streets lined with adobe buildings are a few of this small town's attractions. Nearby, Taos Pueblo and Taos Ski Valley are major draws.

5 Northwestern New Mexico. Red-rock canyons shelter ancient hamlets and high, fortresslike plateaus crowned by Native American villages. Can't-miss places: El Morro National Monument, Chaco Canyon, Zuni Pueblo, Aztec Ruins, and Acoma Pueblo.

6 Northeastern New Mexico. The brilliantly clear light of northeastern New Mexico—the area east of the Sangre de Cristo range that includes parts of Carson National Forest and a large portion of the Santa Fe Trail—illuminates seemingly endless high-desert plains. The small city of Las Vegas is the best hub for dining, shopping, and accommodations.

7 Southeastern New Mexico. This region contains Carlsbad Caverns National Park; Roswell, which draws UFO enthusiasts from far and wide; the lush, high-elevation Lincoln National Forest; and the surreal gypsum wonderland of White Sands National Monument.

8 Southwestern New Mexico. Near Silver City, the ore-rich mountains are dotted with old mining ghost towns. Fish, swim, or boat along the miles of lake water at Elephant Butte Reservoir, near Truth or Consequences. And check out the arts scene in Old Mesilla, adjacent to the largest city in the southern part of the state, Las Cruces.

9 Carlsbad Caverns National Park. Carlsbad is one of the world's most prominent cave systems. The nearby town of Carlsbad also has a handful of notable attractions and a landscaped riverwalk.

NEW MEXICO PLANNER

When to Go	Flying in and Getting Around

When to Go

The cool, dry climates of Santa Fe and Taos are as much a lure in summer as the skiing in Taos and Santa Fe is in winter. Christmas is a wonderful time to be in New Mexico because of Native American ceremonies as well as the Hispanic religious folk plays, special foods, and musical events. Santa Fe is at its most festive at this time, with incense and piñon smoke sweetening the air and the darkness of winter illuminated by thousands of *farolitos* (glowing paper-bag lanterns), which line walkways, doorways, and rooftops. Most ceremonial dances at the pueblos occur in summer, early fall, and at Christmas and Easter. Other major events—including the Santa Fe Opera, Chamber Music Festival, and Native American and Spanish markets—are geared to the heavy tourist season of July and August. The Santa Fe Fiesta and New Mexico State Fair in Albuquerque are held in September, and the Albuquerque International Balloon Fiesta in October. Hotel rates are generally highest during the peak summer season but fluctuate less than those in most major resort areas. If you plan to come in summer, be sure to make reservations in advance. Avoid the heaviest crowds by coming in spring or fall.

Flying in and Getting Around

New Mexico is easy to reach by plane but a full day's drive from major metro areas in the neighboring states of Arizona, Utah, Colorado, Oklahoma, and Texas. Unless you're a big fan of long road trips (the scenery getting here is spectacular, especially coming from Arizona, Utah, and Colorado), it generally makes the most sense to fly here.

Northern and central New Mexico's main air gateway is Albuquerque International Sunport (ABQ), which is served by virtually all of the nation's major domestic airlines as well as some smaller regional ones; there are direct flights from all major West Coast and Midwest cities and a number of big East Coast cities. From here it's an easy 60-minute drive to Santa Fe, or a 2½-hour drive to Taos (shuttle services are available). Santa Fe Municipal Airport (SAF) also has daily service on American Airlines to Dallas and Los Angeles. To reach southern New Mexico, it's more convenient to fly into El Paso International Airport (ELP), 50 mi southeast of Las Cruces, 160 mi southeast of Silver City, 135 mi southwest of Ruidoso, and 160 mi southwest of Carlsbad. El Paso's airport is smaller but still has direct flights from many major carriers. There are also flights between El Paso and Albuquerque, and a handful of cities around the state (Ruidoso, Carlsbad, Alamogordo) have regional air service.

A car is your best way to get around the region, whether traveling among New Mexico's main cities, or even exploring them in depth. You can see much of Downtown Santa Fe, Taos, Ruidoso, and Silver City on foot or using buses, but in Albuquerque and Las Cruces a car is really a necessity for any serious touring and exploring.

For more flight information and ground transportation options, see the Travel Smart section at the back of this book.

WHAT'S NEW IN NEW MEXICO

Happy Anniversary

Santa Fe celebrated its 400th anniversary in 2010, and Albuquerque enjoyed its tricentennial in 2006. The entire state gets into the action in 2012, when New Mexico ushers in 100 years of statehood—it had been a territory before that, dating to when the United States took possession following the 1848 Treaty of Guadalupe Hidalgo. Many events, from museum exhibits to arts presentations, are being planned to take place throughout the year. You can learn more at ⊕ *www.nmcentennial.org.*

History in a New Light

Santa Fe's venerable **Palace of the Governors**, the oldest public building in America, is the site of the state's newest major attraction, the **New Mexico History Museum**, which opened in 2009. The sleek facility lies adjacent to and behind the palace. Exhibits here tell the rich and complex story of the state's founding through an incredible collection of artifacts that, up to this point, only made brief appearances in temporary exhibits at the Palace of the Governors. The 20,000-square-foot facility uses interactive, state-of-the-art audio and visual technology to bring New Mexico's heritage to life—a refreshing contrast to the sometimes static methods many of the state's museums employ in their exhibits (in fairness, some of the museums occupy extremely old, historic buildings).

Albuquerque's Hotel Renaissance

The Duke City's lodging landscape has been mostly dominated by predictable chains over the years, but three hip, elegant, and distinctive new properties have shaken things up considerably. Two of these hotels are historic and situated Downtown: the glamorous Andaluz is a LEED-certified, arty makeover of the historic La Posada with a swanky restaurant (Lucia), while the Hotel Parq Central, opened in late 2010 in Downtown's funky EDo section, is inside a completely reimagined 1920s hotel. The rooftop Apothecary bar is a sly nod to the building's medical legacy. A 10-minute drive south of the airport on the Isleta Pueblo, the Hard Rock Casino & Resort is an upscale, stylish addition to the growing selection of hotels that have opened on Indian pueblos around the state in recent years (Buffalo Thunder, Hyatt Regency Tamaya, Sandia, and Inn of the Mountain Gods are a few others).

New Trails to Santa Fe

Well, contrails anyway. After years of little or no commercial air service, Santa Fe Municipal Airport (SAF) has finally ushered in daily service from two of the nation's busiest airports, DFW in Dallas and LAX in Los Angeles, on American Eagle (the regional carrier of American Airlines). The service has been highly popular, making it not just easier to reach Santa Fe from many parts of the country, but also points north, such as Las Vegas and Taos, as Santa Fe's small, convenient airport is an hour closer to these areas than Albuquerque. The service comes on the heels of the expansion of **New Mexico Railrunner Express** rail service, from Albuquerque to Santa Fe's newly developed **Railyard District**. New businesses keep popping up here, including a massive branch of REI, a much-anticipated outpost of the wildly popular Flying Star restaurant-coffeehouse empire, and numerous galleries and boutiques. The district's fantastic farmers' market was named one of the nation's best by CNN in 2010.

QUINTESSENTIAL NEW MEXICO

Ancient Peoples

Nowhere in the United States will you find communities that have been continuously inhabited for a longer period than the oldest pueblos of New Mexico, Acoma and Taos. Acoma has been a living, working community for more than 1,000 years—the cliff-top city here is perhaps the most dramatically situated pueblo in the state, and a must-see attraction, especially since the tribe opened a stunning cultural center and museum in 2006. Taos Pueblo, which contains the largest collection of multistory pueblo dwellings in the country, also dates back more than a millennium.

But these are just two of the state's 19 pueblos, not to mention the Indian Pueblo Cultural Center (which was dramatically expanded in 2008) in Albuquerque, and outstanding museums on Native American arts and culture in Santa Fe. Ancient, now-deserted sites, such as Chaco and Aztec, offer further opportunities to explore and learn about New Mexico's thriving indigenous culture.

The Cradle of Creativity

New Mexico draws all kinds of vibrant spirits, both to visit and relocate, but the state is particularly a magnet for artists. Santa Fe, with its dozens of prestigious galleries and art museums, claims the third-largest art market in the nation, after New York City and Los Angeles. The much smaller town of Taos claims a similarly exciting gallery scene, and the state's largest city, Albuquerque, is no slouch when it comes to the arts—galleries have popped up all over the city in recent years.

Although New Mexico's prestigious gallery scene is concentrated in its cities, many of the state's most talented artists live in small, scenic villages and work out of their home studios. Some of these studios are open year-round, but the best way to visit them—and also discover

If you want to get a sense of New Mexico culture, and indulge in some of its pleasures, start by familiarizing yourself with the rituals of daily life. These are a few highlights that you can take part in with relative ease.

some of the most charming and distinctive communities in the state—is to participate in a Studio Tour Weekend. More than 40 of these events are held year-round, most of them from early fall through December, with others taking place in the spring. During tour weekends, the private studios in a given town open their doors to visitors—it's a great time to converse with artists, shop for their creations, and get off the beaten path. Some particularly noteworthy studio tours include those in Galisteo (late October), a funky little village near Santa Fe; Silver City (late May), which combines its studio tour with a rollicking blues festival; Ruidoso (mid-June), whose cool-climate Art in the Pines event features 25 artists; and Abiquiu (mid-October), where Georgia O'Keeffe lived and some 70 artists participate.

Peak Experiences

With nearly 50 peaks towering higher than 12,000 feet, New Mexico is a wonderland for people who love the mountains—it's partly this vertiginous topographical feature that gives the state its unparalleled beauty. The southern spine of the Rocky Mountains range, known as the Sangre de Cristos, runs right through the center of the state, looming over Taos and Santa Fe. The stunning Sandia Mountains face the city of Albuquerque, and similarly beautiful peaks dot the landscape as far south as Cloudcroft. Much of the Land of Enchantment's high country is accessible. Hiking trails lead to some of the highest points in the state, and several first-rate ski areas have been carved out of New Mexico's mountains, including Taos Ski Valley, Angel Fire, and Ski Santa Fe to the north, and Ski Apache in Ruidoso.

IF YOU LIKE

Historic Sites

There's no state in the Union with a richer historical heritage than New Mexico, which contains not only buildings constructed by Europeans well before the Pilgrims set foot in Massachusetts but also still-inhabited pueblos that date back more than a millennium.

The entire state can feel like one massive archaeological dig, with its mystical Native American ruins and weathered adobe buildings. Stately plazas laid out as fortifications by the Spanish in the 17th century still anchor many communities, including Albuquerque, Las Cruces, Las Vegas, Santa Fe, and Taos. And side trips from these cities lead to ghost towns and deserted pueblos that have been carefully preserved by historians. Here are some of the top draws for history buffs.

One of the most well-preserved and fascinating ruin sites on the continent, the ancient **Chaco Culture National Historical Park** in Chaco Canyon was home to the forerunners of today's Pueblo Indians more than 1,000 years ago.

Santa Fe's **San Miguel Mission** is a simple, earth-hue adobe structure built in about 1625—it's the oldest church still in use in the continental United States.

A United Nations World Heritage Site, the 1,000-year-old **Taos Pueblo** has the largest collection of multistory pueblo dwellings in the United States.

The oldest public building in the United States, the Pueblo-style **Palace of the Governors** anchors Santa Fe's historic Plaza and has served as the residence for 100 Spanish, Native American, Mexican, and American governors; it's now the state history museum.

Hiking Adventures

At just about every turn in the Land of Enchantment, whether you're high in the mountains or low in a dramatic river canyon, hiking opportunities abound. Six national forests cover many thousands of acres around New Mexico, as do 34 state parks and a number of other national and state monuments and recreation areas. The ski areas make for great mountaineering during the warmer months, and the state's many Native American ruins are also laced with trails.

Hiking is a year-round activity in New Mexico, as you can virtually always find temperate weather somewhere in the state. Consider the following areas for an engaging ramble.

About midway between Santa Fe and Albuquerque, **Kasha-Katuwe Tent Rocks National Monument** is so named because its bizarre rock formations look like tepees rising over a narrow box canyon. The hike here is relatively short and only moderately challenging, offering plenty of bang for the buck.

One of the more strenuous hiking challenges in the state is **Wheeler Peak**. The 8-mi trek to New Mexico's highest point (elevation 13,161 feet) rewards visitors with stunning views of the Taos Ski Valley.

From the northeastern fringes of Albuquerque, **La Luz Trail** winds 9 mi (with an elevation gain of more than 3,000 feet) to Sandia Crest.

Gila National Forest's short **Catwalk Trail**, in the southwestern corner of the state, is a metal walkway that clings to the sides of the soaring cliffs in White Water Canyon.

Burger Joints

In a state with plenty of open ranching land and an appreciation for no-nonsense, homestyle eating, it's no surprise that locals debate intensely about where to find the best burger in town.

In New Mexico, the preferred meal is a green-chile cheeseburger—a culinary delight that's available just about anyplace that serves hamburgers. Burgers served in tortillas or sopaipillas also earn kudos, and increasingly, you'll find establishments serving terrific buffalo, lamb, turkey, and even tuna and veggie burgers.

With about 75 locations throughout the state, the New Mexico chain **Blake's Lotaburger** has become a cult favorite for its juicy Angus beef burgers. Just order at the counter, take a number, and wait for your meal (which is best accompanied by a bag of seasoned fries).

A friendly and funky little roadhouse about a 15-minute drive south of Santa Fe, **Bobcat Bite** is a much-loved source of outstanding green-chile burgers. Loyalists order them rare.

Feasting on a burger at the **Mineshaft Tavern** is a big reason to stop in the tiny village of Madrid, as you drive up the fabled Turquoise Trail from Albuquerque to Santa Fe. This rollicking bar serves hefty patties.

Dramatic Photo Ops

New Mexico's spectacular landscapes and crystal-clear atmosphere can help just about any amateur with a decent camera produce professional-quality photos. Many of the common scenes around the state seem tailor-made for photography sessions: terra-cotta-hued adobe buildings against azure blue skies, souped-up lowrider automobiles cruising along wide-open highways, and rustic fruit and chile stands by the side of the road. In summer, dramatic rain clouds contrast with vermilion sunsets to create memorable images. Come fall, shoot the foliage of cottonwood and aspen trees, and in winter, snap the state's snowcapped mountains.

The **High Road to Taos,** a stunning drive from Santa Fe with a rugged alpine backdrop, encompasses rolling hillsides studded with orchards and tiny villages.

More than 1,000 balloons lift off from the **Albuquerque International Balloon Fiesta,** affording shutterbugs countless opportunities for great photos—whether from the ground or the air. And there are year-round opportunities to soar above the city.

The dizzyingly high **Rio Grande Gorge Bridge,** near Taos, stands 650 feet above the Rio Grande—the reddish rocks dotted with green scrub contrast brilliantly against the blue sky.

White Sands National Monument, near Alamogordo, is a huge and dramatic expanse of 60-foot-high shifting sand dunes—it's the largest deposit of gypsum sand in the world, and one of the few landforms recognizable from space.

FAQS

Just how spicy is New Mexican food? Compared with food served in most parts of the country, traditional New Mexico fare—green- and red-chile sauces, the salsa that comes with chips—ranks pretty high on the fire meter. If you've spent a bit of time in Louisiana, Texas, or elsewhere in the Southwest, you've likely encountered plenty of kick in the local cuisine. In New Mexico, on average, the heat factor is even a tad higher. If you're averse to spicy fare, it's easy enough to request milder salsa with your meal, or to ask the staff at restaurants for recommendations about which foods pack the least heat. In less touristy areas, however, or in restaurants that cater primarily to locals, expect food that's considerably spicier than what you may be used to.

Should I visit New Mexico in the winter for a warm getaway, and avoid it in summer because of excessive heat? Actually, New Mexico doesn't conform to the stereotypes of hot desert destinations. Much of the state (including its largest city, Albuquerque) sits a mile above sea level, and popular destinations like Ruidoso, Santa Fe, and Taos all have elevations of around 7,000 feet. Although New Mexico is sunny and quite beautiful all winter, it's nevertheless extremely cold in many parts of the state—the average January low temperature in Santa Fe is 15°F, which is actually lower than you'll find in Chicago or Boston during this time of year. It does often warm up considerably during the day, but you still shouldn't come to New Mexico in winter expecting a toasty break from Old Man Winter: remember, this is a prime skiing destination. In summer, these same high-elevation communities remain consistently cool and dry—in Ruidoso, which is at the same latitude as Phoenix and Dallas, the average high in July is just 83°F, which is comparable to the temperature in Minneapolis.

What's the best strategy for including New Mexico as part of a larger Southwestern road trip? If you have at least 10 days, and ideally a bit more, road-tripping through New Mexico and into the adjoining states that make up the famed Four Corners region (Arizona, Utah, and Colorado) is a fantastic way to experience the Southwest. Just keep in mind that distances are vast, and you'll spend a lot of time driving, albeit through some of the country's most amazing scenery. An excellent strategy is to fly into Albuquerque and drive in a counterclockwise loop into north-central Arizona (Flagstaff, Sedona, Grand Canyon), southern Utah (Bryce and Zion national parks, Moab), southwestern Colorado (Mesa Verde, Durango), and return through New Mexico to visit Farmington, Taos, and Santa Fe. A drive like this can easily run close to 2,000 mi, but the incredible scenery will leave you wanting more.

TOP ATTRACTIONS

Carlsbad Caverns National Park
The only member of the national park system in New Mexico with full—and prestigious—"park" status, Carlsbad offers visitors the chance to descend some 75 stories underground to view massive caverns filled with wild-shaped stalactites and stalagmites.

Gila National Forest
The first parcel set aside as protected wilderness by the U.S. Forest Service in 1924 is remote and enormous (it's slightly larger than Connecticut). But make the effort to visit, and you'll be rewarded with some of the Southwest's best hiking and camping, plus a chance to view the ancient Gila Cliff Dwellings National Monument, and to tour several ghost towns.

Museum of International Folk Art
A case could be made for almost any museum in Santa Fe as the most noteworthy one in New Mexico, but it's this distinct facility on Museum Hill that stands out not only for its regional exhibits but also for having one of the world's most acclaimed collections of folk art. Collections here appeal equally to kids and adults, and the two shops on-site carry an astounding array of crafts and books.

Bandelier National Monument
An easy and scenic drive from both Santa Fe and Taos, this 23,000-acre expanse of deep canyons, rushing waterfalls, and high-desert mesas contains remarkably well-preserved cliff dwellings and ceremonial kivas that trace the past millennium of the region's thriving indigenous life and culture.

White Sands National Monument
The cool, jarringly bright white dunes—some as high as 60 feet—contained within this eerie 145,344-acre landscape have long captured the imagination of children, and brought out the inner-children of adults. Be sure to get out of your car and scamper up a few of these fine-gypsum dunes.

Taos Art Museum and Fechin House
Northern New Mexico's reputation as an internationally renowned arts center began with the establishment of an artists' colony in Taos in 1900, and this former home of one of the movement luminaries—Nicolai Fechin—provides a rich overview of the era. More than 50 Taos masters are represented here.

Acoma Pueblo
Just an hour west of Albuquerque, this fabled pueblo has continuously occupied the same soaring mesa-top perch, some 367 feet above the valley floor, for more than 1,000 years. You can tour the village and visit the stunning, contemporary Haak'u Museum, with art and exhibits documenting the community's legacy.

Chaco Culture National Historical Park
This fascinating site is one of the world's seminal archaeological treasures—the dozens of painstakingly excavated ruins held a complex community with as many as 5,000 inhabitants during its apex around 1,000 AD to 1,200 AD.

National Hispanic Cultural Center
With a mix of architecturally prominent performance centers, a terrific art museum, and an excellent restaurant serving authentic regional cuisine, this comprehensive facility in a historic Albuquerque neighborhood showcases Latino arts and culture throughout the Western Hemisphere, but with a decided New Mexico emphasis.

TOP EXPERIENCES

Ski the Southern Rockies

It may sound like a mere novelty—skiing less than 100 mi from the Mexican border, which, indeed, you can do at the relatively small and casual downhill facility in **Cloudcroft**. But the Land of Enchantment offers some of the most difficult and breathtaking ski terrain in the country, and is home to several outstanding facilities. The southern spine of the Rockies, with elevations topping out at 13,000 feet and well over 250 inches of annual snowfall in some places, runs right down the center of New Mexico. Often recognized by major ski magazines for its first-rate ski school and demanding trails, **Taos Ski Valley** is the state's most famous winter-sports destination—it comprises a friendly, handsomely developed village of condos and restaurants. Other nearby northern New Mexico venues with great alpine and cross-country skiing, snowboarding, snowshoeing, and snowmobiling include **Red River, Angel Fire, Pajarito** (an underrated gem in Los Alamos), **Santa Fe,** and **Sandia** (just east of Albuquerque). And down in the state's southern reaches, in addition to Cloudcroft, you can tackle some 750 well-groomed acres at **Ski Apache**, just outside the resort town of Ruidoso.

Browse the Art Markets of Santa Fe

New Mexico's most popular destination, Santa Fe is also one of the great cultural treasures of the Southwest, packed as it is with first-rate museums. The best season for appreciating the arts is summer, when the **Santa Fe Opera** comes into full swing, as does the **Santa Fe Chamber Music Festival**. But the biggest weekends of summer are when the legendary Indian and Spanish markets come to town, and there's no more exciting time to take in Santa Fe. The **Spanish Market** dominates the city's historic Plaza the last weekend of July and draws more than 250 local artisans versed in the traditional regional practices of straw appliqué, hide painting, metalwork, *retablo* and santo carving, weaving, and furniture making. During the third weekend in August, more than 1,200 artists representing some 100 tribes throughout North America display their jewelry, textiles, paintings, and other fine works during the **Santa Fe Indian Market**. Additional antiques-related markets take place in mid-August, and the city hosts a smaller but still excellent **Spanish Winter Market** in December.

Sample New Mexico's Wines

You might think beer would be the state's most celebrated drink, given the laid-back nature of New Mexicans and the fiery nature of the local cuisine. In fact, the region has developed into an increasingly fruitful (pardon the pun) and critically acclaimed wine producer, its soil and climate perfect for growing a number of varietals, from Pinot Noir in the cooler upper elevations to Chardonnay and Cabernet Sauvignon in warmer areas. There are about two-dozen vineyards in the state, and half have tasting rooms. Albuquerque's **Gruet Winery** now ranks among the nation's most esteemed producers of Champagne-style sparkling wines, and others around the state—**Black Mesa, La Chiripada, Casa Rondena, St. Clair**—have garnered prominent awards. But you can also try local vintages during several popular festivals. The **Southern New Mexico Wine Festival** in Las Cruces and the **Albuquerque Wine Festival** both take place in late May. Las Cruces then hosts the **Harvest Wine Festival** over Labor Day weekend, which is when Bernalillo holds its **New Mexico Wine Festival**. Other communities with wine events include Ruid-

oso (mid-June), Santa Fe (early July), and Alamogordo (late September).

Usher in the Holidays, New Mexico Style

The piñon-scented air, cozy adobe architecture, and traditional Native American and Spanish festivals have long made New Mexico a great place to visit during the December holiday season. In Carlsbad, boats cruise by lighted holiday displays during the town's Christmas on the Pecos celebration. Christmas in Santa Fe is perhaps the city's most festive time of year. During the 10 days of **Las Posadas Novena at San Miguel Mission**, the story of Mary and Joseph's journey to Bethlehem is reenacted. **The Feast Day of Our Lady of Guadalupe**, December 12, is grandly celebrated at the Santuario de Guadalupe, and **Christmas at the Palace** resounds with hours of festive music emanating from the Palace of the Governors in mid-December. The traditional Christmas Eve stroll down Canyon Road, complete with snacks and costumed carolers, is the way to celebrate the night before Christmas when in Santa Fe. Christmas Native American dances take place at most pueblos. The Spanish-inspired dance-drama *Los Matachines* is performed at Picurís Pueblo. There are also pine-torch processions and kachina dances at Taos Pueblo and Basket, Buffalo, Deer, Harvest, Rainbow, and Turtle dances at Acoma, Cochiti, San Ildefonso, Santa Clara, and Taos pueblos.

Take the Tramway to Albuquerque's Sandia Peak

Take the aerial tramway to the top of the Sandia Mountains for an incomparable view over Albuquerque. You can ride the world's longest aerial tram (it climbs over 5,000 feet in elevation, and covers nearly 3 mi in distance) to the top, take in the soaring panoramas of the entire Rio Grande Valley from Santa Fe down toward Socorro, and enjoy drinks plus lunch or dinner at the lofty **High Finance Restaurant & Tavern**, which clings precipitously to the sheer edge of Sandia Peak. But if you have time, use the tram as a means to an exhilarating outdoor adventure—at the top you can access the **Sandia Peak Ski Area** in winter for fun in the snow, or for challenging mountain biking down these very slopes in summer. You can hike on short and easy trails or choose far more challenging ones, including the famed **La Luz trail**, which descends down the face of the Sandias back into Albuquerque's Northeast Heights neighborhood. You can also drive to the ski area and ranger station (and then hike or take the chairlift to the tram station)—this beautiful drive takes about 45 minutes.

GREAT ITINERARIES

ALBUQUERQUE TO TAOS: NEW MEXICO MOUNTAIN HIGH

Day 1: Albuquerque

Start out by strolling through the shops of Old Town Plaza, then visit the New Mexico Museum of Natural History and Science. Also be sure to check out the Albuquerque Museum of Art and History, and try to make your way over to the Albuquerque Biological Park, which contains the aquarium, zoo, and botanic park. For lunch, try the atmospheric Church Street Café or the sophisticated St. Clair Winery and Bistro, both in Old Town.

Later in the afternoon, you'll need a car to head east a couple of miles along Central to reach the University of New Mexico's main campus and the nearby Nob Hill District. Start with a stroll around the UNM campus with its many historic adobe buildings; if you have time, pop inside either the Maxwell Museum of Anthropology or the University Art Museum. When you're finished here, walk east along Central into Nob Hill and check out the dozens of offbeat shops. If it's summer, meaning that you still have some time before the sun sets, it's worth detouring from Old Town to Far Northeast Heights (a 15-minute drive), where you can take the Sandia Peak Aerial Tramway 2.7 mi up to Sandia Peak for spectacular sunset views of the city. Either way, plan to have dinner back in Nob Hill, perhaps at Zinc or Flying Star. If you're still up for more fun, check out one of the neighborhood's lively lounges; head back Downtown for a bit of late-night barhopping.

Days 2 and 3: Santa Fe

On Day 2, head to Santa Fe early in the morning by driving up the scenic Turquoise Trail; once you arrive in town, explore the adobe charms of the Downtown central Plaza. Visit the Palace of the Governors and check out the adjacent New Mexico History Museum. At the nearby Museum of Fine Arts you can see works by Southwestern artists, and a short drive away at the Museum of International Folk Art you can see how different cultures in New Mexico and elsewhere in the world have expressed themselves artistically. Give yourself time to stroll the narrow, adobe-lined streets of this charming Downtown, and treat yourself to some authentic New Mexican cuisine in the evening, perhaps with a meal at La Choza or Maria's.

On your second day in town, plan to walk a bit. Head east from the Plaza up to Canyon Road and peruse the galleries. Have lunch at one of the restaurants midway uphill, such as Geronimo or El Farol. From here, you can either continue walking 2 mi up Canyon, and then Upper Canyon, roads to the Randall Davey Audubon Center, or you can take a cab there. If you're up for some exercise, hike the foothills—there are trails within the center's property and also from the free parking area (off Cerro Gordo Road) leading into the Dale Ball Trail Network. You might want to try one of Santa Fe's truly stellar, upscale restaurants your final night in town, either La Boca or the restaurant at the Inn of the Anasazi.

Day 4: Abiquiu

From Santa Fe, drive north up U.S. 285/84 through Española, and then take U.S. 84 from Española up to Abiquiu, the fabled community where Georgia O'Keeffe lived and painted for much of the final five decades of her life. On your way up, before you reach Española, make the detour toward Los Alamos and spend the morning visiting Bandelier National Monument. In Abiquiu, plan to tour Georgia O'Keeffe's home.

Days 5 and 6: Taos

Begin by strolling around Taos Plaza, taking in the galleries and crafts shops. Head south two blocks to visit the Harwood Museum. Then walk north on Paseo del Pueblo to the Taos Art Museum and Fechin House. In the afternoon, drive out to the Rio Grande Gorge Bridge. Return the way you came to see the Millicent Rogers Museum on your way back to town. In the evening, stop in at the Adobe Bar at the Taos Inn and plan for dinner at Graham's Grille. On the second day, drive out to Taos Pueblo in the morning and tour the ancient village while the day

is fresh. Return to town and go to the Blumenschein Home and Museum, lunching afterward at the Dragonfly Café. After lunch drive out to La Hacienda de los Martinez for a look at early life in Taos and then to Ranchos de Taos to see the San Francisco de Asís Church.

Day 7: The High Road

On your final day, drive back down toward Albuquerque and Santa Fe via the famed High Road, which twists through a series of tiny, historic villages—including Peñasco, Truchas, and Chimayó. In the latter village, be sure to stop by El Santuario de Chimayó. Have lunch at Léona's Restaurante or Rancho de Chimayó, and do a little shopping at Ortega's Weaving Shop. From here, it's a 30-minute drive to Santa Fe.

FLAVORS OF NEW MEXICO

CHILE TIME

Chile peppers, which have been locally grown since ancient times, are a defining ingredient of New Mexican cuisine. Combined with corn tortillas, beans, tomatoes, and potatoes, chiles bind together the New Mexico that for centuries sustained indigenous people, the Spanish, and subsequent arrivals. A fan will travel any distance—down any highway—in pursuit of a great chile sauce (which is referred to in these parts as simply "chile"). From Chope's south of Las Cruces to M&J's Sanitary Tortilla Factory in Albuquerque and JoAnn's Ranch-o-Casados in Española (to name a few classic hot spots), the pursuit of the most flavorful—but not necessarily the hottest—chile remains a personal quest akin to proving one's honor.

How chiles first arrived in New Mexico is the subject of debate. Some believe the Spanish introduced them to the Pueblo Indians on their travels north from Mexico. Others say they were grown in New Mexico centuries prior to the arrival of the Spanish, having been introduced through trade with the peoples of Mexico and South America.

The source of the chile's heat is the chemical capsaicin, found in the pepper's heart and membrane. In addition to providing a culinary delight to chile lovers, capsaicin has been used medicinally since prehistoric times; it's thought to prevent blood clots and heart attacks, and has been found to hinder cholesterol absorption. Low in fat and high in vitamins A and C and beta-carotene, it also speeds up metabolism and helps digestion. When you eat chile, or even touch it, endorphins (the "hormones of pleasure") are released in the brain. The same chemical reaction that produces "chile addiction" also blunts pain.

The green variety of chile, generically called "Hatch" (for the New Mexico town that produces the bulk of the state's crop), is the commercially developed type known as New Mexico 6–10 and the Big Jim. The best red chiles are said to be grown from the old stock cultivated in Chimayó and other high mountain villages of the north—Española, Dixon, Velarde, and Peñasco.

By far the state's most important vegetable crop, New Mexico chiles are grown on 30,000 acres, mostly in Luna and Doña Ana counties. Sixty percent of the nation's chile crop comes from the Land of Enchantment.

From mid-August through the fall, the New Mexican air is scented with the warm, enticing fragrance of chiles roasting outdoors in large, wire, propane-fired cages. Around State Fair time in September, people head for their favorite roadside stand to buy a sack of fresh-roasted green chiles. Once stored in the freezer, they're used all winter long, in stews, enchiladas, salsas, and burritos.

As the season progresses into October, it's time to buy a red-chile *ristra*, a string of chiles, to hang full, heavy, and sweet, near the front door, a sign of warmth and welcome. It's said the ristra brings good luck—and it certainly is convenient to have the makings of soul-warming red-chile salsa right at hand.

—Sharon Niederman

MENU GUIDE

Aguacate: Spanish for avocado, the key ingredient of guacamole.

Albóndigas: Meatballs, usually cooked with rice in a meat broth.

Bizcochitos: Buttery cookies flavored with cinnamon and anise seeds and served typically at Christmas but available throughout the year.

Burrito: A warm flour tortilla wrapped around meat, beans, and vegetables and smothered in chiles and cheese; many New Mexicans also love breakfast burritos (filled with any combination of the above, along with eggs and, typically, bacon or sausage and potatoes).

Calabacitas: Summer squash, usually served with corn, chiles, and other vegetables.

Carne adovada: Red-chile-marinated pork (or, occasionally, chicken).

Chalupa: A corn tortilla deep-fried in the shape of a bowl, filled with pinto beans (sometimes meat), and topped with cheese, guacamole, sour cream, lettuce, tomatoes, and salsa.

Chicharrones: Fried pork rinds.

Chilaquiles: Often served at breakfast, this casserole-like dish consists of small pieces of fried tortillas baked with red or green chiles, bits of chicken or cheese, and sometimes eggs.

Chile relleno: A poblano pepper peeled, stuffed with cheese or a special mixture of spicy ingredients, dipped in batter, and fried.

Chile: A stewlike dish with Texas origins that typically contains beans, beef, and red chile.

Chiles: New Mexico's infamous hot peppers, which come in an endless variety of sizes and in various degrees of hotness, from the thumb-size jalapeño to the smaller and often hotter serrano. They can be canned or fresh, dried or cut up into salsa. Most traditional New Mexican dishes are served either with green, red, or both types of chiles (ask for "Christmas" when indicating to your server that you'd like both red and green). Famous regional uses for green chile include green-chile stew (usually made with shredded pork), green-chile cheeseburgers, and green-chile-and-cheese tamales.

Chimichanga: The same as a burrito, only deep-fried and topped with a dab of sour cream or salsa. (The chimichanga was allegedly invented in Tucson, Arizona.)

Chipotle: A dried smoked jalapeño with a smoky, almost sweet, chocolaty flavor.

Chorizo: Well-spiced Spanish sausage, made with pork and red chiles.

Enchilada: A rolled or flat corn tortilla filled with meat, chicken, seafood, or cheese, an enchilada is covered with chile and baked. The ultimate enchilada is made with blue Native American corn tortillas. New Mexicans order them flat, sometimes topped with a fried egg.

Fajitas: A Tex-Mex dish of grilled beef, chicken, fish, or roasted vegetables and served with peppers, onions, and pico de gallo, served with tortillas; traditionally known as *arracheras*.

Flauta: A tortilla filled with cheese or meat and rolled into a flutelike shape ("flauta" means flute) and lightly fried.

Frijoles refritos: Refried beans, often seasoned with lard or cheese.

Frito Pie: Originally from Texas but extremely popular in New Mexican diners

and short-order restaurants, this savory, humble casserole consists of Fritos snack chips layered with chile, cheese, green onions, and pinto beans.

Guacamole: Mashed avocado, mixed with tomatoes, garlic, onions, lemon juice, and chiles, used as a dip, a side dish, or a topping.

Hatch: A small southern New Mexico town in the Mesilla Valley, known for its outstanding production and quality of both green and red chiles. The "Hatch" name often is found on canned chile food products.

Huevos rancheros: New Mexico's answer to eggs Benedict—eggs doused with chile and sometimes melted cheese, served on top of a corn tortilla (they're best with a side order of chorizo).

Nopalitos: The pads of the prickly pear cactus, typically cut up and served uncooked in salads or baked or stir-fried as a vegetable side dish. (The tangy-sweet, purplish-red fruit of the prickly pear is often used to make juice drinks and margaritas.)

Posole: Resembling popcorn soup, this is a sublime marriage of lime, hominy, pork, chiles, garlic, and spices.

Quesadilla: A folded flour tortilla filled with cheese and meat or vegetables and warmed or lightly fried so the cheese melts.

Queso: Cheese; an ingredient in many Mexican and Southwestern recipes (cheddar or Jack is used most commonly in New Mexican dishes).

Ristra: String of dried red chile peppers, often used as decoration.

Salsa: Finely chopped concoction of green and red chile peppers, mixed with onion, garlic, and other spices.

Sopaipilla: Puffy deep-fried bread that's similar to Navajo fry bread (found in Arizona and western New Mexico); it's served either as a dessert with honey drizzled over it or savory as a meal stuffed with pinto beans or meat.

Taco: A corn or flour tortilla served either soft, or baked or fried and served in a hard shell; it's then stuffed with vegetables or spicy meat and garnished with shredded lettuce, chopped tomatoes, onions, and grated cheese.

Tacos al carbón: Shredded pork cooked in a mole sauce and folded into corn tortillas.

Tamale: Ground corn made into a dough, often filled with finely ground pork and red chiles; it's steamed in a corn husk.

Tortilla: A thin pancake made of corn or wheat flour, a tortilla is used as bread, as an edible "spoon," and as a container for other foods. Locals place butter in the center of a hot tortilla, roll it up, and eat it as a scroll.

Trucha en terra-cotta: Fresh trout wrapped in corn husks and baked in clay.

Verde: Spanish for "green," as in chile verde (a green chile sauce).

KIDS AND FAMILIES

New Mexico is an underrated family destination. It doesn't have the major theme parks or obvious family attractions of some places, and artsy places like Santa Fe and Taos are seemingly adult-oriented. But much of the state, from cities to secluded parks and wilderness areas, offer plenty for kids and teenagers. The Land of Enchantment is rife with museums with interactive, high-tech exhibits, as well as historic sites—from ancient pueblos to the mountain villages in which Billy the Kid and Pat Garrett tussled. It's also a mecca for skiing, hiking, mountain biking, and plenty of other family-friendly activities.

Choosing a Place to Stay

You'll find a good variety of midpriced chain accommodations throughout the state's most visited regions—places that typically have pools, rooms that can be combined to become family suites, and helpful perks like refrigerators, microwaves, free breakfast buffets, and kids-stay-free policies. A more recent statewide development has been the opening of several large resorts operated by Indian Pueblos, most of them around Albuquerque and Santa Fe (the Hyatt Tamaya, Buffalo Thunder, Sandia, Hard Rock). Although these properties all feature casinos, they also abound with kids' attractions, including sprawling pools and athletic facilities. The Hard Rock has a bowling alley, arcade, and Laser Tag, while the Hyatt Tamaya offers horseback rides and presents family-oriented cultural activities like storytelling and bread-baking demonstrations. Also, the state's many inns and B&Bs often have at least one or two units well suited to families. Many of these smaller accommodations comprise a series of separate casitas, some with multiple bedrooms, kitchens, and extensive sitting areas.

What to See and Do

In the state's heavily visited north-central Rio Grande Valley, from Albuquerque to Taos, you'll find dozens of attractions popular with visitors of all ages. Albuquerque has the best variety: **Albuquerque BioPark** (with its aquarium and zoo), **¡Explora!** interactive science museum, the Indian Pueblo Cultural Center, the hands-on **New Mexico Museum of Natural History and Science**, the **National Hispanic Cultural Center**, the **International Balloon Museum**, and the **Sandia Peak Aerial Tramway.** You could easily keep kids entertained here for several days.

The museums of Santa Fe and Taos are better-suited to adults or older kids, although Santa Fe's **Museum of International Folk Art** and **New Mexico History Museum** have plenty of exhibits geared to all ages, and **El Rancho de las Golondrinas** living history museum is a must. What families also appreciate in these parts are the many outdoorsy pursuits—horseback rides and skiing, and opportunities to explore Native American culture at **Bandelier National Monument** and **Taos Pueblo** (**Acoma Pueblo,** an hour west of Albuquerque, also shouldn't be missed).

Elsewhere in the state, the regions with the greatest family appeal tend to be dominated as well by outdoorsy activities. **White Sands National Monument** and **Carlsbad Caverns** are favorites in the southern part of the state, and kids also love the Wild West culture of **Lincoln, Fort Sumner, Ruidoso,** and **Cloudcroft.**

A LAND APART

Almost every New Mexican has a tale or two to tell about being perceived as a "foreigner" by the rest of the country. There's the well-documented case of the Santa Fe man who tried to purchase tickets to the 1996 Olympic Games in Atlanta, only to be shuffled over to the department handling international requests. Even the U.S. Postal Service occasionally returns New Mexico–bound mail to its senders for insufficient "international" postage.

Though annoying to residents, such cases of mistaken identity are oddly apt (keep an ear open to how often New Mexicans themselves refer to their state, one of the nation's poorest, as a Third World country). New Mexico is, in many ways, an anomaly: it has its own cuisine, architecture, fashion, and culture, all of these an amalgam of the designs and accidents of a long and intriguing history. In prehistoric times indigenous peoples hunted game in New Mexico's mountains and farmed along its riverbanks. Two thousand years ago Pueblo Indians began expressing their reverence for the land through flat-roofed earthen architecture, drawings carved onto rocks, and rhythmic chants and dances. The late 16th and early 17th centuries brought the Spanish explorers who, along with the Franciscan monks, founded Santa Fe as a northern capital of the empire of New Spain, a settlement that was contemporaneous with the Jamestown colony of Virginia.

Although the Spanish brutally enslaved and mistreated the Native Americans, during the course of several hundred years tolerance has grown and traditions have commingled. Pueblo Indians passed on the use of chiles, beans, and corn, and the Spanish shared their skill at metalwork, influencing the Native American jewelry that has become symbolic of the region. The Spanish also shared their architecture, which itself had been influenced by 700 years of Arab domination of Spain, and the acequia method of irrigation still in use in the villages of northern New Mexico.

The last of the three main cultures to make its mark was that of the Anglo (any nonindigenous, non-Hispanic person in New Mexico is considered an Anglo—even groups who don't normally identify with the Anglo-Saxon tradition). Arriving throughout the 19th century, Anglos mined the mountains for gold, other precious metals, and gemstones and uncovered vast deposits of coal, oil, and natural gas. Their contributions to New Mexican life include the railroad, the highway system, and—for better or worse—the atomic bomb.

The resulting mélange of cultures has produced a character that's uniquely New Mexican: Spanish words are sprinkled liberally through everyday English parlance; Spanish itself, still widely spoken in the smaller villages, contains numerous words from the Pueblo Indian dialects. Architectural references and culinary terms in particular tend to hew to the original Spanish: you can admire the vigas and *bancos* that adorn the restaurant where you can partake of posole or sopaipilla.

But beyond the linguistic quirks, gastronomic surprises, and cultural anomalies that make New Mexico unique, there remains the most distinctive feature of all—the landscape. At once subtle and dramatic, the mountains and mesas seem almost surreal as they glow gold, terracotta, and pink in the clear, still air of the high desert. The shifting clouds overhead cast rippling shadows across the

land, illuminating the delicate palette of greens, grays, and browns that contrast with a sky that can go purple or dead black or eye-searingly blue in a matter of seconds. It's a landscape that has inspired writers (such as D. H. Lawrence and Willa Cather), painters (such as Georgia O'Keeffe and Peter Hurd), and countless poets, dreamers, filmmakers, and assorted creative spirits for centuries.

Indeed, watching the ever-changing sky is something of a spectator sport here, especially during the usual "monsoons" of summer. So regular that you could almost set your watch by them, the thunderheads start to gather in late afternoon, giving visual warning before the inevitable downpour. In the meantime, the sky dazzles with its interplay of creamy white clouds edged by charcoal, sizzling flashes of lightning, and dramatic shafts of light shooting earthward from some ethereal perch.

The mountains absorb and radiate this special illumination, transforming themselves daily according to the whims of light and shadow. The very names of the major ranges attest to the profound effect their light show had on the original Spanish settlers. The Franciscan monks named the mountains to the east of Santa Fe *Sangre de Cristo,* or "Blood of Christ," because of their tendency to glow deep red at sunset. To the south, east of Albuquerque, the Sandia ("Watermelon" in Spanish) Mountains also live up to their colorful name when the sun sets. Georgia O'Keeffe once joked about the Pedernal mesa in the Jemez range, "It's my private mountain, it belongs to me. God told me if I painted it enough, I could have it."

The awe-inspiring beauty of the landscape renders New Mexico's tag lines more than just marketing clichés. The state is truly a "Land of Enchantment," and Santa Fe is indeed "the City Different." Surrounded by mind-expanding mountain views and filled with sinuous streets that promote foot over car traffic, Santa Fe welcomes with characteristic adobe warmth. Rapid growth and development have prompted many local residents to worry about becoming too much like everywhere else, but the surfeit of trendy restaurants, galleries, and boutiques that tout regional fare and wares, both authentic and commercial, are still distinctly Santa Fean. Commercialism notwithstanding, Santa Fe's deeply spiritual aura affects even nonreligious types in surprising ways, inspiring a reverence probably not unlike that which inspired the Spanish monks to name it the City of Holy Faith. (Its full name is La Villa Real de la Santa Fe de San Francisco de Asís, or the Royal City of the Holy Faith of St. Francis of Assisi.) A kind of mystical Catholicism blended with ancient Native American lore and beliefs flourishes throughout northern New Mexico in tiny mountain villages that have seen little change through the centuries. Tales of miracles, spontaneous healings, and spiritual visitations thrive in the old adobe churches that line the High Road that leads north of Santa Fe to Taos.

If Santa Fe is spiritual, sophisticated, and occasionally snobby, Taos, 65 mi away, is very much an outpost despite its relative proximity to the capital. Compared with Santa Fe, Taos is smaller, feistier, quirkier, tougher, and very independent. Taoseños are a study in diverse convictions, and most anyone will share his or hers with you if you lend an ear. Rustic and comfortably unpretentious, the town contains a handful of upscale restaurants with cuisines and wine lists as innovative as what you might find in New York. It's a haven for aging hippies, creative geniuses, cranky misanthropes, and anyone else who wants a good quality of life in a place that accepts new arrivals without a lot of questions—as long as they don't offend longtime residents with their city attitudes.

Sixty miles south of Santa Fe, Albuquerque adds another distinctive perspective to the mix. New Mexico's only big city, it shares many traits with cities its size elsewhere: traffic, noise, crime, and sprawl. But what sets it apart is its dogged determination to remain a friendly small town, a place where pedestrians still greet one another as they pass and where Downtown's main street is lined with angle parking (a modern-day version of the hitching post). Old Town, a congenial district whose authentic historical appeal is tempered by the unabashed pursuit of the tourist buck, is a typical example of how traditional small-town New Mexico flourishes amid a larger, more demanding economy without sacrificing the heart and soul of the lifestyle. San Felipe de Neri Catholic Church, built in 1793, is still attended by local worshippers.

The unifying factor among these and other towns and the terrain around them is the appeal of the land and the people. From the stunning natural formations of Carlsbad Caverns to the oceanic sweep of the "badlands" north of Santa Fe, it's the character of the residents and respect for the land that imbue New Mexico with its enchanted spirit. First-time visitors discover the unexpected pleasures of a place where time is measured not only by linear calculations of hours, days, weeks, and years but also by the circular sweep of crop cycles, gestation periods, the rotation of generations, and the changing of seasons.

Summer is traditionally the high season, when the arts scene explodes with gallery openings, performances at Santa Fe's open-air opera house, and a variety of festivals and celebrations. In autumn the towering cottonwoods that hug the riverbanks turn gold, days are warm and sunny, and the nights are crisp. Those beehive-shaped kiva fireplaces get a workout in winter, a time when life slows down to accommodate occasional snowstorms, and the scent of aromatic firewood like piñon and cedar fill the air like an earthy incense.

Even after you leave, New Mexico will sneak into your consciousness in unexpected ways. As much a state of mind as it is a geographic entity, a place where nature can be glimpsed simultaneously at its most fragile and most powerful, New Mexico truly is a land of enchantment.

—Nancy Zimmerman

Albuquerque

WORD OF MOUTH

"Absolutely rent a car! Public transportation is available [bus] but it isn't the easiest or most convenient for visitors wanting to go to popular sites in and around ABQ. Most of the busses are really for locals going to and from work, etc. There is a rail line that runs from ABQ to Santa Fe and would work well. But to have the most flexibility, rent a car."

–DebitNM

Updated
by Andrew
Collins

A bird's-eye view of Albuquerque reveals a typical Sun Belt city, stretching more than 100 square mi with no grand design, architectural or otherwise, to hold it together. The city's growth seems as free-spirited as the hot-air balloons that take part in the Albuquerque International Balloon Fiesta. This is true, to a degree, of the city's somewhat nebulous, suburban-looking, outer neighborhoods, especially the West Side, which continues to sprawl farther west because few natural boundaries stand in the way.

On the ground, however, you'll discover a vibrant, historic urban landscape that's been inhabited for more than 300 years. In Old Town, Nob Hill, and some of the other older neighborhoods along the Central Avenue (Historic Route 66 corridor), you'll notice a vibrant mix of Spanish, Mexican, Native American, and Anglo architectural and design influences. In these areas, you can actually park the car and walk around a bit, and you'll discover increasingly dynamic and distinctive clusters of retail, dining, and mixed-use development. Downtown has even seen a spate of higher-density condos in recent years, many in converted historic buildings.

Albuquerque is the center of New Mexico's educational institutions and financial, manufacturing, and medical industries. It's an unpretentious, practical city with a metro population of nearly 850,000. Many who live here have come from outside New Mexico, giving Albuquerque a more diverse and cosmopolitan demographic than most communities in the state. The city's rich arts scene is proudly distinct from those of Santa Fe and Taos. Significant museums and galleries draw much local support, and feed off the creative energy of the many artists, writers, poets, filmmakers, and musicians who call this area home. Albuquerque has also become increasingly popular with Hollywood filmmakers in recent years because its outlying districts seem indistinctly and generically "western U.S."—they could pass for any number of locales. Recent hit movies filmed in Albuquerque include *The Book of Eli, No Country for Old Men, Transformers, The Men Who Stare at Goats,* and *Crazy Heart.*

Outdoors enthusiasts and seekers of places off the beaten path will also find plenty to see and do both in town and a very short drive away. The city's dining scene has improved markedly over the past few years, as local farmers' markets continue to grow in popularity and several local wineries have begun earning national acclaim. And the once generic supply of hotels has been bolstered by a new spate of elegant resorts opened on Native American pueblos just beyond city limits as well as a pair of hip boutique hotels Downtown. Albuquerque's star is slowly, but very clearly, rising.

ORIENTATION AND PLANNING

GETTING ORIENTED

2

Albuquerque contains a relatively compact and well-defined core comprising just a handful of neighborhoods—Downtown, Old Town, the University of New Mexico (UNM) district and adjacent Nob Hill—that's encircled by a somewhat sprawling and less clearly defined region. Colorful Historic Route 66 unifies the older, central neighborhoods, cutting west to east through the center of the city. Visitors tend to spend most of their time in this corridor (from Old Town to Nob Hill), as it contains the majority of the city's notable dining, lodging, shopping, and sightseeing. The more vast outlying neighborhoods are mostly residential and lack distinct boundaries: in clockwise order: the West Side, Los Ranchos/North Valley, Northeast Heights, Uptown/East Side, Airport, and Barelas/South Valley. They include a smattering of farther-afield attractions and worthwhile restaurants and hotels.

ALBUQUERQUE NEIGBHORHOODS

Old Town. As its name suggests, this historic neighborhood contains the earliest buildings in the city. Today it's home to numerous galleries, shops, boutiques, and museums, plus a few hotels, and it's one of the key destinations for visitors. It's just west of and adjacent to Downtown.

Downtown. A handful of modern office towers loom over Downtown, which is bisected by Central Avenue, the city's most important thoroughfare. This relatively compact district has few formal attractions but is home to a number of noteworthy hotels, restaurants, and shops. It's within walking distance of Old Town, which lies just to the west. The eastern edge of Downtown contains an up-and-coming subneighborhood called EDo (East of Downtown).

Barelas/South Valley. Extending just south of Downtown and Old Town, historic Barelas is home to the acclaimed National Hispanic Cultural Center and is an otherwise mostly residential area. It gradually gives way to the broad South Valley, a somewhat downcast area with a mix of residential and light-industrial blocks.

UNM/Nob Hill. Off-campus life is focused directly to the south and east of the University of New Mexico, stretching along Central Avenue from University Boulevard east through the Nob Hill neighborhood. Low-budget eateries, specialty shops, and music and arts venues are tightly clustered within the college-named streets just to the south of Central; things get more upscale as you head farther east.

Los Ranchos/North Valley. The North Valley (along with its sister South Valley) is the agrarian heart of Albuquerque. It is here, where generations of Hispanic families have resided, that you will experience the deepest sense of tradition.

Northeast Heights. This is quite a large neighborhood, taking in the area north of Interstate 40 and rising steadily east into the foothills of the Sandias, where there's great hiking and an incredible aerial tram to

TOP REASONS TO GO

Drive up the Camino Real (North 4th Street) or south into Barelas where you'll glimpse vintage shops and taquerias with hand-painted signage in idiosyncratic script and blazing-hot colors. Be sure to pause for a bite at Red Ball, Barelas Coffee House, or Mary & Tito's.

Visit the KiMo Theatre, in the center of Downtown right on old Route 66.

Walk or bike the Paseo del Bosque along the Rio Grande. The scenery along the 16-mi trail is a menagerie of cottonwoods, migrating birds, and the ever-present river rippling quietly at your side.

Explore the National Hispanic Cultural Center, a one-of-a-kind music and arts venue.

Witness the sunset over the volcanoes in the Western desert—a brilliant pink flood that creeps over the valley, making its way east to illuminate the Sandias before disappearing. It's even better in late August when the scent of roasting green chiles fills the air.

the top of the peak. You'll mostly find houses and shopping centers in this part of town, but it's worth driving up here just for the city views.

Uptown/East Side. This eclectic part of the city, ranging from the somewhat shady neighborhoods east of Nob Hill to the upscale shopping of Uptown, is a mixed bag. There are few attractions (the new National Museum of Nuclear Science & History being one exception), but Uptown has a good selection of hotels, as well as mostly chain restaurants and shops.

Airport. The mesa-top neighborhood immediately southwest of the airport has a lot of hotels, but little to see or do. It is, however, a short drive from Downtown, UNM, and Nob Hill.

West Side. This expansive, rapidly growing section of the city is mostly residential, but it is home to the fascinating and underrated Petroglyph National Monument.

ALBUQUERQUE PLANNER

WHEN TO GO

Albuquerque is sunny and relatively pleasant year-round. Fall is by far the most popular time to visit. On just about any day in late-August through November, big balloons sail across the sharp blue sky and the scent of freshly roasting green chiles permeates the air. Balloon Fiesta brings enormous crowds for nearly two weeks in early October (book hotels at this time as far in advance as possible). But shortly after, the weather's still great and hotel prices plummet. Albuquerque's winter days (usually 10°F warmer than those in Santa Fe) are usually mild enough for golf, hiking, or simply strolling around Old Town or Nob Hill. The occasional frigid spike usually thaws by morning. Spring brings winds, though plenty of sunshine, too, and rates stay low until the summer crowds flock in. Mid-May through mid-July can be brutally hot though dry, with high temperatures often soaring into the high 90s.

This is followed by roughly six to eight weeks of cooler temperatures, a bit more humidity, and the spectacular late-afternoon cloud formations that herald the brief "monsoon" season.

GETTING HERE AND AROUND

AIR TRAVEL

The major gateway to New Mexico is **Albuquerque International Sunport** (*ABQ* ☎ *505/244–7700* ⊕ *www.cabq.gov/airport*), a well-designed and attractive facility that's just 5 mi southeast of Downtown and just 3 mi south of UNM/Nob Hill. There's a free ABQ Rapid Ride bus shuttle service (⇨ *Bus Travel, below)* on weekdays from the airport to Downtown's Alvarado Transportation Center, where you can connect with Rail Runner service (⇨ *Train Travel, below)*.

BUS TRAVEL

If you're only visiting for a couple of days and not planning to explore beyond Old Town, Downtown, Nob Hill, and Uptown, the city's public bus system is a practical if somewhat slow-going option. The ABQ Rapid Ride Red Line service plies the Central Avenue corridor and runs until about 9 pm Monday through Saturday and until 6 pm Sunday. The service is extended until about 2:30 am on Friday and Saturday nights June through September. Rapid Ride also has a Blue Line that runs from UNM to the West Side, and a Green Line that can get you from Downtown into Northeast Heights. You can obtain a customized trip plan at the city's public bus service, ABQ Ride.

The Alvarado Transportation Center Downtown is Rapid Ride's central hub and offers direct connections to the NM Rail Runner train service north to Santa Fe (via Bernalillo) and to the South Valley suburbs. Buses accept bicycles, although space is limited. Service is free on the Downtown Circulator shuttle route (available only on weekdays), or if you are transferring (to any route) from the Rail Runner; otherwise, the fare is $1 (bills or coins, exact change only; 25¢ transfers may be requested on boarding). Bus stops are well marked. *See also Bus Travel in the Travel Smart chapter.*

Bus Contact: **ABQ Rapid Ride** (☎ *505/243-7433* ⊕ *www.cabq.gov/transit)*.

CAR TRAVEL

Although the city's public bus service, ABQ Ride, provides good coverage, a car is the easiest and most convenient way to get around. Albuquerque sprawls in all directions, but getting around town is not difficult. The main highways through the city, north–south Interstate 25 and east–west Interstate 40, converge just northeast of Downtown and generally offer the quickest access to outlying neighborhoods and the airport. Rush-hour jams are common in the mornings and late afternoons, but they're still far less severe than in most big U.S. cities. All the major car-rental agencies are represented at Albuquerque's Sunport airport.

Because it's a driving city, most businesses and hotels have free or inexpensive off-street parking, and it's easy to find metered street parking in many neighborhoods as well as affordable garages Downtown. Problems usually arise only when there's a major event in town, such as a concert near the University of New Mexico or a festival Downtown or in Old Town, when you may want to arrive on the early side to get a space.

TAXI TRAVEL

Taxis are metered in Albuquerque, and service is around-the-clock. Given the considerable distances around town, cabbing it can be expensive; figure about $9 from Downtown to Nob Hill, and about $20 from the airport to an Uptown hotel. There's also a $1 airport fee.

Taxi Contacts: **Albuquerque Cab** (☎ 505/883–4888 ⊕ www.albuquerquecab. com). **Yellow Cab** (☎ 505/247–8888).

TRAIN TRAVEL

The New Mexico Rail Runner, a commuter-train line, provides a picturesque, hassle-free way to make a day trip to Santa Fe. These sleek bi-level trains with large windows run south for about 35 mi to the suburb of Belén (stopping in Isleta Pueblo and Los Lunas), and north about 65 mi on a scenic run right into the historic heart of Santa Fe, with stops in Bernalillo, Sandoval, and a few other spots. Albuquerque stops are Downtown, at the Alvardo Transportation Center (where ABQ Ride offers free bus service to the airport), and at the north end of town at Journal Center/Los Ranchos. On weekdays, the trains run about eight or nine times per day, from about 4 am until 6:30 pm. There are also a few trains on Saturdays and a morning and late-afternoon run on Sundays. Fares are zone-based (one-way from $2 to $8), but day passes are just $1 more; bicycles ride free. Connections to local bus service are available at most stations. *For information on Amtrak service, see Train Travel in the Travel Smart chapter.*

Train Contact: **New Mexico Rail Runner Express** (☎ 866/795–7245 ⊕ www. nmrailrunner.com).

VISITOR INFORMATION

The Albuquerque Convention and Visitors Bureau operates tourism information kiosks at the airport (on the baggage-claim level) and in Old Town on Plaza Don Luis, across from San Felipe de Neri church.

Albuquerque Convention and Visitors Bureau (✉ Box 2686687125 ☎ 505/842–9918 or 800/284–2282 ⊕ www.itsatrip.org).

GUIDED TOURS

Established in 2009, the **ABQ Trolley Co** (☎ 505/240–8000 ⊕ www. abqtrolley.com) whisks guests on an 18-mi, 75-minute tour of the city's top attractions and neighborhoods, using colorful open-air trolleys. These narrated rides—which are offered April through October, Tuesday through Sunday—are a great way to gain an overview of the city.

The**Albuquerque Museum of Art and History** (☎ 505/243–7255 ⊕ www. cabq.gov/museum) leads free, hour-long historical walks through Old Town, beginning at 11 am Tuesday through Sunday, mid-March through mid-December.

Backcountry and local-history expert Roch Hart, owner of **NM Jeep Tours** (☎ 505/252–0112 ⊕ http://nmjeeptours.com),offers Jeep tours and guided hikes that start from Albuquerque and go as far as time and permits allow. He can suggest an itinerary (ghost towns, rock formations, petroglyphs), or tailor one to your interests and time frame.

Tours of Old Town (☎ *505/246–8687* ⊕ *http://nmjeeptours.com*) offers guided walking strolls around Old Town. The standard tour lasts about 75 minutes and is offered Friday through Wednesday, four times daily. Longer ghost-hunting and moonlight tours are also offered on occasion—check for times.

PLANNING YOUR TIME

Although the city sprawls, it does contain a handful of neighborhoods well suited to exploring on foot. In both Downtown and Old Town, you'll find plenty of garages and parking lots, and good areas to get out of the car and explore on foot. The same is true of the adjoining Nob Hill and UNM neighborhoods. For a short visit to the city, you could focus your time on these two areas.

The rest of the city stretches pretty far, and it can take anywhere from 10 to 30 minutes to get from one part of town to the other. Notable attractions, such as those along the Rio Grande Corridor and up in the Sandia Mountains, take at least a couple of hours and as much as a full day to explore. A helpful strategy is to bunch together geographically outlying attractions that interest you, perhaps hitting Gruet Winery and the Balloon Museum the same day you head up into nearby Corrales or Bernalillo, or combining a visit to the Sandia Peak Tram with an excursion east out of town, either toward Santa Fe via the Turquoise Trail or out to the historic sites in Mountainair (*as described in the Side Trips section later in this chapter*).

Most visitors to Albuquerque combine a stay here with some explorations of the entire northern Rio Grande Valley. If you're looking for the perfect regional tour, combine the short Albuquerque itinerary below with those provided in the Side Trips section below, which covers several great areas within a 60- to 90-minute drive of Albuquerque, as well as covering Isleta Pueblo and the towns of Corrales and Bernalillo, just on the outskirts of Albuquerque.

EXPLORING ALBUQUERQUE

Albuquerque's terrain is diverse. Along the river in the North and South valleys, the elevation hovers at about 4,800 feet. East of the river, the land rises gently to the foothills of the Sandia Mountains, which rise to over 6,000 feet; the 10,378-foot summit is a grand spot from which to view the city below. West of the Rio Grande, where Albuquerque is growing most aggressively, the terrain rises abruptly in a string of mesas topped by five volcanic cones. The changes in elevation from one part of the city to another result in corresponding changes in temperature, as much as 10°F at any time. It's not uncommon for snow or rain to fall on one part of town but for it to remain dry and sunny in another, and because temperatures can rise and fall considerably throughout the day and evening, it's a good idea to bring along a couple of layers when exploring large areas or for several hours.

ALBUQUERQUE IN A DAY

One of the best places to kick off the day is the Downtown branch of Flying Star restaurant, where you can enjoy breakfast in the heart of Downtown before checking out the handful of shops and galleries on Gold and Central avenues. From here, it's a short drive or 30-minute walk west along Central to reach Old Town, where you can explore the shops and museums of the neighborhood. This isn't the prettiest stretch of road, and another option for reaching Old Town is to walk north on 11th or 12th streets and then west on Mountain Road, perhaps stopping for cookies and coffee at legendary Golden Crown Panaderia. This takes an extra 20 minutes but will take you through a historic and rather humble residential area that's seen a lot of sprucing up in recent years as increasing numbers of artists and professionals have begun moving Downtown.

Once in Old Town, check out the Albuquerque Museum of Art and History, and also try to make your way over to the Albuquerque BioPark, which contains the aquarium, zoo, and botanic park. For lunch, try the atmospheric Monica's or the sophisticated St. Clair Winery & Bistro, both near the Old Town center.

Later in the afternoon, drive or take the Red Line bus a couple of miles east along Central to reach the University of New Mexico's main campus and the nearby Nob Hill District. Start with a stroll around the UNM campus with its many historic adobe buildings; if you have time, pop inside either the Maxwell Museum of Anthropology or the UNM Art Museum. When you're finished here, walk east along Central into Nob Hill and check out the dozens of offbeat shops. If it's summer, meaning that you still have some time before the sun sets, it's worth detouring from Old Town to Far Northeast Heights (a 15-minute drive), where you can take the Sandia Peak Aerial Tramway 2.7 mi up to Sandia Peak for spectacular sunset views of the city. Either way, plan to have dinner back in Nob Hill, perhaps at Nob Hill Bar and Grill or El Patio. If you're still up for more fun, check out one of the neighborhood's lively lounges or head back Downtown for a bit of late-night barhopping.

OLD TOWN

Albuquerque's social and commercial anchor since the settlement was established in 1706. Old Town and the surrounding blocks contain the wealth of the city's top cultural attractions, including several excellent museums. The action extends from the historic Old Town Plaza for several blocks in all directions—most of the museums are north and east of the plaza. In this area you'll also find a number of restaurants and scads of shops. Some of these places are touristy and can be missed, *but the better ones are included in the Where to Eat and Shopping sections of this chapter*. The artsy Saw Mill and Wells Park/Mountain Road neighborhoods extend just east of Old Town's museum row; the Los Duranes section, where the Indian Pueblo Cultural Center commands attention, is just a bit beyond walking distance to the northeast of Old Town.

From Old Town to Albuquerque's up-and-coming Downtown, it's a rather drab (though quick) 1¼-mi bus ride, walk, or drive southeast along Central Avenue.

WHAT TO SEE

Albuquerque BioPark. The city's foremost outdoor attraction and nature center, the park comprises the restored Tingley Beach as well as three distinct attractions, Albuquerque Aquarium, Rio Grande Botanic Garden, and Rio Grande Zoo. The garden and aquarium are located together (admission gets you into both facilities); the zoo is a short drive southeast. You can also ride the scenic Rio Line vintage narrow-gauge railroad between the zoo and gardens and the aquarium complex; rides are free if you purchase a combination ticket to all of the park's facilities.

Two main components of the Albuquerque BioPark, **Albuquerque Aquarium** and **Rio Grande Botanic Garden** (⊠ *2601 Central Ave. NW, west of Old Town, north of Central Ave. and just east of the Central Ave. bridge*) are a huge draw with kids but also intrigue adult visitors. At the aquarium, a spectacular shark tank with floor-to-ceiling viewing is among the most popular of the marine exhibits. The Spanish-Moorish garden is one of three walled gardens near the entrance of the 36-acre botanic garden. The exquisite Sasebo Japanese Garden joins other specialty landscapes including the Curandera Garden, exhibiting herbs used by traditional Spanish folk-medicine practitioners; Rio Grande Heritage Farm, which re-creates a '30s-era local farm and features canning, quilting, and other demonstrations; and the Children's Fantasy Garden, complete with walk-through pumpkin, a 14-foot dragon, and giant bees. As of this writing, a Bugarium, which will contain open-air displays about insects, is currently under construction and expected to open in 2011. The seasonal PNM Butterfly Pavilion is open late May through mid-October and, year-round, the glass conservatory holds desert and Mediterranean plantings. In summer, concerts are given on Thursday at the botanic garden. From late November through late December, the botanic garden comes alive each evening from 6 to 9 pm for the River of Lights festival, a walk-through display of holiday lights and decorations.

The 64-acre **Rio Grande Zoo** (⊠ *903 10th St. SW*) is an oasis of waterfalls, cottonwood trees, and naturalized animal habitats. More than 250 species of wildlife from around the world live here, including giraffes, camels, polar bears, elephants, zebras, and koalas. The Tropical America exhibit offers a bit of contrast for dry Albuquerque, replicating a jungle rain forest and containing toucans, spider monkeys, and brilliant orchids and bromeliads. The zoo has established captive-breeding programs for more than a dozen endangered species. Concerts are performed on the grounds on summer Friday evenings. There's a café on the premises. The Thunderbird Express is a ¾-scale train that runs in a nonstop loop within the zoo, and during the 20-minute ride conductors talk in depth about the creatures and their habitats. Running Tuesday through Sunday, it's free with combo tickets, or $2 otherwise (buy tickets onboard or at the Africa exhibit). **Tingley Beach** (⊠ *1800 Tingley Dr. SW, south of Central Ave. and just east of Central Ave. bridge*) is

Albuquerque

26 ←

448

Coors Rd.

22 **23** →

24

Griegos Rd.

Rio Grande
Nature Center
State Park

25

LOS RANCHOS/
NORTH VALLEY

Valley
Park

Candelaria Rd.

12th St.

4th St.

Campbell Rd.

Mathew Blvd.

Garfield
Park

Claremont

Rio Grande Blvd.

Gabaldon Dr.

WEST
SIDE

Rio Grande

Indian School
Rd.

40

Coronado Fwy.

Haines Ave.

Broadway

RIO
GRANDE
VALLEY
STATE
PARK

**See Albuquerque
Old Town Detail Map**
1 - **9** OLD TOWN

Mountain Rd.

Mill Pond Rd.

6th St.

5th St.

4th St.

Mountain Rd.

Tiguex
Park

Old Town
Bridge

Albuquerque
Country
Club

Lomas Blvd.

Central Ave.

14th St.

Fruit Ave.

Tileras

Marquette

**Convention
Center**

Atrisco Rd.

Laguna Blvd.

Kit Carson

11 DOWNTOWN
Special Collections
Library ♦

Central Ave.

Gold Ave.

12 ♦ **Amtrak**

Gold Ave.

Sunset Rd.

Lead Ave.

10th St.

Coal Ave.

Silver Ave.

**Bus
Terminal**

Sunset Gardens Rd.

Rio
Grande Zoo

Santa Fe Ave.

Santa Fe Ave.

3rd St.

4th St.

6th St.

2nd St.

Cromwell Ave.

Galewood Ave.

Rio Grande

Lewis Ave.

Atrisco Dr.

Barelas
Bridge

Stadium Blvd.

Bridge Blvd.

13

Broadway

San Ygnacio Rd.

Golf Blvd.

BARELAS/
SOUTH VALLEY

Anderson

Isleta Blvd.

Sunset Rd.

Riverside

William St.

3rd St.

Wheeler

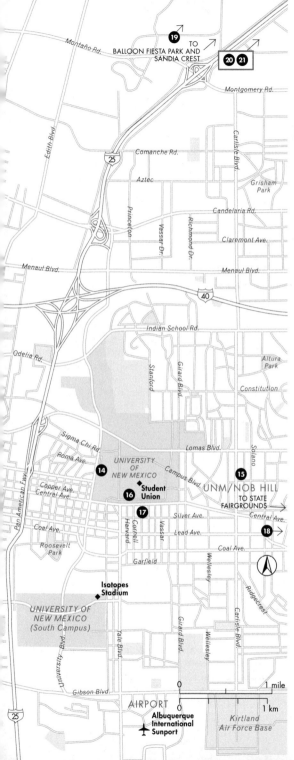

2

a recreational arm of the biological park that consists of three ponds, created in the 1930s by diverting water from the Rio Grande. You can rent paddleboats (or bicycles; both seasonally), fish the trout-stocked ponds (gear and fishing licenses can be purchased at the fishing-tackle shop on-site), or sail your model electric or wind-powered boats. To the west of the ponds, the cottonwood Bosque (wetlands forest) fringes the river. Ecological tours of the Bosque are given in summer. It's part of the popular 16-mi Paseo del Bosque bike path, which is open year-round. There's also a snack bar and a Rio Line station; the ¾-scale passenger trains make a stop here en route between the aquarium and garden complex and the zoo. ⊠ *903 10th St. SW, Old Town* ☏ *505/764–6200* ⊕ *www.cabq.gov/biopark* ☜ *Tingley Beach and grounds free, Albuquerque Aquarium and Rio Grande Botanic Garden $7 (combined ticket), Rio Grande Zoo $7; combination ticket for all attractions, including unlimited rides on the Rio Line and Thunderbird Express trains $12* ⊗ *Aquarium, botanic garden, and zoo Sept.–May daily 9–5; June–Aug. weekdays 9–5, weekends 9–6. Tingley Beach daily sunrise–sunset. No trains Mon.*

Fodor'sChoice **Albuquerque Museum of Art and History.** This modern structure houses
★   the largest collection of Spanish-colonial artifacts in the nation, along with a superb photo archive and other relics of the city's birth and development. The Common Ground galleries represent an important permanent collection of primarily 20th-century paintings, all by world-renowned artists with a New Mexico connection. Changing exhibits also reveal a commitment to historically important artists and photographers of the 20th and 21st centuries. The centerpiece, *Four Centuries: A History of Albuquerque,* is a pair of life-size models of Spanish conquistadors in original chain mail and armor. Perhaps the one on horseback is Francisco Vásquez de Coronado, who, in search of gold, led a small army into New Mexico in 1540—a turning point in the region's history. A multimedia presentation chronicles the development of the city since 1875. The sculpture garden contains more than 50 contemporary works by Southwestern artists that include Glenna Goodacre, Michael Naranjo, and Luis Jiménez. Visitors may also take advantage of three 45-minute, free (with museum admission) tours. **Slate at the Museum,** a casual eatery operated by Downtown's excellent Slate Street Cafe, serves soups, salads, espresso drinks, desserts, and other tasty light fare. ⊠ *2000 Mountain Rd. NW, Old Town* ☏ *505/243–7255 museum, 505/242–0434 shop, 505/242–5316 café* ⊕ *www.cabq.gov/museum* ☜ *$4 (free Sun. 9–1)* ⊗ *Tues.–Sun. 9–5.*

☾   **American International Rattlesnake Museum.** Included in the largest collection of different species of living rattlers in the world are such rare and unusual specimens as an albino western diamondback. From the outside the museum looks for all the world like a plain old shop, but inside, the museum's exhibits, its engaging staff, and a video supply visitors with the lowdown on these venomous creatures—for instance, that they can't hear their own rattles and that the human death rate from rattlesnake bites is less than 1%. The mission here is to educate the public on the many positive benefits of rattlesnakes, and to contribute to their conservation. ⊠ *202 San Felipe St. NW, just off the southeast*

A GOOD TOUR: OLD TOWN

Soak up the history in **Old Town Plaza**, and then cross the street and visit **San Felipe de Neri Catholic Church**. Then take a five-minute (or longer if the shops or smaller museums beckon) stroll over to two of the city's grandest cultural institutions, the **Albuquerque Museum of Art and History** and the **New Mexico Museum of Natural History and Science**. Kids also enjoy **¡Explora!**, which is next door.

From here, choose one of these options (all short rides away—the first two are on primary bus routes):

1. West on Central, along a historic section of Route 66 lined with shabby vintage motels, is the **Albuquerque BioPark**, which consists of the Albuquerque Aquarium, Botanic Garden, Rio Grande Zoo, and Tingley Beach.

2. East on Central to Downtown, and a gawk at (or tour of) the **KiMo Theatre** and some neon viewing and gallery hopping. **516 Arts** is the place to start (⇨ *Art Galleries, in Shopping, below*). Detour farther east to EDo (East of Downtown) and walk by the impressive old main library

(now Special Collections Library & the Center for the Book, **but currently closed for renovations**) and its exhibits, or go directly south on 4th Street to the **National Hispanic Cultural Center**.

3. Drive east along Mountain Road and enjoy a taste of old Albuquerque neighborhoods. Stop at **Harwood Art Center,** then backtrack a few blocks turning north on 12th Street to the **Indian Pueblo Cultural Center**.

TIMING
The best time to visit Old Town is in the morning, before the stores open at 10 and the daily rush of activity begins. In the beaming morning light, the echoes of the past are almost palpable (and you might find parking). Plan to spend an hour in the plaza area, and, depending on your interests, another hour or two in the Albuquerque Museum of Art and History and the New Mexico Museum of Natural History and Science. The BioPark easily fills an afternoon by itself (allow about two hours for the gardens and aquarium; an hour or so for the zoo).

corner of the plaza, Old Town ☎ *505/242–6569* ⊕ *www.rattlesnakes. com* ✉ *$5* ⊙ *June–Sept., Mon.–Sat. 10–6, Sun. 1–5; Oct.–May, weekdays 11:30–5:30, Sat. 10–6, Sun. 1–5.*

🅒 **¡Explora!** This imaginatively executed science museum—its driving concept is "Ideas You Can Touch"—is right across from the New Mexico Museum of Natural History and Science. ¡Explora! bills itself as an all-ages attraction (and enthralled adults abound), but there's no question that many of the innovative hands-on exhibits such as a high-wire bicycle and a kinetic sculpture display are geared to children. They offer big fun in addition to big science (and a good dose of art as well). While its colorful Bucky dome is immediately noticeable from the street, ¡Explora! also features a playground, theater, and a freestanding staircase that appears to "float" between floors. ✉ *1701 Mountain Rd. NW, Old Town* ☎ *505/224–8300* ⊕ *www.explora.us* ✉ *$7* ⊙ *Mon.– Sat. 10–6, Sun. noon–6.*

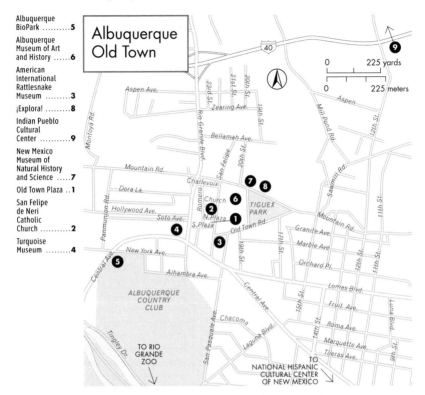

Albuquerque
Old Town

Indian Pueblo Cultural Center. The multilevel semicircular design at this museum was inspired by Pueblo Bonito, the prehistoric ruin in Chaco Canyon in northwestern New Mexico. The elegant design emphasizes the relationship between the two sites, with the museum entryway facing east, providing sacred exposure. Start by watching the museum's video about the region's Pueblo culture. Then move to the upper-level alcove, where changing exhibits feature aspects of the arts and crafts of each of the state's 19 pueblos. Lower-level exhibits trace the history of the Pueblo people. Youngsters can touch Native American pottery, jewelry, weaving, tools, and dried corn at the Hands-On Corner, draw petroglyph designs, and design pots. Paintings, sculptures, jewelry, leather crafts, rugs, souvenir items, drums, beaded necklaces, painted bowls, and fetishes are for sale. Ceremonial dances are performed on weekends at 11 and 2, and there are arts-and-crafts demonstrations each weekend. The **Pueblo Harvest Café, which is open two to three hours later than the museum,** is a great spot to try such Native American fare as blue-corn pancakes and Indian tacos, or Native Fusion items like grilled lamb "lollipops" crusted in red-chile piñons, and elk tenderloin with blackberry-sage compote. Note that technically the museum lies a bit north of Old Town, in the Los Duranes neighborhood—it's a 25-minute walk or five-minute drive. ⊠ *2401 12th St. NW, Old Town*

☎ *505/843–7270 or 800/766–4405* ⊕ *www.indianpueblo.org* ✉ *$6* ☉ *Daily 9–5.*

✿ **New Mexico Museum of Natural History and Science.** The wonders at Albuquerque's most popular museum include the simulated volcano (with a river of bubbling hot lava flowing beneath the see-through glass floor), the frigid Ice Age cave, and "Dawn of the Dinosaurs." The only Triassic exhibit in North America, this permanent hall features some of the state's own rare finds. The Evolator—short for Evolution Elevator—a six-minute high-tech ride, uses video, sound, and motion to whisk you through 35 million years of New Mexico's geological history. A film in the Extreme Screen DynaTheater makes viewers feel equally involved. Arrive via the front walkway, and you'll be greeted by life-size bronze sculptures of a 21-foot-long horned Pentaceratops and a 30-foot-long carnivorous Albertosaur. Then, on the flip side of time, the Paul Allen–funded Start-Up! galleries explore the silicon age. Detailing of the birth of the PC here in the Duke City (Allen and a very young Bill Gates came here in the mid-1970s to create software for the Altair kits that Ed Roberts designed on the south end of town, and the rest, well, you know), these exhibitions are a fascinating tour through the early garage days of many such start-ups. It's also done a fair job with the Apple side of the story. Also at the museum is the LodeStar Science Center, whose state-of-the-art planetarium is home of the wildly popular First Friday Fractals show (tickets available online only). ✉ *1801 Mountain Rd. NW, Old Town* ☎ *505/841–2800* ⊕ *www.nmnaturalhistory.org* ✉ *Museum $7, DynaTheater $7, planetarium $7; combination ticket for any 2 attractions $12, for any 3 attractions $15* ☉ *Daily 9–5.*

Fodor's Choice **Old Town Plaza.** Don Francisco Cuervo y Valdés, a provincial governor
★ of New Mexico, laid out this small plaza in 1706. No slouch when it
✿ came to political maneuvering, he named the town after the duke of Alburquerque, viceroy of New Spain. He hoped flattery would induce the duke to waive the requirement that a town have 30 families before a charter was issued—there were only 15 families living here in 1706. The duke acquiesced. (Albuquerque is nicknamed the Duke City, so he's hardly been forgotten.) Today the plaza is tranquil, with shade trees, wrought-iron benches, and a graceful white gazebo. Roughly 200 shops, restaurants, cafés, galleries, and several cultural sites in *placitas* (small plazas) and lanes surround Old Town Plaza. During fiestas Old Town comes alive with mariachi bands and dancing señoritas. ■**TIP→** **Seasonally, the Albuquerque Museum of Art and History** (⇨ *above*) **offers an excellent guided walking tour that details local history and the historic architecture that remains intact here.** Mostly dating back to the late 1800s, styles from Queen Anne to Territorial and Pueblo Revival, and even Mediterranean, are apparent in the one- and two-story (almost all adobe) structures. Event schedules and maps, which contain a list of public restrooms and many (but by no means all) Old Town shops and sights are available at the **Old Town Visitors Center** (✉ *303 Romero St. NW, Old Town* ☎ *505/243–3215* ⊕ *www.itsatrip.org*), an outpost of the Albuquerque CVB that's somewhat hidden in the rear of Plaza Don Luis, across the street from the San Felipe de Neri Catholic Church. It is open daily, typically 9–4:30 but usually a bit later in summer.

San Felipe de Neri Catholic Church. More than two centuries after it first welcomed worshippers, this structure, erected in 1793, is still active. The building, which replaced Albuquerque's first Catholic church, has been expanded several times, but its adobe walls and other original features remain. Small gardens front and flank the church; the inside is a respite from the tourism bustle beyond its doorstep—the painting and iconography is simple, authentic, and lovely, the atmosphere hushed. Next to it is a shop and small museum that displays relics—vestments, paintings, carvings—dating from the 17th century. ■ TIP→ **There's a hidden treasure behind the church: inside the gnarled tree is a statue that some speculate depicts the Virgin Mary.** ⊠ *2005 Plaza NW, Old Town* ☎ *505/243–4628* ⊕ *www.sanfelipedeneri.org* ☻ *Church open to public daily 8 am–dusk; museum Mon.–Sat. 9:30–5.*

Turquoise Museum. Just west of the hubbub of Old Town, this museum inside a small strip mall focuses on the beauty, mythology, and physical properties of turquoise, a semiprecious but adored gemstone that many people associate with the color of New Mexico's skies. A self-guided tour, entered via a simulated mine shaft, leads to one-of-a-kind show-pieces and examples from more than 65 mines on four continents. Displays show how turquoise forms, the importance of individual mines, and highlight its uses by Native Americans in prehistoric times. At the education center you can learn to distinguish the real McCoy from plastic. The museum's proprietors are a multigenerational family of longtime traders, and know whereof they speak; if you retain nothing else, do remember that only turquoise specified as "natural" is the desirable, unadulterated stuff. There is an active silversmith's shop adjacent to the display area; a small gift shop sells historic and contemporary pieces. ⊠ *2107 Central Ave. NW, Old Town* ☎ *505/247–8650* ⊕ *www. turquoisemuseum.com* ⊡ *$4* ☻ *Weekdays 9:30–5, Sat. 9:30–4 (last entrance is one hour before closing).*

DOWNTOWN

Although Downtown doesn't have many formal attractions short of its anchor (and destination-worthy) art gallery scene, this bustling neighborhood is one of the West's developing urban-comeback stories. It's a diverting place to wander, gallery hop, shop, snack (or dine), or simply soak in some fine remnants from its Route 66–era boom years for a couple of hours. Farther east is another revitalizing section: now known as EDo (East of Downtown), which encompasses the historic Huning Highland District. This is where Albuquerque's Old Main Library—an architectural gem—and Gothic Revival high school (now condos) still stand, and several notable restaurants and shops have sprouted up.

Fodor'sChoice
★

KiMo Theatre. When the KiMo was built, in 1927, Route 66 was barely established and running on its original alignment: north–south on 4th Street. Downtown was the center of activity, and movie palaces were the national rage. Local merchant Oreste Bachechi saw his moment, and hired architect Carl Boller to design a theater that would reflect the local zeitgeist. And that he did. Decorated with light fixtures made from buffalo skulls (the eye sockets glow amber in the dark), Navajo symbols, and nine spectacular Western-themed wall murals by Carl Von Hassler, the KiMo represents Pueblo Deco at its apex. Luckily, it was saved from the wrecking ball in 1977, and now, fully restored, it stands—one of the few notable early-20th-century structures

remaining in Downtown Albuquerque. The self-guided tour is a must (guided tours can also be arranged by appointment), or, even better, catch a live performance. ⊠ *423 Central Ave. NW, at 5th St., Downtown* ☎ *505/768–3522 theater, 505/768–3544 event info* ⊕ *www.cabq.gov/ kimo* ✉ *Free self-guided tours* ☉ *Tues.–Fri. 8:30–4:30, Sat. 11–5.*

New Mexico Holocaust & Intolerance Museum. Reestablished in a larger and more attractive Downtown space in 2009, this moving museum packs plenty of punch with its poignant exhibits that document genocide and persecution throughout history, with special emphasis placed upon the Holocaust carried out by the Nazis before and during World War II. Exhibits inside touch on child slave labor, the rescue of Bulgarian and Danish Jews, the Nuremburg Trials, and include a re-created gate from a concentration camp and many artifacts related to Holocaust survivors and the Nazis. There are also exhibits describing genocides throughout history such as the infamous Bataan Death March. ⊠ *616 Central Ave. SW, Downtown* ☎ *505/247–0606* ⊕ *www.nmholocaustmuseum. org* ✉ *Donations accepted* ☉ *Tues.–Sat. 11–3:30.*

BARELAS/SOUTH VALLEY

The historic Barelas neighborhood, to the south of Old Town and Downtown, features the must-see National Hispanic Cultural Center. Otherwise it's mostly a residential neighborhood that gradually gives way to the broad South Valley, a rough-around-the-edges area that contains modest homes in some sections, and light industry in others.

WHAT TO SEE

Fodor's Choice
★
☾
National Hispanic Cultural Center. A showpiece for the city, and a showcase for Latino culture and genealogy in Albuquerque's old Barelas neighborhood, this exciting contemporary space contains a museum and art galleries, multiple performance venues, a 10,000-volume genealogical research center and library, a restaurant, and an education center. Exhibits include dynamic displays of photography and paintings by local artists as well as by internationally known names. The center mounts performances of flamenco dancing, bilingual theater, traditional Spanish and New Mexican music, world music, the symphony, and more. This is the largest Latino cultural center in the country, and with a $10 million programming endowment, the center provides top-notch entertainment in its stunning and acoustically superb Roy E. Disney Center for Performing Arts and smaller Albuquerque Journal Theatre, and hosts major traveling art exhibits in its first-rate museum, which also houses an esteemed permanent collection with more than 2,000 works. Architecturally, the center borrows from a variety of Spanish

cultures, from Moorish Spain (including a re-creation of a defensive tower, or Torreón; the finely detailed fresco that embellishes the interior's 45-foot-tall walls and ceiling depicts Hispanic cultural heritage through time) to Mexico and the American Southwest. There's a vintage WPA-era school that now contains the research library and **La Fonda del Bosque restaurant** ($$, no dinner), which serves tasty New Mexican fare indoors and out on the patio; Sunday brunch, live music included, draws a big family crowd. The gift shop, La Tiendita, has a well-chosen and impeccably sourced selection of books, pottery, and artwork. ⊠ *1701 4th St. SW, at Avenida César Chavez (Bridge Blvd.), Barelas* ☎ *505/246–2261 cultural center, 505/247–9480 restaurant, 505/766–6604 gift shop, 505/724–4771 box office* ⊕ *www.nhccnm. org* ⊠ *$3* ☉ *Tues.–Sun. 10–5.*

UNM/NOB HILL

Established in 1889, the University of New Mexico (UNM) is the state's leading institution of higher education, with internationally recognized programs in anthropology, biology, Latin American studies, and medicine. Its many outstanding galleries and museums are open to the public free of charge. The university's Pueblo Revival–style architecture is noteworthy, particularly the old wing of Zimmerman Library and the Alumni Chapel, both designed by John Gaw Meem, a Santa Fe–based architect whose mid-20th-century work dominates the campus.

WHAT TO SEE

Maxwell Museum of Anthropology. Many of the more than 2½ million artifacts at the Maxwell, the first public museum in Albuquerque (established in 1932), come from the Southwest. Two permanent exhibitions chronicle 4 million years of human history and the art and cultures of 11,500 years of human settlement in the Southwest. The photographic archives contain more than 250,000 images, including some of the earliest photos of Pueblo and Navajo cultures. The museum shop sells traditional and contemporary Southwestern Native American jewelry, rugs, pottery, basketry, and beadwork, along with folk art from around the world. In the children's section are inexpensive books and handmade tribal artifacts. Parking permits for adjacent UNM lots are available inside the museum. ⊠ *University of New Mexico, Redondo West Dr., west end of campus, just east of University Blvd. NE, between Las Lomas Rd. NE and Dr. Martin Luther King Blvd. NE, UNM/Nob Hill* ☎ *505/277–4405* ⊕ *www.unm.edu/~maxwell* ⊠ *Free* ☉ *Tues.–Sat. 10–4.*

Fodor's Choice ★ **Nob Hill.** The heart of Albuquerque's Route 66 culture and also its hippest, funkiest retail and entertainment district, Nob Hill is the neighborhood just east of UNM, with its commercial spine extending along Central Avenue (old Route 66). Along this stretch you'll find dozens of offbeat shops, arty cafés, and student hangouts, and on the blocks just north and south of Central Avenue, you'll see an eclectic assortment of building styles. Most of the more noteworthy businesses are along the stretch of Central between UNM and Carlisle Boulevard, but the activity is gradually moving east. Old art deco strip malls and vintage motels along this stretch are slowly being transformed into new restaurants

A GOOD WALK: DOWNTOWN

The impeccably landscaped grounds of the University of New Mexico surround a central area containing knolls, a duck pond, fountains, waterfalls, and benches. As you begin a counterclockwise route from the school's southeast corner, your first stop is for a map at the nearby Welcome Center. Then stroll north past the Student Union Building, then left into the plaza. Zimmerman Library will be on your right; stop in and take a look at the old section, yet another one of John Gaw Meem's memorable campus buildings. Directly ahead is the oasis-like Duck Pond. Loop around the pond to the west, and the Alumni Chapel comes into view. Just beyond it is the **Maxwell Museum of Anthropology**, in the Anthropology Building on the western edge of the campus. Meander southeast now to Northrup Hall and the Meteoritics Museum within. A short distance farther east you will find yourself at the Center for the Arts, just across from the parking structure where you began. Stop in at the Center, heading past Popejoy Hall to the **UNM Art Museum**, which contains the Raymond Jonson Gallery. As you exit, turn right past the UNM bookstore (Lobo gear alert!), noting

sleek and striking George Pearl Hall, which was built in 2007 to house the UNM School of Architecture and Planning, and cross Central Avenue. A half-block down on Cornell Drive is the **Tamarind Institute**. Detour nine blocks south of Central along Girard Boulevard (five blocks east of Cornell) to the **Ernie Pyle Library.** Back on Central, you're a two-minute walk from campus to the edge of **Nob Hill**, where you can shop, café hop, and admire the historic residential and commercial architecture.

TIMING

Seeing the University of New Mexico could take as little as an hour or two for the basics, and a solid half-day if you visit all the museums. If you've driven here, park the car in the Cornell Parking Structure near the southeast end of campus; it's the side adjacent to Nob Hill and is the ideal place to start—and end—a loop around the university. Spend an hour strolling the grounds, maybe catching some rays by the duck pond. Allot up to an hour for each subsequent stop. All facilities are open year-round, but some are closed from Saturday to Monday. Save Nob Hill for late afternoon or evening, when this neighborhood really comes alive.

and shops. The neighborhood was developed during the 1930s and '40s, peaked in prosperity and popularity during the 1950s, and then fell into a state of decline from the 1960s through the mid-'80s. It was at this time that a group of local business and property owners formed a neighborhood group and banded together to help turn the neighborhood around, and Nob Hill has been enjoying great cachet and popularity ever since. ⊠ *Central Ave., from University of New Mexico campus east to Washington St., UNM/Nob Hill.*

NEED A BREAK? An airy storefront café with a few tables on the sidewalk overlooking bustling Nob Hill, cheerful **Ecco Gelato & Espresso** (⊠ 3409 Central Ave. NE ☎ 505/268–0070 ⊕ www.eccogelato.com) began in Santa Fe and has quickly become a huge hit in the Duke City. The artisan gelato comes in a variety of refreshing, inventive flavors—consider coconut-lime, fig-and-walnut, rhubarb-orange, and chocolate-cherry.

OFF THE BEATEN PATH

Ernie Pyle Library. After several visits to New Mexico, Ernie Pyle, a Pulitzer Prize–winning news reporter, built a house in 1940 that now contains the smallest branch of the Albuquerque Public Library. On display are photos, handwritten articles by Pyle, and news clippings about his career as a correspondent during World War II and his death from a sniper's bullet on April 18, 1945, on the Pacific island of Ie Shima. ⊠ *900 Girard Blvd. SE, UNM/Nob Hill* ☎ *505/256–2065* ⊕ *www.cabq. gov/library* ☒ *Free* ☉ *Tues. and Thurs.–Sat. 10–6, Wed. 11–7.*

Tamarind Institute. This world-famous institution played a major role in reviving the fine art of lithographic printing, which involves working with plates of traditional stone and modern metal. Tamarind certification is to a printer what a degree from Juilliard is to a musician. A small gallery within the facility exhibits prints and lithographs by well-known masters like Jim Dine, and up-and-comers in the craft as well. Guided tours (reservations essential) are conducted on the first Friday of each month at 1:30. The Tamarind moved around the corner to a spacious, contemporary space in the old UNM architecture building in summer 2010. ⊠ *2500 Central Ave. SE, UNM/Nob Hill* ☎ *505/277–3901* ⊕ *http://tamarind.unm.edu* ☒ *Free* ☉ *Weekdays 9–5.*

UNM Art Museum. A handsome facility inside the UNM Center for the Arts, the museum holds New Mexico's largest collection of fine art. Works of old masters share wall space with the likes of Picasso and O'Keeffe, and many photographs and prints are on display. Lectures and symposia, gallery talks, and guided tours are regularly scheduled. On the museum's lower level, the **Raymond Jonson Gallery** is dedicated to the work of Raymond Jonson (1891–1982), a pioneering modernist (and founder, in 1938, of the Transcendental Painting Group) whose paintings and drawings focus on mass and form. The gallery moved here in fall 2010, and previously occupied Jonson's former home and studio, designed by John Gaw Meem in 1950, whose impressive exterior you can still view at 1909 Las Lomas Road. Each summer the gallery mounts a major Jonson retrospective and also exhibits 21st-century works of sculpture, video, and photography, as well as maintaining an important archive on the founding artist and his contemporaries. ⊠ *University of New Mexico Center for the Arts, north of Central Ave. entrance opposite Cornell Dr. SE, UNM/Nob Hill* ☎ *505/277–4001* ⊕ *http://unmartmuseum.unm.edu* ☒ *$5 donation suggested* ☉ *Tues.–Fri. 10–4, weekends 1–4.*

LOS RANCHOS/NORTH VALLEY

Many attractions lie north of Downtown, Old Town, and the University of New Mexico. Quite a few, including the Anderson and Casa Rodeña wineries and the Rio Grande Nature Center, are clustered in two of the city's longest-settled areas: the more rural and lush cottonwood-lined North Valley, and Los Ranchos, along the Rio Grande. Early

Spanish settlers made their homes here, building on top of even earlier Pueblo homesteads. Historic adobe houses abound. This area is a natural gateway to the West Side. Drive across the lovely Montaño Road bridge and Petroglyph National Monument is moments away, as is

> **DID YOU KNOW?**
>
> Franciscan monks first planted their grapevines in New Mexico before having more success in northern California.

the highly recommended side-trip destination, Corrales (⇨ *Side Trips from Albuquerque, below*).

WHAT TO SEE

☺ **Anderson-Abruzzo International Balloon Museum.** This dramatic museum celebrates the city's legacy as the hot-air ballooning capital of the world. The dashing, massive facility is named for Maxie Anderson and Ben Abruzzo, who pioneered ballooning in Albuquerque and were part of a team of three aviators who made the first manned hot-air balloon crossing of the Atlantic Ocean in 1978. You'll understand why this museum is so large when you see the exhibits—including several historic balloons, and both large- and small-scale replicas of balloons and zeppelins. You'll also see vintage balloon baskets, china and flatware from the ill-fated *Hindenburg* and an engaging display on that tragic craft, and dynamic displays that trace the history of the sport, dating back to the first balloon ride, in 1783. Kids can design their own balloons at one creative interactive exhibit. There's a large museum shop offering just about any book or product you could imagine related to hot-air ballooning.

The museum anchors Albuquerque's Balloon Fiesta Park, home to the legendary **Albuquerque International Balloon Fiesta** (☎ *505/821–1000 or 888/422–7277 ⊕ www.balloonfiesta.com*), which began in 1972 and runs for nearly two weeks in early October. Albuquerque's history of ballooning dates from 1882, when Professor Park A. Van Tassel, a saloon keeper, ascended in a balloon at the Territorial Fair. During the fiesta, the largest hot-air-balloon gathering anywhere, you can watch the Special Shapes Rodeo, when hundreds of unusual balloons, including depictions of the old lady who lived in the shoe, the pink pig, and dozens of other fanciful characters from fairy tales and popular culture, soar high above more than a million spectators. There are night flights, obstacle races, and many other surprising balloon events. Book your hotel far in advance if you plan to attend, and note that hotel rates also rise during the fiesta. ✉ *9201 Balloon Museum Dr. NE, off Alameda Blvd., Los Ranchos/North Valley* ☎ *505/768–6020 ⊕ www.balloonmuseum.com* ✉ *$4* ⊗ *Tues.–Sun. 9–5.*

Anderson Valley Vineyards. A low-key winery that was established in 1973 and enjoys a dramatic, pastoral Los Ranchos setting not far from the Rio Grande, Anderson Valley specializes in Chardonnay and Cabernet Sauvignon. The staff in the intimate tasting room is friendly and knowledgeable, and you can sip your wine while relaxing on an enchanting patio with wonderful views of the Sandia Mountains in the distance. In this agrarian, tranquil setting, it's hard to imagine that you're just a little more than 3 mi north of the bustle of Old Town and

Downtown. ✉ *4920 Rio Grande Blvd. NW, between Montaño and Chavez Rds. NW, Los Ranchos/North Valley* 🕾 *505/344–7266* 🖃 *Free* ⊗ *Wed.–Sun. noon–5.*

Fodor'sChoice **Casa Rondeña Winery.** Perhaps the most architecturally stunning of New
★ Mexico's wineries, Casa Rondeña—which is technically in Los Ranchos de Albuquerque, not the Duke City proper—resembles a Tuscan villa, with its green-tile roof and verdant grounds laced with gardens and fountains. It's hard to believe that most of the structures here went up with the winery's founding in 1995. Casa Rondeña produces a superb Meritage red blend as well as a terrific Viognier. You can see a vintage oak fermentation tank and a great hall with soaring ceilings, where tastings are conducted. The winery hosts many events including a chamber music festival with wine receptions and dinners. ✉ *733 Chavez Rd. NW, between Rio Grande Blvd. and 4th St. NW, Los Ranchos/North Valley* 🕾 *505/344–5911 or 800/706–1699* ⊕ *www.casarondena.com* 🖃 *Free* ⊗ *Mon.–Sat. 10–6, Sun. noon–6.*

☙ **Rio Grande Nature Center State Park.** Along the banks of the Rio Grande, this year-round 270-acre refuge in a portion of the Bosque (about midway up on the Paseo del Bosque trail) is the nation's largest cottonwood forest. If bird-watching is your thing, you've come to the right place: this is home to all manner of birds and migratory waterfowl. Constructed half aboveground and half below the edge of a pond, the park's glass-walled interpretive center (an interesting small-scale building by noted New Mexico architect Antoine Predock) has viewing windows that provide a look at what's going on at both levels, and speakers that broadcast the sounds of the birds you're watching into the room. You may see birds, frogs, ducks, and turtles. The park has active programs for adults and children and trails for biking, walking, and jogging. ∎**TIP➔** **Keep your eye out for what appears to be a game of jacks abandoned by giants: these jetty jacks were built in the 1950s to protect the Rio Grande levees from flood debris.** ✉ *2901 Candelaria Rd. NW, Los Ranchos/North Valley* 🕾 *505/344–7240* ⊕ *www.rgnc.org* 🖃 *$3 per vehicle, grounds free* ⊗ *Nature center daily 10–5, park daily 8–5.*

☙ **Unser Racing Museum.** Albuquerque is home to the illustrious auto-racing family, the Unsers, whose four generations of drivers have dominated the sport since the early 20th century—the most famous members include Bobby Unser Sr. and Al Unser Sr. Exhibits at this spiffy museum include a display on Pikes Peak, Colorado, and the legendary hairpins where the Unser family first got serious about racing; a study of their legacy at the Indianapolis 500; and a good selection of vintage racers, including a few you can test-drive (virtually, that is). ✉ *1776 Montaño Rd. NW, just east of the Rio Grande Blvd. overpass, near the Montaño Road bridge, Los Ranchos/North Valley* 🕾 *505/341–1776* ⊕ *www. unserracingmuseum.com* 🖃 *$10* ⊗ *Daily 10–4.*

NORTHEAST HEIGHTS

In Northeast Heights you are in the foothills of the Sandia Mountains, in upscale neighborhoods that surprise you with the sudden appearance of piñon and ponderosa. Trips to this area can easily be combined with more north-central venues like the Balloon Museum and the North Valley wineries.

Gruet Winery. It's hard to imagine a wine-tasting venue with less curb appeal. Gruet Winery sits along an ugly access road paralleling Interstate 25, sandwiched between an RV showroom and a lawn-furniture store. But behind the vaguely chaletlike exterior of this otherwise modern industrial building, you're afforded the chance to visit one of the nation's most acclaimed producers of sparkling wines (to see its actual vineyards you'll have to head south to Truth or Consequences). Gruet (pronounced *grew*-eh) had been famous in France since the 1950s for its Champagnes. In New Mexico, the Gruet family has been producing wine since 1984, and it's earned nationwide kudos for its Methode Champenoise (employing traditional Champagne-making methods for its sparkling wine), as well as for impressive Pinot Noirs, Syrahs, and Chardonnays. Most of the state's top restaurants carry Gruet vintages, as do many leading wine cellars around the country. Tastings include five wines and a souvenir glass. ✉ *8400 Pan American Freeway (I–25) NE, on the north frontage road for I–25, between Alameda Blvd. and Paseo del Norte, Northeast Heights* ☎ *505/821–0055 or 888/857–9463* ⊕ *www.gruetwinery.com* ✉ *Winery free, 5-wine tasting $6* ⊗ *Weekdays 10–5, Sat. noon–5; tours Mon.–Sat. at 2.*

FodorsChoice **Sandia Peak Aerial Tramway.** Tramway cars climb 2.7 mi up the steep western face of the Sandias, giving you a close-up view of red rocks and tall trees—it's the world's longest aerial tramway. From the observation deck at the 10,378-foot summit you can see Santa Fe to the northeast and Los Alamos to the northwest—about 11,000 square mi of spectacular scenery. Tram cars leave from the base at regular intervals for the 15-minute ride to the top. You may see birds of prey soaring above or mountain lions roaming the cliff sides. An exhibit room at the top surveys the wildlife and landscape of the mountain. Narrators point out what you're seeing below, including the barely visible remnants of a 1953 plane crash that killed all 16 passengers onboard. If you want to add a meal to the excursion, there's the upscale **High Finance Restaurant** (☎ *505/243–9742* ⊕ *www.sandiapeakrestaurants.com*) on top of the mountain, serving steaks, lobster tail, and good burgers at lunch). High Finance affords clear views from every table, making it a favorite destination for a romantic dinner—the food isn't bad, but it's more about the scenic experience here. A more casual spot, **Sandiago's** (☎ *505/856–6692* ⊕ *www.sandiapeakrestaurants.com*), is at the tram's base. ∎TIP➔ **It's much colder and windier at the summit than at the tram's base, so pack a jacket.** You can also use the tram as a way to reach the Sandia Peak ski and mountain-biking area (⇨ *Sandia Park, in Side Trips from Albuquerque, below*). ✉ *10 Tramway Loop NE, Far Northeast Heights* ☎ *505/856–7325* ⊕ *www.sandiapeak.com* ✉ *$20* ⊗ *Memorial Day–Labor Day, daily 9–9; Sept.–May, Wed.–Mon. 9–8, Tues. 5 pm–8 pm.*</

UPTOWN/EAST SIDE

Just east of Nob Hill and south of Northeast Heights, Uptown and the East Side bridge the older and historic parts of Route 66 with the newer, somewhat suburban-looking parts of the city. The only attraction in these parts is the new National Museum of Nuclear Science & History. Few visitors spend time here, except to check out the shopping and dining at ABQ Uptown and Coronado Mall, which are also close to a few hotels.

ℭ **National Museum of Nuclear Science & History.** Renamed in 2009 following a move from its temporary former location in Old Town, this impressive museum traces the history of the atomic age and how nuclear science has dramatically influenced the course of modern history. Exhibits include replicas of Little Boy and Fat Man (the bombs dropped on Japan at the end of World War II), a compelling display about the difficult decision to drop atomic bombs, and a look at how atomic culture has dovetailed with pop culture. There are also children's programs and an exhibit about X-ray technology. This new facility also contains the 9-acre Heritage Park, which has a B-29 and other mega-airships, plus rockets, missiles, cannons, and even a nuclear sub sail. One highlight is the restored 1942 Plymouth that was used to transport the plutonium core of "the Gadget" (as that first weapon was known) down from Los Alamos to the Trinity Site for testing. ⊠ *601 Eubank Blvd. SE, a few blocks south of I–40Uptown/East Side* ☎ *505/245–2137* ⊕ *www. atomicmuseum.org* ⊡ *$8* ⊙ *Daily 9–5.*

WEST SIDE

The fastest-growing part of Albuquerque lies on a broad mesa high above the Rio Grande Valley. The West Side is primarily the domain of new suburban housing developments and strip malls, some designed more attractively than others. Somewhat controversially, growth on the West Side has seemed to occur below, above, and virtually all around the archaeologically critical Petroglyph National Monument. Allow a 20-minute drive from Old Town and the North Valley to reach the monument.

ℭ **Petroglyph National Monument.** Beneath the stumps of five extinct volcanoes, this park encompasses more than 25,000 ancient Native American rock drawings inscribed on the 17-mi-long West Mesa escarpment overlooking the Rio Grande Valley. For centuries, Native American hunting parties camped at the base, chipping and scribbling away. Archaeologists believe most of the petroglyphs were carved on the lava formations between 1100 and 1600, but some images at the park may date back as far as 1000 BC. A paved trail at **Boca Negra Canyon** (north of the visitor center on Unser Boulevard, beyond Montaño Road) leads past several dozen petroglyphs. The trail at **Rinconado Canyon** (south of the visitor center on Unser) is unpaved. The rangers at the visitor center will supply maps and help you determine which trail is best for the time you have. ⊠ *Visitor center, 6001 Unser Blvd. NW, at Western Trail Rd., 3 mi north of I–40 Exit 154; from I–25 take Exit 228 and proceed west on Montaño Rd. across the bridge, then south on Unser*

1 mi, West Side ☎ 505/899–0205 ⊕ www.nps.gov/petr ⚏ $1 weekdays, $2 weekends for parking at Boca Negra Canyon; access to rest of monument is free ⊙ Daily 8–5.

WHERE TO EAT

The Duke City has long been a place for hearty home-style cooking in big portions, and to this day, it's easy to find great steak-and-chops houses, retro diners, and authentic New Mexican restaurants. The trick is finding them amid Albuquerque's miles of chain options and legions of dives, but if you look, you'll be rewarded with innovative food, and generally at prices much lower than in Santa Fe or other major Southwestern cities.

Albuquerque's dining scene has evolved considerably of late. In Nob Hill, Downtown, and Old Town many notable new restaurants have opened, offering swank decor and complex and artful variations on modern Southwest, Mediterranean, Asian, and other globally inspired cuisine. A significant Vietnamese population has made that cuisine a star, but Indian, Japanese, Thai, and South American traditions all have a presence, making this New Mexico's best destination for ethnic fare.

WHAT IT COSTS				
¢	$	$$	$$$	$$$$
Restaurants	under $10	$10–$15	$16–$22	$23–$30	over $30

Prices are per person for a main course at dinner, excluding 8.25% sales tax.

Use the coordinate (✛ A2) at the end of each listing to locate a site on the corresponding map.

OLD TOWN

$$$ ╳ **Antiquity.** Within the thick adobe walls of this darkly lighted, romantic
CONTINENTAL space on the plaza in Old Town, patrons have been feasting on rich, elegantly prepared American classics for more than 50 years. This isn't the edgy, contemporary restaurant to bring an adventuresome foodie—Antiquity specializes in classics, from starters of French onion soup and escargot to main courses like Australian lobster tail with drawn butter and black angus New York strip-loin steak with horseradish sauce. But the consistently well-prepared food and charming service make it a winner. ⊠ *112 Romero St. NW, Old Town* ☎ *505/247–3545* ⊟ *AE, D, MC, V* ⊙ *No lunch* ✛ *B3.*

$ ╳ **Church Street Café.** Built in the early 1700s, this structure is among
NEW MEXICAN the oldest in New Mexico. Renovations have preserved the original adobe bricks to ensure that this spacious eatery remains as authentic as its menu, which features family recipes spanning four generations—with fresh, local ingredients and spirits employed to satiate streams of hungry tourists and locals. Request the courtyard for alfresco dining amid trellises of sweet grapes and flowers, and where classical and flamenco guitarist José Salazar often performs. Buttery guacamole, with

BEST BETS FOR ALBUQUERQUE DINING

With hundreds of restaurants to choose from, how will you decide where to eat? Fodor's writers and editors have selected their favorite restaurants by price and cuisine in the Best Bets lists below. Find specific details about a restaurant in the full reviews, listed below.

 Fodor's Choice ★

Casa Vieja $$$, 91
El Patio ¢, 61
Farina Pizzeria & Wine Bar $, 58
Grove Cafe & Market ¢ , 59
Jennifer James 101 $$$, 64
Range Cafe & Bakery $, 93

By Price

¢

Duran's Central Pharmacy, 55
El Patio, 61
Grove Cafe & Market, 59
Mary & Tito's, 63
Mineshaft Tavern, 96
Viet Taste, 64

$

Flying Star, 61
Farina Pizzeria & Wine Bar, 58
Nob Hill Bar and Grill, 62
Range Cafe & Bakery, 93

San Marcos Cafe, 97
Sophia's Place, 63

$$

Brasserie La Provence, 60
Seasons Rotisserie & Grill, 55
Slate Street Cafe, 59
Standard Diner, 60

$$$

Antiquity , 53
Artichoke Café, 58
Casa Vieja, 91
Jennifer James 101, 64
Prairie Star, 92
Zinc Wine Bar & Bistro, 62

$$$$

Bien Shur, 63
Corn Maiden, 92
Rancher's Club, 59

By Cuisine

AMERICAN

66 Diner ¢, 60
Bien Shur $$$$, 63

Gold Street Caffè $, 58
Frontier Restaurant ¢, 62
Mineshaft Tavern ¢, 96
Standard Diner $$, 60

CAFÉ

Flying Star $, 61
Golden Crown Panaderia ¢, 55
Grove Cafe & Market ¢, 59
Range Cafe & Bakery $, 93
San Marcos Cafe $, 97
Sophia's Place $, 63

ASIAN

Crazy Fish $, 61
Viet Taste ¢, 64

CONTEMPORARY

Casa Vieja $$$, 91
Jennifer James 101 $$$, 64
Nob Hill Bar and Grill $, 62
Prairie Star $$$, 92
Slate Street Cafe $$, 59

Zinc Wine Bar & Bistro $$$, 62

FRENCH/ITALIAN/MEDITERRANEAN

Artichoke Café $$$, 58
Brasserie La Provence $$, 60
Farina Pizzeria & Wine Bar $, 58
Lucia $$$, 59
Yanni's Mediterranean Grill $$, 62
Village Pizza ¢, 91

NEW MEXICAN

Barelas Coffee House ¢, 60
Church Street Café $, 53
Duran's Central Pharmacy ¢, 55
El Patio ¢, 61
Los Cuates ¢, 64
Mary & Tito's ¢, 63

just a bit of bite, is the perfect appetizer to prep one's palate for tender carne asada, redolent and sumptuously spiced. Try the house specialty, chiles rellenos stuffed with beef and cheese, or a portobello-and-bell-pepper fajita. Traditional desserts and hearty breakfast choices are also offered. ⊠ *2111 Church St. NW, Old Town* ☎ *505/247–8522* ⊕ *www. churchstreetcafe.com* ⊟ *AE, D, MC, V* ☾ *No dinner Sun* ✛ *B3.*

¢ ✕ **Duran's Central Pharmacy.** This expanded Old Town lunch counter
NEW MEXICAN with a dozen tables and a tiny patio just might serve the best tortillas in town. A favorite of old-timers who know their way around a blue-corn enchilada, Duran's is an informal place whose patrons give their food the total attention it deserves. Be sure to leave some browsing time for the pharmacy's book section: Duran's has a good selection of not easily found history and coffee-table volumes covering the Duke City and its storied environs. ⊠ *1815 Central Ave. NW, Old Town* ☎ *505/247–4141* ⊟ *No credit cards* ☾ *No dinner* ✛ *B4.*

¢ ✕ **Golden Crown Panaderia.** On the eastern fringe of Old Town, in a
CAFÉ nascent arts district, this aromatic, down-home-style bakery is known for two things: the ability to custom-design and bake artful breads in the likeness of just about any person or place, and hearty green-chile bread (made with tomatoes, cilantro, Parmesan, green chile, and onions). You can order hot cocoa, cappuccino, *bizcochito* (the official state cookie, also known as New Mexican wedding cookies), pumpkin-filled empanadas, plenty of other sweets and sandwiches (ask what bread is fresh and hot), and wonderfully spicy and aromatic pizzas made with green-chile crusts. There's seating on a small patio. ⊠ *1103 Mountain Rd. NW, Old Town* ☎ *505/243–2424 or 877/382–2924* ⊕ *www. goldencrown.biz* ⊟ *MC, V* ☾ *Closed Mon* ✛ *C3.*

$ ✕ **Monica's El Portal.** Locals in the know favor this rambling, authentic
NEW MEXICAN New Mexican restaurant on the west side of Old Town over the more famous, though less reliable, standbys around Old Town Plaza. Monica's has a prosaic dining room plus a cute tiled patio, and the service is friendly and unhurried. If you've never had *chicharrones* (fried pork skins), try them here with beans stuffed inside a flaky sopaipilla. Or consider the traditional blue-corn chicken or beef enchiladas, and the savory green-chile stew. This is honest, home-style food, and lunch here may just fill you up for the rest of the day. ⊠ *321 Rio Grande Blvd. NW, Old Town* ☎ *505/247–9625* ⊟ *AE, D, MC, V* ☾ *Closed Mon. No dinner weekends* ✛ *B3*

$$ ✕ **Seasons Rotisserie & Grill.** Upbeat yet elegant, this Old Town eatery
CONTEMPORARY is an easy place to have a business lunch or a dinner date, and oenophiles will revel in its well-chosen cellar. The kitchen serves innovative grills and pastas, such as wood-roasted duck breast with Gorgonzola–sweet-potato gratin and grilled Colorado lamb with Moroccan couscous, sautéed haricots verts, and cherry-mint demi-glace; great starters include pan-seared crab cakes with cilantro-lime aioli, and sweet-corn griddle cakes with marsala-fig chutney and almond-pepper tapenade. The rooftop patio and bar provides evening cocktails and lighter meals. ⊠ *2031 Mountain Rd. NW, Old Town* ☎ *505/766–5100* ⊕ *www.seasonsonthenet.com* ⊟ *AE, D, DC, MC, V* ☾ *No lunch weekends* ✛ *B3.*

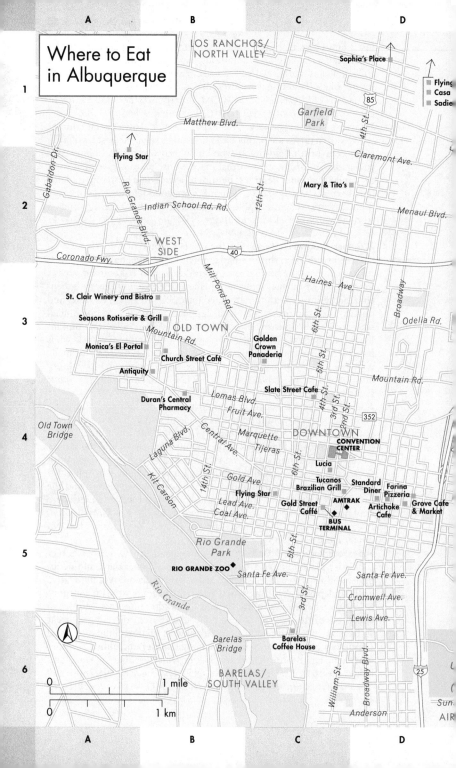

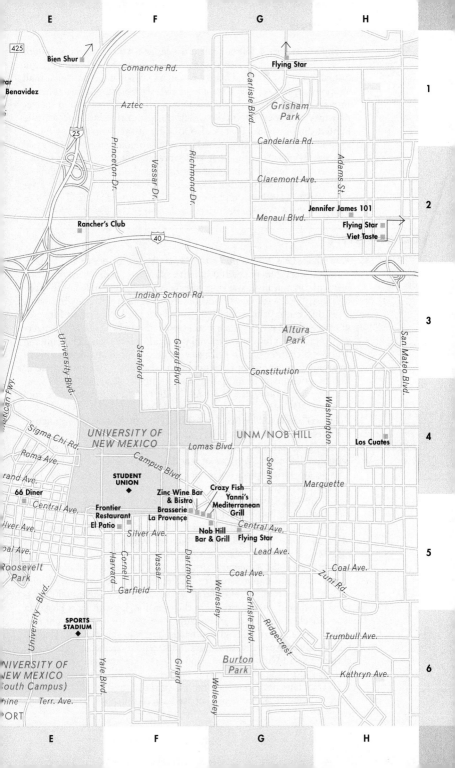

$ ✕ **St. Clair Winery & Bistro.** The state's largest winery, in the southern
CONTINENTAL   New Mexico town of Deming, St. Clair Winery has a charming and
affordable restaurant and tasting room in Old Town. It's part of a small
shopping center on the west side of the neighborhood, just south of
Interstate 40. You enter a shop with a bar for wine tasting and shelves
of wines and gourmet goods, which leads into the dark and warmly
lighted dining room. There's also a large, attractive patio. At lunch,
sample the panini sandwich of New Mexico goat cheese and roasted
peppers. Dinner treats include crab-and-artichoke dip, garlic chicken
slow-cooked in Chardonnay, and pork tenderloin cooked in Nebbiolo
wine with raspberry-chipotle sauce. St. Clair serves a popular Sunday brunch. ⊠ *901 Rio Grande Blvd., Old Town* ☎ *505/243–9916 or
888/870–9916* ⊕ *www.stclairvineyards.com* ▭ *AE, D, MC, V* ⊹ *B3.*

DOWNTOWN

$$$ ✕ **Artichoke Café.** Locals praise the Artichoke for its service and French,
CONTEMPORARY   contemporary American, and Italian dishes prepared, whenever possi-
ble, with organically grown ingredients. Specialties include house-made
ravioli stuffed with ricotta and butternut squash with a white wine,
sage, and butter sauce; and pan-seared sea scallops wrapped in pro-
sciutto with red potatoes, haricots verts, and wax beans. The appetizers
are so tasty you may want to make a meal out of them. The building
is about a century old, in the historic Huning Highland district in the
emerging EDo section of Downtown, but the decor is Uptown modern.
The two-tier dining room spills out into a small courtyard. ⊠ *424 Cen-
tral Ave. SE, Downtown* ☎ *505/243–0200* ⊕ *www.artichokecafe.com*
▭ *AE, D, DC, MC, V* ⊗ *No lunch weekends* ⊹ *D5.*

$ ✕ **Farina Pizzeria & Wine Bar.** The team at the Artichoke Café, just across
PIZZA   the street, has opened this stellar pizza lounge inside an ancient former
Fodor's Choice   grocery store with hardwood floors, exposed-brick walls, pressed-tin
★   ceiling, and a couple of rows of wooden tables along with a long bar.
This noisy, spirited place doles out exceptionally tasty pizzas with blis-
tering-hot crusts and imaginative toppings; the Salsiccia, with sweet-
fennel sausage, roasted onions, and mozzarella, has plenty of fans.
Finish with rich butterscotch *budino* (Italian pudding), and take note of
the extensive, fair-priced list of wines by the glass. ⊠ *510 Central Ave.
SE, Downtown* ☎ *505/243–0130* ⊕ *www.farinapizzeria.com* ▭ *AE, D,
DC, MC, V* ⊗ *No lunch weekends* ⊹ *D4.*

$ ✕ **Gold Street Caffè.** A culinary cornerstone of Downtown Albuquerque's
CAFÉ   renaissance, this dapper storefront café with exposed-brick walls and
high ceilings serves breakfast fare that is a cut above, plus equally satis-
fying lunch and dinner entrées. In the morning, go with Eggs Eleganza
(two poached eggs atop a green-chile brioche with local goat cheese),
along with a side of chile-glazed bacon. Later in the day, consider the
Dungeness crab cakes with almond-crusted goat cheese, or seared-beef
chopped salad with fried rice noodles and chile-lime vinaigrette. You
can also just hang out among the hipsters and office workers, sipping
a caramel latte and munching on one of the tasty desserts, or enjoy a
glass of wine from the short but well-selected list. ⊠ *218 Gold Ave.*

SW, Downtown ☎ *505/765–1633* 🍴 *MC, V* ⊘ *No dinner Sun. and Mon* ✥ *C5.*

¢   ✕ **Grove Cafe & Market.** On the east side of Downtown in the historic
CAFÉ   Huning Highland district (an area now commonly called EDo), this airy,
Fodor's Choice   modern establishment is a local favorite that features locally grown,
★   seasonal specials at reasonable prices. Enjoy such fresh, quality treats
as Grove Pancakes with fresh fruit, crème fraîche, local honey, and
real maple syrup; a Farmers Salad with roasted golden beets, Marcona
almonds, goat cheese, and lemon-basil vinaigrette; or an aged Genoa
salami sandwich with olive tapenade, arugula, and provolone on an
artisanal sourdough bread. You can dine on the arbored patio. Or
come by for a loose-leaf tea or latte with a cupcake. The market sells an
impressive mix of chocolates, cheeses, and gourmet foods. ✉ *600 Central Ave. SE, Downtown* ☎ *505/248–9800* ⊕ *www.thegrovecafemarket.com* 🍴 *AE, D, MC, V* ⊘ *Closed Mon. No dinner* ✥ *D5.*

$$$ ✕ **Lucia.** Lucia provides Albuquerque with a much-needed dose of
MEDITERRANEAN   style. The angular, spare dining room with mod overhanging lights
and contemporary furnishings is downright edgy and unexpected for
a dining venue inside the historic Hotel Andaluz. The menu pushes
the envelope, too, with pricey (by local standards) and creative Mediterranean fare with nary a hint of green chiles. You might start with
grilled baby artichokes with caper-saffron butter, followed by Catalonian-herb-crusted rack of lamb with oil-poached tomatoes, chickpea
compote, and roasted-garlic asparagus. There are no weak links on
this ambitious menu. Breakfast and lunch are served, too. The patio
area is dog-friendly. ✉ *Hotel Andaluz, 125 2nd St. NW, Downtown* ☎ *505/923–9080* ⊕ *www.hotelandaluz.com/lucia* 🍴 *AE, D, DC, MC, V* ✥ *C4.*

$$$$ ✕ **Rancher's Club.** Few hotel restaurants in Albuquerque merit serious
STEAK   culinary consideration, but this clubby, old-world steak house in the
Albuquerque Hilton earns raves among deep-pocketed carnivores for
its delicious aged steaks and ribs. The dining room is hung with saddles,
mounted bison heads, and ranching-related art. If you want to impress
a date or clients, order the fillet of Wagyu Kobe beef with creamed
spinach, lobster-mashed potatoes, and morel-mushroom jus. Other
standouts include elk chops, Alaskan wild salmon, and porterhouse
steak. ✉ *Albuquerque Hilton, 1901 University Blvd. NE, Downtown* ☎ *505/889–8071* ⊕ *http://theranchersclubofnm.com* 🍴 *AE, D, DC, MC, V* ⊘ *No lunch* ✥ *E2*

$$ ✕ **Slate Street Cafe.** A high-energy, high-ceiling dining room with a semi-
ECLECTIC   circular, central wine bar and modern lighting, this stylish restaurant
sits amid pawn shops and bail-bond outposts on a quiet, unprepossessing side street Downtown. But once inside, you'll find a sophisticated, colorful space serving memorable, modern renditions of classic
American fare, such as fried chicken and meat loaf. The starters are
notable, including grilled sesame-crusted ahi with wasabi cream, and
bruschetta topped with honey-cured ham and Brie. Banana-stuffed brioche French toast is a favorite at breakfast and weekend brunch. More
than 25 wines by the glass are served. ✉ *515 Slate St. NW, Downtown*

☎ *505/243–2210* ⊕ *www.slatestreetcafe.com* ▤ *AE, D, MC, V* ☺ *No dinner Sun.* ✠ *C4.*

$$ ✕ **Standard Diner.** In the historic Huning Highlands district, aka EDo (for
CONTEMPORARY   East of Downtown), the Standard occupies a 1930s Texaco station with
high ceilings, massive plate-glass windows, and rich tile floors—it's at
once elegant yet casual, serving upscale yet affordable takes on tradi-
tional diner standbys. The extensive menu dabbles in meal-size salads
(try the tempura-lobster Caesar salad), burgers (including a terrific one
topped with bourbon butter), sandwiches, and traditional diner entrées
given nouvelle flourishes (fish tacos with fresh bay scallops, bacon-
wrapped meat loaf with red-wine gravy). Kick everything up with a
side of truffle-pecorino french fries, and save room for the fancy milk
shakes in novel flavors such as apricot–crème brûlée and espresso Guin-
ness. ⊠ *320 Central Ave. SE, Downtown* ☎ *505/243–1440* ⊕ *www.
standarddiner.com* ▤ *AE, D, MC, V* ✠ *D4.*

$$ ✕ **Tucanos Brazilian Grill.** There isn't much point in going to Tucanos if
BRAZILIAN   you don't love meat. Sure, they serve some vegetables, but the real focus
is on *churrasco*, South American–style grilled skewers of beef, chicken,
pork, and turkey that parade endlessly out of the open kitchen on the
arms of enthusiastic waiters. Carnivore-centrism aside, one unexpected
treat, if it's available, is the grilled pineapple. The noisy, high-ceiling
spot next to the Century 14 Downtown movie theater is a good place
to go for drinks, too, and if you're looking for either a stand-alone
cooler or a liquid partner for your hearty fare, look no further than a
bracing *caipirinha*, the lime-steeped national cocktail of Brazil. ⊠ *110
Central Ave. SW, Downtown* ☎ *505/246–9900* ⊕ *www.tucanos.com*
▤ *AE, D, MC, V* ✠ *C4.*

BARELAS/SOUTH VALLEY

¢ ✕ **Barelas Coffee House.** Barelas may look like a set in search of a script,
NEW MEXICAN   but it's the real deal: diners come from all over the city to sup in this
old-fashioned chile parlor in the Hispanic Historic Route 66 neighborhood south of Downtown. You may notice looks of quiet contentment
on the faces of the many dedicated chile eaters as they dive into their
bowls of Barelas's potent red. There's also tasty breakfast fare. The staff
treats everybody like an old friend—indeed, many of the regulars who
come here have been fans of Barelas for decades. ⊠ *1502 4th St. SW,
Barelas/South Valley* ☎ *505/843–7577* ☙ *Reservations not accepted*
▤ *D, MC, V* ☺ *Closed Sun. No dinner* ✠ *C6.*

UNM/NOB HILL

¢ ✕ **66 Diner.** Dining at this '50s-style art deco diner is a must for fans of
AMERICAN   Route 66 nostalgia, and the upbeat decor and friendly service also make
it a hit with families. The specialties here are many: chicken-fried steak,
burgers, malted milk shakes, enchiladas. Plenty of breakfast treats are
available, too. ⊠ *1405 Central Ave. NE, UNM/Nob Hill* ☎ *505/247–
1421* ⊕ *www.66diner.com* ▤ *AE, D, MC, V* ✠ *E4.*

$$ ✕ **Brasserie La Provence.** You'll find classic French bistro dishes—*moules
FRENCH   frites,* couscous *merguez* (spicy lamb sausage), and *croque madame*

(grilled ham, egg, and cheese sandwich)—and a nice wine list in this amiable corner spot on the west edge of Nob Hill, steps from UNM campus. Service is good, and the food—which is very good—is improved by the congenial atmosphere. Try the patio when the weather is fair, or the lemon-colored back room when it's not. There are specials each day, and the less-expected menu items such as *Poulet du Midi* (seared chicken breast stuffed with chèvre and figs) are palate- and budget-pleasing as well. ☒ *3001 Central Ave. NE, UNM/Nob Hill* ☎ *505/254–7644* ⊕ *www.laprovencenobhill.com* ⊟ *AE, D, MC, V* ✢ *F5.*

$ ╳ **Crazy Fish.** A good bet for relatively straightforward sushi and
JAPANESE sashimi, Crazy Fish is an attractive, upbeat storefront space with minimal fuss and gimmickry—just clean lines and a black-and-gray color scheme. Friendly young servers whisk out plates of fresh food to a mix of students and yuppies. In addition to sushi, the kitchen prepares such favorites as crispy chicken, garlic-peppered beef, and seared-albacore salad with a ginger-soy dressing. Tempura-fried bananas with chocolate ice cream make for a sweet ending. ☒ *3015 Central Ave. NE, UNM/ Nob Hill* ☎ *505/232–3474* ⊕ *www.crazyfishabq.com* ⊟ *AE, D, MC, V* ☽ *Closed Mon. No lunch weekends* ✢ *F5.*

¢ ╳ **El Patio.** A university-area hangout, this sentimental favorite serves
NEW MEXICAN consistently exemplary New Mexican food on a funky patio and inside
Fodor's Choice a cozy dining room. The service is sometimes pokey, but always friendly.
★ Go for the green-chile-chicken enchiladas or any of the heart-healthy and vegetarian selections. But watch out for the fiery green chiles served at harvesttime—this is spicy food even by local standards. Note that liquor isn't served, but beer and wine are—you can get decent-tasting "margaritas" made with wine. ☒ *142 Harvard St. NE, UNM/Nob Hill* ☎ *505/268–4245* ⊕ *www.elpatiodealbuquerque.com* ⚐ *Reservations not accepted* ⊟ *MC, V* ✢ *F5.*

$ ╳ **Flying Star.** Flying Star has become a staple and miniphenom here,
★ and although it's a chain, it's locally owned and—just as at its Satel-
CAFÉ lite Coffee spots around town—each outpost offers something a little different. The cavernous Downtown branch is a favorite for its striking setting inside the historic Southern Union Gas Co. building and its unexpected modernist motif; the newer Corrales and Bernalillo locales are notable for their shaded outdoor patio and indoor fireplaces. At the original Nob Hill space, the crowd is youthful and bohemian, and the space tighter. The concept works on many levels: it's a newsstand, late-night coffeehouse (there's free Wi-Fi), and an order-at-the-counter restaurant serving a mix of creative Asian, American, and New Mexican dishes (plus several types of wine and beer). Options include Greek pasta with shrimp, green-chile cheeseburgers, Thai-style tofu salad with tangy lime dressing, turkey-and-Jack-cheese-melt sandwiches, and an egg- and chile-packed "graburrito." Desserts change often, but count on a tantalizing array. For a winning pick-me-up, employ some strong hot coffee to wash down a tall slice of the fantastic coconut cream pie. We list a few of our favorite locations. ☒ *3416 Central Ave. SE, UNM/Nob Hill* ☎ *505/255–6633* ☒ *723 Silver Ave., Downtown* ☎ *505/244–8099* ☒ *10700 Corrales Rd., Corrales* ☎ *505/938–4717* ☒ *200 S. Camino del Pueblo, Bernalillo* ☎ *505/404–2100* ⊕ *www.flyingstarcafe.com* ⊟ *AE, D, MC, V.* ✢ *A2; C4; D1; G5; G1; H2.*

¢   ✕ **Frontier Restaurant.** This definitive student hangout across from UNM
CAFÉ   is open daily until late 1 am for inexpensive diner-style American and
New Mexican chow. A notch up from a fast-food joint, it's open later
than most such spots in town, and the breakfast burritos are terrific.
Featured along with the John Wayne and Elvis artwork in this sprawl-
ing '70s spot are oversize cinnamon buns. We won't fault you if you
cave and order one. ⊠ *2400 Central Ave. SE, at Cornell Dr. SE, UNM/
Nob Hill* ☎ *505/266–0550* ⊕ *www.frontierrestaurant.com* ▭ *AE, D,
MC, V* ✛ *F5.*

$ ✕ **Nob Hill Bar and Grill.** This elegant, centrally situated space in Nob Hill
NEW AMERICAN   has been the site of two failed yet very good restaurants in recent years,
but the latest occupant—the dapper and nearly always packed Nob Hill
Bar and Grill—appears to be succeeding. The staff's youthful and energetic personality, and the dining room and bar's swanky yet still unfussy
decor are big plusses, as are the consistently delicious modern takes
on American classics. Tuck into a plate of applewood-smoked chicken
wings with Coca-Cola barbecue sauce, or nachos topped with ahi tuna,
before feasting on hearty mains like steak-frites with garlic-parsley fries,
and a terrific veggie burger fashioned out of *edamame* (green soy beans)
and wild mushrooms, and served with ginger-lime mayo. ⊠ *3128 Central Ave. SE, UNM/Nob Hill* ☎ *505/266–4455* ⊕ *www.upscalejoint.
com* ▭ *AE, D, MC, V* ☉ *Closed Mon* ✛ *F5*

$$ ✕ **Yanni's Mediterranean Grill.** Yanni's is a convivial place where the food
GREEK   can run second to its refreshing azure-tiled ambience. Serving mari-
nated grilled lamb chops with lemon and oregano, grilled yellowfin
sole encrusted with Parmesan, *pastitsio* (a Greek version of mac and
cheese), and spinach, feta, and roasted garlic pizzas, Yanni's also offers
a vegetarian plate with good meatless moussaka, tabbouleh, spanako-
pita, and stuffed grape leaves. There's a huge patio off the main dining
room, and next door you can sip cocktails and mingle with locals at
Opa Bar. ⊠ *3109 Central Ave. NE, UNM/Nob Hill* ☎ *505/268–9250*
⊕ *www.yannisandopabar.com* ▭ *AE, D, MC, V* ✛ *F5.*

$$$ ✕ **Zinc Wine Bar & Bistro.** A snazzy spot in lower Nob Hill, fairly close
CONTEMPORARY   to UNM, Zinc captures the essence of a San Francisco neighborhood
bistro with its high ceilings, hardwood floors, and white tablecloths and
dark-wood straight-back café chairs. You can sample wine from the
long list or listen to live music downstairs in the Cellar Bar. Consider
the starter of crispy duck-confit eggrolls with curry-chile-lime dipping
sauce; or the main dish of seared scallops with wild-rice–cranberry pilaf
and a tarragon-crayfish beurre blanc. The kitchen uses organic ingredients whenever available. Don't miss the exceptional weekend brunch.
⊠ *3009 Central Ave. NE, UNM/Nob Hill* ☎ *505/254–9462* ⊕ *www.
zincabq.com* ▭ *AE, D, MC, V* ✛ *G5*

LOS RANCHOS/NORTH VALLEY

$ ✕ **Casa de Benavidez.** The fajitas at this sprawling local favorite with a
NEW MEXICAN   romantic patio are among the best in town, and the *carne adovada* is
faultless; the burger wrapped inside a sopaipilla is another specialty, as
are the chimichangas packed with beef. The charming restaurant occupies a late-19th-century Territorial-style house. ⊠ *8032 4th St. NW, Los*

Ranchos/North Valley ☎ *505/898–3311* ⊕ *www.casadebenavidez.com* ⊟ *AE, D, MC, V* ☉ *No dinner Sun* ✛ *D1.*

¢ ✕ **Mary & Tito's.** Locals do go on about who's got the best chile, red or
NEW MEXICAN green. What they don't dispute is that Mary & Tito's—an institution for decades, and run by the same family since it opened—is as tasty as it comes. It's casual, friendly, and the real deal. Grab a booth and try the rellenos or the enchiladas. A bonus: the chile is vegetarian, and the red is always sm-o-o-o-th. Although open for dinner nightly, the kitchen closes at 6 pm Monday through Thursday. ✉ *2711 4th St. NW, 2 blocks north of Menaul Blvd. NW, Los Ranchos/North Valley* ☎ *505/344–6266* ⌘ *Reservations not accepted* ⊟ *AE, D, MC, V* ☉ *Closed Sun* ✛ *D2*

$ ✕ **Sadie's.** One of the city's longtime favorites for simple-but-spicy,
NEW MEXICAN no-nonsense, New Mexican fare, Sadie's—remembered fondly by old-timers for the era when it made its home in the Lucky 66 bowling alley next door—now occupies a long, fortresslike adobe building. Specialties include carne adovada, spicy beef burritos, and chiles rellenos. The service is always prompt, though sometimes there's a wait for a table. While you're waiting, try one of the excellent margaritas. Sadie's salsa is locally renowned and available by the jar for takeout. ✉ *6230 4th St. NW, Los Ranchos/North Valley* ☎ *505/345–5339* ⊕ *www. sadiesofnewmexico.com* ⊟ *AE, D, MC, V* ✛ *D1*

$ ✕ **Sophia's Place.** Devotees can't get enough of the *muy buenos* berry
NEW MEXICAN pancakes with real maple syrup, breakfast burritos (with the *papas*— or potatoes—inside, so ask if you'd like them out instead), enchiladas sprinkled with *cotija* (a mild, crumbly cow's milk cheese), and just about anything the kitchen whips up. Dishes range from creative and generous salads and chipotle-chile bacon cheeseburgers to udon noodles and fish tacos. In Los Ranchos de Albuquerque, in the heart of the North Valley, Sophia's (named after the Alice Waters–trained chef-owner's daughter) is a simple neighborhood spot, yet one that people drive out of their way for—especially for the weekend brunch. Everything is fresh, often organic, prettily presented, and always made-to-order. ✉ *6313 4th St. NW, Los Ranchos/North Valley* ☎ *505/345–3935* ⌘ *Reservations not accepted* ⊟ *AE, D, MC, V* ☉ *No dinner Sun.* ✛ *D1.*

NORTHEAST HEIGHTS

$$$$ ✕ **Bien Shur.** The panoramic city and mountain views are an essential
AMERICAN part of this quietly refined restaurant on the ninth floor of the Sandia Casino complex, but Bien Shur also aspires to be one of the most sophisticated restaurants in the city. Alas, the service can be uneven at times, and although the food is usually on the mark, it's quite pricey for Albuquerque. You might start with a panfried crab cake with cilantro oil, saffron aioli, and tomato salsa. Among the several stellar entrées, skip the seafood and go right for the steaks and chops, such as buffalo tenderloin, or the prodigious 20-ounce porterhouse steak. ✉ *Sandia Resort & Casino, Tramway Rd. NE, east of I–25, Northeast Heights* ☎ *505/798–3700* ⊕ *www.sandiacasino.com* ⊟ *AE, D, MC, V* ☉ *Closed Sun. and Mon. No lunch* ✛ *E1.*

UPTOWN/EAST SIDE

$$$
ECLECTIC
Fodor's Choice
★

~~Closed~~

✕ **Jennifer James 101.** Helmed by and named for one of New Mexico's most respected chefs, this small Uptown eatery is known mostly by foodies, locals, and fans of Jennifer James' previous restaurants around town. The menu is limited, and reservations are a must, but once you take your seat in the simple, high-ceilinged dining room in an unassuming shopping center, you're in for a treat. The menu changes often and focuses on seasonal ingredients; perhaps an appetizer of salt-cured foie gras with mâche and a balsamic-pomegranate reduction, or a main dish featuring wild boar braised with red wine and rosemary and served with polenta, grilled radicchio, and Gorgonzola. There's also a carefully considered wine list that includes several surprisingly affordable, good bottles. ⊠ *4615 Menaul Blvd. NE, Uptown/East Side* ☎ *505/884–3860* ⊕ *http://web.me.com/jenniferjames101* ⌃ *Reservations essential* ☰ *AE, MC, V* ⊗ *No lunch Sun. and Mon.* ✣ *H2.*

¢
NEW MEXICAN

✕ **Los Cuates.** A short drive northeast of Nob Hill and UNM, Los Cuates (a three-location local minichain) doesn't get as much attention as some of the city's more touristy New Mexican restaurants, but the food here is reliable, and prepared with pure vegetable oil rather than lard, which is one reason it's never as greasy as at some competitors. The green-chile stew is vegetarian (unless you request meat). All the usual favorites are served here, but top picks include the roast-beef burrito covered with melted cheese, and the tostada *compuesta* (a corn tortilla stuffed with beef, beans, rice, potatoes, carne adovada, and *chile con queso*—chile cheese sauce). ⊠ *4901 Lomas Blvd. NE, Uptown/East Side* ☎ *505/255–5079* ⊕ *www.loscuatesrestaurants.com* ⌃ *Reservations not accepted* ☰ *AE, D, MC, V* ✣ *H4.*

¢
VIETNAMESE

✕ **Viet Taste.** Come here for another side of spicy hot. Excellent, authentic Vietnamese food is served up in this compact, modern, bamboo-accented restaurant. Ignore the fact that it's within one of Albuquerque's ubiquitous strip malls. Consider the popular *pho* (noodle soup) variations, order the tofu (or chicken or shrimp) spring rolls with tangy peanut sauce, dig into the spicy lemongrass with chicken, and all will be well. ⊠ *5721 Menaul Blvd. NE, Uptown/East Side* ☎ *505/888–0101* ☰ *AE, D, MC, V* ✣ *H2.*

WHERE TO STAY

With a few exceptions, Albuquerque's lodging options fall into two categories: modern chain hotels and motels, and distinctive and typically historic inns and B&Bs. You won't find many larger hotels that are independently owned, historic, or rife with personality, although Central Avenue—all across the city—is lined with fascinating old motor courts and motels from the 1930s through the '50s, many with original neon signs and quirky roadside architecture. Alas, nearly all of these are run-down and substandard; they should be avoided unless you're extremely adventurous and can't resist the super-low rates (often as little as $18 a night).

If you're seeking charm and history, try one of the many excellent inns and B&Bs, or the Andaluz and Parq Central hotels, which are both Downtown and quite new, but set inside distinctive historic buildings. Although the chain hotels may appear interchangeable, there are several that stand out, and many of these are described below. Two parts of the city with an excellent variety of economical, plain-Jane, franchise hotels (Hampton Inn, Comfort Inn, Courtyard Marriott, etc.) are the airport area and the north Interstate 25 corridor. Albuquerque's airport is convenient to attractions and Downtown, and the north Interstate 25 corridor offers easy access to sightseeing, dining, and Balloon Fiesta Park. Wherever you stay in Albuquerque, you can generally count on finding rates considerably lower than the national average, and much cheaper than those in Santa Fe.

WHAT IT COSTS					
	¢	$	$$	$$$	$$$$
Hotels	under $70	$70–$120	$121–$175	$176–$250	over $250

Prices are for two people in a standard double room in high season, excluding 12%–13% tax.

Use the coordinate (✛ A2) at the end of each listing to locate a site on the corresponding map.

OLD TOWN

$
HOTEL
  Best Western Rio Grande Inn. Although part of the Best Western chain, this contemporary four-story low-rise just off Interstate 40—a 10-minute walk from Old Town's plaza—has an attractive Southwestern design and furnishings, plus such modern touches as free Wi-Fi. The heavy, handcrafted wood furniture, tin sconces, and artwork in the rooms come from local suppliers and artisans. The quite decent Albuquerque Grill serves three meals daily. It's a good value. **Pros:** free shuttle to airport and around town within 1-mi radius; excellent value. **Cons:** it's a hike from the rear rooms to the front desk; a bit close to the interstate. ⊠ *1015 Rio Grande Blvd. NW, Old Town* ☎ *505/843–9500 or 800/959–4726* ⊕ *www.riograndeinn.com* ↩ *173 rooms* ⌂ *In-room: a/c, refrigerator, Wi-Fi. In-hotel: restaurant, room service, bar, pool, gym, laundry facilities, parking (free), some pets allowed* ⊟ *AE, D, DC, MC, V* ✛ *F4*

$$
BED & BREAKFAST
  Böttger Mansion of Old Town. Charles Böttger, a German immigrant, built this pink two-story mansion in 1912. The lacy, richly appointed rooms vary greatly in size and decor; some have four-poster beds, slate floors, claw-foot tubs, or pressed-tin ceilings. All have down comforters, fluffy pillows, and terry robes—and a few are said to be haunted by a friendly ghost or two. The Wine Cellar Suite, in the basement, can accommodate up to six guests and has a kitchenette. A grassy courtyard fronted by a patio provides an escape from the Old Town crowds. Breakfast might consist of stuffed French toast or perhaps burritos smothered in green chile, which you can also enjoy in your room. **Pros:** balloon, golf, and tour packages are available; very handy location to dining and

BEST BETS FOR ALBUQUERQUE LODGING

Fodor's offers a selective listing of quality lodging experiences in every price range, from the city's best budget beds to its most sophisticated luxury hotels. Here, we've compiled our top recommendations by price and experience. The very best properties—in other words, those that provide a particularly remarkable experience in their price range—are designated in the listings with the Fodor's Choice logo.

Fodor'sChoice ★

Andaluz $$$, 67

Downtown Historic Bed & Breakfasts of Albuquerque $$, 70

Hyatt Regency Tamaya $$$, 93

Los Poblanos Inn $$$, 73

Mauger Estate B&B Inn $$, 72

By Price

$

Chocolate Turtle B&B, 91

Cinnamon Morning B&B, 72

Holiday Inn Hotel & Suites Albuquerque Airport, 75

Hotel Blue, 71

Nativo Lodge Hotel, 73

Shaffer Hotel, 90

$$

Casas de Sueños, 67

Downtown Historic Bed & Breakfasts of Albuquerque, 70

Embassy Suites Hotel Albuquerque, 70

Hard Rock Hotel & Casino, 88

Hotel Albuquerque at Old Town, 67

Mauger Estate B&B Inn, 72

$$$

Andaluz, 67

High Feather Ranch, 98

Hotel Parq Central, 71

Hyatt Regency Tamaya, 93

Los Poblanos Inn, 73

Sandia Resort & Casino, 74

By Experience

BEST FOR KIDS

Best Western Rio Grande Inn $, 65

Embassy Suites Hotel Albuquerque $$, 70

Hard Rock Hotel & Casino $$, 88

Hyatt Regency Tamaya $$$, 93

Shaffer Hotel $, 90

ROMANTIC

Andaluz $$$, 67

Downtown Historic Bed & Breakfasts of Albuquerque $$, 70

High Feather Ranch $$$, 98

Hyatt Regency Tamaya $$$, 93

Los Poblanos Inn $$$, 73

Mauger Estate B&B Inn $$, 72

BEST SERVICE

Chocolate Turtle B&B $, 91

Cinnamon Morning B&B $, 72

Hyatt Regency Tamaya $$$, 93

Los Poblanos Inn $$$, 73

Sandia Resort & Casino $$$, 74

HISTORIC SIGNIFICANCE

Andaluz $$$, 67

Hotel Parq Central $$$, 71

Böttger Mansion of Old Town $$, 65

Mauger Estate B&B Inn $$, 72

Shaffer Hotel $, 90

SCENIC VIEWS

Albuquerque Marriott $$, 74

Elaine's, A Bed and Breakfast $$, 95

High Feather Ranch $$$, 98

Hyatt Regency Albuquerque $$$, 71

Hyatt Regency Tamaya $$$, 93

Sandia Resort & Casino $$$, 74

BEST-KEPT SECRET

Casas de Sueños $$, 67

High Feather Ranch $$$, 98

Hotel Parq Central $$$, 71

Mauger Estate B&B Inn $$, 72

Nativo Lodge Hotel $, 73

Shaffer Hotel $, 90

attractions. **Cons:** not for the floral-and-frilly phobic. ⊠ *110 San Felipe St. NW, Old Town* ☎ *505/243–3639 or 800/758–3639* ⊕ *www.bottger. com* ⇆ *7 rooms, 1 2-bedroom suite* ⚿ *In-room: a/c, kitchen (some), Wi-Fi. In-hotel: parking (paid)* ☐ *AE, MC, V* ❑ *BP* ⊹ *F5.*

\$\$

BED & BREAKFAST

▦ **Casas de Sueños.** This historic compound of 1930s- and '40s-era adobe casitas is perfect if you're seeking seclusion and quiet, yet seek proximity to museums, restaurants, and shops. Casas de Sueños (*sueños* means dreams in Spanish) is a few blocks south of Old Town Plaza, but on a peaceful residential street fringing the lush grounds of Albuquerque Country Club. The individually decorated units, which open onto a warren of courtyards and gardens, come in a variety of shapes and configurations. Typical features include Saltillo-tile floors, wood-burning kiva-style fireplaces, leather or upholstered armchairs, skylights, and contemporary Southwestern furnishings. Many rooms have large flat-screen TVs with DVD players and CD stereos, and some sleep as many as four adults. The full breakfast is served outside in the garden when the weather permits, and inside a lovely artists' studio at other times. **Pros:** charming and tucked away; some private patios. **Cons:** rooms vary greatly in amenities and configuration—some are more enchanting than others. ⊠ *310 Rio Grande Blvd. SW, on the south side of Central Ave., Old Town* ☎ *505/247–4560 or 800/665–7002* ⊕ *www.casasdesuenos. com* ⇆ *21 casitas* ⚿ *In-room: a/c, kitchen (some), DVD (some), Wi-Fi. In-hotel: parking (free)* ☐ *AE, MC, V* ❑ *BP* ⊹ *F5.*

\$\$

HOTEL

▦ **Hotel Albuquerque at Old Town.** This 11-story Southwestern-style hotel rises distinctly above Old Town's ancient structures. The large rooms have elegant, contemporary desert-color appointments, hand-wrought furnishings, and tile bathrooms; most rooms have a small balcony with no patio furniture but nice views. Cristobal's serves commendable Spanish-style steaks and seafood; Café Plazuela & Cantina offers more casual American and New Mexican food; and a fine flamenco guitarist entertains in the Q-Bar & Gallery Lounge. Spa treatments and facials are available. **Pros:** the high-ceiling, rustically furnished, Territorial-style lobby is a comfy place to hang out; hotel employs many eco-friendly practices. **Cons:** rather unattractive from the outside. ⊠ *800 Rio Grande Blvd. NW, Old Town* ☎ *505/843–6300 or 877/901–7666* ⊕ *www.hhandr.com/albuquerque* ⇆ *168 rooms, 20 suites* ⚿ *In-room: a/c, refrigerator (some), Wi-Fi. In-hotel: 2 restaurants, room service, bar, pool, gym, spa, parking (free)* ☐ *AE, D, DC, MC, V* ⊹ *F4.*

DOWNTOWN

\$\$\$

HOTEL

Fodor'sChoice

★

▦ **Andaluz.** Opened in 1939 by Conrad Hilton (who honeymooned here with Zsa Zsa Gabor), this glamorous 10-story hotel on the National Register of Historic Places was known as La Posada de Albuquerque until it was reinvented (and completely redone inside)—at a cost of \$30 million—as a high-end boutique hotel in 2009. Its new name, Andaluz, and its stunning decor reflect the Moroccan and Spanish-colonial influences of the original Hilton design. Its pursuit of Silver LEED certification reflects the hotel's commitment to eco-friendly practices. The restaurant's beautiful two-story lobby is a wonderful spot to soak up the building's rich ambience, perhaps before grabbing cocktails in the

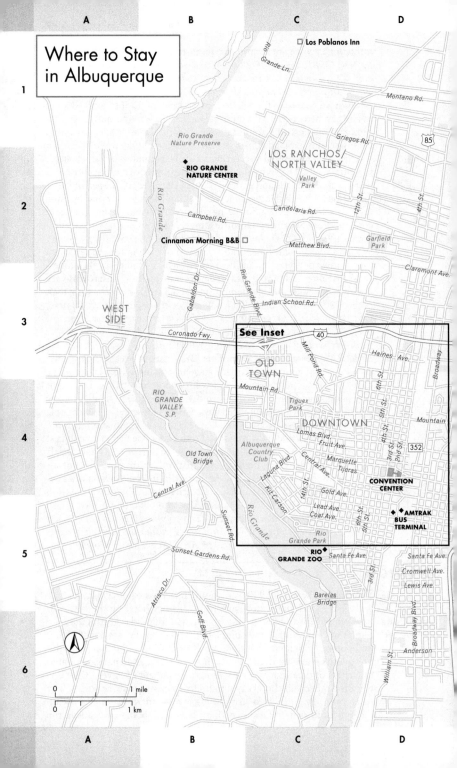

Where to Stay in Albuquerque

A B C D

1

□ Los Poblanos Inn

Rio Grande Ln.

Montano Rd.

Griegos Rd.

85

Rio Grande
Nature Preserve

◆ RIO GRANDE
NATURE CENTER

LOS RANCHOS/
NORTH VALLEY

Valley
Park

2

Campbell Rd.

Candelaria Rd.

12th St.

4th St.

Cinnamon Morning B&B □

Matthew Blvd.

Garfield
Park

Claremont Ave.

Rio Grande

Gabaldon Dr.

Rio Grande Blvd.

Indian School Rd.

3

WEST
SIDE

Coronado Fwy.

40

See Inset

Haines Ave.

Broadway

RIO
GRANDE
VALLEY
S.P.

OLD
TOWN

Mill Pond Rd.

Mountain Rd.

6th St.

5th St.

Tiguex
Park

DOWNTOWN

Mountain

4

Old Town
Bridge

Albuquerque
Country
Club

Lomas Blvd.

Fruit Ave.

4th St.

3rd St.

2nd St.

352

Central Ave.

Marquette

Laguna Blvd.

Central Ave.

Tijeras

CONVENTION
CENTER

Kit Carson

4th St.

Gold Ave.

Sunset Rd.

Rio Grande

Lead Ave.
Coat Ave.

6th St.

◆ ◆ AMTRAK
BUS
TERMINAL

5

Sunset Gardens Rd.

Rio
Grande Park

RIO ◆
GRANDE ZOO

Santa Fe Ave.

Santa Fe Ave.

3rd St.

Cromwell Ave.

Lewis Ave.

Atrisco Dr.

Goff Blvd.

Barelas
Bridge

Broadway Blvd.

William St.

Anderson

6

0   1 mile

0   1 km

A B C D

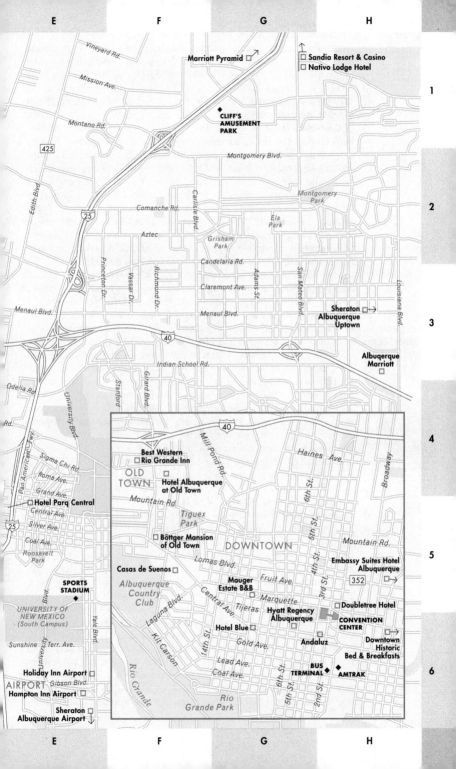

swank Ibiza bar or dinner in acclaimed Lucia restaurant. **Pros:** historic cachet aesthetic but with plenty of modern perks. **Cons:** priciest rooms in town. ⊠ *125 2nd St. NW, Downtown* ☎ *505/242–9090 or 800/777–5732* ⊕ *www.hotelandaluz.com* ↵ *107 rooms, 7 suites* ⟨ *In-room: a/c, Wi-Fi. In-hotel: restaurant, room service, bar, laundry service, Wi-Fi hotspot, parking (paid)* ☰ *AE, D, DC, MC, V* ✚ *H6*

$$
HOTEL

Doubletree Hotel. A two-story waterfall splashes down a marble backdrop in the sleek, contemporary lobby of this 15-story Downtown hotel, with attractive, pale-gold rooms that contain mid-20th-century-inspired furnishings and art—larger units have wet bars, sitting areas, and sofa beds. Popular with business travelers, the hotel offers some very attractive rates on weekends, when occupancy is often a bit higher. The restaurant at the foot of the waterfall is called, appropriately, La Cascada (The Cascade). **Pros:** Old Town shuttle service available; nicely updated rooms and amenities; free Wi-Fi. **Cons:** not all rooms have mountain views; not enough spaces in parking lot when hotel is full. ⊠ *201 Marquette Ave. NW, Downtown* ☎ *505/247–3344 or 800/222–8733* ⊕ *www.doubletree.com* ↵ *295 rooms* ⟨ *In-room: a/c, Internet. In-hotel: restaurant, room service, bar, pool, gym, laundry service, Wi-Fi hotspot, parking (paid)* ☰ *AE, D, DC, MC, V* ✚ *H5.*

$$
BED & BREAKFAST
Fodor's Choice
★

Downtown Historic Bed & Breakfasts of Albuquerque. Comprising a pair of grand early-20th-century homes as well as a private carriage house and one other cottage in the Huning Highland Historic District, this stunning property exudes romance. Rooms come in many shapes and sizes, from cozier and less-pricey units to spacious cottages with full kitchens and private exterior entrances. Antiques fill the rooms, which have hardwood floors, bathrobes, modern bathrooms, and free Wi-Fi. A lavish full breakfast is included, and the accommodations open onto neatly tended gardens. **Pros:** exquisite furnishings; intimate property but where guests have plenty of privacy and independence; central Downtown location. **Cons:** some my find the decor to be excessively antique. ⊠ *207 High St., Downtown* ☎ *505/842–0223 or 888/342–0223* ⊕ *www.albuquerquebedandbreakfasts.com* ↵ *8 rooms, 2 cottages* ⟨ *In-room: a/c, kitchen (some), refrigerator, Wi-Fi. In-hotel: parking (free)* ☰ *AE, D, MC, V* ✚ *H6.*

$$
HOTEL

Embassy Suites Hotel Albuquerque. This all-suites high-rise with a striking contemporary design sits on a bluff alongside Interstate 25, affording guests fabulous views of the Downtown skyline and vast desert mesas to the west, and the verdant Sandia Mountains to the east. Rooms are large and done in soothing Tuscan colors; the living areas have pull-out sleeper sofas, refrigerators, dining and work areas, microwaves, and coffeemakers. You'll also find two phones and two TVs in each suite. Included in the rates is a nightly reception with hors d'oeuvres and cocktails, and a full breakfast each morning. With so much living and sleeping space and a great location accessible to Downtown, Nob Hill, and the airport, this is a great option if you're staying in town for a while or traveling with a family. **Pros:** quiet but convenient location adjacent to Interstate 25 and just south of Interstate 40; congenial staff. **Cons:** suites attract families in addition to business travelers; the occasional child run rampant may not appeal to all. ⊠ *1000*

Woodward Pl. NE, Downtown ☎ *505/245–7100 or 800/362–2779*
⊕ *www.embassysuitesalbuquerque.com* ⇥ *261 suites* ⚷ *In-room: a/c,*
refrigerator, Wi-Fi. In-hotel: restaurant, bar, gym, spa, parking (free)
⊟ *AE, D, MC, V* ⑩ *BP* ⚓ *H5.*

$ ⊞ **Hotel Blue.** The reasonable rates here draw a party crowd, and the
HOTEL art deco–inspired rooms can pick up street noise as well; based on the
(fairly basic) services alone it would be a stretch to call this place hip or
boutique. Still, people rave about the beds and 40-inch flat-screen TVs,
and it is ideally located, especially for those with business Downtown. It
overlooks a small park, is a short stroll from Downtown's music clubs
and restaurants, and it's a short drive, bus ride, or 15-minute walk from
Old Town. In summer, a lively Saturday growers' market (including arts
vendors, music, and more) sets up in Robinson Park next door. **Pros:**
comfortable Tempur-Pedic beds; complimentary shuttle to the airport,
convention center, and Old Town from 7 am until 10 pm. **Cons:** this
part of Downtown can feel a little unsettling and desolate at night.
⊠ *717 Central Ave. NW, Downtown* ☎ *505/924–2400 or 877/878–*
4868 ⊕ *www.thehotelblue.com* ⇥ *125 rooms, 10 suites* ⚷ *In-room: a/c,*
refrigerators, Internet. In-hotel: bar, pool, gym, parking (free) ⊟ *AE,*
D, MC, V ⑩ *CP* ⚓ *G6.*

$$$ ⊞ **Hotel Parq Central.** One of the more imaginative—and handsomely
HOTEL executed—adaptations of a disused building into a fine hotel, the Parq
Central opened in late 2010 inside a striking three-story former hospi-
tal that dates to 1926. In the up-and-coming EDo neighborhood, the
hotel is just off I–25, a short drive west of UNM and Nob Hill. The
designers had fun with this project, creating the Apothecary rooftop
bar in which vintage 1920s cocktails are served, and utilizing many of
the building's original features, from clay tiles to original windows. The
spacious rooms have high-quality Fretté linens, terry robes, 37-inch
LCD flat-screen TVs, iPod consoles, and free Wi-Fi. In-room mas-
sage services can be arranged by the solicitous staff. **Pros:** wonder-
fully historic building; beautifully designed rooms; hip clientele. **Cons:**
within earshot of busy I–25; the building's medical past may creep
some people out. ⊠ *806 Central Ave. SE, Downtown* ☎ *505/242–0040*
⊕ *www.hotelparqcentral.com* ⇥ *56 rooms, 18 suites* ⚷ *In-room: a/c,*
safe, refrigerator, Wi-Fi. In-hotel: restaurant, bar, gym, laundry service,
parking (free), some pets allowed ⊟ *AE, D, MC, V* ⚓ *E5.*

$$$ ⊞ **Hyatt Regency Albuquerque.** Adjacent to the Albuquerque Convention
HOTEL Center, this upscale high-rise comprises a pair of soaring, desert-color
towers that figure prominently in the city's skyline. The gleaming art
deco–inspired interior is refined and not overbearing. The contemporary
rooms, done in mauve, burgundy, and tan, combine Southwestern style
with all the amenities you'd expect of a high-caliber business-oriented
hotel, including Wi-Fi, iPod docking stations, flat-screen TVs, plush
pillow-top mattresses, and fluffy bathrobes. McGrath's Bar and Grill
serves steaks, chops, chicken, and seafood (and breakfast to the power
crowd), and there's also a Starbucks on-site. Bigwigs of all stripes stay
in the penthouse. **Pros:** easy walking distance from the KiMo Theatre and Downtown's art galleries and restaurants, and a quick cab
(or bus) ride elsewhere; the views, lap pool, and well-equipped 24/7

fitness center. **Cons:** until you get your bearings the layout can seem somewhat mazelike; no views on lower floors. ⊠ *330 Tijeras Ave. NW, Downtown* ☎ *505/842–1234 or 800/233–1234* ⊕ *www.albuquerque. hyatt.com* ↩ *395 rooms, 14 suites* ♿ *In-room: a/c, Wi-Fi. In-hotel: restaurant, bar, pool, gym, laundry service, parking (paid)* ⊟ *AE, D, DC, MC, V* ✛ *G6.*

$$

BED & BREAKFAST

Fodor's Choice

★

Mauger Estate B&B Inn. This 1897 Queen Anne–style mansion—on the National Register of Historic Places—was the first home in Albuquerque to have electricity. While the mercantile Mauger (pronounced *major*) family is long gone (and the electricity long since upgraded, along with a detailed restoration throughout), this well-run B&B has retained many of the building's original architectural elements, including oval windows with beveled and "feather-pattern" glass, hardwood floors, high ceilings, a redbrick exterior, and a front veranda. Rooms—clean and contemporary with a restrained Victorian touch (seen best in the dark woods)—have refrigerators and baskets stocked with munchies, triple-sheeted beds with soft feather duvets, irons and boards, and fresh flowers. There's also a two-bedroom, two-bathroom town house next door. Guests have access to a full-service health club a few blocks away. **Pros:** pleasant common room, with a library and a late-afternoon cookies-and-wine spread; responsive and informed innkeeper; good breakfasts, which they will pack to go on request. **Cons:** at night, on the western fringe of Downtown, it can feel a bit sketchy for walking, but parking is secure. ⊠ *701 Roma Ave. NW, Downtown* ☎ *505/242–8755 or 800/719–9189* ⊕ *www.maugerbb.com* ↩ *8 rooms, 1 2-bedroom town house* ♿ *In-room: a/c, refrigerator, Wi-Fi. In-hotel: parking (free), some pets allowed* ⊟ *AE, D, MC, V* ⦾ *BP* ✛ *G5.*

LOS RANCHOS/NORTH VALLEY

$

BED & BREAKFAST

Cinnamon Morning B&B. A private, beautifully maintained, pet-friendly compound set back from the road and a 10-minute drive north of Old Town, Cinnamon Morning is just south of Rio Grande Nature Center State Park and a perfect roost if you want to be close to the city's wineries and the launching areas used by most hot-air-ballooning companies. Three rooms are in the main house, a richly furnished adobe home with colorful decorations and a lush garden patio. There's also a secluded two-bedroom guesthouse with a bath, full kitchen, private entrance, living room, and fireplace; and a colorfully painted one-bedroom casita with a private patio, Mexican-style furnishings, a viga ceiling, and a living room with a sleeper sofa. The full breakfasts here are filling and delicious, served by a roaring fire in winter or in the courtyard in summer. **Pros:** hosts will gladly help with travel ideas and planning. **Cons:** cancellations must be made 14 days ahead; you need a car to get around town from here. ⊠ *2700 Rio Grande Blvd. NW, Los Ranchos/North Valley* ☎ *505/345–3541 or 800/214–9481* ⊕ *www.cinnamonmorning. com* ↩ *3 rooms, 1 casita, 1 guesthouse* ♿ *In-room: kitchen (some), Wi-Fi. In-hotel: parking (free), some pets allowed* ⊟ *AE, D, MC, V* ⦾ *BP* ✛ *C2.*

$$$ **Los Poblanos Inn.** Designed by acclaimed architect John Gaw Meem,
INN this rambling, historic inn lies outside of Albuquerque's sprawl, on 25
Fodor'sChoice acres of organic farm fields, lavender plantings, and gardens in Los
★ Ranchos on the town's north side, near the Rio Grande and just across
the street from Anderson Valley Vineyards—with all the greenery and
the quiet pace of life here, you'd never know you're in the desert, or
in the middle of a large city. You reach the inn via a spectacular tree-
lined lane. Accommodations, including 12 new rooms added in 2010,
contain folk paintings, painted viga ceilings, and high-quality linens.
Rooms also contain bath products made on-site, including lavender
soap and oils; all have kiva fireplaces, too. The property also includes
the 15,000-square-foot La Quinta Cultural Center, with dramatic
fresco by Peter Hurd. There's also a library with beautiful artwork
and a farm shop selling gifts and gourmet goods, and rates include
a stellar breakfast using organic eggs and produce (also available to
nonguests by reservation). **Pros:** pastoral setting amid lovely lavender
fields; superb breakfast. **Cons:** 10-minute drive from Old Town and
Downtown. ⊠ *4803 Rio Grande Blvd. NW, Los Ranchos/North Val-
ley* ☎ *505/344–9297 or 866/344–9297* ⊕ *www.lospoblanos.com* ⤳ *12
rooms, 8 suites, 2 guesthouses* ⚹ *In-room: a/c, kitchen (some), refrig-
erator (some), DVD (some), Wi-Fi. In-hotel: gym, pool, parking (free)*
⊟ *AE, MC, V* ⦿ *BP* ⊹ *C1.*

NORTHEAST HEIGHTS

$$ **Marriott Pyramid.** This curious ziggurat-shaped 10-story building fits
HOTEL in nicely with the other examples of postmodern architecture that have
sprung up in northern Albuquerque. It's among the more upscale chain
hotels in the north Interstate 25 corridor, and it's an excellent base for
exploring Northeast Heights and the North Valley—plus it's a bit closer
to Santa Fe than Downtown or airport hotels. Rooms have sponge-
painted walls, dapper country-French decor, large flat-screen TVs, and
open onto a soaring atrium lobby. Perks include evening turndown
service and newspapers delivered to the room each morning. **Pros:** easy
access to Interstate 25. **Cons:** the lobby layout is a bit confusing; setting is by a busy interstate with a fairly bland view; a bit of a drive
from Downtown. ⊠ *5151 San Francisco Rd. NE, Northeast Heights*
☎ *505/821–3333 or 800/466–8356* ⊕ *www.albuquerquemarriottnorth.
com* ⤳ *248 rooms, 54 suites* ⚹ *In-room: a/c, refrigerator, Wi-Fi. In-
hotel: restaurant, room service, bar, pool, gym, laundry facilities, laundry service, parking (free)* ⊟ *AE, D, DC, MC, V* ⊹ *G1.*

$ **Nativo Lodge Hotel.** Although it's priced similarly to a number of
HOTEL generic midrange chain properties on the north side, this five-story
property has more character than most, especially in the expansive
public areas, bar, and restaurant, which have an attractive Southwestern
motif that includes hand-carved panels depicting symbols from Native
American lore and river-rock walls. Rooms at this eco-conscious property have wing chairs, work desks, Wi-Fi, and dual-line phones. The
hotel is just off Interstate 25, but set back far enough to avoid highway noise; several movie theaters and a bounty of mostly chain restaurants are nearby. **Pros:** personable service; relaxing atmosphere. **Cons:**

if your primary business is Downtown, this is a bit far north. ⊠ *6000 Pan American Freeway NE, Northeast Heights* ☎ *505/798–4300 or 888/628–4861* ⊕ *www.hhandr.com/nativo.php* ↩ *146 rooms, 2 suites* △ *In-room: a/c, refrigerator (some), Wi-Fi. In-hotel: restaurant, room service, bar, pool, gym, laundry facilities, parking (free), some pets allowed* ⊟ *AE, D, DC, MC, V* ⊹ *H1.*

$$$ 📷 **Sandia Resort & Casino.** On a bluff with sweeping views of the San-

RESORT   dia Mountains and Rio Grande Valley, this seven-story casino-resort sets a standard for luxury in Albuquerque; unfortunately the service here doesn't always quite match the promise. Nevertheless, appoint-ments like 32-inch plasma TVs, handcrafted wooden furniture, lou-vered wooden blinds, and muted, natural-color palettes lend elegance to the spacious rooms. The 700-acre grounds, which are in the Far Northeast Heights, just across Interstate 25 from Balloon Fiesta Park, ensure privacy and quiet and include a superb golf course and an amphi-theater that hosts top-of-the-line music and comedy acts. The Green Reed Spa offers a wide range of treatments, many using local clay and plants. One of the city's best restaurants, Bien Shur, occupies the casino's top floor, and there are three other places to eat on-site. The casino is open 24 hours. **Pros:** 24/7 room service; lots to see and do on the grounds. **Cons:** smoking is allowed on premises; pool not open year-round. ⊠ *Tramway Rd. NE, just east of I–25Northeast Heights* ☎ *505/796–7500 or 800/526–9366* ⊕ *www.sandiacasino.com* ↩ *198 rooms, 30 suites* △ *In-room: Wi-Fi. In-hotel: 4 restaurants, room ser-vice, bars, golf course, pool, gym, spa, laundry service, parking (free)* ⊟ *AE, D, DC, MC, V* ⊹ *H1.*

UPTOWN/EAST SIDE

$$ 📷 **Albuquerque Marriott.** This 17-story, upscale, Uptown property draws

HOTEL   a mix of business and leisure travelers; it's close to three shopping malls and not too far from Nob Hill. Kachina dolls, Native American pot-tery, and other regional artworks decorate the elegant public areas. The rooms are traditional American, with walk-in closets, 32-inch LCD TVs, armoires, and crystal lamps, and a few Southwestern accents. Rooms—which have floor-to-ceiling windows—enjoy staggering views (the higher the floor the better), either of Sandias to the east or the vast mesas to the west. Cielo Sandia specializes in steaks and contemporary New Mexican fare. **Pros:** cozy lobby lounge; close to upscale shopping and dining. **Cons:** a little far from Downtown; a large property that can feel a bit impersonal. ⊠ *2101 Louisiana Blvd. NE, Uptown/East Side* ☎ *505/881–6800 or 800/228–9290* ⊕ *www.marriott.com/abqnm* ↩ *405 rooms, 6 suites* △ *In-room: a/c, refrigerator, Internet. In-hotel: restaurant, room service, bar, pool, gym, laundry facilities, laundry service, parking (free)* ⊟ *AE, D, DC, MC, V* ⊹ *H3*

$$ 📷 **Sheraton Albuquerque Uptown.** Within walking distance of two noted

HOTEL   shopping malls, this 2008-renovated property meets the consistent Sheraton standard with a pleasant lobby with a cozy bar area. Earthy and muted reds, oranges, and sand-shaded colors accent the lobby and functional but ample rooms, whose nicer touches include a second sink outside the bathroom, 37-inch LCD TVs, comfy mattresses, and

2

bathrobes. **Pros:** close to Northeast Heights attractions and with easy interstate (and shopping) access. **Cons:** at a busy intersection; a bit far from Downtown. ☒ *2600 Louisiana Blvd. NE, Uptown* ☎ *505/881–0000 or 866/716–8134* ⊕ *www.sheratonabq.com* ⌑ *295 rooms* ⌂ *In-room: a/c, refrigerator, Wi-Fi. In-hotel: 2 restaurants, room service, bar, pool, gym, parking (free)* ▤ *AE, D, DC, MC, V* ✛ *H3.*

CAMPING

¢ ⛺ **Albuquerque Central KOA.** At town's edge, in the foothills of the Sandia Mountains, this well-equipped campground has expansive views, a dog run, and Wi-Fi, but only a few trees. Reservations are essential during Balloon Fiesta in October. ☒ *12400 Skyline NE, Exit 166 off I-40, Uptown/East Side* ☎ *505/296–2729 or 800/562–7781* ⊕ *www.koakampgrounds.com* ⌂ *Flush toilets, full hookups, partial hookups (electric and water), dump station, drinking water, guest laundry, showers, fire grates, grills, picnic tables, electricity, public telephone, general store, service station, play area, swimming (pool)* ⌑ *206 sites, 100 with full hookups* ▤ *AE, D, MC, V.*

AIRPORT

$ 🏨 **Hampton Inn Airport.** One of the better midprice options near the airport, the Hampton Inn can be counted on for clean, updated rooms with plenty of perks (free Wi-Fi, a pool, on-the-run breakfast bags to take with you to the airport or wherever you're off to that day). **Pros:** easy in, easy out. **Cons:** though convenient, neighborhood isn't especially scenic or pleasant. ☒ *2231 Yale Blvd. SE, Airport* ☎ *505/246–2255 or 800/426–7866* ⊕ *www.hamptoninn.com* ⌑ *62 rooms, 9 suites* ⌂ *In-room: a/c, Wi-Fi. In-hotel: restaurant, bar, pool, gym, laundry facilities, parking (free)* ▤ *AE, D, DC, MC, V* ✛ *E6.*

$ 🏨 **Holiday Inn Hotel & Suites Albuquerque Airport.** Just west of the airport, this upscale, four-story hotel sits high on a bluff, affording nice views of Downtown and the western mesa as well as the Sandia Mountains. Some suites have whirlpool tubs. The indoor pool and a small, 24/7 fitness room, along with a 24-hour business center, make this a favorite with business travelers. **Pros:** work areas are well lit, a plus for the business traveler. **Cons:** bland neighborhood—you'll need to drive or take cab to get to Downtown or Nob Hill. ☒ *1501 Sunport Pl. SE, Airport* ☎ *505/944–2255 or 800/465–4329* ⊕ *www.holidayinnabq.com* ⌑ *110 rooms, 20 suites* ⌂ *In-room: a/c, Wi-Fi. In-hotel: a/c, restaurant, room service, bar, pool, gym, laundry facilities, parking (free)* ▤ *AE, D, DC, MC, V* ✛ *E6.*

$$ 🏨 **Sheraton Albuquerque Airport Hotel.** Only 350 yards from the airport, this 2010-renovated 15-story hotel sits up high on a mesa with vast views of the Sandia Mountains to the east and Downtown Albuquerque to the northwest. It's handy being so close to the terminal, and the Southwest-accented rooms have cushy Sheraton Sweet Sleeper beds, large work desks, Wi-Fi, and coffeemakers. Rojo Grill ranks among the better hotel restaurants in town. Ask for a room on an upper floor for the best view. **Pros:** short walk from airport; sleek, contemporary room decor. **Cons:** bland neighborhood—you'll need to drive or take

cab to get Downtown or to Nob Hill. ⊠ *2910 Yale Blvd. SE, Airport* ☎ *505/843–7000 or 800/325–3535* ⊕ *www.starwoodhotels.com* ⬅ *276 rooms, 2 suites* ⏶ *In-room: a/c, Wi-Fi. In-hotel: restaurant, room service, bar, pool, gym, parking (free), some pets allowed (paid)* ⊟ *AE, D, DC, MC, V* ⊕ *E6.*

NIGHTLIFE AND THE ARTS

For the 411 on arts and nightlife, consult the "Venue" section of the Sunday edition of the *Albuquerque Journal* (⊕ *www.abqjournal.com*), the freebie weekly *Alibi* (⊕ *www.alibi.com*), and the Arts Alliance's inclusive Arts & Cultural Calendar (⊕ *www.abqarts.org*). For highlights on some of the best music programming in town, go to ⊕ *http://ampconcerts.org.*

NIGHTLIFE

BARS AND LOUNGES

Atomic Cantina (⊠ *315 Gold Ave. SW, Downtown* ☎ *505/242–2200* ⊕ *www.atomiccantina.com*), a funky-hip Downtown lounge popular for its cool juke box and extensive happy hours, draws a mix of students, yuppies, and music fans. Many nights there's live music, from punk to rockabilly to trance.

Like its neighbor, Atomic Cantina, **Burt's Tiki Lounge** (⊠ *313 Gold Ave. SW, Downtown* ☎ *505/247–2878* ⊕ *www.burtstikilounge.com*) is a place to mingle with unpretentious locals.

With more than 20 beers on tap and an airy patio out back, **Copper Lounge** (⊠ *1504 Central Ave. SE, UNM/Nob Hill* ☎ *505/242–7490* ⊕ *www.thecopperlounge.com*) is a friendly neighborhood bar near UNM. It's a favorite of students, artists, and workers from nearby Downtown looking to relax after work.

Albuquerque's sizable gay and lesbian community rejoiced with the 2010 opening of **Effex** (⊠ *100 5th St. NW, UNM/Nob Hill* ☎ *505/842–8870*) an impressive, centrally located, two-level nightclub with a huge rooftop bar and an even larger downstairs dance floor.

Graham Central Station (⊠ *4770 Montgomery Blvd. NE, Northeast Heights* ☎ *505/883–3041* ⊕ *www.grahamcentralstationalbuquerque. com*), part of a rowdy regional chain of massive nightclubs, consists of four distinct bars under one roof: country-western, rock, dance, and Latin. It's open Wednesday through Saturday.

Fodor's Choice ★ Distinctive craft brews like hoppy Imperial Red and rich Oatmeal Stout draw fans of artisan beer to Downtown's **Marble Brewery** (⊠ *111 Marble Ave. NW, Downtown* ☎ *505/243–2739* ⊕ *www.marblebrewery.com*). The elegant tasting room and pub, with an expansive outdoor patio, contains a beautiful 40-foot bar and serves tasty apps and sandwiches—there's live music some evenings, and the owners have opened a taproom on the Plaza in Santa Fe, too.

O'Niell's Pub (⊠ *4310 Central Ave. SE, UNM/Nob Hill* ☎ *505/256–0564*) occupies a handsome space on the eastern edge of Nob Hill, where it serves good Mexican and American comfort food and presents jazz, bebop, and other music. The expansive patio is perfect for afternoon beer and snacks.

CASINOS

If you love to gamble, the area surrounding Albuquerque has a surfeit of options, including Santa Ana, San Felipe, Isleta, Laguna, and Acoma pueblos. Sandia is the one resort that's right within city limits.

Sandia Resort & Casino (⊠ *Tramway Rd. NE at I–25, Northeast Heights* ☎ *505/796–7500 or 800/526–9366* ⊕ *www.sandiacasino.com*) is a light, open, airy resort with an enormous gaming area brightened by soaring ceilings and big windows. In addition to 2,100 slot machines, you'll find craps, blackjack, mini baccarat, and several versions of poker. The 4,200-seat casino amphitheater hosts rock-circuit stalwarts such as the B-52s, and has hosted B.B. King, Kenny Rogers, Chicago, the occasional big-name comedian, and other acts.

LIVE MUSIC

For a city its size, Albuquerque has a rich and varied music scene—and at reasonable prices to boot. You can find world-class world-music festivals like ¡Globalquerque! and the NM Jazz Festival, Norteño roots music, heartstring-tearing country, blues, folk, and the latest rock permutations—and all manner of venues in which to hear (or dance to) them. There's even room for the big-arena warhorses, who mostly play the casinos these days.

¡Globalquerque! (⊕ *www.globalquerque.com*), a two-day world-music festival held at the National Hispanic Cultural Center, has been running annually in late September since 2005, and the acts and auxiliary programming just keep getting better. Festival producer AMP Concerts is also the organization that lures acts like David Byrne and the Cowboy Junkies to intimate Downtown venues.

The 15,000-seat **Hard Rock Pavilion** (⊠ *5601 University Blvd. SE, Airport* ☎ *505/452–5100* ⊕ *www.hardrockpavilion.com*) amphitheater attracts big-name acts such as Green Day, Nine Inch Nails, Cher, and Rhianna. Formerly known as Journal Pavilion, the venue was expanded and rebranded in 2010 by the new Hard Rock Resort, 7 mi south on Isleta Pueblo.

Outpost Performance Space (⊠ *210 Yale Blvd. SE, UNM/Nob Hill* ☎ *505/268–0044* ⊕ *www.outpostspace.org*) programs an inspired, eclectic slate, from local *nuevo*-folk to techno, jazz, and traveling East Indian ethnic. Some big names—especially in the jazz world—show up at this special small venue.

THE ARTS

Albuquerque has a remarkable wealth of local talent, but it also draws a surprising number of world-class stage performers from just about every discipline imaginable. Check the listings mentioned at the introduction to this section for everything from poetry readings, impromptu chamber music recitals, folk, jazz, and blues festivals, and formal symphony performances to film festivals, Flamenco Internacional, and theater.

MUSIC

The well-respected **New Mexico Symphony Orchestra** (☎ *505/881–8999 or 800/251–6676* ⊕ *www.nmso.org*) plays pops, Beethoven, and, at Christmas, Handel's *Messiah*. Most performances are at 2,000-seat Popejoy Hall.

Popejoy Hall (✉ *University of New Mexico Center for the Arts, North of Central Ave. entrance opposite Cornell Dr. SE, UNM/Nob Hill* ☎ *505/925–5858 or 877/664–8661* ⊕ *www.popejoyhall.com*) presents concerts, from rock and pop to classical, plus comedy acts, lectures, and national tours of Broadway shows. UNM's Keller Hall, also in the Center for the Arts, is a small venue with fine acoustics, a perfect home for the university's excellent chamber music program.

THEATER

Albuquerque Little Theatre (✉ *224 San Pasquale Ave. SW, Old Town* ☎ *505/242–4750* ⊕ *www.albuquerquelittletheatre.org*) is a nonprofit community troupe that's been going strong since 1930. Its staff of professionals teams up with local volunteer talent to produce comedies, dramas, musicals, and mysteries. The company theater, across the street from Old Town, was built in 1936 and designed by John Gaw Meem. It contains an art gallery, a large lobby, and a cocktail lounge.

Fodor's Choice
★
The stunning **KiMo Theatre** (✉ *423 Central Ave. NW, Downtown* ☎ *505/768–3544* ⊕ *www.cabq.gov/kimo*), an extravagantly ornamented 650-seat Pueblo Deco movie palace, is one of the best places in town to see anything. Jazz, dance—everything from traveling road shows to local song-and-dance acts—might turn up here. Former Albuquerque resident Vivian Vance of *I Love Lucy* fame once performed on the stage; today you're more likely to see Wilco or a film-festival screening.

While Popejoy Hall draws them in with huge Broadway touring shows, UNM's **Rodey Theater** (✉ *North of Central Ave. entrance opposite Cornell Dr. SE, UNM/Nob Hill* ☎ *505//925–5858 or 877/664–8661* ⊕ *www.unmtickets.com*), a smaller, 400-seat house in the same complex, stages experimental and niche works throughout the year, including student and professional plays and dance performances such as the acclaimed annual Summerfest Festival of New Plays during July and the June Flamenco Festival.

The **Teatro Nuevo México** (✉ *107 Bryn Mawr Dr. SE, UNM/Nob Hill* ☎ *505/362–6567* ⊕ *www.teatronuevomexico.com*) is dedicated to presenting works created by Latino artists. In addition to plays by the likes of Federico García Lorca and Nilo Cruz, notable in their production roster is a revival of the Spanish operetta form known as zarzuela. These crowd-pleasing pieces may be comedies or drama, and are presented in collaboration with NHCC and the New Mexico Symphony Orchestra.

In January and February, theater fans of the fresh and new flock to the Revolutions International Theatre Festival, presented by the **Tricklock Company** (✉ *1705 Mesa Vista Dr. NE, UNM/Nob Hill* ☎ *505/254–8393* ⊕ *www.tricklock.com*). Recognized internationally, Tricklock's productions tour regularly and emphasize works that take it—and the audience—to the edge of theatrical possibility.

SHOPPING

Albuquerque's shopping strengths include a handful of cool retail districts, such as Nob Hill, Old Town, and the rapidly gentrifying Downtown. These are good neighborhoods for galleries, antiques, and home-furnishing shops, bookstores, and offbeat gift shops. Otherwise, the city is mostly the domain of both strip and indoor malls, mostly filled with ubiquitous chain shops, although you can find some worthwhile independent shops even there.

SHOPPING NEIGHBORHOODS AND MALLS

The **Uptown** (✉ *Louisiana Blvd. NE, between I–40 and Menaul Blvd. NE, Uptown/East Side*) neighborhood is Albuquerque's hub of chains and mall shopping. The older traditional mall is Coronado (at Louisiana Blvd. NE and Menaul Blvd. NE), which has a big Barnes & Noble and a new Sephora. New and upscale ABQ Uptown is an attractive outdoor village containing an Apple Store, Borders, Coldwater Creek, Lucky Brand Jeans, and Williams-Sonoma.

On the far northwest outskirts of town, **Cottonwood Mall** (✉ *10000 Coors Blvd. NW at Coors Bypass, West Side* ☎ *505/899–7467* ⊕ *www. simon.com/mall/?id=214*) is anchored by Dillard's, Macy's, JCPenney, and Sears, and has about 135 midrange to upscale shops, including Williams-Sonoma, Aveda, Cache, and Abercrombie & Fitch. There are a dozen restaurants and food stalls, plus a 14-screen theater.

Albuquerque's **Downtown** (✉ *Central and Gold Aves. from 1st to 10th Sts., Downtown*) has had its highs and lows, but local developers are only renting to independent businesses in an effort to keep Downtown from turning into a collection of chain outlets. Stroll along Central and Gold avenues (and neighboring blocks) to admire avant-garde galleries, cool cafés, and curious boutiques.

Fodor'sChoice   Funky **Nob Hill** (✉ *Central Ave. from Girard Blvd. to Washington St., UNM/Nob Hill*), just east of the University of New Mexico and anchored by old Route 66, pulses with colorful storefronts and kitschy signs. At night, neon-lighted boutiques, galleries, and performing-arts spaces encourage foot traffic. Many of the best shops are clustered inside or on the blocks near Nob Hill Business Center, an art deco structure containing several intriguing businesses and La Montañita Natural Foods Co-op, an excellent spot for a snack. There are also branches of the popular clothing chains Urban Outfitters and Buffalo Exchange.

Old Town (✉ *Central Ave. and Rio Grande Blvd., Old Town*) has the city's largest concentration of one-of-a-kind retail shops, selling clothing, home accessories, Native American art, and Mexican imports—and the predictable schlock targeted at tourists.

ART GALLERIES

In addition to Tamarind Institute and Jonson Gallery, both at UNM (⇨ *UNM/Nob Hill section in Exploring Albuquerque, above*), Albuquerque has a solid and growing gallery scene. For comprehensive gallery listings, pick up a copy of the free annual *Collector's Guide* (⊕ *www.collectorsguide.com*); for current shows and ArtsCrawl schedules, look up the Arts & Cultural Calendar online (⊕ *www.abqarts.org*).

516 Arts (⊠ *516 Central Ave. SW, Downtown* ☎ *505/242–1445* ⊕ *www.516arts.org*) holds a special place in the Duke City's art world. They offer world-class contemporary art in changing shows that often cross media boundaries. Exhibits mine the work of local and national artists, and are as likely to speak to issues as they are to offer a powerfully appealing visual presence.

DSG (⊠ *510 14th St. SW, Old Town* ☎ *505/266–7751 or 800/474–7751* ⊕ *www.dsg-art.com*), owned by John Cacciatore, handles works of paint, tapestry, sculpture, and photography by leading regional artists, including Frank McCulloch, Carol Hoy, Leo Neufeld, Larry Bell, Angus Macpherson, Jim Bagley, Nancy Kozikowski, and photographer Nathan Small.

Harwood Art Center (⊠ *1114 7th St. NW, off Mountain Rd., Old Town* ☎ *505/242–6367* ⊕ *www.harwoodartcenter.org*), on the fringe of Downtown and Old Town in the Sawmill/Wells Park neighborhood, is a remarkable resource for its huge roster of community-oriented art classes, and a gallery in its own right. Shows—predominantly of New Mexico–based artists working in nontraditional forms—take place in their historic brick school building and change monthly.

Mariposa Gallery (⊠ *3500 Central Ave. SE, UNM/Nob Hill* ☎ *505/268–6828* ⊕ *www.mariposa-gallery.com*) sells contemporary fine crafts, including jewelry, sculptural glass, works in mixed media and clay, and fiber arts. The changing exhibits focus on upcoming artists; its buyer's sharp eyes can result in real finds for the serious browser.

A 2,000-square-foot space specializing in works by some of the state's most acclaimed current artists, **Matrix Fine Art** (⊠ *3812 Central Ave. SE, UNM/Nob Hill* ☎ *505/268–8952* ⊕ *www.matrixfineart.com*) carries an impressive collection of paintings and photography.

★ **Weyrich Gallery** (⊠ *2935–D Louisiana Blvd. NE, Uptown/East Side* ☎ *505/883–7410* ⊕ *www.weyrichgallery.com*) carries distinctive jewelry, fine art, Japanese tea bowls, woodblocks, hand-colored photography, and other largely Asian-inspired pieces.

SPECIALTY STORES

ANTIQUES

Classic Century Square Antique Mall (⊠ *4516 Central Ave. SE, UNM/Nob Hill* ☎ *505/265–3161*) is a three-story emporium of collectibles and antiques. The emphasis is on memorabilia from the early 1880s to the 1950s. (When the set designers for the television miniseries *Lonesome Dove* needed props, they came here.) Items for sale include art deco and art nouveau objects, retro-cool '50s designs, Depression-era glass, Native American goods, quilts and linens, vintage clothes, and Western memorabilia.

Cowboys & Indians (✉ *4000 Central Ave. SE, UNM/Nob Hill* ☎ *505/255–4054* ⊕ *www.cowboysandindiansnm.com*) carries Native American and cowboy art and artifacts.

BOOKS

One of the last of the great independents, **Bookworks** (✉ *4022 Rio Grande Blvd. NW, Los Ranchos/North Valley* ☎ *505/344–8139* ⊕ *www.bkwrks.com*), maintains an eclectic stock of regional coffee-table books, a well-culled selection of modern fiction and nonfiction, architecture and design titles, and a (small) playground's worth of kids' books. Regular signings and readings draw some very big guns to this tiny treasure.

Massive **Page One** (✉ *11018 Montgomery Blvd. NE, Northeast Heights* ☎ *505/294–2026* ⊕ *www.page1book.com*), arguably the best bookstore in Albuquerque, specializes in technical and professional titles, maps, globes, children's titles, and 150 out-of-state and foreign newspapers. Book signings, poetry readings, and children's events are frequently scheduled.

GIFTS, FOOD, AND TOYS

Beeps (✉ *Nob Hill Shopping Center, 3500 Central Ave. SE, UNM/Nob Hill* ☎ *505/262–1900*), a Nob Hill favorite, carries cards, T-shirts, and amusing, if bawdy, novelties.

Candy Lady (✉ *Mountain Rd. at Rio Grande Blvd., Old Town* ☎ *505/224–9837 or 800/214–7731* ⊕ *www.thecandylady.com*) is known as much for its scandalous adult novelty candies as for its tasty red- and green-chile brittle, plus the usual fudge, chocolates, piñon caramels, and candies. A small room, to the right as you enter, displays the "adult" candy.

La Casita de Kaleidoscopes (✉ *Poco A Poco Patio, 326–D San Felipe St. NW, Old Town* ☎ *505/247–4242* ⊕ *www.casitascopes.com*) carries both contemporary and vintage kaleidoscopes of all styles, by more than 80 top artists in the field.

Fodor's Choice ★ **Los Poblanos Farm Shop** (*4803 Rio Grande Blvd. NW, Los Ranchos/North Valley* ☎ *505/344–9297 or 866/344–9297* ⊕ *www.lospoblanos.com*), beside the beautiful country inn of the same name, carries books, culinary gadgets, organic house-made lavender products, and a considerable variety of artisan jams, vinegars, sauces, and gourmet goodies. It overlooks a fragrant lavender field.

Theobroma Chocolatier (✉ *12611 Montgomery Blvd. NE, Northeast Heights* ☎ *505/293–6545,* ⊕ *www.theobromachocolatier.com*) carries beautiful, handcrafted, high-quality chocolates, truffles, and candies (most of them made on premises), as well as Taos Cow ice cream.

HISPANIC IMPORTS AND TRADITIONS

An Old Town stalwart since the late 1970s, **Casa Talavera** (✉ *621 Rio Grande Blvd., Old Town* ☎ *505/243–2413* ⊕ *www.casatalavera.com*) is just outside the plaza area, across Rio Grande Boulevard. Do go peruse the wide selection of hand-painted Mexican Talavera tiles. Prices are reasonable, making the colorful geometrics, florals, mural patterns, and solids, close to irresistible. Tin lighting fixtures as well as ceramic sink and cabinet knobs fill in the rest of the space in this DIY-inspiring shop.

Hispaniae (✉ *410 Romero St. NW, Old Town* ☎ *505/244–1533* ⊕ *www. hispaniae.com*) is like the Jackalope of yore, and then some. Sure it has every permutation of Our Lady of Guadalupe imaginable (on switch plates, tin tokens, etc.), but Nuestra Señora is just the tip of it. This long narrow space is packed with finds of the Latino craft kind, from inexpensive cake toppers in the shape of sweet little pigs to painted tin Christmas ornaments and hand-carved hardwood furnishings.

La Piñata (✉ *No. 2 Patio Market, 206 San Felipe St. NW, Old Town* ☎ *505/242–2400*) specializes in piñatas and papier-mâché products, plus Native American jewelry and leather goods.

Saints & Martyrs (✉ *404A San Felipe NW, Old Town* ☎ *505/224–9323* ⊕ *www.saints-martyrs.com*) has almost a gallery feel. The hand-painted *retablos* and other saintly images are displayed so well that it's easy to imagine how one might look in your house. There's also a high-quality selection of sterling-silver *milagros*.

HOME FURNISHINGS

Fodor's Choice ★ **A** (✉ *3500 Central Ave. SE, UNM/Nob Hill* ☎ *505/266–2222* ⊕ *www. theastore.com*) is a Nob Hill stop for housewares, soaps, candles, body-care products, and jewelry.

A branch of a popular regional chain, **El Paso Import Co.** (✉ *3500 Central Ave. SE, UNM/Nob Hill* ☎ *505/265–1160* ⊕ *www.elpasoimportco. com*) carries distressed and "peely-paint" antique-looking chests and tables loaded with character. If you love the shabby-chic look, head to this Nob Hill furniture shop.

Hey Jhonny (✉ *3418 Central Ave. SE, UNM/Nob Hill* ☎ *505/256–9244* ⊕ *www.heyjhonny.com*) is an aromatic store full of exquisite candles, soaps, pillows, fountains, and other soothing items for the home; there's also a branch that carries more furniture and larger pieces around the corner, at 118 Tulane Street.

Objects of Desire (✉ *3225 Central Ave. NE, UNM/Nob Hill* ☎ *505/232–3088* ⊕ *www.objectsofdesireabq.com*) is the place to find that special lamp or table from a whimsical and worldly collection of furnishings.

Qué Chula del Corazón (✉ *3410 Central Ave. NE, UNM/Nob Hill* ☎ *505/255–0515* ⊕ *www.quechulastyle.com*) imports brightly colored (and displayed) folk art, glassware, tooled leather bags, *equipale* furniture, textiles, and pottery from throughout Mexico.

Peacecraft (✉ *3215 Central Ave. NE, UNM/Nob Hill* ☎ *505/255–5229* ⊕ *www.peacecraft.org*) supports fair trade and stocks handmade folk art and crafts from around the world—wooden boxes from Kenya, clothing from Guatemala, hats from Honduras. The store employs university students in work-study programs.

NATIVE AMERICAN ARTS AND CRAFTS

Andrews Pueblo Pottery (✉ *303 Romero St. NW, Suite 116, Old Town* ☎ *505/243–0414 or 877/606–0543* ⊕ *www.andrewspp.com*) carries a terrific selection of Pueblo pottery, fetishes, kachina dolls, and baskets for the beginning and seasoned collector.

Bien Mur Indian Market Center (⊠ *100 Bien Mur Dr. NE, off Tramway Rd. NE east of I–25, Northeast Heights* ☎ *505/821–5400 or 800/365–5400* ⊕ *www.sandiapueblo.nsn.us/bienmur.html*) in Sandia Pueblo showcases the best of the best in regional Native American rugs, jewelry, and crafts of all kinds. You can feel very secure about what you purchase at this trading post, and prices are fair.

Gertrude Zachary (⊠ *1501 Lomas Blvd. NW, Old Town* ☎ *505/247– 4442* ⊠ *3300 Central Ave. SE, UNM/Nob Hill* ☎ *505/766–4700* ⊕ *www.gertrudezachary.com*) dazzles with its selection of Native American jewelry. Don't let the screaming billboards around town deter you—this may be the best place to get a bargain on a good bracelet or ring. Locals buy here, too.

To understand what it takes to make Native American jewelry (or if you want to learn the craft yourself), a stop at the fascinating **Indian Jewelers Supply** (⊠ *2105 San Mateo Blvd. NE, 1 block south of Indian School Rd. NE, at Haines Ave. NE, Uptown/East Side* ☎ *505/265–3701* ⊕ *www.ijsinc.com*) is a must. Trays of gemstones (finished and not), silver sold by weight, findings, and the tools to work them with, fill this large space. It's open 8 to 5 (closed Sunday)—go midmorning to avoid the early rush.

Margaret Moses Gallery (⊠ *326 San Felipe St. NW, Old Town* ☎ *505/842– 1808 or 888/842–1808* ⊕ *www.margaretmoses.com*) stocks Pueblo pottery, including the black earthenware pottery of San Ildefonso, as well as the work of potters from Acoma, Santa Clara, Isleta, and Zía. Rare Zuni and Navajo jewelry is on display, as are Navajo weavings from 1900 to the present.

SPORTS AND THE OUTDOORS

Albuquerque is blessed with an exceptional setting for outdoor sports, backed by a favorable, if unpredictable, climate. Usually 10°F warmer than Santa Fe's, Albuquerque's winter days are often mild enough for most outdoor activities. The Sandias tempt you with challenging mountain adventures *(see Sandia Park in the Side Trips from Albuquerque section, below, for details on mountain biking and skiing in the Sandia Mountains above Albuquerque)*; the Rio Grande and its cottonwood forest, the Bosque, provide settings for additional outdoors pursuits.

PARTICIPANT SPORTS

The **City of Albuquerque** (☎ *505/768–5300* ⊕ *www.cabq.gov/living.html*) maintains diverse cultural and recreational programs. Among the city's assets are more than 20,000 acres of open space, four golf courses, 200 parks, more than 400 mi of tracks for biking and jogging, as well as swimming pools, tennis courts, ball fields, playgrounds, and a shooting range.

AMUSEMENT PARK

Drive down San Mateo Northeast in summer and you may see a roller coaster smack in the middle of the city. **Cliff's Amusement Park** (⊠ *4800 Osuna Rd. NE, off I–25 at San Mateo Blvd. NE, Northeast Heights* ☎ *505/881–9373* ⊕ *www.cliffsamusementpark.com*) is a clean, well-run attraction for everyone from two-year-olds on up. It features a wooden-track roller coaster as well as rides for all ages and state-fair-type games of chance. The park also has a large water-play area. Cliff's is open early April through September, but days and hours vary, so call first.

BALLOONING

Albuquerque's high altitude, mild climate, and steady but manageable winds, make it an ideal destination for ballooning. A wind pattern known as the Albuquerque Box, created by the city's location against the Sandia Mountains, makes Albuquerque a great place to fly.

If you've never been ballooning, you may picture a bumpy ride, where changes in altitude produce the queasy feeling you get in a tiny propeller plane. But the experience is far calmer than that. The balloons are flown by licensed pilots (don't call them operators) who deftly turn propane-fueled flames on and off, climbing and descending to find winds blowing the way they want to go—there's no real steering involved, which makes the pilots' control that much more admirable. Pilots generally land balloons where the wind dictates, so chase vehicles pick you up and return you to your departure point, so particularly skilled pilots can use conditions created by the Box to land precisely where you started. Even without door-to-door service, many visitors rank a balloon ride over the Rio Grande Valley as their most memorable experience.

Several reliable companies around Albuquerque offer tours. A ride costs about $160 to $180 per person.

Fodor's Choice One of the best balloon tours is with **Rainbow Ryders** (☎ *505/823–1111* ★ *or 800/725–2477* ⊕ *www.rainbowryders.com*), an official ride concession for the Albuquerque International Balloon Fiesta. As part of the fun, you get to help inflate and pack away the balloon. In case you missed breakfast prior to your flight, a Continental breakfast and glass of champagne await your return.

BICYCLING

With the creation of many lanes, trails, and dedicated bike paths, Albuquerque's city leaders are recognized for their bike-friendly efforts—a serious challenge given the committed car culture of its residents. The city's public works department produces a detailed **bike map**, which can be obtained free by calling ☎ *505/768–3550* or downloaded from ⊕ *www.cabq.gov/bike*.

Albuquerque has miles of bike lanes and trails through and around the city as well as great mountain-biking trails at Sandia Peak Ski Area (⇨ *Sandia Park, in Side Trips from Albuquerque, below*).

Although mountain bikes may be rented in the Sandias, bike-rental sources are scarce around town. **Northeast Cyclery** (⊠ *8305 Menaul Blvd. NE, Northeast Heights* ☎ *505/299–1210*) has a good range of road and mountain bikes for rent. Most are unisex styles, and they carry kid sizes as well.

Seasonally, at **Tingley Beach** (⊕ *www.cabq.gov*) balloon-tire and mountain bikes are available by the hour *(⇨ Albuquerque BioPark, in Exploring Albuquerque, above)*.

★   The **Paseo del Bosque Bike Trail** (⊕ *www.cabq.gov*) runs right through Tingley. It's flat for most of its 16-mi run, and it's one of the loveliest rides in town.

BIRD-WATCHING

The Rio Grande Valley, one of the continent's major flyways, attracts many migratory bird species. Good bird-viewing locales include the **Rio Grande Nature Center State Park** (⊠ *2901 Candelaria Rd. NW, Los Ranchos/ North Valley* ☎ *505/344–7240* ⊕ *www.nmparks.com*).

GOLF

Most of the better courses in the region—and there are some outstanding ones—are just outside town *(⇨ Side Trips from Albuquerque, below, for details)*. The four courses operated by the city of Albuquerque have their charms, and the rates are reasonable. Each course has a clubhouse and pro shop, where clubs and other equipment can be rented. Weekday play is first-come, first-served, but reservations are taken for weekends. Contact the **Golf Management Office** (☎ *505/888–8115* ⊕ *www.cabq.gov/ golf*) for details. Of the four city courses, **Arroyo del Oso** (⊠ *7001 Osuna Rd. NE, Northeast Heights* ☎ *505/884–7505*) earns high marks for its undulating 27-hole layout; greens fees are $22 to $29 for 18 holes. The 18-hole **Los Altos Golf Course** (⊠ *9717 Copper Ave. NE, Northeast Heights* ☎ *505/298–1897*), one of the region's most popular facilities, has $22 to $29 greens fees. There's also a short, par-3, 9-hole executive course.

Sandia Golf Club (⊠ *Tramway Rd. NE just east of I–25, Northeast Heights* ☎ *505/798–3990* ⊕ *www.sandiagolf.com*), at the swanky Sandia Resort & Casino, offers 18 holes set amid lush hilly fairways, cascading waterfalls, and desert brush. Greens fees are $53 to $65.

The University of New Mexico has two superb courses. Both are open daily and have full-service pro shops, instruction, and snack bars. Greens fees for out-of-staters run about $35 to $45 without a cart. **UNM North** (⊠ *2201 Tucker Rd. NE, at Yale Blvd., UNM/Nob Hill* ☎ *505/277–4146*) is a first-class 9-hole, par-36 course on the north side of campus. The 18-hole facility at **UNM South** (⊠ *3601 University Blvd., just west of airport off I–25, Airport* ☎ *505/277–4546* ⊕ *www. unmgolf.com*) has garnered countless awards from major golf magazines and hosted PGA and LPGA qualifying events; there's also a short par-3 9-hole course.

HIKING

Fodor's Choice ★   In the foothills in Albuquerque's Northeast Heights, you'll find great hiking in **Cibola National Forest,** which can be accessed from Tramway Road Northeast, about 4 mi east of Interstate 25 or 2 mi north of Paseo del Norte. Just follow the road into the hillside, and you'll find several parking areas (there's a daily parking fee of $3). This is where you'll find the trailhead for the steep and challenging **La Luz Trail,** which rises some 9 mi (an elevation gain of more than 3,000 feet) to the top of Sandia Crest. You can take the Sandia Peak Aerial Tram *(⇨ Exploring*

Albuquerque, above) to the top and then hike down the trail, or vice versa (keep in mind that it can take up to six hours to hike up the trail, and four to five hours to hike down). Spectacular views of Albuquerque and many miles of desert and mountain beyond that are had from the trail. You can also enjoy a hike here without going the whole way—if your energy and time are limited, just hike a mile or two and back. No matter how far you hike, however, pack plenty of water.

SPECTATOR SPORTS

BASEBALL
The city hosts Triple A minor league baseball's **Albuquerque Isotopes** (⊠ *1601 Avenida César Chavez SE, UNM/Nob Hill* ☎ *505/924–2255* ⊕ *www.albuquerquebaseball.com*), the farm club of the major league Los Angeles Dodgers; the season runs April through August.

BASKETBALL
It's hard to beat the excitement of home basketball games of the **University of New Mexico Lobos** (⊠ *University Ave., at Avenida César Chavez, UNM/Nob Hill* ☎ *505/925–5858 or 877/664–8661* ⊕ *www.golobos. com*), when 18,000 rabid fans crowd into the school's arena, "the Pit," from November to March. Both the women's and men's teams have enjoyed huge success in past years.

FOOTBALL
The competitively ranked **University of New Mexico Lobos** (⊠ *University Ave., at Avenida César Chavez, UNM/Nob Hill* ☎ *505/925–5858 or 877/664–8661* ⊕ *www.golobos.com*) play at the 40,000-seat University Stadium in the fall.

SIDE TRIPS FROM ALBUQUERQUE

It takes only a few minutes of driving in any direction to leave urban Albuquerque behind and experience some of New Mexico's natural and small-town beauty. Rivers, valleys, canyons, and peaks are just outside the city's limits, and amid them are many villages worth a stop. If you're headed up to Santa Fe, definitely consider traveling there by way of the rambling and tortuous Turquoise Trail, a charming alternative to speedy Interstate 25.

SOUTH OF ALBUQUERQUE

When Francisco Vásquez de Coronado arrived in what is now New Mexico in 1540, he found a dozen or so villages along the Rio Grande in the ancient province of Tiguex, between what is now Bernalillo to the north of Albuquerque and Isleta to the south. Of those, only Sandia and Isleta survive today. The Salinas Pueblo Missions ruins, about 65 mi southeast of Albuquerque, remain a striking example of the Spanish penchant for building churches on sites inhabited by native people.

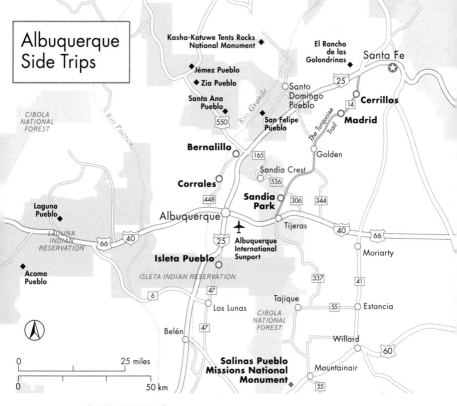

ISLETA PUEBLO

13 mi south of Albuquerque, via I–25 (Exit 213) and NM 47.

Of the pueblos in New Mexico when the Spanish first arrived, Isleta Pueblo is one of two Tiwa-speaking communities left in the middle of the Rio Grande Valley. It was also one of a handful of pueblos that didn't participate in the Pueblo Revolt of 1680, during which Isleta was abandoned. Some of the residents fled New Mexico with the Spanish to El Paso, where their descendants live to this day on a reservation called Ysleta del Sur. Other members went to live with the Hopi of Arizona but eventually returned and rebuilt the pueblo.

Facing the quiet plaza is Isleta's church, **St. Augustine,** built in 1629. One of the oldest churches in New Mexico, it has thick adobe walls, a viga-crossed ceiling, and an austere interior. Legend has it that the ground beneath the floor has the odd propensity to push church and community figures buried under the floor back up out of the ground; bodies have been reburied several times, only to emerge again.

Polychrome pottery with red and black designs on a white background is a specialty here. The pueblo celebrates its feast days on August 28 and September 4, both in honor of St. Augustine. The tribal government maintains picnicking and camping facilities, several fishing ponds, and a renowned 18-hole golf course. It also runs the **Hard Rock Casino &**

Resort (✉ *11000 Broadway SE [NM 47]* ☎ *505/724–3800 or 877/475–3827* ⊕ *www.hardrockcasinoabq.com*), which ranks among the state's most popular gaming facilities. It was known as Isleta Casino up until summer 2010, when the tribe formed a branding agreement with the popular Hard Rock hospitality brand and reopened the entire resort with a sleek new look. It's a large and handsome space with more than 1,600 slots and myriad gaming tables; the concert hall hosts a mix of oldies, pop stars, and country-and-western acts—past numbers have included Tom Jones, Vince Gill, and Tony Bennett. There's also boxing held throughout the year, and local bands as well as comedy acts often perform at the resort's two nightspots, Fusion and Lucha. Additionally, Hard Rock operates Albuquerque's largest rock-concert venue, the Hard Rock Pavilion (⇨ *Nightlife and the Arts, above*). The resort also includes a snazzy, 201-room Hard Rock Hotel, with a full-service spa, making Isleta more competitive with other high-profile Native American resorts in the region (i.e., Sandia Resort & Casino; Santa Ana Pueblo, with its Hyatt Regency Tamaya; and Pojoaque, with Buffalo Thunder Resort). Although Isleta is wonderfully picturesque—beehive ovens stand beside adobe homes bedecked with crimson chiles—camera use is restricted here. Only the church may be photographed. ✉ *Tribal Rd. 40* ☎ *505/869–3111* ⊕ *www.isletapueblo.com.*

WHERE TO STAY

$$

RESORT

📺 **Hard Rock Hotel & Casino.** Opened in 2010 as one of the newest properties in the gaming-driven Hard Rock hotel chain, this full-service resort is a bit more reasonably priced than others in the region and is also a bit more kid-friendly, with a huge pool and a family-fun center with a bowling alley, billiards, Laser Tag, an arcade. Rooms come in a wide range of configurations, some with sitting areas, wet bars, whirlpool tubs, and balconies overlooking the high-desert scenery. All have large flat-screen TVs, iPod docking stations, and good-size bathrooms with soaking tubs and rain showerheads. Adults will find plenty of keep them occupied here, too, from an extensive full-service spa to a slew of casual bars, restaurants, and gaming areas. **Pros:** sleek and attractive rooms with cushy furnishing; closer to airport than other casino resorts in the area; a bit less pricy than other Albuquerque casino resorts. **Cons:** somewhat isolated from Albuquerque and not much to see or do in area; few places to eat nearby. ✉ *11000 Broadway SE (NM 47)* ☎ *505/724–3800 or 877/475–3827* ⊕ *www.hardrockcasinoabq.com* ⇨ *201 rooms* ⚒ *In-room: a/c, Wi-Fi. In-hotel: 5 restaurants, room service, bars, golf course, pool, gym, spa, parking (free)* ☰ *AE, D, DC, MC, V.*

SPORTS AND THE OUTDOORS

One of the most esteemed facilities in the state, **Isleta Eagle Golf Course** (✉ *4001 NM 47 SE* ☎ *505/848–1900 or 866/475–3822* ⊕ *www. hardrockcasinoabq.com*) consists of three 9-hole layouts set around three lakes; greens fees are $50 to $65 for 18 holes.

SALINAS PUEBLO MISSIONS NATIONAL MONUMENT

58 mi (to Punta Agua/Quarai) from Albuquerque, east on I–40 (to Tijeras Exit), south on NM 337 and NM 55; 23 mi from Punta Agua to Abó, south on NM 55, west (at Mountainair) on U.S. 60, and north on NM 513; 34 mi from Punta Agua to Gran Quivira, south on NM 55.

Salinas Pueblo Missions National Monument is made up of three sites— **Quarai, Abó, and Gran Quivira**—each with the ruins of a 17th-century Spanish-colonial Franciscan missionary church and an associated pueblo. The sites represent the convergence of two Native American peoples, the Anasazi and the Mogollon, who lived here for centuries before the Spanish arrived. Quarai, the nearest to Albuquerque, was a flourishing Tiwa pueblo whose inhabitants' pottery, weaving, and basket-making techniques were quite refined. On the fringe of the Great Plains, all three of the Salinas pueblos were vulnerable to raids by nomadic Plains Indians. Quarai was abandoned about 50 years after its mission church, **San Purísima Concepción de Cuarac,** was built in 1630. If you can arrange it, arrive in time for the late-afternoon light—the church's red sandstone walls still rise 40 feet out of the earth, and are a powerful sight. At Abó are the remains of the three-story church of San Gregorio and a large unexcavated pueblo. (The masonry style at Abó, also built of red stone, bore some similarity to that at Chaco Canyon, which has led some archaeologists to speculate that the pueblo was built by people who left the Chaco Canyon area.) Gran Quivira contains two churches and some excavated Native American structures. There are walking trails and small interpretive centers at each of the pueblos, and expanded exhibits at the monument headquarters in the old cow town cum arts center of Mountainair. You'll come to Quarai first via this route, and this is the loveliest of the three; Abó—which you can swing by easily enough if you loop back to Albuquerque via U.S.60 west (through Mountainair), then north on either NM 47 (for the scenic back route through Isleta) or Interstate 25—is a close second. Gran Quivira is more a detour, and you might find yourself wanting to take a little time to stroll down Mountainair's quaint main street then getting a bite at Pop Shaffer's Café (⇨ *below*) instead. ⊠ *N. Ripley Ave., at W. Broadway (U.S. 60), Mountainair* ☎ *505/847–2585* ⊕ *www.nps. gov/sapu* 🎫 *Free* ☉ *Late May–early Sept., daily 9–6; early Sept.–late May, daily 9–5.*

WHERE TO STAY

$ 🏠 **Casa Manzano.** Tucked about a mile up a dirt-and-gravel forest road,
INN Casa Manzano rewards its guests with intimate views of the Manzano Mountains, and accommodations that warrant its reputation as a retreat. Designed by cohost Bert Herrman, this thoughtfully laid-out modern property is beautifully detailed with red-tile roofs, Saltillo-tile floors, courtyard garden with a hot tub, hand-plastered *nichos*, hand-crafted woodwork, and finely impressed tinwork. And it's as environmentally up-to-date as can be. A case study of solar-powered elegance, the property contains two wings, each with two separate guest rooms and one bathroom (both rooms in each wing are ever only rented to families or friends traveling together, and who don't mind sharing a bath). **Pros:** breakfast is sumptuous—and often includes offerings from

the lovingly tended garden. **Cons:** other meals require a drive, either into town or down to Mountainair. ✉ *103 Forest Rd. 321, 29 mi south from Tijeras on NM 337 and NM 55, Tajique* ☎ *505/384–9767* ⊕ *www. home.earthlink.net/~casa.manzano* ⇄ *4 rooms with shared bath* ⚲ *In-room: no a/c, no TV, Internet. In-hotel: gym, some pets allowed* ▭ *MC, V* ⎰⊙⎱ *BP* ⊘ *Closed Dec.–Apr.*

$ ⊞ **Shaffer Hotel.** One of the nation's few remaining structures built in
HOTEL   the Pueblo Deco style, the Shaffer was restored and reopened as a hotel in 2005 after many years of neglect. The 1923 building, in the heart of historic—if modest—Downtown Mountainair, offers a wide range of accommodations. The simple "cowboy rooms" share a community bathroom but have rates starting at just $28—all others have private baths, some with original claw-foot tubs. All are done with 1920s and '30s deco antiques and tile bathrooms; they're not fancy, but they are comfortable. Try for a side room facing the park—you'll still hear the freight trains rumbling by much of the night, but it's worse in the back. The lobby's a tin-ceiling period gem (original owner Pop Shaffer himself did all the woodwork), and from it you can step right into **Pop Shaf-fer's Café** ($). The homemade pie (pecan, mmm), breakfast burritos, and bizcochito cookies are all highly commendable, as is the hand-painted true-to-era Native American–inspired decor. **Pros:** rife with his-tory, this place is a real slice. **Cons:** service can be a bit spotty and the rooms a bit sterile. ✉ *103 W. Main St., Mountainair* ☎ *505/847–2888 or 888/595–2888* ⊕ *www.shafferhotel.com* ⇄ *11 rooms, 9 with bath; 8 suites* ⚲ *In-room: no a/c, Internet. In-hotel: restaurant, gym, Wi-Fi hotspot* ▭ *AE, D, MC, V.*

NORTH OF ALBUQUERQUE

CORRALES

2 mi north of Albuquerque. Take Paseo Del Norte (NM 423) or Alam-eda Blvd. (NM 528) west from I–25 and head north on Corrales Rd. (NM 448).

This sweet village just north of Albuquerque is a little bit cooler, a little bit greener, and a lot more pastoral than the city. Drive slowly through Bernalillo and Corrales, and you're bound to see lots of horses, cows, and llamas.

Serene Corrales is an ancient agricultural community now inhabited by artists, craftspeople, and the affluent—plus a few descendants of the old families. Small galleries, shops, and places to eat dot the town, and in fall, roadside fruit and vegetable stands open. Bordered by Albuquer-que and Rio Rancho, Corrales makes a pleasant escape to winding dirt roads, fields of corn, and apple orchards. On summer weekends visit the Corrales Farmers' Market; in October, the village holds a Harvest Festival. The village's main drag, NM 448, is one of New Mexico's offi-cial scenic byways, lined with grand estates and haciendas and shaded by cottonwoods. Just off the byway, you can break for a stroll through Corrales Bosque Preserve, a shaded sanctuary abutting the Rio Grande that's a favorite spot for bird-watching—some 180 species pass through here throughout the year. You can also catch a glimpse of historic hacienda life when you take a tour of the exquisitely restored 19th-century adobe compound of **Casa San Ysidro** (✉ *973 Old Church Rd.* ☎ *505/898–3915* ⊕ *www.cabq.gov* ⊡ *$4* ☉ *Wed.–Sun., call for times*).

WHERE TO EAT AND STAY

$$$
ECLECTIC
Fodor's Choice
★

✕**Casa Vieja.** Set in a rambling early-18th-century compound along the Corrales Scenic Byway, this purportedly haunted hacienda had bounced among a couple of different owners in recent years before falling into the very capable hands of talented chef and slow-food proponent Josh Gerwin. The atmospheric restaurant, with a large patio that's ideal in warm weather, earns raves for its creatively prepared, sustainable cuisine, which mixes local ingredients with global preparations, and top-notch wine list. You might start with a duck-confit tamale cooked in mole and served with a cilantro-chive-crème-fraîche sauce, before tucking into cast-iron-seared scallops with garlic-potato-and-scallion croquettes, cauliflower soup, and sorrel puree. The chipotle-buttermilk flan makes for a terrific ending. ✉ *4541 Corrales Rd.* ☎ *505/898–7489* ⊕ *www.casaviejanm.com* ▭ *AE, D, MC, V* ☉ *No lunch weekdays.*

¢
PIZZA

✕**Village Pizza.** A Chicago native with a knack for baking runs this ordinarily named joint that serves extraordinarily good pizza. Crusts come in different styles (including Chicago-style deep dish), and a wide range of toppings is offered, including such gourmet fixings as artichoke hearts and smoked oysters. In back is an adobe-walled courtyard with a couple of big leafy trees and lots of seating. There's a bargain-priced all-you-can-eat pizza buffet at lunchtime and on Monday and Tuesday nights, and you get a 10% discount if you ride in on horseback. ✉ *4266 Corrales Rd.* ☎ *505/898–0045* ⊕ *www.villagepizzacorrales.com* ▭ *AE, D, MC, V.*

$
BED & BREAKFAST

⌂**Chocolate Turtle B&B.** Hosts Nancy and Dallas Renner run this light-filled four-room hideaway in a quiet neighborhood in West Corrales. It's a short drive from Rio Rancho and 20 minutes from Downtown Albuquerque, but the setting is as peaceful as can be. This Territorial-style home's large windows and neatly landscaped grounds afford sweeping views of the Sandia Mountains. Fresh flowers further brighten the colorfully painted Southwestern-themed rooms, which range from a cozy single to three more substantial doubles, the most desirable with its own private terrace. **Pros:** friendly and knowledgeable hosts. **Cons:** no TVs or phones in room; it's a 20-minute walk to the nearest restaurants. ✉ *1098 W. Meadowlark La.* ☎ *505/898–1800 or 877/298–1800* ⊕ *www.chocolateturtlebb.com* ⇨ *4 rooms* ⚄ *In-room: a/c, no phone, no TV, Wi-Fi. In-hotel: Internet terminal.* ▭ *AE, D, MC, V* ⎮⎮ *BP.*

BERNALILLO

17 mi north of Albuquerque via I–25, 8 mi north of Corrales via NM 448 to NM 528.

Once a rather tranquil Hispanic village, Bernalillo is today one of New Mexico's fastest-growing towns—it's increasingly absorbing the suburban growth northward from Albuquerque. The town holds a Wine Festival each Labor Day weekend, but the most memorable annual event is the Fiesta of San Lorenzo, which has honored the town's patron saint for nearly 400 years. On August 10, San Lorenzo Day, the entire town takes to the streets to participate in the traditional masked *matachine* dance. Matachines, of Moorish origin, were brought to this hemisphere by the Spanish. In New Mexico various versions are danced to haunting fiddle music, in both Native American pueblos and old Spanish villages at different holidays. Though interpretations of the matachines are inexact, one general theme is that of conquest. One dancer, wearing a devil's mask and wielding a whip, presides over the others. A young girl, dressed in white, is also present.

WHAT TO SEE

The town's leading attraction, **Coronado State Monument,** is named in honor of Francisco Vásquez de Coronado, the leader of the first organized Spanish expedition into the Southwest, from 1540 to 1542. The prehistoric **Kuaua Pueblo,** on a bluff overlooking the Rio Grande, is believed to have been the headquarters of Coronado and his army, who were caught unprepared by severe winter weather during their search for the legendary Seven Cities of Gold. A worthy stop, the monument has a museum in a restored kiva, with copies of magnificent frescoes done in black, yellow, red, blue, green, and white. The frescoes depict fertility rites, rain dances, and hunting rituals. The original artworks are preserved in the small visitor center. Adjacent to the monument is **Coronado State Park,** which has campsites and picnic grounds, both open year-round. In autumn the views at the monument and park are especially breathtaking, with the trees turning russet and gold. There's also overnight camping at the adjacent Coronado Campground (☎ *505/980–8256).* ⊠ *485 Kuaua Rd., off NM 44/U.S. 550* ☎ *505/867–5351* ⊕ *www.nmstatemonuments.org* ⊡ *$3* ☽ *Wed.–Mon. 8:30–5.*

WHERE TO EAT AND STAY

$$$$ ✕ **Corn Maiden.** The upscale dining option at the posh Hyatt Regency
ECLECTIC Tamaya resort, this art-filled dining room with large windows taking in views of the Sandias is also one of the great special-occasion venues in greater Albuquerque (albeit with lofty prices). Many seats view the bustle of the open kitchen, where a talented culinary team mix Native American, Mexican, and global ingredients to lavish effect. Share-worthy starts include crostini topped with grilled buffalo and poached quail eggs, and jicama-wrapped lobster ravioli with tomato relish. The specialty among main dishes is a mixed grill of chorizo, organic chicken, and chile-rubbed beef rib-eye. Friends may consider splitting the decadent sampler of four luscious desserts. ⊠ *Hyatt Regency Tamaya, 1300 Tuyuna Trail, Santa Ana Pueblo* ☎ *505/771–6037* ⊕ *www.tamaya. hyatt.com* ⚞ *Reservations essential* ⊟ *AE, D, DC, MC, V* ☽ *Closed Sun. and Mon. No lunch.*

$$$ ✕ **Prairie Star.** Residents from as far as Santa Fe have been known to
ECLECTIC make the drive to this 1920s Pueblo Revival hacienda, renowned for
★ the sunset views from its patio. The menu combines contemporary American, Southwestern, and Asian cuisine, including duck-confit crepes with red-chile-infused blueberries, lemon chèvre, mint, and pistachios, and coriander-rubbed ahi tuna with ginger-jasmine rice cakes and seaweed slaw. The lamb chops, from Chama Valley, are also delicious. The culinary quality has become consistently outstanding over

the years, the wine list is among the best in the state, and the setting is gorgeous. Prairie Star is on the Santa Ana reservation, overlooking the acclaimed Santa Ana Golf Course. ⊠ *288 Prairie Star Rd., Santa Ana Pueblo* ☎ *505/867–3327* ⊕ *www.santaanagolf.com* ▭ *AE, D, DC, MC, V* ⊘ *Closed Mon. No lunch.*

$ ✕ **Range Cafe & Bakery.** Banana pancakes, giant cinnamon rolls, Asian
ECLECTIC   spinach salad, grilled portobello burgers, homemade meat loaf with
Fodor'sChoice   garlic mashed potatoes, steak-and-enchilada platters, and the signature
★   dessert, Death by Lemon, are among the highlights at this quirky spot known for down-home fare with creative touches. All the above, plus a full complement of rich, decadent Taos Cow ice cream, is served in a refurbished mercantile building with a dead-center view of the Sandia Mountains. You can order breakfast fare until 3 pm. There are also two newer branches in Albuquerque (the one near Downtown is nicest), but the original has the best ambience. ⊠ *925 Camino del Pueblo* ☎ *505/867–1700* ✉ *2200 Menaul Blvd. NE, Downtown* ☎ *505/888–1660* ✉ *4401 Wyoming Blvd. NE, Northeast Heights* ☎ *505/293–2633* ⊕ *www.rangecafe.com* ⌖ *Reservations not accepted* ▭ *AE, D, MC, V.*

$$$ ⊞ **Hyatt Regency Tamaya.** This spectacular large-scale resort, on 500 acres
RESORT   on the Santa Ana Pueblo, includes a top-rated golf course, state-of-the-
Fodor'sChoice   art spa, and cultural museum and learning center. Most rooms, swathed
★   in natural stone, wood, and adobe and filled with pueblo-inspired textiles and pottery, overlook the Sandia Mountains or cottonwood groves; many have balconies or patios. Cultural events include bread-baking demonstrations (in traditional adobe ovens), storytelling, and live tribal dance and music performances. Other amenities include waterslides over two of the outdoor pools, atmospheric bars, guided nature walks, and hot-air ballooning nearby. Three restaurants all serve consistently excellent food. The Santa Ana Star Casino is a free shuttle ride away. And if you're looking for an exceptional horseback ride, arrange one with the Tamaya stables. As you drink in eyefuls of the spectacular pueblo backcountry and weave among trees and plantings, you'll wonder why you ever settled for the dull nose-to-butt riding experiences of yesteryear. **Pros:** this is *the* place to come to get away; it's in the direction of Santa Fe, making it a good base for day trips to that area. **Cons:** it's way out there—factor in a 15-minute drive even into Downtown Bernalillo. ⊠ *1300 Tuyuna Trail, Santa Ana Pueblo* ☎ *505/867–1234 or 800/633–7313* ⊕ *www.tamaya.hyatt.com* ⤸ *331 rooms, 19 suites* ⌂ *In-room: a/c, refrigerator, Wi-Fi. In-hotel: 3 restaurants, room service, bars, golf course, tennis courts, pools, gym, spa, children's programs (ages 2–14)* ▭ *AE, D, DC, MC, V.*

THE TURQUOISE TRAIL

Fodor'sChoice   Etched out in the early 1970s and still well traveled is the scenic Tur-
★   quoise Trail (or more prosaically, NM 14), a National Scenic Byway which follows an old route between Albuquerque and Santa Fe that's dotted with ghost towns now being restored by writers, artists, and other urban refugees. This 70 mi of piñon-studded mountain back road along the eastern flank of the sacred Sandia Mountains is a gentle roller coaster that also affords panoramic views of the Ortiz, Jémez,

and Sangre de Cristo mountains. It's believed that 2,000 years ago Native Americans mined turquoise in these hills. The Spanish took up turquoise mining in the 16th century, and the practice continued into the early 20th century, with Tiffany & Co. removing a fair share of the semiprecious stone. In addition, gold, silver, tin, lead, and coal have been mined here. There's plenty of opportunity for picture taking and picnicking along the way. The pace is slow, the talk is about the weather, and Albuquerque might as well be on another planet. The entire loop of this trip takes a day, the drive up the Sandia Crest a half day. Two Web sites offer good information: ⊕ *www.turquoisetrail.org* and ⊕ *www.byways.org.*

SANDIA PARK

7 mi north of Tijeras. From Tijeras, take I–40 east and exit north on the Turquoise Trail (NM 14); proceed 6 mi and turn left onto NM 536.

Driving east from Albuquerque, before you head up the Turquoise Trail, drop down south from Interstate 40 first, and stop at the **Sandia Ranger Station** for a bit of orientation on the Cibola National Forest and the mountains you're about to drive through. Pick up pamphlets and trail maps, and—if there are enough kids in the audience—witness a fire-prevention program with a Smokey the Bear motif. From here you can also embark on a short self-guided tour to the nearby **fire lookout tower** and **Tijeras Pueblo ruins,** and head out on the trails throughout the forest. ⊠ *11776 NM 337, Tijeras, south of I–40, off Exit 175* ☎ *505/281–3304* ⊕ *www.fs.fed.us/r3/cibola/districts/sandia.shtml* ☒ *Ranger station free, parking in Cibola National Forest $3* ⊗ *Mon.–Sat. 8–4:30.*

In Cedar Crest, just off NM 14 a couple of miles south of Sandia Park, the modest but nicely laid-out **Museum of Archaeology & Material Culture** chronicles archaeological finds and contains artifacts dating from the Ice Age to the Battle of Wounded Knee. Exhibits shed light on prehistoric man, buffalo hunting, a history of turquoise mining in north-central New Mexico, and the 1930s excavations of Sandia Cave (about 15 mi away) that offered evidence of some of the earliest human life in North America. ⊠ *22 Calvary Rd.; turn west 5 mi north of I–40 Exit 175 in Cedar Crest* ☎ *505/281–2005* ☒ *$3* ⊗ *May–Oct., daily noon–7.*

☾ It may take months for this odyssey of a place to completely sink in: quirky and utterly fascinating, **Tinkertown Museum** contains a world of miniature carved-wood characters. The museum's late founder, Ross Ward, spent more than 40 years carving and collecting the hundreds of figures that populate this cheerfully bizarre museum, including an animated miniature Western village, a Boot Hill cemetery, and a 1940s circus exhibit. Ragtime piano music, a 40-foot sailboat, and a life-size general store are other highlights. The walls surrounding this 22-room museum have been fashioned out of more than 50,000 glass bottles pressed into cement. This homage to folk art, found art, and eccentric kitsch tends to strike a chord with people of all ages. As you might expect, the gift shop offers plenty of fun oddities. ⊠ *121 Sandia Crest Rd. (NM 536); take Cedar Crest Exit 175 north off I–40 east and follow signs on NM 14 to Sandia Crest turnoff* ☎ *505/281–5233* ⊕ *www. tinkertown.com* ☒ *$3* ⊗ *Apr.–Oct., daily 9–6.*

Fodor's Choice
★

For awesome views of Albuquerque and half of New Mexico, take NM 536 up the back side of the Sandia Mountains through Cibola National Forest to **Sandia Crest.** At the 10,378-foot summit, explore the foot trails along the rim (particularly in summer) and take in the breathtaking views of Albuquerque down below, and of the so-called Steel Forest—the nearby cluster of radio and television towers. Always bring an extra layer of clothing, even in summer—the temperature at the crest can be anywhere from 15 to 25 degrees cooler than down in Albuquerque. If you're in need of refreshments or are searching for some inexpensive souvenirs, visit the **Sandia Crest House Gift Shop and Restaurant** (☏ 505/243–0605), on the rim of the crest.

As you continue north up NM 14 from Sandia Park, after about 12 mi you pass through the sleepy village of **Golden,** the site of the first gold rush (in 1825) west of the Mississippi. It has a rock shop and a mercantile store. The rustic adobe church and graveyard are popular with photographers. Be aware that locals are very protective of this area and aren't known to warm up to strangers.

WHERE TO STAY

$$ ☐ **Elaine's, A Bed and Breakfast.** This antique-filled three-story log-and-
BED & BREAKFAST   stone home is set in the evergreen folds of the Sandia Mountain foot-hills. Four acres of wooded grounds beckon outside the back door. The top two floors have rooms with balconies and big picture windows that bring the lush mountain views indoors. The third-floor room also has cathedral ceilings and a brass bed; some rooms have fireplaces, and one has its own outside entrance. Breakfast, served in a plant-filled room or outside on a patio with a fountain, often includes fresh fruit, pancakes, or waffles with sausage. ⊠ *Snowline Estate, 72 Snowline Rd.* ☐ *Box 444, Cedar Crest 87008* ☏ *505/281–2467 or 800/821–3092* ⊕ *www.elainesbnb.com* ↬ *5 rooms* ♿ *In-room: no a/c, no phone, no TV, Wi-Fi* ⊟ *AE, D, MC, V* ♉ *BP.*

CAMPING

¢   ⛺ **Turquoise Trail Campground and RV Park.** Pine and cedar trees dot this 14-acre park in the Sandias, which has hiking trails with access to the Cibola National Forest. Adjacent to the premises is the Museum of Archaeology & Material Culture. Campsite rates are calculated per person; you will need reservations in October when spots fill up quickly. ⊠ *22 Calvary Rd., 5 mi north of I–40 Exit 175 in Cedar Crest* ☏ *505/281–2005* ⊕ *www.turquoisetrailcampground.com* ♿ *Flush toilets, full hookups, partial hookups (electric and water), dump station, drinking water, guest laundry, showers, fire grates, fire pits, grills, picnic tables, public telephone, general store, play area* ↬ *57 sites, 45 with hookups* ⊟ *AE, D, MC, V.*

SPORTS AND THE OUTDOORS

Fodor'sChoice   The 18-hole **Paa-Ko Ridge Golf Course** (⊠ *1 Club House Dr.* ☏ *505/281–*
★   *6000 or 866/898–5987* ⊕ *www.paakoridge.com*) has been voted New Mexico's best place to play golf by *Golf Digest.* Golfers enjoy vistas of the mesas and the Sandia Mountains from any of five tee placements on each hole. Greens fees are $89 to $114, and tee-time reservations may be made a month ahead. The course is just off NM 14, 3½ mi north of the turnoff for Sandia Crest (NM 536).

Although less extensive and challenging than the ski areas farther north in the Sangre de Cristos, **Sandia Peak** (✉ *NM 536* ☎ *505/242–9052 ski area, 505/857–8977 snow conditions* ⊕ *www.sandiapeak.com*) is extremely popular with locals from Albuquerque and offers a nice range of novice, intermediate, and expert downhill trails; there's also a ski school. Snowboarding is welcome on all trails, and there's cross-country terrain as well, whenever snow is available. Snowfall can be sporadic, so call ahead to check for cross-country; Sandia has snowmaking capacity for about 30 of its 200 acres of downhill skiing. The season runs from mid-December to mid-March, and lift tickets cost $43. Keep in mind that you can also access the ski area year-round via the Sandia Peak Aerial Tramway (⇨ *Exploring Albuquerque*, above), which is faster from Albuquerque than driving all the way around. In summer, the ski area converts into a fantastic mountain-biking and hiking terrain. The ski area offers a number of packages with bike and helmet rentals and lift tickets. Other summer activities at Sandia Peak include sand volleyball, horseshoes, and picnicking.

MADRID

37 mi northeast of Albuquerque, 12 mi north of Golden on NM 14.

Totally abandoned when its coal mine closed in the 1950s, Madrid (locals put the emphasis on the first syllable: *mah*-drid) has gradually been rebuilt and is now—to the dismay of some longtime locals—on the verge of trendiness (some would say it's already there). The entire town was offered for sale for $250,000 back then, but there were no takers. Finally, in the early 1970s, a few artists fleeing big cities settled in and began restoration. Weathered houses and old company stores have been repaired and turned into boutiques and galleries, some of them selling high-quality furniture, paintings, and crafts. Big events here include Old Timers Days on July 4th weekend, and the Christmas open house, held weekends in December, when galleries and studios are open and the famous Madrid Christmas lights twinkle brightly.

OFF THE BEATEN PATH

Aged hippies, youthful hipsters, and everyone in between congregate at **Java Junction** (✉ *2855 NM 14* ☎ *505/438–2772 or 877/308–8884* ⊕ *www.java-junction.com*) for lattes, chai, sandwiches, breakfast burritos, pastries, and other toothsome treats. You can also pick up a number of house-made gourmet goods, from hot sauces to jalapeño-raspberry preserves. Upstairs there's a pleasantly decorated room for rent that can sleep up to three guests.

WHERE TO EAT

¢ ✕ **Mineshaft Tavern.** A rollicking old bar and restaurant adjacent to the
CAFÉ Old Coal Mine Museum, this boisterous place—there's live music many nights—was a miners' commissary back in the day. Today it serves what many people consider the best green-chile cheeseburger (available with beef or buffalo) in New Mexico, along with 12 ice-cold beers on tap and a selection of other pub favorites and comfort foods—the Cobb salad, for one, is excellent. Although open daily, the kitchen closes around 7:30 pm on weekdays. ✉ *2846 NM 14* ☎ *505/473–0743* ⊕ *www.themineshafttavern.com* ▱ *D, MC, V.*

SHOPPING

The town of Madrid has only one street, so the three-dozen-or-so shops and galleries are easy to find.

You can watch live glassblowing demonstrations at **Al Leedom Studio** (☎ *505/473–2054* ⊕ *www.alleedom.com*) ; his vibrant vases and bowls are sold alongside the beautiful handcrafted jewelry of wife Barbara Leedom. The Leedoms' friendly cat and dancing dog are also big crowd pleasers. In a pale blue cottage in the center of town, the **Ghost Town Trading Post** (☎ *505/471–7605* ⊕ *www.wildhogsmadridnm.com*) is a great bet for fine Western jewelry fashioned out of local gemstones (not just turquoise, but opal, amber, and onyx). **Johnsons of Madrid** (☎ *505/471–1054*) ranks among the most prestigious galleries in town, showing painting, photography, sculpture, and textiles created by some of the region's leading artists. You could spend hours browsing the fine rugs and furnishings at **Seppanen & Daughters Fine Textiles** (☎ *505/424–7470* ⊕ *www.finetextiles.com*), which stocks custom Zapotec textiles from Oaxaca, Navajo weavings, Tibetan carpets, and fine Arts and Crafts tables, sofas, and chairs.

CERRILLOS

3 mi northeast of Madrid on NM 14.

Cerrillos was a boomtown in the 1880s—its mines brimmed with gold, silver, and turquoise, and eight newspapers, four hotels, and 21 taverns flourished. When the mines went dry the town went bust. Since then, Cerrillos has served as the backdrop for feature-film and television Westerns, among them *Young Guns* and *The Hi-Lo Country*. Today, it might easily be mistaken for a ghost town, which it's been well on the way to becoming for decades. Time has left its streets dry, dusty, and almost deserted, although it is home to a number of artists, and the occasional Amtrak roars through to remind you what century you're in.

Casa Grande (✉ *17 Waldo St.* ☎ *505/438–3008* ⊕ *www.casagrandetradingpost. com*), a 28-room adobe (several rooms of which are part of a shop), has a small museum ($2) with a display of early mining exhibits. There's also a clean and neat, but oddly out-of-place petting zoo ($2) with about 20 animals, and a genuinely scenic overlook. Casa Grande is open daily 8 am–sunset.

Pack rats and browsers alike ought not to miss the **What-Not Shop** (✉ *15B 1st St.* ☎ *505/471–2744*), a venerable secondhand-antiques shop of a half-century's standing packed floor to ceiling with Native American pottery, cut glass, rocks, political buttons, old postcards, clocks, and who knows what else.

WHERE TO EAT AND STAY

$ ✕ **San Marcos Cafe.** In Lone Butte, about 6 mi north of Cerrillos (and CAFÉ actually quite a lot closer to Santa Fe than to Albuquerque but nevertheless a fixture on the Turquoise Trail), this restaurant is known for its creative fare and nontraditional setting—an actual feed store, with roosters, turkeys, and peacocks running about outside. In one of the two bric-a-brac–filled dining rooms, sample rich cinnamon rolls and such delectables as burritos stuffed with roast beef and potatoes and topped with green chile, and the classic eggs San Marcos: tortillas stuffed with scrambled eggs and topped with guacamole, pinto beans, melted Jack cheese, and red chile. Hot apple pie à la mode with rum sauce is a favorite. Expect a wait on weekends unless you make a reservation. ✉ *3877 NM 14* ☎ *505/471–9298* ▭ *MC, V* ☯ *No dinner*.

$$$

BED & BREAKFAST

⊡ **High Feather Ranch.** A grand adobe homestead and B&B, plush High Feather Ranch anchors 130 wide-open acres with breathtaking mountain views. It feels completely removed from civilization but is, in fact, within an hour's drive of both Santa Fe and Albuquerque. Although built in the late 1990s, the sprawling inn contains reclaimed 19th-century timber, antique gates, and fine vintage furnishings. Rooms have high ceilings and plenty of windows, and you're never far from a portal or patio; one room has an outdoor shower in a private courtyard. Rates include an impressive full breakfast. **Pros:** between Madrid and Cerrillos, you're alone with the scenery and certain to leave relaxed and well fed. **Cons:** there's a 1-mi stretch of dirt road to get to the door, but it's nothing to fret about. ✉ *29 High Feather Ranch; 2 mi north of Madrid, turn right onto CR 55/Gold Mine Rd.* ☎ *505/424–1333 or 800/757–4410* ⊕ *www.highfeatherranch.com* ⇆ *2 rooms, 1 suite* ♨ *In-room: no a/c, no phone, no TV, Wi-Fi. In-hotel: some pets allowed* ▭ *AE, D, MC, V* |◎| *BP.*

SPORTS AND THE OUTDOORS

Fodor's Choice
★

Rides with **Broken Saddle Riding Co.** (✉ *Off NM 14, Cerrillos* ☎ *505/424–7774* ⊕ *www.brokensaddle.com*) take you around the old turquoise and silver mines the Cerrillos area is noted for. On a Tennessee Walker or a Missouri Fox Trotter you can explore the Cerrillos hills and canyons, 23 mi southeast of Santa Fe. This is not the usual nose-to-tail trail ride.

Santa Fe

WORD OF MOUTH

"Lunch at Tia Sophia's (good and simple), and then a little more shopping. Then back to the lower part of Canyon Road for more galleries. So much art, so little time! We spent our last evening polishing off the leftovers from our wonderful Thursday night dinner before our early departure on Sunday. All in all we had a great time; Santa Fe is a wonderful place for a girl's get-a-way."

–PaigeS

Updated by
Georgia de
Katona

On a plateau at the base of the Sangre de Cristo Mountains—at an elevation of 7,000 feet—Santa Fe is brimming
with reminders of nearly four centuries of Spanish and Mexican rule, and of the Pueblo cultures that have been here for
hundreds more.

The town's placid central Plaza, which dates from the early 17th century, has been the site of bullfights, gunfights, political rallies, prom-
enades, and public markets over the years. A one-of-a-kind destination,
Santa Fe is fabled for its rows of chic art galleries, superb restaurants,
and diverse shops selling everything from Southwestern furnishings and
cowboy gear, to Tibetan textiles and Moroccan jewelry.

La Villa Real de la Santa Fe de San Francisco de Asísi (the Royal City of
the Holy Faith of St. Francis of Assisi) was founded in the early 1600s
by Don Pedro de Peralta, who planted his banner in the name of Spain.
During its formative years, Santa Fe was maintained primarily for the
purpose of bringing the Catholic faith to New Mexico's Pueblo Indians.
In 1680, however, the Indians rose in revolt and the Spanish colonists
were driven out of New Mexico. The tide turned 12 years later, when
General Don Diego de Vargas returned with a new army from El Paso
and recaptured Santa Fe. To commemorate de Vargas's recapture of the
town in 1692, Las Fiestas de Santa Fe have been held annually since
1712. The nation's oldest community celebration takes place on the
weekend after Labor Day, with parades, mariachi bands, pageants, and
the burning of Zozóbra—a must-see extravaganza held in Fort Marcy
Park just blocks north of the Plaza.

Following de Vargas's defeat of the Pueblos, the then-grand Camino
Real (Royal Road), stretching from Mexico City to Santa Fe, brought
an army of conquistadors, clergymen, and settlers to the northernmost reaches of Spain's New World conquests. In 1820 the Santa Fe
Trail—a prime artery of U.S. westward expansion—spilled a flood of
covered wagons from Missouri onto the Plaza. A booming trade with
the United States was born. After Mexico achieved independence from
Spain in 1821, its subsequent rule of New Mexico further increased
this commerce.

The Santa Fe Trail's heyday ended with the arrival of the Atchison,
Topeka & Santa Fe Railway in 1880. The trains, and later the nation's
first highways, brought a new type of settler to Santa Fe—artists who
fell in love with its cultural diversity, history, and magical color and
light. They were especially drawn to the area because eccentricity was
embraced not discouraged, as it often was in the social confines of the
East Coast. Their presence attracted tourists, who quickly became a
primary source of income for the proud, but largely poor, populace.

Cosmopolitan visitors from around the world are consistently surprised
by the city's rich and varied cultural offerings despite its relatively small
size. Often referred to as the "City Different," Santa Fe became the first

TOP REASONS TO GO

A winter stroll on Canyon Road. There are few experiences to match walking this ancient street on Christmas Eve when it's covered with snow, scented by piñon fires burning in luminarias along the road, and echoing with the voices of carolers and happy families.

A culinary adventure. Start with rellenos for breakfast and try tapas for dinner. Enjoy some strawberry habanero gelato or sip an Aztec Warrior Chocolate Elixir. Take a cooking lesson. Santa Fe is an exceptional dining town, the perfect place to push the frontiers of your palate.

Into the wild. Follow the lead of locals and take any one of the many easy-access points into the incredible, and surprisingly lush, mountains that rise out of Santa Fe. Raft the Rio Grande, snowboard, snowshoe, or try mountain biking.

Market mashup. Summer offers the phenomenal International Folk Art Market, the famed Indian Market, and the two-for-one weekend of Traditional Spanish Market and Contemporary Hispanic Market. The offerings are breathtaking and the community involvement yet another aspect of Santa Fe to fall in love with.

American city to be designated a UNESCO Creative City, acknowledging its place in the global community as a leader in art, crafts, design, and lifestyle.

ORIENTATION AND PLANNING

GETTING ORIENTED

Humorist Will Rogers said on his first visit to Santa Fe, "Whoever designed this town did so while riding on a jackass, backwards, and drunk." The maze of narrow streets and alleyways confounds motorists; however, pedestrians delight in the vast array of shops, restaurants, flowered courtyards, and eye-catching galleries at nearly every turn. Park your car, grab a map, and explore the town on foot.

Interstate 25 cuts just south of Santa Fe, which is 62 mi northeast of Albuquerque. U.S. 285/84 runs north–south through the city. The NM 599 bypass, also called the Santa Fe Relief Route, cuts around the west side of the city from Interstate 25's Exit 276, southwest of the city, to U.S. 285/84, north of the city; it's a great shortcut if you're heading from Albuquerque to Española, Abiquiu, Taos, or other points north of Santa Fe. The modest flow of water called the Santa Fe River runs west, parallel to Alameda Street, from the Sangre de Cristo Mountains to the open prairie southwest of town, where it disappears into a narrow canyon before joining the Rio Grande. There's a *dicho*, or saying, in New Mexico: "*agua es vida*"—water is life—and every little trickle counts.

SANTA FE NEIGHBORHOODS

The Plaza. The heart of historic Santa Fe, the Plaza has been the site of a bullring, fiestas, and fandangos. Despite the buildup of tourist shops, the Plaza retains its old-world feel and is still the center of many annual festivities and much of the town's activity.

East Side and Canyon Road. One of the city's oldest streets, Canyon Road is lined with galleries, shops, and restaurants housed in adobe compounds, with thick walls, and lush courtyard gardens. The architectural influence of Old Mexico and Spain, and the indigenous Pueblo cultures, makes this street as historic as it is artistic.

Old Santa Fe Trail and South Capitol. In the 1800s wagon trains from Missouri rolled into town from the Old Santa Fe Trail, opening trade into what had been a very insular Spanish colony and forever changing Santa Fe's destiny. This street joins the Plaza on the south side after passing the state capitol and some of the area's oldest neighborhoods.

Museum Hill. What used to be the outskirts of town became the site of gracious, neo-Pueblo style homes in the mid-20th century, many of them designed by the famed architect John Gaw Meem. Old Santa Fe Trail takes you to Camino Lejo, aka Museum Hill, where you'll find four excellent museums and a café.

The Railyard District. This bustling area, also known as the Guadalupe District, has undergone a major transformation in the last decade. The new Railyard Park is a model for urban green space and is across the street from a permanent new home for the vibrant farmers' market. The redevelopment along Guadalupe Street has added dozens of shops, galleries, and restaurants to the town's already rich assortment.

SANTA FE PLANNER

WHEN TO GO

The city's population, an estimated 72,000, swells by many thousands in summer. In winter, skiers and snowboarders arrive, lured by the challenging slopes and fluffy, powdery snow of Ski Santa Fe and—within a two-hour drive—Angel Fire and Taos Ski Valley (⇨ *chapter 4*). Prices are highest June through August. Between September and November and in April and May they're lower, and (except for the major holidays) from December to March they're the lowest.

Santa Fe has four distinct seasons, though the sun shines nearly every day of the year. June through August temperatures are high 80s to low 90s during the day, 50s at night, with afternoon rain showers—monsoons—cooling the air. During this season it's advisable to keep a lightweight, waterproof jacket with you. The monsoons come suddenly and can quickly drench you. September and October bring beautiful weather and a marked reduction in crowds. Temperatures—and prices—drop significantly after Halloween. December through March is ski season. Spring comes late at this elevation. April and May are blustery, with daily warm weather (70s and above) finally arriving in May. ■TIP→ **The high elevation here catches people unawares and altitude sickness** can utterly ruin a day of fun. Drink water, drink more water, and then have a little more.

GETTING HERE AND AROUND

AIR TRAVEL

Among the smallest state capitals in the country, Santa Fe has only a small airport. Albuquerque's is the nearest major one, about an hour away. Tiny Santa Fe Municipal Airport is served by one commercial airline, American Eagle, with daily flights to Dallas (DFW) and Los Angeles (LAX). The airport is 9 mi southwest of Downtown.

Airport Contacts Albuquerque International Sunport (*ABQ* ☎ *505/244–7700* ⊕ *www.cabq.gov/airport*). **Santa Fe Municipal Airport** (*SAF* ✉ *Airport Rd. and NM 599* ☎ *505/473–4118*).

BUS TRAVEL

The city's bus system, Santa Fe Trails, covers 10 major routes through town and is useful for getting from the Plaza to some of the outlying attractions. Route M is most useful for visitors, as it runs from Downtown to the museums on Old Santa Fe Trail south of town, and Route 2 is useful if you're staying at one of the motels out on Cerrillos Road and need to get into town (if time is a factor for your visit, a car is a much more practical way to get around). Individual rides cost $1, and a daily pass costs $2. Buses run about every 30 minutes on weekdays, every hour on weekends. Service begins at 6 am and continues until 11 pm on weekdays, 8 to 8 on Saturday, and 10 to 7 (limited routes) on Sunday.

Bus Contacts Santa Fe Trails (☎ *505/955–2001* ⊕ *www.santafenm.gov*).

CAR TRAVEL

Santa Fe is served by several national rental car agencies, including Avis, Budget, and Hertz. Additional agencies with locations in Santa Fe include Advantage, Enterprise, Sears, and Thrifty. *See Car Travel in the Travel Smart chapter for national rental agency phone numbers.*

Car Rental Contacts Advantage (☎ *505/983–9470* ⊕ *www.advantage.com*). **Enterprise** (☎ *505/473–3600* ⊕ *www.enterprise.com*). **Sears** (☎ *505/984–8038* ⊕ *www.sears.avis.com*). **Thrifty** (☎ *505/474–3365 or 800/367–2277* ⊕ *www. thrifty.com*).

TAXI TRAVEL

Capital City Cab Company controls all the cabs in Santa Fe. The taxis aren't metered; you pay a flat fee based on how far you're going, usually $6 to $10 within the Downtown area. There are no cabstands; you must phone to arrange a ride.

Taxi Contact Capital City Cab (☎ *505/438–0000*).

TRAIN TRAVEL

Amtrak's Southwest Chief stops in Lamy, a short drive south of Santa Fe, on its route from Chicago to Los Angeles via Kansas City; other New Mexico stops include Raton, Las Vegas, Albuquerque, and Gallup daily. In 2006, the state's first-ever commuter train line, the New Mexico Rail Runner Express, began serving the north-central part of the state. Service is from Belén, south of Albuquerque, to Santa Fe, with numerous stops in between. The Rail Runner offers a scenic, efficient alternative to reaching Santa Fe from the airport in Albuquerque (a shuttle bus operates between Albuquerque's Downtown train station and the airport).

Train Contacts Amtrak (☎ 800/872-7245 ⊕ www.amtrak.com). **New Mexico Rail Runner Express** (☎ 866/795-7245 ⊕ www.nmrailrunner.com).

GUIDED TOURS
GENERAL INTEREST

Custom Tours by Clarice (☎ 505/438-7116 ⊕ www.santafecustomtours. com) are guided open-air tram excursions that run four times a day from the corner of Lincoln Avenue and West Palace Avenue. These 90-minute tours don't require reservations and offer a nice overview of Downtown; the company also gives bus and shuttle tours of Bandelier and Taos, and shuttle services from town to the Santa Fe Opera (reservations required).

Great Southwest Adventures (☎ 505/455-2700 ⊕ www.swadventures. com) conducts guided tours in 7- to 35-passenger van and bus excursions to Bandelier, O'Keeffe country, the High Road and Taos, and elsewhere in the region. Guides are avid outdoors enthusiasts; in addition to their regular tour offerings, the company arranges eye-opening single- and multiday custom hikes and photography trips.

Rojo Tours (☎ 505/474-8333 ⊕ www.rojotours.com) designs specialized trips—to view wildflowers, pueblo ruins and cliff dwellings, galleries and studios, Native American arts and crafts, and private homes—as well as adventure activity tours.

Santa Fe Detours (☎ 505/983-6565 or 800/338-6877 ⊕ www.sfdetours. com) offers a more limited selection of tours, by reservation only.

Santa Fe Guides (☎ 505/466-4877 ⊕ www.santafeguides.org) is an organization of about 15 respected independent tour guides—its Web site lists each member and his or her specialties.

MAKING THE MOST OF YOUR TIME

It's best to explore Santa Fe one neighborhood at a time and arrange your activities within each. If you've got more than two days, be sure to explore the northern Rio Grande Valley. For the best tour, combine your adventures in Santa Fe with some from the Side Trips section (⇨ *below*), which highlights several trips within a 60- to 90-minute drive of town.

Plan on spending a full day wandering around Santa Fe Plaza, strolling down narrow streets, under portals, and across ancient cobbled streets. Sip coffee on the Plaza, take in a museum or two (or three) and marvel

---

PEDICABS

Santa Fe Pedicabs offer a great alternative to getting around the heart of town, especially if your restaurant is a ways from your hotel. Friendly drivers can regale you with all sorts of information and trivia about Santa Fe as they whisk you along in bicycle carriages. Sit back and enjoy watching the crowds and the sights go by. Cost is $1 per minute. ✉ Santa Fe Plaza, Canyon Rd., Railyard District ☎ 505/577-5056 ⊕ www. santafepedicabs.com.

at the cathedral. The **New Mexico History Museum** and **Palace of the Governors** are great places to start to gain a sense of the history and cultures influencing this area. ■ TIP→ **Take one of the docent-led tours offered by the museums.** Almost without exception the docents are engaging and passionate about their subjects. You gain invaluable insight into the collections and their context by taking these free tours. Inquire at the front desk of the museums for more information.

On a stretch called Museum Hill, you'll find four world-class museums, all quite different and all highly relevant to the culture of Santa Fe and northern New Mexico. Start at the intimate gem, the **Museum of Spanish Colonial Art,** where you'll gain a real sense of the Spanish empire's influence on the world beyond Spain. The **Museum of International Folk Art** is thoroughly engaging for both young and old. If you have the stamina to keep going, have lunch at the tasty Museum Café and then visit the **Museum of Indian Arts and Culture** and then move on to the **Wheelwright Museum of the American Indian.** There is a path linking all these museums together, and the walk is easy. The museum shops at these four museums are outstanding—if you're a shopper you could easily spend an entire day in the shops alone.

An easy walk from any of the Downtown lodgings, Canyon Road should definitely be explored on foot. Take any of the side streets and stroll amongst historical homes and ancient *acequias* (irrigation ditches). If you really enjoy walking, keep going up Canyon Road past Cristo Rey Church, where the street gets even narrower and is lined with residential compounds. At the top is the **Randall Davey Audubon Center,** where bird-watching abounds.

Another enjoyable day can be spent exploring the hip Railyard District, which is bursting with energy and development from the new Railyard Park and the various businesses surrounding it. The **Santuario de Guadalupe** is a great place to start. Head south from there and enjoy shops, cafés, art galleries, the farmers' market, and the fun new Railyard Park. If you enjoy ceramics, don't miss a stop at **Santa Fe Clay,** an amazing gallery, supply store, and studio where dozens of artists are busy at work. The venerable **SITE Santa Fe** is also here, with its cutting-edge modern art installations.

There are more galleries and shops in Downtown Santa Fe than can be handled in one day. If you've got the time, or if you don't want to spend hours in multiple museums, take a look at our shopping recommendations (⇨ *Shopping, below*) and go from there.

VISITOR INFORMATION

New Mexico Department of Tourism visitor center (⊠ *Lamy Building, 491 Old Santa Fe Trail* ☎ *505/827–7400* ⊕ *www.newmexico.org*). **Santa Fe Convention and Visitors Bureau** (⊠ *201 W. Marcy St.* ☎ *505/955–6200 or 800/777–2489* ⊕ *www.santafe.org*).

EXPLORING SANTA FE

Five Santa Fe museums participate in the Museum of New Mexico pass (four state museums and the privately run Museum of Spanish Colonial Art) and it is by far the most economical way to visit them all. The four-day pass costs $20 and is sold at all five museums, which include the New Mexico History Museum/Palace of the Governors, Museum of Fine Arts, Museum of Indian Arts and Culture, Museum of International Folk Art, and Museum of Spanish Colonial Art.

THE PLAZA

Much of the history of Santa Fe, New Mexico, the Southwest, and even the West has some association with Santa Fe's central Plaza, which New Mexico governor Don Pedro de Peralta laid out in 1607. The Plaza was already well established by the time of the Pueblo revolt in 1680. Freight wagons unloaded here after completing their arduous journey across the Santa Fe Trail. The American flag was raised over the Plaza in 1846, during the Mexican War, which resulted in Mexico's loss of all its territories in the present southwestern United States. For a time the Plaza was a tree-shaded park with a white picket fence. In the 1890s it was an expanse of lawn where uniformed bands played in an ornate gazebo. Particularly festive times on the Plaza are the weekend after Labor Day, during Las Fiestas de Santa Fe, and at Christmas, when all the trees are filled with lights, and rooftops are outlined with *farolitos,* votive candles lit within paper-bag lanterns.

TOP ATTRACTIONS

★ **Georgia O'Keeffe Museum.** One of many East Coast artists who visited New Mexico in the first half of the 20th century, O'Keeffe returned to live and paint here, eventually emerging as the demigoddess of Southwestern art. O'Keeffe's innovative view of the landscape is captured in *From the Plains,* inspired by her memory of the Texas plains, and *Jimson Weed,* a study of one of her favorite plants. Special exhibitions with O'Keeffe's modernist peers are on view throughout the year—many of these are exceptional, sometimes even more interesting than the permanent collection. ⊠ *217 Johnson St.* ☎ *505/946–1000* ⊕ *www. okeeffemuseum.org* 🖾 *$8, free 5–8 pm first Fri. of the month* ⊙ *Mon.– Thur. and Sat.–Sun. 10–5; Fri. 10–7.*

ℭ **The New Mexico History Museum.** The new museum is the anchor of a campus that encompasses the **Palace of the Governors,** the **Museum of New Mexico Press,** the **Fray Angélico Chávez History Library,** and **Photo Archives** (an assemblage of more than 750,000 images dating from the 1850s). Behind the palace on Lincoln Avenue, the museum thoroughly encompasses the early history of indigenous people, Spanish colonization, the Mexican Period, and travel and commerce on the legendary Santa Fe Trail. Opened in May 2009, the museum has permanent and changing exhibits, such as "Jewish Pioneers of New Mexico," which explores the vital role Jewish immigrants played during the late 19th and early 20th centuries in the state's civic, economic, and cultural development. With advance permission, students and researchers have

Fodor's Choice
★

access to the comprehensive Fray Angélico Chávez Library and its rare maps, manuscripts, and photographs (more than 120,000 prints and negatives). The Museum of New Mexico Press, which prints books, pamphlets, and cards on antique presses, also hosts bookbinding demonstrations, lectures, and slide shows. The Palace of the Governors is a humble one-story neo-Pueblo adobe on the north side of the Plaza, and is the oldest public building in the United States. Its rooms contain period furnishings and exhibits illustrating the building's many functions over the past four centuries. Built at the same time as the Plaza, circa 1610 (scholars debate the exact year), it was the seat of four regional governments—those of Spain, Mexico, the Confederacy, and the U.S. territory that preceded New Mexico's statehood, which was achieved in 1912. The building was abandoned in 1680, following the Pueblo Revolt, but resumed its role as government headquarters when Don Diego de Vargas successfully returned in 1692. It served as the residence for 100 Spanish, Mexican, and American governors, including Governor Lew Wallace, who wrote his epic *Ben Hur* in its then drafty rooms, all the while complaining of the dust and mud that fell from its earthen ceiling.

Dozens of Native American vendors gather daily under the portal of the Palace of the Governors to display and sell pottery, jewelry, bread, and other goods. With few exceptions, the more than 500 artists and craftspeople registered to sell here are Pueblo or Navajo Indians. The merchandise for sale is required to meet strict standards: all items are handmade or hand-strung in Native American households; silver jewelry is either sterling (92.5% pure) or coin (90% pure) silver; all metal jewelry bears the maker's mark, which is registered with the Museum of New Mexico. Prices tend to reflect the high quality of the merchandise but are often significantly less that what you'd pay in a shop. Please remember not to take photographs without permission.

There's an outstanding gift shop and bookstore with many high-quality, New Mexico–produced items. ✉ *Palace Ave., north side of Plaza, Lincoln Ave., west of the Palace* ☎ *505/476–5100* ⊕ *www. nmhistorymuseum.org* ✉ *$9, 4-day pass $20 (good at all 4 state museums and Museum of Spanish Colonial Art), free Fri. 5–8* ☉ *Tues.–Thurs. and weekends 10–5, Fri. 10–8 (also Mon. 10–5 June–early Sept.)*

★ **St. Francis Cathedral Basilica.** The iconic cathedral, a block east of the Plaza, is one of the rare significant departures from the city's nearly ubiquitous Pueblo architecture. Construction was begun in 1869 by Jean Baptiste Lamy, Santa Fe's first archbishop, who worked with French architects and Italian stonemasons. The Romanesque style was popular in Lamy's native home in southwest France. The circuit-riding cleric was sent by the Catholic Church to the Southwest to change the religious practices of its native population (to "civilize" them, as one period document puts it) and is buried in the crypt beneath the church's high altar. He was the inspiration behind Willa Cather's novel *Death Comes for the Archbishop* (1927). In 2005 Pope Benedict XVI declared St. Francis the "cradle of Catholicism" in the Southwestern United States, and upgraded the status of the building from mere cathedral to cathedral basilica—it's one of just 36 in the country.

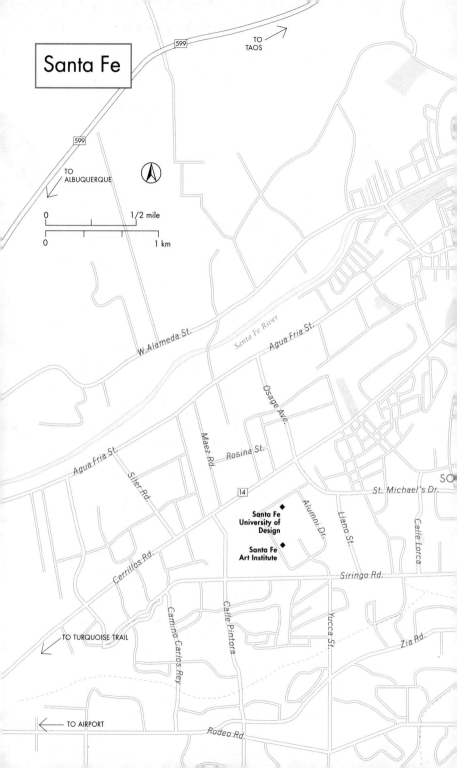

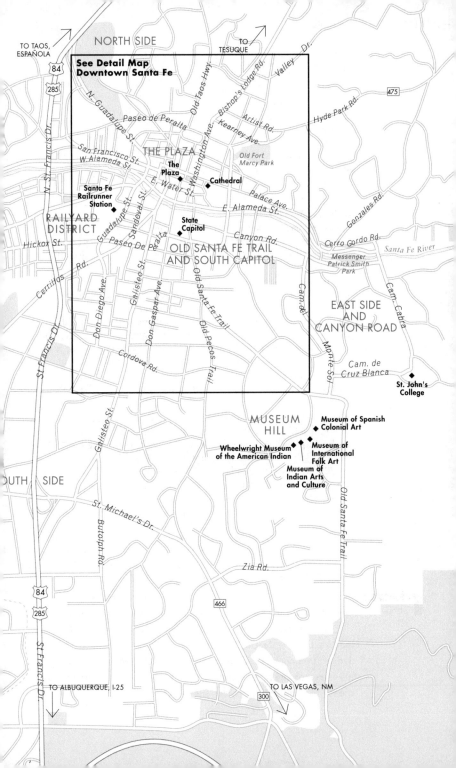

Just south of the cathedral, where the parking lot meets Paseo de Peralta, is the **Archdiocese of Santa Fe Museum** (☎ *505/983–3811*), a small museum where many of the area's historic, liturgical artifacts are on view. ✉ *231 Cathedral Pl.* ☎ *505/982–5619* ⊙ *Mon.–Sat. 6–6, Sun. 7–7, except during Mass. Mass Mon.–Sat. at 7 am and 5:15 pm and Sun. at 8 am, 10 am, noon, and 7 pm. Museum weekdays 8:30–4:30.*

> **FLAME ON!**
>
> Every weekend after Labor Day thousands gather to watch a groaning, flailing, 50-foot bogey-man-puppet known as Zozóbra go up in flames amidst an incredible display of fireworks—taking troubles of the past year with him. It's wildly pagan and utterly Santa Fe.

WORTH NOTING

Institute of American Indian Arts (IAIA) Museum. This fascinating museum just a block from the Plaza contains the largest collection of contemporary Native American art in the United States. The collection of paintings, photography, sculptures, prints, and traditional crafts was created by past and present students and teachers. In the 1960s and 1970s it blossomed into the nation's premier center for Native American arts and its alumni represent almost 600 tribes around the country. The museum continues to showcase the cultural and artistic vibrancy of indigenous people and expands what is still an often limited public perception of what "Indian" art is and can be. Artist Fritz Scholder taught here, as did sculptor Allan Houser. Among their disciples was the painter T. C. Cannon. ✉ *108 Cathedral Pl.* ☎ *505/983–1777* ⊕ *www.iaia.edu* ⬚ *$5* ⊙ *June–Oct., Mon.–Sat. 10–5, Sun. noon–5; Nov.–May, Wed.–Sat. and Mon. 10–5, Sun. noon–5.*

La Fonda. A *fonda* (inn) has stood on this site, southeast of the Plaza, for centuries. Architect Isaac Hamilton Rapp, who put Santa Fe style on the map, built this area landmark in 1922. Remodeled in 1926 by architect John Gaw Meem, the hotel was sold to the Santa Fe Railway in 1926 and remained a Harvey House hotel until 1968. Because of its proximity to the Plaza and its history as a gathering place for everyone from cowboys to movie stars (Errol Flynn stayed here), it's referred to as "The Inn at the End of the Trail." Step inside to browse the shops on the main floor or to eat at one of the restaurants (La Plazuela or the French Bakery). The dark, cozy bar draws both locals and tourists and has live music many nights. For a real treat: Have a drink at the fifth-floor Bell Tower Bar (open late spring–early fall), which offers tremendous sunset views. ✉ *E. San Francisco St., at Old Santa Fe Trail* ☎ *505/982–5511.*

NEED A BREAK?

Ecco Gelato (✉ *105 E. Marcy St.* ☎ *505/986–9778*) is a clean, contemporary café across from the Downtown public library with large plate-glass windows, and brushed-metal tables inside and out on the sidewalk under the portal. Try the delicious and creative gelato flavors (strawberry-habanero, saffron-honey, minty white grape, chocolate-banana) or some of the espressos and coffees, pastries, and sandwiches (roast beef and blue cheese, tuna with dill, cucumber, and sprouts).

A GOOD WALK: THE PLAZA

To get started, drop by the information booth at the Plaza's northwest corner, across the street from the clock, where Palace Street meets Lincoln Street (in front of the bank) to pick up a free map. From there, begin your walk around the Plaza. You can get an overview of the history of Santa Fe and New Mexico at the **Palace of the Governors** on the campus of the just-opened **New Mexico History Museum,** which borders the northern side of the Plaza on Palace Avenue. Outside, under the palace portal, dozens of Native American artisans sell handcrafted wares. From the palace, round the corner to Lincoln Street to the **New Mexico Museum of Art,** where the works of regional masters are on display. The **Georgia O'Keeffe Museum,** on nearby Johnson Street, exhibits the works of its namesake, New Mexico's best-known painter.

From the O'Keeffe Museum, return to the Plaza and cut across to its southeast corner to Old Santa Fe Trail, where you can find the town's oldest hotel, **La Fonda,** a good place to soak up a little of bygone Santa Fe. One block east on Cathedral Place looms the imposing facade of **St. Francis Cathedral Basilica.** Across from the cathedral is the **Institute of American Indian Arts,** with its wonderful museum of contemporary Native art. A stone's throw from the museum is cool, quiet Sena Plaza, accessible through two doorways on Palace Avenue.

TIMING

It's possible to zoom through this compact area in about five hours—two hours exploring the Plaza and the Palace of the Governors, two hours seeing the Museum of Fine Arts and the Museum of the Institute of American Indian Arts, and an hour visiting the other sites.

New Mexico Museum of Art *(Museum of Fine Arts).* Designed by Isaac Hamilton Rapp in 1917, the museum contains one of America's finest regional collections. It's also one of Santa Fe's earliest Pueblo Revival structures, inspired by the adobe structures at Acoma Pueblo. Split-cedar *latillas* (branches set in a crosshatch pattern) and hand-hewn vigas form the ceilings. The 8,000-piece permanent collection, of which only a fraction is exhibited at any given time, emphasizes the work of regional and nationally renowned artists, including the early modernist Georgia O'Keeffe; realist Robert Henri; the Cinco Pintores (five painters) of Santa Fe (including Fremont Elis and Will Shuster, the creative mind behind Zozóbra); members of the Taos Society of Artists (Ernest L. Blumenschein, Bert G. Phillips, Joseph H. Sharp, and E. Irving Couse, among others); and the works of noted 20th-century photographers of the Southwest, including Laura Gilpin, Ansel Adams, and Dorothea Lange. Rotating exhibits are staged throughout the year. Many excellent examples of Spanish-colonial-style furniture are on display. An interior *placita* (small plaza) with fountains, WPA murals, and sculpture, and the St. Francis Auditorium, where concerts and lectures are often held, are other highlights. ⊠ *107 W. Palace Ave.* ☎ *505/476–5072* ⊕ *www. mfasantafe.org* ⊠ *$9, 4-day pass $20 (good at 4 state museums and the*

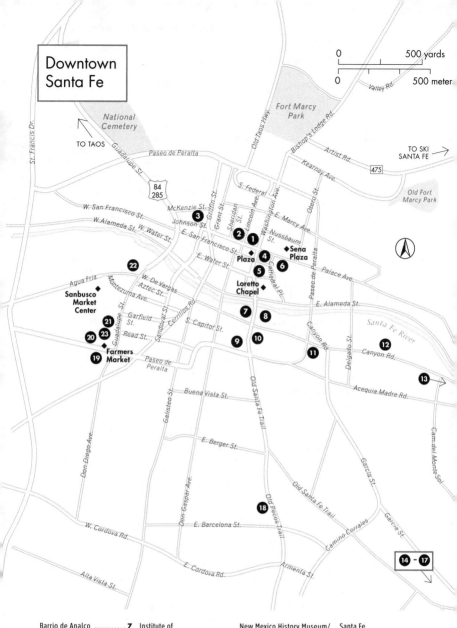

Downtown Santa Fe

National Cemetery

TO TAOS

Paseo de Peralta

St. Francis Dr.

Guadalupe St.

84 285

W. San Francisco St.

W. Alameda St.   W. Water St.

McKenzie St.

Johnson St.

E. San Francisco St.

E. Water St.

Grant St.

Sheridan St.

Griffin St.

S. Federal

Lincoln Ave.

Washington Ave.

E. Marcy Ave.

Nussbaum St.

Plaza

Sena Plaza

Cathedral Pl.

Loretto Chapel

Paseo de Peralta

Palace Ave.

E. Alameda St.

Fort Marcy Park

Old Taos Hwy.

Bishop's Lodge Rd.

Artist Rd.

Kearney Ave.

Otero St.

475

TO SKI SANTA FE

Old Fort Marcy Park

Santa Fe River

Canyon Rd.

Delgado St.

El Zaguan

Cam.-del-Monte Sol

Acequia Madre Rd.

Garcia St.

Agua Fria

Montezuma Ave.

Sanbusco Market Center

Garfield St.

Read St.

Farmers Market

Paseo de Peralta

W. De Vargas St.

Aztec St.

Cerrillos Rd.

S. Capitol St.

Sandoval St.

Guadalupe St.

Buena Vista St.

Galisteo St.

Don Diego Ave.

E. Berger St.

Old Santa Fe Trail

Old Pecos Trail

Don Gaspar Ave.

W. Cordova Rd.

E. Barcelona St.

E. Cordova Rd.

Alta Vista St.

Armenta St.

Camino Corrales

Garcia St.

14 - 17

0   500 yards

0   500 meter

Valley Rd.

New Mexico Art & Architecture: Glossary of Terms

Perhaps more than any other region in the United States, New Mexico has its own distinctive cuisine and architectural style, both heavily influenced by Native American, Spanish-colonial, Mexican, and American frontier traditions. The brief glossary that follows explains terms used frequently in this book.

ART AND ARCHITECTURE

Adobe: A brick of sun-dried earth and clay, usually stabilized with straw; a structure made of adobe.

Banco: A small bench, or banquette, often upholstered with handwoven textiles, that gracefully emerges from adobe walls.

Bulto: Folk-art figures of a santo (saint), usually carved from wood.

Camposanto: A graveyard.

Capilla: A chapel.

Casita: Literally "small house," this term is generally used to describe a separate guesthouse.

Cerquita: A spiked, wrought-iron, rectangular fence, often marking grave sites.

Coyote fence: A type of wooden fence that surrounds many New Mexico homes; it comprises branches, usually from cedar or aspen trees, arranged vertically and wired tightly together.

Farolito: Small votive candles set in paper-bag lanterns, farolitos are popular at Christmastime. The term is used in northern New Mexico only. People in Albuquerque and points south call the lanterns *luminarias,* which in the north is the term for the bonfires of Christmas Eve.

Heishi: Technically the word means "shell necklace," but the common usage refers to necklaces made with rounded, thin, disc-shaped beads in various materials, such as turquoise or jet.

Hornos: Domed outdoor ovens made of plastered adobe or concrete blocks.

Kiva: A circular ceremonial room, built at least partially underground, used by Pueblo Indians of the Southwest. Entrance is gained from the roof.

Kiva fireplace: A corner fireplace whose round form resembles that of a kiva.

Nicho: A built-in shelf cut into an adobe or stucco wall.

Placita: A small plaza.

Portal: A porch or large covered area adjacent to a house.

Pueblo Revival (also informally called Pueblo style): Most homes in this style, modeled after the traditional dwellings of the Southwest Pueblo Indians, are cube or rectangle shaped. Other characteristics are flat roofs, thick adobe or stucco walls, small windows, rounded corners, and viga beams.

Retablo: Holy image painted on wood or tin.

Santero: Maker of religious images.

Terrones adobes: Adobe cut from the ground rather than formed from mud.

Viga: Horizontal roof beam made of logs, usually protruding from the side of the house.

3

A GOOD WALK: CANYON ROAD

Begin on Paseo de Peralta at the **Gerald Peters Gallery,** which has an enormous collection. Continue a half block north to Canyon Road. Turn right (east) and follow the road, which unfolds in shadows of undulating adobe walls. Street parking is at a premium, but there's a city-owned pay lot at the corner of Camino del Monte Sol, a few blocks up. Between visits to galleries and shops, take a break at one of the courtyards or fine restaurants. Be sure to stop by the beautiful gardens outside **El Zaguan.** At the intersection of Upper Canyon and Cristo Rey, you'll find the massive **Cristo Rey**

Church. Wear good walking shoes and watch out for the irregular sidewalks, which can get icy in winter.

TIMING

A tour of Canyon Road could take a whole day or as little as a few hours. If art is more than a curiosity to you, you may want to view the Gerald Peters Gallery apart from your Canyon Road tour. There's so much to see there that visual overload could hit before you get halfway up the road. Even on a cold day the walk is a pleasure, with massive, glistening icicles hanging off roofs and a silence shrouding the side streets.

Museum of Spanish Colonial Art), free Fri. 5–8 pm ☉ Tues.–Thurs and weekends 10–5, Fri. 10–8 (also Mon. 10–5 June–early Sept.).

Sena Plaza. Two-story buildings enclose this courtyard, which can be entered only through two small doorways on Palace Avenue or the shops facing Palace Avenue. Surrounding the oasis of flowering fruit trees, a fountain, and inviting benches are a variety of locally owned shops. The quiet courtyard is a good place for repose or to have lunch at La Casa Sena. The buildings, erected in the 1700s as a single-family residence, had quarters for blacksmiths, bakers, farmers, and all manner of help. ⊠ *125 E. Palace Ave.*

EAST SIDE AND CANYON ROAD

Once a trail used by indigenous people to access water and the lush forest in the foothills east of town, then a route for Hispanic woodcutters and their burros, and for most of the 20th century a prosaic residential street with only a gas station and a general store, Canyon Road is now lined with upscale art galleries, shops, and restaurants. The narrow road begins at the eastern curve of Paseo de Peralta and stretches for about 2 mi at a moderate incline toward the base of the mountains. Lower Canyon Road is where you'll find the galleries, shops, and restaurants. Upper Canyon Road (above East Alameda) is narrow and residential, with access to hiking and biking trails along the way, and the Randall Davey Audubon Center at the very top.

Most establishments are in authentic, old adobe homes with thick, undulating walls that appear to have been carved out of the earth. Within those walls is art ranging from cutting-edge contemporary to traditional and even ancient works. Some artists are internationally renowned, like Fernando Botero, others' identities have been lost with time, like the weavers of magnificent Navajo rugs.

There are few places as festive as Canyon Road on Christmas Eve, when thousands of farolitos illuminate walkways, walls, roofs, and even trees. In May the scent of lilacs wafts over the adobe walls, and in August red hollyhocks enhance the surreal color of the blue sky on a dry summer day.

Cristo Rey Church. Built in 1940 and designed by legendary Santa Fe architect John Gaw Meem to commemorate the 400th anniversary of Francisco Vásquez de Coronado's exploration of the Southwest, this church is the largest Spanish adobe structure in the United States and is considered by many the finest example of Pueblo-style architecture anywhere. The church was constructed in the old-fashioned way by parishioners, who mixed the more than 200,000 mud-and-straw adobe bricks and hauled them into place. The 225-ton stone reredos (altar screen) is magnificent. ⊠ *1120 Canyon Rd., at Cristo Rey* ☎ *505/983–8528* ⊗ *Daily 8–5.*

NEED A BREAK?

Kakawa (⊠ *1050 Paseo de Peralta, across the street from Gerald Peters Gallery* ☎ *505/982–0388* ⊕ *www.kakawachocolates.com*) is the place to go if chocolate—very good chocolate—is an essential part of your day. Proprietor Mark Sciscenti is a self-described chocolate historian and chocolate alchemist, and you're unlikely to ever have tasted anything like the divine, agave-sweetened, artisanal creations that emerge from his kitchen. Historically accurate chocolate drinks, like the Aztec Warrior Chocolate Elixir, divine caramels, and agave-sweetened, gluten-free chocolate baked goods are served in this cozy, welcoming shop that's as much a taste experience as an educational one.

El Zaguan. Headquarters of the **Historic Santa Fe Foundation (HSFF)**, this 19th-century Territorial-style house has a small exhibit on Santa Fe architecture and preservation, but the real draw is the small but stunning garden abundant with lavender, roses, and 160-year-old trees. You can relax on a wrought-iron bench and take in the fine views of the hills northeast of town. An HSFF horticulturist often gives free tours and lectures in the garden on Thursday at 1 in summer (call to confirm). Tours are available of many of the foundation's properties on Mother's Day. ⊠ *545 Canyon Rd.* ☎ *505/983–2567* ⊕ *www.historicsantafe.org* ⊠ *Free* ⊗ *Foundation office weekdays 9–noon and 1:30–5; gardens Mon.–Sat. 9–5.*

Gerald Peters Gallery. While under construction, this 32,000-square-foot building was dubbed the "ninth northern pueblo," its scale supposedly rivaling that of the eight northern pueblos around Santa Fe. The suavely designed Pueblo-style gallery is Santa Fe's premier showcase for American and European art from the 19th century to the present. It feels like a museum, but all the works are for sale. Pablo Picasso, Georgia O'Keeffe, Charles M. Russell, Deborah Butterfield, George Rickey, and members of the Taos Society are among the artists represented, along with nationally renowned contemporary ones. ⊠ *1011 Paseo de Peralta* ☎ *505/954–5700* ⊕ *www.gpgallery.com* ✉ *Free* ⊙ *Mon.–Sat. 10–5.*

NEED A BREAK?

Locals congregate in the courtyard or on the front portal of **Downtown Subscription** (⊠ *376 Garcia St.* ☎ *505/983–3085*), a block east of Canyon Road. A great, friendly spot to people-watch, this café-newsstand sells coffees, snacks, and pastries, plus one of the largest assortments of newspapers and magazines in New Mexico. It has lovely outdoor spaces to sit and sip during warm weather. A delightful spot toward the end of gallery row on Canyon Road, right at the intersection with East Palace Avenue, the **Teahouse** (⊠ *821 Canyon Rd.* ☎ *505/992–0972*) has several bright dining rooms throughout the converted adobe home, and a tranquil outdoor seating area in a rock garden. In addition to fine teas from all over the world, you can find extremely well-prepared breakfast and lunch fare. The service tends to be leisurely but friendly.

OLD SANTA FE TRAIL AND SOUTH CAPITOL

It was along the Old Santa Fe Trail that wagon trains from Missouri rolled into town in the 1800s, forever changing Santa Fe's destiny. This street, off the south corner of the Plaza, is one of Santa Fe's most historic and is dotted with houses, shops, markets and the state capitol several blocks down.

TOP ATTRACTIONS

★ **New Mexico State Capitol.** The symbol of the Zía Pueblo, which represents the Circle of Life, was the inspiration for the capitol, also known as the Roundhouse. Doorways at opposing sides of this 1966 structure symbolize the four winds, the four directions, and the four seasons. Throughout the building are artworks from the outstanding collection of the Capitol Art Foundation, historical and cultural displays, and handcrafted furniture—it's a superb and somewhat overlooked array of fine art. The **Governor's Gallery** hosts temporary exhibits. Six acres of imaginatively landscaped gardens shelter outstanding sculptures. ⊠ *Old Santa Fe Trail at Paseo de Peralta* ☎ *505/986–4589* ⊕ *www.newmexico. gov* ✉ *Free* ⊙ *Weekdays 7–6; tours weekdays by appt.*

Fodor's Choice
★ **San Miguel Mission.** The oldest church still in use in the United States, this simple earth-hue adobe structure was built in the early 17th century by the Tlaxcalan Indians of Mexico, who came to New Mexico as servants of the Spanish. Badly damaged in the 1680 Pueblo Revolt, the structure was restored and enlarged in 1710. On display in the chapel are priceless statues and paintings and the San José Bell, weighing nearly 800 pounds, which is believed to have been cast in Spain in 1356. In winter the church sometimes closes before its official closing hour. Mass is held on Sunday at 5 pm. Next door in the back of the Territorial-style dormitories of the old St. Michael's High School, a **Visitor Information Center** can help you find your way around northern New Mexico. ⊠ *401 Old Santa Fe Trail* ☎ *505/983–3974* ✉ *$1* ⊙ *Mon.–Sat. 9–4:30, Sun. 10–4.*

A GOOD TOUR: MUSEUM HILL

This museum tour begins 2 mi southeast of the Plaza, an area known as Museum Hill that's best reached by car or via one of the city buses that leaves hourly from near the Plaza. Begin at the **Museum of Indian Arts and Culture**, which is set around Milner Plaza, an attractively landscaped courtyard and gardens with outdoor art installations. On some summer days the Plaza hosts Native American dances, jewelry-making demonstrations, kids' activities, and other interactive events; there's also the Museum Hill Cafe, which is open for lunch (and Sunday brunch) and serves delicious and reasonably priced salads, quiche, burgers, sandwiches and wraps, ice cream, and other light fare. To get here from Downtown, drive uphill on Old Santa Fe Trail to Camino Lejo. Across Milner Plaza is the **Museum of International Folk Art (MOIFA)**. From Milner Plaza, a pedestrian path leads a short way to the **Museum of Spanish Colonial Art**. Return to Milner Plaza, from which a different pedestrian path leads west a short way to the **Wheelwright Museum of the American Indian**. To reach the **Santa Fe Children's Museum**, you need to drive back down the hill or ask the bus driver to let you off near it.

TIMING

Set aside a full day to see all the museums on the Upper Santa Fe Trail/Museum Hill. Kids usually have to be dragged from the Children's Museum, even after an hour or two.

WORTH NOTING

Barrio de Analco. Along the south bank of the Santa Fe River, the barrio—its name means "District on the Other Side of the Water"—is one of America's oldest neighborhoods, settled in the early 1600s by the Tlaxcalan Indians (who were forbidden to live with the Spanish near the Plaza) and in the 1690s by soldiers who had helped recapture New Mexico after the Pueblo Revolt. Plaques on houses on East De Vargas Street will help you locate some of the important structures. Check the performance schedule at the **Santa Fe Playhouse** on De Vargas Street, founded by writer Mary Austin and other Santa Feans in the 1920s.

Loretto Chapel. A delicate Gothic church modeled after Sainte-Chapelle in Paris, Loretto was built in 1873 by the same French architects and Italian stonemasons who built St. Francis Cathedral. The chapel is known for the "Miraculous Staircase" that leads to the choir loft. Legend has it that the chapel was almost complete when it became obvious that there wasn't room to build a staircase to the choir loft. In answer to the prayers of the cathedral's nuns, a mysterious carpenter arrived on a donkey, built a 20-foot staircase—using only a square, a saw, and a tub of water to season the wood—and then disappeared as quickly as he came. Many of the faithful believed it was St. Joseph himself. The staircase contains two complete 360-degree turns with no central support; no nails were used in its construction. The chapel closes for services and special events. Adjoining the chapel are a small museum and gift shop. ✉ *207 Old Santa Fe Trail* ☎ *505/982–0092* ⊕ *www.lorettochapel.com* 🎫 *Donations accepted* 🕙 *Mon.–Sat. 9–6, Sun. 10:30–5.*

The Oldest House. More than 800 years ago, Pueblo people built this structure out of "puddled" adobe (liquid mud poured between upright wooden frames). This house, which contains a gift shop, is said to be the oldest in the United States. ⊠ *215 E. De Vargas St.*

MUSEUM HILL

TOP ATTRACTIONS

★ **Museum of Indian Arts and Culture.** An interactive, multimedia exhibition tells the story of Native American history in the Southwest, merging contemporary Native American experience with historical accounts and artifacts. The collection has some of New Mexico's oldest works of art: pottery vessels, fine stone and silver jewelry, intricate textiles, and other arts and crafts created by Pueblo, Navajo, and Apache artisans. Changing exhibitions feature arts and traditions of historic and contemporary Native Americans. You can also see art demonstrations and a video about the life and work of Pueblo potter Maria Martinez. ⊠ *710 Camino Lejo* ☎ *505/476-1250 or 505/476-1269* ⊕ *www. indianartsandculture.org* ⊠ *$9, 4-day pass $20, good at all 4 state museums and the Museum of Spanish Colonial Art* ☉ *Tues.–Sun. 10–5 (also Mon. 10–5 June–early Sept.).*

Fodor's Choice **Museum of International Folk Art** (MOIFA). A delight for adults and children alike, this museum is the premier institution of its kind in the world. In the Girard Wing you'll find thousands of amazingly inventive handmade objects—a tin Madonna, a devil made from bread dough, dolls from around the world, and miniature village scenes galore. The Hispanic Heritage Wing contains art dating from the Spanish-colonial period (in New Mexico, 1598–1821) to the present. The 5,000-piece exhibit includes religious works—particularly *bultos* (carved wooden statues of saints) and retablos, as well as textiles and furniture. The exhibits in the Neutrogena Wing rotate, showing subjects ranging from outsider art to the magnificent quilts of Gee's Bend. Lloyd's Treasure Chest, the wing's innovative basement section, provides a behind-the-scenes look at this collection. You can rummage through storage drawers, peer into microscopes, and, on occasion, speak with conservators and other museum personnel. Check the Web site or call to see if any of the excellent children's activities are scheduled for the time of your visit. Allow time to visit the incredible gift shop and bookstore. ⊠ *706 Camino Lejo* ☎ *505/476-1200* ⊕ *www.moifa.org* ⊠ *$9, 4-day pass $20, good at all 4 state museums and the Museum of Spanish Colonial Art* ☉ *Tues.–Sun. 10–5 (also Mon. 10–5 June–early Sept.).*

Fodor's Choice **Museum of Spanish Colonial Art.** This 5,000-square-foot adobe museum occupies a classically Southwestern former home designed in 1930 by acclaimed regional architect John Gaw Meem. The Spanish Colonial Art Society formed in Santa Fe in 1925 to preserve traditional Spanish-colonial art and culture, and the museum, which sits next to the Museum of International Folk Art and the Museum of Indian Arts and Culture complex, displays the fruits of the society's labor—one of the most comprehensive collections of Spanish-colonial art in the world. Objects here, dating from the 16th century to the present, include *retablos* (holy images painted on wood or tin), elaborate santos, tinwork, straw appliqué, furniture, ceramics, and ironwork. The contemporary collection of works by New Mexico Hispanic artists of the 20th century helps put all this history into regional context. ✉ *750 Camino Lejo* ☎ *505/982–2226* ⊕ *www.spanishcolonial.org* 🎫 *$6, 4-day pass $20, good at all 4 state museums and the Museum of Spanish Colonial Art* ⊙ *Tues.–Sun. 10–5 (also Mon. 10–5 June–Sept.).*

WORTH NOTING

☾ **Santa Fe Children's Museum.** Stimulating hands-on exhibits, a solar greenhouse, oversize geometric forms, and an 18-foot indoor rock-climbing wall all contribute to this museum's popularity with kids. Outdoor gardens with climbing structures, forts, and hands-on activities are great for whiling away the time in the shade of big trees. Puppeteers and storytellers perform often. ✉ *1050 Old Pecos Trail* ☎ *505/989–8359* ⊕ *www.santafechildrensmuseum.org* 🎫 *$9* ⊙ *Sept.–May, Wed.–Sat. 10–5, Sun. noon–5; June–Aug., Tues.–Sat. 10–5, Sun. noon–5.*

Wheelwright Museum of the American Indian. A private institution in a building shaped like a traditional octagonal Navajo hogan, the Wheelwright opened in 1937. Founded by Boston scholar Mary Cabot Wheelwright and Navajo medicine man Hastiin Klah, the museum originated as a place to house ceremonial materials. Those items were returned to the Navajo in 1977, but what remains is an incredible collection of 19th- and 20th-century baskets, pottery, sculpture, weavings, metalwork, photography, paintings, including contemporary works by Native American artists, and typically fascinating changing exhibits. The Case Trading Post on the lower level is modeled after the trading posts that dotted the southwestern frontier more than 100 years ago. It carries an extensive selection of books and contemporary Native American jewelry, kachina dolls, weaving, and pottery. ✉ *704 Camino Lejo* ☎ *505/982–4636 or 800/607–4636* ⊕ *www.wheelwright.org* 🎫 *Free* ⊙ *Mon.–Sat. 10–5, Sun. 1–5; gallery tours weekdays at 2, Sat. at 1.*

> ### IFAM
>
> The **International Folk Art Market** (☎ *505/476–1197* ⊕ *www.folkartmarket.org*), held the second full weekend in July on Milner, is *a truly remarkable* art gathering. Master folk artists from every corner of the planet come together to sell their work amidst a festive array of huge tents, colorful banners, music, food, and delighted crowds. There is a feeling of fellowship and celebration here that enhances the satisfaction of buying wonderful folk art.

RAILYARD DISTRICT

The most significant development in Santa Fe in recent years has taken place in the Railyard District, a neighborhood just south of the Plaza that was for years called the Guadalupe District (and occasionally still known as that). Comprising a few easily walked blocks along Guadalupe Street between Agua Fria and Paseo de Peralta, the district has been revitalized with a snazzy new park and outdoor performance space,

A GOOD TOUR: THE RAILYARD DISTRICT

From the Plaza, head west on San Francisco Street, and then take a left onto Guadalupe Street toward **Santuario de Guadalupe,** two blocks up on your right. After you visit the Santuario, take your time browsing through the shops and eating lunch in one of the restaurants lining Guadalupe Street or around the corner, to the right on Montezuma Street, at the Sanbusco Market Center, a massive, converted warehouse full of boutiques and a Borders bookstore. Check out the great shops and the photographic history on the walls near the market's main entrance. Back on Guadalupe, head south to the historic Gross Kelly Warehouse, one of the earliest Santa Fe–style buildings. Note Santa Fe's two train depots—one is now the site of popular, but touristy, Tomasita's Restaurant; the other, set farther back, is the Santa Fe Depot, where the **Santa Fe Southern Railway** trains and the New Mexico Rail Runner depart. Continue a short distance south on Guadalupe until you reach **SITE Santa Fe** gallery and performance space, set inside a former bottling warehouse. Across the street, spend some time wandering the aisles, or picking up picnic supplies, at the friendly, bustling **Santa Fe Farmers' Market.** It's amazing both the amount of produce and goods coming from this high desert region and the huge crowds that pack the market. Just beyond the Farmers' Market is the Railyard Park, where you can stroll, or lounge, and enjoy your edible goodies amidst green grass, lovely trees, and great stonework. Catercorner from SITE Santa Fe, **El Museo Cultural de Santa Fe** is one of the state's more unusual museums, a combination performance space, classroom, gallery, and event venue that promotes Hispanic culture and education in the City Different. Be sure to visit the gallery at Santa Fe Clay, next door to El Museo, where you'll find world-class ceramic sculpture and working studios.

TIMING

A visit to the Santuario de Guadalupe can take 15 minutes to an hour, depending on whether or not there's an art show in progress. If you like shopping and visiting art galleries, and decide to eat in this area, you might spend hours in this diverse and exciting neighborhood.

a shopping complex, a new permanent indoor-outdoor home for the farmers' market, and several new restaurants and galleries.

This historic warehouse and rail district endured several decades of neglect after the demise of the train route through town. But rather than tearing the buildings down (this is a city where 200-year-old mud-brick buildings sell at a premium, after all), developers gradually converted the low-lying warehouses into artists' studios, antiques shops, bookstores, indie shops, and restaurants. The restored scenic train to Lamy and the Rail Runner commuter train to Albuquerque have put the rail tracks as well as the vintage mission-style depot back into use.

A central feature of the district's redevelopment is the Railyard Park, at the corner of Cerrillos Road and Guadalupe Street, which was designed to highlight native plants and provide citizens with a lush, urban space.

The adjoining buildings contain the vibrant Santa Fe Farmers' Market, the teen-oriented community art center Warehouse21, SITE Santa Fe museum, art galleries, shops, restaurants, and live-work spaces for artists. This dramatic development reveals the fascinating way Santa Feans have worked to meet the needs of an expanding city while paying strict attention to the city's historic relevance.

WHAT TO SEE

El Museo Cultural de Santa Fe. More an arts, educational, and community gathering space than a museum, El Museo celebrates Santa Fe's—and New Mexico's—rich Hispanic heritage by presenting a wide range of events, from children's theater, to musical concerts, to a great Dia de Los Muertos celebration at the beginning of November. The facility sponsors the Contemporary Hispanic Market just off the Plaza each July (held the same time as Spanish Market), and the Contemporary Hispanic Artists Winter Market, held at the center in late November. There's a small gallery showing contemporary art by Hispanic artists. A great resource to visitors who plan ahead are the many classes and workshops, which touch on everything from guitar and Mexican folkloric dance to children's theater and art. ⊠ *1615 Paseo de Peralta* ☎ *505/992–0591* ⊕ *www.elmuseocultural.org* ⊡ *Free; prices vary for events and shows* ⊙ *Tues.–Fri. 1–5, Sat. 10–5.*

Santa Fe Southern Railway. For a leisurely tour across the Santa Fe plateau and into the vast Galisteo Basin, where panoramic views extend for up to 120 mi, take a nostalgic ride on the antique cars of the Santa Fe Southern Railway. The train once served as a spur of the Atchison, Topeka & Santa Fe Railway. Today the train takes visitors on 36-mi round-trip scenic trips to Lamy, a sleepy village with the region's only Amtrak service, offering picnics under the cottonwoods (bring your own or buy one from the caterer that meets the train) at the quaint rail station. Aside from day trips, the railway offers special events such as a Friday-night "High Desert High Ball" cash bar with appetizers and a Saturday Night Barbecue Train ($58). Trains depart from the Santa Fe Depot, rebuilt in 1909 after the original was destroyed in a fire. Reservations are essential. ⊠ *410 S. Guadalupe St. 888/989–8600* ⊕ *www.sfsr.com* ⊡ *Day trips from $32* ⊙ *Call for schedule.*

Santuario de Guadalupe. A massive-walled adobe structure built by Franciscan missionaries between 1776 and 1795, this is the oldest shrine in the United States to Our Lady of Guadalupe, Mexico's patron saint. The church's adobe walls are nearly 3 feet thick, and among the sanctuary's religious art and artifacts is a beloved image of Nuestra Virgen de Guadalupe, painted by Mexican master Jose de Alzibar in 1783. Highlights are the traditional New Mexican carved and painted altar screen called a reredo, an authentic 19th-century sacristy, a pictorial-history archive, a library devoted to Archbishop Jean Baptiste Lamy that is furnished with many of his belongings, and a garden with plants from the Holy Land. ⊠ *100 Guadalupe St.* ☎ *505/988–2027* ⊡ *Donations accepted* ⊙ *May–Oct., Mon.–Sat. 9–4; Nov.–Apr., weekdays 9–4.*

★ **SITE Santa Fe.** The events at this nexus of international contemporary art include lectures, concerts, author readings, performance art, and gallery shows. The facility hosts a biennial exhibition every even-numbered year. Exhibitions are often provocative, and the immense, open space is ideal for taking in the many larger-than-life installations. ⊠ *1606 Paseo de Peralta* ☎ *505/989–1199* ⊕ *www.sitesantafe.org* 🖾 *$10, free Fri., free Sat. 10–noon during Santa Fe Farmers' Market* ⊙ *Wed., Thurs., and Sat. 10–5, Fri. 10–7, Sun. noon–5.*

WHERE TO EAT

Eating out is a major pastime in Santa Fe and it's well worth coming here with a mind to join in on the fun. Restaurants with high-profile chefs stand beside low-key joints, many offering unique and intriguing variations on regional and international cuisine. You'll find restaurants full of locals and tourists alike all over the Downtown and surrounding areas. Although Santa Fe does have some high-end restaurants where dinner for two can easily exceed $200, the city also has plenty of reasonably priced dining options.

Waits for tables are very common during the busy summer season, so it's a good idea to call ahead even when reservations aren't accepted, if only to get a sense of the waiting time. Reservations for dinner at the better restaurants are a must in summer and on weekends the rest of the year.

So-called Santa Fe–style cuisine has so many influences that the term is virtually meaningless. Traditional, old-style Santa Fe restaurants serve New Mexican fare, which combines both Native American and Hispanic traditions and is quite different from Americanized or even authentic Mexican cooking. Many of the better restaurants in town serve a contemporary regional style of cooking that blends New Mexican ingredients and preparations with those of interior and coastal Mexico, Latin America, the Mediterranean, East Asia, and varied parts of the United States.

For a city this small, there is a delightful array of cuisines available aside from the delicious and spicy food of northern New Mexico: Middle Eastern, Spanish, Japanese, Italian, East Indian, and French, to name just a few. More and more restaurants, from casual lunch joints to the finest dining establishments, are focusing on using local and regional ingredients, from meats, to cheeses, to produce. Smoking was recently banned in all bars and restaurants in the city, infuriating some and thrilling many.

WHAT IT COSTS				
	¢	$	$$	$$$	$$$$
Restaurants	under $10	$10–$17	$18–$24	$25–$30	over $30

Prices are per person for a main course at dinner, excluding 8.25% sales tax.

BEST BETS FOR SANTA FE DINING

With hundreds of restaurants to choose from, how will you decide where to eat? Fodor's writers and editors have selected their favorite restaurants by price, cuisine, and experience in the Best Bets lists below. Find specific details about a restaurant in the full reviews, listed alphabetically in the chapter.

3

Fodor's Choice ★

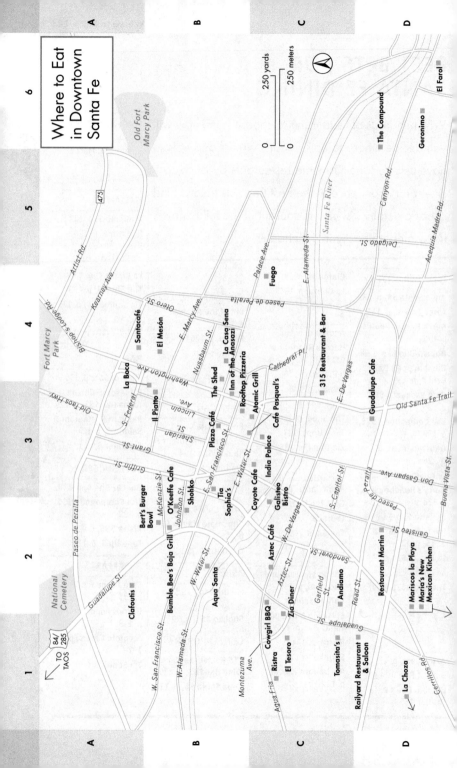

Where to Eat in Downtown Santa Fe

0   250 yards
0   250 meters

A

National Cemetery

Clafoutis

Aqua Santa

Ristra   El Tesoro

Cowgirl BBQ

Zia Diner

Tomasita's

Railyard Restaurant & Saloon

La Choza

B

Bert's Burger Bowl

O'Keeffe Cafe

Bumble Bee's Baja Grill

Shohko

Tia Sophia's

Coyote Cafe

Aztec Café

Galisteo Bistro

Maria's New Mexican Kitchen

Mariscos la Playa

Andiamo

C

Santacafé

El Mesón

La Boca

Il Piatto

Plaza Café

The Shed

Inn of the Anasazi   La Casa Sena

Rooftop Pizzeria

Atomic Grill

Café Pasqual's

India Palace

315 Restaurant & Bar

Guadalupe Cafe

Restaurant Martin

Fuego

D

Old Fort Marcy Park

The Compound

Geronimo

El Farol

Fort Marcy Park

Paseo de Peralta

Guadalupe St.

Old Taos Hwy.

Artist Rd.

Bishop's Lodge Rd.

Kearney Ave.

Otero St.

E. Marcy Ave.

Washington Ave.

Nussbaum St.

Lincoln Ave.

Grant St.

Sheridan St.

E. San Francisco St.

E. Water St.

Cathedral Pl.

Palace Ave.

Paseo de Peralta

E. Alameda St.

Santa Fe River

Delgado St.

Canyon Rd.

Acequia Madre Rd.

E. De Vargas

Old Santa Fe Trail

Don Gaspar Ave.

S. Capitol St.

Paseo de Peralta

Buena Vista St.

Galisteo St.

Read St.

Sandoval St.

Garfield St.

Aztec St.

W. De Vargas

Montezuma Ave.

Agua Fria

W. Water St.

W. San Francisco St.

W. Alameda St.

Griffin St.

McKenzie St.

Johnson St.

S. Federal

Cerrillos Rd.

Guadalupe St.

TO TAOS   84/285

475

TO TAOS

1   2   3   4   5   6

THE PLAZA

Use the coordinate (✛ A1) at the end of each listing to locate a site on the corresponding map.

¢ ✕ **Atomic Grill.** Burgers, salads, pizzas, sandwiches, and other light fare
AMERICAN are served at this tiny café a block off the Plaza. The food is decent but the service can be brusque. The best attributes are the comfy patio overlooking pedestrian-heavy Water Street, the huge list of imported beers, and the late hours (it's open until 3 most nights)—an extreme rarity in Santa Fe. You'll be glad this place exists when the bars let out and you're famished. ⊠ *103 Water St.* ☎ *505/820–2866* ⊕ *http:// theatomicgrill.com* ⊟ *MC, V* ✛ *C3.*

$$$ ✕ **Cafe Pasqual's.** A perennial favorite, this cheerful cubbyhole dishes up
CONTEMPORARY Southwestern and Nuevo Latino specialties for breakfast, lunch, and
Fodor's Choice dinner. Don't be discouraged by lines out front—it's worth the wait.
★ The culinary muse behind it all is Katharine Kagel, who championed organic, local ingredients, and whose expert kitchen staff produces mouthwatering breakfast and lunch specialties like the breakfast relleno (a big, cheese-stuffed chile with eggs and a smoky tomato salsa served with beans and tortillas), huevos motuleños (eggs in a tangy tomatillo salsa with black beans and fried bananas), and the sublime grilled free-range chicken sandwich. Dinner is a more formal, though still friendly and easygoing, affair: char-grilled lamb with pomegranate-molasses glaze, steamed sugar snap peas, and pan-seared potato cakes is a pleasure; the kicky starter of the Thai mint salad with chicken is a revelation. Mexican folk art, colorful tiles, and murals by Oaxacan artist Leovigildo Martinez create a festive atmosphere. Try the chummy communal table, or go late morning or after 1:30 pm to (hopefully) avoid the crush. ⊠ *121 Don Gaspar Ave.* ☎ *505/983–9340* ⊕ *www.pasquals. com* ⊟ *AE, MC, V* ⌦ *No reservations for breakfast and lunch* ✛ *C3.*

$$$$ ✕ **Coyote Cafe.** In 2007 Eric DiStefano took over Coyote Cafe with three
CONTEMPORARY other local industry veterans and the results have been mixed. Adding to—or detracting from, depending on who you ask—the challenges at Coyote is the fact that DiStefano has also resumed the position as executive chef at Geronimo—with many of the same items appearing on both menus. Coyote Cafe is reliable for taste variations on the beloved green chile, but the menu has evolved to include the flavors of French and Asian cuisine. Menu offerings include griddled buttermilk corn cakes with chipotle prawns, DiStefano's signature dish; a peppery elk tenderloin; and the five-spice rotisserie rock hen with green-chile "mac 'n' cheese." Service and food quality vary widely—not an encouraging trend considering the high cost of dining here. Your best bet may be to head to the adjacent Rooftop Cantina (open April through October), a fun outdoor gathering spot with a loud and lively social scene where you can enjoy cool cocktails and flavorful under-$15 fare like burgers and Mexico-inspired fish tacos. ⊠ *132 W. Water St.* ☎ *505/983–1615* ⊕ *www.coyotecafe.com* ⊟ *AE, D, DC, MC, V* ☾ *No lunch at Coyote Cafe (Rooftop Cantina only)* ✛ *C3.*

$$$ ✕ **El Mesón & Chispa Tapas Bar.** This place is as fun for having drinks and
SPANISH tapas or catching live music (from tango nights to Sephardic music) as for enjoying a full meal. The dining room has an old-world feel

with simple dark-wood tables and chairs, creamy plastered walls, and a wood-beam ceiling—unpretentious yet elegant. The Chispa bar is livelier and feels like a Spanish *taberna*. The delicious tapas menu includes dishes like Serrano ham and fried artichoke hearts stuffed with Spanish goat cheese over *romesco* sauce. Among the more substantial entrées are a stellar paella as well as cannelloni stuffed with veal, smothered with béchamel sauce, and topped with Manchego au gratin. ⊠ *213 Washington Ave.* ☎ *505/983–6756* ▤ *AE, MC, V* ⊕ *http://elmeson-santafe. com* ⊘ *Closed Sun. and Mon. No lunch* ⊹ *B4.*

$$$$
CONTEMPORARY

✕ **Fuego.** An elegant yet comfortable dining room inside the oasis of La Posada resort, Fuego has become a local favorite for fantastic, inventive food and flawless service. It is one of Santa Fe's top culinary secrets, albeit with sky-high prices. You might start with seared foie gras with apple pie au poivre before trying free-range *poussin* (young chicken) over a nest of braised leeks and salsify, or roast rack of Colorado elk with parsnip dumplings and a dried-cherry mole. Perhaps the most astounding offering is the artisanal cheese plate—Fuego has one of the largest selections of cheeses west of Manhattan. The wine list is similarly impressive and the helpful sommelier is always on hand to advise. Le Menu Découverte allows you to sample a five-course meal of chef's specialties for $125 (additional $65 for wine pairing). The spectacular Sunday Rancher's Brunch, at $45 per person, is a bargain. ⊠ *La Posada de Santa Fe Resort and Spa, 330 E. Palace Ave.* ☎ *505/986–0000* ⊕ *www. laposadadesantafe.com* ▤ *AE, D, DC, MC, V* ⊹ *C4.*

$$
ECLECTIC
Fodor's Choice
★

✕ **Galisteo Bistro.** Walk into this inviting space a few blocks from the Plaza—with its open kitchen, stacked stone walls, and high ceiling—and you'll likely hope that the food tastes as good as the room feels. Thankfully, it does. The crab cakes are stellar; leading entrées include chicken saltimbocca, grass-fed beef cooked á la béarnaise or Roberto-style (with sautéed marsala mushrooms and roasted green chiles), and mandarin mango pasta with pan-roasted chicken, fresh vegetables, and curried orange-mango sauce over semolina penne. The beautiful desserts often favor chocolate. There's a nice selection of wines, plus a limited offering of locally brewed beers. ⊠ *227 Galisteo St.* ☎ *505/982–3700* ⊕ *www.galisteobistro.com* ▤ *AE, D, MC, V* ⊘ *Closed Mon. and Tues. No lunch* ⊹ *C3.*

$
ITALIAN
Fodor's Choice
★

✕ **Il Piatto.** Chef Matt Yohalem continues to charm the legions of local fans and lucky visitors who dine at his place with creative pasta dishes like *pappardelle* with braised duckling, caramelized onions, sun-dried tomatoes, and mascarpone-duck au jus or homemade pumpkin ravioli with pine nuts and sage brown butter. Entrées include grilled salmon with spinach risotto and tomato-caper sauce, and a superb pancetta-wrapped trout with rosemary, wild mushrooms, and polenta. The menu changes seasonally and emphasizes locally sourced ingredients. It's a crowded but enjoyable trattoria with informal ambience, reasonable prices, and a snug bar. For about $30, the prix-fixe dinner, with an appetizer, main dish, and dessert, is a steal. Add a glass of wine from the reputable list of Italians and both your stomach and your wallet will leave happy. ⊠ *95 W. Marcy St.* ☎ *505/984–1091* ⊕ *www.ilpiattosantafe.com* ▤ *AE, D, MC, V* ⊘ *No lunch weekends* ⊹ *B3.*

$ ✕ **India Palace.** The kitchen prepares fairly traditional recipes—tandoori
INDIAN chicken, lamb vindaloo, *saag paneer* (spinach with farmer cheese),
shrimp *biryani* (tossed with cashews, raisins, almonds, and saffron
rice)—but the presentation is always flawless and the ingredients fresh.
Meals are cooked as hot or mild as requested. Try the Indian buffet at
lunch. ⊠ *227 Don Gaspar Ave., enter from parking lot on Water St.*
☎ *505/986–5859* ⊕ *www.indiapalace.com* ▭ *AE, MC, V* ✛ *C3.*

$$$$ ✕ **Inn of the Anasazi.** Executive chef Oliver Ridgeway takes a global
CONTEMPORARY approach and uses locally and seasonally available ingredients in cre-
Fodor's Choice ating dishes like mole-glazed veal medallions with white and green
★ asparagus, Oregon morels, and elephant garlic or Hawaiian tuna with
wasabi-nut crust. Fare served on the patio (open in summer) and the
bar is lighter and just as interesting—the ahi tuna gyro and the fennel
salad with kalamata tapenade are terrific. The romantic, 90-seat restaurant with hardwood floors, soft lighting, smooth-plastered walls, and
beam ceilings feels slightly less formal than the other big-ticket dining
rooms in town. The patio makes for fun street-side people-watching
and the bar is a cozy, convivial nook. Sunday brunch is superb. ⊠ *113
Washington Ave.* ☎ *505/988–3030* ⊕ *www.innoftheanasazi.com* ▭ *AE,
D, DC, MC, V* ✛ *B3.*

$$ ✕ **La Boca.** This little restaurant, a clean, bright room within an old
SPANISH adobe building, earns rave reviews and has become a local favorite
Fodor's Choice for its intriguingly prepared Spanish food and excellent wine list. Chef
★ James Campbell Caruso has created a menu just right for Santa Fe's
eating style; a wide, changing array of delectable tapas and an edited
selection of classic entrées, like the paella. The friendly, efficient staff is
happy to advise on wine and food selections. The chef's tasting menu
for $55 per person (additional $25 for wine or sherry pairings) is a fun
way to experience Caruso's well-honed approach to his food. Desserts,
like the rich chocolate pot-au-feu, are sumptuous. The room tends to
be loud and can get stuffy during winter when the Dutch door and
windows are closed, but crowds are friendly and you never know who
you'll end up next to in this town of low-key luminaries and celebri-
ties. Half-price tapas, during Tapas en la Tarde, from 3 to 5 during the
week, make a perfect and economical late lunch. ⊠ *72 W. Marcy St.,
The Plaza* ☎ *505/982–3433* ⊕ *www.labocasf.com* ▭ *AE, D, DC, MC,
V* ☉ *No lunch Sun.* ✛ *B3.*

$$$ ✕ **La Casa Sena.** The Southwestern-accented and Continental fare served
ECLECTIC at La Casa Sena is beautifully presented if not consistently as delicious
as it appears. Weather permitting, get a table on the patio surrounded by
hollyhocks, flowering shrubs, and centuries-old adobe walls. A favorite
entrée is the braised Colorado lamb shank with chipotle-*huitlacoche*
demi-glace, roasted purple- and Yukon-gold potatoes, braised *cipol-
lini* onions, and orange *gremolata*. There's a knockout lavender crème
brûlée as well as a tantalizingly spicy-sweet chocolate–red chile soup
served with strawberries, whipped cream, and honey-sugared piñons on
the dessert menu. For a musical meal (evenings only), sit in the restau-
rant's adjacent, less-pricey Cantina ($$), where the talented and perky
staff belt out Broadway show tunes. An on-site wine shop sells many
of the estimable vintages offered on the restaurant's wine list. ⊠ *Sena*

Plaza, 125 E. Palace Ave. ☎ *505/988–9232* ⊕ *www.lacasasena.com* ▤ *AE, D, DC, MC, V* ✛ *B4.*

$$$$　✕ **O'Keeffe Cafe.** This swanky but low-key restaurant next to the Geor-
CONTEMPORARY　gia O'Keeffe Museum turns out some delicious and creative fare with
generous influences from Basque and French traditions. This is much
more than a typical museum café, although the lunches do make a
great, if expensive, break following a jaunt through the galleries. Dinner is the main event, however, showcasing such tempting and tasty
selections as sweetbreads with shallots and cherry demi-glace; cashew-
encrusted mahimahi over garlic-mashed potatoes with a mango–citrus
butter sauce; and Colorado lamb chops with red chile–honey glaze
and mint-infused couscous. Chef Leo Varos's prix-fixe dinner menu,
when offered, is a fantastic deal at around $35. The wine selection is
incredibly extensive, with a number of highly prized international offerings. Patios shaded by leafy trees are great dining spots during warm
weather. Free, validated parking is available at the Eldorado Hotel.
✉ *217 Johnson St.* ☎ *505/946–1065* ⊕ *www.okeeffecafe.com* ▤ *AE,
D, MC, V* ✛ *B2.*

$　✕ **Plaza Café.** Run with homespun care by the Razatos family since
ECLECTIC　1947, this café has been a fixture on the Plaza since 1918. The decor—
★　red leather banquettes, black Formica tables, tile floors, a coffered tin
ceiling, and a 1940s-style service counter—hasn't changed much in
the past half century. The food runs the gamut, from cashew mole
enchiladas to New Mexico meat loaf to chile-smothered burritos to
a handful of Greek favorites, but the ingredients tend toward Southwestern. You'll be hard put to find a better tortilla soup. You can cool
it off with an old-fashioned ice-cream treat from the soda fountain or
a slice of one of the delicious, homemade pies. It's a good, tasty stop
for breakfast, lunch, or dinner. ✉ *54 Lincoln Ave.* ☎ *505/982–1664*
⊕ *http://thefamousplazacafe.com* ⌂ *Reservations not accepted* ▤ *AE,
D, MC, V* ✛ *B3.*

$　✕ **Rooftop Pizzeria.** For sophisticated pizza, head to this slick indoor-
PIZZA　outdoor restaurant atop the Santa Fe Arcade. The kitchen here scores
★　high marks for its rich and imaginative pizza toppings: consider the
one topped with lobster, shrimp, mushrooms, apple-smoked bacon,
caramelized leeks, truffle oil, Alfredo sauce, and four cheeses on a blue-
corn crust. Antipasti and salads are impressive, too, as there's a wonderful smoked-duck-confit-and-peppercorn spread, or the smoked-salmon
Caesar salad. There's also an extensive beer and wine list. Although the
Santa Fe Arcade's main entrance is on the Plaza, it's easier to access
the restaurant from the arcade's Water Street entrance, a few doors up
from Don Gaspar Avenue. ✉ *60 E. San Francisco St.* ☎ *505/984–0008*
⊕ *www.rooftoppizzeria.com* ▤ *AE, D, MC, V* ✛ *B3.*

$$$　✕ **Santacafé.** Southwest minimalist elegance marks the interior of Santa-
CONTEMPORARY　café, one of Santa Fe's vanguard "food as art" restaurants, two blocks
★　north of the Plaza in the historic Padre Gallegos House. Seasonal ingre-
dients are used in the inventive dishes, which might include Alaskan
halibut with English peas, saffron couscous, capers, and preserved
lemon. Shiitake-and-cactus spring rolls with ponzu sauce make a terrific
starter, as does the sublime crispy-fried calamari with a snappy lime-chile

dipping sauce. The latter is big—add a salad for a few dollars and you've got a meal. The shady patio is a joy in summer, and the bar is a snazzy spot to meet friends for drinks just about any time of year. If you're on a tight budget, consider the reasonably priced and equally delicious lunch menu. Sunday brunch is a favorite among locals. ⊠ *231 Washington Ave.* ☎ *505/984–1788* ⊕ *www.santacafe.com* ⊟ *AE, MC, V* ✢ *A4.*

$ ✕ **The Shed.** The lines at lunch attest to the status of this Downtown New
NEW MEXICAN Mexican eatery. The rambling, low-doored, and atmospheric adobe
Fodor$Choice dating from 1692 is decorated with folk art, and service is downright
★ neighborly. Even if you're a devoted green-chile sauce fan, you must try the locally grown red chile the place is famous for; it is rich and perfectly spicy. Specialties include red-chile enchiladas, green-chile stew with potatoes and pork, comforting posole, and their charbroiled Shed-burgers. The mushroom bisque is a surprising and delicious offering. Homemade desserts, like the mocha cake, are a yummy way to smooth out the spice. There's a full bar, too. ⊠ *113½ E. Palace Ave.* ☎ *505/982–9030* ⊕ *www.sfshed.com* ⊟ *AE, DC, MC, V* ☺ *Closed Sun.* ✢ *B4.*

$$$ ✕ **Shohko.** After a brief hiatus Shohko and her family have returned
JAPANESE and once again this is the place for the freshest, best-prepared sushi
★ and sashimi in town. On any given night there are two-dozen or more varieties of fresh fish available. The soft-shell crab tempura is feather-light, and the Kobe beef with Japanese salsa is tender and delicious. Sit at the sushi bar and watch the expert chefs, including Shohko, work their magic, or at one of the tables in this old adobe with whitewashed walls, dark-wood vigas, and Japanese decorative details. Table service is friendly, but can be slow. ⊠ *321 Johnson St., The Plaza* ☎ *505/982–9708* ⊕ *www.shohkocafe.com* ⊟ *AE, D, DC, MC, V* ☺ *No lunch weekends* ✢ *B2.*

¢ ✕ **Tia Sophia's.** This Downtown joint serves strictly New Mexican break-
NEW MEXICAN fasts and lunches (open until 2 pm). You're as likely to be seated next
★ to a family from a remote village in the mountains as you are to a legislator or lobbyist from the nearby state capitol. Tia's ("Auntie's") delicious homemade chorizo disappears fast on Saturdays; if you're an aficionado, get there early. Order anything and expect a true taste of local tradition, including perfectly flaky, light sopaipillas. Mammoth chile-smothered breakfast burritos will hold you over for hours on the powdery ski slopes during winter. Be warned, though: the red and green chiles are spicy and you're expected to understand this elemental fact of local cuisine. Alcohol is not served here. ⊠ *210 W. San Francisco St.* ☎ *505/983–9880* ⊟ *MC, V* ☺ *No dinner. Closed Sun.* ✢ *B3.*

EAST SIDE AND CANYON ROAD

Use the coordinate (✢ A1) at the end of each listing to locate a site on the corresponding map.

$$$$ ✕ **The Compound.** Chef Mark Kiffin has transformed this gracious,
CONTEMPORARY folk-art-filled old restaurant into one of the state's culinary darlings.
Fodor$Choice No longer white-glove formal, it's still a fancy place, thanks to decor
★ by famed designer Alexander Girard and a highly attentive staff, but it maintains an easygoing, distinctly Santa Fe feel. From chef Kiffin's

oft-changing menu, devoted to ingredients based on those introduced to the area by the Spanish, consider a starter of warm flan of summer sweet corn, with lobster succotash and radish sprouts. Memorable entrées include Alaskan halibut with orange lentils, summer squash, and *piquillo* peppers in a smoked ham hock broth; and buttermilk roast chicken with creamed fresh spinach and foie gras pan gravy. The extensive and carefully chosen wine list will please the most discerning oenophile. Lunch is as delightful as dinner, while considerably less expensive—about $14 per person. ⊠ *653 Canyon Rd.* ☎ *505/982–4353* ⊕ *www.compoundrestaurant.com* ⊟ *AE, D, DC, MC, V* ⊗ *No lunch weekends* ✠ *D6.*

$$$ ✕ **El Farol.** In this crossover-cuisine town, owner David Salazar sums up
SPANISH   his food in one word: "Spanish." Order a classic entrée like paella or make a meal from the nearly 30 different tapas—from tiny fried squid to wild mushrooms. Dining is indoors and out. Touted as the oldest continuously operated restaurant in Santa Fe, El Farol (built in 1835) has a relaxed ambience, a unique blend of the Western frontier and contemporary Santa Fe. People push back the chairs and start dancing at around 9:30. The restaurant books live entertainment seven nights a week, from blues and Latin to rock, and there's a festive flamenco performance on Wednesday. End a long day of sightseeing by grabbing a table on the porch in the late afternoon and sipping a refreshing margaritas. ⊠ *808 Canyon Rd.* ☎ *505/983–9912* ⊕ *www.elfarolsf.com* ⊟ *AE, D, MC, V* ✠ *D6.*

$$$$ ✕ **Geronimo.** At this bastion of high cuisine, the complex dishes range
CONTEMPORARY   from pan-roasted Kurobuta pork tenderloin with spicy soy apricot glaze
Fodor's Choice   and scallion black pepper risotto, to fiery sweet-chile-and-honey-grilled
★   Mexican sweet prawns with jasmine-almond rice cakes, frisée-and-red-onion salad, and *yuzu* (Japanese citrus fruit)-and-basil aioli. Chef Eric Di Stefano's peppery elk tenderloin remains a perennial favorite. Desserts are artful and rich, and the Sunday brunch is well regarded. Located in the Borrego House, a massive-walled adobe dating from 1756, the intimate, white dining rooms have beamed ceilings, wood floors, fireplaces, and cushioned *bancos* (banquettes). The restaurant is renowned for both its cuisine and its highly refined service. In summer you can dine under the front portal; in winter the bar with fireplace is inviting. For a less formal experience, dine in the dark, seductive bar—the cocktails are excellent. ⊠ *724 Canyon Rd.* ☎ *505/982–1500* ⊕ *www. geronimorestaurant.com* ⊟ *AE, MC, V* ⊗ *No lunch Mon.* ✠ *D6.*

OLD SANTA FE TRAIL AND SOUTH CAPITOL

Use the coordinate (✠ A1) at the end of each listing to locate a site on the corresponding map.

$$$ ✕ **315 Restaurant & Wine Bar.** As if it were on a thoroughfare in Paris
CONTEMPORARY   rather than on Old Santa Fe Trail, 315 has a Continental, white-table-
★   cloth sophistication, but the offbeat wall art gives it a contemporary feel. Chef-owner Louis Moskow, who also owns the popular Railyard Restaurant *(⇨ below)*, uses traditional techniques to prepare innovative yet simple fare using organic vegetables and locally raised meats. Daily

specialties on the ever-evolving menu might include squash-blossom beignets with local goat cheese, basil-wrapped shrimp with apricot chutney and curry sauce, or grilled boneless lamb loin with crispy polenta, spring vegetables, and green peppercorn sauce. The garden patio opens onto the street scene. There's also a wine bar with an exceptional list of vintages; ask for Moskow's pairing advice. ⊠ *315 Old Santa Fe Trail* ☎ *505/986–9190* ⊕ *www.315santafe.com* ⊟ *AE, MC, V* ⊗ *Closed Sun. No lunch Mon* ✛ *C3.*

¢ ✕ **Body Cafe.** There is a world of things to do inside the contemporary, Asian-inspired Body. At this holistically minded center five minutes from Downtown, you'll find a spa offering a full range of treatments, a yoga studio (with a good range of classes open to visitors), a child-care center, and a boutique selling a wide range of beauty, health, and lifestyle products, plus jewelry, clothing, music, tarot cards, and all sorts of interesting gifts. The café uses mostly organic, local ingredients and serves three meals a day, with an emphasis on vegan and raw food. The breakfast smoothies and homemade granola are delicious. At lunch try soba noodles with peanuts and ginger-soy vinaigrette, or the raw enchiladas (really!), and at dinner there's an unbelievably good raw vegan lasagna layered with basil-sunflower pesto, portobello mushrooms, spinach, squash, tomatoes, nut cheese, and marinara sauce. Beer and wine are served. ⊠ *333 W. Cordova Rd.* ☎ *505/986–0362* ⊕ *www.bodyofsantafe.com* ⊟ *AE, D, MC, V* ✛ *E4.*

CAFÉ

3

$ ✕ **Guadalupe Cafe.** Come to this informal café for hefty servings of New Mexican favorites like enchiladas—vegetarian options are delicious—and quesadillas, or burritos smothered in green or red chile, topped off with sopaipilla and honey. The seasonal raspberry pancakes are one of many breakfast favorites as are eggs Benedict with green-chile hollandaise sauce. Service is hit-or-miss and the wait for a table considerable—but the spicy food keeps 'em coming back for more. ⊠ *422 Old Santa Fe Trail* ☎ *505/982–9762* ⌕ *Reservations not accepted* ⊟ *DC, MC, V* ⊗ *Closed Mon. No dinner Sun.* ✛ *D3.*

NEW MEXICAN

$ ✕ **Maria's New Mexican Kitchen.** Creaky wood floors and dark-wood vigas set the scene for some quite good local cuisine. Serving more than 100 kinds of margaritas is but one of this rustic restaurant's claims to fame. The house margarita is one of the best in town (and you may have surmised that we take our margaritas seriously here). Get the SilverCoin if you want to go top-shelf and leave the rest of the super tequilas to sip on without intrusion of other flavors. The place holds its own as a reliable, supertasty source of authentic New Mexican fare, including chiles rellenos, blue-corn enchiladas, and green-chile tamales. The Galisteo chicken, parboiled and covered in red chiles, is simple and satisfying. Don't be surprised to have to wait for a table, and don't worry, the line moves quickly. ⊠ *555 W. Cordova Rd.* ☎ *505/983–7929* ⊕ *www.marias-santafe.com* ⊟ *AE, D, DC, MC, V* ✛ *E4.*

NEW MEXICAN

★

$ ✕ **Mariscos la Playa.** Yes, even in landlocked Santa Fe it's possible to find incredibly fresh and well-prepared seafood served in big portions. This cheery, colorful Mexican restaurant surrounded by strip malls is just a short hop south of Downtown. Favorite dishes include the absolutely delicious shrimp wrapped in bacon with Mexican cheese and *caldo*

SEAFOOD

★

vuelve a la vida ("come back to life"), a hearty soup of shrimp, octopus, scallops, clams, crab, and calamari. There's also shrimp soup in a tomato broth, fresh oysters on the half shell, and *pescado a la plancha,* super-tender trout cooked with butter and paprika. The staff and service are delightful. ⊠ *537 W. Cordova Rd.* ☎ *505/982–2790* ⊟ *AE, DC, MC, V* ⊹ *E4.*

$ ✕ **Pyramid Cafe.** Tucked into a strip mall five minutes south of the Plaza,
MIDDLE EASTERN   this casual restaurant—with photos of Tunisia, kilim rugs, and North African textiles on the walls—delights locals with flavors not available anywhere else in town. The Tunisian owner and his staff are adept at preparing classic dishes with the Mediterranean flavors of Lebanon and Greece, but when they turn their attention to home flavors, and those of neighboring Morocco, your taste buds will sing. Try the specials, like the Moroccan *tajin,* with chicken, prunes, raisins, and spices served with rice in a domed terra-cotta dish. The *brik a l'oeuf,* a turnover-like Tunisian specialty in phyllo dough with an egg and creamy herbed mashed potatoes tucked inside, is as wonderful as it is unusual. The Tunisian Plate, a sampler, is incredible. Local, organic ingredients are used, and there are excellent vegetarian options. The lunch buffet is fresh and satisfying. ⊠ *505 W. Cordova Rd.* ☎ *505/989–1378* ⊟ *AE, MC, V* ⊹ *E4.*

$$$ ✕ **Restaurant Martin.** After cooking at some of the best restaurants in
CONTEMPORARY   town (Geronimo, the Old House, Anasazi), acclaimed chef Martin Rios is finally flexing his culinary muscles in his own place. Martin and his savvy wife, Jennifer, took a ramshackle old building on a big lot behind the capitol and have created a simple, elegant restaurant with a gorgeous patio. Martin prepares progressive American cuisine, which is heavily influenced by his French culinary training. Lunch favorites include his superb Caesar salad, and a deftly prepared Atlantic salmon BLT sandwich. The crispy coconut-chicken-and-glass-noodle salad is both hot and tangy. Dinner entrées include a delicious vegetarian tasting plate with spring pea ravioli, sweet potato puree, asparagus, carrots, and goat cheese and a grilled Kurobuta pork striploin with *guajillo* chile–and–plum glaze with sweet potato and crispy young vegetables. The brunch menu on the weekends includes classic huevos rancheros prepared with typical Martin flair, and crispy Alaskan halibut Baja fish tacos. ⊠ *526 Galisteo St.* ☎ *505/820–0919* ⊕ *www.restaurantmartinsantafe.com* ⊟ *AE, MC, V* ⊙ *Closed Mon* ⊹ *D2.*

RAILYARD DISTRICT

Use the coordinate (⊹ A1) at the end of each listing to locate a site on the corresponding map.

$ ✕ **Andiamo.** A longtime locals' favorite, Andiamo scores high marks for
ITALIAN   its friendly staff, consistently good food, and comfortable dining room.
★   Produce from the farmers' market down the street adds to the seasonal surprises of this intimate northern Italian restaurant set inside a sweet cottage in the Railyard District. Start with the addictively delectable crispy polenta with rosemary and Gorgonzola sauce; move on to the white pizza with roasted garlic, fontina, grilled radicchio, pancetta, and rosemary; and consider such hearty entrées as crispy duck legs

with grilled polenta, roasted turnips, and sautéed spinach; or linguine with spicy grilled shrimp and olives in a white wine tomato cream sauce. There's a super wine list with varied prices. Save room for the chocolate *pot de crème.* ⌧ *322 Garfield St.* ☎ *505/995–9595* ⊕ *www. andiamoonline.com* ⊟ *AE, DC, MC, V* ⊗ *No lunch weekends* ✛ *C2.*

$$ ✕ **Aqua Santa.** Brian Knox, the charming, gregarious chef at the helm
CONTEMPORARY of this locals' favorite, is a devotee of the Slow Food philosophy. His
Fodor's Choice love and appreciation of food is palpable; some of the finest, simplest,
★ yet most sophisticated dishes in town come from the open kitchen in this tiny, one-room gem of a restaurant. The creamy plastered walls of the intimate dining room are hung with art from local artists, and the ramada-covered patio open in summer feels like dining at a chic friend's house. Diners enjoy dishes like the fabulously tangy Caesar salad, pan-fried oysters with bitter honey and a balsamic reduction, Tuscan bean soup with white-truffle oil, and braised organic New Mexico lamb with olives and summer squash. Brian can be spotted shopping around town for fresh, local ingredients, and the menu changes regularly based on his gastronomic discoveries. Save room for dessert; the silky *panna cotta* (Italian custard) may be the best on the continent. There's an extensive, reasonable wine list, too; ask the friendly staff for their current favorites. ⌧ *451 W. Alameda St. (entrance off Water St.)* ☎ *505/982–6297* ⊟ *MC, V* ⊗ *Closed Sun. and Mon. No lunch Tues. or Sat.* ✛ *B2.*

¢ ✕ **Aztec Cafe.** If a cup of really tasty, locally roasted, noncorporate coffee
CAFÉ in a funky, creaky-wood-floored old adobe sounds like nirvana to you,
Fodor's Choice then this is the place. Cozy, colorful rooms inside are lined with local
★ art (and artists), the staff is laid-back and friendly, and the shady patio outside is a busy meeting ground for locals. Food is homemade, healthy, and flavorful. The menu includes sandwiches such as the Martin-roast turkey, green apples, and Swiss cheese; fabulous, fluffy quiches; soups, breakfast burritos, and superyummy homemade ice cream in the warm season. Brunch happens on the weekends. It's open until 7 (6 pm Sundays) in case you get late-afternoon munchies. There's free Wi-Fi and a public computer with Internet access, and beer and wine are available. ⌧ *317 Aztec St., Railyard District* ☎ *505/820–0025* ⊕ *www.azteccafe. com* ⊘ *Reservations not accepted* ⊟ *AE, MC, V* ✛ *C2.*

$ ✕ **Cowgirl BBQ.** A rollicking, popular bar and grill with several rooms
AMERICAN overflowing with Old West memorabilia, Cowgirl has reasonably priced
☺ Southwestern, Tex-Mex, barbecue, and Southern fare. Highlights include barbecue, buffalo burgers, chiles rellenos, and salmon tacos with tomatillo salsa. A real treat for parents is the outdoor-but-enclosed Kiddie Corral where kids have swings, a climbing structure, and various games to entertain themselves. If you catch one of the nightly music acts—usually rock or blues—you're likely to leave smiling. When the weather is good, grab a seat on the spacious patio out front, order a delicious margarita and some green-chile cheese fries, and settle in for great people-watching. The attached pool hall has a great jukebox to keep toes tapping. Alas, service can be spotty. ⌧ *319 S. Guadalupe St.* ☎ *505/982–2565* ⊕ *www.cowgirlsantafe.com* ⊟ *AE, D, MC, V* ✛ *C1.*

¢ ✕ **El Tesoro.** One of the Railyard District's better-kept secrets, this small
LATIN café occupies a spot in the high-ceilinged center of the Sanbusco Center,

steps from several chic boutiques. The tiny kitchen turns out a mix of Central American, New Mexican, and American dishes, all of them reliable. Grilled tuna tacos with *salsa fresca*, black beans, and rice; and Salvadorian chicken tamales wrapped in banana leaves are among the tastiest treats. El Tesoro also serves pastries, gelato, lemon bars, hot cocoa, and other snacks, making it a perfect break from shopping. ⊠ *Sanbusco Market Center, 500 Montezuma Ave.* ☎ *505/988–3886* ➡ *MC, V* ⊗ *No dinner* ✛ *C1*.

¢ ╳ **La Choza.** The harder-to-find, and less expensive sister to the Shed, La Choza (which means "the shed" in Spanish), serves supertasty, super-traditional New Mexican fare. It's hard to go wrong here: chicken or pork *carne adovada* (marinated in red chile and slow-cooked until tender) burritos, white clam chowder spiced with green chiles, and the classic huevos rancheros are exceptional. The dining rooms are dark and cozy, with vigas across the ceiling and local art on the walls. The staff is friendly and competent, and the addition of a full liquor license has been a boon for dedicated regulars who formerly rued the absence of margaritas. ⊠ *905 Alarid St., near Cerrillos Rd. at St. Francis Dr., around the corner from the Railyard Park* ☎ *505/982–0909* ➡ *AE, DC, MC, V* ⊗ *Closed Sun.* ✛ *D1*.

NEW MEXICAN

ᵔ

Fodor's Choice

★

$ ╳ **Railyard Restaurant & Saloon.** Set inside a bustling, handsome warehouse in the Railyard District, this trendy spot operated by the same owner of 315 Restaurant & Wine Bar serves American favorites that have been given nouvelle twists. Good bets include steamed black mussels in fresh tomato-and-basil broth, fried buttermilk-chicken strips with Creole rémoulade dipping sauce, sesame-and-panko-crusted tuna with a soy-honey sauce, and barbecued baby back ribs. If the softshell crab is available, order it. Many patrons sit in the casual bar, where both the full and bar menus are available, and sip on pomegranate margaritas or well-chosen wines by the glass. The patio out front, with breathtaking views of the Sangre de Cristo Mountains, is a great spot to sit in the summer. Lunch prices average about $10. Service and food quality have been an issue in recent years. ⊠ *530 S. Guadalupe St.* ☎ *505/989–3300* ⊕ *www.railyardrestaurantandsaloon.com* ➡ *AE, D, MC, V* ⊗ *No lunch Sun.* ✛ *D1*.

AMERICAN

$$$ ╳ **Ristra.** This unprepossessing restaurant, set in an old house on the edge of the trendy Railyard District, presents a first-rate menu of Southwestern-influenced modern French cooking. You might start with chorizo-stuffed calamari with watercress and smoked-tomato sauce; roasted rack of lamb with couscous, minted tomatoes, preserved lemon, and Niçoise olives is a tempting main dish. Top off your meal with an almond-butter cake served with warm spiced apples and a mascarpone-caramel sauce. The wines are well selected, and the service is generally good. There's a hip, stylish cocktail bar with its own menu of lighter dishes, including a great burger. ⊠ *548 Agua Fria St.* ☎ *505/982–8608* ⊕ *www. ristrarestaurant.com* ➡ *AE, MC, V* ⊗ *No lunch Sun. and Mon.* ✛ *C1*.

CONTEMPORARY

¢ ╳ **Tomasita's.** Open for years and almost always crowded, this cavernous place serves up reliable—if unspectacular—and spicy, New Mexican food and margaritas. Located in one of the old railroad depots, the interior is nondescript, with vinyl-seated booths and tables packed

NEW MEXICAN

in—though the yellow-glass windows cast a strange light over the place. The full bar is an interesting place to watch a local, not-for-tourists, scene unfold. ✉ *500 S. Guadalupe St., Railyard District* ☎ *505/983– 5721* ⚛ *Reservations not accepted* ▭ *AE, D, DC, MC, V* ✛ *C1.*

$ ✕ **Zia Diner.** Located in a renovated coal warehouse from the 1880s, this

AMERICAN   slick diner with a low-key, art-deco-style interior serves comfort food with a twist (green-chile-piñon meat loaf, for example). Stop in for a full meal or just snack on their classic banana split with homemade hot fudge sauce. Zia's Cobb salad is one of the best in town, and the amazingly fluffy corn, green chile, and Asiago pie served with a mixed green salad is hard to match. Service is friendly, and the food is fresh with lots of local ingredients. There's a small patio and a friendly bar known for its tasty mixed drinks and personable bartenders. Breakfast here is great start to the day: try the Nutty New Mexican, a take on eggs Benedict with green-chile corned beef hash, poached eggs, and hollandaise sauce. Yum! ✉ *326 S. Guadalupe St.* ☎ *505/988–7008* ⊕ *www. ziadiner.com* ▭ *AE, MC, V* ✛ *C2.*

WEST OF PLAZA

Use the coordinate (✛ A1) at the end of each listing to locate a site on the corresponding map.

¢   ✕ **Bert's Burger Bowl.** This unassuming, old-fashioned burger stand has

AMERICAN   brought fans back year after year for the past 55 years with favorites

☺   like their flame-broiled green-chile cheeseburgers (veggie burgers are

Fodor'sChoice   available, too), crispy onion rings, and hand-mixed cherry-lime Cokes.

★   More recently, they've added higher-end burger options like Kobe beef, organic local lamb, and buffalo (these all come with specific toppings). French fries, tacos, and breakfast burritos are also served. The T-shirts here proudly proclaim: ONE LOCATION WORLDWIDE. ✉ *235 N. Guadalupe St.* ☎ *505/982–0215* ▭ *MC, V* ✛ *B2.*

¢   ✕ **Bumble Bee's Baja Grill.** A bright, vibrantly colored restaurant with

MEXICAN   closely spaced tables, piñatas, and ceiling fans wafting overhead,

Fodor'sChoice   Bumble Bee's (it's the nickname of the ebullient owner, Bob) delights

★   locals with its super-fresh Cal Mex–style food. If you like fish tacos, the mahimahi ones with creamy, nondairy slaw are outstanding; try them with a side of salad instead of beans and rice—and *hijole!* (wow!) What a meal! Mammoth burritos with a wide range of fillings (including asparagus—yum!), roasted chicken with cilantro-lime rice, char-grilled trout platters, and a wide variety of vegetarian options keep folks pouring through the doors. You order at the counter, grab some chips and any one of a number of freshly made salsas from the bar, and wait for your number to come up. Beer, wine, and Mexican soft drinks are served. Try a homemade Mexican chocolate brownie for dessert. There's live jazz on Saturday nights. ✉ *301 Jefferson St.* ☎ *505/820–2862* ⊕ *www.bumblebeesbajagrill.com* ✉ *3701 Cerrillos Rd.* ☎ *505/988–3278* ▭ *AE, D, MC, V* ✛ *B2.*

¢   ✕ **Clafoutis.** Undeniably French, this bustling café serves authentic, deli-

CAFÉ   cious food. Walk through the door of this bright, open space and you'll

★   almost certainly be greeted with a cheery *"bonjour"* from Anne-Laure,

SANTA FE COOKING

If you'd like to bring the flavors of the Southwest to your own kitchen, consider taking one or more of the wildly popular and fun cooking classes at the **Santa Fe School of Cooking** (✉ 116 W. San Francisco St., The Plaza ☎ 505/983–4511 ⊕ www.santafeschoolofcooking.com) Regular classes are taught during days and evenings, and more elaborate courses include the Insider's

Culinary Adventure, a meeting-and-eating tour with some of Santa Fe's most notable chefs, or the multiday New Mexico Culture & Cuisine Tour that introduces participants to the chefs, restaurants, and farmers whose passionate devotion to food has made Santa Fe the culinary hot spot that it is. It offers courses that are kid-friendly, too. Reservations are a must.

who owns it with her husband, Philippe. Start your day with a crepe, one of their fluffy omelets, or *les gauffres* (large house waffles). Lunch offers quiches with perfectly flaky crusts, an enticing selection of large salads (the *salade de la maison* has pears, pine nuts, blue cheese, Spanish chorizo, tomatoes, and cucumbers atop mixed greens), and savory sandwiches, like the classic *croque madame* (grilled ham, egg, and cheese) on homemade bread. The classic onion soup is amazingly comforting on a cold day. The café's namesake dessert, clafoutis, is worth saving room for. Their baguettes and pastries are perfectly prepared—no small feat at this elevation. ✉ 402 N. Guadalupe St., near The Plaza ☎ 505/988–1809 ⌛ *Reservations not accepted* ▤ *AE, MC, V* ⊘ *No dinner. Closed Sun.* ✛ A2.

SOUTH SIDE

Use the coordinate (✛ A1) at the end of each listing to locate a site on the corresponding map.

$ ✕ **Chocolate Maven.** Although the name of this cheery bakery suggests
CAFÉ   sweets, and it does sweets especially well, Chocolate Maven produces
★   impressive savory breakfast and lunch fare. Dinner is "farmers' market–inspired" and features seasonal dishes. Favorite treats include wild-mushroom-and-goat-cheese focaccia sandwiches, eggs ménage à trois (one each of eggs Benedict, Florentine, and Madison—the latter consisting of smoked salmon and poached egg), and Caprese salad of fresh mozzarella, basil, and tomatoes. Pizzas are thin-crusted and delicate. Some of the top desserts include Belgian chocolate fudge brownies, mocha-buttercream torte with chocolate-covered strawberries, and French lemon-raspberry cake. Don't let the industrial building put you off; the interior is light, bright, and cozy. Try the Mayan Mocha, espresso mixed with steamed milk and a delicious combo of chocolate, cinnamon, and red chiles—heavenly! ✉ 821 W. San Mateo St. ☎ 505/984–1980 ⊕ www.chocolatemaven.com ▤ AE, D, MC, V ✛ D5.

$ ✕ **Jambo.** In a town where self-professed foodies discuss restaurants and
AFRICAN   dishes ardently, it really says something when a newcomer like Jambo instantly becomes a hot topic. Ahmed Obo, the Kenyan-born owner,

3

who's been in Santa Fe for years, applies great skill and enthusiasm to the food he loves. Afro-Caribbean flavors of coconut, peanuts, and curry influence everything from shrimp to goat stew. Vegetarian choices like the coconut lentil stew are rich and comforting. The restaurant is in a strip mall, but don't let that throw you. Venture inside this casual, homey eatery and enjoy the world-beat music, African art, and the friendly waiters who will happily mention their favorite dishes. ⊠ *2010 Cerrillos Rd.* ☎ *505/473–1269* ⊕ *www.jambocafe.net* ▤ *AE, MC, V* ☉ *Closed Sun.* ✦ *B5.*

$$ ╳ **Mu Du Noodles.** This warm and cozy eatery on a busy stretch of Cer-
ASIAN   rillos Road excels both in its friendly and helpful staff and its interesting pan-Asian fare. Book ahead on weekends—this place fills up fast. Dinner specials are always good, though if you're fond of spicy food be sure to ask for "hot" as their food tends to the mild. Sample sweet-and-sour rockfish with water chestnuts, smoked bacon, and jasmine rice; Vietnamese spring rolls with peanut-hoisin sauce; or stir-fried tenderloin beef with whole scallions, sweet peppers, bean sprouts, and fat rice noodles. The Malaysian *loksa* (a spicy noodle soup) is especially good. Mu, the proprietor, is a strong advocate of cooking with local, organic ingredients. On Sundays, only a light tapas-style menu is served. ⊠ *1494 Cerrillos Rd.* ☎ *505/988–1411* ⊕ *www.mudunoodles.com* ▤ *AE, MC, V* ☉ *Closed Mon. No lunch* ✦ *C4..*

¢   ╳ **Tecolote Cafe.** The mantra here is "no toast," and you won't miss it.
ECLECTIC   Since 1980, the bellies of locals and tourists alike have been satisfied with delicious breakfasts and lunches founded primarily on northern New Mexican cuisine. The simple rooms and comfortable seating allow you to focus on such dishes as the Sheepherder's Breakfast (red potatoes browned with jalapeños and topped with red and green chiles and two eggs), delicious carne adovada (lean pork slow-cooked in their homemade red chile), and a green-chile stew that locals swear by to cure colds. French toast is prepared with homemade breads. When the server asks if you'd like a tortilla or the bakery basket, go for the basket—it's full of warm, fresh muffins and biscuits that are out of this world. ⊠ *1203 Cerrillos Rd.* ☎ *505/988–1362* ⊕ *www.tecolotecafe.com* ⌲ *Reservations not accepted* ▤ *AE, D, DC, MC, V* ☉ *No dinner* ✦ *D4.*

$ ╳ **Tune Up.** The local favorite formerly known as Dave's Not Here is a
ECLECTIC   cozy spot with colorful walls and wood details, booths, a few tables, and a community table. The shaded patio out front is a great summertime spot to enjoy the toothsome breakfasts and lunches served. Start the day with savory, and surprisingly delicate, breakfast rellenos, fluffy buttermilk pancakes, or the *huevos salvadoreños* (eggs scrambled with scallions and tomatoes, served with refried beans, panfried bananas, and a tortilla). Lunch offerings include the super-juicy Dave Was Here burger served with crispy home-cut fries, a ginger-chicken sandwich on ciabatta bread, and Salvadoran treats called *pupusas,* which are most like griddled, flattened, soft tamales—delicious! Dinner offers Yucatecan fish tacos, the succulent Salvadoran combo (with a tamale and a pupusa with roasted tomato salsa and *curtido*—cabbage salad), or an organic flatiron steak. Homemade baked goods include a peanut-butter-cookie sandwich filled with Nutella, and a variety of pies. The staff is

friendly and efficient and the care taken by the owners, Chuy and Charlotte Rivera, is evident. ⊠ *115 Hickox St.* ☎ *505/983–7060* ⊕ *www. tuneupcafe.com* ⌦ *Reservations not accepted* ▤ *AE, MC, V* ✛ *D3.*

OLD LAS VEGAS HIGHWAY

Use the coordinate (✛ A1) at the end of each listing to locate a site on the corresponding map.

¢ ✗ **Bobcat Bite.** It'll take you 15 easy minutes from Downtown to drive
AMERICAN to this tiny roadhouse southeast of town—and it's worth it. Folks drive
Fodor'sChoice a lot farther for Bobcat Bite's steaks and chops ($17) but come espe-
★ cially for one thing: the juiciest burgers in the area. Locals prefer them topped with cheese and green chiles. Only early dinners are available (and no dessert is served), as the place closes by 8 most nights; you'll want to arrive early to get a seat. ⊠ *Old Las Vegas Hwy., 4½ mi south of Old Pecos Trail exit off I–25* ☎ *505/983–5319* ⊕ *www.bobcatbite. com* ⌦ *Reservations not accepted* ▤ *No credit cards* ☉ *Closed Sun. and Mon. (also closed Tues. in winter)* ✛ *F6.*

$ ✗ **Harry's Roadhouse.** This busy, friendly, art-filled compound just south-
ECLECTIC east of town consists of several inviting rooms, from a diner-style space
☾ with counter seating to a cozier nook with a fireplace—there's also an
Fodor'sChoice enchanting courtyard out back with juniper trees and flower gardens.
★ The varied menu of contemporary diner favorites, pizzas, New Mexican fare, and bountiful salads is supplemented by a long list of daily specials—which often include delicious ethnic dishes. Favorites include smoked-chicken quesadillas and grilled-salmon tacos with tomatillo salsa and black beans. Breakfast is fantastic. On weekends, if you're there early, you might just get a chance at one of owner–pastry chef Peyton's phenomenal cinnamon rolls. Desserts here are homey favorites, from the chocolate pudding to the blueberry cobbler. Many gluten-free and veggie options are available, and Harry's is also known for stellar margaritas. The owners are committed to recycling and sustainable business practices. ⊠ *96-B Old Las Vegas Hwy., 1 mi east of Old Pecos Trail exit off I–25* ☎ *505/989–4629* ⊕ *www.harrysroadhousesantafe. com* ▤ *AE, D, MC, V* ✛ *F6.*

WHERE TO STAY

In Santa Fe you can ensconce yourself in quintessential Southwestern style or anonymous hotel-chain decor, depending on how much you want to spend—the city has costlier accommodations than anywhere in the Southwest. Cheaper options are available on Cerrillos (pronounced sir-*ee*-yos) Road, the rather unattractive business thoroughfare southwest of Downtown. Quality varies greatly on Cerrillos, but some of the best-managed, most attractive properties are (from most to least expensive) the Holiday Inn, the Courtyard Marriott, and the Motel 6. You generally pay more as you get closer to the Plaza, but for many visitors it's worth it to be within walking distance of many attractions. Some of the best deals are offered by bed-and-breakfasts—many of those near the Plaza offer much better values than the big, touristy hotels. Rates drop, often from 30% to 50%, from November to April (excluding Thanksgiving and Christmas).

In addition to the usual array of inns and hotels here, Santa Fe has a wide range of **long- and short-term vacation rentals**, some of them available through the **Management Group** (☎ *866/982–2823* ⊕ *www. santaferentals.com*). Rates generally range from $100 to $300 per night for double-occupancy units, with better values at some of the two- to four-bedroom properties. Many have fully stocked kitchens. Another route is to rent a furnished condo or casita at one of several compounds geared to travelers seeking longer stays. The best of these is the luxurious **Campanilla Compound** (☎ *505/988–7585 or 800/828–9700* ⊕ *www.campanillacompound.com*), on a hill just north of Downtown; rates run from about $1,400 to $1,800 per week in summer. Another good, similarly priced bet is **Fort Marcy Suites** (☎ *888/570–2775* ⊕ *www.allseasonsresortlodging.com/santa_fe/fortmarcy*), on a bluff just northeast of the Plaza with great views. The individually furnished units accommodate two to six guests and come with full kitchens, wood fireplaces, VCRs, and CD stereos—these can be rented nightly or weekly.

WHAT IT COSTS					
	¢	$	$$	$$$	$$$$
Hotels	under $70	$70–$130	$131–$190	$191–$260	over $260

Prices are for a standard double room in room in high season, excluding 13.5%–14.5% tax.

THE PLAZA

Use the coordinate (✛ A1) at the end of each listing to locate a site on the corresponding map.

$$$
HOTEL

Eldorado Hotel & Spa. Because it's the closest thing Santa Fe has to a convention hotel, the Eldorado sometimes gets a bad rap, but it's actually quite inviting, with individually decorated rooms and stunning mountain views. Rooms are stylishly furnished with carved Southwestern-style desks and chairs, large upholstered club chairs, and art prints; many have terraces or kiva-style fireplaces. The rooftop pool and gym are great fun, and there's music nightly, from classical Spanish guitar to piano, in the comfortable lobby lounge. A full slate of treatments, from Vichy rain showers to High Mesa salt scrubs, is offered by the hotel's luxe Nidah Spa. The Old House restaurant has been a solid contender in the local restaurant scene for years. **Pros:** serviceable accommodations three blocks from Santa Fe Plaza. **Cons:** staff's attention to service varies considerably. ✉ *309 W. San Francisco St.* ☎ *505/988–4455 or 800/955–4455* ⊕ *www.eldoradohotel.com* ⥌ *213 rooms* ⌕ *In-room: a/c, kitchen (some), Wi-Fi. In-hotel: restaurant, room service, bar, pool, gym, spa, laundry service, parking (paid)* ▭ *AE, D, DC, MC, V* ✛ *B3*.

$$$
HOTEL

Hotel St. Francis. Listed on the National Register of Historic Places, this three-story building, parts of which were constructed in 1923, has walkways lined with turn-of-the-20th-century lampposts and is one block south of the Plaza. The hotel recently underwent a dramatic

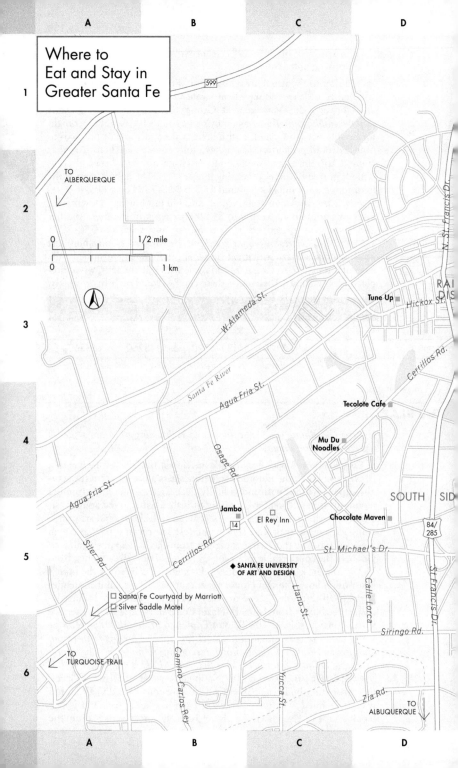

Where to Eat and Stay in Greater Santa Fe

599

TO ALBERQUERQUE

0   1/2 mile

0   1 km

W. Alameda St.

RAIL DIST

Tune Up

Hickox St.

Cerrillos Rd.

Santa Fe River

Agua Fria St.

Tecolote Cafe

Osage Rd.

Mu Du Noodles

SOUTH SID

Agua Fria St.

Jambo

El Rey Inn

Chocolate Maven

84/285

14

Cerrillos Rd.

St. Michael's Dr.

Siler Rd.

◆ SANTA FE UNIVERSITY OF ART AND DESIGN

Llano St.

Cattle Lorca

St. Francis Dr.

Siringo Rd.

Santa Fe Courtyard by Marriott
Silver Saddle Motel

TO TURQUOISE TRAIL

Camino Carlos Rey

Yucca St.

Zia Rd.

TO ALBUQUERQUE

A   B   C   D

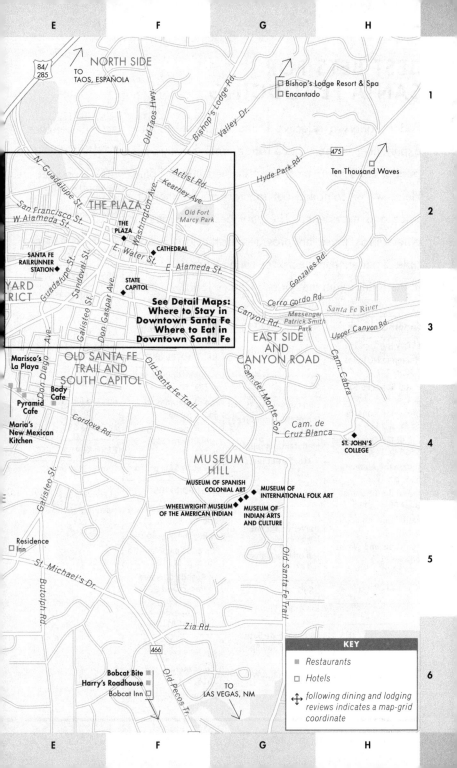

BEST BETS FOR SANTA FE LODGING

Fodor's offers a selective listing of quality lodging experiences in every price range, from the city's best budget beds to its most sophisticated luxury hotels. Here, we've compiled our top recommendations by price and experience. The very best properties—in other words, those that provide a particularly remarkable experience in their price range—are designated in the listings with the Fodor's Choice logo.

renovation and is now reminiscent of a Tuscan monastery, with expansive stone floors, plaster walls, and spare furnishings lit by massive pillar candles at night. The simple, elegant rooms with high ceilings, and casement windows have rustic Mexican furnishings and beautiful, custom linens. The modern New Mexican restaurant, Tabla de Los Santos ($$$), has popular local chef Esteban Garcia at the helm. **Pros:** highly distinct ambience; two blocks from the Plaza and near many shops. **Cons:** service can be spotty; many of the rooms (and especially bathrooms) are quite small. ⊠ *210 Don Gaspar Ave.* ☎ *505/983–5700 or 800/529–5700* ⊕ *www.hotelstfrancis.com* ⇥ *80 rooms, 2 suites* ⚷ *In-room: a/c, refrigerator, Wi-Fi. In-hotel: restaurant, room service, bar, gym, laundry service, parking (paid)* ⊟ *AE, D, DC, MC, V* ✛ *B3.*

$$$$ **⌂ Inn of the Anasazi.** Unassuming from the outside, this first-rate bou-
HOTEL   tique hotel is one of Santa Fe's finest, with superb architectural detail.
Fodor's Choice   The prestigious Rosewood Hotel manages the property and has steadily
★   and carefully upgraded the already sumptuous linens and furnishings over the years. Each room has a beamed viga-and-latilla ceiling, kiva-style gas fireplace, antique Navajo rugs, handwoven fabrics, and organic toiletries (including sunblock). Other amenities include full concierge services, twice-daily maid service, exercise bikes upon request, and a library. Especially nice touches in this desert town are the humidifiers in each guest room. A few deluxe rooms have balconies. The restaurant and bar are excellent. **Pros:** staff is thorough, gracious, and highly professional. **Cons:** standard rooms tend to be small for the price; few rooms have balconies; no hot tub or pool. ⊠ *113 Washington Ave.* ☎ *505/988–3030 or 800/688–8100* ⊕ *www.innoftheanasazi.com* ⇥ *58 rooms* ⚷ *In-room: a/c, safe, Wi-Fi. In-hotel: restaurant, bar, parking (paid), some pets allowed* ⊟ *AE, D, DC, MC, V* ✛ *B4.*

$$$ **⌂ Inn of the Governors.** This rambling hotel by the Santa Fe River is
HOTEL   staffed by a polite, enthusiastic bunch. Rooms have a Mexican theme,
★   with bright colors, hand-painted folk art, feather pillows, Southwestern fabrics, and handmade furnishings; deluxe rooms also have balconies and fireplaces. Perks include a complimentary tea-and-sherry social each afternoon and a quite extensive breakfast buffet along with free Wi-Fi and newspapers. New Mexican dishes and lighter fare like wood-oven pizzas are served in the very popular and very reasonably priced bar-restaurant, Del Charro (¢). **Pros:** close to Plaza; friendly, helpful staff. **Cons:** standard rooms are a bit small and cramped. ⊠ *101 W. Alameda St.* ☎ *505/982–4333 or 800/234–4534* ⊕ *www.innofthegovernors. com* ⇥ *100 rooms* ⚷ *In-room: a/c, refrigerator, Wi-Fi. In-hotel: restaurant, room service, bar, pool, parking (free)* ⊟ *AE, D, DC, MC, V* ⦿ *CP* ✛ *C3.*

$$$$ **⌂ Inn and Spa at Loretto.** This plush, oft-photographed, pueblo-inspired
HOTEL   property attracts a loyal clientele, many of whom swear by the friendly
⟳   staff and high decorating standards. The lobby opens up to the gardens and large pool, and leather couches and high-end architectural details make the hotel a pleasure to relax in. Rooms are among the largest of any Downtown property and contain vibrantly upholstered, handcrafted furnishings and sumptuous slate-floor bathrooms—many have large balconies overlooking Downtown. Other nice touches include an

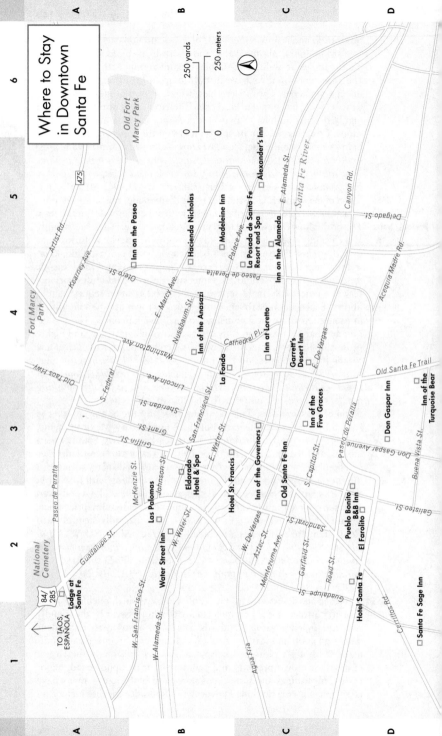

Where to Stay in Downtown Santa Fe

0 250 yards
0 250 meters

Old Fort Marcy Park

Fort Marcy Park

National Cemetery

TO TAOS, ESPAÑOLA

□ Lodge at Santa Fe

□ Inn on the Paseo

■ Hacienda Nicholas

□ Madeleine Inn

□ La Posada de Santa Fe Resort and Spa

■ Alexander's Inn

□ Inn on the Alameda

■ Inn of the Anasazi

□ Inn at Loretto

La Fonda

Garrett's Desert Inn

□ Las Palomas

Eldorado Hotel & Spa

Water Street Inn

Hotel St. Francis □

□ Inn of the Governors

□ Old Santa Fe Inn

□ Inn of the Five Graces

□ Don Gaspar Inn

□ Inn of the Turquoise Bear

Pueblo Bonito B&B Inn □
El Farolito □

Hotel Santa Fe

□ Santa Fe Sage Inn

Santa Fe River

Canyon Rd.
E. Alameda St.
Acequia Madre Rd.
Delgado St.
Old Santa Fe Trail
E. De Vargas
Paseo de Peralta
Don Gaspar Avenue
Buena Vista St.
Galisteo St.
Cerrillos Rd.
Read St.
Garfield St.
Montezuma Ave.
Aztec St.
Sandoval St.
S. Capitol St.
W. De Vargas
E. Water St.
Johnson St.
W. Water St.
W. Alameda St.
Agua Fría
Guadalupe St.
W. San Francisco St.
McKenzie St.
Paseo de Peralta
Griffin St.
Grant St.
Sheridan St.
Lincoln Ave.
E. San Francisco St.
Washington Ave.
E. Marcy Ave.
Nussbaum St.
Otero St.
Kearney Ave.
Artist Rd.
S. Federal
Old Taos Hwy.
Cathedral Pl.
Palace Ave.
Paseo de Peralta

475
84/ 285

iPod dock and a complimentary newspaper each day. The restaurant, Luminaria, serves creative Southwestern fare and the lounge, the Living Room, offers a number of specialty cocktails in a sophisticated but relaxed room. The spa offers a wide range of Balinese and Thai-style treatments and services. **Pros:** the location, two blocks from the Plaza, is ideal; gorgeous grounds. **Cons:** expensive parking and resort fees; rooms tend to be dark. ✉ *211 Old Santa Fe Trail* ☎ *505/988–5531 or 800/727–5531* ⊕ *www.hotelloretto.com* ↪ *134 rooms, 5 suites* ♨ *In-room: a/c, Wi-Fi, refrigerator. In-hotel: restaurant, bar, gym, spa, parking (paid)* ▭ *AE, D, DC, MC, V* ✛ *C4.*

3

$ 🏨 **Inn on the Paseo.** This inn is on a busy road, but at least this stretch
INN of Paseo de Peralta is two lanes wide and is in a semiresidential neighborhood a short walk from the Plaza. Rooms are fairly simple, and can be small, but clean and light, some with hardwood floors and all with pleasing Southwestern furnishings and color schemes—some have fireplaces and private patios. The staff is laid-back and friendly. The two historic main buildings are joined by a modern lobby with a pitched ceiling, where the Continental breakfast is served—in warm weather you can dine on the sundeck. **Pros:** just a few blocks from the Plaza. **Cons:** you need a room away from the road to avoid traffic noise. ✉ *630 Paseo de Peralta* ☎ *505/984–8200 or 800/457–9045* ⊕ *www.innonthepaseo. com* ↪ *16 rooms, 2 suites* ♨ *In-room: a/c, Internet. In-hotel: parking (free), no kids under 8* ▭ *MC, V* ⵣ*CP* ✛ *B4.*

$$$ 🏨 **La Fonda.** History and charm are more prevalent in this sole Plaza-
HOTEL front hotel than first-class service and amenities. Though there has been an inn on this corner for centuries, the pueblo-inspired structure you see today was redesigned in 1922 by famed regional architect John Gaw Meem and has since been enlarged many times. Antiques and Native American art decorate the tiled lobby, and each room has hand-decorated wood furniture, wrought-iron light fixtures, beamed ceilings, and high-speed wireless. Some suites have fireplaces. The 14 rooftop suites are the most luxurious and include Continental breakfast and private concierge services; there's also an exercise room, garden, and outdoor hot tub there. La Plazuela Restaurant, with its hand-painted glass tiles, serves good and creative Southwestern food. Folk and R&B bands rotate nightly in the bar. **Pros:** great building and location; steeped in history. **Cons:** for the price, facilities don't stand up to comparison with other Downtown properties. ✉ *100 E. San Francisco St.* ☎ *505/982– 5511 or 800/523–5002* ⊕ *www.lafondasantafe.com* ↪ *143 rooms, 14 suites* ♨ *In-room: a/c, Wi-Fi. In-hotel: restaurant, bars, pool, gym, laundry service, parking (paid)* ▭ *AE, D, DC, MC, V* ✛ *B4.*

EAST SIDE AND CANYON ROAD

Use the coordinate (✛ A1) at the end of each listing to locate a site on the corresponding map.

$$$ 🏨 **Alexander's Inn.** Once a bed-and-breakfast, Alexander's now rents two
COTTAGES two-story cottages. It remains an excellent lodging option. Located just
★ a few blocks from the Plaza and Canyon Road, it exudes the charm of old Santa Fe. Cottages are cozy, with Southwest- and American

Santa Fe: Spa Mecca of the Southwest

Santa Fe has established itself as a major spa destination. From day spas to resorts where you can spend days ensconced in beautiful surroundings with endless treatment options, there is a spa and a specialty for everyone in this town. There are spas at most of the better hotel resorts, but the spas listed here stand out for their highly trained therapists, specialized treatments, and overall experience.

Absolute Nirvana lives up to its name with its lush, peaceful Indo-Asian setting and the sumptuous treatments it offers. Master-level massage therapists use all-organic, delectable food-grade ingredients. Most treatments finish with home-made snacks and a rose-petal bath in a massive stone tub. Eco-friendly Nirvana is certified by the non-profit Green Spa Network. ✉ *Madeleine Inn, 106 Faithway St., The Plaza* 🕾 *505/983–7942* ⊕ *www.absolutenirvana.com.*

Body is a day spa just south of the Guadalupe District offering Thai, Swedish, and Japanese massage in addition to Rolfing, Reiki, and prenatal massage. Facials focus on rehydrating skin. A café, boutique, and child-care are on the premises. ✉ *333 Cordova Rd.* 🕾 *505/986–0362* ⊕ *www.bodyofsantafe.com.*

La Posada Resort & Spa offers a wide range of treatments, many with regional ingredients, in this historic Downtown resort. Hair and nail services and a fitness center are also in the spa complex. ✉ *330 E. Palace Ave., The Plaza* 🕾 *505/986–0000* ⊕ *www.laposadadesantafe.com.*

Spa Samadhi at Sunrise Springs Resort offers art-strewn walls and waterfalls, fruit and tea, and a profusion of treatments to move one's chi. Earthy cedar sauna and outdoor hot tubs are at your disposal. Transformative sessions, such as holographic and polarity therapies, sound healing, nutritional counseling, and lymphatic release are also available. This ecoresort unfolds over 70 green and serene acres, 15 mi southwest of Downtown Santa Fe. ✉ *242 Los Piños Rd.* 🕾 *505/471–3600* ⊕ *www.sunrisesprings.com.*

Ten Thousand Waves is a renowned Japanese-style spa with outstanding facilities and treatments, 10 minutes north of Santa Fe toward the ski basin. Primarily a day spa—the hot tubs are a popular option—it has a limited number of suites available for longer stays. ✉ *3451 Hyde Park Rd.* 🕾 *505/992–5025* ⊕ *www.tenthousandwaves.com.*

country–style furnishings, ethnic heirlooms, skylights, tall windows, and fireplaces. Each has a kitchen, fireplace, full bathroom, and private bedroom upstairs. The grounds are dotted with tulips, hyacinths, lilac, and apricot trees. Guests receive discounts at the nearby Absolute Nirvana Spa (⇨ *"Santa Fe: Spa Mecca of the Southwest" box, below*) and full access to El Gancho Health Club, a 10-minute drive away. You'll find a generous welcome basket with wine and snacks, and attentive service. **Pros:** private, homey retreat in the heart of historic Santa Fe; an excellent value. **Cons:** shares open yard with private home. ✉ *529 E. Palace Ave.* 🕾 *505/986–1431 or 888/321–5123* ⊕ *www.alexanders-inn.*

com ↪ *2 cottages* ♿ *In-room: kitchen. In-hotel: Wi-Fi hotspot, parking (free), some pets allowed* ⊟ *D, MC, V* ⊺⏀⎮ *CP* ⊹ *C5.*

$$$
INN
Fodor'sChoice
★

Hacienda Nicholas. It is rare to find classic Santa Fe accommodations—this actually *is* an old hacienda—blocks from the Plaza for reasonable prices. This is one such place. The thick adobe walls surrounding the building create a peace and solitude that belies its central location. Southwest decor mixes with French country and Mexican details to create an ambience perfectly suited to this city. Homemade, organic breakfasts are deluxe; afternoon snacks will leave you begging for the recipes (which they'll cheerfully provide). The rooms are extremely comfortable and quiet, with details like plush comforters and sheets, and cozy robes. Several rooms open on to the interior courtyard, which has a kiva fireplace and offers a perfect respite after a long day of exploring. This is a real find. **Pros:** rates are significantly lower than one would expect for the level of service and amenities here; the inn is one of the most eco-friendly in town. **Cons:** no hot tub or pool, though guests have privileges at El Gancho Health & Fitness Club 15 minutes away. ✉ *320 E. Marcy St., The Plaza* ☎ *505/986–1431 or 888/284–3170* ⊕ *www.haciendanicholas.com* ↪ *7 rooms* ♿ *In-rooms: Wi-Fi. In-hotel: Wi-Fi hotspot, parking (free)* ⊟ *AE, D, MC, V* ⊹ *B4.*

$$$
HOTEL
Fodor'sChoice
★

Inn on the Alameda. Near the Plaza and Canyon Road is one of the Southwest's best small hotels. *Alameda* means "tree-lined lane," and this one perfectly complements the inn's location by the gurgling Santa Fe River. The adobe architecture and enclosed courtyards strewn with climbing rose vines combine a relaxed New Mexico country atmosphere with the luxury and amenities of a top-notch hotel, from afternoon wine and cheese to free local and toll-free calls to triple-sheeted beds with luxurious Egyptian cotton bedding. Rooms have a Southwestern color scheme, handmade armoires and headboards, and ceramic lamps and tiles—many have patios and kiva fireplaces. **Pros:** the solicitous staff is first-rate; excellent, expansive breakfast buffet with lots of extras. **Cons:** rooms closest to Alameda can be noisy; no pool. ✉ *303 E. Alameda St.* ☎ *505/984–2121 or 888/984–2121* ⊕ *www.innonthealameda.com* ↪ *59 rooms, 10 suites* ♿ *In-room: a/c, refrigerator (some), Wi-Fi. In-hotel: bar, gym, laundry facilities, parking (free), some pets allowed* ⊟ *AE, D, DC, MC, V* ⊺⏀⎮ *CP* ⊹ *C5.*

$$$$
HOTEL
☾

La Posada de Santa Fe Resort and Spa. Rooms on the beautiful, quiet grounds of this hotel vary, but extensive renovations have enhanced all rooms to a level of luxury befitting the steep rates. Many have fireplaces, all have flat-screen TVs, CD players, leather couches, marble bathrooms, and Navajo-inspired rugs. The main building contains a handful of luxurious, high-ceiling Victorian rooms. The property boasts excellent bar, spa, and common areas, including the fantastic contemporary restaurant Fuego *(⇨ Where to Eat, above)*, the casual Viga restaurant (which has indoor and outdoor seating), and the Staab House Lounge. Guests are offered numerous complimentary events throughout the week, like Margarita Monday, wine-and-cheese pairings on Wednesday, and chef's receptions on Friday. **Pros:** numerous amenities; two blocks from Plaza and similarly close to Canyon Road. **Cons:** resort can sometimes feel overrun with tour-bus crowds; $30 daily resort fee. ✉ *330 E. Palace Ave.* ☎ *505/986–0000 or 866/331–7625* 🌐 *www.laposadadesantafe.com* *120 rooms, 39 suites* *In-room: a/c, Wi-Fi. In-hotel: restaurant, bar, pool, gym, spa, parking (paid)* *AE, D, DC, MC, V* ✣ *C4.*

$$ INN Fodor's Choice ★ **Madeleine Inn.** Santa Fe hasn't always been a town of pseudopueblo buildings and this lovely Queen Anne Victorian is living proof. Built by a railroad tycoon in 1886, this beautifully maintained B&B is nestled amongst mature trees and gardens just four blocks from the Plaza. Plush beds, lovely antiques and art adorn the rooms. Fireplaces grace four rooms and the smells of freshly baked goodies welcome you in the afternoon. Homemade organic breakfasts with too many options to list here are worth sticking around for, and the staff is professional and gracious. The amazing Absolute Nirvana spa is on the premises. Guests have privileges to El Gancho Health & Tennis Club 15 minutes away. **Pros:** excellent value; great service; eco-friendly. **Cons:** steep stairs; no elevators in this three-story Victorian. ✉ *106 Faithway St., The Plaza* ☎ *505/982–3465 or 888/877–7622* 🌐 *www.madeleineinn.com* *7 rooms* *In-hotel: Wi-Fi hotspot, parking (free)* *AE, D, MC, V* ✣ *B5.*

OLD SANTA FE AND SOUTH CAPITOL

Use the coordinate (✣ A1) at the end of each listing to locate a site on the corresponding map.

$$ INN **Don Gaspar Inn.** One of the city's best-kept secrets, this exquisitely landscaped and attractively decorated compound is on a pretty residential street a few blocks south of the Plaza. Its three historic houses have three distinct architectural styles: Arts and Crafts, Pueblo Revival, and Territorial. Floral gardens and aspen and cottonwood trees shade the tranquil paths and terraces, and both Southwest and Native American paintings and handmade furnishings enliven the sunny rooms and suites. The Arts and Crafts main house has two fireplaces, two bedrooms, and a fully equipped kitchen. Staff is attentive without hovering. Considering the setting and amenities, it's a great value. **Pros:** beautiful decor; delicious and generous breakfasts; lush gardens. **Cons:** some rooms close to elementary school can be noisy in the morning when school is in. ✉ *623 Don Gaspar Ave.* ☎ *505/986–8664 or 888/986–8664* 🌐 *www.dongaspar.com* *4 rooms, 3 suites, 2 casitas, 1 house* *In-room: kitchen (some), refrigerator, Wi-Fi. In-hotel: parking (free)* *MC, V* *BP* ✣ *D3.*

$$$ INN **El Farolito.** All the beautiful Southwestern and Mexican furniture in this small, upscale compound is custom-made, and all the art and photography original. Rooms are spacious and pleasant with fireplaces and separate entrances; some are in their own little buildings. El Farolito has a peaceful Downtown location, just steps from the capitol and a few blocks from the Plaza. The same owners run the smaller Four Kachinas inn, which is close by and has one handicapped-accessible room (rare among smaller Santa Fe properties). The breakfast here is a real treat, featuring a tempting range of delicious baked goods. **Pros:** attentive service; special dietary requests accommodated. **Cons:** no on-site pool or hot tub. ✉ *514 Galisteo St.* ☎ *505/988–1631 or 888/634–8782* 🌐 *www.*

farolito.com ⇨ *7 rooms, 1 suite* △ *In-room: a/c, Wi-Fi. In-hotel: parking (free)* ⊟ *AE, D, MC, V* ⏀ *BP* ✢ *D2.*

$ 🖼 **Garrett's Desert Inn.** This sprawling, U-shaped motel may surround a
MOTEL   parking lot and offer relatively little in the way of ambience, but it's fairly well maintained and you can't beat its location just a few blocks from the Plaza, smack in the middle of historic Barrio de Analco. The clean, no-frills rooms are done in earthy tones with a smattering of Southwest touches, and there's a pleasant pool and patio as well. **Pros:** The restaurant, Ze French Bistro, offers delicious French food with chef Laurent Rea at the helm. **Cons:** $8 per night parking fee; not much curb appeal. ⊠ *311 Old Santa Fe Trail* ☎ *505/982–1851 or 800/888–2145* ⊕ *www.garrettsdesertinn.com* ⇨ *83 rooms* △ *In-room: a/c, Wi-Fi. In-hotel: restaurant, pool, gym, laundry facilities, parking (paid)* ⊟ *AE, D, MC, V* ✢ *C4.*

$$$$ 🖼 **Inn of the Five Graces.** There isn't another property in Santa Fe to
HOTEL   compare to this sumptuous yet relaxed inn with an unmistakable East-
Fodor's Choice meets-West feel. The management and staff at this Relais & Chateaux
★   hotel have created a property that fits right in with the kind of memorable properties you hear about in Morocco and Bali. The decor differs from the cliché Santa Fe style, yet locals would tell you that this melding of styles is what true Santa Fe style is all about. The suites have Asian and Latin American antiques and art, kilim rugs, jewel-tone throw pillows, and mosaic-tile bathrooms; most have fireplaces, and many have soaking tubs or walk-in steam showers. The personal service stands out: treats are left on your pillow, refrigerators are stocked, and afternoon margarita and wine-and-cheese spreads, an exquisite breakfast, and even daily walking tours are all available. A new spa treatment room has been added with several luxe treatments to salve the skin from the high, dry mountain climate. Management continues to improve the gardens and outdoor areas, with more lush, flowering plants, gurgling fountains and cozy nooks to relax into. **Pros:** tucked into a quiet, ancient neighborhood; the Plaza is only minutes away; fantastic staff, attentive but not overbearing. **Cons:** very steep rates. ⊠ *150 E. DeVargas St.* ☎ *505/992–0957 or 866/992–0957* ⊕ *www.fivegraces.com* ⇨ *22 suites 1 house* △ *In-room: kitchen (some), refrigerator, Wi-Fi. In-hotel: parking (free), some pets allowed* ⊟ *AE, D, MC, V* ⏀ *BP* ✢ *C3.*

$$ 🖼 **Inn of the Turquoise Bear.** In the 1920s, poet Witter Bynner played host
INN   to an eccentric circle of artists and intellectuals, as well as some wild
Fodor's Choice parties in his mid-19th-century Spanish–Pueblo Revival home, which
★   is now a bed-and-breakfast. Rooms are simple, traditional Southwestern style with heavy wood furniture and plush linens. The inn's style preserves the building's historic integrity, starting with the ranchlike lobby and extending throughout the rambling ambience-thick public rooms. You might sleep in the room where D.H. Lawrence or Willa Cather slept, or perhaps in Robert Oppenheimer's room. The lush, terraced flower gardens provide plenty of places to repose away from the traffic on Old Santa Fe Trail, which borders the property. This is the quintessential Santa Fe inn. **Pros:** gorgeous grounds and a house steeped in local history; gracious, knowledgeable staff; generous Continental breakfasts. **Cons:** no pool or hot tub on-site; quirky layout of some

rooms isn't for everyone. ⊠ *342 E. Buena Vista* ☏ *505/983–0798 or 800/396–4104* ⊕ *www.turquoisebear.com* ⟲ *8 rooms, 2 with shared bath; 3 suites* ⟳ *In-room: Wi-Fi. In-hotel: parking (free), some pets allowed* ⊟ *AE, D, MC, V* |○| *CP* ✛ *D3.*

$$ ⊞ **Pueblo Bonito B&B Inn.** Rooms in this 1873 adobe compound have
BED AND   handmade and hand-painted furnishings, Navajo weavings, brick and
BREAKFAST   hardwood floors, sand paintings and pottery, locally carved santos (Catholic saints), and Western art. All have kiva fireplaces and private entrances, and many have kitchens. A breakfast buffet is served in the convivial main dining room with lots of fresh fruits and yogurt, baked goods, cereals, coffee and teas. Afternoon tea also offers complimentary margaritas. The Plaza is a five-minute walk away. **Pros:** intimate, cozy inn on peaceful grounds; hot tub. **Cons:** bathrooms tend to be small; breakfast is Continental. ⊠ *138 W. Manhattan Ave.* ☏ *505/984–8001 or 800/461–4599* ⊕ *www.pueblobonitoinn.com* ⟲ *13 rooms, 5 suites* ⟳ *In-room: kitchen (some), refrigerator (some), Wi-Fi. In-hotel: restaurant, laundry facilities, parking (free)* ⊟ *AE, DC, MC, V* |○| *CP* ✛ *D3.*

RAILYARD DISTRICT

Use the coordinate (✛ A1) at the end of each listing to locate a site on the corresponding map.

$$ ⊞ **Hotel Santa Fe.** Picurís Pueblo has controlling interest in this hand-
HOTEL   some Pueblo-style three-story hotel on the Railyard District's edge and
Fodor's Choice   a short walk from the Plaza. The light, airy rooms and suites are tradi-
★   tional Southwestern, with locally handmade furniture, wooden blinds, and Pueblo paintings; many have balconies. The hotel gift shop, Santa Fe's only tribally owned store, has lower prices than many nearby retail stores. The 35 rooms and suites in the posh Hacienda wing have corner fireplaces and the use of a London-trained butler. Amaya is one of the better hotel restaurants in town. Informal talks about Native American history and culture are held in the lobby, and Native American dances take place May through October. **Pros:** professional, helpful staff; lots of amenities. **Cons:** standard rooms are fairly small. ⊠ *1501 Paseo de Peralta* ☏ *505/982–1200 or 800/825–9876* ⊕ *www.hotelsantafe.com* ⟲ *40 rooms, 91 suites* ⟳ *In-room: a/c, Wi-Fi. In-hotel: restaurant, bar, pool, laundry service, parking (free)* ⊟ *AE, D, DC, MC, V* ✛ *D2.*

$$ ⊞ **Old Santa Fe Inn.** This contemporary motor-court-style inn looks like
HOTEL   an attractive, if fairly ordinary, adobe motel, but it has stunning and
★   spotless rooms with elegant Southwestern furnishings. Tile baths, high-quality linens, and upscale furnishings fill every room, along with two phone lines and CD stereos; many have kiva fireplaces, or balconies and patios. A small business center and gym are open 24 hours. Most rooms open onto a gravel courtyard parking lot, although chile *ristras* hanging outside each unit brighten things up. The make-your-own-breakfast-burrito buffet is a nice touch. **Pros:** rooms are more inviting than several more-expensive Downtown hotels and it's a short walk to the Plaza; some rooms have Jacuzzi tubs. **Cons:** minimal, though friendly and professional, staffing. ⊠ *320 Galisteo St.* ☏ *505/995–0800 or 800/745–9910* ⊕ *www.oldsantafeinn.com* ⟲ *34 rooms, 9 suites* ⟳ *In-room: a/c,*

refrigerator (some), Wi-Fi. In-hotel: gym, parking (free) ⊟ AE, D, DC, MC, V ⫴ CP ✛ C2.

$ ⚏ **Santa Fe Sage Inn.** On the southern edge of the Railyard District,
MOTEL this smartly renovated motel offers affordable comfort and surprisingly
⚉ attractive (given the low rates) Southwestern decor within walking dis-
★ tance of the Plaza (six blocks). Special packages are available for three-
and four-day stays during peak-season events. Get a room upstairs and
in one of the rear buildings for the most privacy and quiet. Continental
breakfast is included. **Pros:** comfortable; affordable; close to Plaza and
train station. **Cons:** rooms on corner of Cerrillos and Don Diego can be
noisy. ⊠ *725 Cerrillos Rd.* ☎ *505/982–5952 or 866/433–0335* ⊕ *www.
santafesageinn.com* ⥹ *156 rooms* ⚐ *In-room: a/c, Wi-Fi. In-hotel: gym,
pool, laundry facilities, parking (free), some pets allowed* ⊟ *AE, DC,
MC, V* ⫴ *CP* ✛ *D1.*

WEST OF PLAZA

*Use the coordinate (✛ A1) at the end of each listing to locate a site on
the corresponding map.*

$$$ ⚏ **Las Palomas.** It's a pleasant 10-minute walk west of the Plaza to reach
VACATION this group of properties, consisting of two historic, luxurious com-
COTTAGES pounds, one of them Spanish Pueblo–style adobe, the other done in the
Territorial style, with a Victorian ambience, as well as the 15 rooms in
the recently acquired La Tienda & Duran House compound. A network
of brick paths shaded by mature trees leads past the casitas, connect-
ing them with secluded courtyards and flower gardens. Each casita has
a bedroom, full kitchen, living room with pull-out sofa, and fireplace,
and each opens onto a terrace or patio. Locally handcrafted wood-and-
leather sofas, desks, and tables fill these spacious accommodations,
along with Native American artwork and sculptures. It's an elegant
alternative to the city's upscale full-service hotels, affording guests a
bit more privacy and the feel of a private cottage rental—though it is
managed by the Hotel Santa Fe. **Pros:** kid-friendly, with swings and a
play yard; on-site fitness center. **Cons:** big variation in accommodations;
no hot tub or pool on-site (guests may use pool at the Hotel Santa Fe).
⊠ *460 W. San Francisco St.* ☎ *505/982–5560 or 877/982–5560* ⊕ *www.
laspalomas.com* ⥹ *38 units* ⚐ *In-room: kitchen, Wi-Fi. In-hotel: gym,
parking (free)* ⊟ *AE, D, DC, MC, V* ⫴ *CP* ✛ *B2.*

$$ ⚏ **Water Street Inn.** The large rooms in this restored adobe 2½ blocks
INN from the Plaza are decorated with reed shutters, antique pine beds,
viga-beam ceilings, hand-stenciled artwork, and a blend of cowboy, Hispanic, and Native American art and artifacts. Most have fireplaces, and
all have flat-screen TVs with DVD players and CD stereos. Afternoon
hors d'oeuvres are served in the living room; breakfasts are ample and
tasty. A patio deck is available for relaxing. Many of the guests here
return year after year. **Pros:** elegant décor; gracious, noteworthy staff.
Cons: grounds are restricted—the inn overlooks a parking lot. ⊠ *427 W.
Water St.* ☎ *505/984–1193 or 800/646–6752* ⊕ *www.waterstreetinn.
com* ⥹ *8 rooms, 4 suites* ⚐ *In-room: a/c, DVD, Wi-Fi. In-hotel: parking (free)* ⊟ *AE, DC, MC, V* ⫴ *BP* ✛ *B2.*

SOUTH SIDE

Use the coordinate (✛ A1) at the end of each listing to locate a site on the corresponding map.

$ ✦ **El Rey Inn.** The kind of place where Lucy and Ricky might have stayed
HOTEL during one of their cross-country adventures, the El Rey was built in
Fodor's Choice 1936 but has been brought gracefully into the 21st century, its rooms
★ and bathrooms handsomely updated without losing any period charm.
♻ Rooms are individually decorated and might include antique television armoires, beamed ceilings, upholstered wing chairs and sofas; some have kitchenettes. Each unit has a small covered front patio with wrought-iron chairs. Beautifully landscaped grounds are covered with flowers in the summer and towering trees shade the parking lot. There's a landscaped courtyard with tables and chairs by the pool. **Pros:** excellent price for a distinctive, charming property. **Cons:** rooms closest to Cerrillos can be noisy; some rooms are quite dark. ⊠ *1862 Cerrillos Rd.* ☎ *505/982–1931 or 800/521–1349* ⊕ *www.elreyinnsantafe.com* ➫ *86 rooms* ♿ *In-room: a/c, kitchen (some), Wi-Fi. In-hotel: pool, gym, laundry facilities, parking (free)* ▭ *AE, DC, MC, V* ⧦*CP* ✛ *C5.*

$$$ ✦ **Residence Inn.** This compound consists of clusters of three-story adobe
TOWN HOUSES town houses with pitched roofs and tall chimneys. Best bets for families or up to four adults traveling together are the one-room suites, which each have a loft bedroom and a separate sitting area (with a curtain divider) that has a Murphy bed. All units have wood-burning fireplaces. It's right off a major intersection about 3 mi south of the Plaza, but it's set back far enough so that there's no traffic noise. Ask for one of the second-floor end units for the best mountain views. **Pros:** complimentary full breakfast; evening socials; grocery-shopping service. **Cons:** not within easy walking distance of many restaurants or attractions. ⊠ *1698 Galisteo St.* ☎ *505/988–7300 or 800/331–3131* ⊕ *www.marriott.com/ safnm* ➫ *120 suites* ♿ *In-room: a/c, kitchen, Internet. In-hotel: pool, gym, laundry facilities, Wi-Fi hotspot, parking (free)* ▭ *AE, D, DC, MC, V* ⧦*BP* ✛ *E5.*

$$ ✦ **Santa Fe Courtyard by Marriott.** Of the dozens of chain properties along
HOTEL prosaic Cerrillos Road, this is the only bona fide gem, even though it looks like all the others: clad in faux adobe and surrounded by parking lots and strip malls. Don't fret—it's easy to forget about the nondescript setting once inside this polished miniature resort, which comprises several buildings set around a warren of lushly landscaped interior courtyards. Aesthetically, the rooms look Southwestern, with chunky carved-wood armoires, desks, and headboards reminiscent of a Spanish-colonial hacienda. **Pros:** rooms have the usual upscale-chain doodads: mini-refrigerators, coffeemakers, hair dryers, and clock radios. **Cons:** hotel lacks character; Cerrillos Road is unattractive; a 10-minute drive from Plaza. ⊠ *3347 Cerrillos Rd.* ☎ *505/473–2800 or 800/777–3347* ⊕ *www.santafecourtyard.com* ➫ *209 rooms* ♿ *In-room: a/c, refrigerator, Wi-Fi. In-hotel: restaurant, room service, bar, pool, gym, laundry facilities, parking (free)* ▭ *AE, D, DC, MC, V* ✛ *A5.*

¢   ✦ **Silver Saddle Motel.** This low-slung adobe property transcends the gen-
MOTEL erally sketchy quality of the several other budget motels along Cerrillos
★ Road, thanks to the tireless efforts of a new owner. There's a kitschy,

Western aspect to the place—rooms are named for icons of the West (Annie Oakley, Wyatt Earp) and contain related plaques with colorful biographies and local cowboy art. Furnishings are decidedly Southwest: Mexican-tile bathrooms, serape tapestries, built-in bancos, and *equipale* chairs ("seat of the gods" made of woven wood and leather) are present in most. Recent improvements include new carpets, mattresses, a breakfast patio, and a big dose of general TLC. The popular home-furnishings and gift emporium, Jackalope, is next door. The motel is across the street from the town's one strip club, which could be either a pro or a con. **Pros:** superaffordable; good-sized rooms, some with refrigerators; friendly, helpful staff. **Cons:** rooms toward the front get noise from Cerrillos Boulevard; fairly basic. ⊠ *2810 Cerrillos Rd.* 📠 *505/471–7663* ⊕ *www.santafesilversaddlemotel.com* 🔊 *27 rooms* ⚑ *In-room: a/c, kitchen (some), Wi-fi. In-hotel: parking (free)* ▭ *D, MC, V* ⦿*CP* ✛ *A5.*

OLD LAS VEGAS HIGHWAY

Use the coordinate (✛ A1) at the end of each listing to locate a site on the corresponding map.

$

INN

★

🛏 **Bobcat Inn.** A delightful, affordable, country hacienda that's a 15-minute drive southeast of the Plaza, this adobe bed-and-breakfast sits amid 10 secluded acres of piñon and ponderosa pine, with grand views of the Ortiz Mountains and the area's high-desert mesas. John and Amy Bobrick run this low-key retreat and prepare expansive full breakfasts as well as high tea on Saturday during the summer high season (these are by reservation only). Arts and Crafts furniture and Southwest pottery fill the common room, in which breakfast is served and guests can relax throughout the day. The individually decorated rooms are brightened by Talavera tiles, folk art, and colorful blankets and rugs; some have kiva fireplaces. The Lodge Room is outfitted with handcrafted Adirondack furniture, and its bathroom has a whirlpool tub. Guests have access to El Gancho Health & Fitness center (fee) nearby. **Pros:** gracious, secluded inn; wonderful hosts. **Cons:** located outside town, and a drive is required for all activities except eating at Bobcat Bite, which is right next door; no pets; no children under age six. ⊠ *442 Old Las Vegas Hwy.* 📠 *505/988–9239* ⊕ *www.nm-inn.com* 🔊 *5 rooms* ⚑ *In-room: no TV, Wi-Fi. In-hotel: parking (free), no kids under 6* ▭ *D, MC, V* ⦿*BP* ✛ *F6.*

NORTH SIDE

Use the coordinate (✛ A1) at the end of each listing to locate a site on the corresponding map.

$$$

RESORT

☙

🛏 **Bishop's Lodge Resort and Spa.** Although this historic resort is just a five-minute drive from the Plaza, its setting in a bucolic valley at the foot of the Sangre de Cristo Mountains makes it feel worlds apart. Outdoor activities abound including hiking, horseback riding, skeet shooting, tennis (professional lessons available) and trapshooting. History runs deep here with the nearly 150-year-old chapel built by Archbishop Jean Baptiste Lamy—a figure lionized by writer Willa Cather—at the resort's center. Rooms have antique and reproduction Southwestern furnishings—shipping chests, Mexican tinwork, and Native American and Western art. Many offer balconies or patios with spectacular mountain vistas. The Las Fuentes Restaurant & Bar specializes in inventive Nuevo Latino fare, and the kitchen uses produce and herbs from the property's heritage garden. Recently, they've replanted the vineyard with vines descended from those brought to America by Bishop Lamy and intend soon to produce wine. Locals often descend on the excellent Sunday brunch. The tranquil SháNah Spa and the beautiful grounds make this place a special getaway only minutes from Downtown. **Pros:** staff is friendly and well-trained. **Cons:** resort is spread out over 700 acres and some rooms seem rather far-flung. ⊠ *Bishop's Lodge Rd., 2½ mi north of Downtown* ☎ *505/983–6377 or 800/419–0492* ⊕ *www. bishopslodge.com* ⟳ *91rooms, 12 suites 7 villas* ⎈ *In-room: a/c, refrigerator, Internet. In-hotel: 2 restaurants (one open in summer only), bar, tennis courts, pool, gym, spa, children's programs (ages 5–13), parking (free)* ⊟ *AE, D, MC, V* ✛ *G1.*

$$$$
RESORT
　Encantado. Sister to California's famed Auberge du Soleil and Cabo's Esperanza Resort, Encantado provides over-the-top luxury while respecting the region's distinct architectural style. Taking advantage of Santa Fe's endless supply of sunshine, villa-style casitas are contemporary, airy, and earthy. Kitted with adobe fireplaces, deep soaking tubs, heated bathroom floors and spacious dressing areas, rooms exemplify comfortable cushiness. Local products in the minibar (Cap Rock Organic Grape Vodka and C. G. Higgins Caramel Corn) are a thoughtful touch. Detox at the spa with regionally inspired treatments like Mountain Spirit Purification, or take a Pilates class in the movement studio before enjoying a sunset cocktail at the bar and a sumptuous globe-spanning culinary adventure at the restaurant, Terra. Complimentary shuttles run regularly into town and guests have access to Encantado's Downtown concierge center. **Pros:** freestanding couples spa suites; complimentary minibar (nonalcoholic beverages only); stunning rooms. **Cons:** several of the private terraces overlook parking lots; service, though friendly and eager, doesn't always live up to expectation; remote location. ⊠ *198 NM 592* ☎ *877/262–4666* ⊕ *www.encantadoresort. com* ⟳ *65 rooms* ⎈ *In-room: a/c, safe, refrigerator, DVD, Wi-Fi. In-hotel: restaurant, room service, bar, pool, gym, spa, laundry service, Wi-Fi hotspot, parking (free), some pets allowed* ⊟ *AE, MC, V* ✛ *G1.*

$$
HOTEL
　Lodge at Santa Fe. Rooms at this midprice property have pleasant Southwestern furnishings and earth-tone fabrics, though some of the furnishings and facilities are showing wear. The hilltop location offers spectacular views east toward the Sangre de Cristo Mountains and south toward the Sandias—but only from certain rooms, so ask when reserving. The Plaza is a five-minute drive (they offer free shuttle service), the Santa Fe Opera just a bit farther. Las Mañanitas restaurant serves decent Spanish and Southwestern fare, and the adjacent cabaret is home in summer to flamenco dancer Maria Benitez's troupe. **Pros:** guests have free access to the Santa Fe Spa health club next door, away from the crowds and noise of the Plaza. **Cons:** service is sometimes lackluster; no restaurants or attractions within walking distance. ⊠ *750*

N. St. Francis Dr. ☎ *505/992–5800 or 888/563–4373* ⊕ *www.hhandr. com* ⋑ *103 rooms, 25 suites* ⅄ *In-room: a/c, Wi-Fi. In-hotel: restaurant, room service, bar, pool, parking (free)* ▭ *AE, D, DC, MC, V* ⊹ *A1.*

$$$

COTTAGES

Fodor'sChoice

★

⚏ **Ten Thousand Waves.** Devotees appreciate the authentic *onsen* (Japanese-style baths)atmosphere of this health spa and small hotel a few miles northeast of town. Twelve light and airy hillside cottages are settled down a piñon-covered hill below the first-rate spa, which is tremendously popular with day visitors. The sleek, uncluttered accommodations have marble or stone wood-burning fireplaces, CD stereos, fine woodwork, low-slung beds or futons, and courtyards or patios; two come with full kitchens. There's also a cozy, vintage Airstream Bambi trailer available at much lower rates ($139 nightly)—with its ultramod interior, it's a kitschy, fun alternative to the much pricier cottages. The facility has private and communal indoor and outdoor hot tubs and spa treatments. Overnight guests can use the communal tubs for free. The snack bar serves sushi and other healthful treats. Ask about the Japanese movie nights. **Pros:** artful furnishings; peaceful setting; warm service. **Cons:** a bit remote, especially considering lack of a restaurant. ✉ *3451 Hyde Park Rd., 4 mi northeast of the Plaza* ⬧ *Box 10200, 87504* ☎ *505/982–9304* ⊕ *www.tenthousandwaves.com* ⋑ *12 cottages, 1 trailer* ⅄ *In-room: no a/c, kitchen (some), refrigerator, no TV (some), Wi-Fi (some). In-hotel: spa, parking (free), some pets allowed* ▭ *D, MC, V* ⊹ *H2.*

NIGHTLIFE AND THE ARTS

Few, if any, small cities in America can claim an arts scene as thriving as Santa Fe's—with opera, symphony, and theater in splendid abundance. The music acts here tend to be high-caliber, but rather sporadic. Nightlife, as in dance clubs, is considered fairly "bleak." When popular acts come to town the whole community shows up and dances like there's no tomorrow. A super, seven-week series of music on the Plaza bandstand runs through the summer with performances four nights a week. Gallery openings, poetry readings, plays, and dance concerts take place year-round, not to mention the famed opera and chamber-music festivals. Check the arts and entertainment listings in Santa Fe's daily newspaper, the *New Mexican* (⊕ *www.santafenewmexican.com*), particularly on Friday, when the arts and entertainment section, "Pasatiempo," is included, or check the weekly *Santa Fe Reporter* (⊕ *www. sfreporter.com*) for shows and events. As you suspect by now, activities peak in the summer.

NIGHTLIFE

Culturally endowed though it is, Santa Fe has a pretty mellow nightlife scene; its key strength is live music, which is presented at numerous bars, hotel lounges, and restaurants. Austin-based blues and country groups and other acts wander into town, and members of blockbuster bands have been known to perform unannounced at small clubs while vacationing in the area. But on most nights your best bet might be quiet cocktails beside the flickering embers of a piñon fire or under the stars out on the patio.

BARS AND LOUNGES

Corazón (⊠ *401 S. Guadalupe St., Railyard District* ☎ *505/983–4559* ⊕ *www.corazonsantafe.com*) has reinvented a well-known space in the Railyard District with great success. Depending on the night, it's hard to predict whether you'll be shaking your booty to hip-hop, poundin' blues, rock music, or sweet Americana. The local veterans of the music and bar scene who created Corazón book varied lineups in this often-packed space, which serves satisfying pub grub, too.

★ **The Cowgirl** (⊠ *319 S. Guadalupe St., Railyard District* ☎ *505/982–2565*) is one of the most popular spots in town for live blues, country, rock, folk, and even comedy, on occasion. The bar is friendly and the $3.50 happy hour margaritas provide a lot of bang for the buck. The pool hall is fun and can get wild as the night gets late.

Dragon Room (⊠ *406 Old Santa Fe Trail, Old Santa Fe Trail and South Capitol* ☎ *505/983–7712*), at the Pink Adobe restaurant, long a hot spot in town, has been tidied up and, consequently, it's no longer the fun, lively destination for colorful locals and curious tourists. Good drinks and bar food, though.

Eldorado Court and Lounge (⊠ *309 W. San Francisco St., The Plaza* ☎ *505/988–4455*), in the lobby of the classy Eldorado Hotel, is a gracious lounge where classical guitarists and pianists perform nightly. It has the largest wines-by-the-glass list in town.

★ **El Farol** (⊠ *808 Canyon Rd., East Side and Canyon Road* ☎ *505/983–9912*), with its big front porch, is a particularly choice spot to enjoy the afternoon and evenings of summer. The roomy, rustic bar has a true Old West atmosphere—there's been a bar on the premises since 1835—and you can order some fine Spanish brandies and sherries in addition to cold beers and tasty mixed drinks (particularly those margaritas locals are so fond of). It's a great place to see a variety of music; the dance floor fills up with a friendly crowd.

Evangelo's (⊠ *200 W. San Francisco St., The Plaza* ☎ *505/982–9014*) is an old-fashioned, street-side bar, with pool tables downstairs, 200 types of imported beer, and rock bands on many weekends.

Matador (⊠ *116 W. San Francisco St., Suite 113, enter downstairs on Galisteo St., The Plaza* ☎ *No phone*) is a dark, subterranean dive bar close to the Plaza. Owners Frank and César, both entertaining characters, have banished any notions of Southwest-style decor by painting the place black and covering the walls with old punk posters, and locals love it. You'll find a decent selection of beers, stiff mixed drinks, and some fine tequilas (this is Santa Fe, after all). The early crowd is older, and gets younger and hipper as the night goes on.

Milagro 139 (⊠ *139 W. San Francisco St., The Plaza* ☎ *505/995–0139* ⊕ *www.milagro139.com*) draws a friendly, mixed-age crowd thanks to great DJs on Friday and Saturday nights. It's one of the liveliest dance spots in town.

Fodor's Choice
★

Secreto Lounge (✉ *210 Don Gaspar Ave., The Plaza* ☎ *505/983–5700* ⊕ *www.hotelstfrancis.com*) is the beautifully redesigned bar inside the dramatically renovated Hotel St. Francis. Bar staff here make the best and most interesting drinks in town, including a classic Manhattan with clove tincture spritzed over the top. When the weather is good, try to get a seat on the portal out front.

Santa Fe Brewing Company (✉ *35 Fire Pl., on NM 14, the Turquoise Trail, South Side* ☎ *505/424–3333* ⊕ *www.santafebrewing.com*) hosts all sorts of music and serves fine microbrews and food (and Taos's Cow ice cream!) from its location about 15 minutes south of the Plaza. Recent acts have included the BoDeans, Sierra Leone's Refugee All Stars, Delbert McClinton, and local stars Hundred-Year Flood and Goshen. Very kid-friendly, the venue has an indoor room for the cold months, and a great outdoor stage where the performers, and the sunset, are on full view.

Second Street Brewery (✉ *1814 2nd St., South Side* ☎ *505/982–3030* ✉ *1607 Paseo de Peralta, beside farmers' market building, Railyard District* ☎ *505/989–3278*) packs in an eclectic, easygoing bunch for its own microbrewed ales, pub fare, live rock, folk, and some great local DJs. There's an expansive patio at the original 2nd Street location, and the staff is friendly. A newer branch opened in the Railyard District, steps from the train station, in 2009.

Tin Star Saloon (✉ *411B W. Water St., near West of the Plaza* ☎ *505/984– 5050* ⊕ *www.tinstarsaloon.com*) is a welcome addition to Santa Fe's nightlife, with a great bar in a cozy room and live music almost every night. They book a wide range of music, from hard rock to R&B. The crowd here likes to dance.

Tiny's (✉ *Cerrillos Rd. and St. Francis Dr., South Side* ☎ *505/983–9817*), a retro-fabulous restaurant serving steaks and New Mexican fare, is a legend in this town with politicos, reporters, and deal makers. The real draw is the kitsch-filled '50s cocktail lounge.

THE ARTS

The performing arts scene in Santa Fe blossoms in summer when the calendar is filled with classical or jazz concerts, Shakespeare on the grounds of St. John's campus, experimental theater at Santa Fe Stages, or flamenco. . . . "Too many choices!" is the biggest complaint. The rest of the year is a bit quieter, but an increasing number of off-season venues have developed in recent years. The "Pasatiempo" section of the *Santa Fe New Mexican*'s Friday edition or the *Santa Fe Reporter*, released on Wednesday, are great sources for current happenings.

The city's most interesting multiuse arts venue, the **Center for Contemporary Arts (CCA)** (✉ *1050 Old Pecos Trail, Old Santa Fe Trail and South Capitol* ☎ *505/982–1338* ⊕ *www.ccasantafe.org*) presents indie and foreign films, art exhibitions, provocative theater, and countless workshops and lectures.

CONCERT VENUES

Santa Fe's vintage Downtown movie house was fully restored and converted into the 850-seat **Lensic Performing Arts Center** (✉ *211 W. San Francisco St., The Plaza* ☎ *505/988–1234* ⊕ *www.lensic.com*) in 2001. The grand 1931 building, with Moorish and Spanish Renaissance influences, hosts the Santa Fe Symphony, theater, classic films, lectures and readings, noted world, pop, and jazz musicians, and many other noteworthy events.

The **St. Francis Auditorium** (✉ *Museum of Fine Arts,107 W. Palace Ave., northwest corner of the Plaza*) is the scene of cultural events such as theatrical productions and varied musical performances.

MUSIC

★ The acclaimed **Santa Fe Chamber Music Festival** (☎ *505/983–2075* ⊕ *www. sfcmf.org*) runs mid-July through late August, with performances nearly every night at the St. Francis Auditorium, or, occasionally, the Lensic Performing Arts Center. There are also free youth-oriented concerts given on several summer mornings. You can also attend many rehearsals for free; call for times.

Performances by the **Santa Fe Desert Chorale** (☎ *505/988–2282 or 800/244–4011* ⊕ *www.desertchorale.org*) take place throughout the summer at a variety of intriguing venues, from the Cathedral Basilica St. Francis to Loretto Chapel. This highly regarded singing group, which was started in 1982, also performs a series of concerts during the December holiday season.

Fodor's Choice **Santa Fe Opera** (☎ *505/986–5900 or 800/280–4654* ⊕ *www. ★ santafeopera.org*) performs in a strikingly modern structure—a 2,126-seat, indoor-outdoor amphitheater with excellent acoustics and sight lines. Carved into the natural curves of a hillside 7 mi north of the city on U.S. 285/84, the opera overlooks mountains, mesas, and sky. Add some of the most acclaimed singers, directors, conductors, musicians, designers, and composers from Europe and the United States, and you begin to understand the excitement that builds every June. The company, which celebrated its 65th anniversary in 2011, presents five works in repertory each summer—a blend of seasoned classics, neglected masterpieces, and world premieres. Many evenings sell out far in advance, but inexpensive standing-room tickets are often available on the day of the performance. A favorite pre-opera pastime is tailgating in the parking lot before the evening performance—many guests set up elaborate picnics of their own, but you can also preorder picnic meals ($32 per meal) by calling (☎ *505/983–2433*) 24 hours in advance; pick up your meal up to two hours before the show, at the Angel Food Catering kiosk on the west side of the parking lot. Or you can dine at the Preview Buffet, set up 2½ hours before each performance by the Guilds of the Santa Fe Opera. These meals include a large spread of very good food along with wine, held on the opera grounds. During dessert, a prominent local expert on opera gives a talk about the evening's performance. The Preview Buffet is by reservation only, by calling the opera box office number listed above, and the cost is $50 per person.

The **Santa Fe Symphony** (☎ *505/983–1414 or 800/480–1319* ⊕ *www. sf-symphony.org*) performs seven concerts each season (October to April) in the Lensic Performing Arts Center.

THEATER

Santa Fe Performing Arts (☎ *505/984–1370* ⊕ *www.sfperformingarts. org*), running since 1986, has become a local favorite for its professional productions and adult resident company as well as its commitment to outreach education in the schools and for community youth in its after-school programs. The theater is committed to developing new works; call or check the Web site for the current schedule.

The oldest extant theater company west of the Mississippi, the **Santa Fe Playhouse** (✉ *142 E. De Vargas St., Old Santa Fe Trail and South Capitol* ☎ *505/988–4262* ⊕ *www.santafeplayhouse.org*) occupies a converted 19th-century adobe stable and has been presenting an adventurous mix of avant-garde pieces, classical drama, and musical comedy since 1922. The Fiesta Melodrama—a spoof of the Santa Fe scene—runs late August to mid-September.

SHOPPING

Santa Fe has been a trading post for eons. Nearly a thousand years ago the great pueblos of the Chacoan civilizations were strategically located between the buffalo-hunting tribes of the Great Plains and the Indians of Mexico. Native Americans in New Mexico traded turquoise and other valuables with Indians from Mexico for metals, shells, parrots, and other exotic items. After the arrival of the Spanish and the West's subsequent development, Santa Fe became the place to exchange silver from Mexico and natural resources from New Mexico for manufactured goods, whiskey, and greenbacks from the United States. With the building of the railroad in 1880, Santa Fe had access to all kinds of manufactured goods as well as those unique to the region via the old trade routes.

The trading legacy remains, but now Downtown Santa Fe caters to those looking for handcrafted goods. Sure, T-shirt outlets and a few major retail clothing shops have moved in, but shopping in Santa Fe consists mostly of one-of-a-kind independent stores. Canyon Road, packed with art galleries, is the perfect place to find unique gifts and collectibles. The Downtown district, around the Plaza, has unusual gift shops, clothing, and shoe stores that range from theatrical to conventional, curio shops, and art galleries. The funky, revitalized Railyard District, less touristy than the Plaza, is on Downtown's southwest perimeter and includes the Sanbusco Market Center and the Design Center, both hubs of unique and wonderful boutiques.

ART GALLERIES

The following are only a few of the nearly 200 galleries in greater Santa Fe—with the best of representational, nonobjective, Native American, Latin American, cutting-edge, photographic, and soulful works that defy categorization. The Santa Fe Convention and Visitors Bureau (⇨ *Visitor Information, in the Santa Fe Planner, above*) has a more extensive listing. *The Collectors Guide to Santa Fe, Taos, and Albuquerque* is a good resource and is available in hotels and at some galleries, as well as on the Web at ⊕ *www.collectorsguide.com*. Check the "Pasatiempo" pullout in the *Santa Fe New Mexican* on Friday for a preview of gallery openings.

Fodor's Choice ★ **Andrew Smith Gallery** (⊠ *122 Grant Ave., The Plaza* ☎ *505/984–1234* ⊕ *www.andrewsmithgallery.com*) is a significant photo gallery dealing in works by Edward S. Curtis and other 19th-century chroniclers of the American West. Other major figures are Ansel Adams, Edward Weston, O. Winston Link, Henri Cartier-Bresson, Eliot Porter, Laura Gilpin, Dorothea Lange, Alfred Stieglitz, Annie Liebovitz, and regional artists like Barbara Van Cleve.

Bellas Artes (⊠ *653 Canyon Rd., East side andCanyon Road* ☎ *505/983– 2745* ⊕ *www.bellasartesgallery.com*), a sophisticated gallery and sculpture garden, has a captivating collection of ceramics, paintings, photography, and sculptural work, and represents internationally renowned artists like Judy Pfaff, Phoebe Adams, and Olga de Amaral. The vanguard modernist work of sculptor Ruth Duckworth is also well-represented.

Charlotte Jackson Fine Art (⊠ *554 S. Guadalupe St., Railyard District* ☎ *505/989–8688* ⊕ *www.charlottejackson.com*) focuses primarily on monochromatic "radical" painting and sculpture and is set in a fantastic, open space in a renovated Railyard warehouse. Many of the pieces here are large scale, with "drama" the guiding force. Florence Pierce, Joe Barnes, William Metcalf, Anne Cooper, and Joseph Marioni are among the artists producing minimalist works dealing with light and space.

Fodor's Choice ★ **evo Gallery** (⊠ *554 S. Guadalupe St., Railyard District* ☎ *505/982–4610* ⊕ *www.evogallery.org*) is another gallery that affirms Santa Fe's reputation as a leading center of contemporary art. Powerhouse artists like Jenny Holzer, Ed Ruscha, Donald Judd, Jasper Johns, and Agnes Martin, as well as emerging artists, are represented in this huge space in the Guadalupe District.

Fodor's Choice ★ **Gerald Peters Gallery** (⊠ *1011 Paseo de Peralta, East Side and Canyon Road* ☎ *505/954–5700* ⊕ *www.gpgallery.com*) is Santa Fe's leading gallery of American and European art from the 19th century to the present. It has works by Max Weber, Albert Bierstadt, the Taos Society, the New Mexico modernists, and Georgia O'Keeffe, as well as contemporary artists.

Fodor's Choice ★ **James Kelly Contemporary** (⊠ *1601 Paseo de Peralta, Railyard District* ☎ *505/989–1601* ⊕ *www.jameskelly.com*) mounts sophisticated, high-caliber shows by international and regional artists, such as Johnnie Winona Ross, Nic Nicosia, Peter Sarkisian, Tom Joyce, and Sherrie Levine in a renovated warehouse directly across from SITE Santa Fe. James Kelly has been instrumental in transforming the Railyard District into Santa Fe's hub for contemporary art.

LewAllen Contemporary (⊠ *129 W. Palace Ave., The Plaza* ☎ *505/988– 8997* ⊕ *www.lewallencontemporary.com*) is a leading center for a variety of contemporary arts by both Southwestern and other acclaimed artists, among them Judy Chicago and Janet Fish; sculpture, photography, ceramics, basketry, and painting are all shown in this dynamic space near the Plaza.

Fodor's Choice ★ **Linda Durham Contemporary Art** (⊠ *1807 2nd St., No. 1107, South Side* ☎ *505/466–6600* ⊕ *www.lindadurham.com*) has showcased paintings, sculpture and photography of, primarily, New Mexico–based artists. This community-minded gallery has become well-regarded and its artists highly sought. The new space is bright and open, better suited to the myriad works held within.

3

Monroe Gallery (⊠ *112 Don Gaspar Ave., The Plaza* ☎ *505/992–0800* ⊕ *www.monroegallery.com*) showcases works by the most celebrated black-and-white photographers of the 20th century, from Margaret Bourke-White to Alfred Eisenstaedt. The focus is on humanist and photojournalist style photography, and many iconic images are sold here.

Fodor's Choice ★ **Nedra Matteucci Galleries** (⊠ *1075 Paseo de Peralta, East Side and Canyon Road* ☎ *505/982–4631* ⊠ *555 Canyon Rd.* ⊕ *www.matteucci.com.* ☎ *505/983–2731*) exhibits works by California regionalists, members of the early Taos and Santa Fe schools, and masters of American impressionism and modernism. Spanish-colonial furniture, Indian antiquities, and a fantastic sculpture garden are other draws of this well-respected establishment. The old adobe building that the gallery is in is a beautifully preserved example of Santa Fe–style architecture.

Peyton Wright (⊠ *237 E. Palace Ave., The Plaza* ☎ *505/989–9888* ⊕ *www.peytonwright.com*), tucked inside the historic Spiegelberg house, represents some of the most talented emerging and established contemporary artists in the country, such as Dorothy Brett and Jozef Bakós as well as antique and even ancient New Mexican, Russian, and Latin works.

Photo-eye Gallery (⊠ *376–A Garcia St., East Side and Canyon Road* ☎ *505/988–5159* ⊕ *www.photoeye.com*) shows contemporary and historic photography in styles ranging from representational to ephemeral. This gallery and bookstore's dedication to the medium is staggering, with a stellar selection of new and out-of-print editions, and special auctions for especially rare editions or pieces.

Pushkin Gallery (⊠ *550 Canyon Rd., East Side and Canyon Road* ☎ *505/982–1990* ⊕ *www.pushkingallery.com*) provides yet more evidence that Santa Fe's art scene is about so much more than regional work—here you can peruse works by some of Russia's leading 19th- and 20th-century talents, with an emphasis on impressionism.

Riva Yares Gallery (⊠ *123 Grant St., The Plaza* ☎ *505/984–0330* ⊕ *www.rivayaresgallery.com*) specializes in contemporary artists of Latin American descent. There are sculptures by California artist Manuel Neri, color field paintings by Esteban Vicente, and works by Santa Feans Elias Rivera, Rico Eastman, and others—plus paintings by such international legends as Hans Hofmann, Milton Avery, and Helen Frankenthaler.

Santa Fe Art Institute (⊠ *1600 St. Michael's Dr., South Side* ☎ *505/424–5050*), a nonprofit educational art organization that sponsors several artists in residence and presents workshops, exhibitions, and lectures, has a respected gallery whose exhibits change regularly. The institute is set inside a dramatic contemporary building designed by Mexican modernist architect Ricardo Legorreta. Past artists in residence have included Richard Diebenkorn, Larry Bell, Moon Zappa, Henriette Wyeth Hurd, and Judy Pfaff.

Shidoni Foundry and Galleries (⊠ *B1508 Bishop's Lodge Rd., 5 mi north of Santa Fe, North of the Plaza, Tesuque* ☎ *505/988–8001* ⊕ *www. shidoni.com*) casts work for established and emerging artists from all over North America. On the grounds of an old chicken ranch, Shidoni has a rambling sculpture garden and a gallery. Self-guided foundry tours are permitted Saturday 9 to 5 and weekdays noon to 1, but the sculpture garden is open daily during daylight hours; you can watch bronze pourings most Saturday afternoons. This is a dream of a place to expose your kids to large-scale art and enjoy a lovely and, in this area, rare expanse of green grass at the same time.

Eight Modern (⊠ *231 Delgado St., East Side and Canyon Road* ☎ *505/995–0231* ⊕ *www.eightmodern.net*), in an unassuming building just off of Canyon Road, showcases modern and contemporary painting, photography, and sculpture by established artists from around the world. Eight Modern has staked a notable claim in Santa Fe's art world by bringing a number of internationally acclaimed artists here for the first time.

SPECIALTY STORES

ANTIQUES AND HOME FURNISHINGS

At **Asian Adobe** (⊠ *310 Johnson St., The Plaza* ☎ *505/992–6846* ⊕ *www. asianadobe.com*) browse porcelain lamps, ornate antique baby hats and shoes, red-lacquer armoires, and similarly stunning Chinese and Southeast Asian artifacts and antiques. The jewelry selection often includes hard-to-find ethnic Chinese pieces as well as exceptional one-of-a-kind finds from the owner's travels.

Casa Nova (⊠ *530 S. Guadalupe St., The Railyard District* ☎ *505/983–8558* ⊕ *www.casanovagallery.com*) sells functional and decorative art from around the world, deftly mixing colors, textures, and cultural icons—old and new—from stylish pewter tableware from South Africa to vintage hand-carved ex-votos (votive offerings) from Brazil. There is a major emphasis here on goods produced by artists and cooperatives focused on sustainable economic development.

The **Design Center** (⊠ *418 Cerrillos Rd., Railyard District*), which occupies a former Chevy dealership in the Railyard District, contains some of the most distinctive antique and decorative-arts shops in town, plus a couple of small restaurants. Be sure to browse the precious Latin American antiques at **Claiborne Gallery** (☎ *505/982–8019*), along with the artful contemporary desks, tables, and chairs created by owner Omer Claiborne. **Gloria List Gallery** (☎ *505/982–5622*) specializes in rare 17th- and 18th-century devotional and folk art, chiefly from South America, Italy, Spain, and Mexico. At **Sparrow & Magpie Antiques**

(☎ 505/982–1446), look mostly for East Coast and Midwest folk art and textiles, although the shop carries some Southwestern pieces, too.

Design Warehouse (✉ 101 W. Marcy St., The Plaza ☎ 505/988–1555 ⊕ www.designwarehousesantafe.com), a welcome antidote to Santa Fe's preponderance of shops selling Native American and Spanish-colonial antiques, stocks hip, contemporary furniture, kitchenware, home accessories, and other sleek knickknacks, such as those made by the Italian firm Alessi. Note the select collection of amusing books for kids and adults.

Doodlet's (✉ 120 Don Gaspar Ave., The Plaza ☎ 505/983–3771) has an eclectic collection of stuff: pop-up books, silly postcards, tin art, hooked rugs, and stringed lights. Wonderment is in every display case, drawing the eye to the unusual. There's something for just about everyone at this delightfully quirky shop, and often it's affordable.

Jackalope (✉ 2820 Cerrillos Rd., South Side ☎ 505/471–8539 ⊕ www.jackalope.com), a legendary if somewhat overpriced bazaar, sprawls over 7 acres, incorporating several pottery barns, a furniture store, endless aisles of knickknacks from Latin America and Asia, and a huge greenhouse. There's also an area where craftspeople, artisans, and others sell their wares—sort of a mini flea market.

★ **La Mesa** (✉ 225 Canyon Rd., East Side and Canyon Road ☎ 505/984–1688 ⊕ www.lamesaofsantafe.com) has become well-known for showcasing contemporary handcrafted, mostly functional, works by more than 50, mostly local, artists including Kathy O'Neill, Gregory Lomayesva, and Melissa Haid. Collections include dinnerware, glassware, pottery, lighting, fine art, and accessories.

★ **Montez Gallery** (✉ Sena Plaza Courtyard, 125 E. Palace Ave., The Plaza ☎ 505/982–1828) sells Hispanic works of religious art and decoration, including *retablos* (holy images painted on wood or tin), *bultos* (carved wooden statues of saints), furniture, paintings, pottery, weavings, and jewelry. You'll find works by a number of award-winning local artists here.

Pachamama (✉ 223 Canyon Rd., East Side and Canyon Road ☎ 505/983–4020) carries a diverse and captivating collection of Latin American folk art, including small tin or silver *milagros,* the stamped metal images used as votive offerings, and gorgeous jewelry. The shop also carries weavings, Spanish-colonial antiques, and other delightful trinkets.

Sequoia (✉ 201 Galisteo St., The Plaza ☎ 505/982–7000) shows the sleek, imaginative, furniture creations of its owner, who was born in India. The natural glow of the materials in massive wood slab tables and chairs is remarkable. Curvaceous glass shelves, lamps, and candlesticks mix with paintings and fine linens.

BOOKS

More than a dozen shops in Santa Fe sell used books, and a handful of high-quality shops carry the latest releases from mainstream and small presses.

ALLÁ (✉ 102 W. San Francisco St., upstairs, The Plaza ☎ 505/988–5416) is one of Santa Fe's most delightful small bookstores. It focuses on hard-to-find Spanish-language books and records, including limited-edition handmade books from Central America. It also carries Native American books and music, as well as English translations.

Fodor's Choice
★
Collected Works Book Store (✉ *202 Galisteo St., The Plaza* ☎ *505/988–4226* ⊕ *www.collectedworksbookstore.com*) carries art and travel books, including a generous selection of books on Southwestern art, architecture, and general history, as well as the latest in contemporary literature. In the new, expanded space still close to the Plaza, you can now enjoy organic coffees, snacks, and sandwiches. The patio invites long, leisurely reads. The proprietress, Dorothy Massey, and her staff are well-loved for their knowledge and helpfulness.

Garcia Street Books (✉ *376 Garcia St., East Side and Canyon Road* ☎ *505/986–0151* ⊕ *www.garciastreetbooks.com*) is an outstanding independent shop strong on art, architecture, cookbooks, literature, and regional Southwestern works—it's a block from the Canyon Road galleries. It hosts frequent talks by authors under its portal during the summer.

Nicholas Potter (✉ *211 E. Palace Ave., The Plaza* ☎ *505/983–5434*) specializes in used, rare, and out-of-print books with an extensive collection of Southwest art, culture, and history. Modern first editions and photography are other areas of focus. The quixotic shop also stocks used jazz and classical CDs. Potter is an amazing resource for those looking for a specific book or subject and his knowledge is encyclopedic.

Photo-eye Books (✉ *376 Garcia St., East Side and Canyon Road* ☎ *505/988–5152* ⊕ *www.photoeye.com*) has an almost unbelievable collection of new, rare, and out-of-print photography books and a staff of photographers who are excellent sources of information and advice on great spots to shoot in and around Santa Fe.

Travel Bug (✉ *839 Paseo de Peralta, The Plaza* ☎ *505/992–0418*) has a huge array of guidebooks and books about travel, and USGS and other maps. You'll also find all sorts of gadgets for hikers and backpackers. There's also a cozy coffeehouse (excellent java) with Wi-Fi.

CLOTHING AND ACCESSORIES

Many tourists arrive in clothing from mainstream department stores and leave bedecked in Western garb looking like they've stepped from a bygone era. If you simply cannot live without a getup Annie Oakley herself would envy, you will find shopping options beyond your wildest dreams. But take a look around at the striking and highly individualized styles of the locals and you'll see that Western gear is mixed with pieces from all over the globe to create what is the real Santa Fe style. There are few towns where you'll find more distinctive, sometimes downright eccentric, expressions of personal style on every age and every shape. Indians, cowboys, hipsters, students, artists, yogis, immigrants from all over the world, and world travelers all bring something to the style mix of this town and you'll find plenty of shops that will allow you to join in the fun.

It is worth asking specifically to see the work of locals during your wanderings. There are artists of every bent in this town and the surrounding areas, not only putting paint to canvas, but creating jewelry, clothing, accessories, and more. Informed by cultural traditions but as cutting-edge and innovative as anything you'll find in New York or San Francisco, the contemporary jewelry coming from Native American artists like Cody Sanderson and Pat Pruitt is incredible. The shops at IAIA Downtown and the Museum of Indian Arts and Culture on Museum Hill are good places to see these artists and many others.

Fodor's Choice ★ **Back at the Ranch** (⌧ *209 E. Marcy St., The Plaza* ☎ *505/989–8110 or 888/962–6687*) is the place for cowboy boots. The cozy space in an old, creaky-floored adobe is stocked with perhaps the finest handmade cowboy boots you will ever see—in every color, style, and embellishment imaginable. Other finds, like funky ranch-style furniture, 1950s blanket coats, jewelry, and belt buckles are also sold. The staff is top-notch and the boots are breathtaking.

Cupcake Clothing. (⌧ *328 Montezuma Ave., Railyard District* ☎ *505/988–4744* ⊕ *www.cupcakeclothing.net*) is a hip store just off Guadalupe Street in the busy Railyard District. This cozy little shop has all sorts of stylish clothing, shoes, and accessories for women and a very friendly staff to boot. The clientele is pretty evenly split between tourists and locals.

Fodor's Choice ★ **Double Take at the Ranch** (⌧ *321 S. Guadalupe St., Railyard District* ☎ *505/820–7775*) ranks among the best consignment stores in the West, carrying elaborately embroidered vintage cowboy shirts, hundreds of pairs of boots, funky old prints, and amazing vintage Indian pawn and Mexican jewelry. The store adjoins its sister consignment store, also called Double Take, which carries a wide range of contemporary clothing and accessories for men and women; and Santa Fe Pottery, which carries the works of local artists.

Maya (⌧ *108 Galisteo St., The Plaza* ☎ *505/989–7590*) is a groovy assemblage of unconventional and fun women's clothing, jewelry, accessories, select books, shoes, handbags, global folk art, hats, and a small selection of housewares. It's a funky shop with many lines from small design houses and local jewelers. Check out the selection of *relicario*-style (tiny images of saints in silver frames) jewelry from Wanda Lobito. The staff isn't always terribly helpful, but they aren't unfriendly.

Mirá (⌧ *101 W. Marcy St., The Plaza* ☎ *505/988–3585*) clothing for women is hip, eclectic, and funky, combining the adventurous spirit of New Mexico with global contemporary fashion. The shop has jewelry, accessories, and collectibles from Latin America, the Flax line of natural-fiber clothing, and knockout dresses and separates not sold anywhere else in town.

Nathalie (⌧ *503 Canyon Rd., East Side and Canyon Road* ☎ *505/982–1021* ⊕ *www.nathaliesantafe.com*) has long been the destination for those who've come to love Parisian-born owner Nathalie Kent's distinctive style and carefully curated collection of vintage and new pieces. Though Kent's passion clearly leans toward traditional Western wear, from cowboy boots to velvet skirts to exquisite Old Pawn jewelry, you'll also find gorgeous pieces from all over the globe—antique Moroccan treasures line up next to 100-year-old Navajo bracelets like long lost pals. Her home furnishings are stupendous, too.

Fodor's Choice **O'Farrell Hats** (✉ *111 E. San Francisco St., The Plaza* ☎ *505/989–9666*
★ ⊕ *www.ofarrellhatco.com*) is the domain of America's foremost hat-
making family. Founder Kevin O'Farrell passed away in 2006, but the
legacy continues with his son Scott and the highly trained staff. This
quirky shop custom crafts one-of-a-kind beaver-felt cowboy hats that
make the ultimate Santa Fe keepsake. This level of quality comes at a
cost, but devoted customers—who have included everyone from cattle
ranchers to U.S. presidents—swear by O'Farrell's artful creations.

Origins (✉ *135 W. San Francisco St., The Plaza* ☎ *505/988–2323*) bor-
rows from many cultures, carrying pricey women's wear like antique
kimonos and custom-dyed silk jackets, with the overall look of artsy
elegance. One-of-a-kind accessories complete the spectacular look that
Santa Fe inspires.

Fodor's Choice For gear related to just about any outdoors activity you can think of,
★ check out **Sangre de Cristo Mountain Works** (✉ *328 S. Guadalupe St.,
Railyard District* ☎ *505/984–8221* ⊕ *www.sdcmountainworks.com*), a
well-stocked shop that both sells and rents hiking, climbing, camping,
trekking, snowshoeing, and skiing equipment. There's a great selection
of clothing and shoes for men and women. The superactive, knowledgeable staff here can also advise you on the best venues for local
recreation.

FOOD AND COOKWARE

In the DeVargas shopping center, **Las Cosas Kitchen Shoppe** (✉ *De Vargas
Mall, N. Guadalupe St. at Paseo de Peralta, North Side* ☎ *505/988–
3394 or 877/229–7184* ⊕ *www.lascosascooking.com*) carries a fantastic
selection of cookery, tableware, and kitchen gadgetry and gifts. The
shop is also renowned for its cooking classes, which touch on everything
from high-altitude baking to Asian-style grilling.

★ **The Spanish Table** (✉ *109 N. Guadalupe St., West of the Plaza* ☎ *505/986–
0243* ⊕ *www.spanishtable.com*) stands out as a destination for all Spanish culinary needs. With its Spanish meats and cheeses, cookware and
beautiful Majolica pottery, books, dry goods, and wonderful world-
music selection, you will be challenged to leave empty-handed. The staff
is always ready to help advise on a recipe or gift idea and will ship your
purchases anywhere you like.

Fodor's Choice **Todos Santos** (✉ *125 E. Palace Ave., The Plaza* ☎ *505/982–3855*) is a
★ tiny candy shop in the 18th-century courtyard of Sena Plaza, carry-
ing must-be-seen-to-be-believed works of edible art, including chocolate milagros and altar pieces gilded with 23-karat gold or silver leaf.
Truffles come in exotic flavors, like tangerine chile, rose caramel, and
lemon verbena. The buttery, spicy, handmade chipotle caramels melt
in your mouth—buy several bags so you won't end up eating the gifts
you intend to give. Amidst the taste sensations and quirky folk art are
amazing and delightful customized Pez dispensers from Albuquerque
folk artist Steve White and astonishing, intricate recycled paper creations from local phenom Rick Phelps.

JEWELRY

Eidos (✉ *500 Montezuma Ave., inside Sanbusco Center, Railyard District* ☎ *505/992–0020* ⊕ *www.eidosjewelry.com*) features "concept-led" minimalist contemporary jewelry from European designers and Deborah Alexander and Gordon Lawrie, who own the store. It's a lovely, contemporary space with a fascinating array of materials, good range of prices, and helpful staff.

Golden Eye (✉ *115 Don Gaspar St., The Plaza* ☎ *505/984–0040* ⊕ *www. goldeneyesantafe.com*) is a pint-size shop (even by Santa Fe standards) that features fine, handcrafted jewelry in high-karat gold, often paired with gemstones. Its experienced, helpful staff of artisans can help you pick out something beautiful and unusual.

Jett (✉ *110 Old Santa Fe Trail, The Plaza* ☎ *505/988–1414*) showcases jewelers and artists, many local, who are remarkable for creative, original approaches to their work. Intriguing selection of surprisingly affordable silver and gold jewelry, modern artistic lighting, and delightful miniature objects like vintage trailers and circus tents made from recycled metal.

LewAllen & LewAllen Jewelry (✉ *105 E. Palace Ave., The Plaza* ☎ *800/988–5112* ⊕ *www.lewallenjewelry.com*) is run by father-and-daughter silversmiths Ross and Laura LewAllen. Handmade jewelry ranges from whimsical to mystical inside their tiny shop just off the Plaza. There is something for absolutely everyone in here, including delightful charms for your pet's collar.

Fodor's Choice ★ **Patina** (✉ *131 W. Palace Ave., The Plaza* ☎ *505/986–3432 or 877/877–0827* ⊕ *www.patina-gallery.com*) presents outstanding contemporary jewelry, textiles, and sculptural objects of metal, clay, and wood, in an airy, museum-like space. With a staff whose courtesy is matched by knowledge of the genre, artists-owners Ivan and Allison Barnett have used their fresh curatorial aesthetic to create a showplace for more than 110 American and European artists they represent—many of whom are in permanent collections of museums such as MoMA.

MARKETS

Pueblo of Tesuque Flea Market (✉ *U.S. 285/84, 7 mi north of Santa Fe, Tesuque* ☎ *505/983–2667* ⊕ *www.pueblooftesuqueﬂeamarket.com*) was once considered the best flea market in America by its loyal legion of bargain hunters. The Tesuque Pueblo took over the market in the late '90s and raised vendor fees, which increased the presence of predictable, often pricey goods brought in by professional flea-market dealers. In recent years, however, the pueblo has brought in a nice range of vendors, and this market may have hundreds of vendors showing their goods in peak season. The 12-acre market is next to the Santa Fe Opera and is open Friday to Sunday, mid-March to December.

Fodor's Choice ★ Browse through the vast selection of local produce, meat, flowers, honey, and cheese—much of it organic—at the thriving **Santa Fe Farmers' Market** (✉ *1607 Paseo de Peralta, Railyard District* ☎ *505/983–4098* ⊕ *www.santafefarmersmarket.com*). The market is now housed in its new, permanent building in the Railyard and it's open year-round. It's a great people-watching event, with entertainment for kids as well as a snack bar selling terrific breakfast burritos and other goodies. With the growing awareness of the importance and necessity of eating locally grown and organic food, this market offers living testimony to the fact that farming can be done successfully, even in a high-desert region like this one.

NATIVE AMERICAN ARTS AND CRAFTS

Morning Star Gallery (⊠ *513 Canyon Rd., East Side and Canyon Road* ☏ *505/982–8187* ⊕ *www.morningstargallery.com*) is a veritable museum of Native American art and artifacts. An adobe shaded by a huge cottonwood tree houses antique basketry, pre-1940 Navajo silver jewelry, Northwest Coast Native American carvings, Navajo weavings, and art of the Plains Indians. Prices and quality prohibit casual purchases, but the collection is magnificent.

Niman Fine Arts (⊠ *125 Lincoln Ave., The Plaza* ☏ *505/988–5091* ⊕ *www.namingha.com*) focuses on the prolific work of contemporary Hopi artists Arlo, Dan, and Michael Namingha. Arlo is a sculptor working in bronze, wood, and stone; Dan paints and sculpts; and Michael works with digital imagery.

Packard's on the Plaza (⊠ *61 Old Santa Fe Trail, The Plaza* ☏ *505/983–9241* ⊕ *www.packards-santafe.com*), the oldest Native American arts-and-crafts store on Santa Fe Plaza, also sells Zapotec Indian rugs from Mexico and original rug designs by Richard Enzer, old pottery, saddles, kachina dolls, and an excellent selection of coral and turquoise jewelry. Local favorite Lawrence Baca, whose iconic jewelry has made him a regular prizewinner at Spanish Market, is featured here. Prices are often high, but so are the standards. There's also an extensive clothing selection.

Fodor's Choice ★ The **Rainbow Man** (⊠ *107 E. Palace Ave., The Plaza* ☏ *505/982–8706* ⊕ *www.therainbowman.com*), established in 1945, does business in an old, rambling adobe complex, part of which dates from before the 1680 Pueblo Revolt. The shop carries early Navajo, Mexican, and Chimayó textiles, along with photographs by Edward S. Curtis, a breathtaking collection of vintage pawn and Mexican jewelry, Day of the Dead figures, Oaxacan folk animals, New Mexican folk art, kachinas, and contemporary jewelry from local artists. The friendly staff possesses an encyclopedic knowledge of the art here.

Fodor's Choice ★ **Robert Nichols Gallery** (⊠ *419 Canyon Rd., East Side and Canyon Road* ☏ *505/982–2145* ⊕ *www.robertnicholsgallery.com*) represents a remarkable group of Native American ceramics artists doing primarily nontraditional work. Diverse artists such as Glen Nipshank, whose organic, sensuous shapes would be right at home in MoMA, and Diego Romero, whose Cochiti-style vessels are detailed with graphic-novel-style characters and sharp social commentary, are right at home here. It is a treat to see cutting-edge work that is clearly informed by indigenous traditions.

Fodor's Choice ★ "Eclectic Modern Vintage" is **Shiprock Santa Fe's** (⊠ *53 Old Santa Fe Trail, The Plaza* ☏ *505/982–8478* ⊕ *www.shiprocksantafe.com.*) tagline, and it accurately sums up their incredible collection of pottery, textiles, painting, furniture, and sculpture. The gallery is notable for its dedication to showcasing exquisite vintage pieces alongside vanguard contemporary works.

Trade Roots Collection (⊠ *411 Paseo de Peralta, The Plaza* ☎ *505/982–8168* ⊕ *www.traderoots.com*) sells Native American ritual objects, such as fetish jewelry and Hopi rattles, and magnificent strands of turquoise from famed American mines. Contemporary silver pieces using top-quality genuine stones are also popular. Open by appointment only, this store is an excellent source of fine ethnic crafts materials for artists.

Trader's Collection (⊠ *218 Galisteo St., The Plaza* ☎ *505/992–0441*) was created by several key staff members when the venerable Shush Yaz gallery closed in August 2007. In this new showplace of American Indian arts and crafts, antique pieces commingle with contemporary works by artists such as Nocona Burgess and jeweler Kim Knifechief. The staff is friendly and knowledgeable.

SPORTS AND THE OUTDOORS

The Santa Fe National Forest is right in the city's backyard and includes the Dome Wilderness (5,200 acres in the volcanically formed Jémez Mountains) and the Pecos Wilderness (223,333 acres of high mountains, forests, and meadows at the southern end of the Rocky Mountains chain). The 12,500-foot Sangre de Cristo Mountains (the name translates as "Blood of Christ," for the red glow they radiate at sunset) fringe the city's east side, constant and gentle reminders of the mystery and power of the natural world. To the south and west, sweeping high desert is punctuated by several less formidable mountain ranges. The dramatic shifts in elevation and topography around Santa Fe make for a wealth of outdoor activities. Head to the mountains for fishing, camping, and skiing; to the nearby Rio Grande for kayaking and rafting; and almost anywhere in the area for bird-watching, hiking, and biking.

For a report on general conditions in the forest, contact the **Santa Fe National Forest Office** (⊠ *11 Forest La., South Side* ☎ *505/438–5300* ⊕ *www.fs.fed.us/r3/sfe*). For a one-stop shop for information about recreation on public lands, which include national and state parks, contact the **New Mexico Public Lands Information Center** (⊠ *301 Dinosaur Trail, South Side* ☎ *505/954–2002* ⊕ *www.publiclands.org*). It has maps, reference materials, licenses, permits—just about everything you need to plan an adventure in the New Mexican wilderness.

BICYCLING
You can pick up a map of bike trips—among them a 30-mi round-trip ride from Downtown Santa Fe to Ski Santa Fe at the end of NM 475—from the New Mexico Public Lands Information Center, or at the bike shops listed below. One excellent place to mountain bike is the Dale Ball Trail Network, which is accessed from several points.

Fodor's Choice ★ **Mellow Velo** (⊠ *638 Old Santa Fe Trail, Old Santa Fe Trail and South Capitol* ☎ *505/995–8356* ⊕ *www.melovelo.com*) is a friendly, neighborhood bike shop offering group tours, privately guided rides, bicycle rentals ($35 per day—make reservations), and repairs. The helpful staff at this well-stocked shop offers a great way to spend a day—or seven!

New Mexico Bike N' Sport (⌧ *524C W. Cordova Rd., Old Santa Fe Trail and South Capitol* ☎ *505/820–0809* ⊕ *www.nmbikensport.com*) is a big shop that provides rentals and a large selection of bikes, clothing, and all necessary gear.

Santa Fe Mountain Sports (⌧ *1221 Flagman Way, Suite B1, South Side* ☎ *505/988–3337* ⊕ *www.santafemountainsports.com*) has a good selection of bikes for rent.

BIRD-WATCHING

☾
Fodor's Choice
★

At the end of Upper Canyon Road, at the mouth of the canyon as it wends into the foothills, the 135-acre **Randall Davey Audubon Center** harbors diverse birds and other wildlife. Guided nature walks are given many weekends; there are also two major hiking trails that you can tackle on your own. The home and studio of Randall Davey, a prolific early Santa Fe artist, can be toured on Monday afternoons in summer. There's also a nature bookstore. ⌧ *1800 Upper Canyon Rd., East Side and Canyon Road* ☎ *505/983–4609* ⊕ *http://nm.audubon.org/center/index.html* ⌧ *Center $2, house tour $5* ☾ *Weekdays 9–5, weekends 10–4; grounds daily dawn–dusk; house tours Mon. at 2.*

For a knowledgeable insider's perspective, take a tour with **WingsWest Birding Tours** (☎ *800/583–6928* ⊕ *www.wingswestnm.com*). Gregarious and knowledgeable guide Bill West leads four- to eight-hour early-morning or sunset tours that venture into some of the region's best bird-watching areas, including Santa Fe Ski Basin, Cochiti Lake, the Jémez Mountains, the Upper Pecos Valley, and Bosque del Apache National Wildlife Refuge. West also leads popular tours throughout Mexico.

GOLF

Marty Sanchez Links de Santa Fe (⌧ *205 Caja del Rio Rd., off NM 599, the Santa Fe Relief Route, South Side* ☎ *505/955–4400* ⊕ *www.linksdesantafe.com*), an outstanding municipal facility with beautifully groomed 18- and 9-hole courses, sits on high prairie west of Santa Fe with fine mountain views. It has driving and putting ranges, a pro shop, and a snack bar. The greens fees are $35 for the 18-hole course, $25 on the par-3 9-holer.

HIKING

Hiking around Santa Fe can take you into high-altitude alpine country or into lunaresque high desert as you head south and west to lower elevations. For winter hiking, the gentler climates to the south are less likely to be snow packed, while the alpine areas will likely require snowshoes or cross-country skis. In summer, wildflowers bloom in the high country, and the temperature is generally at least 10 degrees cooler than in town. The mountain trails accessible at the base of the Ski Santa Fe area (end of NM 475) stay cool on even the hottest summer days. Weather can change with one gust of wind, so be prepared with extra clothing, rain gear, food, and lots of water. Keep in mind that the sun at 10,000 feet is very powerful, even with a hat and sunscreen. *See the Side Trips from Santa Fe section, below, for additional hiking areas near the city.*

For information about specific hiking areas, contact the New Mexico Public Lands Information Center. Any of the outdoor gear stores in town can also help with guides and recommendations. The **Sierra Club** (⊕ *www.riogrande.sierraclub.org*) organizes group hikes of all levels of difficulty; a schedule of hikes is posted on the Web site.

Fodor's Choice
★
Aspen Vista is a lovely hike along a south-facing mountainside. Take Hyde Park Road (NM 475) 13 mi, and the trail begins before the ski area. After walking a few miles through thick aspen groves you come to panoramic views of Santa Fe. The path is well marked and gently inclines toward Tesuque Peak. The trail becomes shadier with elevation—snow has been reported on the trail as late as July. In winter, after heavy snows, the trail is great for intermediate-advanced cross-country skiing. The round-trip is 12 mi and sees an elevation gain of 2,000 feet, but it's just 3½ mi to the spectacular overlook. The hillside is covered with golden aspen trees in late September.

Spurring off the Dale Ball trail system, the steep but rewarding (and dog-friendly) **Atalaya Trail** runs from the visitor parking lot of St. John's College (off Camino de Cruz Blanca, on the east side), up a winding, ponderosa pine–studded trail to the peak of Mt. Atalaya, which affords incredible 270-degree views of Santa Fe. The nearly 6-mi round-trip hike climbs nearly 2,000 feet (to an elevation of 9,121 feet), so pace yourself. The good news: the return to the parking area is nearly all downhill.

A favorite spot for a ramble, with a vast network of trails, is the **Dale Ball Foothills Trail Network** (⊕ *www.santafenm.gov/index.aspx?NID=1059*), a network of some 20 mi of paths that winds and wends up through the foothills east of town and can be accessed at a few points, including Hyde Park Road (en route to the ski valley) and the upper end of Canyon Road, at Cerro Gordo. There are trail maps and signs at these points, and the trails are very well marked.

HORSEBACK RIDING
New Mexico's rugged countryside has been the setting for many Hollywood Westerns. Whether you want to ride the range that Gregory Peck and Kevin Costner rode or just head out feeling tall in the saddle, you can do so year-round. Rates average about $20 an hour. *See the Side Trips from Santa Fe section for additional horseback listings in Galisteo and Española.*

Bishop's Lodge (⊠ *1297 Bishop's Lodge Rd., North Side* ☎ *505/983–6377*) provides rides and guides year-round. Call for reservations.

MULTIPURPOSE SPORTS CENTER
★ The huge **Genoveva Chavez Community Center** (⊠ *3221 Rodeo Rd., South Side* ☎ *505/955–4001* ⊕ *www.chavezcenter.com*) is a reasonably priced (adults $5 per day) facility with a regulation-size ice rink (you can rent ice skates for the whole family), an enormous gymnasium, indoor running track, 50-meter pool, leisure pool with waterslide and play structures, aerobics center, fitness room, two racquetball courts, and a child-care center.

RIVER RAFTING

If you want to watch birds and wildlife along the banks, try the laid-back Huck Finn floats along the Rio Chama or the Rio Grande's White Rock Canyon. The season is generally between April and September. Most outfitters have overnight package plans, and all offer half- and full-day trips. Be prepared to get wet, and wear secure water shoes. For a list of outfitters who guide trips on the Rio Grande and the Rio Chama, contact the **Bureau of Land Management (BLM), Taos Resource Area Office** (⊠ *226 Cruz Alta Rd., Taos* ☎ *505/758–8851* ⊕ *www.nm.blm. gov*), or stop by the BLM visitor center along NM 68, 16 mi south of Taos in Pilar.

Kokopelli Rafting Adventures (⊠ *551 W. Cordova Rd., #540, Old Santa Fe Trail and South Capitol* ☎ *505/983–3734 or 800/879–9035* ⊕ *www. kokopelliraft.com*) will take you on half-day to multiday river trips down the Rio Grande and Rio Chama. **New Wave Rafting** (⊠ *Mile 21 Hwy. 68, Embudo* ☎ *800/984–1444* ⊕ *www.newwaverafting.com*) conducts full-day, half-day, and overnight river trips, as well as fly-fishing trips, from its new location in Embudo, 21 mi north of Española. **Santa Fe Rafting Company and Outfitters** (⊠ *1000 Cerrillos Rd., South Side* ☎ *505/988–4914 or 888/988–4914* ⊕ *www.santaferafting.com*) leads day trips down the Rio Grande and the Chama River and customizes rafting tours. Tell them what you want—they'll figure out a way to do it.

SKIING

To save time during the busy holiday season you may want to rent skis or snowboards in town the night before hitting the slopes so you don't waste any time waiting during the morning rush. **Alpine Sports** (⊠ *121 Sandoval St., South Side* ☎ *505/983–5155* ⊕ *www.alpinesports-santafe.com*) rents downhill and cross-country skis and snowboards. **Cottam's Ski Rentals** (⊠ *3451 Hyde Park Rd., 7 mi northeast of Downtown, toward Ski Santa Fe* ☎ *505/982–0495 or 800/322–8267*) rents the works, including snowboards, sleds, and snowshoes.

★ **Santa Fe Mountain Sports** (⊠ *1221 Flagman Way, Suite B1, South Side* ☎ *505/988–3337* ⊕ *www.santafemountainsports.com*) is a family-owned specialty mountain shop that rents boots, skis, and snowboards for the whole family in the winter, as well as bicycles in the summertime. The super-helpful staff is great to work with.

Ski Santa Fe (⊠ *End of NM 475, 18 mi northeast of Downtown* ☎ *505/982–4429 general info, 505/983–9155 conditions* ⊕ *www. skisantafe.com*), open roughly from late November through early April, is a fine, midsize operation that receives an average of 225 inches of snow a year and plenty of sunshine. It's one of America's highest ski areas—the 12,000-foot summit has a variety of terrain and seems bigger than its 1,700 feet of vertical rise and 660 acres. There are some great powder stashes, tough bump runs, and many wide, gentle cruising runs. The 44 trails are ranked 20% beginner, 40% intermediate, and 40% advanced; there are seven lifts. Snowboarders are welcome, and there's the Norquist Trail for cross-country skiers. Chipmunk Corner provides day care and supervised kids' skiing. The ski school is excellent. Rentals, a good restaurant, a ski shop, and Totemoff Bar and Grill round out the amenities.

SIDE TRIPS FROM SANTA FE

Take even a day or two to explore the areas around Santa Fe and you'll start to get a sense of just how ancient this region is and how deeply the modern culture has been shaped by the Pueblo and Spanish people who have been here for centuries. If you're a geology buff or just happy to wander through this dramatic environment, you'll see things you couldn't possibly expect. *Each of the excursions below can be accomplished in a day or less.* The High Road to Taos trip makes for a very full day, so start early or plan to spend the night near or in Taos.

SOUTH OF SANTA FE

The most prominent side trip south of the city is along the fabled Turquoise Trail, an excellent—and leisurely—alternative route to Albuquerque that's far more interesting than Interstate 25; *it's covered in the Side Trips from Albuquerque section, in chapter 2.* Although the drive down Interstate 25 offers some fantastic views of the Jémez and Sandia mountains, the most interesting sites south of town require hopping off the interstate. From here you can uncover the region's history at El Rancho de las Golondrinas and enjoy one of New Mexico's most dramatic day hikes at Tent Rocks canyon. Conversely, if you leave Santa Fe via Interstate 25 north and then cut down in a southerly direction along U.S. 285 and NM 41, you come to tiny Galisteo, a little hamlet steeped in Spanish colonial history.

PECOS NATIONAL HISTORIC PARK

★ *25 mi east of Santa Fe on I–25.*

Pecos was the last major encampment that travelers on the Santa Fe Trail reached before Santa Fe. Today the little village is mostly a starting point for exploring the Pecos National Historic Park, the centerpiece of which is the **ruins of Pecos,** once a major pueblo village with more than 1,100 rooms. Twenty-five hundred people are thought to have lived in this structure, as high as five stories in places. Pecos, in a fertile valley between the Great Plains and the Rio Grande Valley, was a trading center centuries before the Spanish conquistadors visited in about 1540. The Spanish later returned to build two missions.

The pueblo was abandoned in 1838, and its 17 surviving occupants moved to the Jémez Pueblo. Anglo travelers on the Santa Fe Trail observed the mission ruins with a great sense of fascination (and relief—for they knew it meant their journey was nearly over). A couple of miles from the ruins, **Andrew Kozlowski's Ranch** served as a stage depot, where a fresh spring quenched the thirsts of horses and weary passengers. The ranch now houses the park's law-enforcement corps and is not open to the public. You can view the mission ruins and the excavated pueblo on a ¼-mi self-guided tour in about two hours.

The pivotal Civil War battle of Glorieta Pass took place on an outlying parcel of parkland in late March 1862; a victory over Confederate forces firmly established the Union army's control over the New Mexico Territory. The Union troops maintained headquarters at Kozlowski's Ranch during the battle. Guided park tours ($2 per person, in summer only) to the battle site, Greer Garson's home (the late actress lived in the area for a time), and outlying ruins start at the park visitor center. ⊠ *NM 63, off I–25 at Exit 307, Pecos* ☎ *505/757–7200 park info, 505/757–7241 visitor center* ⊕ *www.nps.gov/peco* ☞ *$3* ⊘ *Late May–early Sept., daily 8–6; early Sept.–late May, daily 8–4:30.*

GALISTEO
25 mi south of Santa Fe via I–25 north to U.S. 285 to NM 41 south.

South of Santa Fe lie the immense open spaces and subtle colorings of the Galisteo Basin and the quintessential New Mexican village of Galisteo—a blend of multigenerational New Mexicans and recent migrants who protect and treasure the bucolic solitude of their home. The drive from Santa Fe takes about 30 minutes and offers a panoramic view of the low, sculpted landscape of the Galisteo Basin, which is an austere contrast to the alpine country of the Sangre de Cristos. It's a good place to go for a leisurely lunch or a sunset drive to dinner, maybe with horseback riding. Aside from these options, there really isn't anything more to do here except enjoy the surroundings.

Founded as a Spanish outpost in 1614, with original buildings constructed largely with stones from the large pueblo ruin nearby that had once housed 1,000 people, Galisteo has attracted a significant number of artists and equestrians (trail rides and rentals are available at local stables) to the otherwise very traditional community. Cottonwoods shade the low-lying Pueblo-style architecture, a premier example of vernacular use of adobe and stone. The small church is open only for Sunday services.

SPORTS AND THE OUTDOORS
Galarosa Stable (⊠ *NM 41, Galisteo* ☎ *505/466–4654 or 505/670–2467*) offers two-hour horseback rides starting at $70 per person, south of Santa Fe in the panoramic Galisteo Basin.

EL RANCHO DE LAS GOLONDRINAS
★ *15 mi south of Santa Fe off I–25 Exit 276 in La Cienega.*

The "Williamsburg of the Southwest," El Rancho de las Golondrinas ("Ranch of the Swallows") is a reconstruction of a small agricultural village with buildings from the 17th to 19th century. Travelers on El Camino Real would stop at the ranch before making the final leg of the journey north, a half-day ride from Santa Fe in horse-and-wagon time. By car, the ranch is only a 25-minute drive from the Plaza. From Interstate 25, the village is tucked away from view, frozen in time. Owned and operated by the Paloheimo family, direct descendants of those who owned the ranch when it functioned as a *paraje*, or stopping place, the grounds maintain an authentic character without compromising history for commercial gain. Even the gift shop carries items that reflect ranch life and the cultural exchange that took place there.

Self-guided tours survey Spanish colonial lifestyles in New Mexico from 1660 to 1890: you can view a molasses mill, threshing grounds, and wheelwright and blacksmith shops, as well as a mountain village and a *morada* (meeting place) of the order of Penitentes (a religious fraternity known for its reenactment during Holy Week of the tortures suffered by Christ). Farm animals roam through the barnyards on the 200-acre complex. Wool from the sheep is spun into yarn and woven into traditional Rio Grande–style blankets, and the corn grown is used to feed the animals. During the spring and harvest festivals, on the first weekends of June and October, respectively, the village comes alive with Spanish-American folk music, dancing, and food and crafts demonstrations. The ranch hosts a wine festival over the weekend of July 4th, and the increasingly popular Viva Mexico! celebration in mid-July celebrates the two regions' interconnected relationship through demonstrations by Mexican master artisans, musicians, craftspeople, and the famed *voladores*—men who spin gracefully from ropes off 60-foot poles—perform a vibrant and daredevil show. There are ample picnic facilities, and a snack bar serves a limited number of items on weekends only. ⊠ *334 Los Pinos Rd.* ☎ *505/471–2261* ⊕ *www.golondrinas.org* ✏ *$5* ☽ *June–Sept., Wed.–Sun. 10–4; some additional weekends for special events.*

KASHA-KATUWE TENT ROCKS NATIONAL MONUMENT
☾ *40 mi south of Santa Fe via I–25 Exit 264.*

Fodor's Choice
★

This is a terrific hiking getaway, especially if you have time for only one hike. The sandstone rock formations look like stacked tents in a stark, water- and wind-eroded box canyon. Located 45 minutes south of Santa Fe, near Cochiti Pueblo, Tent Rocks offers excellent hiking year-round, although it can get hot in summer, when you should bring extra water. The drive to this magical landscape is equally awesome, as the road heads west toward Cochiti Dam and through the cottonwood groves around the pueblo. It's a good hike for kids. The round-trip hiking distance is only 2 mi, about 1½ leisurely hours, but it's the kind of place where you'll want to hang out for a while. Take a camera, but leave your pets at home—no dogs are allowed. There are no facilities here, just a small parking area with a posted trail map and a self-pay admission box; you can get gas and pick up picnic supplies and bottled water at Cochiti Lake Convenience Store. ⊠ *1405 Cochiti Hwy.* ⊹ *Take I–25 south to Cochiti Exit 264; follow NM 16 for 8 mi, turning right onto NM 22; continue approximately 3½ more mi past Cochiti Pueblo entrance; turn right onto BIA 92, which after 2 mi becomes Forest Service Rd. 266, a rough road of jarring, washboard gravel that leads 5 mi to well-marked parking area* ☎ *505/761–8700* ⊕ *www.nm.blm. gov* ✏ *$5 per vehicle* ☽ *Apr.–Oct., daily 7–7; Nov.–Mar., daily 8–5.*

SPORTS AND THE OUTDOORS
The 18-hole, par-72 **Pueblo de Cochiti Golf Course** (⊠ *5200 Cochiti Hwy., Cochiti Lake* ☎ *505/465–2239*), set against a backdrop of steep canyons and red-rock mesas, is a 45-minute drive southwest of Santa Fe. Cochiti was designed by Robert Trent Jones Jr. and offers one of the most challenging and visually stunning golfing experiences in the state. Greens fees are $62 (Friday) and include a cart. A number of special deals throughout the week make this course a good value.

PUEBLOS NEAR SANTA FE

For a pleasant side trip, visit several of the state's 19 pueblos, including San Ildefonso, one of the state's most picturesque, and Santa Clara, whose lands harbor a dramatic set of ancient cliff dwellings. Between the two reservations sits the striking landmark called Black Mesa, which you can see from NM 30 or NM 502. The solitary butte has inspired many painters, including Georgia O'Keeffe, and it is from this mesa that deer dancers descend at dawn during winter ceremonial dances. Both of these pueblos are home to outstanding potters and it is well worth visiting open studios to watch the process and see what is available. Plan on spending one to three hours at each pueblo, and leave the day open if you're there for a feast day, when dances are set to an organic rather than mechanical clock. Pueblo grounds and hiking areas do not permit pets.

POJOAQUE PUEBLO
17 mi north of Santa Fe on U.S. 285/84.

There's not much to see in the pueblo's plaza area, but the state visitor center and adjoining **Poeh Cultural Center and Museum** on U.S. 285/84 are well worth a visit. The latter is an impressive complex of traditional adobe buildings, including the three-story Sun Tower; the facility comprises a museum, a cultural center, and artists' studios. The museum holds some 8,000 photographs, including many by esteemed early-20th-century photographer Edward S. Curtis, as well as hundreds of works of both traditional and contemporary pottery, jewelry, textiles, and sculpture. There are frequent demonstrations by artists, exhibitions, and, on Saturday from May through September, traditional ceremonial dances. By the early 20th century the pueblo was virtually uninhabited, but the survivors eventually began to restore it. Pojoaque's feast day is celebrated with dancing on December 12. The visitor center is one of the friendliest and best stocked in northern New Mexico, with free maps and literature on hiking, fishing, and the area's history. The crafts shop in the visitor center is one of the most extensive among the state's pueblos; it carries weaving, pottery, jewelry, and other crafts by both Pojoaque and other indigenous New Mexicans. ⊠ *78 Cities of Gold Rd., off U.S. 285/84, 17 mi north of Santa Fe* ☎ *505/455–3460* ⊕ *www. poehmuseum.com* ✉ *Donations accepted.*

$ ✕ **Gabriel's.** This restaurant has location (convenient for pre-opera and
NEW MEXICAN   post-high-road tours), a gorgeous setting (the Spanish colonial–style art, the building, the flower-filled courtyard, and those mountain views!), and the made-to-order guacamole going for it. The margaritas aren't too shabby either. The caveat? The quality of the entrées tends to be wildly uneven. Service is generally friendly, but as uneven as the food. If you're content with a gorgeous setting and making the stellar guacamole and margaritas your mainstay, this is a fine place to go for sunset. Prices are reasonable and the views truly are spectacular. ⊠ *U.S. 285/84, Exit 176, just south of Buffalo Thunder Resort, 5 mi north of Santa Fe Opera* ☎ *505/455–7000* ⊟ *AE, D, DC, MC, V.*

$$$ 🏨 **Buffalo Thunder Resort & Casino.** Managed by Hilton, this expansive,
RESORT   upscale gaming and golfing getaway is the closest full-service resort to

Santa Fe—it's just 15 mi north. The rooms are spacious and airy, all with large windows and some with full balconies taking in the surrounding vistas. The property offers plenty of leisure amenities: an extensive slate of treatments in the 16,000-square-foot Wo' P'in Spa, access to a pair of championship 18-hole layouts at the adjacent Towa Golf Resort, a concert venue, and good mix of upscale and casual restaurants and bars. There's also an enormous casino, but it's set well away from the lobby and public areas on a separate level, making it easy to ignore if gaming isn't your thing. Hilton also operates a less pricey but also quite nice Homewood Suites next door. **Pros:** Snazziest hotel between Santa Fe and Taos, convenient to opera and Los Alamos, panoramic mountain and mesa views. **Cons:** Just off of a busy highway, lobby is noisy and crowded with gamers on many evenings, nothing much within walking distance. ⊠ *30 Buffalo Thunder Rd.,off U.S. 285/84, Exit 177Pojoaque* ☎ *505/455–5555 or 877/455–7775* ⊕ *www. buffalothunderresort.com* ⤵ *290 rooms, 85 suites* ⌂ *In-room: a/c, safe, Wi-Fi. In-hotel: 5 restaurants, room service, bars, golf courses, tennis, pools, gym, spa, parking (free).* ⊟ *AE, D, DC, MC, V.*

NAMBÉ PUEBLO
4 mi east of Pojoaque on NM 503, 20 mi north of Santa Fe.

Nambé Pueblo (which means "People of the Round Earth") has no visitor center, so the best time to visit is during the October 4th feast day of St. Francis celebration or the very popular July 4th celebration. If you want to explore the landscape surrounding the pueblo, take the drive past the pueblo until you come to **Nambé Falls and Nambé Lake Recreation Area** (☎ *505/455–2304*). There's a shady picnic area and a large fishing lake that's open March to November (the cost is $15 for fishing, and $20 for boating—no gas motors are permitted). The waterfalls are about a 15-minute hike in from the parking and picnic area along a rocky, clearly marked path. The water pours over a rock precipice—a loud and dramatic sight given the river's modest size. Overnight RV ($35) and tent ($25) camping are also offered. The area is closed Monday. ⊠ *Nambé Pueblo Rd., off NM 503* ☎ *505/455–4444 info, 505/455–2304 ranger station* ⊕ *www.nambefalls.com* ⤳ *$10 per car.*

SAN ILDEFONSO PUEBLO
23 mi north of Santa Fe via U.S. 285/84 to NM 502 west.

Maria Martinez, one of the most renowned Pueblo potters, lived here. She first created her exquisite "black on black" pottery in 1919 and in doing so sparked a major revival of pueblo arts and crafts. She died in 1980, and the 26,000-acre San Ildefonso Pueblo remains a major center for pottery and other arts and crafts. Many artists sell from their homes, and there are trading posts, a visitor center, and a museum where some of Martinez's work can be seen on weekdays. San Ildefonso is also one of the more visually appealing pueblos, with a well-defined plaza core and a spectacular setting beneath the Pajarito Plateau and Black Mesa. The pueblo's feast day is January 23, when unforgettable buffalo, deer, and Comanche dances are performed from dawn to dusk. Cameras are not permitted at any of the ceremonial dances but may be used at other times with a permit. ⊠ *NM 502* ☎ *505/455–3549* ⤳ *$7 per vehicle,*

Pueblo Etiquette

When visiting pueblos and reservations, you're expected to follow a certain etiquette. Each pueblo has its own regulations for the use of still and video cameras and video and tape recorders, as well as for sketching and painting. Some pueblos, such as Santo Domingo, prohibit photography altogether. Others, such as Santa Clara, prohibit photography at certain times; for example, during ritual dances. Still others allow photography but require a permit, which usually costs from $10 to $20, depending on whether you use a still or video camera. The privilege of setting up an easel and painting all day will cost you as little as $35 or as much as $150 (at Taos Pueblo). Associated fees for using images also can vary widely, depending on what kind of reproduction rights you might require. **Be sure to ask permission before photographing anyone in the pueblos;** it's also customary to give the subject a dollar or two for agreeing to be photographed. Native American law prevails on the pueblos, and violations of photography regulations could result in confiscation of cameras.

Specific restrictions for the various pueblos are noted in the individual descriptions. Other rules are described below.

■ Possessing or using drugs and/or alcohol on Native American land is forbidden.

■ Ritual dances often have serious religious significance and should be respected as such. Silence is mandatory—that means no questions about ceremonies or dances while they're being performed. Don't walk across the dance plaza during a performance, and don't applaud afterward.

■ Kivas and ceremonial rooms are restricted to pueblo members only.

■ Cemeteries are sacred. They're off-limits to all visitors and should never be photographed.

■ Unless pueblo dwellings are clearly marked as shops, don't wander or peek inside. Remember, these are private homes.

■ Many of the pueblo buildings are hundreds of years old. Don't try to scale adobe walls or climb on top of buildings, or you may come tumbling down.

■ Don't litter. Nature is sacred on the pueblos, and defacing land can be a serious offense.

■ Don't bring your pet or feed stray dogs.

■ Even off reservation sites, state and federal laws prohibit picking up artifacts such as arrowheads or pottery from public lands.

still-camera permit $10, video-recorder permit $20, sketching permit $25 ⊙ *Apr.–Oct., daily 8–5; museum, weekdays, Apr.–Oct. 8–4:30.*

SANTA CLARA PUEBLO

27 mi northwest of Santa Fe, 10 mi north of San Ildefonso Pueblo via NM 30.

Santa Clara Pueblo, southwest of Española, is the home of a historic treasure—the awesome **Puyé Cliff Dwellings,** believed to have been built in the 13th to 14th centuries. They can be seen by driving 9 mi up a gravel road through a canyon, south of the village off NM 502. You can tour the cliff dwellings, topped by the ruins of a 740-room pueblo, on your own or with a guide—several special tours are available for additional fees. Pay your entrance fees and arrange for tours at the Puyé Cliffs Welcome Center, at the Valero gas station on the corner of NM 30 and Puyé Cliffs Road. ⊠ *NM 30, Santa Clara Pueblo, Española* 🕾 *505/747–2455* ⊕ *www.puyecliffs.com* 🖃 *$7* ⊙ *Daily 8:30–6. Closed the week before Easter, June 13, Aug. 12, and Christmas day.*

The village's shops sell burnished red pottery, engraved blackware, paintings, and other arts and crafts. All pottery is made via the coil method, not with a pottery wheel. Santa Clara is known for its carved pieces, and Avanyu, a water serpent that guards the waters, is the pueblo's symbol. Other typical works include engagement baskets, wedding vessels, and seed pots. The pueblo's feast day of St. Claire is celebrated on August 12. The pueblo also contains four ponds, miles of stream fishing, and picnicking and camping facilities. Permits for the use of trails, camping, and picnic areas, as well as for fishing in trout ponds, are available at the sites. ⊠ *NM 30, off NM 502, Española* 🕾 *505/753–7326* 🖃 *Pueblo free, cliff dwellings $5, still-camera permits $5* ⊙ *Daily 9–4:30.*

JÉMEZ COUNTRY

In the Jémez region, the 1,000-year-old Ancestral Puebloan ruins at Bandelier National Monument present a vivid contrast to Los Alamos National Laboratory, birthplace of the atomic bomb. You can easily take in part of Jémez Country in a day trip from Santa Fe.

On this tour you can see terrific views of the Rio Grande Valley, the Sangre de Cristos, the Galisteo Basin, and, in the distance, the Sandias. There are places to eat and shop for essentials in Los Alamos and a few roadside eateries along NM 4 in La Cueva and Jémez Springs. There are also numerous turnouts along NM 4, several that have paths leading down to the many excellent fishing spots along the Jémez River.

The 48,000-acre Cerro Grande fire of 2000 burned much of the pine forest in the lower Jémez Mountains, as well as more than 250 homes in Los Alamos. Parts of the drive are still scarred with charcoaled remains, but vegetation has returned, and many homes have been rebuilt in the residential areas.

LOS ALAMOS

35 mi from Santa Fe via U.S. 285/84 north to NM 502 west.

Look at old books on New Mexico and you rarely find a mention of Los Alamos, now a busy town of 19,000 that has the highest per capita income in the state. Like so many other Southwestern communities, Los Alamos was created expressly as a company town; only here the workers weren't mining iron, manning freight trains, or hauling lumber—they were busy toiling at America's foremost nuclear research facility, Los Alamos National Laboratory (LANL). The facility still employs some 8,000 full-time workers, most living in town but many others in the Española Valley and even Santa Fe. The lab has experienced some tough times over the years, from the infamous Wen Ho Lee espionage case in the late '90s to a slew of alleged security breaches in 2003 and 2004. The controversies have shed some doubt on the future of LANL.

A few miles from ancient cave dwellings, scientists led by J. Robert Oppenheimer built Fat Man and Little Boy, the atom bombs that in August 1945 decimated Hiroshima and Nagasaki, respectively. LANL was created in 1943 under the auspices of the intensely covert Manhattan Project, whose express purpose was to expedite an Allied victory during World War II. Indeed, Japan surrendered—but a full-blown cold war between Russia and the United States ensued for another four and a half decades.

LANL works hard today to promote its broader platforms, including "enhancing global nuclear security" but also finding new ways to detect radiation, fighting pollution and environmental risks associated with nuclear energy, and furthering studies of the solar system, biology, and computer sciences. Similarly, the town of Los Alamos strives to be more well-rounded, better understood, and tourist-friendly.

The **Bradbury Science Museum** is Los Alamos National Laboratory's public showcase, and its exhibits offer a balanced and provocative examination of such topics as atomic weapons and nuclear power. You can experiment with lasers; witness research in solar, geothermal, fission, and fusion energy; learn about DNA fingerprinting; and view exhibits about World War II's Project Y (the Manhattan Project, whose participants developed the atomic bomb). ⊠ *Los Alamos National Laboratory, 15th St. and Central Ave.* ☎ *505/667–4444* ⊕ *www.lanl.gov/museum* ⊠ *Free* ☉ *Tues.–Fri. 9–5, Sat.–Mon. 1–5.*

New Mexican architect John Gaw Meem designed **Fuller Lodge,** a short drive up Central Avenue from the Bradbury Science Museum. The massive log building was erected in 1928 as a dining and recreation hall for a small private boys' school. In 1942 the federal government purchased the school and made it the base of operations for the Manhattan Project. Part of the lodge contains an art center that shows the works of northern New Mexican artists; there's a picturesque rose garden on the grounds. This is a bustling center with drop-in art classes, nine art shows per year, and a gallery gift shop featuring 70 local artisans. ⊠ *2132 Central Ave.* ☎ *505/662–9331* ⊕ *www.artfulnm.org* ⊠ *Free* ☉ *Mon.–Sat. 10–4.*

NEED A BREAK? Join the ranks of locals, Los Alamos National Laboratory employees, and tourists who line up each morning at **Chili Works** (⊠ *1743 Trinity Dr.* ☎ *505/662–7591*) to sample one of the state's best breakfast burritos. This inexpensive, simple takeout spot is also worth a stop to grab breakfast or lunch before heading off for a hike at Bandelier. The burritos are stellar and the chile is *hot*.

The **Los Alamos Historical Museum,** in a log building beside Fuller Lodge, displays exhibits on the once-volatile geological history of the volcanic Jémez Mountains, the 700-year history of human life in this area, and more on—you guessed it—the Manhattan Project. It's rather jarring to observe ancient Puebloan potsherds and arrowheads in one display and photos of an obliterated Nagasaki in the next. ✉ *1921 Juniper St.* ☎ *505/662–4493* 🌐 *www.losalamoshistory.org* 🎟 *Free* ⏲ *Mon.–Sat. 9:30–4:30, Sun. 1–4.*

WHERE TO EAT AND STAY

$ ECLECTIC ★ ✕ **Blue Window Bistro.** Despite its relative wealth, Los Alamos has never cultivated much of a dining scene, which makes this cheerful and elegant restaurant all the more appreciated by foodies. The kitchen turns out a mix of New Mexican, American, and Continental dishes, from a first-rate Cobb salad to steak topped with Jack cheese and green chile to double-cut pork chops with mashed potatoes, applewood-smoked bacon, and red-onion marmalade. In addition to the softly lighted dining room with terra-cotta walls, there are several tables on a patio overlooking a lush garden. ✉ *813 Central Ave.* ☎ *505/662–6305* 💳 *AE, D, DC, MC, V* ⏲ *Closed Sun.*

$ HOTEL 🏨 **Best Western Hilltop House Hotel.** Minutes from the Los Alamos National Laboratory, this three-story hotel hosts both vacationers and scientists. It's standard chain-hotel decor here: rooms are done with contemporary, functional furniture and have microwaves, refrigerators, and coffeemakers; deluxe ones have kitchenettes. The La Vista Restaurant on the premises serves tasty, if predictable, American fare. The very good Blue Window Bistro is next door. **Pros:** great proximity to the restaurants and shops in town; friendly, easygoing staff. **Cons:** this isn't a property with much character; but it's sufficient for business travelers and those wanting to use Los Alamos as a jumping-off point for excursions beyond Santa Fe. ✉ *400 Trinity Dr.* ☎ *505/662–2441 or 800/462–0936* 🌐 *www.bwhilltop.com* 🛏 *73 rooms, 19 suites* 👍 *In-room: a/c, kitchen (some), refrigerator, Wi-Fi. In-hotel: restaurant, room service, bar, pool, gym, laundry facilities, some pets allowed* 💳 *AE, D, DC, MC, V* 🍽 *CP.*

BANDELIER NATIONAL MONUMENT

Fodor's Choice ★ *10 mi south of Los Alamos via NM 501 south to NM 4 east; 40 mi north of Santa Fe via U.S. 285/84 north to NM 502 west to NM 4 west.*

Seven centuries before the Declaration of Independence was signed, compact city-states existed in the Southwest. Remnants of one of the most impressive of them can be seen at **Frijoles Canyon in Bandelier National Monument.** At the canyon's base, near a gurgling stream, are the remains of cave dwellings, ancient ceremonial kivas, and other stone structures that stretch out for more than a mile beneath the sheer walls of the canyon's tree-fringed rim. For hundreds of years the ancestral Puebloan people, relatives of today's Rio Grande Pueblo Indians, thrived on wild game, corn, and beans. Suddenly, for reasons still undetermined, the settlements were abandoned.

Wander through the site on a paved, self-guided trail. Steep wooden ladders and narrow doorways lead you to the cave dwellings and cell-like rooms. There is one kiva in the cliff wall that is large, and tall enough to stand in. Don't forget to look up, sometimes way up, into the nooks and crevices of the canyon wall above the dwellings to view the remarkable, mysterious petroglyphs left behind by the Ancestral Puebloans.

Bandelier National Monument, named after author and ethnologist Adolph Bandelier (his novel *The Delight Makers* is set in Frijoles Canyon), contains 23,000 acres of backcountry wilderness, waterfalls, and wildlife. Sixty miles of trails traverse the park. A small museum in the visitor center focuses on the area's prehistoric and contemporary Native American cultures, with displays of artifacts from 1200 to modern times as well as displays on the forest fires that have devastated parts of the park in recent years. There is a small café in the wonderful, 1930s CCC-built stone visitors complex. It is worth getting up early to get here when there are still shadows on the cliff walls because the petroglyphs are fantastic and all but disappear in the bright light of the afternoon. If you are staying in the area, ask about the night walks at the visitor center, they're stellar! Pets are not allowed on any trails. ☎ *505/672–0343* ⊕ *www.nps.gov/band/index.htm* 🖃 *$12 per vehicle, good for 7 days* ⊘ *Late May–early Sept., daily 8–6; early Sept.–Oct. and Apr.–late May, daily 8–5:30; Nov.–Mar., daily 8–4:30.*

VALLES CALDERA NATIONAL PRESERVE
15 mi southwest of Los Alamos via NM 4.

⟳

Fodor's Choice

★

A high-forest drive brings you to the awe-inspiring Valles Grande, which at 14 mi in diameter is one of the world's largest calderas and which became Valles (say *vah*-yes) Caldera National Preserve in 2000. The caldera resulted from the eruption and collapse of a 14,000-foot peak over 1 million years ago; the flow out the bottom created the Pajarito Plateau and the ash from the eruption spread as far east as Kansas. You can't imagine the volcanic crater's immensity until you spot what look like specks of dust on the lush meadow floor and realize they're elk. The Valles Caldera Trust manages this 89,000-acre multiuse preserve with the aim to "protect and preserve the scientific, scenic, geologic, watershed, fish, wildlife, historic, cultural, and recreational values of the Preserve, and to provide for multiple use and sustained yield of renewable resources within the Preserve."

The preserve is open to visitors for hiking, cross-country skiing, horseback riding, horse-drawn carriage rides, van wildlife photography tours, mountain-bike tours, bird-watching, and fly-fishing. Some of the activities require reservations and a fee, although there are two free, relatively short hikes signposted from the parking area along NM 4, and no reservations are needed for these. Drive into the Caldera to the check-in station to gain access to other short hikes, guided tours, and information about events. Their Web site is the best source to plan a visit to this breathtaking area. Fishing and hunting (elk and turkeys) permits are given out based on a lottery system; lottery "tickets" are sold for a nominal fee. 🖃 *18161 NM 4* ☎ *505/661–3333 or 866/382–5537* ⊕ *www.vallescaldera.gov.*

JÉMEZ SPRINGS
20 mi west of Valles Caldera on NM 4.

The funky mountain village of Jémez (say *hay*-mess) Springs draws outdoorsy types for hiking, cross-country skiing, and camping in the nearby U.S. Forest Service areas. The town's biggest tourist draws are

Jémez State Monument and Soda Dam, but many people come here for relaxation at the town's bathhouse.

The geological wonder known as **Soda Dam** was created over thousands of years by travertine deposits—minerals that precipitate out of geothermal springs. With its strange mushroom-shaped exterior and caves split by a roaring waterfall, it's no wonder the spot was considered sacred by Native Americans. In summer it's popular for swimming. ⊠ *NM 4, 1 mi north of Jémez State Monument.*

Jémez State Monument contains impressive Spanish and Native American ruins set throughout a 7-acre site and toured via an easy 1/3-mi loop trail. About 700 years ago ancestors of the people of Jémez Pueblo built several villages in and around the narrow mountain valley. One of the villages was Guisewa, or "Place of the Boiling Waters." The Spanish colonists built a mission church beside it, San José de los Jémez, which was abandoned by around 1640. ⊠ *NM 4* ☎ *575/829–3530* ⊕ *www. nmstatemonuments.org* ✉ *$3* ☉ *Wed.–Mon. 8:30–5.*

★ Now owned and operated by the village of Jémez Springs, the original structure at the **Jémez Spring Bath House** was erected in the 1870s near a mineral hot spring. Many other buildings were added over the years, and the complex was completely renovated into an intimate Victorian-style hideaway in the mid-1990s. It's a funky, low-key spot that's far less formal and fancy than the several spa resorts near Santa Fe. You can soak in a mineral bath for $12 (30 minutes) or $17 (60 minutes). Massages cost between $42 (30 minutes) and $98 (90 minutes). An acupuncturist is available with advance notice. Beauty treatments include facials, manicures, and pedicures. The Jémez Package ($95) includes a half-hour bath, an herbal blanket wrap, and a one-hour massage. You can stroll down a short path behind the house to see where the steaming hot springs feed into the Jémez River. The tubs are not communal, but individual, and there are no outdoor tubs. Children under 14 are not allowed. ⊠ *062 Jémez Springs Plaza, off NM 4 Jémez Springs* ☎ *575/829–3303 or 866/204–8303* ⊕ *www.jemezsprings.org/ bathhouse.html* ✉ *Free* ☉ *June–early Nov., daily 10–8; early Nov.–May, daily 10–6.*

Giggling Springs offers a large, outdoor, natural-mineral hot spring. Right across the street from the Laughing Lizard, this is a good option for the soakers who want hot water but don't want the individualized treatments at the Bath House. The staff is very accommodating. Children under 14 are not permitted. Pool capacity is limited to eight at a time; reservations are recommended. ⊠ *040 Abousleman Loop* ☎ *575/829–9175* ⊕ *www.gigglingsprings.com* ✉ *$15 per hour, $25 for two hours, $35 for the day* ☉ *Closed Mon. and Tues.*

WHERE TO STAY

$ ⌂ **Cañon del Rio.** On 6 acres along the Jémez River beneath towering mesas, this light-filled, contemporary adobe inn has rooms with cove ceilings, tile floors, and Native American arts and crafts. All have French doors and open onto a courtyard with a natural-spring fountain. Wellness packages include massage, acupuncture, and aromatherapy. Breakfasts are a big deal here and they're delicious. **Pros:** property has an abundance of water—a real treat in New Mexico. **Cons:** though rooms are comfortable, the decor looks like that of a Southwestern chain hotel. ⊠ *16445 NM 4* ☏ *575/829–4377* ⊕ *www.canondelrio.com* ➹ *6 rooms, 1 suite* ♿ *In-room: a/c, kitchen (some), no TV. In-hotel: Wi-Fi hotspot* ◻ *AE, D, MC, V* ﺀ ◯︙ *CP.*

¢ ⊡ **Laughing Lizard Inn and Cafe.** Consisting of a simple four-room motel-style inn and a cute adobe-and-stone café with a corrugated-metal roof, the Laughing Lizard makes for a sweet and cheerful diversion—it's right in the center of the village. Rooms are cozy and simple with white linens, dressers, books, and porches that look out over the rugged mesa beyond the river valley. Tasty, eclectic fare—great salads, freshly ground burgers, super calzones and pizzas, and a lineup of New Mexican favorites—is served in the homey café, which has a Saltillo-tile screened porch and an open-air wooden deck. This hub of friendly energy is owned and operated by the Lagan family, and their care and attention shows. **Pros:** great staff; beautiful location. **Cons:** rooms are fairly small; no a/c. ⊠ *NM 4* ☏ *575/829–3108* ⊕ *www.thelaughinglizard.com* ➹ *4 rooms* ♿ *In-room: no a/c. In-hotel: restaurant, some pets allowed* ◻ *D, MC, V.*

JÉMEZ PUEBLO

12 mi south of Jémez Springs via NM 4; 85 mi west of Santa Fe via U.S. 285/84 and NM 4; 50 mi north of Albuquerque via I–25, U.S. 550, and NM 4.

As you continue southwest along NM 4, the terrain changes from a wooded river valley with high mesas on either side to an open red-rock valley, the home of the Jémez Pueblo, which is set along the Jémez River. After the pueblo at Pecos (⇨ *Pecos National Historic Park, above)* was abandoned in 1838, Jémez was the state's only pueblo with residents who spoke Towa (different from Tiwa and Tewa). The Jémez Reservation encompasses 89,000 acres, with two lakes, Holy Ghost Springs and Dragonfly Lake (off NM 4), open for fishing by permit only, April to October on weekends and holidays. The only part of the pueblo open to the public is the **Walatowa Visitor Center,** a fancy Pueblo Revival building that contains a small museum, an extensive pottery and crafts shop, and rotating art and photography exhibits; there's a short nature walk outside. The pueblo is sometimes open to the public for special events, demonstrations, and ceremonial dances—call for details. The pueblo is noted for its polychrome pottery. The Walatowa gas and convenience store, on NM 4 next to the visitor center, is one of the few such establishments between Los Alamos and Bernalillo. Photographing, sketching, and video recording are prohibited. ⊠ *7413 NM 4* ☏ *575/834–7235* ⊕ *www.jemezpueblo.org* 🎟 *Free* ☉ *Daily 8–5.*

GEORGIA O'KEEFFE COUNTRY

It's a 20-minute drive north of Santa Fe to reach the Española Valley, where you head west to the striking mesas, cliffs, and valleys that so inspired the artist Georgia O'Keeffe—she lived in this area for the final 50 years of her life. You first come to the small, workaday city of Española, a major crossroads from which roads lead to Taos, Chama, and

Abiquiu. The other notable community in this area is tiny Ojo Caliente, famous for its hot-springs spa retreat.

ESPAÑOLA

20 mi north of Santa Fe via U.S. 285/84.

This small but growing city midway along the Low Road from Santa Fe to Taos is a business hub for the many villages and pueblos scattered throughout the region north of Santa Fe. The area at the confluence of the Rio Grande and Rio Chama was declared the capital for Spain by Don Juan de Oñate in 1598, but wasn't more than a collection of small settlements until the town was founded in 1880s as a stop on the Denver & Rio Grande Railroad. Lacking the colonial charm of either Santa Fe or Taos, Española is known for being pretty rough-and-tumble. There are many cheap burger joints, New Mexican restaurants, and a few chain motels, but few reasons to stick around for more than a quick meal. The city has become known as the "lowrider capital of the world" because of the mostly classic cars that have been retrofitted with lowered chassis and hydraulics that allow the cars to bump and grind as they cruise the streets on perpetual parade. The cars are often painted with religious murals, homages to dead relatives, and other spectacular scenes.

You may see a number of people wearing white (and sometimes orange or blue) turbans; they are members of the large American Sikh community that settled on the south end of town in the late 60s. Initially viewed with suspicion by the provincial Hispanics of the area, the Sikhs have become integral members of the community, teaching Kundalini yoga, establishing businesses and medical practices, and influencing many local restaurants to add vegetarian versions of New Mexican dishes to their menus.

All the main arteries converge in the heart of town amidst a series of drab shopping centers, so watch the signs on the town's south side. Traffic moves slowly, especially on weekend nights when cruisers bring car culture alive.

NEED A BREAK? **Lovin' Oven** serves delicious homemade donuts, apple fritters, biscochito cookies, turnovers, and hot coffee amidst all the latest news and gossip shared amongst the hordes of locals who pour through the doors at this sweet little shop on Española's south end. Get there early—once the goodies are gone they're gone. ⊠ *107 N. Riverside Dr.* ☎ *505/753-5461.*

The region is known for its longstanding weaving traditions, and one place you can learn about this heritage is the **Española Valley Fiber Arts Center** (⊠ *325 Paseo de Oñate* ☎ *505/747-3577* ⊕ *www.evfac.org* ⊠ *Free* ☉ *Mon. 9–8, Tues.–Sat. 9–5, Sun. noon–5*), a nonprofit, teaching facility set inside an adobe building in the city's historic section. Here you can watch local weavers working with traditional materials and looms and admire (and purchase) their works in a small gallery. There are also classes offered on spinning, weaving, and knitting, which are open to the public and range from one day to several weeks. Emphasis here is placed on the styles of weaving that have been practiced here in the northern Rio Grande Valley since the Spaniards brought sheep and treadle looms here in the late 16th century. The center also celebrates the ancient traditions of New Mexico's Navajo and Pueblo weavers.

WHERE TO EAT AND STAY

$$

MEXICAN

Fodor's Choice

★

✕ **El Paragua Restaurant.** With a dark, intimate atmosphere of wood and stone, this historic place started out as a lemonade-cum-taco stand in the late 1950s but is now known for some of the state's most authentic New Mexican and regional Mexican cuisine. Steaks and fish are grilled over a mesquite-wood fire; other specialties include chorizo enchiladas, panfried breaded trout amandine, and menudo. This restaurant is still a family affair; service is gracious and the food is worth the drive. If you don't have time to sit down for a meal, stop at El Parasol taco stand (¢) in the parking lot next door for excellent, cheap Mexican–New Mexican fare. Vegetarians rejoice! Ask for the Khalsa special, a superdelicious veggie quesadilla created for the local Sikhs (the many folks you may see around the area wearing white turbans), or try the veggie tacos. You'll also find El Parasol restaurants on the 84/285 frontage road in Pojoaque, and at 1833 Cerrillos Road in Santa Fe. ⊠ *603 Santa Cruz Rd., NM 76 just east of NM 68* ☎ *505/753–3211 or 800/929–8226* ⊕ *www.elparagua.com* ☰ *AE, DC, MC, V.*

$$$$

INN AND VILLAS

Fodor's Choice

★

🛏 **Rancho de San Juan.** This secluded 225-acre compound hugs Black Mesa's base. Many of the inn's rooms are self-contained suites, some set around a courtyard and others amid the wilderness. All rooms have Southwestern furnishings, Frette robes, Aveda bath products, and CD stereos; nearly all have kiva fireplaces. The top units have such cushy touches as two bedrooms, 12-foot ceilings, Mexican marble showers, kitchens, Jacuzzis, and private patios. The à la carte menu in the Three Forks restaurant (dinner Tuesday through Saturday, by reservation only) features inventive contemporary cuisine, changes weekly. Past fare has included Texas quail stuffed with corn bread, green chiles, and linguica sausage, and Alaskan halibut with tomatillo-lime salsa, caramelized butternut squash, and creamed spinach. Hike to a beautiful hand-carved sandstone shrine on a bluff above the property. In-suite spa and massage services are available. **Pros:** an ideal secluded getaway close to Ojo Caliente and out of the bustle of Santa Fe. **Cons:** property is a virtual island in rural New Mexico and you must drive to sights and restaurants; service not always as attentive to guests' needs considering the rates. ⊠ *U.S. 285, 3½ mi north of U.S. 84* ⬠ *Box 4140, 87533* ☎ *505/753–6818* ⊕ *www.ranchodesanjuan.com* ⏴ *4 suites, 9 casitas* ♨ *In-room: no a/c (some), kitchen (some), no TV. In-hotel: restaurant, Wi-Fi hotspot, no kids under 8* ☰ *AE, D, DC, MC, V* ¶⦿¶ *MAP.*

HORSEBACK RIDING

Santa Fe Stables (⊠ *115 NM 399, Espanola* ☎ *505/231–7113* ⊕ *www.santaferidingcompany.com*) clearly treats its horses well, and the staff of wranglers are good with people, too. Private rides ensure you're a personal experience as you explore the gorgeous scenery on Santa Clara Pueblo's Black Mesa. Rides are generally two hours; special trips can be arranged in advance.

ABIQUIU

24 mi northwest of Española via U.S. 84.

This tiny, very traditional Hispanic village was originally home to freed *genizaros,* indigenous and mixed-blood slaves who served as house servants, shepherds, and other key roles in Spanish, Mexican, and American households well into the 1880s. Genizaros now make up a significant population of the state. Many descendants of original families still live in the area, although since the late 1980s Abiquiu and its surrounding countryside have become a nesting ground for those fleeing big-city life, among them actresses Marsha Mason and Shirley MacLaine. Abiquiu—along with parts of the nearby Española Valley—is also a hotbed of organic farming, with many of the operations here selling their goods at the Santa Fe Farmers' Market and to restaurants throughout the Rio Grande Valley. Newcomers or visitors may find themselves shut out by locals; it's best to observe one very important local custom: no photography is allowed in and around the village.

A number of artists live in Abiquiu, and several studios showing traditional Hispanic art as well as contemporary works and pottery, are open regularly to the public; many others open each year over Columbus Day weekend (second weekend of October) for the **Annual Abiquiu Studio Tour** (☎ *505/685–4454 ⊕ www.abiquiustudiotour.org*).

Fodor's Choice
★

You can visit **Georgia O'Keeffe's home** through advance reservation (about four months is recommended if you come during high season) with the **Georgia O'Keeffe Museum** (☎ *505/685–4539 ⊕ www.okeeffemuseum. org*), which conducts one-hour tours Tuesday, Thursday, and Friday, mid-March through November for $30, with additional tours on Wednesday in July and August, for $40. In 1945 Georgia O'Keeffe bought a large, dilapidated late-18th-century Spanish-colonial adobe compound just off the plaza. Upon the 1946 death of her husband, photographer Alfred Stieglitz, she left New York City and began dividing her time permanently between this home, which figured prominently in many of her works, and the one in nearby Ghost Ranch. She wrote about the house, "When I first saw the Abiquiu house it was a ruin. As I climbed and walked about in the ruin I found a patio with a very pretty well house and a bucket to draw up water. It was a good-sized patio with a long wall with a door on one side. That wall with a door in it was something I had to have. It took me 10 years to get it—three more years to fix the house up so I could live in it—and after that the wall with the door was painted many times." The patio is featured in *Black Patio Door* (1955) and *Patio with Cloud* (1956). O'Keeffe died in 1986 at the age of 98 and left provisions in her will to ensure that the property's houses would never be public monuments.

WHERE TO STAY

$$
INN

Abiquiu Inn and Cafe Abiquiu. Deep in the Chama Valley, the inn has a secluded, exotic feel—almost like an oasis—with brightly decorated rooms, including several four-person casitas, with woodstoves or fireplaces and tiled baths; some units have verandas with hammocks and open views of O'Keeffe Country. The café ($$) serves commendable New Mexican, Italian, and American fare, from blue-corn tacos stuffed with grilled trout to lamb-and-poblano stew; it's also known for its seasonal fresh-fruit cobblers. The inn is the departure point for O'Keeffe-home tours, where the O'Keeffe Museum has a small office. It has an art gallery featuring local work, crafts shop, and gardens. Two basic but very comfortable rooms are available for $80. The RV park on the property offers full hookups and a dump station for $35 per night. **Pros:** good base for exploring O'Keeffe Country; gorgeous, lush setting **Cons:** service is friendly but fairly hands-off; rooms at the front of the inn get noise from the road. ⊠ *21120 U.S. 84* ⬦ *Box 120, 87510* ☎ *505/685–4378 or 888/735–2902* ⊕ *www.abiquiuinn.com* ↩ *25 rooms, 6 suites, 5 casitas* ⚬ *In-room: a/c, kitchen (some). In-hotel: restaurant, Wi-Fi hotspot* ☰ *AE, D, DC, MC, V.*

SHOPPING

Bode's (⊠ *U.S. 84, look for Phillips 66 gas station sign* ☎ *505/685–4422* ⊕ *www.bodes.com*), pronounced *boh*-dees, across from the Abiqui post office, is much more than a gas station. It's a popular stop for newspapers, quirky gifts, locally made arts and crafts, cold drinks, supplies, fishing gear (including licenses), amazing breakfast burritos, hearty green-chile stew, sandwiches, and other short-order fare. The friendly, busy station serves as general store and exchange post for news and gossip.

GHOST RANCH

10 mi northwest of Abiquiu on U.S. 84.

For art historians, the name Ghost Ranch brings to mind Georgia O'Keeffe, who lived on a small parcel of this 20,000-acre dude and cattle ranch. The ranch's owner in the 1930s—conservationist and publisher of *Nature Magazine,* Arthur Pack—first invited O'Keeffe here to visit in 1934; Pack soon sold the artist the 7-acre plot on which she lived summer through fall for most of the rest of her life.

In 1955 Pack donated the rest of the ranch to the Presbyterian Church, which continues to use Pack's original structures and about 55 acres of land as a conference center.

☾
Fodor'sChoice
★

The **Ghost Ranch Education and Retreat Center,** open to the public year-round, is busiest in summer, when the majority of workshops take place. Subjects range from poetry and literary arts to photography, horseback riding, and every conceivable traditional craft of northern New Mexico. These courses are open to the public, and guests camp or stay in semirustic cottages or casitas. If you're here for a day trip, after registering at the main office, you may come in and hike high among the wind-hewn rocks so beloved by O'Keeffe. The **Florence Hawley Ellis Museum of Anthropology** contains Native American tools, pottery, and other artifacts excavated from the Ghost Ranch Gallina digs. Pioneer anthropologist Florence Hawley Ellis conducted excavations at Chaco Canyon and at other sites in New Mexico. Adjacent to the Ellis Museum, the **Ruth Hall Museum of Paleontology** exhibits the New Mexico state fossil, the *Coelophysis,* also known as the littlest dinosaur (it was about 7 to 9 feet long), originally excavated near Ghost Ranch. For the art lover, or the lover of the New Mexican landscape, Ghost Ranch offers guided O'Keeffe & Ghost Ranch Landscape Tours of the specific sites on the ranch that O'Keeffe painted during the five decades that she summered here. Her original house is not part of the tour and is closed to the public. These one-hour tours are available mid-March through mid-October, on Tuesday, Wednesday, Friday, and Saturday at 1:30 and 3; the cost is $25, and you must call first to make a reservation. The landscape tours are timed to coincide with the tours given at her house in Abiquiu, although they have nothing to do with the O'Keeffe studio tours offered there. Here's a little-known tidbit: limited camping is available on Ghost Ranch for both RVs and tents ($16–$26) and full hookups are available for RVs.

The **Ghost Ranch Piedra Lumbre Education and Visitor Center** (✉ *U.S. 84, just north of main Ghost Ranch entrance* ☎ *505/685–4312*), which is part of the Ghost Ranch organization has a gallery with rotating art presentations, exhibits on New Mexico's natural history, a gift shop, and two museums. ✉ *U.S. 84 , between mileposts 224 and 225, about 13 mi north of Abiquiu* ☎ *505/685–4333* ⊕ *www.ghostranch.org* 🏷 *$3 minimum suggested donation* ✉ *U.S. 84, just north of main Ghost Ranch entrance* ☎ *505/685–4312* ⊕ *www.ghostranch.org* 🏷 *Donations accepted* ☉ *Visitor center Mar.–Oct., daily 9–5. Florence Hawley Ellis Museum of Anthropology and Ruth Hall Museum of Paleantology late May–early Sept., Tues.–Sat. 9–5, Sun. and Mon. 1–5; early Sept.–late May, Tues.–Sat. 9–5.*

OFF THE
BEATEN
PATH
Monastery of Christ in the Desert. Designed by renowned Japanese-American architect and wood carver George Nakashima, this remote rock-and-adobe church—with one of the state's most spectacular natural settings—can be visited for daily prayer or silent overnight retreats (if requested in advance by mail or e-mail); there are basic accommodations for up to 16 guests (10 single and 3 double rooms), and there's a two-night minimum, with most visitors staying for several days. A suggested per-night donation of $50 to $125 is requested, depending on the room, and none have electricity. Day visitors can come anytime and stroll the grounds, visit the gift shop, and participate in different prayer services throughout the day, but are asked to respect the silence practiced at the monastery. The road is rutted in places and becomes impassable during rainy weather—you can definitely get stuck here for a day, or even a few days, during particularly wet periods, such as summer monsoon season. Check weather forecasts carefully if you're only intending to visit for the day. ✛ *Pass Ghost Ranch visitor center and turn left on Forest Service Rd. 151; follow dirt road 13 mi to monastery* 🏠 *Box 270, Abiquiu 87510* ☎ *801/545–8567 messages only* ⊕ *www.christdesert.org.*

CHAMA
95 mi northwest of Taos on U.S. 64, 59 mi north of Abiquiu on U.S. 84.

A railroad town nestled at the base of 10,000-foot Cumbre Pass, lush and densely wooded Chama offers year-round outdoor activities, as well as a scenic railroad. From here, U.S. 84 hugs the Rio Chama and leads southward through monumental red rocks and golden sandstone spires that inspired Georgia O'Keeffe's vivid paintings of creased mountains, stark crosses, bleached animal skulls, and adobe architecture.

The booms and busts of Chama have largely coincided with the popularity of train transportation. The town's earliest boom, which precipitated its founding, occurred in the 1880s when workers piled into town to construct the Denver & Rio Grande Railroad. In those days, narrow-gauge trains chugged over the high mountain tracks carrying gold and silver out from the mines of the San Juan Mountains, which straddle the nearby Colorado–New Mexico border. Gambling halls, moonshine stills, speakeasies, and brothels were a fixture along the main drag, Terrace Avenue. The lumber industry also thrived during the early years, and the town still has quite a few houses and buildings fashioned out of spare hand-hewn railroad ties.

Chama's outdoor recreation opportunities are hard to beat. Vast meadows of wildflowers and aspen and ponderosa pines blanket the entire region. Hunters are drawn here by the abundant wildlife. There's cross-country skiing and snowmobiling in winter; camping, rafting, hiking, and fishing in summer, all in a pristine, green, high-mountain setting that feels like the top of the world. The temperate mountain air means that most lodgings in the area neither have nor need air-conditioning.

The big attraction in Chama is the historic **Cumbres & Toltec Scenic Railroad,** the narrow-gauge coal-driven steam engine that runs through the San Juan Mountains and over the Cumbres Pass. You chug over ancient trestles, around breathtaking bends, and high above the Los Pinos River—if the terrain looks at all familiar, you may have seen this railroad's "performance" in *Indiana Jones and the Last Crusade.* Midway through the trip you break for lunch and can switch to a waiting Colorado-based train to complete the 64 mi to Antonito, Colorado (from which you'll be shuttled back by bus), or return from this point on the same train. ⊠ *15 Terrace Ave.* ☎ *575/756–2151 or 888/286–2737* ⊕ *www.cumbrestoltec.com* ⚏ *$65–$134* ⊙ *Late May–mid.-Oct., daily departures at 10* AM.

LOS OJOS
13 mi south of Chama on U.S. 64/84.

Los Ojos, midway between Tierra Amarilla and Chama, could well serve as a model for rural economic development worldwide. The little town has experienced an economic revival of sorts by returning to its ancient roots—the raising of Churro sheep (the original breed brought over by the Spanish, prized for its wool) and weaving. Ganados del Valle, the community-based, nonprofit economic development corporation headquartered here, has created jobs and increased prosperity by returning to the old ways, with improved marketing. You can also find a smattering of artists' studios, most of them in rustic buildings with corrugated metal roofs.

The cooperative **Tierra Wools** produces some of the finest original weavings in the Southwest. Designs are based on the old Rio Grande styles, and weavers make rugs and capes of superb craftsmanship entirely by hand, using old-style looms. Weaving workshops are offered. ⊠ *91 Main St.* ☎ *575/588–7231 or 888/709–0979* ⊕ *www.handweavers.com* ⊙ *June–Oct., Mon.–Sat. 10–6, Sun. 11–4; Nov.–May, Mon.–Sat. 10–5.*

OJO CALIENTE

28 mi northeast of Abiquiu by way of El Rito via NM 554 to NM 111 to U.S. 285, 50 mi north of Santa Fe on U.S. 285.

Ojo Caliente is the only place in North America where five different types of hot springs—iron, lithium, arsenic, salt, and soda—are found side by side. The town was named by Spanish explorer Cabeza de Vaca, who visited in 1535 and believed he had stumbled upon the Fountain of Youth. Modern-day visitors draw a similar conclusion about the restorative powers of the springs. The spa itself, originally built in the 1920s, comprises a hotel and cottages, a restaurant, a gift shop, massage rooms, men's and women's bathhouses, a chlorine-free swimming pool, and indoor and outdoor mineral-water tubs. The hotel, one of the original bathhouses, and the springs are all on the National Register of Historic Places, as is the adjacent and recently restored Round Barn, from which visitors can take horseback tours and guided hikes to ancient Pueblo dwellings and petroglyph-etched rocks. Spa services include wraps, massage, facials, and acupuncture. The setting at the foot of sandstone cliffs topped by the ruins of ancient Native American pueblos is nothing short of inspiring and is heavily frequented by locals as well as tourists.

WHERE TO STAY

$$ **Ojo Caliente Mineral Springs Spa and Resort.** Accommodations run the gamut from spartan in the unfussy 1916 hotel (no TVs, simple furnishings) to rather upscale in the elegant suites, which were added in recent years. Rooms in the hotel have bathrooms but no showers or tubs—bathing takes place in the mineral springs (it's an arrangement that pleases most longtime devotees but doesn't sit well with others). The cottages are quite comfy, with refrigerators and TVs; some have kitchenettes, with tile showers in the bathrooms. The 12 spacious suites have such luxury touches as kiva fireplaces and patios; half have private, double soaking tubs outside, which are filled with Ojo mineral waters. All lodgers have complimentary access to the mineral pools and *milagro* (miracle) wraps, and the bathhouse has showers. Horseback tours can be prearranged. The Artesian Restaurant ($$) serves world-beat fare in a charming dining room. Four-day and overnight packages are available. There's also camping on-site, beside the cottonwood-shaded Rio Ojo Caliente—double-occupancy camping rates are $20 for tents, $20 for RVs. **Pros:** can feel like a real getaway for fairly reasonable rates. **Cons:** service and treatments can be lackluster. ⊠ *50 Los Baños Dr., off U.S. 285, 30 mi north of Española* ✆ *Box 68, 87549* ☎ *505/583–2233 or 800/222–9162* ⊕ *www.ojocalientesprings.com* ➷ *19 rooms, 19 cottages, 12 suites, 3 3-bedroom houses* ☖ *In-room: no a/c, no phone, kitchen (some), refrigerator (some), no TV (some), Wi-Fi. In-hotel: restaurant, spa* ⊟ *AE, D, DC, MC, V.*

RESORT COTTAGES

LOW ROAD TO TAOS

Widely considered the efficient route to Taos, the Low Road actually offers plenty of dazzling scenery once you get through traffic-clogged Española and into the Rio Grande Gorge. As you emerge from the gorge roughly 25 minutes later, NM 68 cuts up over a plateau that affords utterly stupendous views of Taos, the Rio Grande gorge, and the surrounding mountains. Note that whether you take the Low Road or the High Road *(⇨ below)*, you first follow U.S. 285/84 north from Santa Fe for about 20 mi, where it's a wide, limited-access freeway. Whereas you exit the highway just north of Pojoaque in order to travel the High Road, you remain on U.S. 285/84 all the way to Española to follow the Low Road; once there, you pick up NM 68 north. Just before you enter into the Rio Grande Gorge, where you parallel the river for several scenic miles, you pass through the tiny but lavishly fertile Velarde, which has a number of fruit and vegetable stands worth stopping for. Without stops, it takes 80 to 90 minutes to make it from Santa Fe to Taos via the Low Road, whereas the High Road takes 2 to 2½ hours.

DIXON

45 mi north of Santa Fe via U.S. 285/84 and NM 68, 20 mi south of Taos via NM 68.

The small village of Dixon and its surrounding country lanes are home to a surprising number of artists. Artistic sensitivity, as well as generations of dedicated farmers, account for the community's well-tended fields, pretty gardens, and fruit trees—a source of produce for restaurants and farmers' markets such as the one in Santa Fe. It's simple to find your way around; there's only one main road.

At the enormously popular **Dixon Studio Tour** (⊕ *www.dixonarts.org*), the first full weekend in November, when area artists open up their home studios to the public. The Web site suggests several nearby guesthouse accommodations and provides a detailed map of the village and its participating artists. The Dixon Arts Association has some four dozen members, many represented in a cooperative gallery attached to **Métier Weaving & Gallery** (⊠ *NM 75* ☎ *505/579–4111*), which also has a showroom that sells the textiles and weavings of artists and owners Irene Smith and Lezlie King.

WHERE TO STAY

$ ⊡ **Rock Pool Gardens.** This private guesthouse has two warmly furnished INN two-bedroom suites, one with a kitchenette and a bathroom connecting the bedrooms, the other with a full kitchen. Each has its own access and patio. The rustic walls, Mexican tile work, and country furnishings lend a cozy air to these otherwise contemporary suites, and lush gardens surround the building. There's a Jacuzzi under the trees and an indoor heated pool set in natural rock. Both suites can be rented for a group for $160 per night. **Pros:** one of the few accommodations between Española and Taos, and it's also a good value. **Cons:** no restaurants or sights within walking distance. ⊠ *NM 75* ☎ *505/579–4602* ☞ *2 suites* ⌂ *In-room: a/c, kitchen, refrigerator, Wi-Fi. In-hotel: pool, some pets allowed* ▭ *No credit cards* ⎟⊙⎟ *CP.*

THE HIGH ROAD TO TAOS

Fodor's Choice ★ The main highway to Taos (NM 68) is a good, even scenic, route if you've got limited time, but by far the most spectacular route is what is known as the High Road. Towering peaks, lush hillsides, orchards, and meadows surround tiny, ancient Hispanic villages that are as picturesque as they are historically fascinating. The High Road follows U.S. 285/84 north to NM 503 (a right turn just past Pojoaque), to County Road 98 (a left toward Chimayó), to NM 76 northeast to NM 75 east, to NM 518 north. The drive takes you through the badlands of stark, weathered rock—where numerous Westerns have been filmed—quickly into rolling foothills, lush canyons, and finally into pine forests. Although most of these insular, traditional Hispanic communities offer little in the way of shopping and dining, the region has become a haven for artists.

From Chimayó to Peñasco, you can find mostly low-key but often high-quality art galleries, many of them run out of the owners' homes. During the final two weekends in September each year, more than 100 artists show their work in the **High Road Art Tour** (☎ *866/343–5381* ⊕ *www.highroadnewmexico.com*) ; call or visit the Web site for a studio map.

Depending on when you make this drive, you're in for some of the state's most radiant scenery. In mid-April the orchards are in blossom; summer turns the valleys into lush green oases; and in fall the smell of piñon adds to the sensual overload of golden leaves and red-chile ristras hanging from the houses. In winter the fields are covered with quilts of snow, and the lines of homes, fences, and trees stand out like bold pen-and-ink drawings against the sky. But the roads can be icy and treacherous—if in doubt, stick with the Low Road to Taos. If you decide to take the High Road just one way between Santa Fe and Taos, you might want to save it for the return journey—the scenery is even more stunning when traveling north to south.

CHIMAYÓ

28 mi north of Santa Fe, 10 mi east of Española on NM 76.

From U.S. 285/84 north of Pojoaque, scenic NM 503 winds past horse paddocks and orchards in the narrow Nambé Valley, then ascends into the red-sandstone canyons with a view of Truchas Peaks to the northeast before dropping into the bucolic village of Chimayó. Nestled into hillsides where gnarled piñons seem to grow from bare bedrock, Chimayó is famed for its weaving, its red chiles, and its two chapels.

Fodor'sChoice **El Santuario de Chimayó**, a small, frontier, adobe church, has a fantasti-
★ cally carved and painted reredos (altar screen) and is built on the site where, believers say, a mysterious light came from the ground on Good Friday in 1810 and where a large wooden crucifix was found beneath the earth. The chapel sits above a sacred *pozito* (a small hole), the dirt from which is believed to have miraculous healing properties. Dozens of abandoned crutches and braces placed in the anteroom—along with many notes, letters, and photos—testify to this. The Santuario draws a steady stream of worshippers year-round—Chimayó is considered the Lourdes of the Southwest. During Holy Week as many as 50,000 pilgrims come here. The shrine is a National Historic Landmark. It's surrounded by small adobe shops selling every kind of religious curio imaginable and some very fine traditional Hispanic work from local

Santa Fe Side Trips/ High and Low Roads to Taos

artists. ☒ *Signed lane off CR 98* ☎ *505/351–4889* ⊕ *www.holychimayo. us* ▣ *Free* ☉ *June–Sept., daily 9–5; Oct.–May, daily 9–4.*

A smaller chapel 200 yards from El Santuario was built in 1857 and dedicated to **Santo Niño de Atocha.** As at the more famous Santuario, the dirt at Santo Niño de Atocha's chapel is said to have healing properties in the place where the *Santo Niño* was first placed. The little boy saint was brought here from Mexico by Severiano Medina, who claimed Santo Niño de Atocha had healed him of rheumatism. San Ildefonso pottery master Maria Martinez came here for healing as a child. Tales of the boy saint's losing one of his shoes as he wandered through the countryside helping those in trouble endeared him to the people of northern New Mexico. It became a tradition to place shoes at the foot of the statue as an offering. Many soldiers who survived the Bataan Death March during World War II credit Santo Niño for saving them, adding to his beloved status in this state where the percentage of young people who enlist in the military remains quite high. ☒ *Signed lane off CR 98* ▣ *Free* ☉ *June–Sept., daily 9–5; Oct.–May, daily 9–4.*

WHERE TO EAT AND STAY

$ SOUTHWESTERN ★ ✕**Rancho de Chimayó.** In a century-old adobe hacienda tucked into the mountains, with whitewashed walls, hand-stripped vigas, and cozy dining rooms, the Rancho de Chimayó is still owned and operated by the family that first occupied the house. There's a fireplace in winter and, in summer, a terraced patio shaded by catalpa trees. Serviceable New Mexican fare is served, and it's hard to deny the ambience of the place. Try the signature Chimayó Cocktail with apple cider, premium tequila, and crème de cassis. You can take an after-dinner stroll on the grounds' paths. Lunch entrées are reasonable, about half the price of dinner. The owners also operate the seven-room **Hacienda de Chimayó B&B** (☎ *505/351–2222*) just across the road. ☒ *CR 98* ☎ *505/351–4444* ⊕ *www.ranchodechimayo.com* ▭ *AE, D, DC, MC, V* ☉ *Closed Mon. Nov.–May.*

¢ SOUTHWESTERN ★ ✕**Leona's Restaurante.** This fast-food-style burrito and chile stand under a massive catalpa tree at one end of the Santuario de Chimayó parking lot has only a few tables, and in summer it's crowded—with good reason. Delicious dishes from the kitchen include homemade posole stew, carne adovada, and green-chile-and-cheese tamales. The specialty is flavored tortillas—everything from jalapeño to butterscotch. The tortillas have become so legendary that owner Léona Medina-Tiede opened a tortilla factory in Chimayó's Manzana Center and now does a thriving mail-order business. ☒ *Off CR 98, behind Santuario de Chimayó* ☎ *505/351–4569 or 888/561–5569* ⊕ *www.leonasrestaurante.com* ▭ *AE, D, DC, MC, V* ☉ *Closed Tues. and Wed. No dinner.*

$ BED AND BREAKFAST ★ ⌂**Casa Escondida.** Intimate and peaceful, this adobe inn has sweeping views of the Sangre de Cristo range. The setting makes it a great base for mountain bikers. The scent of fresh-baked strudel wafts through the rooms, which are decorated with antiques and Native American and other regional arts and crafts. Ask for the Sun Room, in the main house, which has a private patio, viga ceilings, and a brick floor. The separate one-bedroom Casita Escondida has a kiva-style fireplace, tile floors, kitchenette, and a sitting area. A large hot tub is hidden in a grove behind wild berry bushes, there are several covered porches, and a massive bird-feeding station that draws dozens and dozens of birds. In-room massage is available by appointment, and special packages—romance or birthday, for example—are also available. **Pros:** very good value, with gracious hosts and in beautiful surroundings; there's not a TV on the entire property. **Cons:** remote setting means you must drive to sights. ⊠ *CR 0100, off NM 76* ⮴ *Box 142, 85722* ☎ *505/351–4805 or 800/643–7201* ⊕ *www.casaescondida.com* ⅄ *In-room: no phone, kitchen (some), no TV, Wi-Fi. In-hotel: Wi-Fi hotspot, some pets allowed (paid)* ⮯ *7 rooms, 1 suite* ⊟ *MC, V* ⱺ *BP.*

$ ⬚ **Rancho Manzana Bed & Breakfast.** Facing Plaza del Cerro, one of the
INN state's best-preserved Spanish-colonial plazas, this eco-conscious, dis-
Fodor's Choice tinctive retreat affords guests the opportunity to stay in a traditional
★ New Mexico village. Rooms are in private casitas and have natural mud walls, high ceilings, and comfortable, homey furnishings. Each has a private deck. Hearty, organic breakfasts are served. Lush gardens, apple orchards, and massive-walled adobe buildings surround a scenic communal garden and acequia. A fire pit and outdoor hot tub invite stargazing; the proprietors offer cooking classes and can provide excellent advice on touring the area. **Pros:** totally secluded yet convenient to Chimayó attractions; beautiful setting. **Cons:** credit cards aren't accepted. ⊠ *26 Camino de Mision* ☎ *505/351–2227 or 888/505–2227* ⊕ *www.ranchomanzana.com* ⮯ *4 rooms* ⅄ *In-room: no a/c, Wi-Fi. In-hotel: no kids under 12* ⊟ *No credit cards.*

SHOPPING

Centinela Traditional Arts (⊠ *NM 76, 1 mi east of junction with CR 98* ☎ *505/351–2180 or 877/351–2180* ⊕ *www.chimayoweavers.com*) continues the Trujillo family weaving tradition, which started in northern New Mexico more than seven generations ago. Irvin Trujillo and his wife, Lisa, are both gifted, award-winning master weavers, creating Rio Grande–style tapestry blankets and rugs, many of them with natural dyes that authentically replicate early weavings. Most designs are historically based, but the Trujillos are never shy about innovating and their original works are as breathtaking as the traditional ones. The shop and gallery carry these heirloom-quality textiles, with a knowledgeable and very friendly staff on hand to demonstrate or answer questions about the weaving techniques.

Ortega's Weaving Shop (⊠ *NM 76 at CR 98* ☎ *505/351–2288 or 877/351–4215* ⊕ *www.ortegasweaving.com*) sells Rio Grande– and Chimayó-style textiles made by the family whose Spanish ancestors brought the craft to New Mexico in the 1600s. The Galeria Ortega, next door, sells traditional New Mexican and Hispanic and contemporary Native American arts and crafts. In winter the shop is closed on Sunday.

In the plaza just outside the Santuario, **Highroad Marketplace** (⊠ *CR 98* ☎ *505/351–1078 or 866/343–5381*) stocks a variety of arts and crafts created all along the High Road, from Chimayó to Peñasco. Be sure to stop into **El Potrero**, a treasure trove of trinkets as well as high-quality arts and crafts from local artists. Don't be surprised if you're helped by one of the acclaimed Spanish Market artists who moonlight here.

CORDOVA

4 mi east of Chimayó via NM 76.

You'll have to turn south off NM 76 to get down into the narrow, steep valley that this lovely village sits it in, but you'll be happy you did. A picturesque mountain village with a small central plaza, a school, a post office, and a church, Cordova is the center of the centuries-old regional wood-carving industry. The town supports more than 30 full-time and part-time carvers. Many of them are descendants of José Dolores López, who in the 1920s created the village's signature unpainted "Cordova style" of carving. Most of the *santeros* (makers of religious images) have signs outside their homes indicating that santos are for sale. Many pieces are fairly expensive, a reflection of the hard work and fine craftsmanship involved—ranging from several hundred dollars for small ones to several thousand for larger figures—but there are also affordable and delightful small carvings of animals and birds. The St. Anthony of Padua Chapel, which is filled with handcrafted retablos (wood tablets painted with saints) and other religious art, is worth a visit.

TRUCHAS

4 mi northeast of Cordova via NM 76.

Truchas (Spanish for "trout") is where Robert Redford shot the movie *The Milagro Beanfield War* (based on the novel written by Taos author John Nichols). This pastoral village is perched dramatically on the rim of a deep canyon beneath the towering Truchas Peaks, mountains high enough to be almost perpetually capped with snow. The tallest of the Truchas Peaks is 13,102 feet, the second-highest point in New Mexico. This is an insular town, and locals aren't oriented toward selling their specialness to outsiders: be friendly, be discreet when taking pictures, and remember you're treading in someone else's paradise. Truchas has been gaining appeal with artsy, independent-minded transplants from Santa Fe and Taos, who have come for the cheaper real estate and the breathtaking setting. There are several galleries in town, most open by chance, as well as a small general store that sells snacks and a few gifts.

Continue 7 mi north on NM 76, toward Peñasco, and you come to the marvelous San José de Gracia Church in the village of Trampas. It dates from circa 1760.

SHOPPING

In the heart of Truchas, **Cordova's Handweaving Workshop** (⊠ *Country Rd. 75* ☎ *505/689–2437*) produces vibrant and colorful contemporary and traditional rugs.

PEÑASCO

15 mi north of Truchas on NM 76.

Although still a modest-size community, Peñasco is one of the "larger" villages along the High Road and a good bet if you need to fill your tank with gas or pick up a snack at a convenience store.

WHERE TO EAT

$ ✕ **Sugar Nymphs Bistro.** It's taken a little time for people to learn about,
CONTEMPORARY   let alone find, this delightful little place set inside a vintage theater in
Fodor's Choice   sleepy Peñasco. You can't miss the vivid murals on the building, it's right
★   on the High Road, and it is hands down the best restaurant along this
entire route. If you get an early start from Santa Fe and get through
Chimayó in the morning, you'll get here right in time for a fabulous
lunch, or an early dinner if you've meandered. Chef-owner Kai Harper
Leah earned her stripes at San Francisco's famed vegetarian restaurant,
Greens, and presents an eclectic menu of reasonably priced, inspired
food: creatively topped pizzas, bountiful salads, juicy bacon cheeseburgers, butternut-squash ravioli. Try the fantastic green-chile bison stew,
with meat from neighboring Picuris Pueblo's bison herd; it comes with
perfectly moist but crumbly corn bread to soak up all the goodness.
Desserts are memorable—consider the chocolate pecan pie. You can
dine on the patio in warm weather. The Sunday brunch is excellent.
⊠ *15046 NM 75* ☎ *505/587–0311* ▤ *MC, V* ⊗ *Closed Mon. and Tues.*

Taos

WORD OF MOUTH

"Just returned from a visit to Taos. There is a visitor's center on the main drag at the south end of town, where you can get maps, info on places to go, river runner outfitters, etc. Definitely go to the Pueblo for a fascinating glimpse at a culture that has inhabited those lands for centuries."

—donnawho

Updated
by Andrew
Collins

Taos casts a lingering spell. Set on a rolling mesa at the base of the Sangre de Cristo Mountains, it's a place of piercing light and spectacular views, where the desert palette changes almost hourly as the sun moves across the sky. Adobe buildings—some of them centuries old—lie nestled amid pine trees and scrub, some in the shadow of majestic Wheeler Peak, the town's (and state's) highest point, at just over 13,000 feet. The smell of piñon-wood smoke rises from the valley from early autumn through late spring; during the warmer months, the air smells of fragrant sage.

The earliest residents, members of the Taos-Tiwa tribe, have inhabited this breathtaking valley for more than a millennium; their descendants still live and maintain a traditional way of life at Taos Pueblo, a 95,000-acre reserve 3 mi northeast of Taos Plaza. Spanish settlers arrived in the 1500s, bringing both farming and Catholicism to the area; their influence remains most pronounced in the diminutive village of Ranchos de Taos, 4 mi south of town, where the massive adobe walls and *camposanto* (graveyard) of San Francisco de Asís Church have been attracting photographers for generations.

In the early 20th century, another population—artists—discovered Taos and began making the pilgrimage here to write, paint, and take photographs. The early adopters of this movement, painters Bert Phillips and Ernest Blumenschein stopped here in 1898 quite by chance to repair a wagon wheel while en route from Denver to Mexico in 1898. Enthralled with the earthy beauty of the region, they abandoned their intended plan, settled near the plaza, and in 1915 formed the Taos Society of Artists. In later years, many illustrious artists—including Georgia O'Keeffe, Ansel Adams, and D. H. Lawrence—frequented the area, helping cement a vaunted arts tradition that thrives to this day. The steadily emerging bohemian spirit has continued to attract hippies, counterculturalists, New Agers, gays and lesbians, and free spirits. Downtown—along with some outlying villages to the south and north, such as Ranchos de Taos and Arroyo Seco—now support a rich abundance of galleries and design-driven shops. Whereas Santa Fe, Aspen, Scottsdale, and other gallery hubs in the West tend toward pricey work, much of it by artists living elsewhere, Taos remains very much an ardent hub of local arts and crafts production and sales. A half-dozen excellent museums here also document the town's esteemed artistic history.

About 5,000 people live year-round within Taos town limits, but another 25,000 reside in the surrounding county, much of which is unincorporated, and quite a few others live here seasonally. This means that in summer and, to a lesser extent, during the winter ski season, the town can feel much larger than you might expect. It also supports a retail, restaurants, and hotel infrastructure that's typical of what you'd find in a much larger town. Still, overall, the valley and soaring mountains of Taos enjoy relative isolation, low population-density, and magnificent scenery, making this an ideal retreat for those aiming to escape, slow down, and embrace a distinct regional blend of art, cuisine, outdoor recreation, and natural beauty.

ORIENTATION AND PLANNING

GETTING ORIENTED

Taos is small and resolutely rustic, but for the prosaic stretch of chain motels and strip malls that greet you as you approach from the south. Persevere to the central plaza, and you'll find several highly walkable blocks of galleries, shops, restaurants, and art museums. Easygoing Taoseños are a welcoming lot, and if you ever lose your orientation, you'll find locals happy to point you where you need to go. It's difficult to reach Taos without a car, and you'll need one to reach those attractions outside the village center (the Rio Grande Gorge, Millicent Rogers Museum, and the area's best skiing and hiking), as well as to many accommodations and restaurants. The narrow, historic streets near the plaza can be choked with traffic in the peak summer and winter seasons, especially on Fridays and Sundays—ask locals about the several shortcuts for avoiding traffic jams, and try walking when exploring the blocks around the plaza.

TAOS NEIGHBORHOODS

Plaza and Vicinity. More than four centuries after it was laid out, the Taos Plaza and adjacent streets remain the community's hub commercial and social activity. Dozens of upscale shops and galleries, along with several notable restaurants, hotels, and museums, thrive in this pedestrian-friendly area. The plaza itself is a bit overrun with mediocre souvenir shops, but you only need to walk a block in any direction—especially north and east—to find worthy offerings.

South Side. The first Spanish settlers were agrarian, and many families continue to till the fertile land south of Taos. Ranchos de Taos, a small village a few miles south of the plaza, is home to the iconic San Francisco de Asís Church, memorialized by Georgia O'Keeffe and photographer Ansel Adams. The main approach road into Taos from the south, NM 68, is low on curb appeal but nonetheless contains plenty of handy services, like gas stations, convenience stores, and chain motels.

Taos Pueblo. The Pueblo is the ancient beating heart of the entire valley, the historic and architectural basis for everything that Taos has become. A small, bland casino aside, this area a short drive northeast of the plaza has been spared commercial development and remains a neighborhood of modest homes and farms. The Pueblo itself is the sole draw for visitors and well worth a visit.

El Prado. As you drive north from Taos toward Arroyo Seco and points north or west, you'll first take the main thoroughfare, Paseo del Pueblo Norte (U.S. 64) through the small village of El Prado, a mostly agrarian

TOP REASONS TO GO

Small-town sophistication. For a tiny, remote community, Taos supports a richly urbane culinary scene, a fantastic bounty of galleries and design shops, and plenty of stylish B&Bs and inns.

Indigenous roots. The Taos Pueblo and its inhabitants have lived in this region for centuries and continue to play a vital role in local art, culture, and civic life.

Desert solitaire. Few panoramas in the Southwest can compare with that of the 13,000-foot Sangre de Cristo Mountains soaring over the adobe homes of Taos, and beyond that, the endless high-desert mesa that extends for miles to the west.

area that's notable for having several of the area's best restaurants, B&Bs, and shops.

West Side. Taos is hemmed in by the Sangre de Cristo mountains on the east, but to the west, extending from Downtown clear across the precipitously deep Rio Grande Gorge (and the famous bridge that crosses it), the landscape is dominated by sweeping, high-desert scrub and wide-open spaces. The west side is mostly residential and makes for a scenic shortcut around the sometimes traffic-clogged plaza (from Ranchos de Taos, just follow NM 240 to Blueberry Hill Road to complete this bypass).

Arroyo Seco. Set on a high mesa north of Taos, this funky yet hip village and arts center is an ideal spot to browse galleries, grab a meal at one of a handful of excellent restaurants, or simply pause to admire the dramatic views before driving on to the Enchanted Circle or Taos Ski Valley. You'll find a few excellent B&Bs here as well.

Taos Ski Valley. Home to New Mexico's most acclaimed ski area, Taos Ski Valley is a fully separate community from Taos proper—it's 20 mi north, via Arroyo Seco, and nestled in a lush, pine-studded valley with a base elevation of 9,200 feet (meaning it can be chilly here even in July). Many businesses here are open only in winter, but a handful of inns and restaurants serve visitors year-round, as this is also the setting off point for some amazing hikes, including the strenuous but popular trek to the state's highest point, Wheeler Peak.

TAOS PLANNER

WHEN TO GO

With more than 300 days of sunshine annually, Taos typically yields good—if often chilly—weather year-round. The summer high season brings warm days (80s) and cool nights (50s), as well as frequent afternoon thunderstorms. A packed arts and festival schedule in summer means hotels and B&Bs sometimes book well in advance, lodging rates are high, restaurants are jammed, and traffic anywhere near the plaza can slow to a standstill. Spring and fall are stunning and favor mild days and cool nights, fewer visitors, and reasonable hotel prices. In winter, especially during big years for snowfall, skiers arrive en masse but tend to stay close to the slopes and only venture into town for an occasional meal or shopping raid.

GETTING HERE AND AROUND
AIRPORTS AND TRANSFERS

Albuquerque International Sunport (*ABQ* ☎ *505/244–7700* ⊕ *www.cabq. gov/airport*), **about 130 mi away** and a 2½-hour drive, is the nearest major airport to Taos. The small **Santa Fe Municipal Airport** (*SAF* ☎ *505/955–2900*), a 90-minute drive, also has daily service on American Airlines from Dallas and Los Angeles.

Alternatively, as Taos is one of the gateway towns to New Mexico if coming from Colorado, some visitors fly into Denver (five-hour drive) or Colorado Springs (four hours) as part of a trip to both states. Taos Municipal Airport, 12 mi west of town, serves only charters and private planes.

By appointment only, Faust's Transportation, Twin Hearts Express, and Taos Shuttle provide shuttle service from Taos, Taos Ski Valley, and nearby towns to Albuquerque and Santa Fe. The cost is about $50 to $60 per person for Albuquerque, and $25 to $35 for Santa Fe. Some companies have a three-person minimum, and it's always a good idea to book your rides at least 48 hours in advance. Given the high cost of shuttle service and relatively reasonable rates for rental cars at Albuquerque's airport, it's more economical and typically more convenient to rent a car. However, if you're coming solely to ski, staying for a week or more, or planning to stick mostly around the plaza, the shuttle option can make more sense (and you can always rent a car at one of the two agencies in Taos if you're planning an occasional trip farther afield).

Shuttle Contacts Faust's Transportation (☎ *575/758–3410* or *888/231–2222* ⊕ *www.newmexiconet.com/trans/faust/faust.html*). Taos Shuttle (☎ *575/779–5641*). Twin Hearts Express (☎ *575/751–1201* or *800/654–9456*).

CAR TRAVEL

A car is your most practical means both for reaching and getting around Taos. The main route from Santa Fe is via U.S. 285 north to NM 68 north, also known as the Low Road, which winds between the Rio Grande and red-rock cliffs before rising to a spectacular view of the plain and river gorge. You can also take the wooded High Road to Taos, which takes longer but offers a wonderfully scenic ride—many visitors come to Taos via the Low Road, which is more dramatic when driven south to north, and then return to Santa Fe via the High Road (⇨ *High Road to Taos, in Side Trips from Santa Fe, chapter 3*), which has better views as you drive south. From Denver, it's a five-hour drive south via I–25, U.S. 160 west (at Walsenburg), and CO 159 to NM 522; from points east or west, take U.S. 64 (keeping in mind that U.S. 64 west of Taos, between Tres Piedras and Tierra Amarilla, is often closed because of snow in winter).

Cottam Walker Ford and Enterprise are the two local car-rental agencies in Taos; rates typically start around $200 per week but vary greatly depending on the season.

Festivals of Tradition

Several yearly festivals celebrate the Native American and Hispanic roots of Taos. During the last weekend in September, La Hacienda de los Martínez hosts the **Old Taos Trade Fair,** a reenactment of autumn gatherings of the 1820s, when Plains Indians and trappers came to Taos to trade with the Spanish and the Pueblo Indians. The two-day event includes demonstrations of blacksmithing, weaving, and other crafts, a chile cook-off, native foods, music, and dancing.

The **Wool Festival** (⊕ www. taoswoolfestival.org), held in early October in Kit Carson Park, commemorates the long tradition of wool growing and weaving begun in the 16th century, when Spanish settlers brought the tough little Churro sheep to northern New Mexico. Every aspect of the craft "from sheep to shawl" is demonstrated, including shearing, spinning, and weaving. Handmade woolen items are for sale, and you can taste favorite lamb dishes.

During the second weekend of July, the **Taos Pueblo Powwow** (⊕ www. taospueblopowwow.com) attracts Native Americans from many Indian nations. Visitors are welcome to watch the traditional drumming and dancing, shop at the arts-and-crafts market, and partake of fry bread, mutton, green-chile sauce, and other local delicacies.

Car Rental Contacts Cottam Walker Ford (✉ 1320 Paseo del Pueblo Sur ☎ 575/751–3200 ⊕ www.forddetaos.com). **Enterprise** (✉ 1354 Paseo del Pueblo Sur ☎ 575/758–5553 ⊕ www.enterprise.com).

TAXI TRAVEL

Taxi service in Taos is sparse, but Faust's Transportation and Taos Shuttle both serve the area. Rates are $5 at pick up, $2.50 per each additional person, and $1 per mile.

Taxi Contacts Faust's Transportation (☎ 575/758–3410 or 888/231–2222 ⊕ www.newmexiconet.com/trans/faust/faust.html). Taos Shuttle (☎ 575/779–5641).

GUIDED TOURS

Taos Art Tours (☎ 575/737–5595 ⊕ www.taosarttours.com), run by knowledgeable guide Marian Bradley Jackson, offers art walks around Taos that cover key museums, and customized tours of several different studios. Tours cost $40.

VISITOR INFORMATION

Taos Visitors Center (✉ 1139 Paseo del Pueblo Sur ⌕ Drawer I, Taos 87571 ☎ 505/758–3873 or 877/587–9007 ⊕ www.taosvisitor.com). **Taos Ski Valley Chamber of Commerce** (☎ 575/776–1413 or 800/517–9816 ⊕ www.taosskivalley.com).

PLANNING YOUR TIME

Whether you've got an afternoon or a week in the area, begin by strolling around Taos Plaza and along Bent Street, taking in the galleries, Native American crafts shops, and eclectic clothing stores. Take Ledoux Street south from the west side of the plaza and walk two blocks to the

Harwood Museum, then walk back to the plaza and cross over to Kit Carson Road, where you can find more shops and galleries as well as the Kit Carson Home and Museum. Return to Paseo del Pueblo and walk north to the Taos Art Museum and Fechin House to complete a tour that takes in the best of the town center's shopping and museums. However, a few of the must-see attractions in the area are a bit farther afield, and you need at least two days and ideally three or four to take in everything. Among the top outlying attractions, it's possible to visit Taos Pueblo, the magnificent Millicent Rogers Museum, the village of Arroyo Seco, and the Rio Grande Gorge Bridge all in one day—you can connect them to make one loop to the north and west of the city. If you're headed south, stop at La Hacienda de los Martínez to gain an appreciation of early Spanish life in Taos and then to Ranchos de Taos to see the stunning San Francisco de Asís Church. If you approach Taos from the south, as most visitors do, you could also visit both these attractions on your way into town, assuming you arrive by early afternoon.

EXPLORING TAOS

The Museum Association of Taos includes five properties: the Harwood Museum, Taos Art Museum, Millicent Rogers Museum, E. L. Blumenschein Home and Museum, and La Hacienda de los Martínez. Each of the museums charges $8 for admission, but you can buy a combination ticket—$25 for all five, valid for one year.

PLAZA AND VICINITY

E. L. Blumenschein Home and Museum. For an introduction to the history of the Taos art scene, start with Ernest L. Blumenschein's residence, which provides a glimpse into the cosmopolitan lives led by the members of the Taos Society of Artists, of which Blumenschein was a founding member. One of the rooms in the adobe-style structure dates from 1797. On display are the art, antiques, and other personal possessions of Blumenschein and his wife, Mary Greene Blumenschein, who also painted, as did their daughter Helen. Several of Ernest Blumenschein's vivid oil paintings hang in his former studio, and works by other early Taos artists are also on display. ✉ *222 Ledoux St.* ☎ *575/758–0505* ⊕ *www.taoshistoricmuseums.org* ✉ *$8, 5-museum Museum Association of Taos combination ticket $25* ⊗ *Apr.–Oct., Mon.–Sat. 10–5, Sun. noon–5; Nov.–Mar., Mon.–Tues. and Thurs.–Sat. 10–4, Sun. noon–4.*

🕓 **Firehouse Collection.** More than 100 works by well-known Taos artists like Joseph Sharp, Ernest L. Blumenschein, and Bert Phillips hang in the Taos Volunteer Fire Department building. The exhibition space adjoins the station house, where five fire engines are maintained at the ready and an antique fire engine is on display. ✉ *323 Camino de la Placita* ☎ *575/758–3386* ✉ *Free* ⊗ *Weekdays 9–4:30.*

🕓 **Governor Bent Museum.** In 1846, when New Mexico became a U.S. possession as a result of the Mexican War, Charles Bent, a trader, trapper, and mountain man, was appointed governor. Less than a year later he was killed in his house by an angry mob protesting New Mexico's

IF YOU LIKE

ARTS AND CRAFTS

If your idea of fun is museum going and gallery hopping, Taos has much to offer you. The creative spirit is strong here, and it's contagious. Even if you begin by just browsing, you might find that you can't go home without a certain painting or pot that captures the region's unmistakable enchantment. At galleries, you can often meet the artists themselves, or join in the flow of creative energy by participating in one of the town's many art workshops. It's easy to visit a lot of galleries in a short time; many are side by side on a few streets around Taos Plaza. Southwestern landscapes and Native American themes are ubiquitous subjects, but many galleries also show abstract and less regionalized work. Look for outstanding weaving, jewelry, tinwork, and other crafts, too.

NEW MEXICAN CUISINE

For a small town, Taos excels when it comes to authentic New Mexican fare, prepared with local chiles and homemade tortillas, but the town also draws raves for outstanding contemporary restaurants with impressive wine lists. The generally eco-conscious, progressive local population has created a demand for fresh, organic cuisine, including plenty of vegetarian options. Pan-Asian, Middle Eastern, and Mediterranean flavors also greatly influence Taos menus.

OUTDOOR ACTIVITIES

The glorious landscape around Taos draws serious athletes as well as those simply up for an adventure beneath northern New Mexico's mesmerizing skies and towering mountain peaks. Cycling is popular, with rallies and races held in summer. The vast Carson National Forest encompasses thousands of acres of prime hiking and camping terrain, from strenuous alpine climbs to simpler scrambles into rocky gorges or pine-shaded glens. A good variety of rivers and lakes yield excellent trout fishing; you can arrange for outings with local expert guides. The waters also invite rafters, especially when spring runoff fills the rivers with white water. If you're really after a thrill or something different, try a hot-air balloon ride into the Rio Grande Gorge or llama trekking in the wilderness. And of course winter brings skiers from all over to the world-class slopes of Taos Ski Valley, Angel Fire, and Red River. Wherever you play outdoors, just remember the region's high altitude and sometimes extreme day-to-night temperature differences can tax and exhaust you—go easy in the beginning, and talk with local experts before setting out on any ambitious endeavors.

annexation by the United States. Governor Bent was married to María Ignacia, the older sister of Josefa Jaramillo, the wife of mountain man Kit Carson. A collection of Native American artifacts, Western Americana, and family possessions is squeezed into five small rooms of the adobe building where Bent and his family lived. ⊠ *117 Bent St.* ☎ *575/758–2376* ☜ *$3* ⊙ *Daily 10–5.*

Fodor'sChoice ★ **Harwood Museum.** The Pueblo Revival former home of Burritt Elihu "Burt" Harwood, a dedicated painter who studied in France before moving to Taos in 1916, is adjacent to a museum dedicated to the works of local artists. Traditional Hispanic northern New Mexican artists, early art-colony painters, post–World War II modernists, and contemporary artists such as Larry Bell, Agnes Martin, Ken Price, and Earl Stroh are represented. Mabel Dodge Luhan, a major arts patron, bequeathed many of the 19th- and early-20th-century works in the Harwoods' collection, including *retablos* (painted wood representations of Catholic saints) and *bultos* (three-dimensional carvings of the saints). In the Hispanic Traditions Gallery upstairs are 19th-century tinwork, furniture, and sculpture. Downstairs, among early-20th-century art-colony holdings, look for E. Martin Hennings's *Chamisa in Bloom,* which captures the Taos landscape particularly beautifully. A tour of the ground-floor galleries shows that Taos painters of the era, notably Oscar Berninghaus, Ernest Blumenschein, Victor Higgins, Walter Ufer, Marsden Hartley, and John Marin, were fascinated by the land and the people linked to it. An octagonal gallery exhibits works by Agnes Martin. Martin's seven large canvas panels (each 5 feet square) are studies in white, their precise lines and blocks forming textured grids. Operated by the University of New Mexico since 1936, the Harwood is the second-oldest art museum in the state. ⊠ *238 Ledoux St.* ☎ *575/758–9826* ⊕ *www.harwoodmuseum.org* ✉ *$8, 5-museum Museum Association of Taos combination ticket $25* ⊙ *Tues.–Sat. 10–5, Sun. noon–5.*

☪ **Kit Carson Home and Museum.** Kit Carson bought this low-slung 12-room adobe home in 1843 for his wife, Josefa Jaramillo, the daughter of a powerful, politically influential Spanish family. Three of the museum's rooms are furnished, as they were when the Carson family lived here. The rest of the museum is devoted to gun and mountain-man exhibits, such as rugged leather clothing and Kit's own Spencer carbine rifle with its beaded leather carrying case, and early Taos antiques, artifacts, and manuscripts. ⊠ *113 Kit Carson Rd.* ☎ *575/758–0505* ✉ *$8* ⊙ *Tues.– Sat. 10–4, Sun. noon–4.*

NEED A BREAK?
Let the aroma of fresh-ground coffee draw you into the tiny **World Cup** (⊠ *102-A Paseo del Pueblo Norte* ☎ *575/737–5299*), where you can sit at the counter or wander outside to a bench on the porch. Locals engage in political rhetoric here, often slanted toward the left, so be prepared for a rousing debate if you dare to dissent.

☪ **Kit Carson Park.** The noted pioneer is buried in the park that bears his name. His grave is marked with a *cerquita* (a spiked, wrought-iron, rectangular fence), traditionally used to outline and protect burial sites. Also interred here is Mabel Dodge Luhan, the pioneering patron of the early Taos art scene. The 32-acre park has swings and slides for recreational breaks. It's well marked with big stone pillars and a gate. ⊠ *211 Paseo del Pueblo Norte* ☎ *575/758–8234* ✉ *Free* ⊙ *Late May–early Sept., daily 8–8; early Sept.–late May, daily 8–5.*

Fodor's Choice ★ **Taos Art Museum and Fechin House.** The interior of this extraordinary adobe house, built between 1927 and 1933 by Russian émigré and artist Nicolai Fechin, is a marvel of carved Russian-style woodwork and furniture. Fechin constructed it to showcase his daringly colorful paintings. The house became host to the Taos Art Museum in 2003,

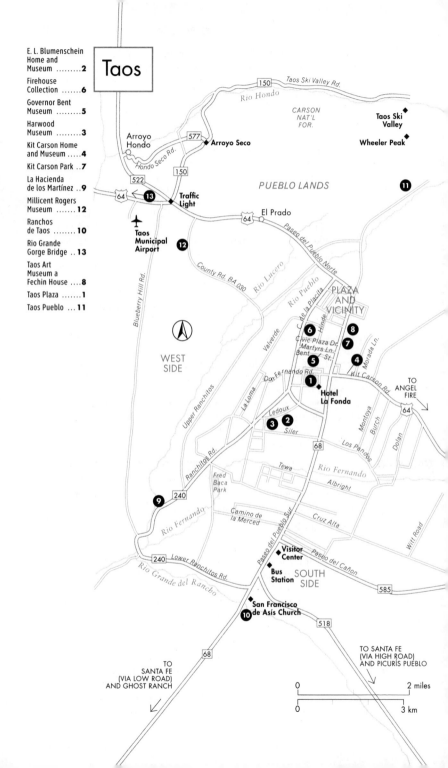

Taos

A GOOD WALK: TAOS PLAZA

Begin at the gazebo in the middle of **Taos Plaza**. After exploring the plaza, head south from its western edge down the small, unmarked alley (its name is West Plaza Drive), crossing Camino de la Placita, to where West Plaza Drive becomes Ledoux Street. Continue south to the **E. L. Blumenschein Home and Museum** and, a few doors farther south, the **Harwood Museum**. (Parking for the Harwood Foundation is at Ledoux and Ranchitos Road.)

From the Harwood Foundation, walk back north on Ranchitos Road a few blocks, make a left on Camino de la Placita, and go right onto Don Fernando Road. Follow it east, crossing the north side of the plaza and then Paseo del Pueblo Norte (NM 68), to where Don Fernando Road becomes Kit Carson Road. You'll soon come to the **Kit Carson Home and Museum**. Then head back to Paseo del Pueblo Norte, turn right (north) and go past the Taos Inn, turning left (west) to browse Bent Street's shops, boutiques, and galleries.

In a tiny plaza is the **Governor Bent Museum**, the modest home of the first Anglo governor of the state. Across the street is the John Dunn House. Once the homestead of a colorful and well-respected Taos gambling and transportation entrepreneur, the Dunn House is now a small shopping plaza. At the western end of Bent Street, head north on Camino de la Placita. In about 2½ blocks you'll come to the Taos Volunteer Fire Department building, which doubles as a fire station and the **Firehouse Collection** exhibition space.

Head east on Civic Plaza and cross Paseo del Pueblo Norte, turning left to reach **Kit Carson Park** and the **Taos Art Museum and Fechin House**, named for the iconoclastic artist Nicolai Fechin.

TIMING
The entire walk can be done in five hours, but allow about eight hours if you stop for lunch along the way and browse in the shops and galleries. You can tour each of the museums in less than an hour.

with a collection of paintings from more than 50 Taos artists, including founders of the original Taos Society of Artists, among them Joseph Sharp, Ernest Blumenschein, Bert Phillips, E. I. Couse, and Oscar Berninghaus. ⊠ *227 Paseo del Pueblo Norte* ☎ *575/758–2690* ⊕ *www. taosartmuseum.org* ⊠ *$8, 5-museum Museum Association of Taos combination ticket $25* ☉ *Tues.–Sun. 10–5.*

Taos Plaza. The first European explorers of the Taos Valley came here with Captain Hernando de Alvarado, a member of Francisco Vásquez de Coronado's expedition of 1540. Basque explorer Don Juan de Oñate arrived in Taos in July 1598 and established a mission and trading arrangements with residents of Taos Pueblo. The settlement developed into two plazas: the plaza at the heart of the town became a thriving business district for the early colony, and a walled residential plaza was constructed a few hundred yards behind. It remains active today, home to a throng of mostly shlocky gift shops. The covered gazebo was donated by heiress and longtime Taos resident Mabel Dodge Luhan. On

A GOOD DRIVE

From Taos Plaza, head southwest 2½ mi on NM 240 (also known as Ranchitos Road) to **La Hacienda de los Martínez**. As you pass by the adobe cottages and modest homes dotting the landscape, you get a sense of the area's rural roots. From the hacienda continue along NM 240, which winds in the shape of a C for another 4 mi to NM 68 and the small farming village of **Ranchos** de Taos. Watch for signs for **San Francisco de Asís Church,** which is on the east side of NM 68. The small plaza here contains several galleries and gift shops worth checking out.

TIMING
Set aside about two hours to tour the hacienda, a bit of Ranchos de Taos, and San Francisco de Asís Church.

the southeastern corner of Taos Plaza is the **Hotel La Fonda de Taos.** Some infamous erotic paintings by D. H. Lawrence that were naughty in his day but are quite tame by present standards can be viewed ($3 entry fee for nonguests) in the former barroom beyond the lobby.

SOUTH SIDE

La Hacienda de los Martínez. Spare and fortlike, this adobe structure built between 1804 and 1827 on the bank of the Rio Pueblo served as a community refuge during Comanche and Apache raids. Its thick walls, which have few windows, surround two central courtyards. Don Antonio Severino Martínez was a farmer and trader; the hacienda was the final stop along El Camino Real (the Royal Road), the trade route the Spanish established between Mexico City and New Mexico. The restored period rooms here contain textiles, foods, and crafts of the early 19th century. There's a working blacksmith's shop, usually open to visitors on Saturday, and weavers create beautiful textiles on reconstructed period looms. ⊠ *708 Hacienda Rd., off Ranchitos Rd. (NM 240)* ☎ *575/758–1000* ⊕ *www.taoshistoricmuseums.org* ✉ *$8, 5-museum Museum Association of Taos combination ticket $25* ☉ *Apr.–Oct., Mon.–Sat. 10–5, Sun. noon–5; Nov.–Mar., Mon.–Tues. and Thurs.–Sat. 10–4, Sun. noon–4.*

Ranchos de Taos. A few minutes' drive south of the center of Taos, this village still retains some of its rural atmosphere despite the highway traffic passing through. Huddled around its famous adobe church and dusty plaza are cheerful, remodeled shops and galleries standing shoulder to shoulder with crumbling adobe shells. This ranching, farming, and budding small-business community was an early home to Taos Native Americans before being settled by Spaniards in 1716. Although many of the adobe dwellings have seen better days, the shops, modest galleries, taco stands, and two fine restaurants point to an ongoing revival.

The massive bulk of **San Francisco de Asís Church** (⊠ *NM 68, 500 yards south of NM 518, Ranchos de Taos* ☎ *575/758–2754* ⊕ *www. nps.gov/nr/travel/amsw/sw44.htm*) is an enduring attraction. The Spanish mission–style church was erected in 1815 as a spiritual and physical refuge from raiding Apaches, Utes, and Comanches. In 1979 the dete-riorated church was rebuilt with traditional adobe bricks by community volunteers. Every spring a group gathers to re-mud the facade. The earthy, clean lines of the exterior walls and supporting bulwarks have inspired generations of painters and photographers. The late-afternoon light provides the best exposure of the heavily buttressed rear of the church—though today's image takers face the challenge of framing the architecturally pure lines through rows of parked cars and a large, white sign put up by church officials; morning light is best for the front. Bells in the twin belfries call Taoseños to services on Sunday and holidays. Monday through Saturday from 9 to 4 you can step inside. In the parish hall just north of the church (and for a $3 fee) you can view a 15-min-ute video presentation every half hour that describes the history and restoration of the church and explains the mysterious painting *Shadow of the Cross,* on which each evening the shadow of a cross appears over Christ's shoulder (scientific studies made on the canvas and the paint pigments cannot explain the phenomenon). The fee also allows you to view the painting.

NEED A BREAK? Join the locals at the north or south location of the **Bean** (⊠ *900 Paseo del Pueblo Norte, El Prado* 🕾 *No phone* ⊠ *1033 Paseo del Pueblo Sur, South Side* 🕾 *575/758–5123*). The Bean roasts its own coffee, and the South Side location—where you can dine on an outside patio—offers good breakfast and lunch fare. The north location, in an adobe building, displays local art-work and is the more atmospheric of the two.

TAOS PUEBLO

Taos Pueblo. For nearly 1,000 years the mud-and-straw adobe walls of Taos Pueblo have sheltered Tiwa-speaking Native Americans. A United Nations World Heritage Site, this is the largest collection of multistory pueblo dwellings in the United States. The pueblo's main buildings, Hlauuma (north house) and Hlaukwima (south house), are separated by a creek. These structures are believed to be of a similar age, prob-ably built between 1000 and 1450. The dwellings have common walls but no connecting doorways—the Tiwas gained access only from the top, via ladders that were retrieved after entering. Small buildings and corrals are scattered about.

Fodor's Choice ★

The pueblo today appears much as it did when the first Spanish explor-ers arrived in New Mexico in 1540. The adobe walls glistening with mica caused the conquistadors to believe they had discovered one of the fabled Seven Cities of Gold. The outside surfaces are continuously main-tained by replastering with thin layers of mud, and the interior walls are frequently coated with thin washes of white clay. Some walls are several feet thick in places. The roofs of each of the five-story structures are supported by large timbers, or vigas, hauled down from the moun-tain forests. Pine or aspen *latillas* (smaller pieces of wood) are placed side by side between the vigas; the entire roof is then packed with dirt.

A GOOD DRIVE

Drive 2 mi north on Paseo del Pueblo Norte (NM 68), and keep your eyes peeled for the signs on the right, beyond the post office, directing you to **Taos Pueblo**. To reach the **Millicent Rogers Museum** next, return to NM 68 to head north about 4½ mi and make a left onto County Road BA030. If you find yourself at the intersection with U.S. 64 and NM 150, you've gone too far. Continue down the county road to the big adobe wall; the sign for the museum is on the right. After exploring the museum, return to NM 68 north; then make a left on U.S. 64 and drive 8 mi west to the **Rio Grande Gorge Bridge**, a stunning marriage of natural wonder and human engineering. If you're up for it, bring along sturdy hiking shoes and plenty of water and snacks for an invigorating walk down into the gorge. But remember, what goes down must come up, and it's an arduous path.

TIMING

Plan on spending 1½ hours at the pueblo. Taos can get hot in summer, but if you visit the pueblo in the morning, you'll avoid the heat and the crowds. If your visit coincides with a ceremonial observance, set aside several hours, because the ceremonies, though they are worth the wait, never start on time. Two hours should be enough time to take in the museum and the grandeur of the Rio Grande Gorge Bridge, but allow another hour or two if you hike down into the gorge.

Even after 400 years of Spanish and Anglo presence in Taos, inside the pueblo the traditional Native American way of life has endured. Tribal custom allows no electricity or running water in Hlauuma and Hlaukwima, where varying numbers (usually fewer than 150) of Taos Native Americans live full-time. About 1,900 others live in conventional homes on the pueblo's 95,000 acres. The crystal-clear Rio Pueblo de Taos, originating high above in the mountains at the sacred Blue Lake, is the primary source of water for drinking and irrigating. Bread is still baked in *hornos* (outdoor domed ovens). Artisans of the Taos Pueblo produce and sell (tax-free) traditionally handcrafted wares, such as mica-flecked pottery and silver jewelry. Great hunters, the Taos Native Americans are also known for their work with animal skins and their excellent moccasins, boots, and drums.

Although the population is about 80% Catholic, the people of Taos Pueblo, like most Pueblo Native Americans, also maintain their native religious traditions. At Christmas and other sacred holidays, for instance, immediately after Mass, dancers dressed in seasonal sacred garb proceed down the aisle of St. Jerome Chapel, drums beating and rattles shaking, to begin other religious rites.

The pueblo **Church of San Geronimo,** or St. Jerome, the patron saint of Taos Pueblo, was completed in 1850 to replace the one destroyed by the U.S. Army in 1847 during the Mexican War. With its smooth symmetry, stepped portal, and twin bell towers, the church is a popular subject for photographers and artists (though the taking of photographs inside is discouraged).

The public is invited to certain ceremonial dances held throughout the year (a full list of these is posted on the pueblo Web site): highlights include the Feast of Santa Cruz Foot Race and Corn Dance (May 3); Taos Pueblo Pow Wow (July 8–10); Feast of San Geronimo Sunset Dance (July 25 and 26, September 29 and 30); Vespers and Bonfire Procession (December 24); and Deer Dance or Matachines Dance (December 25). While you're at the pueblo, respect the RESTRICTED AREA signs that protect the privacy of residents and native religious sites; do not enter private homes or open any doors not clearly labeled as curio shops; do not photograph tribal members without asking permission; do not enter the cemetery grounds; and do not wade in the Rio Pueblo de Taos, which is considered sacred and is the community's sole source of drinking water.

DID YOU KNOW?

The privilege of setting up an easel and painting all day at a pueblo will cost you as little as $35 or as much as $150 (at Taos Pueblo).

The small, rather prosaic, and smoke-free Taos Mountain Casino (open daily) is just off Camino del Pueblo after you turn right off Paseo del Pueblo on your way to the main pueblo. ✉ *Head to right off Paseo del Pueblo Norte just past Best Western Kachina Lodge* ☎ *575/758–1028* ⊕ *www.taospueblo.com* ✉ *Tourist fees $10; guided tours; photography and video permits $6 per camera, cell phone (if you're using it to take pictures), or video-recording device; commercial photography, sketching, or painting only by prior permission from governor's office (*☎ *575/758–1028); fees vary; apply at least 10 days in advance* ☉ *Daily 8–4:30, tours by appointment. Closed for funerals, religious ceremonies, and for 10-week quiet time in late winter or early spring, and last part of Aug.; call ahead before visiting at these times.*

NEED A BREAK?

Look for signs that read FRY BREAD on dwellings in the pueblo: you can enter the kitchen and buy a piece of fresh bread dough that's flattened and deep-fried until puffy and golden brown and then topped with honey or powdered sugar. You also can buy delicious bread that's baked daily in the clay *hornos* (outdoor adobe ovens) that are scattered throughout the pueblo.

WEST SIDE

Fodor'sChoice ★ **Millicent Rogers Museum.** More than 5,000 pieces of spectacular Native American and Hispanic art, many of them from the private collection of the late Standard Oil heiress Millicent Rogers, are on display here. Among the pieces are baskets, blankets, rugs, kachina dolls, carvings, paintings, rare religious artifacts, and, most significantly, jewelry (Rogers, a fashion icon in her day, was one of the first Americans to appreciate the turquoise-and-silver artistry of Native American jewelers). Other important works include the pottery and ceramics of Maria Martinez and other potters from San Ildefonso Pueblo (23 mi north of Santa Fe). Docents conduct guided tours by appointment, and the museum hosts lectures, films, workshops, and demonstrations. The two-room gift shop has exceptional jewelry, rugs, books, and pottery. ✉ *1504 Millicent*

Rogers Rd.; from Taos Plaza head north on Paseo del Pueblo Norte and left at sign for CR BA030 (Millicent Rogers Rd.) ☎ 575/758–2462 ⊕ www.millicentrogers.com ☒ $8, 5-museum Museum Association of Taos combination ticket $25 ⊙ Daily 10–5; closed Mon. in Nov.

Rio Grande Gorge Bridge. It's a dizzying experience to see the Rio Grande 650 feet underfoot, where it flows at the bottom of an immense, steep rock canyon. In summer the reddish rocks dotted with green scrub contrast brilliantly with the blue sky, where you might see a hawk lazily floating in circles. The bridge is the second-highest suspension bridge in the country. Hold on to your camera and eyeglasses when looking down. Shortly after daybreak, hot-air balloons fly above and even inside the gorge. There's a campground with picnic shelters and basic restrooms on the west side of the bridge. ☒ U.S. 64, 12 mi west of town.

ARROYO SECO

Fodor's Choice ★ **Arroyo Seco.** Established in 1834 by local Spanish farmers and ranchers, this charming village has today become a secluded, artsy escape from the sometimes daunting summer crowds and commercialism of the Taos Plaza—famous residents include actress Julia Roberts and former U.S. Defense Secretary Donald Rumsfeld, who own ranches adjacent to one another. You reach the tiny commercial district along NM 150, about 5 mi north of the intersection with U.S. 64 and NM 522 (it's about 9 mi north of the plaza). The drive is part of the joy of visiting, as NM 150 rises steadily above the Taos Valley, offering panoramic views of the Sangre de Cristos—you pass through Arroyo Seco en route to the Taos Ski Valley.

Arroyo Seco is without any formal attractions or museums, and that's partly its charm. The main reasons for making the trip here are to behold the dramatic scenery, grab a bite at one of the handful of excellent restaurants (ice cream from **Taos Cow Cafe** and tamales from **Abe's Cantina** are both revered by locals), and browse the several galleries and boutiques, whose wares tend to be a little more idiosyncratic but no less accomplished than those sold in Taos proper.

TAOS SKI VALLEY

Taos Ski Valley. Skiers and snowboarders from around the world return to the slopes and hospitality of Taos Ski Valley every year. This world-class area is known for its Alpine-village atmosphere, one of the finest ski schools in the country, and the variety of its 72 runs—it's also slowly but surely becoming more of a year-round destination, as the valley attracts outdoors enthusiasts with spectacular, and often challenging, hiking in summer and fall. There aren't many hotels in the valley but most have been converted to ski-in ski-out condos since the early 2000s, further evidence that the once-funky ski area is becoming more of a Colorado-style full-scale resort town. Some of the best trails in Carson National Forest begin at the Village of Taos Ski Valley and traverse dense woodland up to alpine tundra. There are relatively few summer visitors, so you can have the trails up to Bull-of-the-Woods, Gold Hill, Williams

Lake, Italianos, and Wheeler Peak nearly all to yourself. Special events like barn dances and wine tastings occur occasionally throughout the nonskiing seasons.

Taos Ski Valley lies about 10 mi beyond Arroyo Seco—just continue up NM 150, which crosses a high plain, then plunges into the Rio Hondo Canyon to follow the cascading brook upstream through the forest and up into the mountains where NM 150 ends. (The road does not continue to Red River, as some disappointed motorists discover.)

WHERE TO EAT

For a relatively small town many miles from any big city, Taos has a sophisticated and eclectic dining scene. It's as fine a destination for authentic New Mexican fare as any town its size in the state, but you'll also find several upscale spots serving creative fare utilizing mostly local ingredients, a smattering of excellent Asian and Middle Eastern spots, and several very good cafés and coffeehouses perfect for light but bountiful breakfast and lunch fare.

WHAT IT COSTS					
	¢	$	$$	$$$	$$$$
AT DINNER	under $10	$10–$17	$18–$24	$25–$30	over $30

Prices are for a main course, excluding 8.25% sales tax.

Use the coordinate ⊕ B2 at the end of each listing to locate a site on the corresponding map.

PLAZA AND VICINITY

$ ✕ **Antonio's.** Chef Antonio Matus has been delighting discerning diners
MEXICAN   in the Taos area for many years. This rambling, art-filled adobe compound with a delightful redbrick courtyard is the flagship of his three local eateries (the other two are Rellenos Cafe *(⇨ below)* and Sabor, which opened inside La Fonda de Taos hotel inside the old Joseph's Table space in summer 2010). Matus focuses on regional Mexican, as opposed to local New Mexican, specialties, such as *chile en nogada* (poblano peppers stuffed with pork, pears, and raisins and topped with a walnut-cream sauce) and *huachinango a la Veracruzana* (red snapper topped with a tomato-jalapeño-olive sauce), plus a fantastic *tres leches* (three milks) cake and a rich chipotle-chocolate cake. Less conventional options include burgers of locally raised yak and mahimahi ceviche. The Sunday brunch is one of the best in town. ⊠ *122 Dona Luz St.* ☎ *575/751–4800* ⊕ *www.antoniosoftaos.com* ⊟ *MC, V* ⊗ *No dinner Sun.* ⊕ *C4.*

$ ✕ **Bent Street Café & Deli.** Try for a seat on the cheery, covered out-
AMERICAN   door patio next to giant sunflowers, as the interior of this often-packed spot can feel a bit cramped, although service is friendly and helpful wherever you sit. Enjoy breakfast burritos, eggs Benedict, homemade granola, fresh-baked goods, dozens of deli sandwiches, tortilla soup,

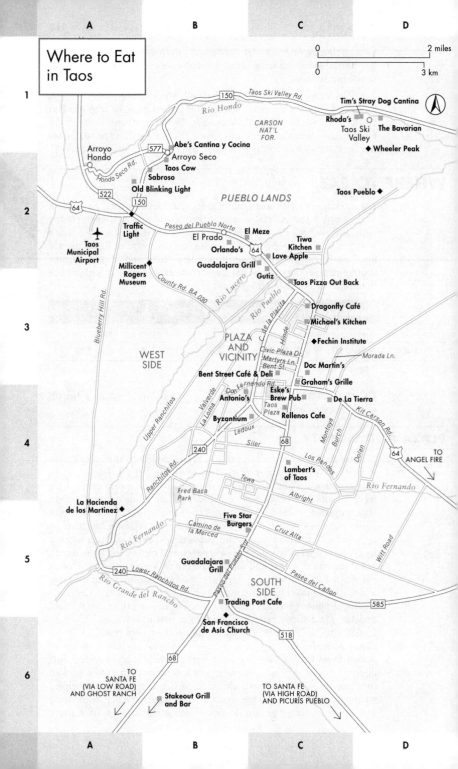

Where to Eat in Taos

0   2 miles

0   3 km

1

Taos Ski Valley Rd.

150

Rio Hondo

CARSON
NAT'L
FOR.

Tim's Stray Dog Cantina

Rhoda's

Taos Ski
Valley

The Bavarian

Wheeler Peak ◆

Arroyo
Hondo

577

Abe's Cantina y Cocina

Arroyo Seco

Hondo Seco Rd.

Taos Cow

Sabroso

Old Blinking Light

522

150

2

64

Traffic
Light

Paseo del Pueblo Norte

El Meze

PUEBLO LANDS

Taos Pueblo ◆

Taos
Municipal
Airport

El Prado

Orlando's

64

Tiwa
Kitchen

Love Apple

Millicent
Rogers
Museum

Guadalajara Grill

Gutiz

County Rd. BA 030

Rio Lucero

Taos Pizza Out Back

3

Rio Pueblo

C. de la Placita

Dragonfly Café

Michael's Kitchen

Hinde

Fechin Institute ◆

Morada Ln.

WEST
SIDE

PLAZA
AND
VICINITY

Civic Plaza Dr.

Martyrs Ln.

Bent St.

Doc Martin's

Blueberry Hill Rd.

Bent Street Café & Deli

Don Fernando Rd.

Graham's Grille

Antonio's

Eske's
Brew Pub

De La Tierra

La Loma

Taos
Plaza

Rellenos Cafe

Upper Ranchitos

Byzantium

Valverde

Ledoux

Kit Carson Rd.

Montoya

Burch

Dolan

64

TO
ANGEL FIRE

4

240

Siler

68

Los Pandos

Rio Fernando

Ranchitos Rd.

Tewa

Lambert's
of Taos

Albright

Witt Road

La Hacienda
de los Martinez ◆

Fred Baca
Park

Rio Fernando

Five Star
Burgers

Camino de
la Merced

Cruz Alta

5

240

Lower Ranchitos Rd.

Guadalajara
Grill

SOUTH
SIDE

Paseo del Cañon

585

Rio Grande del Rancho

Trading Post Cafe

San Francisco
de Asís Church ◆

518

6

68

TO
SANTA FE
(VIA LOW ROAD)
AND GHOST RANCH

Stakeout Grill
and Bar

TO SANTA FE
(VIA HIGH ROAD)
AND PICURÍS PUEBLO

and homemade soups and stews. You might finish your meal with a chocolate-nut brownie. Beer, wine, and gourmet coffees are also served. ✉ *120-M Bent St.* ☎ *575/758–5787* ⊕ *http://johndunnshops.com/ BentStreetDeli.html* ▭ *MC, V* ⊙ *No dinner* ✛ *C3.*

$$ ✕**Byzantium.** Off a grassy courtyard near the Blumenschein and Harwood museums, this quirky locals' favorite defies its traditional-looking adobe exterior to present an eclectic menu with American, Asian, Mediterranean, and Middle Eastern influences. You might start with sesame-steamed ginger-and-chicken dumplings, before moving on to simple but fresh fire-roasted tomatoes and Parmesan over angel-hair pasta, or a hearty mixed grill of strip steak, pork loin, chicken, ribs, and bacon with smoky house-made barbecue sauce. Service is friendly, and the vibe is low-key—this is a spot relatively few tourists discover. ✉ *11–C La Placita* ☎ *575/751–0805* ▭ *AE, MC, V* ⊙ *Closed Tues. and Wed. No lunch* ✛ *C4.*

ECLECTIC

$$$ ✕**De La Tierra.** A dashing, dramatic, high-ceiling restaurant inside the fancifully plush El Monte Sagrado resort, this chic spot presents daring, globally influenced cuisine. Top starters include steamed Thai mussels with lemongrass, coconut milk, and kaffir lime and organic greens with Granny Smith apples, candied walnuts, and blue cheese. Among the mains, you can't go wrong with the chile- and chocolate-rubbed Muscovy duck breast over roasted corn–lima bean–mango succotash— there's also a wide selection of hefty steaks. It's dressy by Taos standards, but you'll still fit in wearing smartly casual threads, and the management has dropped prices considerably in recent years to compete with the town's other comparable restaurants. ✉ *El Monte Sagrado, 317 Kit Carson Rd.* ☎ *575/758–3502* ⊕ *www.elmontesagrado.com* ▭ *AE, D, DC, MC, V* ✛ *C4.*

ECLECTIC

$$ ✕**Doc Martin's.** The stylish restaurant of the Historic Taos Inn takes its name from the building's original owner, a local physician who saw patients in the rooms that are now the dining areas. The creative menu hews toward innovative takes on comforting classics, with an emphasis on sustainable ingredients—try the curious but quite tasty rattlesnake-rabbit sausage with ancho chile–cherry sauce among the starters. Entrées of note include grilled pork loin with green chile–cheese polenta and bacon-fennel salsa, and a juicy elk burger with crisp fries. There's an extensive wine list, and the adjoining Adobe Bar serves up some of the best margaritas in town. In winter ask for a table near the cozy kiva fireplace. ✉ *Historic Taos Inn, 125 Paseo del Pueblo Norte* ☎ *575/758–1977* ⊕ *www.taosinn.com* ▭ *AE, D, MC, V* ✛ *C3.*

SOUTHWESTERN

$ ✕**Dragonfly Café and Bakery.** This charming café bakes its own bread and serves a variety of ethnic specialties including organic Asian salads, Middle Eastern lamb with a Greek salad, hummus and pita bread, curried chicken salad, bison burgers, and Vietnamese chicken salad. You can sit out front on a shaded outdoor patio with a fountain when it's warm and watch the tourists go by. Dragonfly also does a brisk mail-order business with its red-chile–infused truffles, delicious granola, and many other tasty products. Wine and beer are served. ✉ *402 Paseo del Pueblo Norte* ☎ *575/737–5859* ⊕ *www.dragonflytaos.com* ▭ *MC, V* ⊙ *No dinner Sun. Closed Tues.* ✛ *C3.*

ECLECTIC

¢ ✕ **Eske's Brew Pub.** This casual, dining-and-quaffing pub is favored by off-
AMERICAN duty ski patrollers and river guides. The menu mostly covers hearty sandwiches (try the grilled bratwurst and sauerkraut sandwich), soups, and
salads. The microbrewery downstairs produces everything from nutty,
dark stout to light ales, but you shouldn't leave without sampling the
house specialty—Taos green-chile beer. There's live music on weekends,
and in good weather you can relax on the patio. ⊠ *106 Des Georges La.*
☎ *575/758–1517* ⊕ *www.eskesbrewpub.com* ⊟ *MC, V* ✛ *C4.*

$$ ✕ **Graham's Grille.** The folks who frequent this upscale bar and eatery
ECLECTIC tend to be hip and sophisticated—just like the artful, Southwestern-
Fodor's Choice based but cross-cultural food served in this minimalist environment.
★ Local, seasonal produce, cage-free chickens, and homemade stocks are
key to the fresh flavors and creative combinations prepared by chef
Leslie Fay, a long-time Taos restaurateur. Small plates worth sampling
include mac-and-cheese with mild green chiles and hickory-smoked
bacon, duck-breast flatbread with orange-*charmoula* sauce, and black
bean soup with a touch of cumin. The buffalo-brisket sandwich is a
winner at lunch. Main courses range from blue corn–crusted red trout
with cilantro-lime butter to hearty tamale pies. Worthy desserts include
a coconut cake with mango cream and a lemon-and-piñon pound cake
with blueberry coulis. There's a memorable Sunday brunch. ⊠ *106*
Paseo del Pueblo Norte ☎ *575/751–1350* ⊕ *www.thefayway.com/*
dining ⊟ *AE, MC, V* ✛ *C3.*

$ ✕ **Guadalajara Grill.** Some of the tastiest Mexican food this side of the
MEXICAN border makes the well-priced menu of this relaxed and friendly estab-
lishment so popular that there's a location on both the north and south
ends of town. It's ultracasual here (you select your own beer from a
cooler, and order from the counter). The extensive menu includes grilled
fish tacos served in soft homemade tortillas, shrimp with garlic sauce,
bulging burritos smothered in red or green chiles, and for the adventur-
ous, shark enchiladas. ⊠ *822 Paseo del Pueblo Norte* ☎ *575/737–0816*
⊠ *1384 Paseo del Pueblo Sur,South Side* ☎ *575/751–0063* ⊟ *MC, V*
✛ *C2, B5.*

$ ✕ **Gutiz.** This ambitious and consistently terrific favorite for lunch and
ECLECTIC breakfast blends French, Spanish, and South American culinary influ-
ences. Best bets in the morning include cinnamon French toast made
with thick homemade bread and a baked omelet topped with a green
tapenade. Lunch specialties include a warm salad Niçoise and *chicharon*
de pollo—fried chicken tenders topped with hot *aji* Amarillo sauce.
Meals are served on a gravel patio or inside the small lilac-hued din-
ing room with views of the open kitchen. ⊠ *812B Paseo del Pueblo*
Norte ☎ *575/758–1226* ⌦ *Reservations not accepted* ⊟ *No credit cards*
☉ *Closed Mon. No dinner* ✛ *C3.*

$$$ ✕ **Lambert's of Taos.** Superb service and creative cuisine define this Taos
AMERICAN landmark located 2½ blocks south of the plaza. Among starters, don't
miss the marinated roasted-beet salad with warm goat cheese and pumpkin seeds, sautéed lobster and shallots with a vanilla-champagne sauce,
and corn-and-applewood-smoked-bacon chowder. Or have all three
and call it a night. The signature entrées include pepper-crusted lamb
with a red-wine demi-glace and roasted duck with an apricot-chipotle

glaze. Memorable desserts are a warm-apple-and-almond crisp topped with white-chocolate ice cream and a dark-chocolate mousse with raspberry sauce. A small-plate bistro menu is available in the cozy bar or in the spacious dining rooms. The lengthy wine list includes some of California's finest vintages. The owners also operate the Old Blinking Light up near Arroyo Seco (⇨ *below*). ✉ *309 Paseo del Pueblo Sur* ☎ *575/758–1009* ⊕ *www.lambertsoftaos.com* ▭ *AE, DC, MC, V* ⊘ *No lunch* ✚ *C4.*

$ ✕ **Michael's Kitchen.** This casual, homey restaurant serves up a bit of
AMERICAN everything—you can have a hamburger while your friend who can't get enough chile sauce can order up vegetarian cheese enchiladas garnished with lettuce and tomatoes. Brunch is popular with the locals (dig into a plate of strawberry-banana-pecan pancakes), and amusing asides to the waitstaff over the intercom contribute to the energetic buzz. Breakfast and lunch are served daily, with dinner available up until 8 on Friday, Saturday, and Sunday. ✉ *304 Paseo del Pueblo Norte* ☎ *575/758–4178* ⊕ *www.michaelskitchen.com* ⌦ *Reservations not accepted* ▭ *AE, D, MC, V* ✚ *C3.*

$ ✕ **Rellenos Cafe.** Touted as the only organic New Mexican restaurant in
NEW MEXICAN town, this casual eatery from the talented team behind Antonio's and Sabor also offers wheat-free, gluten-free, and vegan menu options. Popular specialties include killer chiles rellenos topped with a brandy-cream sauce, grilled garlic shrimp, and seafood paella. Service is friendly— don't be put off by the bland exterior on a busy stretch of Paseo del Pueblo Sur (there's a nice patio in back). The house drink, a fruity sangria, is served in gargantuan Mexican glasses. ✉ *135 Paseo del Pueblo Sur* ☎ *575/758–7001* ⌦ *Reservations not accepted* ▭ *MC, V* ⊘ *Closed Sun.* ✚ *C4.*

SOUTH SIDE

$ ✕ **Five Star Burgers.** A standout amid the strip of mostly unmemorable
AMERICAN fast-food restaurants along Paseo del Pueblo on the south side of town, this airy, high-ceiling contemporary space serves stellar burgers using hormone-free Angus beef from respected Harris Ranch; turkey, veggie, Colorado lamb, bison, and salmon burgers are also available, and you can choose from an assortment of novel toppings, including fried eggs, wild mushrooms, caramelized onions, and applewood-smoked bacon. Beer and wine are also served. ✉ *1032 Paseo del Pueblo Sur* ☎ *575/758–8484* ⊕ *www.5starburgers.com* ▭ *AE, D, MC, V* ✚ *C5.*

$$$$ ✕ **Stakeout Grill and Bar.** On Outlaw Hill in the foothills of the Sangre
STEAK de Cristo Mountains, this old adobe homestead has 100-mi-long views
Fodor's Choice and sunsets that dazzle. The outdoor patio encircled by a piñon forest
★ has kiva fireplaces to warm you during cooler months. The decadent fare is well prepared, fully living up to the view it accompanies—try filet mignon with béarnaise sauce, buffalo rib eye with chipotle-cilantro butter, almond-crusted wild sockeye salmon with shaved fennel, or fall-off-the-bone braised Colorado lamb shank with orange and port-wine jus. Don't miss the tasty Kentucky bourbon pecan pie and crème brûlée with toasted coconut for dessert. ✉ *Stakeout Dr.; 8 mi south of Taos*

4

Plaza, east of NM 68, look for cowboy sign ☎ *575/758–2042* ⊕ *www. stakeoutrestaurant.com* ▤ *AE, D, DC, MC, V* ☉ *No lunch* ✛ *B6.*

$$ ✕ **Trading Post Cafe.** Local hipsters outnumber tourists at this casual spot
ITALIAN   serving mostly modern Italian fare with regional accents. Intelligent and attentive service along with well-presented contemporary Southwestern art make any meal a pleasure. For starters try the signature noodle soup or minestrone with smoked ham before moving on to an oven-roasted duck with seasonal vegetables and creamy mashed potatoes or any of the traditional pasta dishes. Superb desserts include a coconut-cream pie and rich strawberry shortcake. Parking is just around the back, off NM 518. ⊠ *4179 Paseo del Pueblo Sur, Ranchos de Taos* ☎ *575/758–5089* ⊕ *http://tradingpostcafe.com* ▤ *AE, D, MC, V* ☉ *Closed Mon. No lunch Sun.* ✛ *B5.*

TAOS PUEBLO

¢ ✕ **Tiwa Kitchen.** This one-of-a-kind restaurant, even for Taos, serves
NATIVE   authentic Native American food in a casual setting. Ben White Buffalo
AMERICAN   and his wife Debbie Moonlight Flowers organically grow many of the restaurant's ingredients themselves and use traditional beehive wood-fired ovens just outside the back door for baking corn and roasting peppers. Try the blue-corn taco made with blue-corn fry bread or grilled buffalo sausage served with red or green chile. ⊠ *328 Veterans Hwy. (Taos Pueblo Rd.)* ☎ *575/751–1020* ▤ *No credit cards* ☉ *Closed Tues. and 10 wks in spring during the Pueblo's traditional "quiet time."* ✛ *C2.*

EL PRADO

$$ ✕ **El Meze.** Set back from NM 68 in tiny El Prado, this adobe house
SPANISH   with an expansive back patio that affords unobstructed views of the Sangre de Cristo Mountains reopened in December 2010 following a fire. Tightly spaced tables, polished-wood floors, and bright red adobe walls make it easy to imagine you're tucked away inside a small cafe in the southern Spain countryside, and indeed, El Meze specializes in the flavorful cuisine and wine of this region (along with some more regionally inspired fare). Andalusian-style *chicharrones* (fried pork rinds) and buffalo short ribs *adovada* (marinated in red chile) make terrific starters, while grilled whole trout with preserved lemon, mint, cilantro, and garlic is perfectly prepared. The well-chosen wine list includes Torrontes, Albarino, and fine Rioja blends from throughout Spain. ⊠ *1017 Paseo del Pueblo Norte* ☎ *575/751–3337* ⊕ *www.elmeze.com* ▤ *MC, V* ☉ *Closed Sun. No lunch* ✛ *C2.*

¢ ✕ **Orlando's.** This family-run local favorite is likely to be packed during
NEW MEXICAN   peak hours, while guests wait patiently to devour perfectly seasoned
Fodor's Choice   favorites such as *carne adovada* (red chile–marinated pork), blue-
★   corn enchiladas, and scrumptious shrimp burritos. You can eat in the cozy dining room, outside on the umbrella-shaded front patio, or call ahead for takeout if you'd rather avoid the crowds. Margaritas here are potent. ⊠ *114 Don Juan Valdez La., off Paseo del Pueblo Norte* ☎ *575/751–1450* ⊕ *www.orlandostaos.com* ▤ *MC, V* ✛ *B2.*

$ ✕**Love Apple.** It's easy to drive by the small adobe former chapel that
ECLECTIC houses this delightful restaurant a short drive north of Taos Plaza, just
Fodor's Choice beyond the driveway for Hacienda del Sol B&B. But slow down—you
★ don't want to miss the culinary magic inside. Chef Andrea Meyer uses
organic, mostly local ingredients in the preparation of simple yet sophisticated farm-to-table creations like homemade sweet-corn tamales with
red-chile mole, a fried egg, and crème fraîche, and robustly seasoned
posole stew with grilled lamb sausage, pancetta, caramelized onion, and
radish-lime relish. The price is right, too—just remember it's cash-only.
✉ *803 Paseo del Pueblo Norte* ☎ *575/751–0050* ⊕ *www.theloveapple.
net* ▭ *No credit cards.* ⊘ *Closed Mon. No lunch* ✛ C2.

$ ✕**Taos Pizza Out Back.** Set in a funky timber-frame shack of a building
PIZZA with a large tree-shaded patio hemmed in with coyote fencing, this venerable pizza joint has cultivated a loyal following over the years for its
thick-crust, creatively topped pies (plus very good pastas and salads).
Distinctive pizza combos include the Ranchero, with Italian sausage,
sundried tomatoes, smoked cheddar, and green onions; and the classic
white pizza with fresh tomato, basil, ricotta, Parmesan, and mozzarella.
Everything is available by the slice (they're massive), or in several pie
sizes. Organic ingredients are favored, and there's a good list of beers
and wines. ✉ *712 Paseo del Pueblo Norte* ☎ *575/758–3112* ⊕ *www.
taospizzaoutback.com* ▭ *AE, D, MC, V* ✛ C3.

ARROYO SECO

¢ ✕**Abe's Cantina y Cocina.** Family-owned and -operated since the 1940s,
CAFÉ no-frills Abe's is both a convenience store (nothing special, but okay for
candy or chips) and restaurant—that's the special part. You can have
your breakfast burrito, rolled tacos, or homemade tamales at one of the
small tables crowded next to the canned goods, or take it on a picnic.
✉ *489 NM 150 (Taos Ski Valley Rd.)* ☎ *575/776–8643* ▭ *AE, D, MC,
V* ⊘ *Closed Sun. No dinner* ✛ B1.

$ ✕**Old Blinking Light.** About a mile up NM 150 toward the ski valley from
NEW MEXICAN the landmark "old blinking light" (now a regular stoplight, where U.S.
64, NM 522, and NM 150 meet), this rambling adobe is known for
its steaks, ribs, and enormous (and potent) margaritas. There's also a
long list of tasty appetizers, such as posole stew and chipotle-shrimp
quesadillas. Several huge burgers are available, plus first-rate chicken
mole. In summer you can sit out in the walled garden and take in the
spectacular mountain view. There's a wine shop on the premises, and
the restaurant is owned by the same talented team behind Lambert's
of Taos. ✉ *Mile Marker 1, Taos Ski Valley Rd., between El Prado and
Arroyo Seco* ☎ *575/776–8787* ⊕ *www.oldblinkinglight.com* ▭ *AE,
MC, V* ⊘ *No lunch* ✛ A2.

$$$ ✕**Sabroso.** Reasonably priced, innovative cuisine and outstanding
MEDITERRANEAN wines are served in this 150-year-old adobe hacienda, where you can
Fodor's Choice also relax in lounge chairs near the bar, or on a delightful patio sur-
★ rounded by plum trees. The Mediterranean-influenced contemporary
menu changes regularly, but an evening's entrée might be pan-seared
sea scallops, risotto cakes, and ratatouille, or rib-eye steak topped with
a slice of Stilton cheese. There's live jazz and cabaret in the piano bar

several nights a week. Order from the simpler bar menu if you're seeking something light—the antipasto plate and white-truffle-oil fries are both delicious. ⊠ *470 NM 150 (Taos Ski Valley Rd.)* ☎ *575/776–3333* ⊕ *www.sabrosotaos.com* ⊟ *AE, MC, V* ⊗ *No lunch* ⊹ *B2*.

¢   ✕ **Taos Cow.** Locals, hikers, and skiers headed up to Taos Ski Valley, and
CAFÉ visitors to funky Arroyo Seco flock to this cozy storefront café operated by the famed Taos Cow ice-cream company. This isn't merely a place to sample amazing homemade ice cream (including such innovative flavors as piñon-caramel, lavender, and Chocolate Rio Grande—chocolate ice cream packed with cinnamon-chocolate chunks). You can also nosh on French toast, omelets, turkey-and-Brie sandwiches, black-bean-and-brown-rice bowls, organic teas and coffees, natural sodas, homemade granola, and more. ⊠ *485 NM 150* ☎ *575/776–5640* ⊕ *www.taoscow. com* ⊟ *MC, V* ⊗ *No dinner* ⊹ *B2*.

TAOS SKI VALLEY

$$$ ✕ **The Bavarian.** The restaurant inside the romantic, magically situated
GERMAN alpine lodge, which also offers Taos Ski Valley's most luxurious accom-
Fodor's Choice modations, serves outstanding contemporary Bavarian-inspired cuisine,
★ such as baked artichokes and Gruyère, and braised pork loin with garlic-mashed potatoes and red cabbage. Lunch is more casual and less expensive, with burgers and salads available—in summer this is an excellent spot to fuel up before attempting an ambitious hike, as the restaurant is steps from the trailhead for Wheeler Peak and other popular mountains. There's an extensive wine list, plus a nice range of beers imported from Spaten Brewery in Munich. ⊠ *100 Kachina Rd.* ⌂ *Box 653, Taos Ski Valley 87525* ☎ *575/776–8020* ⊕ *www.thebavarian.net* ⊟ *AE, MC, V* ⊗ *Closed early Apr.–late May and mid-Oct.–late Nov.; closed Mon.–Wed. in summer.* ⊹ *D1*.

$ ✕ **Rhoda's Restaurant.** Rhoda Blake founded Taos Ski Valley with
AMERICAN her husband, Ernie. Her slope-side restaurant serves pasta, burgers, and sandwiches for lunch. Dinner fare is a bit more substantive, such as veal medallions with pancetta and seafood chiles rellenos with ancho chile sauce. ⊠ *Resort Center, on the slope* ☎ *575/776–2291* ⊕ *http://taoswebb.com/menu/rhodas.html* ⊟ *AE, MC, V* ⊗ *Closed June–Sept.* ⊹ *D1*.

$ ✕ **Tim's Stray Dog Cantina.** This wildly popular spot occupies a chalet-
SOUTHWESTERN style building in the heart of the Taos ski area, and it's a favorite spot for breakfast (try the eggs Benedict topped with red chile sauce), lunch, dinner, and après-ski cocktails, including highly refreshing margaritas. Favorites include steak tacos, pork mole enchiladas, huevos rancheros, barbecue-pulled pork sandwiches, and green-chile burgers (both beef and veggie). Hours vary and are more limited outside of ski season—call ahead. ⊠ *105 Sutton Pl.* ☎ *575/776–2894* ⊕ *www.straydogtsv.com* ⊟ *MC, V.* ⊹ *D1*.

WHERE TO STAY

The hotels and motels along NM 68 (Paseo del Pueblo), most of them on the south side of town, suit every need and budget; rates vary little between big-name chains and smaller establishments—Comfort Suites is the best maintained of the chains. Make advance reservations and expect higher rates during ski season (usually from late December to early April, and especially for lodgings on the north side of town, closer to the ski area) and in the summer. Skiers have many lodging choices, from in town to spots nestled beneath the slopes, although several of the hotels up at Taos Ski Valley have been converted to condos in recent years, diminishing the supply of overnight accommodations. Arroyo Seco is a good alternative if you can't find a room right up in the Ski Valley. The area's many B&Bs offer some of the best values, when you factor in typically hearty full breakfasts, personal service, and often roomy casitas with private entrances.

WHAT IT COSTS					
	¢	$	$$	$$$	$$$$
FOR TWO PEOPLE	under $70	$70–$130	$131–$190	$191–$260	over $260

Prices are for a standard double room in high season, excluding 10%–12% tax.

Use the coordinate ✣ B2 at the end of each listing to locate a site on the corresponding map.

PLAZA AND VICINITY

$$
BED & BREAKFAST

🖼 **Adobe & Pines Inn.** Native American and Mexican artifacts decorate the main house of this B&B, which has expansive mountain views. Part of the main adobe building dates from 1830. The rooms and suites contain Mexican-tile baths, kiva fireplaces, and fluffy goose-down pillows and comforters, plus such modern touches as flat-screen TVs, DVD players, Wi-Fi, and CD players. Separate casitas and suites are more spacious and offer plenty of seclusion, with private entrances and courtyard access. The owners serve gourmet breakfasts in a sunny, glass-enclosed patio. **Pros:** quiet rural location; fantastic views; beautiful gardens. **Cons:** a bit of a drive south of town; some bedrooms are small. ✉ 4107 NM 68 ✉ Box 837, Ranchos de Taos 87557 ☎ 575/751–0947 or 800/723–8267 ⊕ www.adobepines.com 🛏 4 rooms, 2 suites, 2 casitas ⌂ In-room: a/c, kitchen (some), refrigerator (some), DVD, Wi-Fi. In-hotel: some pets allowed ☐ MC, V ⧲ BP ✣ B6.

$$$
BED & BREAKFAST

🖼 **Casa de las Chimeneas.** Tile hearths, French doors, and traditional viga ceilings grace the "House of Chimneys" B&B, two-and-a-half blocks from the plaza and secluded behind thick walls. Each room in the 1912 structure has a private entrance, a fireplace, handmade New Mexican furniture, bathrooms with Talavera tiles, and a bar stocked with complimentary beverages. All rooms overlook the gardens, and facilities include a small but excellent spa offering a wide range of treatments. The three-course breakfasts are impressive, and full evening suppers are

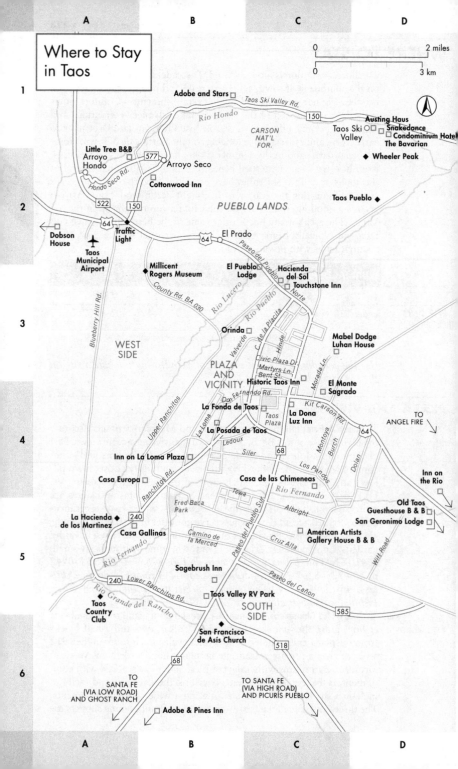

Where to Stay in Taos

	A	B	C	D
1		Adobe and Stars	Taos Ski Valley Rd.	

Rio Hondo

150

CARSON NAT'L FOR.

Austing Haus
Taos Ski Valley — Snakedance
Condominium Hotel
The Bavarian

◆ Wheeler Peak

Little Tree B&B
Arroyo Hondo
577
Arroyo Seco

Cottonwood Inn

Hondo Seco Rd.

PUEBLO LANDS

Taos Pueblo ◆

522
150

2

64
Dobson House

Traffic Light
Taos Municipal Airport

64
El Prado

Paseo del Pueblo

Millicent Rogers Museum

County Rd. BA 030

Rio Lucero

WEST SIDE

El Pueblo Lodge

Hacienda del Sol
Touchstone Inn
Norte

Blueberry Hill Rd.

Rio Pueblo

Orinda
Valverde
C. de la Placita
Hinde

Mabel Dodge Luhan House

3

PLAZA AND VICINITY

Civic Plaza Dr.
Martyrs Ln.
Bent St.
Historic Taos Inn

El Monte Sagrado

Mosada Ln.

Don Fernando Rd.
La Fonda de Taos
La Loma

Taos Plaza

La Dona Luz Inn

Kit Carson Rd.

TO ANGEL FIRE

La Posada de Taos
Ledoux
Siler

Montoya
Burch
Dolan

64

Inn on La Loma Plaza

68

Los Pandos

Inn on the Rio

Casa Europa
Ranchitos Rd.

Fred Baca Park
Tewa

Casa de las Chimeneas

Rio Fernando

Albright

Old Taos Guesthouse B & B
San Geronimo Lodge

La Hacienda de los Martinez ◆
240

Casa Gallinas

Camino de la Merced

Paseo del Pueblo Sur

Cruz Alta

American Artists Gallery House B & B

Witt Road

4

5

Rio Fernando

Upper Ranchitos

Sagebrush Inn

Paseo del Cañon

240
Lower Ranchitos Rd.

Taos Valley RV Park

585

Rio Grande del Rancho

Taos Country Club

SOUTH SIDE

San Francisco de Asís Church

518

6

68

TO SANTA FE (VIA LOW ROAD) AND GHOST RANCH

Adobe & Pines Inn

TO SANTA FE (VIA HIGH ROAD) AND PICURÍS PUEBLO

0 ___ 2 miles
0 ___ 3 km

included in the rates. **Pros:** private setting; on-site spa; walking distance from plaza. **Cons:** 30-day cancellation policy; expensive (rates include dinner, but in a town with so many great restaurants, many guests prefer to eat out). ⊠ *405 Cordoba Rd.* ☎ *575/758–4777 or 877/758–4777* ⊕ *www.visittaos.com* ⟿ *6 rooms, 2 suites* ⚏ *In-room: a/c, refrigerator, Wi-Fi. In-hotel: gym, spa, laundry facilities* ▤ *AE, D, DC, MC, V* ⦿ *MAP* ✛ *C4.*

$ | **BED & BREAKFAST** | **Fodor's Choice** | ★ | ⬕ **Casa Europa.** The main part of this exquisite 18th-century adobe estate has been tastefully expanded to create an unforgettable B&B with old-world romance. Each room has a fireplace and is furnished with handpicked European antiques accented with Southwestern accessories. The two main common areas are light and airy, with comfortable chairs to relax in while the fireplace crackles. Breakfasts are elaborate, and complimentary homemade afternoon baked treats are served. Although the property is less than 2 mi from the plaza, its pastoral setting makes it feel a world away. Innkeepers Lisa and Joe McCutcheon take personal pride in offering their guests every courtesy and assistance. **Pros:** attentive service; memorable setting and sophisticated style; smallest rooms are very affordable. **Cons:** short drive to town. ⊠ *840 Upper Ranchitos Rd.* ☎ *575/758–9798* ⊕ *www.casaeuropanm.com* ⟿ *5 rooms, 2 suites* ⚏ *In-room: a/c, refrigerators, Wi-Fi. In-hotel: some pets allowed* ▤ *MC, V* ⦿ *BP* ✛ *B4.*

$$$ | **RESORT** | ⬕ **El Monte Sagrado.** Although rates have been lowered considerably in recent years, this posh, eco-sensitive, and decidedly quirky small resort—part of Marriott's distinctive, high-end Autograph Collection brand—is still among the priciest properties in the state. Suites and casitas are accented with exotic themes, ranging from Native American designs to foreign flourishes from faraway lands including Japan or Tibet—some have their own outdoor soaking tubs and private courtyards. All units come with flat-screen TVs, iPod docks, and top-of-the-line bath amenities. A popular outdoor area dubbed the Sacred Circle is a patch of grassy land encircled by cottonwoods—this leads to the impressive on-site spa and fitness center, where you might book a lemon-verbena body polish or hot-stone massage. The on-site restaurant, De la Tierra, serves inventive cuisine, and the Anaconda Bar makes a warm and inviting spot to sip and socialize. **Pros:** eco-friendly; imaginative and whimsical decor; terrific spa. **Cons:** unusual decor isn't to everybody's taste; service doesn't always measure up to premium rates. ⊠ *317 Kit Carson Rd.* ☎ *575/758–3502 or 888/213–4419* ⊕ *www. elmontesagrado.com* ⟿ *48 rooms, 6 casitas, 30 suites* ⚏ *In-room: a/c, safe, refrigerator, Wi-Fi. In-hotel: 2 restaurants, room service, bar, pool, gym, spa, bicycles, laundry service, some pets allowed* ▤ *AE, D, DC, MC, V* ✛ *C4.*

$ | **HOTEL** | ⬕ **El Pueblo Lodge.** Among the budget-minded properties in town, this well-maintained adobe-style hotel with a fun retro sign out front and the vibe of an old-school motel comprises several buildings on a peaceful 3-acre spread several blocks north of the plaza. Rooms in the West Building, constructed in the '80s, are a bit more spacious, and some have kiva-style fireplaces. But the original building, a vintage 1940s motor lodge, has more character, with its thick adobe walls and viga

4

ceilings. **Pros:** terrific value; short walk north of the plaza. **Cons:** nothing fancy about the decor. ⊠ *412 Paseo del Pueblo Norte* ☎ *575/758–8700 or 800/433–9612* ⊕ *www.elpueblolodge.com* ⇨ *50 rooms* △ *In-room: a/c, refrigerator, Wi-Fi. In-hotel: pool, some pets allowed* ⊟ *AE, D, MC, V* ⍾⍿ *CP* ⊕ *C3.*

$$ ⍾ **Historic Taos Inn.** A 10-minute walk north of Taos Plaza, this celebrated
INN   property is a local landmark, with some devotees having been regulars here for decades. Spanish-colonial architecture, including decorative alcoves in rooms, lends a warm, distinctive aesthetic to the four buildings, including the upscale Helen's House, which contains some of the fanciest rooms. Older units have thick adobe walls, viga ceilings, and other elements typical of vintage Taos architecture. In summer there's dining alfresco on the patio. The lobby, which also serves as seating for the Adobe Bar, is built around a former town well from which a fountain bubbles forth. Many shops and eateries are within walking distance, and the restaurant, Doc Martin's, is great for people-watching. **Pros:** a short walk from the plaza; lushly furnished rooms, exudes character and history. **Cons:** noise from street traffic and the bar; some rooms are very small. ⊠ *125 Paseo del Pueblo Norte* ☎ *575/758–2233 or 888/518–8267* ⊕ *www.taosinn.com* ⇨ *40 rooms, 3 suites* △ *In-room: a/c (some), Internet. In-hotel: restaurant, bar, Wi-Fi hotspot* ⊟ *AE, DC, MC, V* ⊕ *C3.*

$$$ ⍾ **Inn on La Loma Plaza.** Surrounded by thick walls, this early-1800s
INN   Pueblo Revival building—and the surrounding gardens—capture the spirit and style of Spanish-colonial Taos. The rooms, which are appointed with fresh-cut flowers, have kiva fireplaces, CD stereos, coffeemakers, and Mexican-tile bathrooms, and many have private patios or decks. The living room has a well-stocked library with books on Taos and art. Owners Jerry and Peggy Davis provide helpful advice about the area and serve a generous breakfast, afternoon snacks, and evening coffee. Guests have privileges at the nearby health club (and the inn has its own hot tub). **Pros:** towering trees and lush gardens; inspiring views; extremely comfy rooms and beds. **Cons:** lots of stairs; on a busy street. ⊠ *315 Ranchitos Rd., Box 4159* ☎ *575/758–1717 or 800/530–3040* ⊕ *www.vacationtaos.com* ⇨ *5 rooms, 1 suite, 2 studios* △ *In-room: a/c (some), kitchen (some), DVD, Wi-Fi* ⊟ *AE, D, MC, V* ⍾⍿ *BP* ⊕ *B4.*

$ ⍾ **Inn on the Rio.** This property started as a strip motel, but over the
INN   years it's been transformed with adobe-style decorative touches and hand-painted murals into a charming B&B. If you look hard enough, you can still discern the motel roots of these tastefully furnished rooms with Southwestern art and linens and hand-painted bathrooms, but the rates are very fair. A well-tended garden overflowing with wildflowers and herbs surrounds the pool and hot tub area. Innkeepers Robert and Jules Cahalane prepare homemade bread, green-chile-and-egg casseroles, and cinnamon-infused coffee for breakfast. **Pros:** one of the few outdoor heated pools in town; private entrance to each room. **Cons:** traffic noise; small bathrooms. ⊠ *910 E. Kit Carson Rd.* ☎ *575/758–7199 or 800/737–7199* ⊕ *www.innontherio.com* ⇨ *12 rooms* △ *In-room: no a/c, Wi-Fi. In-hotel: pool, some pets allowed* ⊟ *AE, D, MC, V* ⍾⍿ *BP* ⊕ *D4.*

$

BED & BREAKFAST

🔆 **La Dona Luz Inn.** Paul "Paco" Castillo, who hails from a long line of local Taos artists and curio-shop owners, runs this festive and friendly B&B just a block off of Kit Carson Road and a few minutes' stroll from the plaza. It's one of the best bargains in the neighborhood, and rooms in this 19th-century adobe structure with latilla-and-viga ceilings are decorated with art and antiques from New Mexico, Mexico, and Spain—many have Jacuzzi tubs. The quirkiest and coziest room is also the least expensive room—it's hidden up a spiral staircase and has low ceilings, but there's a nice view of Wheeler Peak to the east. **Pros:** affordable rooms; a short walk from the plaza. **Cons:** in a slightly busy and noisy area (especially in summer). ⊠ *206 Des Georges La.* ☎ *575/758–9000 or 888/758–9060* ⊕ *www.ladonaluz.com* ➷ *6 rooms, 2 suites* ♿ *In-room: a/c, no phone, kitchen (some), refrigerator (some), DVD, Wi-Fi. In-hotel: some pets allowed* ▤ *D, MC, V* ⧗⧘ *CP* ⊕ *C4.*

$$

HOTEL

🔆 **La Fonda de Taos.** This handsomely updated and elegant historic property (there's been a hotel on this location since 1840) is ideal if you wish to be in the heart of the action—it's directly on the plaza. The warm decor, easy proximity to nightlife and dining, and no-children-under-eight policy make this a great choice for a romantic getaway. The rooms are rustic yet elegant and are furnished in neutral colors with luxury linens and hand-tiled bathrooms. A luxury penthouse on the top floor can be joined with other suites into a super-posh four-bedroom retreat. La Fonda also houses the Sabor restaurant, which opened in summer 2010. **Pros:** the most central location of any hotel in town; the building has a great history. **Cons:** less than ideal if you're seeking peace and quiet. ⊠ *108 S. Plaza* ☎ *575/758–2211 or 800/833–2211* ⊕ *www. lafondataos.com* ➷ *19 rooms, 5 suites, 1 penthouse* ♿ *In-room: a/c, kitchen (some), refrigerator, Wi-Fi. In-hotel: 2 restaurants, bar, no kids under 8* ▤ *AE, D, MC, V* ⊕ *C4.*

$$

INN

🔆 **La Posada de Taos.** A couple of blocks from Taos Plaza, this family-friendly 100-year-old inn has beam ceilings, a decorative arched doorway, and the intimacy of a private hacienda. Five guest rooms are in the main house; the sixth unit is a separate cottage with a king-size bed, sitting room, and fireplace. The rooms all have mountain or courtyard garden views, and some open onto private patios. Almost all have kiva-style fireplaces. Breakfasts are hearty. **Pros:** a few blocks from the plaza; historic building. **Cons:** small rooms; not much privacy in the main house. ⊠ *309 Juanita La., Box 1118* ☎ *575/758–8164 or 800/645–4803* ⊕ *www.laposadadetaos.com* ➷ *5 rooms, 1 cottage* ♿ *In-room: no a/c, no phone, Wi-Fi.* ▤ *AE, MC, V* ⧗⧘ *BP* ⊕ *B4.*

$$

INN

🔆 **Mabel Dodge Luhan House.** Quirky and offbeat—much like Taos—this National Historic Landmark was once home to the heiress who drew illustrious writers and artists—including D. H. Lawrence, Willa Cather, Georgia O'Keeffe, Ansel Adams, Martha Graham, and Carl Jung—to Taos. The main house, which has kept its simple, rustic feel, has nine cozy guest rooms; there are eight more in a modern building, as well as two two-bedroom cottages. The house exudes early-20th-century elegance, and the grounds offer numerous quiet corners for private conversations or solo meditation. Guests can stay in what was Mabel's room, in her hand-carved double bed to be precise; or in the solarium, an airy room at the top of the house that is completely surrounded by glass (and accessible by a ladder). For art groupies, nothing can quite compare with sleeping in the elegant room Georgia O'Keeffe stayed in while visiting. The inn is frequently used for artistic, cultural, and educational workshops—hence the tiny, but exceptional, bookstore in the lobby specializing in local authors and artists. **Pros:** historically relevant; rural setting, yet just blocks from the plaza. **Cons:** lots of stairs and uneven paths. ⊠ *240 Morada La.* ☎ *575/751–9686 or 800/846–2235* ⊕ *www.mabeldodgeluhan.com* ➣ *16 rooms, 1 suite, 2 casitas* ⚲ *In-room: a/c, no phone, no TV, Wi-Fi.* ⊟ *AE, MC, V* ⦿ *BP* ⊹ *C3.*

$$
BED & BREAKFAST
▦ **Orinda.** Built in 1947, this adobe estate has spectacular views and country privacy. The rustic rooms have separate entrances, kiva-style fireplaces, traditional viga ceilings, and Mexican-tile baths. Some of the rooms can be combined with a shared living area into a large suite. One has a two-person Jacuzzi. The hearty breakfast is served family-style in the soaring two-story sun atrium amid a gallery of artworks, all for sale. **Pros:** most rooms are spacious; gorgeous views of Taos Mountain. **Cons:** rooms are a little bland; a bit pricey for what is offered. ⊠ *461 Valverde* ☎ *575/758–8581 or 800/847–1837* ⊕ *www.orindabb. com* ➣ *5 rooms* ⚲ *In-room: no a/c (some), refrigerator. In-hotel: Wi-Fi hotspot, some pets allowed* ⊟ *AE, MC, V* ⦿ *BP* ⊹ *C3.*

SOUTH SIDE

$
BED & BREAKFAST
▦ **American Artists Gallery House Bed & Breakfast.** Each of the immaculate adobe-style rooms and suites here is called a "gallery," and owners LeAn and Charles Clamurro have taken care to decorate them with local arts and crafts. Some have Jacuzzis and all have kiva fireplaces; one family-friendly suite has a full kitchen; and all have private entrances, wood-burning fireplaces, and front porches where you can admire the view of Taos Mountain. Sumptuous hot breakfasts—along with conversation and suggestions about local attractions—are served up at a community table in the main house each morning, where you can often see the resident peacock, George, preening outside the windows (keep in mind that George can make a little noise from time to time). **Pros:** private entrances; true gourmet breakfast; reasonable rates. **Cons:** some rooms have small bathrooms; limited common spaces. ⊠ *132 Frontier La., Box 584* ☎ *575/758–4446 or 800/532–2041* ⊕ *www. taosbedandbreakfast.com* ➣ *7 rooms, 3 suites* ⚲ *In-room: a/c, kitchen (some), refrigerator, Wi-Fi. In-hotel: some pets allowed* ⊟ *AE, D, DC, MC, V* ⦿ *BP* ⊹ *C5.*

$$
INN
Fodor'sChoice
★
▦ **Casa Gallinas.** This peaceful compound of three stylishly appointed casitas is out in a rural area near the Hacienda de los Martinez museum—a spot where you can hear the birds sing and enjoy relative isolation, but you're still just a five-minute drive from the restaurants and shopping on the plaza. Each casita is filled with tasteful artwork, painted with vibrant colors, and decorated with one-of-a-kind handcrafted furnishings and fine textiles—one has two bedrooms, and they all have fully equipped kitchens, making them ideal for longer stays. The Bantam Roost has a large deck off the second-floor bedroom. Host Richard Spera is a massage therapist with a studio on the property—he's

happy to help guests plan their days, or to leave them to their own devices. This is really the perfect balance between a vacation rental and an upscale country inn. **Pros:** gorgeous furnishings; pastoral setting; significant discount for stays of a week or more. **Cons:** you're on your own for breakfast, but each unit has a kitchen; not within walking distance of town. ⊠ *613 Callejon* ☎ *575/758–2306* ⊕ *www.casagallina.net* ↘ *3 casitas* ⟲ *In-room: no a/c kitchen, DVD, Wi-Fi* ⊟ *No credit cards* ⊹ *A5.*

$ 🖫 **Old Taos Guesthouse B&B.** Once a ramshackle 180-year-old adobe hacienda, this homey B&B on 7½ verdant acres has been completely and lovingly outfitted with the owners' hand-carved doors and furniture, Western artifacts, and antiques—all have private entrances, and some have fireplaces. There are 80-mi views from the outdoor hot tub, and a shady veranda surrounds the courtyard. The owners welcome families. Breakfasts are healthy and hearty. **Pros:** beautifully appointed; private entrance to each room; serene setting. **Cons:** small bathrooms; some rooms are dark; a short drive from town. ⊠ *1028 Witt Rd., Box 6552* ☎ *575/758–5448 or 800/758–5448* ⊕ *www.oldtaos.com* ↘ *7 rooms, 2 suites* ⟲ *In-room: a/c, no phone (some), kitchen (some). In-hotel: Wi-Fi hotspot, some pets allowed* ⊟ *D, MC, V* ⧉ *BP* ⊹ *D5.*

BED & BREAKFAST

$ 🖫 **Sagebrush Inn.** Georgia O'Keeffe once lived and painted in a third-story room of the original inn. These days it's not as upscale—or expensive—as many other lodging options in Taos, and most rooms are in a newer building, but it has a shaded patio with large trees, a serviceable restaurant, and a collection of antique Navajo rugs. Many of the guest rooms have kiva-style fireplaces; some have balconies. There's country-western music nightly. **Pros:** good value; nightly music. **Cons:** very spread out; many of the rooms are dark; traffic noise. ⊠ *1508 Paseo del Pueblo Sur* ☎ *575/758–2254 or 800/428–3626* ⊕ *www.sagebrushinn. com* ↘ *68 rooms, 32 suites* ⟲ *In-room: a/c, Wi-Fi. In-hotel: 2 restaurants, bar, pool, some pets allowed* ⊟ *AE, D, DC, MC, V* ⧉ *BP* ⊹ *B5.*

HOTEL

$$ 🖫 **San Geronimo Lodge.** Built in 1925, this property was one of the earliest hotels in Taos and sits on 2½ acres that front majestic Taos Mountain and adjoin the Carson National Forest. Owners Charles and Pam Montgomery have worked hard to modernize and brighten rooms while preserving the property's historical charm and appeal. An extensive library, attractive grounds, rooms with gas or wood fireplaces and private decks, and five rooms for guests with pets are among the draws. Hanging Navajo rugs, Talavera-tile bathrooms, and high viga ceilings provide an authentic Southwestern experience. **Pros:** serene inside and out; extensive common rooms. **Cons:** some rooms have small bathrooms; a short drive from town. ⊠ *1101 Witt Rd.* ☎ *575/751–3776 or 800/894–4119* ⊕ *www.sangeronimolodge.com* ↘ *18 rooms* ⟲ *In-room: a/c, DVD, Wi-Fi. In-hotel: pool, some pets allowed* ⊟ *AE, D, MC, V* ⧉ *BP* ⊹ *D5.*

HOTEL

EL PRADO

$$ 🖫 **Hacienda del Sol.** Art patron Mabel Dodge Luhan bought this house about a mile north of Taos Plaza in the 1920s and lived here with her husband, Tony Luhan, while building their main house. It was also their private retreat and guesthouse for visiting notables; Frank

Fodor's Choice
★

Waters wrote *People of the Valley* here—other guests have included Willa Cather and D. H. Lawrence. Most of the rooms contain kiva fireplaces, Southwestern handcrafted furniture, and original artwork, and all have CD players—a few have Jacuzzi tubs. Certain adjoining rooms can be combined into suites. Breakfast is a gourmet affair that might include huevos rancheros or Belgian waffles. Perhaps above all else, the "backyards" of the rooms and the secluded outdoor hot tub have a view of Taos Mountain. **Pros:** cozy public rooms; private setting; some excellent restaurants within walking distance. **Cons:** traffic noise; some rooms are less private than others. ⊠ *109 Mabel Dodge La.* ☎ *575/758–0287 or 866/333–4459* ⊕ *www.taoshaciendadelsol. com* ⇨ *11 rooms* ⌂ *In-room: a/c, refrigerator (some), no TV, Wi-Fi* ⊟ *AE, D, MC, V* ⍟ *BP* ✛ *C3.*

$$ ⬚ **Touchstone Inn.** D. H. Lawrence visited this house in 1929; accord-
BED & BREAKFAST   ingly, the inn's owner, Taos artist Bren Price, has named many of the antique-filled rooms after famous Taos literary figures. The grounds overlook part of the Taos Pueblo lands, about a mile north of Taos Plaza. Some rooms have fireplaces. The enormous Royale Suite has a second-story private deck and large bathroom with Jacuzzi, walk-in shower, and skylight. Early-morning coffee is available in the living room, and breakfasts with inventive vegetarian presentations (such as blueberry pancakes with lemon sauce) are served in the glassed-in patio. The adjacent spa offers a wide range of beauty and skin treatments. **Pros:** extensive common rooms; impeccably furnished rooms; within walking distance of a few excellent restaurants. **Cons:** some highway noise; lots of stairs; a short drive from the plaza. ⊠ *110 Mabel Dodge La.* ☎ *575/758–0192 or 800/758–0192* ⊕ *www.touchstoneinn.com* ⇨ *6 rooms, 3 suites* ⌂ *In-room: a/c, refrigerator, DVD, Wi-Fi. In-hotel: spa* ⊟ *MC, V* ⍟ *BP* ✛ *C3.*

WEST SIDE

$ ⬚ **Dobson House.** Guests who book one of the two private suites at this
BED & BREAKFAST   ecotourist destination can help preserve the environment in style. This eclectic B&B relies primarily on passive heating and cooling and electricity is provided by solar panels. In addition, the 6,000-square-foot residence, within walking distance of the Rio Grande gorge, was built by hand by innkeepers Joan and John Dobson using 2,000 old tires, 20,000 recycled aluminum cans, and 28,000 pounds of dry cement and packed earth. Even so, guests live luxuriously with Ralph Lauren linens, and Joan's full breakfasts of Texas pecan biscuits, chicken-apple sausage, and Mexican baked eggs, plus extensive afternoon snacks and refreshments. The couples' sophisticated art collection adorns the home's authentic adobe walls. **Pros:** environmentally friendly; serene and private; each suite can accommodate up to four. **Cons:** a long drive to town. ⊠ *475 Tune Dr., West Side* ☎ *575/776–5738* ⊕ *www.new-mexico-bed-and-breakfast.com* ⇨ *2 suites* ⌂ *In-room: no a/c, no phone, no TV. In-hotel: no kids under 14* ⊟ *No credit cards* ⍟ *BP* ✛ *A2.*

ARROYO SECO

$$ **Adobe and Stars.** This light-filled adobe-style contemporary inn was
BED & BREAKFAST built in 1996 on a plateau in Arroyo Seco with panoramic views in
all directions—it's directly in the shadows of the Sangre de Cristos, a
quick drive to the ski valley. The eight rooms have beam ceilings and
traditional Southwestern art and furnishings. Those on the upper floors
have the best views, some with private decks. While more affordable
downstairs rooms open to a charming courtyard. All have kiva fire-
places and robes, and guests are treated to a substantial hot break-
fast each morning. **Pros:** big windows in the rooms let in lots of light;
short drive or leisurely stroll from shops and eateries, stunning views.
Cons: a 20-minute drive from the plaza. ⊠ *584 NM 150, 1 mi north of
Arroyo Seco village center* ☎ *575/776–2776 or 800/211–7076* ⊕ *www.
taosadobe.com* ⊅ *8 rooms* ⭗ *In-room: a/c, no phone, no TV (some),
Wi-Fi (some). In-hotel: some pets allowed* ⊟ *D, MC, V* ⊹ *B1.*

$$ **Cottonwood Inn.** This rambling, two-story adobe house with 11 fire-
BED & BREAKFAST places and such classic regional architectural details as *bancos, nichos,*
Fodor's Choice and high latilla-and-viga ceilings is right along the road to the ski val-
★ ley, just a couple of miles south of Arroyo Seco's quaint village center.
Rooms are consistently plush and elegant, with 450-thread-count linens, hand-carved wood furniture, and regional folk art, but they offer
plenty of variety in size and price. The largest have huge bathrooms with
steam shower-baths or Jacuzzi tubs, and the highly popular Mesa Vista
Room has both of these features as well as its own private entrance.
Organic, local ingredients are used in the hearty breakfasts, which
include plenty of fresh-baked pastries, cookies, and scones. **Pros:** closer
to Taos than most accommodations in Arroyo Seco; some of the largest and fanciest bathrooms of any B&Bs in Taos; great views of mesa
and mountains. **Cons:** not within walking distance of any restaurants.
⊠ *NM 230, just beyond junction with NM 150* ☎ *575/776–5826 or
800/324–7120* ⊕ *www.taos-cottonwood.com* ⊅ *8 rooms* ⭗ *In-room:
no a/c, no phone, refrigerator, DVD, Wi-Fi. In-hotel: some pets allowed*
⊟ *AE, MC, V* ⊹ *B2.*

$$ **Little Tree B&B.** In an authentic adobe house in the open country
BED & BREAKFAST between Taos and the ski valley, Little Tree's rooms are built around a
garden courtyard and have magnificent views of Taos Mountain and
the high desert that spans for nearly 100 mi to the west. Some have
kiva fireplaces and Jacuzzis, and all are decorated in true Southwestern
style. **Pros:** rare opportunity to stay in a real adobe (not stucco) home;
spotless and beautifully maintained; incredible views. **Cons:** 15-minute
drive to Taos; isolated. ⊠ *226 Hondo Seco Rd., Arroyo Hondo* ⊡ *Box
509, 87571* ☎ *575/776–8467 or 800/334–8467* ⊕ *www.littletreebandb.
com* ⊅ *4 rooms* ⭗ *In-room: no a/c, Wi-Fi* ⊟ *MC, V* ⊠⊙⊠ *BP* ⊹ *A2.*

TAOS SKI VALLEY

$$ **Austing Haus.** Owner Paul Austing constructed much of this hand-
HOTEL some, glass-sheathed building, 1½ mi from Taos Ski Valley, along
with many of its furnishings. The breakfast room has large picture
windows, stained-glass paneling, and an impressive fireplace. Aromas

of fresh-baked goods, such as Paul's apple strudel, come from the kitchen. Guest rooms are pretty and quiet with harmonious, peaceful colors; some have four-poster beds and fireplaces. In winter the inn offers ski packages. **Pros:** cozy Alpine ambience; close to skiing but slightly removed from crowds of ski area; excellent breakfasts. **Cons:** not directly located at ski slopes. ⊠ *NM 150, Village of Taos Ski Valley* ☎ *575/776–2649 or 800/748–2932* ⊕ *www.austinghaus.net* ↵ *22 rooms, 3 chalets* ⚒ *In-room: Wi-Fi. In-hotel: restaurant* ▭ *AE, DC, MC, V* ⊙| *BP* ✛ *D1.*

$$$$
VACATION LODGE   ⊡ **The Bavarian.** This luxurious, secluded re-creation of a Bavarian lodge has the only midmountain accommodations in the Taos Ski Valley. The King Ludwig suite has a dining room, kitchen, marble bathroom, and two bedrooms with canopied beds. Three suites have whirlpool tubs. Summer activities include hiking, touring with the resident botanist, horseback riding, rafting, and fishing. Seven-night ski packages are offered. The restaurant on-site is one of the most atmospheric in the Taos region. **Pros:** Stunningly plush rooms, only ski-in; ski-out property at midmountain, exceptional onsite dining. **Cons:** Steep rates; difficult driveway to negotiate in winter weather. ⊠ *100 Kachina Rd., Taos Ski Valley* ☎ *575/776–8020* ⊕ *www.thebavarian.net* ↵ *4 suites* ⚒ *In-room: no a/c, kitchen, Wi-Fi. In-hotel: restaurant* ▭ *AE, MC, V* ⊙ *Closed early Apr.–late May and mid-Oct.–late Nov.* ⊙| *BP* ✛ *D1.*

$$$$
VACATION   ⊡ **Snakedance Condominiums Hotel.** This modern condominium resort is
CONDOS   right on the slopes and contains a handsome library where guests can enjoy an après-ski coffee or after-dinner drink next to a fieldstone fireplace. Some units—which range from studios to three-bedroom apartments—have fireplaces. A small spa provides a slew of services, from facials to deep-tissue massages, as well as bodywork aimed specifically to work muscles tested on the ski slopes and hiking trails. In winter, guests can take advantage of the helpful ski valet and ski storage with boot dryers. And in summer the hotel offers weeklong vacation packages, including a cooking school and fitness adventure courses, and rates are a fraction of what they are during ski season. Hondo Restaurant ($$) turns out very good contemporary American fare. **Pros:** Ski-in, ski-out accommodations; handy to have a spa on-site; some great deals in summer. **Cons:** Unless you're a skier, there's little reason to stay here in winter; a good distance from Taos proper, as is true for all hotels in the area. ⊠ *110 Sutton Place Rd., Village of Taos Ski Valley 87525* ☎ *575/776–2277 or 800/322–9815* ↵ *33 condo units* ⚒ *In-room: a/c, kitchen, Wi-Fi. In-hotel: restaurant, bar, gym, spa* ▭ *AE, D, DC, MC, V* ⊙ *Closed mid-Apr.–Memorial Day* ⊙| *CP* ✛ *D1.*

NIGHTLIFE AND THE ARTS

Evening entertainment is modest in Taos. Some motels and hotels present solo musicians or small combos in their bars and lounges. Everything from down-home blues bands to Texas two-step dancing blossoms on Saturday and Sunday nights in winter. In summer things heat up during the week as well. For information about what's going on around town pick up *Taos Magazine.* The weekly *Taos News,* published on

The Taos Hum

Investigations into what causes a mysterious low-frequency sound dubbed the "Taos Hum" are ongoing, although the topic was more popular during a worldwide news media frenzy in the 1990s. Taos isn't the only place where the mysterious hum has been heard, but it's probably the best-known locale for the phenomenon. (The Taos Hum, for example, now has been officially documented in *Encyclopaedia Britannica*.)

Scientists visited Taos during the 1990s in unsuccessful good-faith efforts to trace the sound, which surveys indicated were heard by about 2% of the town's population. Described as a frequency similar to the low, throbbing engine of a diesel truck, the Taos Hum has reportedly created disturbances among its few hearers from mildly irritating to profoundly disturbing. In the extreme, hearers say they experience constant problems, including interrupted sleep and physical effects such as dizziness and nosebleeds.

Speculation about the Taos Hum abounds. Conspiracy theorists believe the sound originates from ominous, secret, government testing, possibly emanating from the federal defense establishment of Los Alamos National Laboratory 55 mi southwest of Taos. The theory correlates with reports of some hearers that the sound began suddenly, as though something had been switched on.

Some investigators say the hearers may have extraordinary sensitivity to low-frequency sound waves, which could originate from all manner of human devices (cell phones, for one) creating constant sources of electromagnetic energy. Still other theorists postulate that low-frequency sound waves may originate in the Earth's lower atmosphere. One intriguing theory says that the hum could be explained by vibrations deep within the Earth, as a sort of precursor to earthquakes (although earthquakes are extremely rare in New Mexico).

Although many believe there's something to the mysterious Taos Hum, less kindly skeptics have dismissed the phenomenon as New Age nonsense linked to mass hysteria. But while you're here, you may as well give it a try (no one need know what you're up to). Find yourself a peaceful spot. Sit quietly. And listen.

Thursday, carries arts and entertainment information in the "Tempo" section. The arts scene is much more lively, with festivals every season for nearly every taste.

NIGHTLIFE

Fodor's Choice The **Adobe Bar** (✉ *Taos Inn, 125 Paseo del Pueblo Norte, Plaza and Vicinity* ☎ *575/758–2233*), a local meet-and-greet spot often dubbed "Taos's living room," books talented acts, from solo guitarists to small folk groups and, two or three nights a week, jazz musicians.

Fodor's Choice **Alley Cantina** (✉ *121 Teresina La., Plaza and Vicinity* ☎ *575/758–2121*) has jazz, folk, and blues—as well as shuffleboard, pool, and board games for those not moved to dance. It's housed in the oldest structure in Downtown Taos.

Caffe Tazza (⌂ *122 Kit Carson Rd., Plaza and Vicinity* ☎ *575/758–8706*) presents free evening performances throughout the week—folk-singing, jazz, belly dancing, blues, poetry, and fiction readings.

The **Kachina Lodge Cabaret** (⌂ *Best Western Kachina Lodge, 413 Paseo del Pueblo Norte, Plaza and Vicinity* ☎ *575/758–2275*) usually brings in an area radio DJ to liven up various forms of music and dancing.

The piano bar at **Sabroso** (⌂ *470 CR 150, Arroyo Seco* ☎ *575/776–3333*) often presents jazz and old standards—the patio out front is a stunning spot to watch sunsets.

The **Sagebrush Inn** (⌂ *1508 Paseo del Pueblo Sur, South Side* ☎ *575/758–2254*) hosts musicians and dancing in its lobby lounge. There's usually no cover charge for country-western dancing.

THE ARTS

Long a beacon for visual artists, Taos is also becoming a magnet for touring musicians, especially in summer, when performers and audiences are drawn to the heady high-desert atmosphere. Festivals celebrate the visual arts, music, poetry, and film.

The **Taos Center for the Arts** (⌂ *133 Paseo del Pueblo Norte, Plaza and Vicinity* ☎ *575/758–2052* ⊕ *http://tcataos.org*), which encompasses the Taos Community Auditorium, presents films, plays, concerts, and dance performances.

The **Taos Fall Arts Festival** (☎ *575/758–21063 or 800/732–8267* ⊕ *www.taosfallarts.com*), from late September to early October, is the area's major arts gathering, when buyers are in town and many other events, such as a Taos Pueblo feast, take place.

The **Taos Spring Arts Celebration** (☎ *575/758–3873 or 800/732–8267*), held throughout May, is a showcase for the visual, performing, and literary arts of the community and allows you to rub elbows with the many artists who call Taos home. The Mother's Day Arts and Crafts weekend during the festival always draws an especially large crowd.

MUSIC

Fodor's Choice ★ From mid-June to early August the Taos School of Music fills the evenings with the sounds of chamber music at the **Taos School of Music Program and Festival** (☎ *575/776–2388* ⊕ *www.taosschoolofmusic.com*). Running strong since 1963, this is America's oldest chamber music summer program and possibly the largest assembly of top string quartets in the country. Concerts are presented a couple of times a week from mid-June through early August, at the Taos Community Auditorium and at Taos Ski Valley. Tickets cost $10 to $20. The events at Taos Ski Valley are free.

Fodor's Choice ★ Solar energy was pioneered in this land of sunshine, and each year in late June the flag of sustainability is raised at the three-day **Taos Solar Music Festival** (⊕ *www.solarmusicfest.com*). Top-name acts appear, and booths promote alternative energy, permaculture, and other eco-friendly technologies.

SHOPPING

Retail options on Taos Plaza consist mostly of T-shirt emporiums and souvenir shops that are easily bypassed, though a few stores carry quality Native American artifacts and jewelry. The more upscale galleries and boutiques are two short blocks north on Bent Street, including the John Dunn House Shops. Kit Carson Road (U.S. 64), has a mix of the old and the new. There's metered municipal parking Downtown, though the traffic can be daunting. Some shops worth checking out are in St. Francis Plaza in Ranchos de Taos, 4 mi south of the plaza near the San Francisco de Asís Church. Just north of Taos off NM 522 you can find Overland Ranch (including Overland Sheepskin Co.), which has gorgeous sheepskin and leather clothing, along with a few other shops and galleries (plus a restaurant), and an outdoor path winding through displays of wind sculptures. You'll find another notable cluster of galleries and shops, along with a few good restaurants, in the village of Arroyo Seco, a 15-minute drive north of Taos toward the ski valley.

ART GALLERIES

For at least a century, artists have been drawn to Taos's natural grandeur. The result is a vigorous art community with some 80 galleries, a lively market, and an estimated 1,000 residents producing art full- or part-time. Many artists explore themes of the Western landscape, Native Americans, and adobe architecture; others create abstract forms and mixed-media works that may or may not reflect the Southwest. Some local artists grew up in Taos, but many—Anglo, Hispanic, and Native Americans—are adopted Taoseños.

Envision Gallery (⊠ *Overland Ranch, NM 522, north of Taos, El Prado* ☎ *505/751–1344* ⊕ *www.envisiongallery.net*) is roughly split between painters—most of them working in contemporary, abstract styles—and sculptors. Many of the latter produce large, outdoor works that are displayed on the open grounds at this impressive gallery that's part of the scenic Overland Ranch complex, in El Prado. About two-dozen artists are represented.

Farnsworth Gallery Taos (⊠ *133 Paseo del Pueblo Norte, Plaza and Vicinity* ☎ *575/758–0776* ⊕ *www.johnfarnsworth.com*) contains the work of artist John Farnsworth, best known for his finely detailed paintings of horses, and also includes colorful local landscapes, large-scale still-lifes, and scenes of Native American kiva dancers.

Inger Jirby Gallery (⊠ *207 Ledoux St., Plaza and Vicinity* ☎ *575/758–7333,* ⊕ *www.jirby.com*) displays Jirby's whimsical, brightly colored landscape paintings. Be sure to stroll through the lovely sculpture garden.

J. D. Challenger Gallery (⊠ *221 Paseo del Pueblo Norte, Plaza and Vicinity* ☎ *575/751–6773 or 800/511–6773*) is the home base of personable painter J. D. Challenger, who has become famous for his dramatically rendered portraits of Native Americans from tribes throughout North America.

Lumina Fine Art & Sculpture Gardens (⊠ *11 NM 230, Arroyo Seco* ☎ *575/776–0123 or 877/558–6462* ⊕ *www.luminagallery.com*) exhibits paintings by worldwide artists and has 3 acres of sculpture gardens, including works of Japanese stone carvers. The setting is beautiful, a short distance off of NM 150 in Arroyo Seco.

Michael McCormick Gallery (⊠ *106-C Paseo del Pueblo Norte, Plaza and Vicinity* ☎ *575/758–1372 or 800/279–0879* ⊕ *www.mccormickgallery. com*) is home to the sensual, stylized female portraits of Miguel Martinez and the iconic portraits of Malcolm Furlow. The gallery also has an extensive collection of Rembrandt etchings.

Mission Gallery (⊠ *138 E. Kit Carson Rd., Plaza and Vicinity* ☎ *575/758–2861*) carries the works of early Taos artists, early New Mexico modernists, and important contemporary artists. The gallery is in the former home of painter Joseph H. Sharp.

Navajo Gallery (⊠ *210 Ledoux St., Plaza and Vicinity* ☎ *575/758–3250*) shows the works of the internationally renowned Navajo painter and sculptor R. C. Gorman, who died in 2005 and who was known for his ethereal imagery—especially his portraits of Native American women.

Nichols Taos Fine Art Gallery (⊠ *403 Paseo del Pueblo Norte, Plaza and Vicinity* ☎ *575/758–2475*) has exhibits of oils, watercolors, pastels, charcoal, and pencils from artists representing many prestigious national art organizations.

Parks Gallery (⊠ *127-A Bent St., Plaza and Vicinity* ☎ *575/751–0343,* ⊕ *www.parksgallery.com*) specializes in contemporary paintings, sculptures, and prints. The late and critically acclaimed mixed-media artist Melissa Zink shows here, as does painter Jim Wagner.

R. B. Ravens Gallery (⊠ *4146 NM 68, South Side* ☎ *575/758–7322 or 866/758-7322* ⊕ *www.rbravens.com*) exhibits paintings by the founding artists of Taos, pre-1930s Native American weavings, and ceramics in a spare museumlike setting. Be sure to admire the beautiful collection of Navajo saddle blankets.

Fodor's Choice ★ **Robert L. Parsons Fine Art** (⊠ *131 Bent St., Plaza and Vicinity* ☎ *575/751–0159 or 800/613–5091* ⊕ *www.parsonsart.com*) is one of the best sources of early Taos art-colony paintings, antiques, and authentic antique Navajo blankets. Inside you'll find originals by such luminaries as Ernest Blumenschein, Bert Geer Phillips, Oscar Berninghaus, Joseph Bakos, and Nicolai Fechin.

Stray Arts Gallery (⊠ *120 Camino de la Placita, Plaza and Vicinity* ☎ *575/758–9780* ⊕ *www.strayhearts.org/stray_arts.php*) sells donated, bargain-priced art to raise funds for the Stray Hearts Animal Shelter. Of course, in a town like Taos, you can find works here by prominent artists (Ouray Meyers, Harriet Green, R. C. Gorman, and many others), making this something of an unexpected find as well as a great cause.

Studio de Colores Gallery (⊠ *119 Quesnel, El Prado* ☎ *575/751–3502 or 888/751-3502* ⊕ *www.decoloresgallery.com*) is home to the work of two artists, Ann Huston and Ed Sandoval, who are married to one another but have extremely distinctive styles. Sandoval is known for his trademark *Viejito* (Old Man) images and swirling, vibrantly colored landscapes; Ann specializes in soft-hue still lifes and scenes of incredible stillness.

Total Arts Gallery (✉ *122-A Kit Carson Rd., Plaza and Vicinity* ☎ *575/758–4667* ⊕ *www.totalartsgallery.com*) comprises several rooms displaying works by some of the area's most celebrated artists, including Barbara Zaring, David Hettinger, Doug Dawson, and Ken Elliott. Themes vary greatly from contemporary paintings and sculptures to more traditional landscapes and regional works.

> **DID YOU KNOW?**
>
> For more than a century, clear mountain light, sweeping landscapes, and a soft desert palette have drawn artists to Taos.

Fodor's Choice
★ At **Two Graces Gallery** (✉ *San Francisco Plaza, South Side* ☎ *575/758–4639*) owner and artist Robert Cafazzo displays an astonishing assortment of traditional Indian pottery and kachinas, contemporary art by local artists, old postcards, and rare books on area artists.

SPECIALTY STORES

BOOKS

Brodsky Bookshop (✉ *226-A Paseo del Pueblo Norte, Plaza and Vicinity* ☎ *575/758–9468* ⊕ *www.taosbooks.com*) has new and used books—contemporary literature, Southwestern classics, children's titles—piled here and there, but amiable proprietor Rick Smith will help you find what you need.

G. Robinson Old Prints and Maps (✉ *John Dunn House, 124-D Bent St., Plaza and Vicinity* ☎ *575/758–2278*) stocks rare books, maps, and prints—some of these priceless and fascinating maps date as far back as the 14th century.

Moby Dickens (✉ *John Dunn House, 124-A Bent St., Plaza and Vicinity* ☎ *575/758–3050* ⊕ *www.mobydickens.com*), a full-service bookstore, specializes in rare and out-of-print books and carries a wide selection of contemporary fiction and nonfiction. It's one of the finest independent bookshops in the state.

CLOTHING

Andean Softwear (✉ *118 Sutton Pl., Taos Ski Valley* ☎ *575/776–2508* ⊕ *www.andeansoftware.com*), which was begun at the Ski Valley in 1984 but has a second location close to the plaza, carries warm, sturdy, but beautifully designed clothing and textiles, as well as jewelry. Much of the wares come from Peru, Bolivia, and Ecuador, as the name of the store implies, but owner Andrea Heckman also imports from Bali, Mexico, Turkey, and plenty of other far-flung locales with distinct arts traditions. Note the deliciously soft alpaca sweaters from Peru.

Artemisia (✉ *115 Bent St., Plaza and Vicinity* ☎ *575/737–9800* ⊕ *www.artemisiataos.com*) has a wide selection of one-of-a-kind wearable art by local artist Annette Randell. Many of her creations incorporate Native American designs. The store also carries jewelry, bags, and accessories by several local artists.

Francesca's (✉ *492 NM 150, Arroyo Seco* ☎ *575/776–8776*) has long been a fixture among the cluster of hip boutiques and galleries in Arroyo

Seco—the boutique is inside the former post office. She specializes in reasonably priced, fanciful, and stylish threads with materials and design inspirations from India, Nepal, and Southeast Asia.

Mariposa Boutique Inc. (✉ *120-F Bent St., Plaza and Vicinity* ☎ *575/758–9028*) sells fanciful handmade women's and children's specialty clothing, including two original lines made in-house.

Fodor's Choice
★
Overland Sheepskin Company (✉ *Overland Ranch, NM 522 , 4 mi north of Taos, El Prado* ☎ *575/758–8820 or 888/754–8352*) carries high-quality sheepskin coats, hats, mittens, and slippers, many with Taos beadwork. This is the original location of what has become a network of about a dozen stores, mostly in the West, and the setting—in the shadows of the Sangre de Cristos, amid a complex of several other shops, is itself a reason for a visit.

Steppin' Out (✉ *120-K Bent St. Plaza and Vicinity* ☎ *575/758–4487*) carries European footwear, distinctive clothing (including the popular Eileen Fisher brand), handmade handbags, and unique accessories.

COLLECTIBLES AND GIFTS

Fodor's Choice
★
Arroyo Seco Mercantile (✉ *488 State Rd. 15, Arroyo Seco* ☎ *575/776–8806* ⊕ *www.secomerc.com*) carries a varied assortment of 1930s linens, handmade quilts, candles, organic soaps, vintage cookware, hand-thrown pottery, decorated crosses, and souvenirs.

Coyote Moon (✉ *120-C Bent St., Plaza and Vicinity* ☎ *575/758–4437*) has a great selection of south-of-the-border folk art, painted crosses, jewelry, and Day of the Dead figurines, some featuring American rock stars.

Horse Feathers (✉ *109-B Kit Carson Rd., Plaza and Vicinity* ☎ *575/758–7457* ⊕ *www.cowboythings.com*) is a fun collection of cowboy antiques and vintage Western wear—boots, hats, buckles, jewelry, and all manner of paraphernalia.

Letherwerks (✉ *124-B Bent St.,Plaza and Vicinity* ☎ *575/758–2778* ⊕ *www.letherwerks.com*) has been making and selling deftly crafted leather belts, bags, wallets, and backpacks since 1969—they also carry quite a few pieces made by other talented local artists around Taos.

Taos Drums (✉ *NM 68, 5 mi south of Plaza, South Side* ☎ *575/758–9844 or 800/424–3786*) is the factory outlet for the Taos Drum Factory. The store, 5 mi south of Taos Plaza (look for the large tepee), stocks handmade Pueblo log drums, leather lamp shades, and wrought-iron Southwestern furniture.

HOME FURNISHINGS

Fodor's Choice
★
Alhambra (✉ *124 Paseo del Pueblo Sur, Plaza and Vicinity* ☎ *575/758–4161*) carries exquisite, high-end antique furniture, rugs, and textiles from India, Tibet, Nepal, Thailand, and China.

At **Antiquarius Imports** (✉ *487 State Road 150, Arroyo Seco* ☎ *575/776–8381* ⊕ *www.antiquariusimports.com*), Ivelisse Brooks's eclectic shop, you'll find rare Indian, Afghan, and African antiques and furniture along with contemporary, naturally dyed carpets made in Pakistan.

Casa Cristal Pottery (✉ *1306 Paseo del Pueblo Norte, El Prado* ☎ *575/758–1530*), 2½ mi north of the Taos Plaza, has a huge stock of stoneware, serapes, clay pots, Native American ironwood carvings, fountains, sweaters, ponchos, clay fireplaces, Mexican blankets, tiles, piñatas, and blue glassware from Guadalajara.

Country Furnishings of Taos (✉ *534 Paseo del Pueblo Norte, Plaza and Vicinity* ☎ *575/758–4633* ⊕ *www.cftaos.com*), which occupies a rambling, picturesque adobe house, sells folk art from northern New Mexico, handmade furniture, metalwork lamps and beds, and colorful accessories.

Starr Interiors (✉ *117 Paseo del Pueblo Norte, Plaza and Vicinity* ☎ *575/758–3065*) has a striking collection of Zapotec Indian rugs and hangings.

Taos Blue (✉ *101-A Bent St., Plaza and Vicinity* ☎ *575/758–3561* ⊕ *www. taosblue.com*) carries jewelry, pottery, and contemporary works by Native Americans (masks, rattles, sculpture), as well as Hispanic santos.

Taos Tin Works (✉ *1204-D Paseo del Pueblo Norte, El Prado* ☎ *575/758–9724* ⊕ *www.taostinworks.com*) sells handcrafted tinwork such as wall sconces, mirrors, lamps, and table ornaments by Marion Moore.

Weaving Southwest (✉ *106A Paseo del Pueblo North, Plaza and Vicinity* ☎ *575/758–0433* ⊕ *www.weavingsouthwest.com*) represents 20 tapestry artists who make beautiful rugs and blankets. The store also sells supplies for weavers, including hand-dyed yarn.

NATIVE AMERICAN ARTS AND CRAFTS

Buffalo Dancer (✉ *103-A E. Plaza, Plaza and Vicinity* ☎ *575/758–8718* ⊕ *www.buffalodancer.com*) buys, sells, and trades Native American arts and crafts, including pottery, belts, kachina dolls, hides, and silver-coin jewelry.

El Rincón Trading Post (✉ *114 E. Kit Carson Rd., Plaza and Vicinity* ☎ *575/758–9188*) is housed in a large, dark, cluttered century-old adobe. Native American items of all kinds are bought and sold here: drums, feathered headdresses, Navajo rugs, beads, bowls, baskets, shields, beaded moccasins, jewelry, arrows, and spearheads. The packed back room contains Native American, Hispanic, and Anglo Wild West artifacts.

SPORTING GOODS

Fodor's Choice ★ **Cottam's Ski & Outdoor** (✉ *207-A Paseo del Pueblo Sur, Plaza and Vicinity* ☎ *575/758–2822,* ⊕ *www.cottamsskishops.com*) carries hiking and backpacking gear, maps, fishing licenses and supplies, and ski and snowboard equipment and rentals, along with related clothing and accessories. There are also shops near the ski lifts at Taos Ski Valley and Angel Fire.

Mudd–n–Flood Mountain Shop (✉ *134 Bent St., Plaza and Vicinity* ☎ *575/751–9100*) has gear and clothing for rock climbers, backpackers, campers, and backcountry skiers.

Taos Mountain Outfitters (✉ *114 S. Plaza, Plaza and Vicinity* ☎ *575/758– 9292* ⊕ *www.taosmountainoutfitters.com*) has supplies for kayakers, skiers, climbers, and backpackers, as well as maps, books, and handy advice.

SPORTS AND THE OUTDOORS

Whether you plan to cycle around town, jog along Paseo del Pueblo Norte, or play a few rounds of golf, keep in mind that the altitude in Taos is higher than 7,000 feet. It's best to keep physical exertion to a minimum until your body becomes acclimated to the altitude—a full day to a few days, depending on your constitution.

BALLOONING

Hot-air ballooning has become nearly as popular in Taos as in Albuquerque, with a handful of outfitters offering rides, most starting at about $225 per person. **Paradise Balloons** (☎ *575/751–6098* ⊕ *www. taosballooning.com*) will thrill you with a "splash and dash" in the Rio Grande River as part of a silent journey through the 600-foot canyon walls of Rio Grande Gorge. **Pueblo Balloon Company** (☎ *575/751–9877* ⊕ *www.puebloballoon.com*) conducts balloon rides over and into the Rio Grande Gorge.

BICYCLING

Taos-area roads are steep and hilly, and none have marked bicycle lanes, so be careful while cycling. The West Rim Trail offers a fairly flat but view-studded 9-mi ride that follows the Rio Grande canyon's west rim from the Rio Grande Gorge Bridge to near the Taos Junction Bridge.

Gearing Up Bicycle Shop (✉ *129 Paseo del Pueblo Sur, Plaza and Vicinity* ☎ *575/751–0365* ⊕ *www.gearingupbikes.com*) is a full-service bike shop that can supply advice on best routes and organized group rides. **Native Sons Adventures** (✉ *1033-A Paseo del Pueblo Sur, South Side* ☎ *575/758–9342 or 800/753–7559,* ⊕ *www.nativesonsadventures. com*) offers guided mountain-biking tours.

FISHING

Carson National Forest has some of the best trout fishing in New Mexico. Its streams and lakes are home to rainbow, brown, and native Rio Grande cutthroat trout.

Reasonably priced and with very knowledgeable guides, **Blue Yonder Fly Fishing** (☎ *575/779–9002* ⊕ *www.blueyonderflyfishing.com*) can customize anything from a casual half-day outing for beginners to an extensive all-day adventure for experienced anglers—gear, instruction, and meals are included. Just south of Taos Plaza, **Cottam's Ski & Outdoor** (✉ *207-A Paseo del Pueblo Sur, Plaza and Vicinity* ☎ *575/758–2822 or 800/322– 8267* ⊕ *www.cottamsoutdoor.com*) provides fishing and bike trips and ski and snowboard rentals. **Solitary Angler** (☎ *575/758–5653 or 866/502– 1700* ⊕ *www.thesolitaryangler.com*) guides fly-fishing expeditions that search out uncrowded habitats. Well-known area fishing guide Taylor

Streit of **Taos Fly Shop & Streit Fly Fishing** (⊠ *308-C Paseo del Pueblo Sur, Plaza and Vicinity* ☎ *575/751–1312* ⊕ *www.taosflyshop.com*) takes individuals or small groups out for fishing and lessons.

GOLF

Views from the course at the **Taos Country Club** (⊠ *54 Golf Course Dr., South Side* ☎ *575/758–7300* ⊕ *www.taoscountryclub.com*) are some of the most dazzling in northern New Mexico. The layout is stunning and quite hilly, and water hazards are few. Greens fees at the 18-hole, par-72 championship course are $62 to $72.

HIKING

Fodor's Choice ★ **Wheeler Peak** is a designated wilderness area of Carson National Forest (⇨ *The Enchanted Circle tour, below*), where travel is restricted to hiking or horseback. Part of the Sangre de Cristo Mountains, this 13,161-foot peak is New Mexico's highest. The most popular and accessible trail to the peak is the Williams Lake Trail, which is about 8-mi round-trip and begins in Taos Ski Valley just east of the Bavarian lodge and restaurant. Only experienced hikers should tackle this strenuous trail all the way to the top, as the 4,000-foot elevation gain is taxing, and the final mile or so to the peak is a steep scramble over loose scree. However, for a moderately challenging and still very rewarding hike, you take the trail to the halfway point, overlooking the shores of rippling Williams Lake. Numerous other rewarding hikes of varying degrees of ease and length climb up the many slopes that rise from the village of Taos Ski Valley—check with rangers or consult the Carson National Forest Web site for details. Trailheads are usually well-signed. Dress warmly even in summer, take plenty of water and food, and pay attention to *all* warnings and instructions distributed by rangers. ⊠ *Parking area for Williams Lake Trail is along Kachina Rd. by the Bavarian lodge and restaurant* ☎ *575/758–6200* ⊕ *www.fs.fed.us/r3/carson*.

LLAMA TREKKING

One of the most offbeat outdoor recreational activities in the Taos area, llama trekking is offered by **Wild Earth Llama Adventures** (☎ *575/586–0174 or 800/758–5262* ⊕ *www.llamaadventures.com*) in a variety of packages, from one-day tours to excursions lasting several days in wilderness areas of the nearby Sangre de Cristo Mountains. Llamas, relatives of the camel, are used as pack animals on trips that begin at $99 for a day hike. Gourmet lunches eaten on the trail are part of the package, along with overnight camping and meals for longer trips.

RIVER RAFTING

Fodor's Choice ★ The Taos Box, at the bottom of the steep-walled canyon far below the Rio Grande Gorge Bridge, is the granddaddy of thrilling white water in New Mexico and is best attempted by experts only—or on a guided trip—but the river also offers more placid sections such as through the Orilla Verde Recreation Area, just south of Taos in the village of Pilar (here you'll also find a small shop and cafe called the Pilar Yacht Club, which caters heavily to rafters and fishing enthusiasts). Spring runoff is the busy season, from mid-April through June, but rafting companies conduct tours March to November. Shorter two-hour options usually cover the fairly tame section of the river. The **Bureau of Land Management, Taos Resource Area Office** (⊠ *226 Cruz Alta* ☎ *575/758–8851* ⊕ *www. blm.gov/nm/st/en.html*) has a list of registered river guides and information about running the river on your own.

Big River Raft Trips (☎ *575/758–9711 or 800/748–3760* ⊕ *www. bigriverrafts.com*) offers dinner float trips and rapids runs. **Far Flung Adventures** (☎ *575/758–2628 or 800/359–2627* ⊕ *www.farflung.com*) operates half-day, full-day, and overnight rafting trips along the Rio Grande and the Rio Chama. **Los Rios River Runners** (☎ *575/776–8854 or 800/544–1181* ⊕ *www.losriosriverrunners.com*) will take you to your choice of spots—the Rio Chama, the Lower Gorge, or the Taos Box. **Native Sons Adventures** (⊠ *1335 Paseo del Pueblo Sur* ☎ *575/758–9342 or 800/753–7559* ⊕ *www.nativesonsadventures.com*) offers several trip options on the Rio Grande.

SKIING

Fodor's Choice
★
With 72 runs—more than half of them for experts—and an average of more than 300 inches of annual snowfall, **Taos Ski Valley** ranks among the country's most respected—and challenging—resorts. The slopes, which cover a 2,600-foot vertical gain of lift-served terrain and another 600 feet of hike-in skiing, tend to be narrow and demanding (note the ridge chutes, Al's Run, Inferno), but 25% (e.g., Honeysuckle) are for intermediate skiers, and 24% (e.g., Bambi, Porcupine) for beginners. Until 2008 it was one of the nation's few resorts that banned snowboarding, but this activity is welcome—and very popular—now. Taos Ski Valley is justly famous for its outstanding ski schools, some of the best in the country. If you're new to the sport, this is a terrific resort to give a try. ⊠ *Village of Taos Ski Valley* ☎ *575/776–2291* ⊕ *www.skitaos. org* 🎟 *Lift tickets $71* ⊙ *Late Nov.–early Apr.*

SIDE TRIPS FROM TAOS

Surrounded by thousands of acres of pristine Carson National Forest and undeveloped high desert, Taos makes an ideal base for roadtripping. Most of the nearby adventures involve the outdoors, from skiing to hiking to mountain biking, and there are several noteworthy campgrounds in this part of the state. Although these side trips can be done in a day, the ski-resort communities mentioned in this section have a decent selection of overnight accommodations.

THE ENCHANTED CIRCLE

Fodor's Choice
★
The Enchanted Circle, an 84-mi loop north from Taos and back, rings Wheeler Peak, New Mexico's highest mountain, and takes you through glorious panoramas of alpine valleys and the towering mountains of the lush Carson National Forest. You can see all the major sights as an ambitious one-day side trip, or take a more leisurely tour and stay overnight.

From Taos, head north about 15 mi via U.S. 64 to NM 522, keeping your eye out for the sign on the right that points to the D.H. Lawrence Ranch and Memorial. You can visit the memorial, which is well-marked from the road, but the other buildings on the ranch are closed to the public. Continue

> **DID YOU KNOW?**
>
> Your best guarantee of authenticity, particularly involving Navajo blankets, is to purchase directly from a reputable reservation outlet.

north a short way to reach Red River Hatchery, and then go another 5 mi to the village of Questa. Here you have the option of continuing north on NM 522 and detouring for some hiking at Wild Rivers Recreation Area, or turning east from Questa on NM 38 and driving for about 12 mi to the unpretentious, family-friendly town of Red River, a noteworthy ski town in winter and an increasingly popular summer-recreation hub during the warmer months.

From here, continue 16 mi east along NM 38 and head over dramatic Bobcat Pass, which rises to just under 10,000 feet. You'll come to the sleepy, old-fashioned village of Eagle Nest, comprising a few shops and down-home restaurants and motels. From here, U.S. 64 joins with NM 38 and runs southeast about 15 mi to one of the state's fastest-growing communities, Angel Fire, an upscale ski resort that's popular for hiking, golfing, and mountain biking in summer. *(See also Northeastern New Mexico, chapter 6, for information on exploring Eagle Nest and Angel Fire by approaching from the east, via Cimarron, or the south, via Mora.)* It's about a 25-mi drive west over 9,000-foot Palo Flechado Pass and down through winding Taos Canyon to return to Taos.

Leave early in the morning and plan to spend the entire day on this trip. Especially during ski season, which runs from late November to early April, but in summer as well you may want to spend a night or more in Red River, which has a number of mostly rustic lodges and vacation rentals, or in Angel Fire, which is becoming increasingly respected as a year-round resort. Watch for snow and ice on the roads from late fall through early spring. A sunny winter day can yield some lovely scenery.

Carson National Forest surrounds Taos and spans almost 200 mi across northern New Mexico, encompassing mountains, lakes, streams, villages, and much of the Enchanted Circle. Hiking (⇨ *Wheeler Peak, in Hiking, above*), cross-country skiing, horseback riding, mountain biking, backpacking, trout fishing, boating, and wildflower viewing are among the popular activities here. The forest is home to big-game animals and many species of smaller animals and songbirds. For canyon climbing, head into the rocky Rio Grande Gorge. The best entry point into the gorge is at the Wild Rivers Recreation Area, north of Questa. You can drive into the forestland at various points along the Enchanted Circle via NM 522, NM 150, NM 38, and NM 578. Carson National Forest also has some of the best trout fishing in New Mexico, with several lakes rife with rainbow, brown, and native Rio Grande cutthroat trout.

The forest provides a wealth of camping opportunities, from organized campgrounds with restrooms and limited facilities to informal roadside campsites and sites that require backpacking in. If mountains, pines, and streams are your goal, stake out sites in Carson National Forest along the Rio Hondo or Red River; if you prefer high-desert country along the banks of the Rio Grande, consider Orilla Verde or Wild Rivers Recreation Area. Backcountry sites are free; others cost up to $7 per night.

If you're coming from a lower altitude, you should take time to acclimatize, and all hikers should follow basic safety procedures. Wind, cold, and wetness can occur any time of year, and the mountain climate produces sudden storms. Dress in layers and wear sturdy footwear; carry water, food, sunscreen, hat, sunglasses, and a first-aid kit. Contact the Carson National Forest's visitor center for maps, safety guidelines, camping information, and conditions (it's open weekdays 8 to 4:30). ⊠ *Forest Service Bldg., 208 Cruz Alta Rd., Taos* ☎ *575/758–6200* ⊕ *www.fs.fed.us/r3/carson.*

The Enchanted Circle Bike Tour takes place in mid-September. The rally loops through the entire 84-mi Enchanted Circle, revealing a brilliant blaze of fall color. In summer you can head up the mountainside via ski lifts in Red River and Angel Fire.

QUESTA
25 mi north of Taos via U.S. 64 to NM 522.

Literally a *questa* (hill) in the heart of the Sangre de Cristo Mountains, Questa is a quiet village nestled against the Red River and amid some of New Mexico's most striking mountain country. **St. Anthony's Church,** built of adobe with 5-foot-thick walls and viga ceilings, is on the main street. Questa's **Cabresto Lake,** in Carson National Forest, is about 8 mi from town. Follow NM 563 northeast to Forest Route 134, then 2 mi of a primitive road (134A)—you'll need a four-wheel-drive vehicle. You can trout fish and boat here from about June to October.

Although it's only a few miles west of Questa as the crow flies, you have to drive about 15 mi north of Questa via NM 522 to NM 378 to reach **Wild Rivers Recreation Area,** which offers hiking access to the dramatic confluence of two national wild and scenic rivers, the Rio Grande and Red River. There are some fairly easy and flat trails along the gorge's rim, including a ½-mi interpretive loop from the visitor center out to La Junta Point, which offers a nice view of the river. But the compelling reason to visit is a chance to hike down into the gorge and study the rivers up close, which entails hiking one of a couple of well-marked but steep trails down into the gorge, a descent of about 650 feet. It's not an especially strenuous trek, but many visitors come without sufficient water and stamina, have an easy time descending into the gorge, and then find it difficult to make it back up. There are also about 30 basic campsites, some along the rim and others along the river. ⊠ *NM 522, follow signed dirt road from hwy., Cerro* ☎ *575/586–1150 visitor center, 575/758–8851 BLM regional field office* ⊕ *www.blm.gov/nm/st/en.html* ⊡ *$3 per vehicle; camping $7 per vehicle* ☉ *Daily 6 am–10 pm; visitor center late May–early Sept., daily 9–6.*

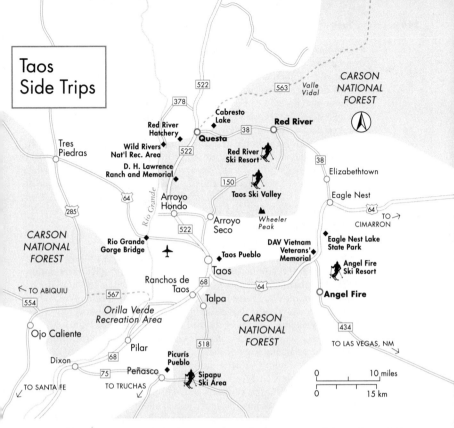

Taos Side Trips

CARSON NATIONAL FOREST

Red River

Questa

Cabresto Lake

Red River Hatchery

Wild Rivers Nat'l Rec. Area

D. H. Lawrence Ranch and Memorial

Tres Piedras

Arroyo Hondo

Rio Grande

Arroyo Seco

Wheeler Peak

Taos Ski Valley

Elizabethtown

Eagle Nest

TO CIMARRON

Eagle Nest Lake State Park

Angel Fire Ski Resort

Angel Fire

Rio Grande Gorge Bridge

Taos Pueblo

DAV Vietnam Veterans' Memorial

CARSON NATIONAL FOREST

Taos

Ranchos de Taos

Talpa

Orilla Verde Recreation Area

TO ABIQUIU

Ojo Caliente

Pilar

Picurís Pueblo

Peñasco

Sipapu Ski Area

CARSON NATIONAL FOREST

TO LAS VEGAS, NM

Dixon

TO SANTA FE

TO TRUCHAS

0   10 miles
0   15 km

NEED A BREAK? Good snacking options are a rarity on the first section of the Enchanted Circle, but the funky **Front Porch Cafe & Ice Cream Shop** (✉ 2322 S. NM 522 ☎ 575/586–1344) is a refreshing stop for coffee, sandwiches, ice cream, and other light treats. It's the perfect place to stock up on food before hiking at Wild Rivers Recreation Area.

At the **Red River Hatchery,** freshwater trout are raised to stock waters in Questa, Red River, Taos, Raton, and Las Vegas. You can feed them and learn how they're hatched, reared, stocked, and controlled. The visitor center has displays and exhibits, a fishing pond, and a machine that dispenses fish food. The self-guided tour can last anywhere from 20 minutes to more than an hour, depending on how enraptured you become. There's a picnic area and camping on the grounds. ✉ NM 522, 5 mi south of town ☎ 575/586–0222 ☜ Free ☉ Daily 8–5.

The influential and controversial English writer David Herbert Lawrence and his wife, Frieda, arrived in Taos at the invitation of Mabel Dodge Luhan, who collected famous writers and artists the way some people collect butterflies. Luhan provided them a place to live, Kiowa Ranch, on 160 acres in the mountains. Rustic and remote, it's now known as the **D. H. Lawrence Ranch and Memorial,** though Lawrence never actually owned it. Lawrence lived in Taos on and off for about 22 months during a three-year period between 1922 and 1925. He wrote his novel *The Plumed Serpent* (1926), as well as some of his finest short stories and poetry, while in Taos and on excursions to Mexico. The houses here, owned by the University of New Mexico, are not open to the public, but you can enter the small cabin where Dorothy Brett, the Lawrences' traveling companion, stayed. You can also visit the D.H. Lawrence Memorial, a short walk up Lobo Mountain. A white shed-like structure, it's simple and unimposing. The writer fell ill while in France and died in a sanatorium there in 1930. Five years later Frieda had Lawrence's body disinterred and cremated and brought his ashes back to Taos. Frieda Lawrence is buried, as was her wish, in front of the memorial. ⊠ *NM 522, follow signed dirt road from highway, San Cristobal* ☎ *575/776–2245* ▣ *Free* ☉ *Daily dawn–dusk.*

RED RIVER
12 mi east of Questa via NM 38.

Home of a major ski resort that has a particularly strong following with visitors from Oklahoma and the Texas panhandle, Red River (elevation 8,750 feet) came into being as a miners' boomtown in 1895, taking its name from the river whose mineral content gives it a rosy color. When the gold petered out, Red River died, only to be rediscovered in the 1920s by migrants escaping the dust storms in the Great Plains. An Old West flavor remains: Main Street shoot-outs, an authentic melodrama, and square dancing and two-stepping are among the diversions. Because of its many country dances and festivals, Red River is affectionately called "The New Mexico Home of the Texas Two-Step." The bustling little Downtown area contains souvenir shops and sportswear boutiques, casual steak and barbecue joints, and about 40 mostly family-oriented, midpriced to economical motels, lodges, and condos. There's good fishing to be had in the Red River itself, and excellent Alpine and Nordic skiing in the surrounding forest.

About 16 mi southeast of Red River, NM 38 leads to the small village of Eagle Nest, the home of **Eagle Nest Lake State Park** (⊠ *42 Marina Way, south of town* ☎ *575/377–1594* ⊕ *www.emnrd.state.nm.us* ▣ *$5* ☉ *Daily 6* AM–9 PM). This 2,400-acre lake is one of the state's top spots for kokanee salmon and rainbow trout fishing as well as a favorite venue for boating; there are two boat ramps on the lake's northwest side. You may also spy elk, bears, mule deer, and even reclusive mountain lions around this rippling body of water, which in winter is popular for snowmobiling and ice fishing. Camping is not permitted.

Thousands of acres of national forest surround rustic Eagle Nest, population 189, elevation 8,090 feet. The shops and other buildings here evoke New Mexico's mining heritage, while a 1950s-style diner, Kaw-Lija's, serves a memorable burger; you can also grab some takeout food in town and bring it to Eagle Nest Lake for a picnic.

WHERE TO EAT
$ ✕ **Sundance.** Always packed with skiers and winter-sports enthusiasts
MEXICAN   during the cooler months, Sundance is a worthy year-round option for huge portions of stick-to-your-ribs Tex-Mex and New Mexican cooking. You won't find any big surprises here, but the pork tamales

and chiles rellenos are both very good, as is the honey-chipotle-glazed barbecue pork tenderloin. If you like your chiles with heat, specify as much—seasoning is generally milder here than in Taos. There's a good beer list, and margaritas are made with agave wine. ✉ *401 High St.* ☎ *575/754–2971* ▭ *MC, V.*

$ ✕**Timbers Steakhouse.** This Wild West-inspired two-story restaurant on
AMERICAN Red River's main drag has a fanciful timber facade and serves best and most varied food in town—it's still tried-and-true American fare, but with high-quality ingredients and occasionally novel preparations. Beyond the excellent chicken-fried and bourbon-glazed steaks, consider breaded catfish with roasted-corn salsa, a first-rate meatloaf with a rich red wine–wild mushroom reduction, and a steak salad over mixed greens with marinated tomatoes and blue cheese. ✉ *402 W. Main St.,* ☎ *575/754–6242* ▭ *AE, D, MC, V* ⊙ *No lunch.*

WHERE TO STAY

$ 🏨 **Best Western Rivers Edge.** This reliable property in the center of
HOTEL Red River has ski-in, ski-out access and rooms equipped with sturdy lodge-inspired furnishings, flat-screen TVs, microwaves and refrigerators. Substantial renovations in 2010 greatly improved the lobby and common areas. As the name indicates, it's set right on the Red River. **Pros:** well-maintained; central location. **Cons:** it's pretty easy to hear noise from adjoining rooms. ✉ *301 W. River St.* ☎ *575/754–1766 or 877/600–9990* ⊕ *www.bestwesternnewmexico.com* ⊅ *30 rooms* ⌂ *In-room: a/c, kitchen (some), refrigerator, DVD (some), Wi-Fi. In-hotel: some pets allowed* ▭ *AE, D, DC, MC, V* ⋈ *CP.*

¢ 🏕 **Roadrunner RV Resort.** The Red River runs right through this woodsy mountain campground set on 25 rugged acres. There are two tennis courts and a video-game room. ✉ *1371 E. Main St., Box 588* ☎ *575/754–2286 or 800/243–2286* ⊕ *www.redrivernm.com/roadrunnerrv* ⌂ *Flush toilets, full hookups, drinking water, guest laundry, showers, picnic tables, electricity, public telephone, general store, play area, swimming (river)* ⊅ *141 RV sites, 2 cabins* ▭ *No credit cards* ⊙ *Closed mid-Sept.–Apr.*

SPORTS AND THE OUTDOORS

At the **Enchanted Forest Cross-Country Ski Area,** 24 mi of groomed trails loop from the warming hut, stocked with snacks and hot cocoa, through 600 acres of meadows and pines in Carson National Forest, 3 mi east of Red River. ✉ *417 W. Main St.* ☎ *575/754–6112* ⊕ *www.enchantedforestxc.com* ⊠ *$15* ⊙ *Late Nov.–Easter, weather permitting.*

The **Red River Ski Area** is in the middle of the historic gold-mining town of Red River, with lifts within walking distance of restaurants and hotels. Slopes for all levels of skiers make the area popular with families, and there's an extensive snowboarding park. There are 57 trails served by seven lifts, and the vertical drop is about 1,600 feet, with annual snowfall averaging about 215 inches. Red River has plenty of rental shops, plus quite a few accommodations and vacation rentals at the base of the slopes or nearby. The resort also books snowmobile tours, and has tubing ($12 per tube). In summer, tubing remains a popular activity on the slopes, along with mountain biking, hiking, disc golf, and chair rides to the top of the mountain. ✉ *400 Pioneer Rd., off NM*

38 ☎ *575/754–2223* ⊕ *www.redriverskiarea.com* ⊠ *Lift tickets $63* ☺ *Late Nov.–late Mar.*

ANGEL FIRE

30 mi south of Red River and 13 mi south of Eagle Nest via NM 38 and U.S. 64.

Named for its blazing sunrise and sunset colors by the Ute Indians who gathered here each autumn, Angel Fire is known these days primarily as a ski resort, generally rated the second best in the state after Taos. In summer there are arts and music events as well as hiking, river rafting, and ballooning. A prominent landmark along U.S. 64, just northeast of town, is the **DAV Vietnam Veterans Memorial** (⊕ *www.angelfirememorial. com*), a 50-foot-high wing-shaped monument built in 1971 by D. Victor Westphall, whose son David was killed in Vietnam.

WHERE TO STAY

$ ▦ **Angel Fire Resort.** The centerpiece of New Mexico's fastest growing and most highly acclaimed four-season sports resort, this mid-range hotel is set at the mountain's base, a stone's throw from the chairlift. Indeed, winter is the busiest season here, but during the warmer months it's a popular retreat with hikers, golfers, and other outdoorsy types who appreciate retiring each evening to spacious digs. Even the standard rooms are 500 square feet, and the larger deluxe units have feather pillows, ski-boot warmers, and fireplaces. The resort also manages a variety of privately owned and somewhat more upscale condo units, from studios to three-bedrooms, which are available nightly or long-term. There are several decent restaurants at the resort, none worth a drive to Angel Fire solely on the merit of their cuisine, but the Roasted Clove is quite good. **Pros:** slope-side location; fantastic views. **Cons:** rooms and public areas need updating. ⊠ *10 Miller La., Box Drawer B* ☎ *575/377–6401 or 800/633–7463* ⊕ *www.angelfireresort.com* ⇥ *139 rooms* ⚹ *In-room: refrigerator, Wi-Fi. In-hotel: 4 restaurants, bars, golf course, tennis courts, bicycles* ▭ *AE, D, MC, V.*

CAMPING

¢ ⛺ **Enchanted Moon Campground.** In Valle Escondido, off U.S. 64 near Angel Fire, this wooded area with a trout pond has views of the Sangre de Cristos. Features include horse stalls, a chuckwagon, and an indoor recreation area with video games. ⊠ *7 Valle Escondido Rd., Valle Escondido* ☎ *575/758–3338* ⊕ *www.emooncampground.com* ⚹ *Flush toilets, full hookups, drinking water, showers, grills, picnic tables, electricity, play area, Wi-Fi* ⇥ *27 RV sites, 22 tent sites* ▭ *No credit cards* ☺ *Closed mid-Oct.–Apr.*

NIGHTLIFE AND THE ARTS

Music from Angel Fire (☎ *575/377–3233 or 888/377–3300* ⊕ *www. musicfromangelfire.org*) is a nightly series of classical (and occasional jazz) concerts presented at venues around Angel Fire and Taos for about three weeks from late August to early September. Tickets cost $20 to $30 per concert, and the festival—begun in 1983—continues to grow in popularity and esteem each year.

SPORTS AND THE OUTDOORS

The 18-hole golf course at the **Angel Fire Country Club** (⊠ *Country Club Dr. off NM 434* ☎ *575/377–3055* ⊕ *www.angelfireresort.com*), one of the highest in the nation, is open May to mid-October, weather permitting. The challenging front 9 runs a bit longer than the back and takes in great views of aspen- and pine-shaded canyons; the shorter back 9 has more water play and somewhat tighter fairways. Greens fees are $65 to $85.

The beautifully maintained **Angel Fire Resort** is a popular ski destination that's not as acclaimed as Taos Ski Valley but has steadily developed cachet as one of the state's better venues. There are 74 runs (about half are intermediate, and a quarter each expert and beginner), five lifts, 16 mi of cross-country trails, and four terrain parks; the vertical drop is about 2,100 feet. Other amenities include a 1,000-foot snow-tubing hill, a ski and snowboard school, snow biking (also taught at the school), ice fishing, a children's ski-and-snowboard center, and superb snow-making capacity (annual snowfall averages about 215 inches). ⊠ *N. Angel Fire Rd., off NM 434* ☎ *575/377–6401 resort, 575/377–4222 snow conditions* ⊕ *www.angelfireresort.com* ☒ *Lift tickets $64* ☽ *Mid-Dec.–late Mar.*

Northwestern
New Mexico

WORD OF MOUTH

"If you are camping, you can spend the night at Chaco; there is no motel/hotel in the park. The closest lodging we have found is in Bloomfield, about a half an hour north of the road into Chaco, an hour or so from the park. Chaco is awesome so do go to it."

—emolloy

Updated by
Lynne Arany

When you catch a New Mexican glibly saying they are "on Indian time," they're referring to a certain relaxed approach to schedules and numbers that is simply part of the way of life in their home state. But once you leave the urban areas of Albuquerque or Santa Fe and start winding your way through the red canyons of the northwestern New Mexican desert, the phrase seems to take on a new significance.

The enormous, silent sweep of plateaus and sky really does seem to form a landscape that's impervious to time—one that conjures the spirits of those who lived here long before recorded history. As you stand on the edge of a sandstone cliff overlooking the San Juan River, walk through Pueblo Bonito in Chaco Canyon, or study the pattern of a handwoven Navajo rug, don't be surprised if you sense the presence of the ancient cultures that inhabited these places, and lived their lives based on the cycles of nature rather than the clock.

The countryside here has a stark and powerful beauty that has been recognized for centuries. The Anasazi people (whose name in Navajo means "Ancient Enemies") first built their cities and roads here more than 1,000 years ago. Today, the region is dominated by the Navajo in the northwest, and the Puebloan descendants of the Anasazi, who live closer to the Rio Grande. The two largest cities in the northwest today, Gallup and Farmington, are the legacy of even later arrivals—the traders, soldiers, homesteaders, and prospectors who made this area their home beginning in the 19th century. Today Gallup is a prime destination for Native American art and jewelry, and Farmington, at the crossroads of the entire Four Corners area, is a hub of energy exploration.

ORIENTATION AND PLANNING

GETTING ORIENTED

Broadly referred to as Indian Country, New Mexico's northwestern region is for most travelers a stop just after or before the Albuquerque, Santa Fe, and Taos regions. This beautiful high-desert area extends about two hours west from Albuquerque on Interstate 40 to Gallup and then the Arizona border, and four hours northwest to Farmington via U.S. 550. Many consider most of the region to be part of the Four Corners area. While drive times between stops may be long—and the roads can be rugged if you venture off the beaten path (as we recommend you do)—these lands will reward you with stunning natural settings of terrain, sky, and cloud; a diversity of cultures; a sense of the sacred; and a timeless sense of history.

Heading West on Route 66. The scent of smoldering piñon, the hypnotic chant of dancers, and the quiet intensity of ancient pueblos combine to

TOP REASONS TO GO

Chaco Canyon: Wander through the finely hewn sandstone ruins in Chaco Canyon and feel a mystic connection to Ancestral Puebloan cultures.

Route 66: Fugitive remnants of signage once brightly painted, now barely visible on a crumbling adobe building in Cubero; the old Puerco bridge; a lunch joint in Gallup—these are a few of the fascinating relics of historic Route 66 that await you.

Ancient Way Trail: The Ancient Way Trail of NM 53 compresses many of northwestern New Mexico's scenic wonders into one journey: Los Gigantes sandstone formations, ponderosa forest, El Malpais badlands, artisans along the trail—and then there's Zuni.

Bisti Badlands: Hoodoos and some of the strangest and most wonderful rock formations in the American Southwest can be found in this multicolored, crumbling landscape.

Acoma: This remarkably picturesque high-mesa landscape is the site of what many archaeologists agree is the oldest continually inhabited city in America.

make this stretch of the legendary highway a truly multisensory journey. Under vibrantly blue skies the pueblos of Laguna, Acoma, and Zuni follow one another as you head into Navajo territory, and remnants of Route 66's storied past (seen in storefronts and signage) punctuate the landscape.

The Four Corners Area. Traveling northwest on the four-lane curves of U.S. 550 through volcanic formations and sandstone striations instills a delicious sense of anticipation. Awaiting the intrepid traveler are monumental Ancestral Pueblo ruins, the surreal Bisti Badlands (for hoodoos and hiking), historic trading posts purveying Navajo silverwork and rugs, and a magical countryside that changes with every shift in light.

NORTHWESTERN NEW MEXICO PLANNER

WHEN TO GO

The best months to tour the Anasazi ruins are from April to early June and from late August to October, but there's no bad time. On rare occasions the roads to Chaco Canyon (or other back-roads locations, like El Malpais or the De-Na-Zin Wilderness area) are closed because of snow or mud in winter (though rain can make the roads extra slick in summer as well), and cold winds can make the going rough in late fall and early spring. The best seasons for attending Pueblo Indian dances are summer and fall, when harvest celebrations take place, and from Thanksgiving through early January. Late June through July are the hottest months, but by August afternoon thunderstorms, called monsoons, begin cooling things down. The trick, as elsewhere in the Southwest, is to simply slow down and relax, Zen-like, into the dry heat.

When visiting pueblos and reservations, you are expected to follow a certain etiquette (⇨ *"Pueblo Etiquette" box, in chapter 3*). Check the pueblos and monuments for dates of feast-day celebrations and fairs; some pueblos are open only on specific days.

GETTING HERE AND AROUND

AIR TRAVEL

Most major airlines provide service to the state's main airport in Albuquerque, 145 mi east of Gallup and 185 mi southeast of Farmington. Some regional carriers fly in and out of Four Corners Regional Airport in Farmington; Great Lakes Airlines flies directly from Denver and with connections from Phoenix, Las Vegas, and Ontario, California (not far from Los Angeles).

Air Contacts Four Corners Regional Airport (*FMN* ⊠ *1300 W. Navajo St., Farmington* ☎ *505/599–1100*). **Great Lakes Airlines** (☎ *800/554–5111* ⊕ *www.flygreatlakes.com*).

BUS TRAVEL

Greyhound (☎ *505/243–4435 or 800/231–2222* ⊕ *www.greyhound.com*) provides service to Grants, Gallup, Farmington, and other towns in northwestern New Mexico.

CAR TRAVEL

A car is your best bet for getting to and around the region. Interstate 40 heads due west from Albuquerque toward Arizona. U.S. 64 leads west from Taos into northwestern New Mexico and east from Arizona. U.S. 550 travels to the northwest from Interstate 25 (15 mi north of Albuquerque), intersecting with U.S. 64 at Bloomfield, 14 mi east of Farmington. Road conditions vary with the seasons. Winter can create snowy, icy roads; summer can bring ferocious thunderstorms, hailstorms, and flash-flood warnings. Any back-roads driving warrants a vehicle with high clearance. You can rent a car from Avis, Budget, or Hertz at the Farmington airport. Budget has an office at the Gallup airport; Enterprise has a location in town.

TRAIN TRAVEL

Amtrak (☎ *800/872–7245* ⊕ *www.amtrak.com*) has daily service between Gallup and Albuquerque, as well as service from Lamy, near Santa Fe, on the Southwest Chief. Taking a train into Gallup (sit in the Observation car) and renting a car there to explore western New Mexico is an alternative.

PLANNING YOUR TIME

This region covers an immense territory—give yourself five to seven days for a thorough exploration. Begin by heading west out of Albuquerque on Interstate 40, planning a night or two in western pueblo country, and then heading north toward Farmington for another night in the Four Corners Region. Allow most of a day for touring Chaco Canyon. On your way back to Albuquerque, take an hour or so to visit the Jémez area. If you're daunted by squeezing so much into a short period, remember that it's easy to visit Acoma, Laguna, and Grants at other times as day trips from Albuquerque or Santa Fe. Some tackle Chaco as a day trip from the Rio Grande Valley, but it's far more practical to spend the night closer by, if not in Cuba then in Bloomfield or Farmington, or even Grants or Gallup (the last two towns being relatively near Chaco's southern entrance). *See also the "Great Itineraries" feature, below.*

ABOUT THE RESTAURANTS

Fast-food and familiar franchise restaurants thrive in this region, but there are also lots of reputable homegrown establishments. The B&Bs here most often serve delicious, homemade breakfasts (and some serve equally tasty dinners). Western favorites like rib-eye steak and barbecue pork and chicken are common menu items, breakfast burritos are ubiquitous, and, as elsewhere in New Mexico, topping everything is red and green chile sauce, commonly referred to simply as "chile." *Vegetarians take note*: chile is often cooked with pork or beef, but many restaurants do offer a meatless version; always ask. Posole is another popular dish usually made with pork, but vegetarian versions do sometimes appear. Other local specialties include Navajo fry bread, which can be served plain, or topped with honey and powdered sugar, or taco-style with meat, beans, lettuce, and cheese; and mutton stew such as you would be served at a pueblo's feast day. Delicious bread and pies, baked in beehive-shaped outdoor *hornos* (ovens), are sold at roadside stands at some pueblos.

ABOUT THE HOTELS

Farmington, Grants, and Gallup are well supplied with chain motels; Cuba also has a couple of decent motels, but Bloomfield has the nicest chain options with relative proximity of Chaco Canyon. There are several appealing B&Bs in the region, including near El Morro on scenic NM 53 south of Grants, and in Farmington. Rooms can fill quickly in spring and fall when weather is ideal, but summer rodeos and other special events—such as the Gallup Inter-Tribal Indian Ceremonial—can also shut you out. Booking ahead in summer, especially for busy Farmington and Bloomfield, which are gateways to destinations in other Four Corner states, is a good idea.

WHAT IT COSTS					
	¢	$	$$	$$$	$$$$
Restaurants	under $10	$10–$15	$16–$22	$23–$30	over $30
Hotels	under $70	$70–$120	$121–$175	$176–$250	over $250

Restaurant prices are per person for a main course at dinner. Hotel prices are for two people in a standard double room in high season, excluding 5%–12% tax.

HEADING WEST ON ROUTE 66

Old Route 66 may be mostly subsumed by the interstate these days, but there are plenty of opportunities for drivers traveling west from Albuquerque to jump off Interstate 40 and explore the remaining sections of the Mother Road.

Drive due west past the historic Puerco River Bridge and the turnoff to the To'hajiilee (pronounced Toe-*hah*-jee-lay) Navajo reservation, and soon the red-rock bluffs loom. If you're lucky, you might catch a glimpse

GREAT ITINERARIES

IF YOU HAVE 2 OR 3 DAYS

The only way to tour this region adequately in two days is if you're incorporating your trip into a journey west into Arizona (via Gallup or Farmington), northwest into Utah (via Farmington), or north into Colorado (via Farmington). In three days, however, you can make a nice loop of the region's top sites: drive west from Albuquerque on Interstate 40, stopping in **Acoma Pueblo** before continuing west to **Gallup**. Spend the late afternoon shopping the old trading posts there, have dinner at Earl's, and stay overnight at the atmospheric **El Rancho**—or, if it's not too late, head south to spend the night in Zuni Pueblo at the special **Inn at Halona**. On Day 2, if you stayed in Gallup, head south on NM 602 to **Zuni**, take a tour of the Middle Village, then head east on NM 53 to **El Morro National Monument** and then **El Malpais**. If you've got a third day, spend the night at a refreshing forest hideaway, **Cimarron Rose Bed & Breakfast**, or at a chain property in **Grants**, then get up early and head north to spend as much time as you can manage in **Chaco Culture National Historical Park** before heading back (exiting via the north entrance) to **Albuquerque**.

IF YOU HAVE 5 TO 7 DAYS

In five to seven days you can get a real sense for the past and present of northwestern New Mexico. On Day 1, drive west on Interstate 40, pause at **Laguna Pueblo,** then continue on to **Acoma Pueblo,** then loop down along NM 53 for short hikes at **El Malpais** or the **Ice Cave and Bandera Crater,** or head to **El Morro National Monument.** Camp there or stay at a nearby B&B. On Day 2, dawdle on the **Ancient Way Trail,** detour to the **Wild Spirit Wolf Sanctuary,** then go on to explore **Zuni Pueblo.** Enjoy the afternoon of Day 3 in **Gallup** by strolling past the murals in historic Downtown, watching Indian dances, and staying at **El Rancho.** On Day 4, follow U.S. 491 (via Shiprock) to **Farmington** and visit some of New Mexico's oldest trading posts en route, or backtrack to NM 371, visiting the **Bisti Wilderness Area** along the way. Day 5 can take you to **Aztec Ruins National Monument, Salmon Ruins,** or **Navajo Lake.** Then plan to spend at least a day exploring **Chaco Culture National Historical Park** from your base in Farmington, and plan a stop at El Bruno's in **Cuba** on your way home.

of the Southwest Chief as it wends its way around the pueblo at Old Laguna on its daily run from Chicago to Los Angeles—this passenger train dates back to the early days and still makes stops in Gallup and Albuquerque. Secluded Acoma Pueblo is next, but not before you pass the remnants of an old Route 66 tourist outpost in Cubero.

Approaching Grants there's La Ventana Arch and El Malpais badlands, both to the south, to consider. And almost immediately after that little 66 hub, you can choose to stay on Interstate 40 and steamroll to Gallup and Navajo lands (or exit at Thoreau and head up to Chaco Canyon via its rougher south entrance), or drop down south onto the

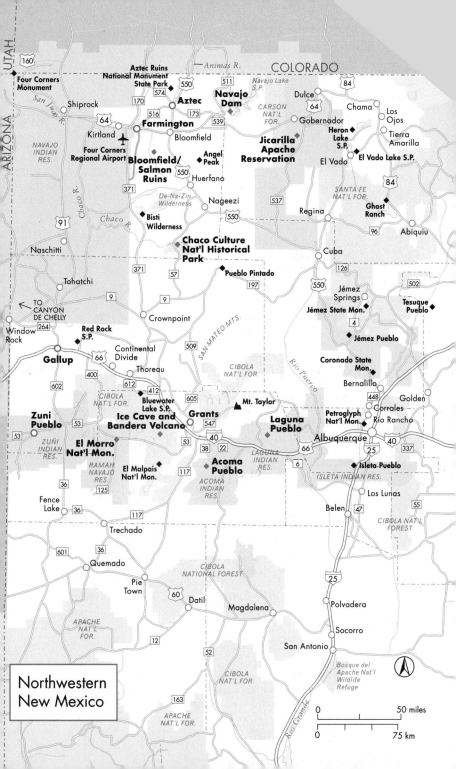

Northwestern
New Mexico

Ancient Way Trail (NM 53), and instead take this gorgeous loop route around—passing through El Morro and Zuni Pueblo on the way.

PUEBLO

46 mi west of Albuquerque on I–40 (Exit 114).

GETTING HERE

To get to Old Laguna, the largest of the six villages that comprise Laguna Pueblo, from Albuquerque, simply head west on Interstate 40 to Exit 114. The exit road looks as though it goes nowhere, but follow the signage directing you to NM 124; continue straight and within less than a mile, you'll wind up right in front of the bright white plaster facade of the San José de Laguna Church. From Grants take Interstate 40 33 mi east to Exit 114.

VISITOR INFORMATION

Laguna Pueblo (⌂ *Box 194, Laguna 87026* ☎ *505/552–6654* ⊕ *www. lagunapueblo.org).*

Laguna Pueblo actually comprises six villages, all traditionally Keres-speaking: Mesita, Seama, Encinal, Paraje, Laguna, and Paguate. (In 1953 one of the world's largest open-pit uranium mines, the Jackpile, began operation in Paguate, bringing with it income and health issues. The mine was shut down in 1982.) But visitors are especially drawn to **Old Laguna**, capped by the eye-catching white facade of San José de Laguna Church, which is visible from Interstate 40. The church, built in 1699, is a National Historic Landmark; its lovely hand-painted and embellished interior may be accessed by special permission. Occasionally—in front of the church or at the scenic overview just west of the Laguna exit—handcrafted silver jewelry and finely painted pottery embellished with Laguna polychrome motifs are available for purchase. The pueblo's villages enjoy many feast days, including St. Ann (July 26, Seama), Virgin Mary (September 8, Encinal), and St. Margaret Mary (October 17, Paraje). Most of the pueblo's residents (and the welcome public) gather at Old Laguna on September 19 to grandly honor St. Joseph with traditional dances; food and fine crafts abound. Feast day dances usually begin at 10 and continue through the afternoon. Except on feast days, visitors may not wander any of the villages unless with a tour. And with the exception of the view from outside the church at Old Laguna, photography is prohibited at all times. ⊠ *Old Laguna: Exit 114 from I–40* ☎ *505/552–6654 tribal office, 505/552–9330 church access, 505/331–6683 tours* ✆ *Church visits are free; fee for tours varies* ☉ *Church 8–3:30 (best to call ahead), village tours by appointment.*

ACOMA PUEBLO

63 mi west of Albuquerque on I–40 (Exit 102) and Indian Route 32/38 south.

GETTING HERE

From Albuquerque, take Interstate 40 west 48 mi to Exit 102. Follow the exit road toward Casa Blanca/Paraje but within 1/3 mi you'll see signs for Highway 22, where you turn left (south). Proceed just over

11 mi to Highway 38 and turn left for ½ mi to the Sky City Cultural Center. Highway 22 is a narrow rural road; although it is paved, you may become distracted by the dazzling scenery, so exercise special care.

VISITOR INFORMATION

Acoma–Sky City Cultural Center (⌖ Box 310, Acoma 87034 ☎ 505/552-6604 or 800/747-0181 ⊕ www.acomaskycity.org).

Fodor's Choice ★ Atop a 367-foot mesa that rises abruptly from the valley floor, **Acoma Pueblo**'s terraced, multistory, multiunit Sky City is like no other pueblo structure. It's one of the oldest continually inhabited spots in North America, with portions believed to be more than 1,500 years old. Captain Hernando de Alvarado, a member of Francisco Vásquez de Coronado's expedition of 1540, was the first European to see Acoma. He reported that he had "found a rock with a village on top, the strongest position ever seen in the world." The Spanish eventually conquered the Acoma people and brutally compelled them to build **San Estéban del Rey**, the immense adobe church that stands to this day. Native American laborers cut the massive vigas for the church's ceiling 30 mi away on Mt. Taylor and physically carried them back to the mesa.

5

About a dozen families live at the mesa-top pueblo full time, with most other Acomas living on Native American land nearby and returning only in summer and for celebrations, such as the feast day of St. Stephen (September 2), and Christmas mass (both are open to the public). Acoma's artisans are known for their thin-walled pottery, hand-painted with intricate black-and-white or polychrome geometrical patterns.

Once you park at the mesa base, plan to spend time in the superb **Haak'u Museum at the Sky City Cultural Center.** Changing exhibits explore traditional and contemporary arts, and are perfectly set in this modernist interpretation of traditional pueblo forms, with fine sandstone detailing and glass panels prepared to evoke historic mica windows. Visitation on the mesa top is by an hour-long guided tour; you're whisked by van up a steep road from behind the center and then led about the mesa community on foot (allow extra time if you choose to walk back down instead, via the ancient staircase carved into the side of the mesa). An Acoma guide will point out kivas, hornos, and unforgettable views toward their sacred sites of **Enchanted Mesa** and **Mt. Taylor,** and describe pueblo history in-depth, as well as direct you to artisan displays throughout the village. (Note: the terrain can be uneven; heeled shoes or flip-flops are not advised.) There's no electricity or running water in the village, but you can see cars parked outside many homes—one wonders what it must have been like to visit Acoma before the road was constructed in 1969. Open hours vary slightly, depending on the weather. Videotaping, sketching, and painting are prohibited, and a permit is required for still photography. Note that the pueblo prohibits photography of the church interior and exterior as well as the adjoining cemetery. As at all indigenous locales, ask permission before photographing residents or their artwork. Regroup back at Haak'u and browse the gallery gift shop and bookstore or enjoy blue-corn pancakes or a grilled chicken wrap with green-chile guacamole at the cozy **Y'aak'a (Corn) Café.** There is shuttle service available if you are staying at the **Sky City Hotel/Casino** (☎ 888/759–2489). Open hours are subject to tribal activities or weather conditions; it is best to check their online calendar or call ahead. ✉ *Indian Rte. 32/38, 16 mi south of I-40 Exit 102 ☎ 505/552–6604 or 800/747–0181* ⊕ *www. acomaskycity.org* ✉ *Pueblo tour $12, Haak'u Museum $4* ⊙ *Apr.–Oct., museum daily 9–6, Pueblo tours daily 9–5 (last full tour leaves at 4); Nov.–Mar., museum daily 9–5, tours daily 8–4. The café closes 1 hr before the museum.*

EN ROUTE

Traveling west on Interstate 40, along the south side of the freeway in the last 10 mi or so before you hit Grants, you'll catch your first glimpse of the stark, volcanic-rock-strewn **El Malpais National Monument and Conservation Area** (✉ *NM 117, 10 mi east of Grants; NM 53, 23 mi south of Grants* ☎ *505/287–7911 BLM* ☎ *505/783–4774 NPS* ⊕ *www.nps. gov/elma*). Take Exit 89, on the east edge of the flow, and travel south on NM 117 about 18 mi to La Ventana, New Mexico's largest natural arch. Before you get to that sandstone wonder, you might pull off at the Bureau of Land Management's (BLM) El Malpais Ranger Station (it's about 9 mi from the exit) for maps and information about the conservation area's miles of hiking trails; the nearby Sandstone Bluffs overlook offers a grand view across El Malpais ("the Badlands"). Alternatively, proceed into Grants, stopping at the comprehensive Northwest New Mexico Visitor Center (Exit 85 ☎ 505/876–2783) for maps and info, then continue west on Interstate 40 to Exit 81, then southwest on NM 53 to the monument area, which is administered by the National Park Service (NPS) and has an information center about 23 mi to the south. El Malpais is not much of an attraction for the just-passing-through visitor, but it's well worth spending a full day or two exploring the park in depth. Popular for hiking as well as caving in the miles of lava tubes—but it's best to venture forth with extremely sturdy soles and lots of water—its some 40 volcanoes dot 114,000 acres. (A quick snapshot of the volcanic landscape may be gained from the Ice Cave and Bandera Crater.) BLM's Joe Skeen Campground has 10 basic sites and a vault toilet; backcountry camping permits are available at the NPS visitor center, though camping is *very* primitive—no facilities exist.

GRANTS

34 mi west of Laguna Pueblo, 29 mi northwest of Acoma via NM 38 north and I-40 west.

The largest community on old Route 66 between Albuquerque and Gallup, little Grants has an intriguing museum and enough chain hotels and inexpensive restaurants to make it a fair base for exploring the eastern half of this region. The night skies here are said to be some of the clearest in the world, making it a worthwhile stop for stargazers. The seat of Cibola County, Grants started out as a farming and ranching center, grew into a rail transport hub, and boomed during the 1950s when uranium was discovered in the nearby mountains. The city has struggled since then to find its economic niche.

GETTING HERE

There are three Grants exits from Interstate 40; from east to west they are Exits 89, 85, and 81. They all feed onto the main drag in town, Santa Fe Avenue, which is also Historic U.S. Route 66. From Albuquerque, to arrive closest to the center of town and the Northwest NM Visitor Center, take Interstate 40 west for 77 mi to Exit 85. If you want to get off sooner, take Exit 89, which is also the turnoff to NM 117 and the eastern extent of El Malpais; if you miss either of these, Exit 81 is a short way past Exit 85 and is also the turnoff to Scenic Byway NM 53, and the western extent of El Malpais.

VISITOR INFORMATION

Grants/Cibola County Chamber of Commerce (✉ *100 N. Iron Ave.* ☎ *800/748–2142* ⊕ *www.grants.org*).

EXPLORING

In the center of sleepy downtown Grants, the small **New Mexico Mining Museum** shares quarters with the chamber of commerce right off the main drag, Santa Fe Avenue. On the ground level are charts, photos, gems, and minerals, and depictions of uranium-mining life in the region—this area is free. After paying admission, an elevator drops you down a few feet into the building's basement, where you can take a self-guided tour of an ersatz mine, and some real mining equipment and related exhibits. ✉ *100 N. Iron Ave.* ☎ *505/287–4802 or 800/748–2142* ⊕ *www.grants.org* 🖃 *Museum free, mine exhibit $3* ⊙ *Mon.–Sat. 9–4.*

Looming 11,301 feet above Grants to the northeast, **Mt. Taylor** is the highest peak in northwestern New Mexico. Its stark presence on the horizon gives a sense of why the mountain is considered sacred not just to the Acoma, but to the Zuni, Laguna, and Navajo as well. You can drive fairly far up the mountain for fine views and hop out to hike on marked trails. On the main road to the peak, about 10 mi northeast of Grants off NM 547 (Exit 85 from Interstate 40), Coal Mine (small fee) and Lobo Canyon (free) campgrounds, both at 7,400 feet elevation, offer first-come, first-served campsites (and restrooms, but no drinking water) amidst ponderosa pines. The campgrounds are closed September 30 through May 15; call the Cibola National Forest/Mt. Taylor Ranger District station (☎ *505/346–3900* ⊕ *www.fs.fed.us*) for information. The annual **Mt. Taylor Winter Quadrathlon** (☎ *505/287–4802 or 800/748–2142* ⊕ *www.mttaylorquad.org*) takes place in mid-February, when some 600 unbelievably fit athletes compete in a highly challenging bicycle, foot, ski, and snowshoe 42-mi race near the summit.

WHERE TO EAT

¢ ✕ **El Cafecito.** Nothing fancy is served here, just big helpings of tasty
NEW MEXICAN regional favorites like enchiladas, stuffed sopaipillas, burgers, and the breakfast of Southwest champions: huevos rancheros, smothered in chile of course. Kids are welcome and happily accommodated. ✉ *820 E. Santa Fe Ave.* ☎ *505/285–6229* 🖃 *MC, V* ⊙ *Closed Sun.*

AND BANDERA CRATER

25 mi southwest of Grants, 1 mi west of El Malpais on NM 53.

GETTING HERE

From Albuquerque, take Interstate 40 west 77 mi to Grants, Exit 81, then turn south onto NM 53. Proceed 25 mi, past the lava fields of El Malpais on the east side of the road; as NM 53 takes a distinct turn west, the Ice Cave signage appears.

Despite its unabashed commercialism (announced by its many somewhat-over-the-top, retro-style billboard advertisements), this roadside curiosity, set squarely on the Continental Divide, easily merits an hour of your time—the short trail from the 1930s trading post (now the gift shop) just off NM 53 affords unusual vistas of blackened lava fields and gnarled juniper and ponderosa stands. It's about a 20-minute moderately strenuous jaunt up to the 1,200-foot-diameter crater of **Bandera Volcano,** which last unleashed a torrent of lava 10,000 years ago. An even shorter walk leads to an old wooden staircase that descends 100 feet into the bowels of a collapsed lava tube, where the **Ice Cave** never rises above 31°F year-round and has a perpetual floor of blue-green ice. The ice remains year after year because of the combination of the air flow patterns in the lava tube and the insulating properties of the lava itself. ⊠ *NM 53, 12000 Ice Caves Rd.* ☎ *888/423–2283* ⊕ *www. icecaves.com* ⊠ *$10* ☉ *May–Aug., daily 8–6; hours vary rest of year, call ahead.*

EL MORRO NATIONAL MONUMENT

43 mi southwest of Grants and 36 mi east of Zuni Pueblo, via NM 53.

From Albuquerque, take Interstate 40 77 mi west to Grants, Exit 81, then turn south onto NM 53. Proceed 43 mi, past the lava fields of El Malpais on the east side of the road; as NM 53 takes a distinct turn west, follow it along and watch for the immense bluff that looms to the south.

EXPLORING

Fodor'sChoice ★ **El Morro National Monument.** When you see the imposing 200-foot-high sandstone bluff that served as a rest stop for Indians, explorers, soldiers, and pioneers, you can understand how El Morro ("the Headland") got its name. The bluff is the famous Inscription Rock, where wayfarers stopped to partake of a waterhole at its base and left behind messages, signatures, and petroglyphs carved into the soft sandstone. The paved Inscription Trail makes a quick ½-mi round-trip from the visitor center and passes that historic water source and numerous inscriptions. Although El Morro is justly renowned for Inscription Rock, try to allow an extra 90 minutes or so to venture along the spectacular, moderately strenuous 2-mi (round-trip) Headland Trail, which meanders past the excavated edge of an extensive field of late-13th-century pueblo ruins, cuts along the precarious rim of a deep box canyon, and affords panoramic views across the Zuni Mountains and El Malpais. The monument's compact museum chronicles 700 years of human history in this region. ⊠ *Visitor center: turnoff is on south side of NM 53*

☎ *505/783–4226* ⊕ *www.nps.gov/elmo* ✉ *$3 per person* ☉ *Late May–early Sept., daily 9–7; early Sept.–early Nov., daily 9–6; early Nov.–late May, daily 9–5. Trails close 1 hr before monument; summer rains and winter ice and snow may close them altogether. Call ahead.*

☺ **Wild Spirit Wolf Sanctuary.** The mystique of wolves is powerful and Wild Spirit is one of the few places where you can see them up close, in large enough enclosures that allow them to behave somewhat naturally. The staff at Wild Spirit are focused on educating the public about the dangers of trying to keep these animals, even hybrid wolf dogs, as pets. Camping is allowed on the premises, if you have a hankering to listen to wolf howls; it's primitive and only $15 a night. The gift shop also sells snacks; it closes after the last tour, about 4:30. The on-site Howling Wolf Grill offers hot food on limited days. ✉ *50 mi southwest of Grants, off NM 53* ✛ *Take NM 53 5 mi west of El Morro National Monument and turn south onto Rte. 125; follow Rte. 125 8 mi south (through Mountainview); turn right onto Rte. 120 (gravel); sanctuary is 4 mi on left* ☎ *505/775–3304* ⊕ *www.wildspiritwolfsanctuary.org* ✉ *$7; additional fee for up-close photo tours, make reservations for these 2 weeks ahead* ☉ *Tours Tues.–Sun. at 11, 12:30, 2, and 3:30; Howling Wolf Grill Thurs.–Sun., during tour times.*

5

WHERE TO EAT AND STAY

¢ 🏠 **Ancient Way Café/El Morro RV Park & Cabins.** This pleasant oasis is
CABINS made up of log-style cabins, a campground, and a café with a great front porch overlooking a gorgeous valley. The old-time wood-lined café serves homemade pies (apple–green-chile–piñon or tart cherry in season) breakfast, lunch, and dinner (the latter only Friday and Saturday nights, with a special-of-the-day menu that might feature apricot habanero ribs or vegetarian pasta with local goat cheese). This would be a find anywhere, but even more so out here on its culinary lonesome between Grants and Zuni on the beautiful Ancient Way Arts Trail. The cabins come in three sizes and provide adequate shelter with private baths, coffeemakers, and refrigerators, and camping (with full hook-ups and showers) is available for tents and RVs. **Pros:** ideal location right off the Trail of the Ancients. **Cons:** cabin decor ranges from '50s frowsy to quaint; no cooking in cabins. ✉ *NM 53, at mile marker 46, 1 mi east of El Morro National Monument* ☎ *505/783–4612* ⊕ *www. elmorro-nm.com* 🛏 *6 cabins* ♿ *In-room: Wi-Fi* ▤ *AE, DC, MC, V.*

$$ 🏠 **Cimarron Rose Bed & Breakfast.** Rustic Southwestern comfort is the
BED AND specialty of the house at this B&B on 20 ponderosa-pine-laden acres.
BREAKFAST Proprietor Sheri McWethy has created a "green" inn, with natural-
Fodor's Choice fiber sheets, no perfumes or dyes in the cleaning products, absolutely
★ no smoking allowed in rooms or anywhere on-site, and a conscientious approach to water use. But Cimarron is lush with amenities and atmosphere, from the discreet private patios and paths winding around the inspired gardens to the detail that makes each suite distinctive and cozy—this is a place you could hole up in and spend your days just wandering the grounds or hiking the nearby trails, or simply dipping into the B&B's library. Full breakfasts are delivered to your door each morning—banana-blue-corn pancakes (with real maple syrup) and Mexican hot chocolate are favorites—and special dietary requests are

accommodated with notice. Day packs and picnic baskets are supplied for those wanting to explore the area. Reservations are required. **Pros:** each accommodation is a suite (including a complete kitchen) with private entry, and a private patio; daily rates decrease for stays over two nights. **Cons:** guests heat up their precooked breakfasts in their rooms; not all pets allowed and an extra fee is charged if accepted. ✉ *689 Oso Ridge Rte. (NM 53), between mile markers 57 and 56* 🕾 *505/783–4770 or 800/856–5776* ⊕ *www.cimarronrose.com* ⇱ *3 suites* ⚷ *In-room: a/c, no phone, kitchen, DVD, no TV, Wi-Fi* ▭ *No credit cards* ❏ *BP.*

¢ ⚠ **El Morro National Monument.** The park has a primitive campground amid the trees ¼ mi from the visitor center. Tap water is turned off between approximately November and April; at those times camping is free. ✉ *NM 53* 🕾 *505/783–4226* ⊕ *www.nps.gov/elmo* ⚷ *Pit toilets, drinking water, picnic tables, public telephone* ⇱ *9 tent sites* ⚶ *Reservations not accepted.*

SHOPPING

Inscription Rock Trading & Coffee Co. (✉ *NM 53, at mile marker 46, 1 mi east of El Morro National Monument, Ramah* 🕾 *505/783–4706* ⊕ *www.inscriptionrocktrading.com*) sells crafts and art, including that of local Zuni artisans and other indigenous people far and wide. Stop by for a caffeine jolt or a fresh fruit smoothie, enjoy the pretty rock garden and the view from the hand-hewn porch, or time your visit to one of their special live music events in summer.

Old Schoolhouse Gallery (✉ *NM 53, at mile marker 46, 1 mi east of El Morro Nat'l Monument, Ramah* 🕾 *505/783–4710* ⊕ *www.elmorro-arts.org* ⊘ *Closed Tues. and Wed.*) is just that—the repurposed old El Morro School, its one-room building now painted brightly in deep orange, pink, and blue hues that draw in passersby. Inside, find changing exhibits (pottery, glass, prints), from a myriad of artful folks who have made the hidden nooks of this verdant area on the edge of the Zuni Mountains their home.

ZUNI PUEBLO

36 mi west of El Morro National Monument on NM 53; 42 mi southwest of Gallup on NM 602.

GETTING HERE

From Albuquerque, take Interstate 40 west 77 mi to Grants, Exit 81, then turn south onto NM 53. Proceed 79 mi into Zuni Pueblo. The Zuni Visitor & Arts Center is on the north side of NM 53, 8.5 mi west of where it intersects NM 602 (or 5.5 mi from alternative Highway 4), the road to Gallup. All visitors are requested to stop at the center for a helpful orientation.

VISITOR INFORMATION

Zuni Visitor & Arts Center (⌖ *1239 NM 53, Box 339, Zuni87327* 🕾 *505/782–7238* ⊕ *www.zunitourism.com or www.ashiwi.org*).

EXPLORING

Zuni Pueblo has been occupied continuously since at least the year 700, and its language—technically A:shiwi, as the Zunis refer to themselves—is unrelated to that of any other pueblo. Hawikku, a Zuni-speaking settlement (now a ruin) 12 mi south of the pueblo, was the first to come in contact with the Spaniards, in 1539. Francisco Vásquez de Coronado came here seeking one of the Seven Cities of Gold. He'd been tipped off by his guide, Estéban, who had seen the setting sun striking the walls of the dwellings and thought the multistoried villages were made of gold.

With a population of more than 10,000, Zuni Pueblo is the largest of New Mexico's 19 Indian pueblos. Zuni—or more correctly in the A:shiwi language, Halona Idiwan'a, or "Middle Place"—has a mix of buildings: modern ones in addition to old adobes, but what is most prevalent are beautifully hewn red-sandstone structures, some more than 100 years old. The artists and craftspeople here are renowned for their masterful stone inlay, Zuni "needlepoint" turquoise and silver jewelry, carved stone animal fetishes, polychrome pottery, and kachina figures. Weavings have become all but impossible to find as old weavers pass on and younger Zunis don't take up the craft, but it's fine work—now mostly seen in belts and sashes for personal use—and worth looking for if textiles are your passion.

The **Zuni Visitor & Arts Center,** where the helpful staff will tell you what your options are for exploring Zuni (and about any special events that might be going on), is also a tribally required stop before you begin to explore this most traditional of the New Mexico pueblos. It is here that you must inquire about photography permits and guidelines (cultural and religious activities are always off-limits). ⊠ *1239 NM 53, on north side of the road as you enter pueblo from east* ☎ *505/782–7238* ⊕ *www.zunitourism.com or www.ashiwi.org* ⊠ *Tours $10 to mission or Middle Village, $15 for both; artists' studios $75 for up to 4 people; Hawikku $50 for up to 2 people* ⊙ *Visitor center weekdays 8:30–5:30, Sat. 10–4, Sun. noon–4. Mission/Middle Village tours Mon.–Sat. at 10, 1, and 3; Sun. at 1 and 3; or by appointment. Closed on tribal holidays.*

The original **Our Lady of Guadalupe Mission,** built in 1629, was destroyed during the Pueblo Revolt of 1680 when Native Americans ousted the Spanish. In 1699 the mission was rebuilt, and in 1966 it was restored. A powerful series of murals by Alex Seowotewa depicting each of the Zuni kachinas now lines the interior walls; the aging adobe structure is again in need of restoration. Visits are by tour only, arranged through the Zuni Visitor & Arts Center. ⊠ *Middle Village* ☎ *505/782–7238* ⊠ *Tours $10* ⊙ *Tours Mon.–Sat. at 10, 1, and 3; Sun. at 1 and 3; hrs sometimes vary, call ahead.*

A:shiwi A:wan Museum and Heritage Center, which celebrates Zuni history and culture through a collection of Hawikku artifacts on loan from the Smithsonian, is housed in the historic Kelsey trading post. The museum's orientation is more toward engaging the community rather than outsiders, but there is much to see here. Historic Zuni pottery and contemporary work is also displayed, as well as documentation from the early-19th-century excavation at Hawikku and a beautiful mural depicting the A:shiwi peoples' emergence story, which starts at the Grand Canyon. ⊠ *02 E. Ojo Caliente Rd., at Pia Mesa Rd.; from NM 53 turn south at Pia Mesa Rd.* 🕾 *505/782–4403* ⊕ *www. ashiwi-museum.org* 🖃 *Donations accepted* ☉ *Weekdays 9–6.*

WHERE TO EAT AND STAY

$ ✕ **Chu Chu's Restaurant.** This locals' favorite is the best place for a full
ECLECTIC   meal (lunch or dinner) in town. It made its reputation on pizza, but now you can fuel up from a broader menu that includes blue corn enchiladas and other New Mexican fare. ⊠ *1344 NM 53, Zuni* 🕾 *505/782–2100* 🖃 *No credit cards.*

$ ▦ **The Inn at Halona.** Your only opportunity to stay right in the heart
Fodor's Choice   of Zuni, this cheery inn is decorated with handwoven rugs, fine Zuni
★   arts and crafts, and locally made furniture. Six of the rooms have private baths; two share a bath. Outside you can relax in the tree-shaded, enclosed, flagstone courtyard or walk the winding streets that surround Zuni's main plaza. Limited room service is available if you order ahead, or you may purchase ingredients at the tribe-staffed Halona Plaza market next door—which is also where Inn guests must go to check in—and prepare a meal in the communal kitchen. The breakfasts (think blue-corn pancakes, made from scratch) are not to be missed. Between the host (the owners come from a historic trading family), the staff, and the comfortable (if a little overstuffed) rooms laden with Indian blankets and pottery, this is a Southwestern standout. **Pros:** one-of-a-kind lodging experience. **Cons:** nearby dinner options are limited. ⊠ *23 Pia Mesa Rd.; from NM 53 turn south at Pia Mesa Rd.* ⑇ *Box 446, Zuni 87327* 🕾 *505/782–4547 or 800/752–3278* 🖷 *505/782–2155* ⊕ *www. halona.com* ➽ *8 rooms, 6 with bath* ⚲ *In-room: a/c, no TV. In-hotel: Wi-Fi hotspot* 🖃 *MC, V* ⑩ *BP.*

SHOPPING

Zuni has experienced an ebb and flow of local outlets for the fine wares of its heavily art-driven community. Art studio tours (⇨ *Zuni Visitor & Arts Center, in Exploring, above*) are another way to get to know more about individual artists and their craft—from fetishes to pottery and silver jewelry—and to see or buy the best. Authenticity, however, is not in question at the larger shops in town. **Zuni Craftsman's Coop** (⊠ *1177 W. NM 53, Zuni* 🕾 *505/782–4425*) specializes in Zuni-made fetishes and jewelry, and occasionally has good examples of their iconic polychrome pottery for sale as well. **Turquoise Village** (⊠ *1184 NM 53, Zuni* 🕾 *505/782–5521 or 800/748–2405* ⊕ *www.turquoisevillage. com*) offers the work of Zuni, Hopi, and Navajo artisans as well as the raw stone, shell, and silver with which much of the work is made. Some historic pieces, such as a 1930s Pima basket, are also sold here. **Pueblo Trading Post** (⊠ *1192 NM 53, Zuni* 🕾 *505/782–4545* ⊕ *www. pueblotradingzuni.com*) dates back "only" to 1980 but is housed in a 1920s carved sandstone building that was once a more traditional trading post and has earned a solid reputation for the quality of its silver and pottery, which is all made by Zuni, Navajo, and Hopi craftspeople from the surrounding region.

GALLUP

138 mi west of Albuquerque on I–40; 42 mi northeast of Zuni via NM 53 and NM 602; 54 mi northwest of El Morro via NM 53 and NM 602.

With a population mix of Navajo, Anglo, and Hispanic—plus a Mormon influence, a strong presence of other tribes, and a richly intertwined culture and history that reflects that mix—Gallup is a place like nowhere else. Known as both the Heart of Indian Country and the Indian Jewelry Capital of the World, with more than 100 trading posts that deal in Native American jewelry, pottery, rugs, and all manner of other arts and crafts, Gallup might just be the best place to acquire that concho belt or squash-blossom necklace you've always wanted. Prices are often better than those you can find in Santa Fe, and the selection is just short of overwhelming. Many of the Navajos, or Diné, selling their wares (and here to shop for more mundane goods themselves) have come in from Window Rock, Arizona, the Navajo Nation's capital, 25 mi northwest of town, or from less accessible rural spots on the surrounding reservation lands. The Navajo Veteran's Memorial Park and the Navajo Nation Museum, both in Window Rock, are an easy drive from Gallup.

Gallup originated in the 1880s as a coal-mining town, and the railroad that followed encouraged a boom. Long strings of freight cars still rumble along the tracks paralleling Historic Route 66, and train whistles hoot regularly. By the '30s, Gallup had become the lucky recipient of more WPA (Works Progress Administration) federal arts program projects than anywhere else in New Mexico; it had also become a fabled stop along Route 66. When you drive down its neon-illuminated main street today, you enter a retro world of pop-culture nostalgia.

GETTING HERE

From Albuquerque, Gallup is most directly reached via Interstate 40. The town stretches east–west for miles, and Gallup's exits start with Exit 26 and end with Exit 16, about 22 mi from the Arizona border. There is no chance of getting lost—all exits lead to Historic U.S. Route 66 (which is also known as NM 118 here), and the entire town may be accessed from this local strip. To reach Downtown Gallup most directly, take Exit 22 and turn left (west) onto Route 66/NM 118.

To reach Gallup from the south via NM 53, take NM 602 north 30 mi. If starting from the center of Zuni, it is an additional 12 mi east on NM 53 to NM 602; from El Morro it is an additional 24 mi west on NM 53 to NM 602.

VISITOR INFORMATION

Gallup Visitors Center (✉ *Gallup-McKinley County Chamber of Commerce, 103 W. Historic Rte. 66, Downtown* ☎ *505/722–2228 or 800/380–4989* ⊕ *www.gallupnm.org*) ; also houses a Navajo Code Talkers exhibit.

EXPLORING

The 12-block Downtown section bounded by Historic Route 66, 1st Street, Hill Avenue, and 4th Street is made for a walking tour. You can browse through the trading posts and get a fine glimpse of modern murals and 19th- and early-20th-century architecture, complete with

Buying Smart: Native Arts and Crafts

When you visit northwestern New Mexico, you'll have numerous opportunities to buy Native American arts, crafts, and souvenirs. But how can you be sure the pieces you buy are authentic? There's a lot of fake merchandise out there, and it's sold by Native Americans and non–Native Americans alike.

Although quality arts and crafts aren't necessarily expensive, if a price for a piece seems too good to be true, it probably is. Still, knowing what you're looking for—and most important, what questions to ask—can help you determine what's worth buying and what isn't. Here are some good rules of thumb:

Goods carrying the IACA (Indian Arts & Crafts Association) symbol are reliably authentic.

When buying jewelry, ask the vendor to tell you about the stones you're looking at and where they came from. The first thing to ask about turquoise is whether it is natural or not ("genuine" won't do—it does not confirm that the stone is its natural color, nor whether it has been treated in any other way). Ask if the turquoise is stabilized, from block, or injected. Hand-polished American turquoise (or Chinese, which is quite common these days and not generally considered a negative by fine artisans—unless it has been treated, of course) is more costly if it hasn't been stabilized or injected with dye to enhance the color, and is uniquely beautiful. Matrix, the brown or black veins in turquoise, is not a flaw, but it often provides clues as to the quality of the stone. Also ask if the jewelry settings, usually silver, are hand fabricated or precast; the former will be

more expensive. And while artists are currently creating quite a lot of very beautiful, clearly contemporary silverwork, be aware of a trend to re-create historic styles—while lovely in their own right, to the untrained eye, these can be difficult to distinguish from genuine period pieces.

If you're interested in pottery, start looking at the wares offered by the renowned potters at Acoma, although the Laguna and Zuni pueblos also have fine potters. Ask whether you're looking at "greenware," precast commercial ceramics that come ready for the artist to apply paint, or hand-coiled pottery. Hand-coiled pots start as coils of hand-gathered clay and are built from the bottom up; feel inside a pot for the telltale unevenness that distinguishes a hand-coiled pot. You can also ask what kind of paint and paintbrush was used to embellish the pottery; traditionally, black designs were rendered with boiled-down bee weed, and yucca-fiber brushes were used to apply it.

In the market for a rug? Beware of imported, foreign-made rugs with Navajo designs. These rugs may be nicely made, but they are entirely different from handwoven Navajo textiles. Authentic pieces usually have tags that identify the weaver; but you can also ask if the yarn is hand spun, hand dyed, and what types of dye were used (commercial or natural or both). A rug that is entirely hand processed will be the most expensive, but it will also be an heirloom. And before complaining about the $5,000 price of a Two Grey Hills rug, remember that it probably took several months to weave.

Pueblo Revival and and WPA details. West Coal Avenue, parallel to and one block south of Route 66, is the main culture strip.

The 1928 **El Morro Theatre** (✉ *207 W. Coal Ave.,Downtown* ☎ *505/726–0050* ⊕ *www.elmorrotheatre.com*) is a shining example of a unique regional building style, Pueblo Deco. El Morro tends to be open sporadically for events and the occasional film fest; on Saturdays it offers a kids matinee—call to find out what's on the schedule. Walk one block south of Route 66 to have a look (while the interior has been refurbished, only the exterior reflects its period glory).

The **Gallup Cultural Center,** a project of the Southwest Indian Foundation, is inside the restored 1918 Atchison, Topeka & Santa Fe Railway station. (A quintessential Fred Harvey House—architect Mary Colter's fabulous El Navajo hotel—was added on to the depot in 1923, but has long since been demolished.) Trains still run in and out of the station (this is where riders pick up Amtrak's historic Southwest Chief on its daily run). The cultural center includes a café (where you can lunch or sip coffee out of replicas of the china used on AT&SF trains), a gift shop that sells the work of Native American artisans (many local), and exhibits that reflect the art and history of area native peoples, westward expansion, and the building of the railroads. Stop to appreciate the statue of revered Navajo chief Manuelito, which stands witness as you enter. ✉ *201 E. Historic Rte. 66, Downtown* ☎ *505/863–4131* ⊕ *www. southwestindian.com* 💲 *Free* ⊙ *Late May–early Sept., weekdays 9–5; early Sept.–late May, weekdays 9–4.*

In summer, Indian dances take place nightly in the artful contemporary surround of the open plaza at the **McKinley County Courthouse and Courthouse Square.** Come in (after a security check) and tour the marvelous array of paintings and murals (by Lloyd Moylan, Gene Kloss, and other period luminaries) inside the lovely multistory 1938 Pueblo Revival court building—they're all products of the WPA federal arts project, even the courthouse itself. ✉ *207 W. Hill Ave., Downtown* ☎ *505/722–2228 info on dances, 505/863–1400 courthouse* ⊕ *www. thegallupchamber.com* 💲 *Free* ⊙ *Murals and other WPA art weekdays 8–5; dances late May–early Sept., daily at 7–8* PM.

Navajo Nation Museum. Here you'll find a complete authentic hogan, as well as small and changing exhibits that explore the culture and history of the tribe. ✉ *Loop Rd. at NM/AZ 264, ¼ mi west of Arizona border (26 mi northwest of Gallup), Window Rock, AZ* ☎ *928/871–7941* ⊕ *www.navajonationmuseum.org* 💲 *Free* ⊙ *Apr.–Oct., Mon. 8–5, Tues.–Fri. 8–7, Sat. 9–5; Nov.–Sept., Mon. 8–5, Tues.–Fri. 8–6, Sat. 9–5.*

The **Octavia Fellin Library,** across the street from the McKinley County Courthouse, further rewards fans of the WPA arts project, with finely crafted woodwork and numerous paintings by Harrison Begay, Allan Houser, and other artists of their caliber casually decorating its walls. ✉ *115 W. Hill Ave., Downtown* ☎ *505/863–1291* 💲 *Free* ⊙ *Mon.–Thurs. 9–8, Fri. 10–6, Sat. 9–6.*

In spring, summer, and early fall, wildflowers add brilliance to the landscape of **Red Rock Park,** which has two popular hiking trails (the 3-mi Pyramid Rock Trail, connecting to the 3½-mi Church Rock Trail, hits an elevation of almost 8,000 feet, and has knockout views of the surrounding red-sandstone formation), campgrounds, and a museum. The park's red-rock amphitheater holds the ever-growing **Gallup Inter-Tribal Indian Ceremonial** (☎ *505/863–3896*), Gallup's premier event since it began in 1922. Over the course of four or five days every August some 50,000 people come to see the dances of more than 50 tribes from across the Americas, watch rodeo events and parades, munch on fry bread, and stroll the native-arts marketplaces. In early December the park hosts the Red Rock **Balloon Rally** (☎ *505/722–2228 or 800/380–4989 ⊕ www.redrockballoonrally.com*) ; although it's smaller in scale than Albuquerque's international extravaganza, some 200 balloons ascending amid the smooth-faced sandstone cliffs makes this one special. The **Red Rock Museum** contains well-mounted exhibits of jewelry, pottery, rugs, architecture, and tools of the Anasazi, Zuni, Hopi, and Navajo, as well as native plantings. ⊠ *NM 566, Exit 26 or 31 from I–40, 7 mi east of Gallup, Church Rock* ☎ *505/722–3839* ⊒ *Park free, museum $1 suggested donation* ⊙ *Park 24 hrs; museum weekdays 8–5, but hrs can vary, so call ahead.*

Clothing, furniture, tools, and typewriters are among the artifacts of the coal-mining era on display at the **Rex Museum,** operated by the Gallup Historical Society inside the former Rex Hotel, a vintage 1900 building with a history of its own. ⊠ *300 W. Historic Rte. 66, Downtown* ☎ *505/863–1363* ⊒ *$2* ⊙ *Weekdays (and some Sat.) 9–3:30, but hrs can vary—call ahead.*

Window Rock Monument & Navajo Veteran's Memorial Park, at the base of an immense, red-sandstone, natural arch—truly a window onto the Navajo landscape—is a compelling exhibit dedicated to all Navajo war veterans, but in particular to the Code Talkers of World War II. Designed in the shape of a sacred Medicine Wheel, the spiritual aspect of this profound memorial is apparent to all. ⊠ *Rte. 12 at NM/AZ 264, ¼ mi west of Arizona border (23 mi northwest of Gallup), Window Rock, AZ* ☎ *928/871–6647 general, 928/871–6417 guided tours* ⊕ *http:// navajonationparks.org* ⊒ *Free* ⊙ *Daily 8–5.*

OFF THE BEATEN PATH

Canyon de Chelly National Monument. Ninety-eight miles northwest of Gallup and situated in the heart of the Navajo Nation, Canyon de Chelly—pronounced de-*shay*—is well worth the drive and a day of exploring. Amid its fascinating Anasazi ruins tucked high into alcoves in the red canyon walls—and spectacular formations like Spider Rock—Diné (Navajo) residents farm and raise sheep on the canyon floor. The visitor center and museum are open all year, and from there, or at nearby Thunderbird Lodge (☎ *928/674–5841 or 800 679–2473* ⊕ *www.tbirdlodge.com*) you can book tours on the canyon bottom—by vehicle or, even more memorably, by horseback—with Navajo guides, or drive the canyon rim and take the self-guided 6-mi hike on White House Trail. A guide will cost about $40 per hour, per vehicle ($15 per hour on horseback), and is well worth hiring if your budget allows. Campgrounds and a couple of chain lodgings are in Chinle; there is also a campground at the monument visitor center. ⊠ *NM/AZ 264 west (through Window Rock), then north on U.S. 191 30 mi, Chinle, AZ* ☎ *928/674–5500* ⊕ *www.nps.gov/cach* ⊒ *Free* ⊙ *Daily 8–5.*

Sixty-three miles west of Gallup and en route to Canyon de Chelly, **Hubbell Trading Post,** in operation since 1878, is still an active purveyor of food staples, clothes, and Navajo rugs, much as it was when John Lorenzo Hubbell was running it (the National Park Service runs it now). With its creaking wood floors, dim lighting, and goods hanging from the rafters, Hubbell provides a palpable sense of what a post was like back in the day; the tours of the Hubbell homestead, complete with original decor intact, offer a glimpse into period home life of a trader of means (who had access to the best Native American handwork). ⊠ *NM/AZ 264, 1 mi west of U.S. 191S, Ganado, AZ* ☎ *928/755–3475* ⊕ *www.nps.gov/hutr* 🖾 *Trading post free, Hubbell home tours $2* ⊘ *Late Apr.–early Sept., daily 8–6 (store 9–6); early Sept.–late Apr., daily 8–5 (store 9–5).*

WHERE TO EAT AND STAY

$$
AMERICAN

✕ **Coal Street Pub.** There are plenty of bars in this town, for sure, but this is a friendly, relaxed pub, locally owned by the Chavez family. A good selection of microbrews is backed up with pub standards like burgers, bratwurst, steaks, salads, fish, and crispy, gooey appetizers. There's live music Tuesday through Saturday evenings. ⊠ *303 W. Coal Ave., Downtown* ☎ *505/722–0117* ⊕ *www.coalstreetpub.com* ⊟ *MC, V* ⊘ *Closed Sun.*

¢
SOUTHWESTERN
★

✕ **Earl's Restaurant.** If you have time for only one meal in Gallup, do as most people do and head to Earl's. The home-style rib-sticking daily specials here include meat loaf and chicken-fried steak, pie, bottomless coffee, and the oversize servings you would expect. Though not in its original location, Earl's has been a family-run institution in the area since 1947. This is a classic diner, grand-scale and Southwestern style, down to the Naugahyde booths and the Western Americana objects hanging on the walls. It's a custom here for Native American jewelry vendors to go table to table displaying their wares. Simply say "No, thank you" if you're not interested and the vendor will leave. ⊠ *1400 E. Historic Rte. 66, Gallup* ☎ *505/863–4201* ⊟ *AE, D, DC, MC, V* ⊘ *No dinner Sun.*

¢
NEW MEXICAN

✕ **El Sombrero.** Open daily, and serving fine traditional New Mexican–style enchiladas and the like, El Sombrero is the cozy alternative to Earl's. ⊠ *1201 W. Historic Rte. 66, Gallup* ☎ *505/863–4554* ⚑ *Reservations not accepted* ⊟ *AE, MC, V* ⊘ *Closed Sun.*

$
HOTEL

🏨 **Comfort Suites.** Everyone from rodeo riders to mining industry suits to mountain-biking tourists stays at this east-side chain property that opened in 2009. High ceilings, a warm taupe and burnt-red color scheme, big flat screens, a cozy couch nook, refrigerators and microwaves in every room, and tea and coffee in the lobby help make this reliable chain outpost appealing. **Pros:** good work desks in the rooms. **Cons:** pool closes at 9 pm; some noise and light from the parking lot. ⊠ *3940 E. U.S. Rte. 66, off I-40 at Exit 26, Gallup* ☎ *505/863–3445 or 800/424–6423* ⊕ *www.choicehotels.com/hotel/nm131* 🛏 *66 rooms* ⚘ *In-room: a/c, refrigerator, DVD (some), Wi-Fi. In-hotel: pool, gym, laundry facilities, laundry service, Internet terminal, parking (free), some pets allowed* ⊟ *AE, D, DC, MC, V* 🍽 *BP.*

5

$ **El Rancho.** For a combination of aging '50s-era nostalgia and Old
HOTEL   West glamour, book a night in El Rancho's Katharine Hepburn or Ron-
Fodor's Choice   ald Reagan room. All units at this 1937 National Register historic
★   property are named for vintage movie stars, many of whom stayed here
back when Hollywood Westerns were shot in the region (the connection goes deeper—El Rancho was built by R.E. Griffith, D.W. Griffith's
brother). Rooms are basic, accented with Western prints and a few other
flourishes. The restaurant ($), open all day, is cozy and serves acceptable
American and Mexican food. You can browse through the on-site shop
for pottery, kachinas, and sand paintings. **Pros:** gorgeously appointed
Western-rustic lobby; at Christmas the lights—and two-story tree—are
a serious throwback, and an assuredly warming sight. **Cons:** rooms
do vary—don't be shy about asking to see a few; no reason to stay in
the attached motel portion of the complex. ✉ *1000 E. Historic Rte.
66,Gallup* ☎ *505/863–9311 or 800/543–6351* ⊕ *www.elranchohotel.
com* ↪ *73 rooms, 3 suites* ☖ *In-room: a/c, Wi-Fi. In-hotel: restaurant,
bar, pool, Wi-Fi hotspot* ⊟ *AE, D, MC, V.*

CAMPING

¢   ⛰ **Red Rock Park.** Red-sandstone formations loom 500 feet over the
park's paved campsites, which are surrounded by red sand and shady
trees. ✉ *NM 566, off I–40 at Exit 26 or 31, 7 mi east of Gallup, Church
Rock* ☎ *505/722–3839* ☖ *Flush toilets, partial hookups, dump station,
drinking water, showers, fire pits, picnic tables, public telephone, ranger
station* ↪ *160 sites* ⊟ *MC, V.*

SHOPPING

As elsewhere, you should be careful when buying Native American jewelry or rugs in Gallup. Generally, if a deal seems too good to be true, it
is. To assure yourself of authenticity and quality, shop at a reputable,
established dealer and ask lots of questions *(⇨ "Buying Smart: Native
Arts and Crafts," above).*

City Electric (✉ *230 W. Coal Ave., Downtown* ☎ *505/863–5252* ⊕ *www.
cityelectricshoe.com*) is a shoe shop Gallup-style, and is definitely worth
a poke around. This purveyor of moccasins, cowboy boots, belts, and
cowboy hats also repairs saddles and shoes and sells leather and fittings
for your own work. This corner shop with a Pueblo Deco facade was
founded by an Italian immigrant in 1924. It has stayed in the Bonaguidi
family ever since.

Coming up from Zuni on NM 602, travelers will come upon **Ellis Tanner Trading Co.** (✉ *1980 NM 602, at Nizhoni Blvd., on the south side of
town; take I–40 Exit 20* ☎ *505/863–4434 or 800/469–4434* ⊕ *www.
etanner.com*), a venerable fourth-generation family operation. **Perry Null
Trading Co.** (✉ *1710 S. 2nd St., on the south side of town; take I–40
Exit 22* ☎ *505/863–5249* ⊕ *http://perrynulltrading.com*) bought out
the 80-year-old Tobe Turpen post in 2005; Perry Null, himself a trader
since the 1970s, continues to sell kachinas, sand paintings, jewelry,
folk art, and more. At **Richardson's Trading Co.** (✉ *222 W. Historic Rte.
66, Downtown* ☎ *505/722–4762* ⊕ *www.richardsontrading.com*), the
great-granddaddy of trading posts, the wooden floors creak under your
feet as you gawk at the knockout array of Navajo and Zuni turquoise

and silver earrings, squash blossoms, concho belts, bracelets, natural-dye handwoven rugs, and beadwork. Richardson's is also a veritable museum of old pawn (the often valuable, unclaimed items pawned by local Native Americans). Another branch of the Tanner trading family runs **Shush Yaz Trading Co.** (⊠ *1304 W. Lincoln Ave., off U.S. 491 just north of I–40 Exit 20* ☎ *505/722–0130* ⊕ *www.shushyaz.com*), which stocks all manner of Native American arts and crafts, including locally made Navajo squaw skirts. The store sells traditional and contemporary jewelry and is a great source of old pawn. The on-site restaurant serves native foods.

EN ROUTE
The drive north toward Shiprock and Farmington on U.S. 491 provides the perfect opportunity to experience two history-laden trading posts that carry on a tradition of bartering that dates back many generations. With intricate geometric designs rendered by master Navajo weavers with hand-spun yarn from local Churro sheep (keeping the natural palette to grays and browns, plus black and white, often to dramatic effect), the works created in this area are known for their unusually tight weave.

Two Grey Hills Trading Post. The fine rugs at this trading post, established in 1897, share space with a variety pack of convenience store goods. ⊠ *Hwy. 19, off U.S. 491, near Newcomb, 59 mi north of Gallup on U.S. 491, then west on Hwy. 19, Toadlena* ☎ *505/789–3270* ⊕ *www.twogreyhills.com* ⊘ *Closed Sun.*

Toadlena Trading Post & Museum. Opened in 1909, Toadlena operates much like the local shop it's always been—and trading goes on daily. A difference now is that its current owner, Mark Winter, has created a small museum that dazzles with its rare early-20th-century rugs and blankets. ⊠ *Hwy. 19, off U.S. 491, near Newcomb, 59 mi north of Gallup on U.S. 491, then west on Hwy. 19, Toadlena* ☎ *505/789–8745 or 888/420–0005* ⊕ *www.toadlenatradingpost.com* ⊘ *Closed Sun.*

SPORTS AND THE OUTDOORS

In addition to its panoramic Pyramid Rock and Church Rock trails at Red Rock Park (⇨ *Red Rock Park, in Exploring, above*), Gallup is a growing resource for mountain bikers, hikers, and rock climbers. The **High Desert Trail System**—a highly competitive 26 mi of stacked loop—begins at Gamerco, a former coal town just north of Gallup, and courses from east to west offer increasingly difficult terrain along a single track. ⊠ *East trailhead 3 mi north of Gallup off U.S. 491* ⊕ *www.galluptrails2010.com.*

The **Mentmore Rock Climbing Area** challenges even the nonvertiginous with bolted top-rope and sports climbs that range from 25 to 45 vertical feet. ⊠ *Mentmore Rd., on the far west end of Gallup, ½ mi west of I–40 Exit 16* ⊕ *www.galluptrails2010.com.*

THE FOUR CORNERS AREA

To gain a sense of the beauty, power, and complexity of the ancient civilizations of the Americas, you can do no better than to travel to Chaco Canyon and the more accessible Salmon Ruins and Aztec Ruins.

Discoveries of the past 30 or 40 years have increased interest in ancient roadways and archaeoastronomy, the study of the ways in which ancient peoples surveyed the skies, kept track of the movement of the planets and stars, and marked their passage within the construction of elaborate stone structures. And it is likely that if you are up this way, you already have it in mind to visit Mesa Verde, in nearby southern Colorado, or Canyon de Chelly (Arizona) in addition to these New Mexico sites.

But the Four Corners region is more than the Ancestral Puebloan ruins of the 12th and 13th centuries. The Navajo Nation covers much of the western portion of the area; the Jicarilla Apache Nation is on the east, and the Ute Mountain reservation is to the north. Near the trout-fishing mecca of Navajo Dam, the Gobernador area, with its striking sandstone formations, is also home to a host of Navajo, or Dinetah, pueblitos which date back to the late 17th and 18th centuries. And everywhere, spectacular hiking, biking, camping, and fishing can be had, along with the opportunity to poke through small towns that are the products of northwestern New Mexico's homesteading era. The best shopping is for antiques, Navajo rugs, and Native American jewelry and pottery.

VISITOR INFORMATION

Indian Country/NM Tourism (⊕ *www.indiancountrynm.org*).

Navajo Nation Tourism Department (⌂ *Box 663, Window Rock, AZ86515* ☎ *928/871–6436 or 928/810–8501* ⊕ *www.discovernavajo.com).*

FARMINGTON

182 mi northwest of Albuquerque via U.S. 550 and U.S. 64; 113 mi northeast of Gallup via U.S. 491 and U.S. 64 or 136 mi northeast of Gallup via I–40 and NM 371.

A rough-and-tumble, unpretentious town full of pickup trucks whose radio dials are programmed with country-and-western stations, Farmington sits in the heart of the Four Corners region (so called because four different states intersect here at one point). Archaeological, recreational, and scenic wonders are within easy driving distance, and its reasonable prices and friendly ways make it an ideal base for exploring the area. (Farmington is also big for the energy biz and major summertime events like the Connie Mack World Series and the National High School Rodeo finals; book ahead accordingly.)

The Navajo gave the name Totah ("Among the Waters") to the land around what is now Farmington, which lies at the confluence of three rivers—the Animas, La Plata, and San Juan. For travelers and locals the presence of these flowing waters gives welcome respite from the surrounding region's dry mesas. Homesteaders began planting farms and orchards on the fertile land in 1879, and the "farming town" eventually became Farmington.

The agricultural economy shifted to one based on oil and gas in the early 1920s, beginning a boom-and-bust cycle tied to the fluctuation of fuel prices. Diversification didn't come until the past decade or so, when Farmington began promoting its historic past with more gusto. Even more revitalizing overall—though it's had a mixed effect on the fortunes of the historic Downtown—was the creation of a regional shopping center, which swells the population by thousands on weekends. People from miles around make their weekly or monthly trip to town to stock up on supplies.

GETTING HERE

To get to Farmington from Albuquerque, take Interstate 25 north 17 mi to Bernalillo Exit 242 (NM 165/U.S. 550). Follow U.S. 550 (older maps may call this NM 44), 150 mi northwest to Bloomfield, then turn west on U.S. 64 and continue 15 mi into Farmington.

From Gallup, travelers may go via U.S. 491 or NM 371. The U.S. 491 route passes through historic trading post territory and is more scenic and about 20 mi shorter; NM 371 is the way to go if Chaco Canyon or the Bisti Badlands are on your agenda. Via U.S. 491 (older maps may call this NM 666): In Gallup, take U.S. 491 north from Interstate 40 Exit 20, and proceed 85 mi to Shiprock, then turn right (east) on U.S. 64 and continue 28 mi into Farmington. Via U.S. 371: Take Interstate 40 east 30 mi to Exit 53 (Thoreau), then take NM 371 north 106 mi. Both routes are highlights of the designated scenic byway, Trail of the Ancients.

VISITOR INFORMATION

Farmington Convention and Visitors Bureau (⊠ 3041 E. Main St. ☎ 505/326–7602 or 800/448–1240 ⊕ www.farmingtonnm.org).

EXPLORING

The **Bolack Electromechanical Museum** is the legacy of former state governor Tom Bolack, who collected wildlife of the taxidermic kind. His son Tommy carries on the collecting tradition, but his museum on the family's B-Square Ranch is a wonder of large-scale, unexpected, electrical items, from aged radio-station transmitters and all the car speakers from the old Rincon Drive-In in Aztec, to a three-stage compressor from a Nevada uranium testing site, a 16-foot-diameter drill bit, and an entire electrical substation. Set back into the bluffs on the south side of town, the spread itself is a sight even if all the objects here don't appeal. Keep an eye out for the peacocks on the road in. Note that you must stop and register at the first buildings you see. ⊠ 3901 Bloomfield Hwy. (U.S. 64) ☎ 505/325–4275 ⊕ www.bolackmuseums.com ☑ Free ☻ By appointment only; 1- to 2-hour guided tours Mon.–Sat. 9–3.

If the kids need some indoor fun, try stopping by the **E3 Children's Museum & Science Center.** The interactive exhibits here include a shadow room, a magnet table, giant floor puzzles, and a role-play area. It's a low-key spot for the younger set to rest and regroup. ⊠ 302 N. Orchard Ave. ☎ 505/599–1425 ⊕ www.farmingtonmuseum.org ☑ Free ☻ Tues.–Sat. 10–5.

You can get an inkling of what the Four Corners area was like during the trading-post days at the **Farmington Museum,** in a modern sandstone building whose stonework is fashioned to echo that found at Aztec and Chaco ruins, and that also houses the Farmington visitor center. Landscaped grounds behind the building extend down to the Animas River—an ideal spot for a picnic. The museum presents art, science, Native American, and regional history exhibits throughout the year (the "Geovator," goofy as it is, simulates a trip deep into the subsurface

BISTI BADLANDS

Dinosaurs roamed the **Bisti Badlands Wilderness areas** when they were part of a shallow sea some 70 million years ago. Hoodoos (mushroom-shaped rock formations in subtle shades of brown, gray, and white) lend the 45,000 acres an eerie, lunar appearance. De-Na-Zin (pronounced duh-*nah*-zen and named for a petroglyph found nearby) is the much larger and less visited of the two sections, and here you can find hillier and more challenging terrain, plus numerous fossils and petrified logs. At Bisti (pronounced *biss*-tye), you can encounter deeply eroded hoodoos whose striations represent layers of sandstone, shale, mudstone, coal, and silt. In many spots you'll climb over mounds of crumbly clay and silt that look a bit like the topping of a coffee cake (but gray). Both sections are ideal for photography, and backcountry camping is permitted—and not to be missed during a full moon, if your timing is good.

The Bureau of Land Management (BLM), which administers the land, stipulates that you remove nothing from either area, preserving its magical appearance for those who follow. The most fascinating terrain is 2 to 3 mi from the parking areas, and there are no trails (or water facilities), so bring a compass and be alert about your surroundings and where you are in relation to the sun—it's relatively easy to get lost in this vast, incredible place. And how 'bout bringing some more water? ✛ *Bisti: 36 mi south of Farmington on NM 371, then 2 mi east on Hwy. 7297 (gravel); De-Na-Zin: unpaved CR 7500, off either NM 371 8 mi south of Bisti entrance or U.S. 550 at Huerfano, 34 mi south of Bloomfield. Roads can be impassable in wet weather, and high-clearance vehicles are advised in all conditions. Contact the BLM Field Office in Farmington for complete information* ☎ *505/599–8900* ⊕ *www.blm.gov.*

stratigraphy of limestone, sandstone, and shale that yields oil and natural gas wealth for the region). Occasionally a traveling exhibit will require an entrance fee; otherwise, admission is free. There's a summertime evening music series on the terrace; call for dates and performers. ⊠ *Farmington Convention and Visitors Bureau, 3041 E. Main St., at Gateway Park* ☎ *505/599–1174* 🖃 *$2 suggested donation* ⊙ *Mon.–Sat. 8–5* ⊕ *www.farmingtonmuseum.org.*

🔿 **Riverside Nature Center,** with its immense colony of Gunnison's prairie dogs and family activities most weekends, anchors the east end of the city's lovely and revivifying **River Corridor.** A 3¼-mi walkway and bike path meanders along the Animas River; hidden, yet right in the center of town, it passes through Animas and Berg parks and ends just behind the Scott Avenue hotel strip on the west. The corridor contains 5½ additional mi of side trails for walkers, runners, cyclists, and wildlife- and bird-watchers, as well as a man-made, 300-yard-long whitewater course. Join them at the center Tuesday mornings at 8 for guided bird-watching walks. ⊠ *Animas Park, off Browning Pkwy. at U.S. 64* ☎ *505/599–1422* ⊙ *Tues.–Sat. 10–6, Sun. 1–5.*

Shiprock Peak. West of Farmington, at U.S. 491 (though the odd map will still refer to this road by its old number, 666) and U.S. 64, just southwest of the town of Shiprock, 1,700-foot Shiprock Peak rises from the desert floor like a massive schooner. It's sacred to the Navajo, who call it Tse'Bit'Ai, or "Rock with Wings." No climbing or hiking is permitted. The formation—sometimes referred to as a pinnacle—is composed of igneous rock flanked by upright walls of solidified lava.

Four Corners Monument. About 30 mi west of Shiprock you can reach the only place in the United States where you can stand in four states at the same time—at the intersection of New Mexico, Arizona, Colorado, and Utah. Wide-open skies—broken occasionally by a distant mesa—surround the site, which was refurbished in 2010 on this very spot, refuting a flock of reports that the original 1912 marker for it might have been a few miles off. Native American artisans sell their wares here nearly every day of the year. Facilities include picnic tables and restrooms, but you must bring your own drinking water. ⊠ *U.S. 160, 6 mi north of Teec Nos Pos, AZ, from U.S. 64* ☎ *928/871–6647* ⊕ *www. navajonationparks.org* ⊠ *$3 per vehicle* ☉ *Fri.–Sun. 8–5.*

WHERE TO EAT

¢ ✕ **Andrea Kristina's Bookstore & Kafé.** Right Downtown, Andrea Kristina's
AMERICAN is a rare find for Farmington: the consummate cozy bookstore-cum-Internet café (free Wi-Fi) that serves fresh, creative, *and* tasty—food throughout the day. Coffee is available, too, of course, or an Oregon chai latte if you prefer. The veggie breakfast burrito is special (the version with chorizo is as well); the lunch-and-dinner menu covers territory like a hot Anaïs Nin sandwich (broiled chicken with pesto, on ciabatta), a range of custom pizzas, and a flock of substantial salads, from Mediterranean spinach to avocado and bacon. The book selection is strong on Southwest titles; fiction and nonfiction options tend to smart and literary. There's live entertainment Thursday through Saturday evenings. ⊠ *218 W. Main St.* ☎ *505/327–3313* ⚅ *Reservations not accepted* ▭ *AE, MC, V* ☉ *Closed Sun.*

$$$ ✕ **K. B. Dillon's.** The punched-tin ceiling and dark-wood furnishings feed
STEAK the appeal of this clubby steak house. The steak-averse can make do with another house specialty, Shrimp Dillon, or a decent pasta, but really, the local grass-fed beef's the thing—and a cold one from the selection of over 30 local microbrews. There's live music on weekend nights. ⊠ *101 W. Broadway* ☎ *505/325–0222* ▭ *AE, MC, V* ☉ *Closed Sun.*

$ ✕ **The Spare Rib.** The decor here is nothing fancy—just plastic tablecloths
SOUTHERN over picnic tables—but the whole family can fill up on generous portions of delicious smoked pork and beef barbecue. Ribs and brisket are as tender as they come, all slow-cooked in house-made sauce. ⊠ *1700 E. Main St.* ☎ *505/325–4800* ⚅ *Reservations not accepted* ▭ *AE, D, MC, V* ☉ *Closed Sun.*

$ ✕ **St. Clair Winery & Bistro.** St. Clair's wines are distilled from grapes
CONTINENTAL grown in Deming, in southern New Mexico. Their labels, Blue Teal, Lescombes, and San Felipe, are well known throughout the state, and their strategically located bistros are pleasant spots for a wine tasting or a full meal—accompanied by live jazz Thurs*day through Sunday evenings*. Dinner treats include crab-and-artichoke dip, garlic chicken

slow-cooked in Chardonnay, and pork tenderloin with Nebbiolo and raspberry-chipotle sauce. ✉ *5150 E. Main St.* ☎ *505/325–0711* ⊕ *www. stclairwinery.com* ▭ *AE, D, MC, V.*

$ ✕ **Three Rivers Eatery & Brewhouse.** In a 1912 onetime drugstore with a
AMERICAN gorgeous pressed-tin ceiling, exposed air ducts, and walls lined with vintage photos, this microbrewery whips up more than 10 kinds of beer (also available to go) with names like Roustabout Stout and Chaco Nut Brown Ale. The brews go well with the enormous portions of tasty soups, salads, burgers, ribs, pizza, and other basic pub grub served here. Stroll down the block a bit to find a friendly local scene at its respectably dingy Tap Room and pool-hall outpost (some of the patina from its original incarnation as Fred Carson's Trading Post remains); occasional live music draws a diverse crowd there. ✉ *101 E. Main St.* ☎ *505/324–2187* ⊕ *www.threeriversbrewery.com* ⚏ *Reservations not accepted* ▭ *AE, MC, V* ⊗ *Closed Sun.*

WHERE TO STAY

$$ ⌂ **Casa Blanca Inn.** Luxury without pretense is the trademark at this
INN mission-style inn, which stands atop a bluff overlooking Farmington. You can relax in the Southwestern-style den or near the patio's fountain, or watch city lights twinkle from the solarium. One room has a two-person hot tub, another has a fireplace, most have porches that face the lovely gardens, some face the bluffs, and all are beautifully appointed. Breakfast—included—is a gourmet affair, and fresh-baked goodies are served in the afternoon. Business travelers seeking a homey atmosphere make it a point to stay in this little oasis. **Pros:** innkeepers are well informed on local doings; they are also rightfully proud of their hand-tended gardens that reap heirloom tomatoes and lavender. **Cons:** hosts' attentiveness might seem intrusive to some. ✉ *505 E. La Plata St.* ☎ *505/327–6503 or 800/550–6503* ⊕ *www.casablancanm.com* ⌦ *5 rooms, 3 suites, 1 cottage* ⌂ *In-room: a/c, kitchen (some), Wi-Fi (some). In-hotel: gym, laundry facilities, Wi-Fi hotspot* ▭ *AE, MC, V* ⦿ *BP.*

$$$$ ⌂ **Kokopelli's Cave.** Carved into the cliff side 250 feet above the La Plata
HOTEL River and surrounded by distant mountains (on a clear day you can see Shiprock and the Chuskas), this man-made cave's exposed sandstone walls trace 70 million years of erosion history. Blasted out in the 1980s and '90s—and originally intended as a getaway office for a local geologist—the decor is generally modern, with a bit of a 1960s "conversation pit" feel. It's laid out like a home, with a fireplace in the den, full kitchen, and a rustic shower that trickles into a hot tub. Two terraces provide breathtaking views, and a trail on the cliff face runs some 70 vertical feet to the parking area. The cave accommodates up to six people and remains a temperate 72°F year-round. Book at least one month in advance. Note: Guests are instructed to stop at the manager's home to check in before going to the cave. Lindy Poole, the congenial manager, will accompany all visitors on their first time out—and fill them in on some of the antics it took to outfit the place. **Pros:** the space is immaculate, and more spacious—tall people will be comfortable—than photos indicate; it is a truly unique experience to stay inside a cave on a cliff dwelling. **Cons:** cave isn't easy to access, especially with large luggage; food supplied is supermarket-deli caliber.

✉ *The cave parking area is about 20 minutes northwest from Downtown Farmington* ☎ *505/325–7855; 505/326–2461 manager* ⊕ *www.bbonline.com/nm/kokopelli* ↪ *1 unit* ♿ *In-room: no a/c. In-hotel: no kids under 12* ⊟ *AE, MC, V* ⊙ *CP.*

$ 🖥 **The Region Inn.** The Region is plain-Jane from the front, and inside the

MOTEL   rooms are a bit dark, but all are updated and comfortable. The three-story motel is independently owned, and the staff's accessibility and responsiveness reflects that. Tequila's restaurant off to the side is quite serviceable and fun for a drink at least. **Pros:** easy-access location with a nonchain demeanor; has dedicated ADA rooms. **Cons:** rooms could use more light. ✉ *601 E. Broadway* ☎ *505/325–1191 or 888/325–1911* ⊕ *www.theregioninn.com* ↪ *75 rooms, 2 suites* ♿ *In-room: a/c, refrigerator, Wi-Fi. In-hotel: pool* ⊟ *AE, D, MC, V* ⊙ *CP.*

$ 🖥 **Silver River Adobe Inn.** Take a deep breath and relax at this red-roof

BED AND   adobe. It's perched on a cottonwood-covered sandstone cliff 30 feet

BREAKFAST   above the junction of the San Juan River and the La Plata. Rough-hewn timbers, fluffy quilts, and complete privacy make this rustic getaway ideal for romance or rumination, though the property and the proprietors are definitely kid-friendly. The proprietors, Diana Ohlson and David Beers, are smart, down-to-earth, and excellent sources of information about adventures and explorations in the area. Organic, home-style breakfasts such as light and puffy Dutch Babies, waffles, crepes, peach *clafoutis*, pumpkin bread, or Tuscan apple cake are a great start to the day. Those interested in sustainability will appreciate the inn's use of solar collectors and the temperature-balancing adobe construction. **Pros:** Diana maintains a massage practice on-site; all rooms have private entrances, baths, and river views. **Cons:** no TV, phone, or Internet; access road is a little quirky—request directions. ✉ *3151 W. Main St., Box 3411,* ☎ *505/325–8219 or 800/382–9251* ⊕ *www.silveradobe.com* ↪ *2 rooms, 1 suite* ♿ *In-room: a/c, no phone, kitchen (some), no TV* ⊟ *AE, MC, V* ⊙ *BP.*

NIGHTLIFE AND THE ARTS

Several Farmington restaurants are popular for a brew or cocktails, notably K. B. Dillon's, and Three Rivers Eatery & Brewhouse. Both have live music on weekend nights. Andrea Kristina's Bookstore & Kafé is a more intimate (though booze-free) setting for acoustic country and jazz on Friday and Saturday nights; there is also an occasional movie on the program.

Summer stock rules at the **Lions Wilderness Amphitheater** (✉ *Lions Wilderness Park, 5700 College Blvd. at Piñon Hills Blvd.* ☎ *877/599–3311 or 505/599–1140* ⊕ *www.fmtn.org/sandstone*) between mid-June and mid-August. Broadway shows are the usual fare of the Sandstone Theatre's series, which is presented outdoors here in a natural sandstone amphitheater. Performances are usually in the evening, Thursday–Sunday; prior to each show, theatergoers may enjoy an optional Southwestern-style dinner. **San Juan College Theater** (✉ *4601 College Blvd.* ☎ *505/566–3430 or 505/327–0076*) presents performances by the San Juan Symphony and other concerts, student recitals, and theatrical performances.

SHOPPING

The historic trading-post district along Main Street Downtown (about a five-block stretch from Auburn Avenue east to Orchard Avenue) is a good place to look for antiques, Native American arts, and remnants of small-town Western architecture from the last century.

In a town with two super-sized Wal-Marts and a Target, a shopping round-up would not be complete without mentioning the gargantuan **Animas Valley Mall** (⊠ *4601 E. Main St.* ☎ *505/326–5465*). Expect the usual chain suspects, plus a multiplex movie theater. To break free from the chains, step out to **Dad's Diner** (⊠ *4395 Largo St.* ☎ *505/564–2516*) ; it's fun, open on Sunday—not much else is in town—and a certain cut above mall food.

Emerson Gallery (⊠ *121 W. Main St.* ☎ *505/599–8597* ⊕ *www. emersongallery.com*) highlights the modern, appealing paintings and prints of Anthony Chee Emerson. His bright yet harmonious palette is decidedly nontraditional, yet his themes speak to Native American history and contemporary issues—sometimes in the same piece.

Detour one block south to **Fifth Generation Trading Co.** (⊠ *232 W. Broadway* ☎ *505/326–3211* ⊕ *www.southwestshowroom.com*), an old trading post run by the Tanner family since 1875. Big and distinctly tourist-driven these days, it has a wealth of Native American wares and is known for sand paintings. About a half-hour drive west of town, in Waterflow, are a number of old-time posts, including the **Hogback Trading Co.** (⊠ *3221 U.S. 64, Waterflow* ☎ *505/598–5154*). A fourth-generation operation in business since 1871, it is especially known for fine, handwoven Navajo rugs.

Shiprock Trading Post (⊠ *301 W. Main St.* ☎ *505/324–0881 or 800/210–7847* ⊕ *www.shiprocktradingpost.com*), established in 1894, came to Farmington in 2007. What sets this location off from its gallery in Santa Fe is its direct connection to the Navajo artisans who come here to buy the richly dyed skeins of wool that collectors will eventually see in their finished rugs. Stop here to view a good selection of topical books, outstanding rugs and jewelry from Indian artists creating contemporary designs from traditional materials, an excellent selection of modern Ganado and Wide Ruins rugs, rare vintage Chiefs blankets, and almost as rare Zuni and Navajo pawn.

SPORTS AND THE OUTDOORS

Fly-fishing is the pre-eminent sport in the San Juan River region. The heart of this prime fishing is at Navajo Dam (⇨ *below*), about 30 mi east of Farmington. Farmington itself draws a goodly group of mountain bikers and golfers, and with good reason.

BIKING   **Cottonwood Cycles** (⊠ *4370 E. Main St.* 87402 ☎ *505/326–0429*). is the local go-to for mountain- (and road-) bike equipment and guidance. All bike styles are available to rent by the day or week; you can reserve online.

The 30-mi Road Apple Rally—around since 1981, it was one of the first of its kind for mountain bikes—takes place in the **Glade Run Recreation Area** every October. During the rest of the year, bikers can traverse over 19,000 challenging acres of slick rock and sandy washes. Trails in the north end of the Glade are marked for mountain- and dirt-bike use only;

the more southerly trails are shared with ATVs. Check at the BLM office or local bike stores for maps and information. ⊠ *1235 La Plata Hwy.* ☎ *505/599–8900* ⊕ *www.blm.gov/nm/* ⊠ *Free* ☉ *Daily, dawn–dusk.*

GOLF Consistently rated one of the best municipal courses in the country, **Piñon Hills Golf Course** (⊠ *2101 Sunrise Pkwy.* ☎ *505/326–6066* ⊕ *www. fmtn.org/pinonhills* ⊠ *18 holes $40–$47* ☉ *Mar.–Oct., daily dawn–dusk; Nov.–Feb., daily 9–5*) offers striking desert views and reasonable greens fees.

WATER SPORTS **Farmington Aquatic Center**, an indoor water wonderland, has a 150-foot-long waterslide and three pools. ⊠ *1151 N. Sullivan Ave.* ☎ *505/599–1167* ⊕ *www.fmtn.org* ⊠ *$5* ☉ *Mon.–Sat. 1–7:30, Sun. 1–4.*

BLOOMFIELD/SALMON RUINS

15 mi east of Farmington on U.S. 64.

GETTING HERE

To get to Bloomfield from Albuquerque, take Interstate 24 north 17 mi to Bernalillo Exit 242 (NM 165/U.S. 550). Follow U.S. 550 (older maps may call this NM 44), 150 mi northwest to Bloomfield.

EXPLORING

Little **Bloomfield** sits at the crossroads of the Four Corners. It's a great place to stay if you're heading south to Chaco Canyon; it's equally good as a stepping-off point to Farmington, Aztec, Navajo Lake, and Mesa Verde. Pick up supplies here, refuel at one of the locally run cafés, and absolutely leave time to tour **Salmon Ruins.**

Salmon (pronounced *sol*-mon) Ruins, which dates from the 11th century, is a large Chacoan Anasazi living complex on the northern edge of the San Juan River. It's a distinctive example of pre-Columbian Pueblo architecture and stonework—the masonry is more finely finished than that at Aztec; the Chaco connection is immediately clear here. The site is named for a homesteader whose family protected the ruins for nearly a century. **Heritage Park** contains the restored George Salmon Homestead, a root cellar, bunkhouse, sweat lodge, hogan, and other types of native housing structures. Salmon also runs off-road and Journey into the Past tours, all amiably guided by field experts; check with them about routes through Chaco Canyon, Bisti Badlands, and the rarely seen Dinétah pueblos, their specialty. ⊠ *6131 U.S. 64, 2 mi west of U.S. 550* ☎ *505/632–2013* ⊕ *www.salmonruins.com* ⊠ *$3* ☉ *May.–Oct., weekdays 8–5, weekends 9–5; Nov.–Apr., weekdays 8–5, Sat. 9–5, Sun. noon–5.*

OFF THE BEATEN PATH **Wines of the San Juan.** Set at the base of a stark sandstone bluff is a surprise oasis that charms the relatively few visitors who venture in. Sit on the well-shaded patio as peacocks and geese make the rounds, enjoy a glass of Girls Are Meaner (a Gewürztraminer) or Dry Blue Winged Olive (a Riesling), and appreciate grapes harvested from NM's own soil (though some of those pressed here are actually grown in the southern part of the state, in Deming). ⊠ *233 NM 511, 14 mi northeast of Bloomfield, Turley* ☎ *505/632–0979* ⊕ *www.winesofthesanjuan.com* ☉ *Closed Tues.*

WHERE TO EAT AND STAY

¢ ✕ **Triangle Café.** This is "where friends meet to eat," and have been doing
AMERICAN so since the late 1950s. Serving three square meals daily (or catch the
brunch buffet on weekends), this is the genuine local article. Come for
homemade pies (coconut cream, cherry, and more), pork chops, burgers,
and solid New Mexican. Sit at the counter, or grab a table or booth.
✉ *506 W. Broadway (U.S. 64), just west of U.S. 550* ☎ *505/632–9918*
🗐 *AE, MC, V.*

$ 🏨 **Best Western Territorial Inn & Suites.** Don't confuse this jackpot find with
HOTEL the run-down Best Western in Farmington. Guests here are not only
Fodor's Choice positioned ideally for Chaco access and the rest of the Four Corners'
★ wonders, but can get a good night's sleep in comfortable, mostly quiet
quarters, and a nice free breakfast spread to boot. A spacious mural-
lined lounge and outdoor patio, plus a well-equipped, if modest, fitness center, Jacuzzi, and lap-style pool complete the scene. **Pros:** clean;
comfortable; well-run. **Cons:** possible road noise makes the rear rooms
a better bet. ✉ *415 S. Bloomfield Blvd. (U.S. 550), just south of U.S.
64* ☎ *505/632–9100* ⊕ *www.bestwesternnewmexico.com* 🛏 *65* 🛆 *In-
room: a/c, refrigerator, Wi-Fi. In-hotel: pool, gym, laundry facilities,
Internet terminal* 🗐 *AE, MC, V* ❗⊙❗ *CP.*

CAMPING

¢ ⚠ **Angel Peak Scenic Area.** The heavenly form of this 7,000-foot-high
sandstone formation is visible for miles, but an up-close view is even
more rewarding. Get the feel of the canyon rim country and enjoy a
hike through badlands formed by an ancient seabed before you pitch
your tent. The last 6 mi of road leading to this primitive site are gravel.
Wood must be brought in; there are no electrical hookups or water.
✉ *CR 7175, off U.S. 550, 15 mi south of Bloomfield* ☎ *505/599–8900*
⊕ *www.blm.gov/nm* 🛆 *Pit toilets, fire grate, picnic tables* 🛏 *9 tent sites.*

AZTEC

*15 mi northeast of Farmington on NM 516, 10 mi north of Bloomfield
on U.S. 550.*

The many Victorian brick buildings and quaint outlying residential
blocks give charming Aztec, the seat of San Juan County, the feeling
of a picture-book hometown. Adding to the allure are the views of the
far-distant snowcapped mountains north of Durango, Colorado.

GETTING HERE

To get to Aztec from Albuquerque, take Interstate 25 north 17 mi to
Bernalillo Exit 242 (NM 165/U.S. 550). Follow U.S. 550 (older maps
may call this NM 44), 160 mi northwest to Aztec.

From Farmington, Aztec is 15 mi northeast on NM 516, at the intersection with U.S. 550.

VISITOR INFORMATION

Aztec Visitors Center ✉ *110 N. Ash St., Aztec* ☎ *505/334–9551* ⊕ *www.
aztecnm.com.*

ON TO COLORADO: MESA VERDE NATIONAL PARK

In the Four Corners area **Mesa Verde National Park** tops the list of must-sees. Spectacular doesn't even begin to describe its 13th-century cliff dwellings; Balcony House, Cliff Palace, and Spruce House are the biggies. Visitors to these Ancestral Puebloan ruins are also in for a rare scenic treat—and the hairpin turns that go with it. Weather can shut this place down. On-site accommodations (☎ 800/449-2288, ⊕ www.visitmesaverde.com) include **Far View Lodge** (late April to late October), near the visitor center, and **Morefield Campground** (early May to early October), 4 mi inside the park. ⊠ Off U.S. 160, between Cortez and Mancos in CO, about 95 mi from Aztec (via U.S. 550) or from Farmington ☎ 970/529-4465 ⊕ www.nps.gov/meve ⌚ Late May–early Sept. $15 per vehicle (good for 7 days), early Sept.–late May $10 per vehicle; ranger-guided tours (seasonal) $3–$15 ⊙ Visitor center daily 8–5; facilities, museum, and tours vary seasonally—call ahead.

EXPLORING

The village part of the **Aztec Museum & Pioneer Village** contains more than a dozen late-19th-century buildings—a blacksmith shop, a schoolhouse, a wooden oil derrick, and a log cabin, among others—that convey a sense of life as it used to be lived in these parts. ⊠ 125 N. Main Ave. (U.S. 550) ☎ 505/334-9829 ⊕ www.aztecmuseum.org ⌚ $3 ⊙ June–Sept., Tues.–Sat. 10–4; Oct.–May, Thurs.–Sat. 10–4.

★ Dating from the early 1100s, North America's largest reconstructed Great Kiva (a partially submerged, circular earthen structure used for ceremonial and community-wide activities) and a pueblo dwelling that once contained more than 500 rooms, **Aztec Ruins National Monument and Museum,** makes for a rewarding stop. The ruins have been designated a World Heritage Site because of their significance in what is known as the Chaco Phenomenon, the extensive multitribal social and economic system that reached far beyond Chaco Canyon. This pueblo was abandoned by the mid-1200s. Early homesteaders thought they'd come across an ancient Aztec ruin, hence the odd name. You only need an hour or so to tour the ruin, which is less spectacular but considerably more accessible than those at Chaco. ⊠ Ruins Rd., ½ mi north of NM 516 ☎ 505/334-6174 ⊕ www.nps.gov/azru ⌚ $5 ⊙ Late May–early Sept., daily 8–6; early Sept.–late May, daily 8–5.

WHERE TO EAT AND STAY

¢ ✕ **Hiway Grill.** There's a blue '50s-era car suspended high on a signpost
AMERICAN outside; inside, the vintage-car photos, art-deco tables, red-vinyl booths, and super friendly staff give this decades-old place the feel of an old-time malt shop. Many of the American and New Mexican dishes, like the Mustang Melt (a burger with grilled onions and melted Swiss on rye with Thousand Island dressing), are named for classic cars. Only order a shake if you've really got an appetite or someone to share it with; chocolate is the local favorite. ⊠ 401 N.E. Aztec Blvd. (NM 516) ☎ 505/334-6533 ⊕ www.hiwaygrill.com ⊟ AE, D, MC, V ⊙ Closed Sun.

¢ ✕ **Main Street Bistro.** When just the thought of one more plate of heavy
AMERICAN food in hot weather makes you want to cry, forestall a meltdown by
coming here. Quiches, soups, frittatas, and delicious sandwiches will set
you straight, as will their excellent coffee. The Bistro Special is a grilled
portobello mushroom sandwich with mixed greens, tomato, sprouts,
and a homemade Italian feta dressing. Also worthwhile is the Ultimate,
a croissant with thin-sliced turkey, avocado, greens, red onion, crispy
bacon, provolone, and creamy avocado dressing. Fresh pastries and
desserts are available daily. And there's free Wi-Fi. ✉ *122 N. Main
Ave. (U.S. 550), across from Aztec Museum* ☎ *505/334–0109* ⊕ *www.
aztecmainstreetbistro.com* ▭ *D, MC, V* ⊗ *No dinner. Closed Sun.*

$ ▦ **Step Back Inn.** Though technically a standard motor hotel, this Victo-
MOTEL rian-style clapboard structure on the north edge of Downtown offers a
more distinctive experience than you can have at any of the countless
chain properties in nearby Farmington, and at similar prices. The public areas are inviting, and individually decorated rooms have a mix of
newer pieces and reproduction antiques, floral wallpaper, and cozy chenille bedspreads. **Pros:** friendly staff; quiet—it's set back from the road.
Cons: getting worn on the edges; Wi-Fi doesn't reach all rooms. ✉ *123
W. Aztec Blvd. (NM 516), 1 mi west of U.S. 550, near intersection with
NM 574* ☎ *505/334–1200 or 800/334–1255* 🖷 *505/334–9858* ⊕ *www.
stepbackinn.com* ➧ *39 rooms* ⚴ *In-room: a/c, Wi-Fi (some)* ⚴ *In-hotel:
Wi-Fi hotspot* ▭ *AE, MC, V* ⊙I *CP.*

NAVAJO DAM

*41 mi east of Farmington via NM 516 and NM 173 or via U.S. 64 and
NM 511. 26 mi east of Aztec via NM 173, or Bloomfield via U.S. 64
and NM 511.*

Navajo Dam is the name of a tiny town a few miles below Navajo Lake
State Park, as well as the name of the dam itself. At the base of the dam
lie the legendary "Quality Waters" of the San Juan River. Exceeding
the hype, this restricted ¾-mi stretch—a portion of which is catch-and-
release only—is one of the country's top five trophy-trout streams. The
next 12 mi of the San Juan are open waters with year-round fishing for
trout, as well as Kokanee salmon, and largemouth and smallmouth
bass. The wildlife-friendly river carves a scenic gorge of stepped cliffs
along cottonwood-lined banks that attract elk, Barbary sheep, golden
and bald eagles, blue herons, and not a few fly fishers in waders.

GETTING HERE

To get to Navajo Dam from Albuquerque, take Interstate 25 north 17
mi to Bernalillo Exit 242 (NM 165/U.S. 550). Follow U.S. 550 (older
maps may call this NM 44), 150 mi northwest to Bloomfield. Then
turn right (east) on U.S. 64 for 9 mi to Blanco; then 17 mi northeast
on NM 511 to the Dam.

From Farmington, Navajo Dam is 24 mi east on U.S. 64 to Blanco, then
17 mi northeast on NM 511.

VISITOR INFORMATION

NM Department of Game & Fish (☎ *877/884–6347* ⊕ *www.thefishphone.com*).

EXPLORING

As you drive up over the dam you will be rewarded with panoramic views down into the San Juan River valley.

Created in 1962 when the dam was built, the eponymous lake at **Navajo Lake State Park** is a popular boating and fishing spot; you can rent boats at two marinas. Short trails lead to the lakeshore, and the 3½-mi-long cottonwood-shaded San Juan River Trail parallels the river down below the dam. Driving the narrow road across the top of the dam, with no guardrails, is a slightly hair-raising, memorable experience. A fishing permit is required. ⊠ *1448 NM 511, off NM 173 or U.S. 64* ☎ *505/632–2278 or 888/667–2757* ⊕ *www.nmparks.com* ⊒ *$5 per vehicle.*

WHERE TO STAY

$$
CABINS
★

Soaring Eagle Lodge. A haven for fly fishers who want casual but upscale accommodations, this lodge houses guests in cabins that are fully furnished, complete with kitchenettes and rod-and-wader racks. You can step out of your cabin to a mile and a half of private river access, or take advantage of the on-site guide service and full fly shop. The food here is excellent, and the location remote, so the package that includes breakfast and dinner is a good choice. **Pros:** fine chefs; comfortably appointed, and fully wired, with an on-site conference center and fly shop. **Cons:** three guests max per cabin; charge for Wi-Fi; pro guides, but they can triple cost. ⊠ *48 CR 4370, off NM 511, 7 mi south of Navajo Dam* ☎ *505/632–3721 or 800/866–2719* ⊕ *www.soaringeaglelodge.net* ⊃ *11 cabins* ⚭ *In-room: a/c, kitchen, Wi-Fi. In-hotel: restaurant, Wi-Fi hotspot* ⊠ *MAP.*

CAMPING

¢ **Navajo Lake State Park.** At the park's three campgrounds some sites sit among piñon and juniper trees and overlook the lake. Hot showers are available at Sims Mesa and Pine campgrounds but not at Cottonwood Campground. ⊠ *1448 NM 511, off NM 173 or U.S. 64* ☎ *505/632–2278 or 888/667–2757 information, 877/664–7787 reservations* ⊕ *www.nmparks.com* ⚭ *Flush toilets, dump station, drinking water, fire pits, picnic tables* ⊃ *200 sites.*

SPORTS AND THE OUTDOORS

Stop by **Abe's Motel & Fly Shop/Born 'n' Raised on the San Juan** (⊠ *1791 NM 173* ☎ *505/632–2194 or 505/632–0492* ⊕ *www.sanjuanriver.com*) to find out what flies you need to snare the wily San Juan rainbows, book a wade or float trip, or just to pick up a cold drink and snacks. There's also lodging here, although it's nothing fancy ($68 to $74 per room, some with kitchenettes—but they are BYO for utensils and cookware; there are 59 rooms, all with Wi-Fi). If you're hungry for more than chips, El Pescador's Restaurant & Lounge is next door. Though revered guide Chuck Rizuto has retired, the now Orvis-endorsed outfitter **Rizuto's Fly Shop & Fisheads San Juan River Lodge** (⊠ *1796 NM 173* ☎ *505/634–0463 shop, 505/632–1411 lodge* ⊕ *www.fisheadsofthesanjuan.com*) offers well-respected guides and lodging too. Stay in one of eight very basic rooms for $94 per night; each has a refrigerator, microwave, and a fly-tying table. "Fish-and-stay" packages start at $275.

CULTURE NATIONAL HISTORICAL PARK

155 mi northwest of Albuquerque via U.S. 550 (north entrance) or 170 mi via I–40 and NM 371 (south entrance); 67 mi southeast of Farmington via U.S. 550 or 115 mi via NM 371; 96 mi northeast of Gallup via I–40 and NM 371.

GETTING HERE

Chaco Canyon may be approached from the north or the south; both routes have unpaved portions, but the route from the north is the better of the two. In either case, vehicles with normal clearance should do fine, but the south is notoriously nasty when it gets wet—it is prone to deep ruts that are especially perilous to RVs, and slick surfaces, which are perilous to everyone. It is always best to check road conditions before you go (☎ 505/786–7014).

From Albuquerque, to the north entrance: Take I–25 north 17 mi to Bernalillo Exit 242 (NM 165/U.S. 550). Follow U.S. 550 (older maps may call this NM 44) northwest about 115 mi to CR 7900 (CR 7900 is 3 mi south of Nageezi and about 50 mi north of Cuba). Turn left (south) onto CR 7900; continue 5 mi to CR 7950 (16 mi, rough dirt), follow signs to the visitor center.

From Albuquerque, to the south entrance: Take I–40 west 103 mi to Thoreau, Exit 53, then north on NM 371; just past Crownpoint (26 mi) turn east onto Navajo 9 to Seven Lakes (12 mi), then north on NM 57 (20 mi, rough dirt) to visitor center. *(Note: NM 57 is marked as Highway 14 on some maps.)*

■TIP➔ The closest gas is 21 mi from the north entrance, at the turn-off from U.S. 550; it is 39 mi from the south entrance, in Crownpoint at NM 371.

Fodor's Choice The roads accessing **Chaco Canyon**, home to Chaco Culture National
★ Historical Park, do a fine job of deterring exploration: they are mostly unpaved and can be very muddy and/or icy during inclement weather (particularly NM 57 from the south). The silver lining is that the roads leading in—and the lack of gas stations, food concessions, or hotels once you get off the highway—keep this archaeological treasure free from the overcrowding that can mar other national park visits: only about 85,000 people visit annually, compared with at least 10 times that number to Canyon de Chelly, which is 80 mi away as the crow flies.

Once past the rough roads you'll see one of the most amazingly well-preserved and fascinating ruin sites on the continent. The excavations here have uncovered what was once the administrative and economic core of a vast community—the locus of a system of over 400 mi of ancient roads that have been identified to date. While there is evidence that people lived in the canyon at least since 400 AD, the majority of these roads, and the buildings and dwellings that make up the canyon site, were constructed from 850 to 1250 AD. Several of the ancient structures—such as an immense Great Kiva, Casa Rinconada, or Pueblo Bonito—are simply astounding, if only for the extreme subtlety and detail of their precisely cut and chinked sandstone masonry. But there's still a shroud of mystery surrounding them. Did 5,000 people really once live here, as some archaeologists believe? Or was Chaco maintained solely as a ceremonial and trade center? The more that's learned about the prehistoric roadways and the outlying sites that they connect, or wondrous creations such as the **Sun Dagger**—an arrangement of stone slabs positioned to allow a spear of sunlight to pass through and bisect a pair of spiral petroglyphs precisely at each summer solstice—the more questions arise about the sophistication of the people that created them.

At the visitor center you can meander through a small museum on Chaco culture, peruse the bookstore, buy bottled water (but no food), and inquire about hiking permits. From here you can drive (or bike) along the 9-mi paved inner loop road to the various trailheads for the ruins; at each you can find a small box containing a detailed self-guided tour brochure (a 50¢ donation per map is requested). Many of the 13 ruins at Chaco require a significant hike, but a few of the most impressive are just a couple of hundred yards off the road. The stargazing here is spectacular: there is a small observatory and numerous telescopes, which are brought out for star parties from April through October; ask about the schedule at the front desk. **Pueblo Bonito** is the largest and most dramatic of the Chaco Canyon ruins, a massive semicircular "great house" that once stood four stories in places and held some 600 rooms (*and* 40 kivas). The park trail runs alongside its fine outer mortar-and-sandstone walls, up a hill that allows a great view over the entire canyon, and then right through the ruin and several rooms. It's the most substantial of the structures—the ritualistic and cultural center of a Chacoan culture that may once have comprised some 150 settlements. ⊠ *NM 57* ⬧ *Box 220, Nageezi87037* ☎ *505/786–7014 x221* ⊕ *www.nps.gov/chcu* ⬧ *$8 per vehicle, good for 7 days* ☉ *Park daily dawn–dusk; visitor center daily 8–5.*

WHERE TO STAY

¢ ⛺ **Chaco Culture National Historical Park.** Not far from the visitor center is the park-service-operated Gallo Campground. The site's primitiveness is its greatest asset: at night the skies come alive with stars, and the only noises you can hear are those of nature. The primary advantage of staying here is waking up in the canyon and having a full day to explore the ruins and perhaps hike some of the backcountry trails. Camping is limited to seven days; vehicles up to 30 feet can park here. Drinking water is available at the visitor center. Starting in early May it's best to arrive as early in the day as possible; the campground fills quickly. Reservations are not accepted, except for groups. ⊠ *North entrance: Take U.S. 550 3 mi south of Nageezi, then turn south onto CR 7900; continue 5 mi to CR 7950 (16 mi, rough dirt), follow signs to the visitor center. South entrance: Take I-40 to Thoreau, Exit 53, then north on NM 371; just past Crownpoint (26 mi) turn east onto Navajo 9 to Seven Lakes (12 mi), then north on NM 57 (20 mi, rough dirt) to visitor center. (Note: NM 57 is marked as Hwy. 14 on some maps.) Call ahead for road conditions.* ☎ *505/786–7014* ⊕ *www.nps.gov/chcu* ⬧ *Flush toilets, fire grates, picnic tables* ⬧ *49 sites.*

EN ROUTE Whether you're coming or going from Chaco's north entrance, or simply heading south on U.S. 550, **Cuba** is a good place to stop for gas and, depending on your inclination and the season, hot coffee or a cold soda.

Remnants of when this route was the notoriously unsafe—and much narrower—NM 44 are gas stations, a convenience store, and **El Bruno's** (⊠ *6453 Main St. [U.S. 550], at NM 126* ☎ *505/289–9429* ⊕ *www. elbrunos.com*), a better-than decent Mexican restaurant that's right on the highway at the far north end of town, plus a handful of inexpensive motels that could serve for a pre- or post-Chaco overnighter; your best bet in this regard is the **Cuban Lodge** (⊠ *6332 Main St. [U.S. 550]* ☎ *505/289–3475*). Continue south on U.S. 550 in daylight if at all possible (late afternoon is perfect): the views only get more spectacular as you go. Watch for Cabezon Peak on your right. But if you've got some time to spare, detour in Cuba to visit **Pueblo Pintado,** about 60 mi west, on Navajo Route 9 via NM 197 from Cuba's south end. Most of it is a very rugged ride, and the Pintado town site is little more than a few houses and a convenience store, but the ruins there—from a Chaco Culture great house—are worth a look and easy to find (for the intrepid, there is an even more rugged back route to Chaco Canyon itself from here).

⌐EN
ROUTE
Heading east on Interstate 40? Usually held on the third Friday of every month, the **Crownpoint Rug Auction** (⊠ *Crownpoint Elementary School, NM 371, 26 mi north of Thoreau at I–40, Exit 53* ☎ *505/786–7386 or 505/786–5302* ⊕ *www.crownpointrugauction.com*) is the foremost place to buy handwoven Navajo rugs—you're bidding with a mix of collectors and dealers, so prices on the some 300 to 400 rugs are sometimes well below what you'd pay at a store. Viewing begins at 4, with the actual auction running from 7 usually until midnight or later. Keep in mind there are no overnight facilities in Crownpoint, though there is a food and drink concession at the auction. Call ahead to confirm auction dates. Cash, traveler's checks, personal checks *only*; no credit cards. ∎**TIP➜ If Chaco Canyon is your next stop (via the south entrance, which is also off NM 371), it is best not drive there after dark.** There are never assurances of space at the campground, and the road can be very bad. Backtrack 26 mi to Interstate 40 and stay overnight in Grants (30 mi east). Note: NM 371 is also a direct route to the Bisti Badlands and to Farmington (80 mi north of Crownpoint).

JICARILLA APACHE NATION

55 mi east of Navajo Dam on U.S. 64; 36 mi west of Chama on U.S. 64.

GETTING HERE

From Farmington, drive 96 mi east on U.S. 64 to get to Dulce, the capital and largest town on the Jicarilla Apache Nation. From Albuquerque, it is 170 mi to Dulce: take Interstate 25 north 17 mi to Bernalillo Exit 242 (NM 165/U.S. 550). Follow U.S. 550 (older maps may call this NM 44), 85 mi northwest to NM 537. Take NM 537 north 56 mi to U.S. 64, then turn right (east) 11 mi into Dulce.

VISITOR INFORMATION

Jicarilla Apache Nation, Tourism Department (⌂ *Box 507, Dulce 87528* ☎ *575/759–3242* ⊕ *www.jicarillaonline.com*).

EXPLORING

Jicarilla Apache Nation. The Spanish named the Jicarilla band of Apaches (pronounced hick-uh-*ree*-ya, meaning "little basket") for their beautiful basketry. For centuries before the arrival of the Spanish, these Native Americans, who as Athabaskan speakers are related to the Navajo and other Apache bands, were a nomadic people who roamed across northeastern New Mexico, southeastern Colorado, and the Oklahoma and Texas panhandles. Their band of 10,000 was reduced to 330 by 1897. The federal government relocated them to this isolated area of almost a million acres a century ago. Since then, the Jicarilla Apaches have made something of a comeback with the sale of timber, oil, and gas development, casino gambling, and savvy investing.

Dulce (pronounced *dull*-say, meaning "sweet" in Spanish) on U.S. 64 is the Jicarilla capital.The tiny but free **Arts & Crafts Museum** (✉ *U.S. 64, ¼ mi west of Downtown Dulce* ☎ *575/759–3242 Ext. 274*) remains the best place to see fine historic and contemporary Jicarilla baskets, beadwork, and pottery. It's also the place to inquire about tours, events, and any tourism restrictions in place because of ceremonial activities. This country is known for fishing, particularly at Stone Lake, and for hunting; contact the **Jicarilla Apache Department of Game & Fish** (☎ *575/759–3255*) for information. You may also hike and camp. As with many pueblos in New Mexico, the casinos have become big draws as well. Some Jicarilla celebrations are open to the public. The Little Beaver Roundup, the third weekend in July, entails a rodeo, powwow, and carnival and draws participants from Native American tribes and pueblos throughout the United States.

WHERE TO STAY

$

HOTEL

⊡ **Best Western Jicarilla Inn & Casino.** The room furnishings here preserve the flavor of the cultural and natural setting, with dark woods, Native American art, and stone fireplaces. The restaurant, the Hill Crest, is a favorite gathering spot for celebration dinners. **Pros:** small fitness center. **Cons:** limited number of nonsmoking rooms. ✉ *13603 Jicarilla Blvd. (U.S. 64), 12 mi west of junction with U.S. 84* ⌾ *Box 233, Dulce 87528* ☎ *505/759–3663 or 800/528–1234* ⊕ *www.bestwesternnewmexico. com* ⤵ *42 rooms* ⌂ *In-room: a/c, Internet. In-hotel: restaurant, gym, Wi-Fi hotspot, some pets allowed* ▭ *AE, D, MC, V.*

Northeastern New Mexico

WORD OF MOUTH

"Is Las Vegas worth taking the time to see?"

—Betsyp

It is a very small town with many interesting houses and buildings. The Rough Riders museum is small, but well done. I would agree . . . that it's probably not worth the trip from Santa Fe, but it's an interesting place to stop if you're going that way. If you do decide to go, check the hours on the museum as I seem to remember them keeping odd hours."

—jbee

Updated
by Andrew
Collins

You'll battle neither crowds nor hype in northeastern New Mexico, one of the most underrated sections of the state, and an area well worth exploring. You can have a wild-flower-strewn trail through alpine meadows and forests of aspen and ponderosa pine all to yourself, or step back in time in small towns that treasure their pasts. The sheer variety of terrain and climate, and the region's storied role in the history of westward expansion, make this a worthwhile short side trip from Santa Fe or Taos, or a memorable way to enter New Mexico from either Colorado or the Plains states. Just beware the sparse population and relative lack of services and luxury trappings—this is a land of simple, authentic pleasures.

Northeastern New Mexico has been inhabited for centuries by such Native American tribes as the Apaches, Comanches, and Utes, but it wasn't until about 1835 that non–Native American populations arrived in any significant numbers. Hispanic settlers moved up into the area at that time from San Miguel del Vado, which is just south of present-day Interstate 25, and established the Las Vegas Land Grant; Las Vegas has remained a Hispanic stronghold ever since. William Becknell had established Las Vegas as the Mexican port of entry when he brought the first pack train west from Missouri to Santa Fe in 1821, in turn creating a pathway—the fabled Santa Fe Trail—for Americans to spread west. The railroad's arrival in the 1870s and '80s brought streams of people and goods into northeastern New Mexico, as did the coal mines. Italians, Mexicans, Greeks, Slavs, Spaniards, and Irish all headed to Raton to work mines that first opened in 1879. German-Jewish merchants opened shops in Las Vegas to serve the miners, the railroads, and the local Hispanic population.

In 1908, an African-American cowboy named George McJunkin found a collection of arrowheads in an arroyo near Folsom where he was looking for lost cattle. They looked different from the other arrowheads he'd seen—and indeed they were. Archaeologists eventually determined that the arrowheads had been made by ancient hominids, now known as Folsom Man, who inhabited northeastern New Mexico at least 10,000 years ago.

During the railroad heyday, Civil War veterans homesteaded in the region, some working for Lucien Maxwell, onetime mountain man and fur trader who came to control the largest landholding (1,714,765 acres) in the Western Hemisphere. Many of New Mexico's large ranches date from the era of the Maxwell Land Grant, territory awarded to the father of Maxwell's wife and another man by the Mexican government in 1841. Modern-day land baron Ted Turner now owns an enormous chunk of open land in these parts. The historic Bell Ranch near Solano still maintains an active cattle operation on 290,100 acres, though it originally held 655,468 acres as the Pablo Montoya Land Grant of 1824; as of fall 2010, the entire tract was on the market for a mere $83 million.

History is very much alive in northeastern New Mexico, in the stories and the way of life of the people who live here, in the architecture, and in the landscape itself. Exploring this land of vast plains, rugged mesas, and wild, crystalline streams may well be the best way to immerse yourself in the American West.

ORIENTATION AND PLANNING

GETTING ORIENTED

Interstate 25 forms the primary north–south corridor through the region, roughly tracing the Old Santa Fe Trail and providing easy access to key towns like Las Vegas and Raton from Albuquerque and Santa Fe to the south, and Colorado to the north. Another key route through the region is east–west U.S. 64, which crosses east over the mountains from Taos into Cimarron and then continues through Raton to Clayton. Otherwise, northeastern New Mexico is mostly traversed by minor state highways and even less-utilized forest and ranch roads, some of these unpaved.

Santa Fe Trail Country. In the mid-19th century, this vast tract of grasslands and prairies, along with the eastern foothills of the Sangre de Cristo range, became the gateway to New Mexico for American settlers headed here from the Midwest. Towns along the Santa Fe Trail's modern offspring, Interstate 25—notably Raton and Las Vegas—remain popular overnight breaks for visitors road-tripping to the Land of Enchantment from Colorado, Kansas, and the Oklahoma and Texas panhandles.

This region has among the lowest population density in the country and is more a linear path of modest, old-time historic sites and lost-in-time hamlets than it is a major vacation destination—most travelers come here on the way to or from Santa Fe, Taos, and Albuquerque, or as meandering daytrips abundant with photo ops, underutilized parks and wildlife refuges, and curious museums.

Off the interstate, villages like Clayton, Cimarron, and Mora seem barely changed over the past few decades and are reached via lone two-lane highways through some of the state's most breathtaking scenery.

NORTHEASTERN NEW MEXICO PLANNER

WHEN TO GO

In a region where the weather is nearly always sunny and dry, if fairly chilly in winter, the only months saddled with consistently harsh conditions are March and April, when "Texas blows through" and you

TOP REASONS TO GO

Historic Hotels. History comes alive at the vintage hotels and saloons of the Santa Fe Trail, whether spending the night at Cimarron's St. James Hotel or Las Vegas's Plaza Hotel, or counting the bullet holes in the ceiling of the Eklund Hotel Dining Room & Saloon.

Wide-open spaces. The high plains give a new meaning to solitude. If you're ever feeling crowded or hemmed in by humanity, try driving across Johnson Mesa via NM 72.

High-mountain majesty. The rocky cliffs, pine-covered valleys, and clear streams that form the eastern flank of the Sangre de Cristos offer respite from big-city life and summer temperatures.

Small-town pleasures. Raton and Las Vegas have lively Downtowns with old-fashioned cafés and antiques shops, while smaller villages like Cimarron, Clayton, and Springer look as though transported from an earlier era.

find yourself dodging tumbleweeds, though this is more applicable to the flatter regions than the mountains. Late spring, when the wildflowers begin to bloom, into late summer is a wonderful time to visit—an occasional afternoon thunderstorm, or "monsoon," often followed by a rainbow, punctuates days that are mostly sunny. Fall brings the gold of aspens, and fishing and hiking are especially spectacular. Temperatures can remain mild through Thanksgiving, and a crisp winter with good snow is a blessing for cross-country skiers. The expansive vistas on snowy days are unforgettable. Roads are well maintained throughout the year, but be alert to storm warnings.

GETTING HERE AND AROUND
AIR TRAVEL
There is no commercial air service directly into the region, but Las Vegas is just an hour from the airport in Santa Fe (SAF), and two hours from Albuquerque International Airport (ABQ) (*see those chapters for airport details*). You might also consider flying into Amarillo, Texas (AMA), which is 2½ hours from Clayton, or Colorado Springs, Colorado (COS), a 2½-hour drive from Raton.

CAR TRAVEL
Without question, a car is the best way both to reach and explore the region, as public transportation options are few and won't get you out to see the parks, attractions, and smaller towns, which are many miles from one another. This is a beautiful region for road-tripping, with little traffic—just remember to always set out with a full tank of gas, as services are few and far between.

Most visitors enter the region via Interstate 25, either driving north from Albuquerque and Santa Fe, where the first major stop is Las Vegas, or driving south from Colorado, where you'll first reach Raton. Less-traveled but still scenic (in a wide-open-spaces kind of way) routes through the region include U.S. 87 up from Amarillo, Texas, to Clayton, and U.S. 64 from the Oklahoma panhandle and southwestern Kansas to Clayton. There are also a few stunningly picturesque routes into the area from the west, over the Sangre de Cristo range: try U.S. 64 from Taos into Cimarron, or NM 518, which you can take from the High Road to Taos (over the mountains from tiny Peñasco to Mora and eventually Las Vegas. These mountain passes see a lot of snow in winter, so check conditions. Finally, a quick and pretty shortcut, if you approach from Texas via Interstate 40, is to head northwest on U.S. 84 from near Santa Rosa to Las Vegas.

TRAIN TRAVEL

Amtrak (☎ *800/872–7245* ⊕ *www.amtrak.com*) operates the Southwest Chief between Chicago and Los Angeles, making stops in Las Vegas and Raton (before moving on to Lamy—near Santa Fe—and Albuquerque). As part of a longer trip along this fabled route, taking Amtrak to Las Vegas or Raton can be interesting—you can get around both towns without a car. But if your aim is to explore anything outside these two towns, train travel isn't practical.

ABOUT THE RESTAURANTS

Las Vegas is the one town in these parts with an especially notable restaurant scene, ranging from some outstanding old-school New Mexican eateries to a few spots serving more creative, higher-end fare. Otherwise, beyond the many fast-food restaurants in Las Vegas and Raton, you'll find just a handful of mostly basic and very casual eateries in the region's other towns. Reservations aren't needed around here, but many restaurants do keep limited hours or close early during slow times—it's a very good idea to call ahead.

ABOUT THE HOTELS

Given the relatively modest numbers of visitors who spend more than a day in this area, lodging options are a bit limited (remember that it's quite easy to visit Las Vegas as a day trip from Santa Fe, or Cimarron as a day trip from Angel Fire or Taos). You'll find a good representation of budget to midprice chain accommodations in Las Vegas and Raton. You'll also find a few historic inns and bed-and-breakfasts throughout the area, all of them with reasonable rates and plenty of character, if not much in the way of luxury. Given the region's considerable natural beauty and its popularity with ardent road-trippers, many visitors camp in these parts, either in tents during the warmer months or at RV parks year-round.

WHAT IT COSTS					
	¢	$	$$	$$$	$$$$
Restaurants	under $10	$10–$15	$16–$22	$23–$30	over $30
Hotels	under $70	$70–$120	$121–$175	$176–$250	over $250

Restaurant prices are per person for a main course at dinner. Hotel prices are for two people in a standard double room in high season, excluding 5%–12% tax.

PLANNING YOUR TIME

It's generally unflattering to refer to a place as a "pass-through" region, but northeastern New Mexico is historically—and to a certain extent presently—just that: Visitors have traditionally explored the area en route from one point or another, first in wagons and then trains along the Old Santa Fe Trail's two routes, and for the past century in automobiles, often following the original roads used by traders and ranchers. These days you can visit the area's most prominent communities, Las Vegas, Cimarron, and Raton, as a day trip from Santa Fe or elsewhere in the Rio Grande Valley.

Set aside a couple of hours to stroll around the Old Town Plaza and Bridge Street in **Las Vegas**. After you've walked the town, drive north on Interstate 25 to **Raton** and visit the Raton Museum and Historic First Street. You can then return west by taking U.S. 64 to **Cimarron**, exploring the heart of yesteryear's Wild West. To give yourself a little more time, spend the night in the allegedly haunted St. James Hotel, or back down in Las Vegas at the Plaza Hotel. It's especially pretty if you return via NM 518 toward the High Road between Santa Fe and Taos. From Cimarron, continue west on U.S. 64, stopping off to fish or walk along the Cimarron River in Cimarron Canyon, and then head south on NM 434 at Angel Fire, stopping off for a visit to Victory Ranch or Salman Ranch in **Mora**. From Las Vegas, just take NM 518 northwest toward Mora.

IF YOU HAVE 3 OR MORE DAYS

With more time, you could retrace either, or even both, of the original Santa Fe Trail routes—Interstate 25 aligns roughly with the original trail, and the shortcut, known as the Cimarron Route, passes through Clayton and rejoins the original trail near Springer. Begin in **Las Vegas**, where you can stay at the Plaza Hotel. Detour for an hour or two to **Fort Union National Monument**. Back at Interstate 25, continue north to **Raton**. On Day 3 head east on NM 72 over starkly captivating Johnson Mesa and visit Capulin Volcano National Monument to view four states from the rim of the volcano. You can stay at the Eklund Hotel Dining Room & Saloon. The following day drive west on U.S. 56 toward **Springer**, a good place to have lunch and browse in the antiques shops Downtown. With or without the Clayton detour, continue west to **Cimarron** (via U.S. 64 from Capulin, or NM 58 from Springer), and from here do the last day of the three-day itinerary given above.

SANTA FE TRAIL COUNTRY

Native American tribes of the Great Plains and Southwest lived and thrived in resource-rich northeastern New Mexico. Throughout the region you can find reminders of them and the pioneers who traveled the Santa Fe Trail, two sections of which passed through the area. The Mountain Route entered New Mexico from southeastern Colorado, crossed through Raton Pass, and passed Cimarron and Rayado before heading on to Fort Union. Because it was so arduous, this route was less subject to attack from the Comanches and Apaches, who were on the defensive warpath because their land was being usurped. The quicker, flatter Cimarron Route (aka Cimarron Cutoff), entering New Mexico from Oklahoma and passing across the dry grasslands, left travelers much more vulnerable. The Mountain Route, which William Becknell followed 900 mi from Franklin, Missouri, during his first successful navigation, also provided an excellent source of water—the Arkansas River—while the Cimarron Route was deathly dry.

LAS VEGAS

64 mi northeast of Santa Fe via I–25.

The antithesis of the Nevada city that shares its name, Las Vegas, elevation 6,470 feet, is a town of about 15,000 that time appears to have passed by. For decades, Las Vegas was actually two towns divided by Rio Gallinas: West Las Vegas, the Hispanic community anchored by the Spanish-style plaza, and East Las Vegas, where German Jews and midwesterners had established themselves around a proper town square. Once an oasis for stagecoach passengers en route to Santa Fe, it became—for a brief period after the railroad arrived in the late 19th century—New Mexico's major center of commerce, and its largest town, where more than a million dollars in goods and services were traded annually.

Booming business and near-total lawlessness characterized the 1870s. Famous characters on both sides of the law passed through the town—including Doc Holliday (who practiced dentistry here), Billy the Kid, and Wyatt Earp. Fierce battles for land—often swindled out of the hands of illiterate Hispanic land-grant holders by ruthless American businessmen—and water rights ensued, with the *Gorras Blancos* ("White Hoods") appearing in 1889 to begin their campaign of cutting fences and setting fire to buildings on lands that had once been community property of the many land grants of the area. Today, the town is considerably more sedate.

The seat of San Miguel County, Las Vegas lies where the Sangre de Cristo Mountains meet the high plains of New Mexico, and its name, meaning "the meadows," reflects its scenic setting. A few funky bookstores, Western-wear shops, restaurants, and coffeehouses line the Old Town Plaza and the main drag, Bridge Street. More than 900 structures here are listed on the National Register of Historic Places, and the town has nine historic districts, many with homes and commercial buildings of ornate Italianate design. In fact, it's often said that Las Vegas provides a glimpse of the Victorian style that would have characterized Santa Fe back in the late 19th century, a few decades before that city was given an idealized adobe makeover in order to attract tourists. Strolling around this very walkable town gives a sense of the area's rough-and-tumble history—Butch Cassidy is rumored to have tended bar here, and miscreants with names like Dirty-Face Mike, Rattlesnake Sam, and Web-Fingered Billy once roamed the streets. You may also recognize some of the streets and facades from films; Las Vegas is where scenes from *Wyatt Earp, No Country for Old Men,* and *All the Pretty Horses* were shot and where Tom Mix shot his vintage Westerns.

Northeastern New Mexico

COLORADO

OKLAHOMA

TEXAS

Sugarite Canyon S.P.

NRA Whittington Center

Raton

Capulin

CARSON NAT'L FOREST

Valle Vidal

Questa

Cimarron Canyon S.P.

Maxwell Nat'l Wildlife Refuge

Eagle Nest Lake

Cimarron

Springer

Clayton

Taos

Rayado

Kiowa Nat'l Grasslands

Coyote Creek S.P.

Guadalapita

Kiowa Nat'l Grasslands

Amistad

Mora

La Cueva

Wagon Mound

Chimayó

SANTA FE NATIONAL FOREST

Watrous

Fort Union Nat'l Mon.

Santa Fe

Las Vegas

Pecos National Historic Park

Las Vegas Nat'l Wildlife Refuge

Trujillo

Mora R.

Mosquero

Conchas Lake

Conchas Dam

0   25 miles

0   50 km

TO SUMNER LAKE STATE PARK

Pecos R.

KEY	
········	Santa Fe Trail, Cimarron Cutoff
- - -	Santa Fe Trail, Mountain Branch

GETTING HERE

Amtrak's Southwest Chief makes daily stops here en route between Albuquerque and the Midwest, but as with most of the region, a car is the most practical way to arrive and explore the surrounding area. Las Vegas is just an hour from Santa Fe via Interstate 25, and two hours south of Taos via the very scenic NM 518.

Contact Amtrak ☎ 800/872-7245 ⊕ www.amtrak.com).

To gain an appreciation of the town's architecture, follow the walking tours described in free brochures available at the **Las Vegas Chamber of Commerce Visitors Center.** Best bets include Stone Architecture of Las Vegas; the Carnegie Park Historic District, with the Carnegie Library; and the Business District of Douglas–6th Street and Railroad Avenue. The latter includes the Mission Revival La Casteneda, a former hotel from the famed Harvey House railroad chain, with a well-preserved grand lobby and dining room. You can also view the tours online at ⊕ http://lasvegasnmcchp.com/tours. ⊠ 701 Grand Ave. ☎ 505/425–8631 or 800/832–5947 ⊕ www.lasvegasnewmexico.com.

EXPLORING

Fodor's Choice ★ About 5 mi northwest of Downtown in the village of Montezuma, students from around the world study language and culture at the **Armand Hammer United World College of the American West.** Looming over the school property is the fantastically ornate, vaguely Queen Anne–inspired Montezuma Castle, a former resort hotel developed by the Santa Fe Railroad and designed by the famous Chicago firm of Burnham and Root. The structure that stands today was the third incarnation of the Montezuma Hotel, which opened in 1886. Student-led tours of the castle are available on certain Saturdays (call ahead). Check in with the guard booth at the campus entrance. ⊠ *NM 65* ☎ *505/454–4200* ⊕ *www.uwc-usa. org/tours.*

Continue another ½ mi past the campus turnoff on NM 65 to reach signs (on the right) for the **hot springs** that inspired Montezuma's tourist boom in the 1880s. Soaking in these relaxing, lithium-laced pools is free, as long as you follow basic rules: no nude bathing, no alcohol, and bathing only between 5 AM and midnight. If crowds allow, try soaking in all three different pools; temperatures vary significantly but the views of the castle and the creek are lovely from each pool.

> ### JULY 4TH IN VEGAS
>
> Las Vegas is especially vibrant and fun during 4th of July weekend, known here as Fiestas de Las Vegas. The town's wildly popular parade begins on the plaza around 9 AM and proceeds down Bridge Street. Proud veterans, civic groups, high school bands, even lowriders, whose elaborately painted cars with amazing hydraulics lift, tilt, and bounce, all join in, and during a greatly anticipated pageant, a Fiestas queen is crowned. There is a craft fair with local artists selling everything from food to tie-dyed clothing, to traditional Hispanic arts.

Las Vegas City Museum & Rough Rider Memorial Collection houses historical photos, medals, uniforms, and memorabilia from the Spanish-American War, documents pertaining to the city's history, and Native American artifacts. Theodore Roosevelt recruited many of his Rough Riders—the men the future president led into battle in Cuba in 1898—from northeastern New Mexico, and their first reunion was held here. ⊠ *727 Grand Ave.* ☎ *505/426–3205* ⊕ *www.lasvegasmuseum.org* ⊡ *$2* ⊗ *Tues.–Sat. 10–4.*

Las Vegas National Wildlife Refuge has the best bird-watching around, with more than 250 known species—including eagles, sandhill cranes, hawks, and prairie falcons—that travel the Central Flyway to this 8,672-acre area of marshes, native grasslands, and forested canyons. Here, where the Sangre de Cristo Mountains meet the Great Plains, the ½-mi-long Gallinas Nature Trail winds beside sandstone cliffs and ruins, and an 8-mi auto tour loops through the most picturesque habitats of the refuge (four-wheel-drive can be necessary following rain or snow). You can get oriented by dropping by the visitor center (free maps and bird species left out for visitors at all times). ⊠ *NM 281; 1½ mi east of Las Vegas on NM 104, then 4½ mi south on NM 281* ☐ *Box 399, Las Vegas 87701* ☎ *505/425–3581* ⊕ *www.fws.gov/refuges* ⊡ *Free* ⊗ *Grounds daily dawn–dusk; visitor center weekdays 8–4:30.*

Las Vegas is the home of **New Mexico Highlands University,** which puts on concerts, plays, sporting events, and lectures. Its tree-shaded campus of largely Spanish-colonial and Romanesque Revival buildings dates to 1893 and anchors the eastern side of Downtown. It houses Depression-era murals by painter Lloyd Moylan. ⊠ *901 University Ave.* ☎ *800/338–6648* ⊕ *www.nmhu.edu.*

A favorite fishing hole for rainbow and German brown trout is **Storrie Lake State Park.** The 1,100-acre lake also draws water-skiers, sailboarders, and windsurfers. The park has both tent and RV campsites. ⊠ *NM 518, 4 mi north of Las Vegas* ☎ *505/425–7278* ⊕ *www.emnrd.state. nm.us* ▭ *$5 per vehicle.*

OFF THE BEATEN PATH

Madison Vineyards & Winery. If you're approaching Las Vegas from Santa Fe via Interstate 25, a side trip down NM 3 is well worth your while. Scenic and loaded with history, the road will also take you to the proud producers of some very respectable New Mexico wines, including the crisp, sweet, white Pecos Wildflower. Madison has picked up quite a few awards over the years. The tasting room in El Barranco is open weekdays (closed Wednesdays) noon to 6, Saturdays 10 to 5, and Sundays noon to 5. ⊠ *NM 3, 6 mi south of I–25 Exit 323, 23 mi southwest of Las Vegas* ☎ *505/421–8028* ⊕ *www.madison-winery.com.*

WHERE TO EAT

¢

NEW MEXICAN

✗ **Charlie's Spic & Span Bakery & Café.** Huevos rancheros and burritos smothered with spicy salsa top the list in this large, simply furnished room that rings with friendly greetings among locals and is a good bet for either breakfast or lunch. You can also pick up cookies, doughnuts, and pastries from the on-site bakery, or a stack of freshly made corn tortillas from the *tortilleria.* ⊠ *715 Douglas Ave.* ☎ *505/426–1921* ▭ *MC, V.*

$$

ECLECTIC

✗ **El Fidel.** Set inside the 1920s Spanish-colonial Revival hotel of the same name (rooms are dated and bleak—don't stay here), this casual restaurant opened in 2009 with an ambitious mission to serve creative, farm-to-market American and Italian fare in a region with few dining options beyond old-school New Mexican joints. The kitchen uses mostly local and organic ingredients to prepare such notable dishes as wild-caught albacore sashimi with spicy-lemon Sriracha sauce, butternut squash soup with candied walnuts, and Mexican white shrimp over lemon-herb capellini with sundried-tomato puree. A worthy brunch is served on weekends. ⊠ *510 Douglas Ave.* ☎ *505/425–6659* ▭ *AE, D, MC, V* ☉ *No lunch Sat.*

$

NEW MEXICAN

✗ **El Rialto Restaurant & Lounge.** The margaritas here will put you in the right mood for huge steaks, stuffed sopaipillas, and tamales. Count on spicy, even by local standards, traditional New Mexican fare—hearty, smothered in sauce, and often deep-fried. The antique bar and historical photos, in addition to an eclectic jumble of friendly locals, make the attached Rye Lounge a fun spot for drinks. Service can be pokey. ⊠ *141 Bridge St.* ☎ *505/454–0037* ▭ *AE, D, MC, V* ☉ *Closed Sun.*

¢

SOUTHWESTERN

Fodor's Choice

★

✗ **Estella's Restaurant.** An old-fashioned, endearingly faded storefront café with a high pressed-tin ceiling, vintage photos, and a Formica counter with swivel stools, Estella's serves simple but memorable New Mexican fare—chicken burritos smothered with green chile, eggs with spicy chorizo, stacked enchiladas—plus a few American favorites like burgers. *Pescado* Veracruz (snapper simmered in a piquant sauce of spices, tomato, red chile, and onion) is a good choice for dinner. ✉ *148 Bridge St.* ☎ *505/454–0048* ▭ *No credit cards* ☉ *Closed Sun. No dinner Sat.–Wed.*

$ ╳ **Landmark Grill.** Popular with locals, hotel guests, and day-trippers, the
AMERICAN   atmospheric restaurant inside the iconic Plaza Hotel serves three meals daily. Cuisine tends toward tried-and-true American (shrimp cocktail, Cobb salad, filet mignon, roasted pork with mushroom-tarragon sauce), with a few New Mexican specialties—blue corn enchiladas, green-chile stew—thrown in. Be sure to enjoy a drink, or perhaps even an after-dinner cigar, at the adjacent Byron T.'s Saloon, with its pressed-tin ceilings and high windows overlooking the plaza. ✉ *Plaza Hotel, 230 Old Town Plaza* ☎ *505/425–3591* ⊕ *www.plazahotel-nm.com/restaurant. html* ▭ *AE, D, DC MC, V.*

WHERE TO STAY

$ ⌂ **Pendaries Village.** The mood here (where the name is pronounced pan-da-*ray*) is budget motel meets Kit Carson, but this secluded retreat and the surrounding mountain hamlet of Rociada provide a relaxing place to enjoy some high-altitude golfing. The beautifully laid out **Pendaries Golf Course** (☎ *505/425–9890) lies* at 7,500 feet altitude and snakes through the eastern edge of the Sangre de Cristo Mountains. Overnight golf packages are available, and daily greens fees are $45 weekdays and $55 weekends (optional golf-cart rental is $15). The rooms here have perfunctory motel-room decor but are clean and comfortable; the on-site Moosehead Restaurant and Saloon (open mid-May to mid-September), with its century-old bar, is usually crowded with locals who come for the steaks and Southwestern food. **Pros:** well-priced; plenty of outdoor activities; secluded setting. **Cons:** bland rooms could use updating; far from civilization. ✉ *1 Lodge Rd., off NM 105, 26 mi northwest of Las Vegas* ⌂ *Box 820, Rociada 87742* ☎ *505/425–3561 or 800/733–5267* ⊕ *www.pendaries.net* ⤳ *18 rooms* ♿ *In-room: no a/c, Internet. In-hotel: restaurant, bar, golf course* ▭ *MC, V* ☉ *Closed Nov.–Mar.*

$ ⌂ **Plaza Hotel.** Rooms at this three-story Italianate hotel, which has
Fodor'sChoice hosted the likes of Doc Holliday and Jesse James, balance the old
★   and the new—they're not overly fancy, but they've been handsomely renovated with high-quality linens, and they've got plenty of space, painted molding, high stamped-tin ceilings, and a sprinkling of charming antiques. Each room also has a modern bath, coffeemaker, and flat-screen TV, with microwaves and refrigerators available on request; and a full breakfast is included. About half the rooms are in the adjacent and similarly historic and also Italianate Ilfeld Building, which the hotel purchased and renovated in 2009. **Pros:** nicest rooms in the region; captures the vibe of the Old West; many shops and eateries within walking distance. **Cons:** moderate street noise; an old property with plenty of quirks. ✉ *230 Old Town Plaza* ☎ *505/425–3591 or 800/328–1882* ⊕ *www.plazahotel-nm.com* ⤳ *67 rooms, 4 suites* ♿ *In-room: a/c, refrigerator (some), Wi-Fi. In-hotel: restaurant, room service, bar, Wi-Fi hotspot, some pets allowed* ▭ *AE, D, DC, MC, V* ⦿ *BP.*

6

CAMPING

¢ ⚠ **Las Vegas New Mexico KOA.** Five miles south of Las Vegas, you can camp and cook out near a piñon-juniper hillside with beautiful views. There's a recreation room, as well as outdoor areas for playing volleyball and horseshoes. The pool feels fantastic after a dry, dusty day of exploring. In addition to the usual KOA accommodations, this site has a one-bedroom apartment available above the main office. ⊠ *I–25, Exit 339, at U.S. 84* 🕾 *HCR 31, Box 1, Las Vegas 87701* 🕾 *505/454–0180 or 800/562–3423* ⊕ *www.koa.com/where/nm/31133* ⚐ *Flush toilets, full hookups, drinking water, guest laundry, showers, picnic tables, general store, play area, swimming (pool), Wi-Fi* 🛒 *5 cabins, 80 tent sites, 54 with hookups* ⊟ *D, MC, V.*

SHOPPING

Paintings, ornate tinwork, contemporary photos, and striking jewelry created by more than a dozen local artists are displayed inside the vintage adobe house that contains **El Zocalo de los Artisanos de Las Vegas** (⊠ *212 Plaza St.* 🕾 *505/718–5515*), just off Old Town Plaza.

New Moon Fashions (⊠ *132 Bridge St.* 🕾 *505/454–0669*) has a well-chosen selection of natural-fiber and imported women's clothing, and comfortable shoes.

Plaza Antiques (⊠ *1805 Old Town Plaza* 🕾 *505/454–9447*) contains several dealers offering a wide range of antiques from different periods; it's in a stunningly restored hip-roof adobe 1870s Victorian.

Rough Rider Antiques (⊠ *501 Railroad St.* 🕾 *505/454–8063*) carries an impressive selection of memorabilia, furniture, glassware, and cowboy and Native American ephemera, much of it dating to the town's Victorian heyday.

Tome on the Range (⊠ *158 Bridge St.* 🕾 *505/454–9944*) is a well-appointed bookstore with good Southwestern and kids' sections.

SPORTS AND THE OUTDOORS

Brazos River Ranch and Outfitters (🕾 *505/453–1212* ⊕ *www.nmoutfitter. com*) can take you on hunting and fly-fishing trips—and they'll do it with the friendliest service this side of the Pecos.

FORT UNION NATIONAL MONUMENT

Fodor's Choice
★   *25 mi north of Las Vegas via I–25 and then northwest 8 mi on NM 161.*

GETTING HERE

The only way to reach Fort Union is by car—it's about a 40-minute drive from Las Vegas, and an hour's drive if you're coming down from Springer.

Fort Union National Monument. The ruins of New Mexico's largest American frontier–era fort sit on an empty windswept plain. It still echoes with the isolation surely felt by the soldiers stationed here between 1851 and 1890, when the fort was established to protect travelers and settlers along the Santa Fe Trail. It eventually became a military supply depot for the Southwest, but with the taming of the West it was abandoned. The visitor center provides historical background about the fort and the

Santa Fe Trail; guided tours are available when volunteers are on hand. ⊠ *Off NM 161,Exit 364 from I–25 Watrous* ☎ *505/425–8025* 💰 *$3* ☺ *Early Sept.–late May, daily 8–4; late May–early Sept., daily 8–6.*

EN ROUTE

As you drive up Interstate 25 from Las Vegas and Fort Union, the high prairie unfolds to the east, an infinite horizon of grassland that's quite breathtaking when the sun sets. **Wagon Mound** (at Exit 387 off Interstate 25) is a butte shaped like a covered wagon, rising from the open plains. The butte is where travelers crossed over from the Cimarron Cutoff to journey south to Fort Union. Local lore tells of mysterious lights, ghosts, and murders committed on top of the butte. The tiny village has few services and is verging on "ghost town" status, with many of its few businesses having closed in recent years and a population dwindling to around 300.

SPRINGER

70 mi north of Las Vegas and 55 mi north of Fort Union via I–25.

A stroll under the shady oaks of Springer's main street is a journey into the past; if it weren't for the modern-day cars driving by, you might think Harry Truman was still president. Indeed, there's not a lot to see and do in this small, sleepy town in which more than a few locals still seem a bit rankled about losing the title of county seat to Raton—in 1897. The main industry of this town of about 1,300 is the Springer Correctional Center, a minimum-security prison. Long ago a shipping center for cattle, sheep, and mining machinery, Springer was founded in 1870 when land baron Lucien Maxwell deeded 320 acres to his lawyer, Frank Springer, for handling the sale of the Maxwell Land Grant to the Dutch East India Company.

GETTING HERE

`A car is the only way to reach tiny Springer, which is just off Interstate 25, Exit 412. Allow about 45 minutes to get here from Raton, and 75 minutes from Las Vegas. From Clayton, it's a 90-minute drive west on U.S. 412/56.

EXPLORING

When Springer was the Colfax County seat, the 1883 structure that houses the **Santa Fe Trail Museum** served as a courthouse. The modest museum has a curious jumble of documents, maps, memorabilia, and other artifacts. The setup is not particularly sophisticated—it takes a bit of patience to wade through the assorted bits and pieces of the past. ⊠ *516 Maxwell St.* ☎ *505/483–5554* 💰 *$2* ☺ *Limited hrs; call ahead.*

Crammed with everything you'd expect to find at a five-and-dime, **Springer Drug** is a local hangout and the site of an ongoing gabfest. The highlight is the old (not old-fashioned, this is the original article) soda fountain, where you can order a sundae, malt, shake, cone, or even a light lunch. ⊠ *825 4th St.* ☎ *575/483–2356.*

OFF THE BEATEN PATH

Dorsey Mansion. In the middle of nowhere (about 35 mi northeast of Springer) stands this curious 36-room log-and-masonry castle built in 1880 by Stephen Dorsey, a U.S. senator from Arkansas. It was once a social gathering place for the rich and powerful. The career of the ambitious senator, who owned the mansion for 15 years, dissolved in a mail-fraud scandal. It's not open to the public, but history buffs may want to drive by. ✉ *Off U.S. 56, 25 mi east of Springer; turn north (left) at rest stop at mile marker 24 and take dirt road 12 mi* ☎ *575/375–2222* ⊕ *www.dorseymansion.com.*

Maxwell National Wildlife Refuge. More than 215 species of migratory waterfowl, including many geese and ducks in fall and winter, stop for a spell at this little-visited 3,700-acre prairie refuge 12 mi northwest of Springer. Sightings of great blue herons are not uncommon in midwinter, and bald eagles are fairly plentiful at this time. Sandhill cranes usually drop by in early fall, Canada geese around December. Deer, prairie dogs, long-tail weasels, jackrabbits, coyotes, bears, and elk live here. The fishing season (Lake 13 is stocked occasionally with rainbows) is between March and October. You can camp (no fee, no facilities) near the fishing areas. ✉ *Off I–25, Exit 426; follow NM 445 north ¾ mi, then NM 505 west 2½ mi to unmarked gravel road 1¼ mi to refuge* ☎ *575/375–2331* ✉ *Free* ☉ *Daily.*

WHERE TO STAY

¢ ⚐ **Brown Hotel & Cafe.** Granny's parlor circa 1924 is the best way to describe the quaintly old-fashioned and warmly welcoming Brown Hotel, where the lobby furnishings include a rocking chair by the fireplace and hooked rugs and doilies. Antiques decorate the basic but very affordable rooms, some of which have chenille bedspreads—note that bathrooms are shared, although each room has its own sink. The café's (¢) claims to fame include the baked goods and made-from-scratch soups (try the yummy broccoli-cheddar); both New Mexican and standard American dishes (tacos, burgers, breakfast burritos, and such) are on the menu. **Pros:** charmingly nostalgic; only real restaurant in town; breakfasts are hearty and well prepared. **Cons:** very few amenities; noise from restaurant and other rooms can be an issue. ✉ *302 Maxwell Ave.* ☎ *575/483–2269* ⇨ *11 rooms with shared bath* ⚐ *In-room: no phone, no a/c, no TV, Wi-Fi. In-hotel: restaurant* ⊟ *MC, V* ⊙ *BP.*

SHOPPING

Fodor'sChoice **Jespersen's Cache** (✉ *403 Maxwell Ave.* ☎ *575/483–2349*), a pack rat's
★ paradise, is a place to get lost for a morning or afternoon. The sheer mass of stuff is astounding—boxed Barbies, railroad lanterns, Depression-era glass, carousel horses. If you've got a collector's eye, you could make your lucky find here.

RATON

40 mi north of Springer via I–25, 95 mi northeast of Taos via U.S. 64.

Raton's appealing setting at the foot of a lush mountain pass provides wide-open views of stepped mesas and sloping canyons from the higher points in town. Because of its rich history, abundance of motels, and convenient location midway between Albuquerque and Denver, it's both a practical and reasonably engaging base for exploring northeastern New Mexico.

As it has for more than a century, Raton (population 7,200), the seat of Colfax County, runs on ranching, railroading, and the industry for which it's most famous, mining. In the early 1900s there were about 35 coal camps around Raton, most of them occupied by immigrants from Italy, Greece, and Eastern Europe. It was hard living in these camps and a tough road out, but a close-knit familial interdependence grew out of mining life—a spirit that still prevails in Raton today. People here are genuinely friendly and have great pride in their town.

Originally a Santa Fe Trail forage station called Willow Springs, Raton was born in 1880 when the Atchison, Topeka & Santa Fe Railway established a repair shop at the bottom of Raton Pass. The town grew up around 1st Street, which paralleled the railroad tracks. Much of the Raton Downtown Historic District, which has 70-odd buildings on the National Register of Historic Places, lies along Historic First Street, which consists of several restored blocks of antiques shops, galleries, and everyday businesses.

The Historic First Street area provides a fine survey of Western architecture from the 1880s to the early 1900s.

GETTING HERE

Although Amtrak's Southwest Chief stops daily in Raton, it's a nearly five-hour train ride from Albuquerque. A car is by far the most practical way to get here and explore the area—Raton lies midway between Albuquerque and Denver, a little less than a four-hour drive from either. It's also a logical stop if you're driving to Taos on U.S. 64 (about 2½ hours away) from the Oklahoma and Texas panhandles—it's about 2 hours from the border.

Contact **Amtrak** (☎ 800/872-7245 ⊕ www.amtrak.com).

VISITOR INFORMATION

Raton Chamber of Commerce Visitor Center (✉ 100 Clayton Rd. [U.S. 64], ½ mi west of I-25 Exit 451) ☎ 575/445-3689 ⊕ www.raton.info).

EXPLORING

Garlands and female figureheads adorn the 1906 **Abourezk Building,** originally a drugstore, later a dry-goods and grocery store, and now the home of the Heirloom Shop. (*See Shopping, below.*) ✉ 132 S. 1st St..

In the early 20th century the **Mission Santa Fe Depot,** a 1903 Spanish Mission Revival structure, serviced several dozen trains daily (Amtrak still stops here). ✉ 1st St. and Cook Ave.

The tiny storefront **Raton Museum,** inside the 1906 Coors Building (the beer manufacturer once used it as a warehouse), brims with artifacts of the coal camps, railroading, ranch life, and the Santa Fe Trail. The museum, which has a large and interesting photo collection, is a good first stop on a visit to the area. The docents enjoy explaining local history. ✉ 108 S. 2nd St. ☎ 575/445-8979 ⊠ Free ⊘ May–Sept., Tues.–Sat. 10–4; Oct.–Apr., Wed.–Sat. 10–4.

Southern California may have its HOLLYWOOD sign, but northeastern New Mexico has its **raton sign**—and this neon-red beauty is completely accessible. From the north end of 3rd Street, head west on Moulton Avenue to Hill Street and follow signs along the twisting road to the parking area at Goat Hill. Here you can walk around the sign, take in 270-degree views of the countryside, or picnic while contemplating the history of Raton Pass—the original Santa Fe Trail ran up Goat Hill clear into Colorado.

Just down a couple of blocks from the train station, the **Scouting Museum,** devoted to all things Boy Scout, is a must-see for anyone planning a visit to Philmont Scout Ranch in Cimarron. Amiable curator Dennis Downing has amassed an exhaustive collection of scouting-related books, badges, films of old jamborees, buttons, and *Boys' Life* magazines. ⊠ *400 S. 1st St.* ☎ *575/445–1413* ◻ *Free* ☉ *June–Aug., daily 10–5, or by appointment.*

Fodor'sChoice
★ More retro 1930s and '40s than Victorian, 2nd Street—Raton's main commercial drag—also has a number of handsome old buildings. The pride and joy of the neighborhood is the **Shuler Theater,** a 1915 European rococo–style structure whose lobby contains WPA murals depicting local history. The Shuler is one of the few remaining stages where all sets, curtains, and scenery are hand-operated with hemp rope and wooden pulleys. On weekdays between 10 and 5 the staff will happily take you on a free tour. ⊠ *131 N. 2nd St.* ☎ *575/445–4746* ⊕ *www.shulertheater. com* ◻ *Tours free* ☉ *By tour only, weekdays between 10 and 5.*

Fodor'sChoice
★
☉ **Sugarite Canyon State Park,** a gem of a park near the Colorado state line, has some of the state's best hiking, camping, wildflower viewing, fishing, and bird-watching ("sugarite" is a corruption of the Comanche word *chicorica,* meaning "an abundance of birds," and is pronounced shug-ur-*eet*). The road to Sugarite twists and turns high up into the canyon to Lake Maloya, a trout-stocked body of water from which a spillway carries overflow down into the canyon. From its 7,800-foot elevation hills rise up the eastern and western canyon walls where miners once dug for ore; you can still see gray slag heaps and remnants of the coal camp, which thrived here from 1910 to 1940, along portions of the park road near the visitor center (the former coal-camp post office) and down near the base of the canyon. The center contains exhibits on the mining legacy, and from here you can hike 1½ mi to the original camp.

Hikes elsewhere in the park range from the easy ½-mi Grande Vista Nature Trail to the pleasant 4-mi jaunt around Lake Maloya to the challenging Opportunity Trail. "Caprock" is the name given to the park's striking basaltic rock columns, which were formed millions of years ago when hot lava from a nearby volcano created the 10- to 100-foot-thick rocks. Climbing is permitted on these sheer cliffs, although it's not recommended for the faint of heart. ⊠ *NM 526, 7 mi northeast of Raton via NM 72* ☎ *575/445–5607* ⊕ *www.emnrd.state.nm.us/ PRD/ sugarite.htm* ◻ *$5 per vehicle* ☉ *Daily 6* AM–*9* PM.

The **Wells Fargo Express Building,** also designed in the Spanish Mission Revival style, was erected in 1910. The building houses both the Raton Arts & Humanities Council and the **Old Pass Gallery** (☎ *575/445– 2052*), which presents exhibits of regional art, books, and jewelry. ⊠ *145 S. 1st St.* ☎ *575/445–2052* ⊕ *www.ratonarts.org.*

**EN
ROUTE**

From the crest of **Capulin Volcano National Monument,** elevation 8,182 feet, you can see four states: Colorado, New Mexico, Texas, and Oklahoma. To the southeast is the vast section of the Santa Fe Trail that includes the Cimarron Cutoff; to the west are the snowcapped Sangre de Cristo Mountains. Unlike much of the dry surrounding territory, Capulin has enough water to support an oasis of trees, shrubs, and wildflowers. A narrow 2-mi paved road leads to the rim of the volcano; from there you can walk the final 0.2 mi into the extinct, and not especially dramatic, crater vent. (An easy-to-hike 1-mi trail circles the rim, so you can see it from different angles.) The cone of Capulin (the word is Spanish for "chokecherry"; these bushes are scattered across the area) rises more than 1,300 feet from its base. The visitor center has books, a brief video about the site, and interpretive exhibits. ✛ *To reach Capulin via scenic NM 72 and NM 325, allow about an hour and 15 minutes; it's a quicker 40-minute drive from Raton if you drive here by way of U.S. 64/87, which passes through ranch country underneath the biggest, bluest skies imaginable. Antelope herds graze alongside cattle. This is the classic West, with old windmills jutting into the sky of the rimrock country. The first 30 mi west from Capulin passes through the Raton-Clayton volcano field, where the cones of quiet volcanoes break the flat, green landscape. From Capulin to Clayton, it's about an hour's drive east on U.S. 64/87.* ✉ *NM 325, 3 mi north of Capulin off U.S. 64* ☎ *575/278–2201* ⊕ *www.nps.gov/cavo* 🖃 *$5 per vehicle* ☉ *Late May–early Sept., daily 8–5; early Sept.–late May, daily 8–4.*

WHERE TO EAT

¢　✕ **Eva's Bakery.** This cheerful sit-down bakery across from the Shuler
BAKERY　Theater has fabulous chocolate-cake doughnuts and oatmeal-raisin cookies—as well as a regular crowd of old-timers who gather here to keep up with town gossip. Breakfast burritos, chile fries, burgers, and Frito pies are big sellers. ✉ *134 N. 2nd St.* ☎ *575/445–3781* ☉ *Closed Sun. No dinner.*

$$　✕ **The Icehouse.** A historic 1909 icehouse near the rail bridge on the
AMERICAN　south end of Downtown is the setting for this restaurant serving steaks and seafood. The high-ceiling brick structure is accented with lots of old wood, historic photos of the icehouse in its working days, local cowboys and beautifully groomed prize bulls. If a memorable steak is what you're after, the prime Angus cuts are prepared to perfection by chef and co-owner Bill Ratliff. ✉ *945 S. 2nd St.* ☎ *575/445–2339* 🖃 *AE, DC, MC, V* ☉ *Closed Sun.*

$$　✕ **Sweet Shop Restaurant.** Don't be put off by the plain storefront; inside
AMERICAN　this long-running restaurant exudes history and nostalgia with its antiques, collectibles, and old-fashioned candies for sale (it was founded by a Greek candy maker named Pappas in the 1920s). Don't expect any surprises from the standard American menu—just reliably prepared dishes like Alaskan king crab legs, porterhouse steak, shrimp fettuccine, and a few surf-and-turf combos. ✉ *1201 S. 2nd St.* ☎ *575/445–9811* 🖃 *AE, D, DC, MC, V* ☉ *Closed Sun.*

6

WHERE TO STAY

¢ ⊞ **Budget Host Melody Motel.** Of the several vintage no-frills motels in northeastern New Mexico, this funky little 27-room lodging on the north side of Downtown Raton offers outstanding value. The rock-bottom-priced rooms are spotless and nicely updated, with sturdy, functional furnishings. You can pull your car right up to your unit at this retro motor court with a fabulous old sign, and the staff is friendly and helpful. **Pros:** walking distance from Shuler and Downtown shops; inexpensive; comfy common area with Wi-Fi and Continental breakfast. **Cons:** no frills. ⊠ *136 Canyon Dr.* ☎ *575/445–3655* ⊕ *www.budgethost.com* ⟿ *27 rooms* ⟡ *In-room: a/c. In-hotel: Wi-Fi hotspot, some pets allowed* ⊟ *AE, D, MC, V.*

$ ⊞ **Hearts Desire Inn Bed & Breakfast.** Gregarious host Barbara Riley, who grew up on a ranch south of Springer, has filled the rooms of her inn with Victorian antiques and collectibles (many for sale). This 1885 former boardinghouse is steps from Downtown dining and the historic district. The top-floor hunting-and-fishing-theme suite has a full kitchen, TV and VCR, and two twin beds. In addition to a hearty breakfast in town, snacks are served in the evening. **Pros:** historical 1885 building; convenient Downtown location. **Cons:** lots of stairs; frilly and old-fashioned decor isn't for everyone; some of the bathrooms are small. ⊠ *301 S. 3rd St.* ☎ *575/445–1000 or 866/488–1028* ⊕ *www.heartsdesireraton.com* ⟿ *3 rooms, 1 suite* ⟡ *In-room: a/c, kitchen (some), Wi-Fi. In-hotel: some pets allowed* ⊟ *AE, D, MC, V* ❘○❘ *BP.*

$ ⊞ **Holiday Inn Express.** The most upscale and contemporary of the hotels in town has clean rooms, fine views of Johnson Mesa and the vast grasslands, and a peaceful location south of Downtown. An extensive Continental breakfast buffet is included, as are snacks in the lobby from 4 to 8. Request one a room in the newer wing for extra legroom. **Pros:** beautiful vistas; plenty of handy in-room amenities. **Cons:** rates can get fairly steep during summer weekends; no restaurant. ⊠ *101 Card Ave., I-25 Exit 450* ☎ *575/445–1500 or 800/465–4329* ⊕ *www.ratonsfinest.com* ⟿ *80 rooms* ⟡ *In-room: a/c, Wi-Fi. In-hotel: pool, laundry facilities, some pets allowed* ⊟ *AE, D, MC, V* ❘○❘ *CP.*

CAMPING

¢ ⛰ **Sugarite Canyon State Park.** Arrive early for the best choice among the fully developed sites at either of this park's two campgrounds, Lake Alice and Soda Pocket. Be sure to follow park warnings regarding the resident brown bears at Soda Pocket. ⊠ *NM 526, 6 mi northeast of Raton* ✆ *HCR 63, Box 386, 87740* ☎ *575/445–5607; 877/664–7787 reservations* ⊕ *www.emnrd.state.nm.us/PRD/sugarite.htm* ⟡ *Flush toilets, full hookups, dump station, drinking water, showers, picnic tables, electricity* ⟿ *40 tent and RV sites, 12 with hookups* ⊟ *MC, V.*

NIGHTLIFE AND THE ARTS

Shuler Theater (⊠ *131 N. 2nd St.* ☎ *575/445–4746*) presents late-summer concerts, Music from Angel Fire (a program that brings world-class chamber music to various venues in northern New Mexico). Children's theater, local college productions, and traveling dance, folk dance, and vocal evenings are scheduled throughout the year. For the better part of this century, locals have popped into the rollicking **White House Saloon**

(✉ *133 Cook Ave.* ☎ *575/445–9992*) for drinks after work and late into the evening. If you get hungry, the adjoining restaurant serves well-prepared steaks and seafood from 6 to 9.

SHOPPING

Hattie Sloan, proprietor of the **Heirloom Shop** (✉ *132 S. 1st St.* ☎ *575/445–8876*), was one of the key figures involved in the restoration of Historic First Street. Hattie and her daughter and co-owner Cathy know their antiques and have packed this highly browse-worthy shop with beautiful selections, from rhinestone necklaces to quilts, china, and linens.

Rubin's Family Clothiers (✉ *113 S. 2nd St.* ☎ *575/445–9492*) sells Pendleton shirts, woolen skirts, and well-made shoes. Its owners, Kathryn and Leon Rubin, can tell you a thing or two about local history—their store has been in the family for almost a century. Given the quality of some of the merchandise, the prices at **Santa Fe Trail Traders** (✉ *100 S. 2nd St.* ☎ *575/445–2888 or 800/286–6975*) are reasonable. Items include earrings, sand paintings, dream catchers, Nambé hand-cast bowls, Navajo rugs old and new, beadwork, and kachinas (many by well-known artists).

Fodor's Choice
★
You can enter **Solano's Boot & Western Wear** (✉ *101 S. 2nd St.* ☎ *575/445–2632* ⊕ *www.solanoswesternwear.com*) a city slicker and exit a cowboy or cowgirl. The enormous space, an experience as much as a store, is full of fashionable, practical Western garb. Check out the collection of cowboy hats.

SPORTS AND THE OUTDOORS

Raton's playground is **Sugarite Canyon State Park.** *(See Exploring, above.)* Sugarite's alpine **Lake Maloya** (✉ *NM 526, 10 mi northeast of Raton* ☎ *575/445–5607*) is generously stocked with rainbow trout. The profusion of wildflowers and flocks of bluebirds make the lake a joy to hike around. Boating and ice-fishing are popular as well.

CLAYTON

43 mi east of Capulin on U.S. 64/87, 83 mi east of Springer on U.S. 56.

Clayton, which lies flat on the high prairie at an elevation of 5,000 feet, seemingly grew up out of nothing. Downtown is sleepy and sunny, with the old-fashioned retro-veneer typical of little Western towns. It's nowhere near an interstate and so lacks the scads of ubiquitous chain properties found in Las Vegas and Raton; mom-and-pop-owned shops dominate. This town of about 2,300 bills itself as the carbon dioxide capital of the world, but the carbon dioxide here isn't hanging in the air but rather underground, embedded in sandstone southwest of town. Cattle graze on the many ranches around Clayton, which is the seat of massive and sparsely populated Union County, which at more than 3,800 square mi is larger than Rhode Island and Delaware combined.

GETTING HERE

There's one and only one way to get to and from Clayton: personal car. It's a quite scenic (because of the mesmerizing blue skies and wide-open mesas) one-hour drive from Capulin on U.S. 64/87, or from Springer

SCENIC DRIVE: NM 72

Fodor's Choice ★ To reach Capulin from Raton, skip U.S. 64 and instead take **NM 72** past Sugarite Canyon State Park, a stunning road that climbs up over Johnson Mesa, from which you have amazing 100-mi views north over the mesa into the plains of eastern Colorado. It's bare and flat up here, as though you're driving across a table straddling the Colorado–New Mexico border. About halfway across the mesa (15 mi from Raton), note the old stone church to your right, which was built by the early farmsteaders and has since been abandoned—it's a beautiful, lonely little building with a presence that illustrates the life of solitude the mesa's settlers must have endured.

Farther along on the right, a historical marker details the 1908 discovery of Folsom Man by George McJunkin, which established the existence of indigenous inhabitants in the area dating back some 10,000 years. The road trails down the eastern side of the mesa and leads into tiny Folsom. Here make a right turn south on NM 325 to reach Capulin Volcano, 6 mi away.

it's a little more than 90 minutes via U.S. 56/412. Clayton is just 10 mi west of the Oklahoma and Texas borders—allow about 2½ hours for the drive to Amarillo, and 4 hours northeast to Dodge City, Kansas (a popular route among fans of the Old West).

VISITOR INFORMATION
Clayton Chamber of Commerce (✉ *1103 S. 1st St.* ☎ *575/374-9253 or 800/390-7858* ⊕ *www.claytonnewmexico.org*).

EXPLORING
The friendly locals here may look at you cockeyed when they learn you've come to sightsee, but Clayton does have a few curious landmarks.

☼ You can view more than 500 fossilized dinosaur tracks along the ½-mi wooden **Dinosaur Trackway at Clayton Lake State Park,** making this one of the few sites of its kind in the world. The tracks, estimated to be 100 million years old, were made when the area was the shore of a prehistoric sea. Eight species of dinosaurs, vegetarian and carnivorous, lived here. The sparkling lake that gives the state park its name is ideal for camping, hiking, and fishing. ✉ *NM 370, 12 mi north of Clayton* ☎ *575/374-8808* ⊕ *www.emnrd.state.nm.us/prd/Clayton.htm* 🖾 *$5 per vehicle* ☼ *Daily 6 AM–9 PM.*

The 1892 **Eklund Hotel Dining Room & Saloon,** whose splendid Victorian dining room has crystal chandeliers, apricot tufted-velvet booths, giltflocked wallpaper, and marble fireplaces, is quite a draw in Clayton. The hunting-lodge atmosphere in the saloon is quite different but no less authentic, with a large raw-rock fireplace, wooden booths, mounted game heads, and historic photos and clippings of Clayton's past. The town's most famous historical character, the notorious train robber Black Jack Ketchum, was hanged just out front in 1901. His last words were "I had breakfast in Clayton, but I'll have dinner in hell!" Put your boot up on the brass rail at the bar (won in a poker game) and order a cold one. ✉ *15 Main St.* ☎ *877/355-8631* ⊕ *www.theeklund.com.*

There are few better places in New Mexico to soak in wide-open prairie vistas, clear skies, and fresh air than in the 230,000-acre **Kiowa and Rita Blanca National Grasslands.** One section of the grasslands is near Clayton and spreads east into Oklahoma and Texas. Another prominent one is about 80 mi west of Clayton, closer to Springer, south of U.S. 56. In the section near Clayton, if you look carefully, you can see ruts made by the wagons that crossed on the Old Santa Fe Trail. The land was drought-stricken during the Dust Bowl of the 1920s and '30s, when homesteaders abandoned their farms. After that, the government purchased the land and rehabilitated it to demonstrate that it could be returned to the tall grassland native to the region.

For an enjoyable loop drive through the grasslands, head east out of Clayton on U.S. 56; at NM 406 head north to just past Seneca, to where NM 406 makes a sharp turn to the east. Take the county gravel road west 3 mi and north 1 mi, noting the interpretive sign about the Santa Fe Trail. Continue a little farther north to the green gate that leads to the trail (following the limestone markers), where you can see ancient wagon ruts. Except for the occasional house or windmill, the view from the trail is not much different from what the pioneers saw. ⊠ *Off U.S. 56, north and south of Clayton* ⊕ *Administrative office: 714 Main St., Clayton 88415* ☎ *575/374–9652* ⊕ *www.fs.fed.us/r3/cibola/districts/kiowa.shtml* ☑ *Free.*

WHERE TO STAY

$ 🖼 **Best Western Kokopelli Lodge.** Locals have long used this Southwestern-style Best Western to house out-of-town guests, where the rooms are spacious and pets are allowed (by prior arrangement). **Pros:** well maintained; large rooms. **Cons:** next to railroad tracks; traffic noise. ⊠ *702 S. 1st St.* ☎ *575/374–2589 or 800/392–6691* 🛏 *44 rooms* ♿ *In-room: a/c, Wi-Fi. In-hotel: pool, some pets allowed* ⊟ *AE, D, MC, V* ⧄*BP.*

$ 🖼 **Eklund Hotel Dining Room & Saloon.** The renovated rooms of this rustic beauty of a building are comfortable and elegant, and each has custom-made furniture and a modern-but-period-style bathroom. Friendly staff help get you situated and will happily tell you about the hotel's history and things to do in the area. American standards and Southwestern fare are served in the dining room and saloon ($–$$). Old West elegance and the house specialty—hand-cut steaks—please locals and visitors alike. **Pros:** Wild West decor and history; friendly staff. **Cons:** furnishings are simple and old-fashioned. ⊠ *15 Main St.* ☎ *575/374–2551 or 877/355–8631* ⊕ *www.theeklund.com* 🛏 *26 rooms* ♿ *In-room: a/c, Wi-Fi. In-hotel: restaurant, bar* ⊟ *MC, V* ⧄*CP.*

CIMARRON

108 mi from Clayton via U.S. 56/412 west to Springer, I–25 north, and NM 58 west; 42 mi southwest of Raton on U.S. 64.

As you approach Cimarron from the south or east, you can't help but notice a massive, grayish-white pinnacle perched atop the mountain at the northwest edge of town. Known as the Tooth of Time, it indicated to Santa Fe Trail travelers that their journey was nearing an end, for Santa Fe was only seven days away by wagon. Today the Tooth of Time is the emblem of the Philmont Scout Ranch, where 21,000 Boy Scouts assemble each summer.

In a land that was once home to Jicarilla Apaches and Utes, Cimarron later became a refuge for gamblers and outlaws and a stopping point for soldiers, gold seekers, and mountain men. (Its name means "untamed" in Spanish.) Founded in the early 1840s, it was the home of land baron Lucien Maxwell. These days, with a population around 900, it's a sleepy little town with some fine old buildings, and a good base from which to do some great fishing on the Cimarron River or in the various rivers flowing through Valle Vidal, and an interesting stopover between Taos and Raton. It's common to see deer grazing on the edge of town—and look out for elk if you're driving at dusk or after dark. They are huge, and hitting one can be deadly.

GETTING HERE

Tiny Cimarron lies at the eastern edge of the Sangre de Cristos and is directly along the popular U.S. 64 route that leads to Taos from Raton (making it a popular route for travelers coming from Colorado, Kansas, Oklahoma, and northern Texas). It's a 45-minute drive from Raton to Cimarron, and another 90 minutes to Taos, passing through scenic Eagle Nest. Personal automobile is the only practical way to reach and explore this area.

VISITOR INFORMATION

Cimarron Chamber of Commerce (✉ 104 N. Lincoln Ave. ☎ 575/376–2417 or 888/376–2417 ⊕ www.cimarronnm.com).

EXPLORING

☾ Costumed reenactments at **Kit Carson Museum** demonstrate 19th-century life on what was then the Maxwell Land Grant, but is now part of the incredible Philmont Ranch. Exhibits include a working *horno* (oven), blacksmith shop, and the Maxwell Trading Post—stocked as it might have been during Santa Fe Trail days. Period crafts are also demonstrated, and free tours are given. ✉ NM 21, 11 mi south of Cimarron, Rayado ☎ 575/376–1136 ☎ Free ☉ Mid-June–mid-Aug., daily 8–5.

★ The workers who toiled inside the sturdy, steep-roofed stone building that holds the **Old Mill Museum** once processed 300 barrels of flour a day for the Maxwell Ranch and the Jicarilla Apache reservation. Now the mill houses four floors of vintage photos, clothing, tools, and memorabilia depicting life in Colfax County from the 1860s into the 20th century. ✉ 220 W. 17th St., 1 block north of St. James Hotel ☎ 575/376–2417 ☎ $2 ☉ Late May–early Sept., hrs vary; call ahead.

The largest scouting venue in the world, 137,000-acre **Philmont Scout Ranch** has hosted nearly 1 million Boy Scouts throughout its history—about 21,000 currently visit every summer, and on any given day about 3,000 of them are out plying the property's miles of rugged trails. Phillips Petroleum magnate and Boy Scouts of American benefactor Waite Phillips established the mountainous ranch. The museums of the Philmont Scout Ranch include **Villa Philmonte,** the restored 1927 Spanish-Mediterranean summer home of Waite Phillips, furnished with European and Southwestern antiques and Native American and Southwestern art. Tours of the mansion are conducted in July and August. Scouting cofounder Ernest Thompson Seton donated most of the holdings of the **Philmont Museum & Seton Memorial Library,** among them New Mexican art and artifacts, Native American rugs and pottery, and books on natural history and the history of the Southwest. ⊠ *17 Deer Run Rd., off NM 21, 4 mi south of Cimarron* ☎ *575/376–2281* ⊕ *www. philmontscoutranch.org* ☜ *Museum free, villa tour $5* ☉ *Museum Sept.–May, Mon.–Sat. 8–5; June–Aug., daily 8–5. Villa tours late May– early Sept. by appointment.*

With 27 bullet holes in the tin dining-room ceiling, resident ghosts profiled on the TV show *Unsolved Mysteries,* and a guest book signed by Jesse James, the **St. James Hotel** (⊠ *617 S. Collison Ave.* ☎ *575/376–2664* ⊕ *www.exstjames.com* ☉ *Tours daily between 10 and 4*) epitomizes the Wild West. Every notable outlaw of the late 19th century is said to have visited the place. Chef to presidents Lincoln and Grant, Frenchman Henri Lambert opened the St. James first as a saloon in 1872 and then eight years later developed it into a hotel. The lobby is filled with Western Victoriana: overstuffed sofas; stuffed heads of bison, elk, deer, and bear on the walls; and fringe on the lamp shades.

EN ROUTE West of Cimarron Canyon State Park, U.S. 64 passes over a high bald ridge, from which you'll be awarded a magnificent view over **Eagle Nest Lake,** the Moreno Valley, and the eastern slope of the Sangre de Cristo Mountains in the distance. Continue down through Eagle Nest Lake village toward Angel Fire (*See also Enchanted Circle in Taos, chapter 4*). Then make a left turn (south) onto NM 434, which passes little Black Lake and offers one final view of the valley before narrowing sharply and plummeting into dark, deep, ponderosa pine–shrouded Guadalupita Canyon. Drive slowly: the road twists and turns and crosses several one-lane bridges over Coyote Creek.

The Rincon Mountains rise to 9,500 feet to the west of NM 434, and to the east (a left turn off the highway) you can stop for a ramble at **Coyote Creek State Park** (☎ *575/387–2328* ⊕ *www.emnrd.state.nm.us/ PRD/CoyoteCreek.htm* ☜ *$5*), which also has exceptionally good trout fishing and some campsites.

South of Coyote Creek State Park on NM 434, you'll pass through tiny, insular **El Turquillo.** Here the highway widens as it opens into a broad sunny valley—to the east you'll spy the red-rock cliffs that form the face of Black Mesa, the land barrier between here and the eastern grasslands.

OFF THE BEATEN PATH **Valle Vidal.** One of New Mexico's great, although quite isolated, scenic routes heads northwest from U.S. 64 toward the town of Costilla (44 mi north of Taos on NM 522), affording great opportunities for sighting elk, deer, wild turkeys, and many other birds. The roughly 80-mi dirt road requires several hours of driving to complete—although it's okay for non–four-wheel-drive vehicles in summer and fall (assuming there hasn't been a major rainfall in a couple of days and you're comfortable driving on some pretty rough roads). The trip passes through the heart of pristine Valle Vidal, a remote 102,000-acre tract of high-mountain grasslands, ponderosa, aspen, and sandstone cliffs. The fishing (season is July to December) in this region is mighty fine—the native Rio Grande cutthroat trout is found only in the rivers here—and there are

SCENIC DRIVE: ROUTE 64

One of the most breathtaking stretches of highway in the state is U.S. 64 west from Cimarron through **Cimarron Canyon State Park** (☎ 575/377–6271 ⊕ www.emnrd. state.nm.us/prd/CimarronCanyon. htm 🖼 $5 per vehicle), which is actually just one small part of the immense 33,000-acre Colin Neblett Wildlife Area. The road passes through a steep and lush canyon banked by 400-foot crenellated granite palisades. Paralleling the road is the sparkling Cimarron River, which is known for its superb trout fishing. Wildlife (including elk, deer, and bear), granite cliff formations, a

natural spring, an abandoned mine, and a visitor center are also draws. There's a campground beneath the pines, too, with spaces for RVs (no hookups) and tents, picnic tables, and pit toilets.

As you come around a bend in NM 434 heading from El Turquillo toward Mora, behold the Sangre de Cristo range, specifically the east side of **Trampas and Truchas peaks**, from an angle few tourists ever see. Just before Mora and the intersection with NM 518 is an intricate network of irrigation ditches that farmers employ to keep this region so fertile.

two campgrounds, Cimarron and McCrystal. The western section of the road is closed May through June for elk-calving season, and the eastern section is closed to protect the elks January through March. ⊠ *Off U.S. 64, turnoff is 8 mi east of Cimarron* ☎ *575/758–6200* ⊕ *www.fs.fed.us/ r3/carson (*for information on conservation efforts and history of Valle Vidal, visit ⊕ *www.vallevidal.org).*

WHERE TO EAT AND STAY

¢ ✗ **Colfax Tavern.** Also known as Cold Beer, New Mexico (which is
AMERICAN painted in huge white letters on the exterior), this little red roadhouse
Fodor's Choice on the way to Cimarron from Raton continues a tradition from the
★ Prohibition era. Among the joint's trademarks are an ongoing card game, excellent green-chile burgers, Shiner Bock (a beloved beer from Shiner, Texas) on tap, Spaghetti Monday, Saturday-night dances, and a winter *Jeopardy!* tournament. The colorful staff and crowd make you feel right at home, especially if you're wearing cowboy boots. Keep in mind that the tavern closes nightly at 8 PM. ⊠ *U.S. 64, 11 mi east of Cimarron, Colfax* ☎ *575/376–2229* ⊟ *No credit cards* ☉ *Closed Tues.*

$ **St. James Restaurant.** Given a fresh makeover and much-improved menu
AMERICAN in 2009, the atmospheric restaurant and bar inside the creaky old St. James Hotel now makes for the town's only notable dining option (and it's open for three meals a day). The kitchen mostly focuses on traditional American favorites, such as T-bone steaks, deep-fried catfish, and chicken-fried steaks, but several New Mexican dishes are offered, too, including hearty stuffed sopaipillas. ⊠ *617 S. Collison Ave.* ☎ *575/376–2664* ⊕ *www.exstjames.com* ⊟ *AE, D, MC, V.*

$ 🏠 **Casa del Gavilan.** On the Santa Fe Trail and directly below the Tooth
Fodor's Choice of Time, this 1912 white adobe compound (the name means "House
★ of the Hawk") on 225 acres is a romantic hideaway of the first order. The original owner, industrialist J. J. Nairn, used to entertain artists

and other creative types here, and writer Zane Grey wrote *Knights of the Range* while he was holed up here. The rooms in the main house are furnished with Southwestern antiques and artworks by the likes of Frederick Remington and Charles Stewart, and the 12-foot ceilings with huge pine vigas (support beams) lend an airy feel to the massive adobe walls. A two-bedroom suite in the adjacent guest cottage is ideal for families or friends traveling together. Tasty breakfasts should be taken on the patio when the weather permits. During the winter months, dinner can be arranged for guests with advanced notice. **Pros:** magnificent architecture; large rooms; breathtaking natural surroundings. **Cons:** remote; no TV. ⊠ *NM 21, 6 mi south of Cimarron 87714* ☎ *575/376–2246 or 800/428–4526* ⊕ *www.casadelgavilan.com* ⊃ *4 rooms, 1 2-bedroom suite* ⚲ *In-room: no a/c, no TV. In-hotel: Wi-Fi hotspot* ☰ *D, MC, V* ⊠ *BP.*

$
Fodor's Choice
★

⊡ **St. James Hotel.** Lace curtains and Victorian-era antiques adorn 12 of the rooms here (there are also 10 modern, more affordable, but less distinctive motel rooms). The entire property underwent an elegant $1.5 million restoration in 2009, and rooms now look better than ever, but there's a bit of a chill in the air—and that's just what the ghost-hunting fans like about this supposedly haunted hotel. An extensive hot breakfast buffet is included, and the restaurant (⇨ *Where to Eat, above*) serves reliably good American fare. **Pros:** quaint; rustic; fun for kids and others with an interest in ghost sightings. **Cons:** newer units have less interesting decor; Wi-Fi only carries to a few rooms because of thick adobe walls. ⊠ *617 S. Collison Ave.* ☎ *575/376–2664 or 888/376–2664* ⊕ *www.exstjames.com* ⊃ *22 rooms, 1 suite* ⚲ *In-room: a/c, Wi-Fi (some). In-hotel: restaurant, bar, Wi-Fi hotspot* ☰ *AE, D, MC, V.*

6

SHOPPING

Just off the main highway to the north is East 9th Street, a street of historic buildings and a few shops. The **Cimarron Art Gallery** (⊠ *337 E. 9th St.* ☎ *575/376–2614 or 800/253–1470*) sells Southwestern odds and ends, and artifacts, and has a 1930s soda fountain for dishing out ice cream, sodas, and coffee drinks. **Blue Moon Eclectics** (⊠ *333 E. 9th St.* ☎ *575/376–9040*) has locally made arts and crafts as well as some Navajo and Zuni jewelry.

MORA

72 mi south from Cimarron on U.S. 64 and NM 434; 30 mi northwest of Las Vegas on NM 518.

Originally settled in 1835 by land grantees, Mora was seen by the Mexican government as a buffer between their territory and encroaching Americans. The town grew rapidly from the get-go, but refused to give up loyalty to Mexico when the U.S. troops took over in 1846. Battles for control of the area raged for more than a year, until the United States finally gained the upper hand on its new territory. One hundred years ago, Mora was a bustling center of commerce and politics, and was known as the breadbasket of New Mexico because of its incredible production of wheat and grains. The wide, curbed streets

Tapetes de Lana

There are few fairy-tale stories of revitalized rural economies in America. Tapetes de Lana is one of them.

Tapetes de Lana ("Wool Tapestry" in Spanish) started as a vocational-training program for weavers in Las Vegas in 1998 with a small grant and the sheer determination of its founder, Carla Gomez. Gomez had supported herself and her three children with her weaving for years and wanted to extend the skill to her community in the hopes that others could do the same rather than leave the area to find work or take minimum-wage jobs in one of the large national chain stores that have begun to populate the area.

What started out as a small group of women working in an old, one-room schoolhouse on the outskirts of Las Vegas has blossomed—considerably. Gomez now runs two weaving centers (one on the Las Vegas plaza, the other in the center of Mora), oversees 40 employees, and is supervising the construction of a spinning mill, theater-arts complex, and commercial kitchen on the Mora property.

The weaving centers offer more than the promise of a new economic base in these relatively sleepy areas—they also represent a revitalization of a traditional art form that in many areas of the country is dying out entirely. Weaving has been a mainstay in New Mexico since 1598, when Don Juan de Oñate brought Spanish colonists and Churro sheep from Spain. Despite struggling to stay vital since the late 1800s, New Mexico's weavers retain a reputation for high-quality, uniquely beautiful products. Tapetes de Lana has become an essential component of that living tradition.

And the result of all this industrious-ness? Gorgeous, handwoven shawls, scarves, rugs, and heirloom *jerga* blankets. Custom-made pillows, coasters, and yarns are available. Silk and alpaca, mohair, wool, and chenille textiles all hang gracefully from the walls and racks in the studios. Weavers study and practice their skills in the same studio where the work is sold.

When you're in Las Vegas or Mora, stop and visit the bustling shops and studios of Tapetes de Lana. You're witnessing rural revitalization in action.

and building fronts, though in need of restoration, attest to the town's past importance.

Today Mora is a sparsely settled, still mostly Hispanic farming village where you can get gas, pick up snacks at the small-town market, and enjoy a few lesser-visited but no less diverting attractions. There are a couple of informal restaurants on the main road serving traditional New Mexican fare as well as the excellent lunch-only café at Salman Ranch (⇨ *La Cueva Historic District, below*), open late summer to midfall.

GETTING HERE

You need a car to visit this relatively remote town, and driving to Mora over the Sangre de Cristo range via the High Road and NM 518 makes an adventurous and highly photogenic back way into northeastern New Mexico from Santa Fe (about 2½ hours) or Taos (about 1½ hours). Pretty much every route into town is beautiful, including the more direct

SCENIC DRIVE: MORA TO PEÑASCO

From Cleveland Roller Mill you can either return via NM 518 to Las Vegas (about 30 mi) or continue north on NM 518 over the gorgeous eastern face of the Sangre de Cristo range. You'll eventually come to Peñasco, on the High Road to Taos, from which you can either go south to Santa Fe or north to Taos. **The drive from Mora to Peñasco** offers spectacular mountain views, and passes by old farmsteads and adobe hamlets slowly being worn down by the wind and weather.

Fodor'sChoice ★ As you head south on NM 518 toward Las Vegas, be sure to stop in the **La Cueva Historic District.** Among the buildings here, which date to the 1850s, is a stone-walled mill that supplied flour to the soldiers of Fort Union. Pioneer rancher Vicente Romero's

mill also supplied power to the area until 1950; at what is now called the **Salman Ranch,** you can pick raspberries mid-August to mid-October, or buy fresh berries, raspberry jam and vinegar, and dried flowers and herbs at the original La Cueva Ranch Store. Brilliantly colored wildflower gardens, and homemade tamales, burgers, and raspberry sundaes served at the café draw families during "U Pick" raspberry season. The historic district's San Rafael Church, dating from the 1870s, is also worth a look. ⊠ *NM 518 at NM 442, 10 mi south of Mora, 20 mi north of Las Vegas* ☎ *575/387-2900 or 866/281-1515* ⊕ *www.salmanraspberryranch.com* ☉ *Store Jan.–June, Thurs.–Mon. 9–4; July–Dec., daily 9–5; café mid-Aug.–mid-Oct., Tues.–Sat. 11–4; U Pick field, mid-Aug.–mid-Oct., Tues.–Sun. 10–4.*

6

45-minute drive up NM 518 from Las Vegas, and the twisting, narrow hour-long drive down NM 434 from Angel Fire.

EXPLORING

At the junction of NM 434 and NM 518, make a right and head a couple of miles north to **Cleveland Roller Mill Museum,** a fixture in Mora Valley, which served as the region's main flour mill in the late 1800s. Milling demonstrations are held over the Labor Day Millfest, and in summer you can visit the artists' cooperative, where local artisans sell their sculpture, weaving, jewelry, and other crafts. The museum is run by the proprietors of surrounding Cassidy Farms, a nursery specializing in native conifers and shrubs. ⊠ *NM 518* ☎ *575/387-2645* ☎ *$2* ☉ *Weekends 10–3, and by appointment.*

Tapetes de Lana Weaving Center (☎ *575/387-2247* ⊕ *www.tapetesdelana.com*), the local weaving collaborative, has a spacious studio and shop on the corner of NM 518 and NM 434, where you can purchase beautiful handwoven textiles and help support the local economy and culture.

☾ If you've got animal-loving kids with you, stop by **Victory Ranch,** a working 1,100-acre alpaca farm. You can pet the high-altitude–loving creatures and join in the feeding three times daily (at 11 am, 1 pm, and 3 pm) as well as visit the gift shop for Peruvian-made hats, sweaters, and mittens. The ranch is handicapped-accessible. ⊠ *NM 434, 1 mi north of NM 518* ☎ *575/387-2254* ⊕ *www.victoryranch.com* ☎ *$3* ☉ *Daily 10–4.*

Southeastern New Mexico

WORD OF MOUTH

"We headed south to White Sands. All I can say is WOW, very unusual place to be in. There is a paved road that turns into a carved-out road-way in the dunes themselves. It is such a wonderful experience but hot even when it is cool . . . lots of places to sled down the dunes, picnic, and bathrooms. You can rent the sleds at the visitors center."

—2dogs

Updated by
Georgia de
Katona

Southeastern New Mexico retains a delicious feeling of wildness. The nearest interstate is generally as far as 200 mi away, and with few lights from strip malls and no urban sprawl, the stargazing here is a treat for the expert and novice alike.

Because of the clarity of the skies and the absence of typical light pollution, Cloudcroft has one of the largest solar observatories in the world, the National Solar Observatory. Alamogordo, at the base of the mountains, uses special lights to minimize glare for optimal night-sky views. Of course, the area's seeming proximity to the heavens is what's made it the subject of an ongoing debate among UFO believers for almost 60 years: what was it, exactly, that fell from the sky over Roswell that night in July of 1947? Drive to Cloudcroft (8,600 feet) from Alamogordo and you will double your altitude and take you into the cool mountain air of the heavily forested Lincoln National Forest. Curious, large-eared mule deer wander amid the juniper and pines, as well as among sand dunes near the Pecos River farther east. The seemingly monotonous Chihuahuan Desert holds the underground wonderland of Carlsbad Caverns, and the hulking El Capitan peak.

For all its beauty, the area seems understandably harsh to strangers. Spanish settlers quickly bypassed the region in the late 1500s, in favor of the more friendly environs around the Rio Grande in the western and northern portions of New Mexico. Yet in this very region—at Black Water Draw near what is now Portales and Clovis—evidence of some of the earliest inhabitants of North America has been found. Artifacts discovered in the region prove that primitive hunters and gatherers lived here as long as 11,000 years ago, alongside fantastic creatures like the woolly mammoth.

Native Americans lived here for hundreds of years before encroachment by the Spanish, and later the Americans. Though Hispanic settlers had established a few scattered communities, the area was primarily the homeland of Mescalero Apaches. In the mid-1800s Fort Sumner and Fort Stanton were erected to offer protection for miners and American settlers during intensified skirmishes with local tribes. Near Ruidoso, in what is left of their traditional homeland in the Sacramento Mountains, the Mescalero Apaches now own a luxury resort and ski area that attract tens of thousands of visitors annually.

The grasslands in southeastern New Mexico came to be ruled by cattle kings like John Chisum in the late 1800s. The baby-faced outlaw Billy the Kid (Henry McCarty) became a living legend here during the infamous Lincoln County War, waged by rival entrepreneurs in 1872. He wasn't the only outlaw to make his mark on the territory, however; in the now-vanished town of Seven Rivers, between Carlsbad and Artesia, shoot-outs were said to be so common around the turn of the 20th century that it was claimed "you could read your newspaper by the light of the gunfire." Things calmed down—a bit—once the discovery of oil and other valuable minerals brought miners to the area in the early 1900s.

ORIENTATION AND PLANNING

GETTING ORIENTED

The wildly rugged Guadalupe and Sacramento mountain ranges cut through the south-central portion of the state, dividing the Pecos River valley to the east from the Mesilla River valley to the west. The major highway south through southeastern New Mexico is U.S. 285, accessible from Interstate 40 at the Clines Corner exit, 59 mi east of Albuquerque. If you're destined for Roswell or Carlsbad from southwestern New Mexico, the best route is U.S. 70 east from Las Cruces or U.S. 62/180 east from El Paso, Texas. To get to Roswell and other points in southeastern New Mexico, drive east from Albuquerque on Interstate 40 for about 60 mi, exit on U.S. 285 heading south, and continue 140 mi to Roswell. From Roswell take U.S. 285 to Carlsbad, about 75 mi away (320 mi from Albuquerque). From El Paso, Texas, take U.S. 62/180 east and north 154 mi to Carlsbad Caverns (187 mi to Carlsbad).

The Southeast Corner. It's a lot more like Texas than other areas of New Mexico, and you'll notice a strong Texas drawl coming from the locals. Stark expanses of land are broken by the dramatic Guadalupe Mountains, and once you've visited Carlsbad Caverns you'll realize why so many passed by them without knowing what amazing things lay below.

East-Central Outposts. Cattle are the name of the game in the grassy plains of this region. You'll see huge open areas in between the small towns and amazing wildflowers if you're lucky enough to drive through after good rains. Tucumcari and Santa Rosa offer amazing displays of vintage neon along the famed Route 66.

Heading to High Country. After visiting the visually stunning and smoldering heat of White Sands, you'll be delightfully surprised by how fast the scenery and the temperature change once you head into the mountains toward Cloudcroft or Ruidoso. The Wild West outpost of Lincoln is but one of the many fun historic towns to visit in the area.

SOUTHEASTERN NEW MEXICO PLANNER

WHEN TO GO

Winters tend to be gentle in the desert regions, but between May and early September blistering heat is not uncommon. Even the mountainous areas can be surprisingly warm during a hot spell. In the lowlands, plan summer outdoor excursions for early morning or late afternoon. Spring is cooler, but it's often accompanied by blustery, dust-laden winds. One of the best times to visit is between September and early November, when skies are clear blue and the weather is usually balmy. The mountains typically get plenty of snow in the winter months, though the roads are well maintained and navigable, and the snow wonderfully powdery and dry.

TOP REASONS TO GO

White Sands National Monument.
Journey to Mars. The otherworldly
landscape of White Sands is an
amazing place any time of day; the
white gypsum sands glisten and
remain surprisingly cooler than
you'd think.

Carlsbad Caverns. Journey to
the center of the Earth. Nothing
can prepare you for the visually
stunning, massive scale of these
incredible natural wonders. The
comfortable subground temperatures
are a delightful respite from the
heat above.

Roswell. Journey beyond. Even if
you aren't an alien enthusiast, visiting Roswell is a fun detour—especially with kids. You'll learn why
rumors and stories persist and see
every variety of alien souvenirs—
even plastic lawn aliens (à la those
beloved pink flamingos).

Cloudcroft and Ruidoso. Journey
to the clouds. Once you've gone
down, head up—way, way up—where
cool alpine breezes greet you. The
towns remind you of their Old West
history while offering all sorts of
delightful respite from the blistering
heat of the lowlands.

GETTING HERE AND AROUND

AIR TRAVEL

Albuquerque International Sunport (✉ *2200 Sunport Blvd. SE, Albuquer-
que* ☎ *505/842–4366*) is 380 mi north of Carlsbad and 295 mi north
of Roswell. **El Paso International Airport** (✉ *6701 Convair Dr., El Paso,
TX* ☎ *915/772–4271*) in Texas is the main gateway to southern New
Mexico. The major airlines with scheduled service to the airport are
America West, American, Continental, Delta, Frontier, and Southwest.
The municipal airport in Roswell has regular service from Dallas-Fort
Worth (DFW) and Los Angeles (LAX) on **American Eagle** (☎ *800/433–
7300* ⊕ *www.aa.com*).

BUS TRAVEL

Greyhound (☎ *800/231–2222* ⊕ *www.greyhound.com*) provides bus
service to Carlsbad, White's City, and other destinations in southern
New Mexico. **Silver Stage Lines** (☎ *800/522–0162*) offers van service
to Carlsbad Caverns National Park and Carlsbad by special charter.

CAR TRAVEL

The quality of the roadways in southeastern New Mexico varies widely,
particularly in remote rural areas. Drive with caution on the region's
narrow highways, which particularly in mountainous areas have no
shoulders. On minor roadways, even if paved, be alert for curves, dips,
and steep drop-offs. You can rent a car at El Paso International Airport and Albuquerque International Sunport. Auto dealerships in some
southeastern New Mexico cities rent cars. Your best bet for finding car
rentals in smaller communities, such as Roswell and Carlsbad, is at
municipal airports. Both Avis and Hertz rent cars at the Roswell airport,
while Hertz has a site at Carlsbad's airport.

ABOUT THE RESTAURANTS

Leave the fancy duds at home—you're unlikely to find a formal dining room to strut into. Casual dress reigns supreme in this part of the world. Although much of southeastern New Mexico is cowboy country, where thick steaks and barbecue make the meal, good Mexican food can be found, too. Food tends to lean heavily toward the old-fashioned American meat-and-potatoes style—generally pretty bland with often surprisingly mild chile. There are a few standout restaurants, and we've noted them.

ABOUT THE HOTELS

You'll find generally reliable chain motels to choose from if that's what suits you, but you can also choose from a luxury resort, numerous quaint cabins, and several charming and beautiful bed-and-breakfasts in the Sacramento Mountains. These private facilities serve some of the tastiest food in the region and can offer amenities like therapeutic massage, horseback riding, and guided fishing and hiking tours.

WHAT IT COSTS					
	¢	$	$$	$$$	$$$$
Restaurants	under $10	$10–$15	$16–$22	$23–$30	over $30
Hotels	under $70	$70–$120	$121–$175	$176–$250	over $250

Restaurant prices are per person for a main course at dinner. Hotel prices are for two people in a standard double room in high season, excluding 10%–12% tax.

PLANNING YOUR TIME

You can explore a cross section of the southeast's attractions in three days by moving quickly. If you start your trip from El Paso, Texas, swing through Guadalupe Mountains and Carlsbad Caverns national parks first. If you're dropping down from Albuquerque, reverse the itinerary and make cities such as Ruidoso and Roswell your first stops before traveling on to the national parks. *See also Great Itineraries, below. For more information on Carlsbad Caverns* see chapter 9.

THE SOUTHEAST CORNER

Some folks refer to the southeast as "Little Texas," and indeed you'll find the easy smiles and small-town graciousness of the neighbor state in great abundance. The biggest attraction—Carlsbad Caverns National Park—is just above the Texas state line. *See chapter 9 for more information.* Cattle and sheep still roam miles of arid pastures, much the way they have for well over a century. During the past two decades a steady migration of newer residents—many of them retirees leaving crowded metropolitan areas for wide-open spaces and clean air—has added significantly to the population and to the availability of such staples as espresso.

LINCOLN NATIONAL FOREST

GETTING HERE

Lincoln National Forest comprises two distinct sections, one with Carlsbad Caverns, the other encompassing the mountains around Ruidoso and Cloudcroft. U.S. 70 runs east–west from Tularosa at Interstate 25, to Ruidoso and through Roswell. U.S. 82 runs east–west from I–25 at Alamogordo, to Cloudcroft and on through Artesia. U.S. 285 runs north–south through Roswell and Artesia. To get to Carlsbad Caverns, take U.S. 285 south and turn southwest onto U.S. 180, in Carlsbad. You'll travel about 18 mi before turning north onto NM 7 at White's City, with 7 mi to go before arriving at the Carlsbad Caverns visitor center.

Covering 1.1 million acres of Eddy, Otero, Chaves, and Lincoln counties, the magnificent **Lincoln National Forest** encompasses two distinct regions: the arid lower elevations near Carlsbad, and the towering pines and mountain peaks of the Ruidoso area. The piñon and juniper of the southernmost region stretch through the Guadalupe Mountains to connect with the Carlsbad Caverns and Guadalupe Mountains national parks. The forestland has many caves, some of which can be accessed with a free permit available at the Guadalupe Ranger District.

Call or visit the **Guadalupe Ranger District** (✉ *Federal Bldg., Room 159, 114 S. Halagueno St., Carlsbad* ☎ *505/885–4181*) for permit information. These caves are not developed, so be prepared for primitive conditions. The only private development you can find other than scattered ranches is at **Queen** (49 mi southwest of Carlsbad, on NM 137). This site consists of a small mobile-home community, restaurant, store, gas station, and church camp. This forested area is hugely popular with hunters lured by ample populations of mule deer.

Fodor's Choice   You truly have to see **Sitting Bull Falls** to believe that a cascading,
★   150-foot-tall waterfall flowing into beautiful, crystal-clear pools exists in southeastern New Mexico. It's no mirage—and you can even swim in the waters of this oasis. A 1-mi hike from the parking lot over a paved trail takes you to a desert riparian area lush with ferns, watercress, and cottonwoods. At the parking lot, the forest service provides rock ramadas for picnics. There are viewing decks and restrooms, and 16 mi of hiking trails lace the area. The park is open for day use only. If you want to camp overnight, drive southwest on NM 137 until you reach the New Mexico–Texas state line and Dog Canyon Campground in Guadalupe Mountains National Park. During extreme drought conditions, call first to make sure the area hasn't been closed.

✉ *From Carlsbad take U.S. 285 north about 12 mi, then turn west on NM 137 for 27 mi* ☎ *575/885–4181* 💲*$5 per vehicle, free Wed.* ☉ *Apr.–Sept., daily 8:30–6; Oct.–Mar., daily 8:30–5.*

The northernmost portion of the Lincoln forest, surrounding the resort community of Ruidoso, is a more traditional sanctuary, with snowy mountain peaks, lakes, and gurgling mountain streams. Developers have capitalized on this beauty, so the forest is interspersed with cabins, resorts, church camps, condos, and ski runs. Still, there are miles of pristine wilderness, many of which can be accessed by hiking trails.

More than 25 camping areas are scattered throughout Lincoln National Forest. Although fishing lakes and streams are available on private, municipal, or tribal lands, there's very little opportunity for the sport on these public forestlands. To obtain more information about hiking, camping, hunting, and other recreation, contact the forest service's main headquarters in Alamogordo (☎ *575/434–7200* ⊕ *www. stateparks.com/lincoln.html*).

ARTESIA

36 mi north of Carlsbad on U.S. 285, 40 mi south of Roswell on U.S. 285, 110 mi west of Alamogordo on U.S. 82.

Artesia got its name from artesian wells that were dug here in the late 1800s to tap the abundant water supply just below the ground's surface. The region's subterranean bounty includes more than water, however; oil and gas were discovered here in the 1920s, and today there are more than 20,000 oil and 4,000 natural-gas wells in the area. Pumping jacks cover the dunes and fields to the east. The Navajo Oil Refinery, alongside U.S. 285, is a major employer for this city of about 12,000.

A Federal Law Enforcement Training Center took over the abandoned campus of a private liberal arts college here in 1989, and thousands of law-enforcement employees from agencies such as the U.S. Bureau of Land Management and U.S. Customs Service now train at its driving and shooting ranges. Other than grabbing a meal, there isn't a great deal to do here. On football-season Fridays you can't miss the array of orange banners and bulldog emblems touting the local high school team, the Bulldogs, in this highly sports-conscious town.

Artesia is a quick 36-mi drive north of Carlsbad. The inns near Carlsbad Caverns National Park (⇨ *chapter 9*), as well as the restaurants, are arguably good reasons to make the drive. They stand out as gems in a little town that doesn't generally draw much tourism and a region that is short on gems.

GETTING HERE

Artesia is easily accessed from Interstate 25 just north of Alamogordo by heading east on U.S. 82 through Cloudcroft. You can also get here from Interstate 40 by driving south on U.S. 84 or U.S. 285. Greyhound is the only bus line serving the area.

Contacts Greyhound (☎ *800/231–2222* ⊕ *www.greyhound.com*).

EN ROUTE For a closer look at the farms and dairies of the Pecos Valley, veer northeast off the main highway (U.S. 285) just north of Artesia and take Alt. U.S. 285. This 40-mi route meanders through quaint farming villages of Lake Arthur, Dexter, and Hagerman and will rejoin the main highway at Roswell.

To view one of the valley's little-known but fascinating attractions, turn east onto Hatchery Road in Dexter. One mile down you'll find the **Dexter National Fish Hatchery & Technology Center** (✉ *7116 Hatchery Rd., Dexter* ☎ *575/734–5910*), a facility with the noble mission of studying, propagating, and possibly salvaging endangered species of warm-water fish like the pike minnow (once known as the Colorado squawfish, and

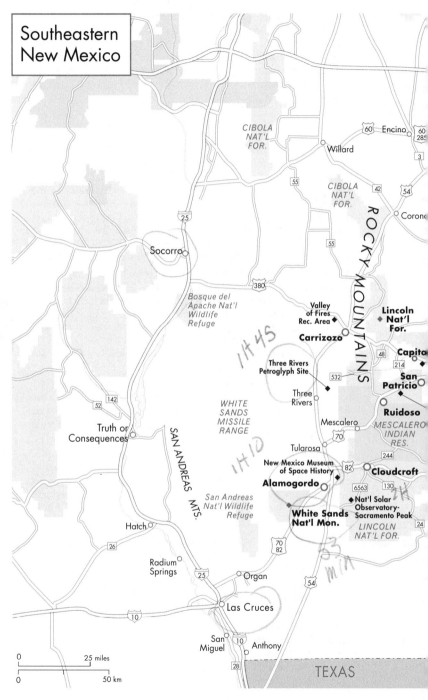

Southeastern New Mexico

Encino
60
285
Willard
3
CIBOLA NAT'L FOR.
55
CIBOLA NAT'L FOR.
42
54
25
Corone
Socorro
55
380
Bosque del Apache Nat'l Wildlife Refuge
Valley of Fires Rec. Area
Lincoln Nat'l For.
Carrizozo
48
Capita
214
Three Rivers Petroglyph Site
532
San Patricio
WHITE SANDS MISSILE RANGE
Three Rivers
Ruidoso
Mescalero
MESCALERO INDIAN RES.
142
52
70
Truth or Consequences
SAN ANDREAS MTS.
Tularosa
244
New Mexico Museum of Space History
82
Cloudcroft
Alamogordo
130
San Andreas Nat'l Wildlife Refuge
6563
Nat'l Solar Observatory-Sacramento Peak
Hatch
White Sands Nat'l Mon.
LINCOLN NAT'L FOR.
24
26
Radium Springs
70 82
25
Organ
54
10
Las Cruces
San Miguel
10
Anthony
0   25 miles
28
0   50 km
TEXAS

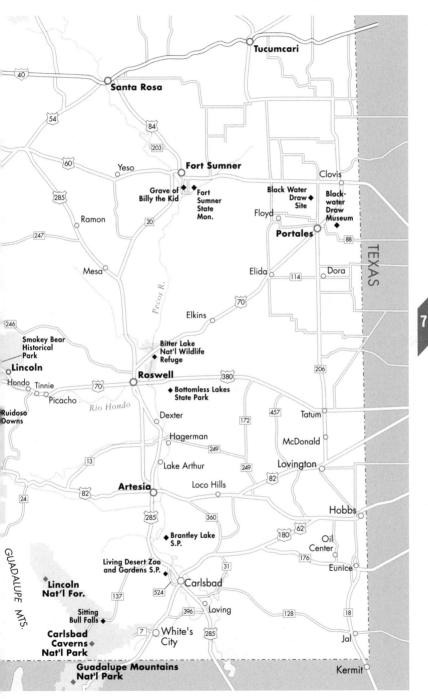

GREAT ITINERARY

It's best to start from the gateway of El Paso, Texas, and make **Carlsbad Caverns National Park** (⇨ chapter 9) your first stop. Take the Big Room Tour in the late morning or early afternoon, and in warmer months, be sure to catch the spectacular evening bat exodus out of the cave's mouth. Afterward you can overnight in **Carlsbad.** On the morning of Day 2, stop by Living Desert Zoo and Gardens State Park before heading north to **Roswell** to learn about alleged alien visitors at the International UFO Museum and Research Center and view the impressive

collections of the Roswell Museum and Art Center, including the Goddard rocketry display and paintings by Southwestern artists. Push on to overnight in **Lincoln.** You awaken in a town of 70, where the ghosts of past gunslingers loom large. Make time for some outdoor activities in the mountains surrounding **Ruidoso.** A ski resort is open in winter and horse racing takes place at Ruidoso Downs in summer. Arrange your schedule so you have at least an hour for **White Sands National Monument,** which is open in summer until 9.

once common to the Colorado River). You can view live exhibits and read all about the center's activities at a small visitor center on-site. A guide will accommodate tour groups if requests are made in advance.

ROSWELL

40 mi north of Artesia on U.S. 285; 205 mi southeast of Albuquerque, south on I–25 and east on U.S. 380; 78 mi southwest of Fort Sumner, via NM 20 and U.S. 285.

The true character of Roswell has been largely obscured over the last few decades by the brouhaha over UFOs. Rather than a hotbed of extraterrestrial activity, Roswell is in reality a simple, conservative city with an economy based on manufacturing, agriculture, oil, and gas. The population of around 50,000 grew out of a farming community founded in the fertile Pecos Valley about a century ago; artesian wells still provide the water used to irrigate crops like alfalfa, hay, and cotton. Residents may sigh over the fact that visitors only come here in search of spaceships—but they've also learned to have fun with it, and to cash in on the tourist trade.

GETTING HERE

You can reach Roswell by heading south from Interstate 40 or north from Interstate 10 (in Texas) on U.S. 285. From Interstate 25, take U.S. 54 via U.S. 70 at Tularosa, north of Alamogordo, or U.S. 380 at Carrizozo. Public transport doesn't exist out here. You're best off renting a car at El Paso or Albuquerque.

VISITOR INFORMATION

Roswell Chamber of Commerce (✉ *131 W. 2nd St.* ☎ *575/623–5695 or 877/849–7679* ⊕ *www.roswellnm.org*).

EXPLORING

Fodor's Choice ★ The **Anderson Museum of Contemporary Art,** which started as a personal collection evolving from founder Don Anderson's patronage of artists, since the 1960s has become an important showcase of contemporary art. This 17,000-square-foot, salon-style museum exhibits sculpture, painting, print, and textiles, and it continues to evolve according to the refined-but-eclectic whims of Anderson, who at 90-plus years of age remains very active in museum operations. Among the 300-odd pieces is an impressive collection of the dramatic, large-scale fiberglass sculptures by recently deceased El Paso artist Luis Jiménez—they're oddly at home with the golf-bag "sharks" by Robbie Barber hung from the ceiling. The remarkable and competitive Roswell Artist-in-Residence program, whose participants' work feeds the ongoing collection, is operated by the museum's foundation and provides a home, studio, supplies and a stipend to five artists at a time over one year. ⊠ *409 E. College Blvd.* ☎ *575/623–5600* ⊕ *www.roswellamoca.org* ⊠ *Free* ۞ *Weekdays 9–noon and 1–4, weekends 9–noon and 1–5.*

★ ۩ The lakes at **Bottomless Lakes State Park** were created when an ancient sea that covered the area 240 million years ago evaporated, leaving behind salt and gypsum deposits. Those deposits then slowly dissolved with accumulations of rain, and ceilings collapsed into sinkholes. Scuba divers, boaters, and swimmers now take advantage of the crystal-clear, spring-fed water. The main Lea Lake facility has a bathhouse with modern showers and restrooms, and paddleboats and paddleboards can be rented from late May to early September. A visitor center has exhibits of park history, geology, and geography; during the peak season, interpretive lectures are given in the evenings. ⊠ *Off U.S. 380, 12 mi east of Roswell, turn south on NM 409 and continue 3 mi* ☎ *575/624–6058* ⊠ *$5 per vehicle* ۞ *Park daily 6 am–9 pm (day use). Visitor center late May–early Sept., daily 9–6; early Sept.–late May, daily 8–5.*

From the viewing platforms along the 8½-mi self-guided tour at the **Bitter Lake National Wildlife Refuge,** you can watch for snow geese, sandhill cranes, and other exotic birds, along with more-familiar species. ⊠ *4065 Bitter Lakes Rd.; from Roswell, head north on U.S. 285, then turn east on Pine Lodge Rd. for 7 mi* ☎ *575/622–6755* ⊠ *Free* ۞ *Daily dawn–dusk.*

۩ Depending on your point of view, the **International UFO Museum and Research Center** will either seem like a display of only-in-America kitsch or a real opportunity to examine UFO documentation and other phenomena involving extraterrestrials. This homespun nonprofit facility is surprisingly low-tech—some of the displays look like they've seen previous duty on B-movie sets (the museum is, coincidentally, inside an old movie house). The blowups of newspaper stories about the 1947 Roswell crash, its fallout, and 1950s UFO mania make interesting reading, and you can view the videotaped recollections of residents who say they saw the crash firsthand. The gift shop sells all manner of souvenirs depicting wide-eyed extraterrestrials, along with books and videos. Though some of the exhibits are whimsical, the portion of the museum devoted to research accumulates serious written collections and investigations of reported UFOs.

7

The museum organizes the UFO Festival (⊕ *www.roswellufofestival. com*) over the first weekend of July each year. Lectures about UFOs and aliens, science fiction writers' workshops, and films are offered, in addition to guest appearances by celebrities—Adrienne Barbeau and Julian Sands were recent luminaries. Vendors and musicians set up in the parking lot, there are parades and costumes galore, and the atmosphere all over Downtown is festive. Five-day passes are $20, otherwise day visits are included with museum entrance. ⊠ *114 N. Main St.* ☎ *575/625–9495 or 800/822–3545* ⊕ *www.roswellufomuseum.com* ▦ *$5* ⊙ *Daily 9–5.*

Fodor's Choice The impressive **Roswell Museum and Art Center** often gets overlooked in
★   favor of alien hoopla, but it contains a very good collection of Southwestern artists, including works by Georgia O'Keeffe, Henriette Wyeth, Peter Hurd, plus early modernist pieces from members of the early Taos and Santa Fe art colonies. The extensive Rogers Aston Collection has displays of Plains Indian artifacts and Spanish armor. Robert H. Goddard's collection exhibits the inventions and journals of the rocketry genius, who conducted some of his early experiments near Roswell. The **Robert H. Goddard Planetarium,** which is part of the museum, is open only occasionally, generally on holiday weekends and for celestial events—call ahead for the schedule. ⊠ *100 W. 11th St.* ☎ *575/624–6744* ⊕ *www.roswellmuseum.org* ▦ *Free* ⊙ *Mon.–Sat. 9–5, Sun. 1–5.*

WHERE TO EAT AND STAY

$$ ✕ **Cattle Baron.** You'll find the standard array of grilled meats and sea-
STEAK   food at this centrally located restaurant, which is part of a regional
☾   chain. While the food and service is merely adequate, the extensive and fresh salad bar is a relief if you're hankering for a big plate of fresh veggies with lots of toppings and tasty dressings. The dark-wood furnishings here are offset by big windows and a skylight. ⊠ *1113 N. Main St.* ☎ *575/622–2465* ⊕ *www.cattlebaron.com* ▤ *AE, D, DC, MC, V.*

¢ ✕ **El Toro Bravo.** Next to the International UFO Museum and Research
MEXICAN   Center, this Mexican restaurant achieves a kitschy flair with matador
★   paintings, piñatas, and wrought-iron wall lamps. Owner Artie Acevas uses family recipes in the preparation of ethnic favorites such as fajitas, enchiladas, tacos, and burritos. Cold beer and wine help cool the delicious fire of the spicy dishes. ⊠ *102 S. Main St.* ☎ *575/622–9280* ▤ *AE, D, MC, V.*

$$ ⊡ **Hampton Inn & Suites.** This contemporary hotel stands out even
☾   among the reliable Hampton Inn chain properties. High ceilings, cozy comforters, and very good beds are bonuses in large, elegant, contemporary rooms. **Pros:** friendly, professional staff; exceptionally clean rooms; walking distance to several reliable chain restaurants. **Cons:** 2 mi from Downtown. ⊠ *3607 N. Main St.* ☎ *575/623–5151* ⊕ *www. roswellsuites.hamptoninn.com* ➫ *70 rooms* ⊘ *In-room: a/c, refrigerator, Wi-Fi. In-hotel: pool, gym, laundry facilities, laundry service* ▤ *AE, D, DC, MC, V* ⊙┃ *CP.*

UFO Over Roswell

Of all the sightings of Unidentified Flying Objects in the world, it's the one that took place more than 50 years ago outside Roswell, New Mexico, that remains most credible in people's minds. Rumors of alien bodies and silenced witnesses are the real-life happenings that inspired fantastical entertainment like the TV series The X-Files and Roswell. The most likely reason so many people refuse to dismiss the Roswell Incident is the undisputed fact that in July 1947 something fell from the sky.

On July 8, 1947, officers at Roswell Army Airfield announced to the Roswell Daily Record that the military had retrieved wreckage of a UFO nearby. The next day U.S. Army Air Force officials retracted the story, saying it was in fact a weather balloon that had crashed. Over the years, theories of a cover-up and suspicions that the military had also recovered alien bodies linked the town of Roswell with aliens as strongly as Loch Ness is with its monster. Backing up the alien-bodies theory is the testimony of people like mortician Glen Dennis, who today works with Roswell's International UFO Museum and Research Center. He maintains that a nurse at the military hospital passed him sketches of aliens and that the military called him in 1947 to ask odd questions about embalming bodies.

In the 1990s a flood of information, including books like UFO Crash at Roswell and accounts from eyewitnesses who claim they were silenced, rekindled the conspiracy theories. The air force responded in 1994 with a report revealing that fragments mistaken for a flying saucer came not from a weather balloon but from an air force balloon used in the top-secret Project Mogul. The true nature of the balloon had to be concealed in 1947 because its purpose was to monitor evidence of Soviet nuclear tests. As this new explanation didn't address the alien-bodies issue, the air force issued a 231-page report, "The Roswell Report, Case Closed," in 1997. This document explains that from 1954 to 1959, life-size dummies were used in parachute drop experiments. That this time frame postdates the 1947 Roswell Incident is immaterial to the air force, which claims people have simply confused dates in their memories.

The holes in every story, whether from the military or eyewitnesses, have allowed the Roswell UFO legend to mushroom extravagantly. It now incorporates tales of captured aliens (alive and dead) that further feed our imaginations, thanks in part to the capitalizing media. You can see depictions of slender, doe-eyed aliens, known as the "Grays," all over storefronts and souvenir shops in Roswell. These spooky, diminutive creatures might even be called the New Mexico version of leprechauns, with only the rare treasure seeker getting to encounter one.

7

CAMPING

¢ 🦥 **Bottomless Lakes State Park**. Lea Lake, 90 feet deep, is the only lake of the group in this park where swimming is allowed. In summer, you can rent paddleboards and paddleboats for a small fee. The lakes stand in stark contrast to the hot, unshaded surroundings, although the campgrounds do have sheltered picnic tables. Rainbow trout are stocked in Devil's Inkwell during the winter months. ✉ *Off U.S. 380, 12 mi east of Roswell; turn south on NM 409 and continue 3 mi* ☎ *877/664–7787* ⚒ *Flush toilets, pit toilets, full hookups, partial hookups (electric and water), dump station, drinking water, showers, grills, picnic tables, electricity, public telephone, ranger station, play area, swimming (lake)* ⤳ *32 RV sites, 27 tent sites* 🚫 *No credit cards.*

EAST-CENTRAL OUTPOSTS

Vast herds of pronghorn (commonly, but erroneously, called antelope) graze alongside roadways in this wide-open area, known as the Eastern Plains of New Mexico. When rains have been generous to this usually parched region, green grass and wildflowers adorn the rolling hills; ordinarily, however, the grasslands struggle to survive the burning heat of the New Mexico summer and take on a golden-brown hue. The many miles of uninhabited prairie create a convenient cattle range, helping the many ranchers in this area continue a century-old tradition.

People in these agricultural and oil communities are busy making a living, so you won't find many touristy stops or shops along the highways. The purity of the rural life seen here is part of its charm, though. A note of caution: pay attention to winter snowstorm warnings. You don't want to get caught in the blinding, blizzardlike conditions that can create huge drifts of snow.

PORTALES

91 mi northeast of Roswell on U.S. 70.

Along with neighboring Clovis, this farming and ranching community bills itself as the world's top producer of Valencia peanuts, a specialty crop ideally suited to red, sandy soil. In October, Portales hosts a peanut festival where nuts are sold in raw form or cooked up in candies and other delicacies. Portales also is home to Eastern New Mexico University, a four-year college.

GETTING HERE

From Roswell, take U.S. 285 north 5 mi and U.S. 70 east 91 mi. Or, if you want a nice drive through sand dunes and rural farmland, from Artesia, take U.S. 82 east 65 mi to Lovington and NM 206 north to Portales 109 mi.

VISITOR INFORMATION

Portales Chamber of Commerce (✉ *100 S. Ave. A* ☎ *575/356–8541 or 800/635–8036* ⊕ *www.portales.com*).

EXPLORING

In the early 1930s, archaeologists in eastern New Mexico unearthed remnants of prehistoric animals like mammoths, camels, and saber-tooth tigers. More important, this was the first site in the contiguous United States that provided conclusive evidence that humans lived here at least 11,300 years ago. The culture and artifacts associated with these earliest inhabitants take their name from the nearby city of Clovis. The **Black Water Draw Museum** contains photographs of early excavations, along with artifacts from Clovis, Folsom, and later Native American civilizations. The museum looks a little lonely on the side of U.S. 70, 8 mi northeast of Portales, but its interior is cheerful, with informative, well-presented exhibits and a "touch and feel" table for children.

The **Black Water Draw Archaeological Site** remains active and is open at regular hours to visitors in summer and on weekends in spring and fall. Self-guided tours on developed trails are well worth the effort for the privilege of viewing work in progress at a major archaeological site. Stay strictly on the trails, which offer options of ¾-mi or ½-mi round-trips with about 20 different interpretive stops with signs describing vegetation and geology (the wildflowers following spring rains can be spectacular). On hot days, wear a hat, use sunscreen, and carry water for these excursions. An exhibit building offers a fascinating look at ongoing excavations of prehistoric animal bones, and an ancient, hand-dug well can be viewed near the exhibit building.

✉ *42987 Highway 70* ☎ *575/356–5235* 🖅 *Site and museum $3* ⊘ *Museum late May–early Sept., Mon.–Sat. 10–5, Sun. noon–5; early Sept.–late May, Tues.–Sat. 10–5, Sun. noon–5. Site June–Aug. and Nov.–Mar., daily 9–5; Sept., Oct., Apr., and May, weekends 9–5.*

The nation's largest **windmill collection** is found on Portales's Kilgore Street (you can't miss it). Resident Bill Dalley has collected the 85-plus windmills in his own backyard. Since he's the past president of the International Windmillers' Trade Fair Association, meetings of the group are sometimes conducted here.

WHERE TO EAT AND STAY

$$
STEAK
✕ **Cattle Baron.** This Portales steak house in the heart of cattle country was the founding establishment for the popular chain that now extends into Roswell, Ruidoso, and Las Cruces. Prime rib is the specialty, and the trademark salad bar doesn't disappoint with its fresh greens, crisp veggies, and homemade soups. The interior is decorated with plenty of wooden accents and skylights. ✉ *1600 S. Ave. D* ☎ *575/356–5587* ⊕ *www.cattlebaron.com* 🖃 *AE, D, DC, MC, V.*

$
AMERICAN
✕ **Mark's Restaurant & Catering.** Tasty breakfast omelets, steaks, and sandwiches attract the hungry college crowd from nearby Eastern New Mexico University. Try the house specialty, a chicken-fried steak dinner. This diner-style hangout has a fun atmosphere. The tables are inlaid with tile, the chairs are covered with brightly colored vinyl, and there are a few exotic parrot decorations. Their house-made salsa is tasty! ✉ *1126 W. 1st St., across from airplane display next to Eastern New Mexico University* ☎ *575/359–0857* 🖃 *D, MC, V.*

$ Holiday Inn Express. Locals send their guests to this updated facility for the clean, comfortable rooms and down-home friendly staff. Rooms contain appealing dark-wood furnishings and comfortable chairs, in addition to great beds. Good-size bathrooms with large showers and adjustable showerhead height are added amenities. **Pros:** a standout among other hotel options in town. **Cons:** no restaurants within walking distance. ⊠ *1901 W. 2nd St.* ☎ *575/356–4723* ⌁ *65 rooms* ⌂ *In-room: refrigerator, Wi-Fi. In-hotel: pool, laundry facilities, laundry service* ▭ *AE, D, DC, MC, V.*

CAMPING

¢ △ **Oasis State Park.** Sand dunes, huge cottonwood and elm trees, and the refreshing air from the 3-acre lake make this state park seem like an oasis. Especially pleasurable activities here include hiking, bird-watching (especially in winter), fishing, and camping. Horseback riding is allowed, although swimming and boating are not. Six miles north of Portales via U.S. 70 and NM 467. ⊠ *Off NM 467, 6 mi north of Portales* ☎ *575/356–5331 park, 877/665–7787 reservations* ⌂ *Flush toilets, pit toilets, partial hookups (electric and water), dump station, drinking water, showers, grills, picnic tables, electricity, ranger station, play area* ⌁ *13 RV sites, 10 tent sites* ▭ *No credit cards.*

FORT SUMNER

83 mi northeast of Roswell.

Besides its historic significance as one of the area's earliest military outposts and the place where Billy the Kid was killed, the town of Fort Sumner is known for its air park, where NASA launches balloons used in scientific research. Nearby Sumner Lake provides irrigation for area farms and ranches, as well as boating and fishing opportunities. In June the De Baca County Chamber of Commerce hosts the annual Old Fort Days here, with living-history demonstrations and mock shoot-outs.

GETTING HERE

Though in the middle of proverbial nowhere, Fort Sumner is easy to reach. It's 75 mi northwest of Portales, north on U.S. 70 and west on U.S. 60/84; 83 mi northeast of Roswell, north on U.S. 285 and northeast on NM 20; 159 mi southeast of Albuquerque, east on Interstate 40 and south on U.S. 84.

EXPLORING

★ The **Billy the Kid Museum** houses 20,000 square feet of exhibits about the young scofflaw, as well as antique wagon trains, guns, household goods, and other artifacts of the frontier era. There's an interesting film about the Kid and the Lincoln County wars he was involved in. The museum is closed the first two weeks of January. ⊠ *1435 E. Sumner Ave. (U.S. 60/84)* ☎ *575/355–2380* ⊕ *www.billythekidmuseumfortsumner.com* ⌁*$5* ⊙ *Mid-May–Sept., daily 8:30–5; Oct.–Dec. and mid-Jan.–mid-May, Mon.–Sat. 8:30–5.*

Artifacts and photographs at **Fort Sumner State Monument** illustrate the history of the fort, which was established in 1862 on the east bank of the Pecos River. From 1863 to 1868 it was the headquarters for a disastrous attempt to force the Navajo people and some Apache bands—after their defeat on various battlefields in the Southwest—to farm the inhospitable land. Natural disasters destroyed crops, wood was scarce, and even the water from the Pecos proved unhealthy. Those who survived the harsh treatment and wretched conditions (3,000 didn't) were returned to reservations elsewhere in 1868. The post was then sold and converted into a large ranch. This is the same ranch where, in 1881, Sheriff Pat Garrett gunned down Billy the Kid. The Kid is now buried in a nearby cemetery, where his headstone is secured in a barred cage (this was erected after the headstone was stolen three times and later recovered). ✉ *Billy the Kid Rd.* ✣ *From town of Fort Sumner, head east on U.S. 60/84 and south on Billy the Kid Rd., parts of which are signed NM 212* ☎ *575/355–2573* 🎟 *$5* ⏲ *Wed.–Mon. 8:30–5.*

The small **Old Fort Sumner Museum**, next to Fort Sumner, has displays about Billy the Kid and ranch life. ✉ *Billy the Kid Rd.* ☎ *575/355–2942* 🎟 *$3.50* ⏲ *Daily 8:30–5.*

At **Sumner Lake State Park** you can boat, fish, camp, picnic, hike, sightsee, swim, and water-ski. ✉ *10 mi north of Fort Sumner on U.S. 84, then west on NM 203 for 6 mi* ☎ *575/355–2541* 🎟 *Day use $5 per vehicle.*

WHERE TO STAY

CAMPING

¢ ⛺ **Sumner Lake State Park.** The choices at this popular recreational site range from primitive, shoreline camping with no facilities to developed sites. Shading in this desert location varies. ✉ *10 mi north of Fort Sumner on U.S. 84, then west on NM 203 for 6 mi* ☎ *575/355–2541 park info, 877/665–7787 reservations* 👍 *Flush toilets, pit toilets, partial hookups (electric and water), dump station, drinking water, showers, fire grates, grills, picnic tables, electricity, ranger station, play area, swimming (lake)* *40 developed sites, 18 sites with partial hookup, 50 primitive sites* 💳 *No credit cards.*

7

SANTA ROSA

32 mi north of Fort Sumner on U.S. 84, at I–40; 117 mi east of Albuquerque on I–40.

A visually charming little town loaded with history, Santa Rosa also has the only body of water in the state—the Blue Hole—where divers can obtain deepwater certification. That spot, along with the Pecos River and other natural bodies of water, were created by ancient sinkholes in the bedrock that drew early peoples and animals as far back as the time of woolly mammoths.

GETTING HERE

Santa Rosa is right along Interstate 40, 117 mi east of Albuquerque; it's 133 mi north of Roswell via U.S. 285 and U.S. 54. Like most smaller towns in New Mexico, this isn't a place to point yourself if you don't have a car because public transport just doesn't exist.

VISITOR INFORMATION

Santa Rosa Visitor Information Center (✉ *486 Historic Rte. 66* ☎ *575/472–3763* 🌐 *www.santarosanm.org*).

DRIVING IN CIRCLES

To continue touring southeastern New Mexico, the easiest route (132 mi) is to backtrack to Roswell via Highway 20 to U.S. 285 and head west on U.S. 70/380 toward Lincoln County. Look for the pronghorns grazing alongside roadways in the flat eastern plains, which is an ideal habitat for these delicate creatures. Sometimes after a summer rain has made grasses and flowers bloom, you'll find more than 100 pronghorn grazing along a short stretch of road.

A more adventurous route (178 mi) to Lincoln County would be a loop west from Fort Sumner on U.S. 60.

At the town of Vaughn, head south on U.S. 54 and travel through the southernmost region of Cibola National Forest to the fringes of the Lincoln National Forest. These areas are mountainous but semiarid, as evidenced by sparse hillsides dotted with brush and junipers. On this route you pass through **Corona,** near where the Roswell UFO is said to have crashed. No signs designate the site. At Carrizozo, head east on U.S. 380. You pass the towns of Capitan and Lincoln before you reach U.S. 70. Cut back west on U.S. 70 to get to San Patricio.

EXPLORING

☺ About 8,000 diving permits are issued per year for folks who strap on
Fodor'sChoice   tanks and plunge into the 80-foot-deep artesian spring–fed pool at the
★   **Blue Hole.** The Blue Hole is open for public swimming during daylight hours (no fee). Cliff diving is great fun here, as is snorkeling and coming face to face with the many koi and goldfish that have been deposited here over the years.

Stella Salazar runs the **dive shop** (☎ 575/472–3370) adjacent to the Blue Hole; hours are generally restricted to the weekends, although the pool is open seven days a week. Tanks, air, weight belts, and a few other basics are available there. Weekly dive permits are $8. The folks from **Sandia Snorkel** (☎ 505/247–8632) in Albuquerque are out at the Hole every second weekend. The shop staff is full of helpful information about diving certification and the conditions of the pool (which remains a constant 62°F year-round). ⊠ Blue Hole Rd. ✛ Turn south off Rte. 66 onto Lake Dr.; turn left onto Blue Hole Rd. just past Park Lake ☎ 575/472–3763

Spanish explorer Francisco Vásquez de Coronado is said to have settled the quaint village of **Puerto de Luna,** 10 mi south of Santa Rosa on NM 91, back in 1541, and the area has been a crossroads of settlers, travelers, and the railroad ever since. The bypassing of Santa Rosa, when Route 66 was replaced by I–40, has clearly impacted the town, although it maintains more vitality and economic activity than many of the towns along the route in this part of the state. There is a real pride among Santa Rosa's residents, and traditions of the town's deep Hispanic roots are still apparent.

Santa Rosa Lake State Park is 7 mi north of town and offers fishing, camping, and access to waterskiing and other water sports. The man-made lake was created to keep the flooding of the Pecos River under control, and it's become a resting spot for many different birds, including a number of gorgeous cormorants.

WHERE TO EAT AND STAY

$ ✕ **Lake City Diner.** In a charming old bank building on the corner of Route 66 and 4th Street, this bright, clean restaurant serves some of the best food in town. The menu contains fairly traditional dishes, and many are notable because of the fresh ingredients from local farms. You'll find rib-eye steak, chicken Milanesa, and a mouthwatering, homestyle, green-chile chicken enchilada casserole. Mixed green salads are a delight in an area where "greens" often means iceberg lettuce. Desserts, such as the Mexican chocolate pie (with cinnamon), are a must. ⊠ *101 4th St.* ☎ *575/472–5253* ⊟ *AE, MC, V* ⊘ *No lunch. Closed Sun.*

AMERICAN

$ ⊡ **La Quinta Inn.** Perched on a high point in Santa Rosa, this motel offers the nicest stay in town, and the wonderful views of the surrounding Pecos River Valley are a treat. The indoor pool is very clean, and relaxing in the outdoor hot tub, nestled amongst boulders, is a nice way to finish a day spent in the car. Rooms are spacious and immaculate, with contemporary furnishings in soft Southwestern colors. The staff is helpful and friendly. **Pros:** the free breakfast, though classified as Continental, is large and offers lots of choices; the view. **Cons:** not within walking distance of the Blue Hole or the historic Downtown. ⊠ *2277 Historic Rte. 66* ☎ *575/472–4800* ⬎ *60 rooms* ⬆ *In-room: refrigerator, Wi-Fi. In-hotel: pool, laundry facilities, some pets allowed* ⊟ *AE, D, DC, MC, V* ¶⚬¶ *CP.*

CAMPING

¢ ⛺ **Santa Rosa Lake State Park.** For travelers wanting to do some fishing, this reservoir and campground is a quick and easy drive just north of Santa Rosa. Aside from fishing, waterskiing and boating are permitted, and there are numerous hiking trails. Weather in spring and fall is almost ideal at about 70°F, although summer tends to be at least 90°F. Beautiful, glossy black cormorants can be spotted on the shores and provide a real treat for bird-watchers. Reservations are allowed but are not generally necessary, even in spring. ⊠ *7 mi north of Santa Rosa via NM 91* ☎ *575/472–3110 park info, 877/664–7787 reservations* ⊕ *www.emnrd.state.nm.us/PRD/santarosa.htm* ⬆ *Showers, picnic tables, electricity (some)* ⬎ *76 developed sites* ⊟ *AE, D, DC, MC, V.*

TUCUMCARI

59 mi east of Santa Rosa on I–40.

Tucumcari is a tumbledown little town with intriguing early- to mid-20th-century architecture. Neat little houses on quiet, tree-shaded streets can keep you peeking around corners and down new streets for quite awhile. Along Route 66—the main, and only, route through town—you'll find low-slung motels in various stages of use and disuse, restaurants, markets, gas stations, curios stores, and, of course, *neon.* As hard as this town tries to develop itself economically, it's those neon signs and the still-living, old-time businesses that keep it alive.

GETTING HERE

Right off of I–40, Tucumcari is 174 mi east of Albuquerque, and 59 mi east of Santa Rosa. Greyhound Bus Lines serves town.

Contacts Greyhound (☎ 800/231–2222 ⊕ www.greyhound.com).

VISITOR INFORMATION

Tucumcari/Quay County Chamber of Commerce (✉ 404 W. Rte. 66 ☎ 575/461–1694 ⊕ www.tucumcarinm.com).

EXPLORING

★ The biggest attraction beyond the miles of neon and the Blue Swallow ☾ Motel is the **Mesalands Community College Dinosaur Museum,** where marvelous full-size bronze dinosaur skeletons are on display. This area was a hotbed of Triassic activity, when dinosaurs emerged in their development, and there are species here—like the Struthiomimus—that you won't find anywhere else in the world. The skeletons are cast in the local foundry, and they *are* touchable. The latest addition, a Parosaurolophus from the Farmington, New Mexico, area even "breathes" through recreated respiratory tubes—talk about realistic! ✉ 222 E. Laughlin Ave., follow signs off Rte. 66 ☎ 575/461–3466 ✍ $6 ☼ Mar.–Labor Day, Tues.–Sat. 10–6; Labor Day–Feb., noon–5.

WHERE TO EAT AND STAY

$ ✕ **Del's.** The huge fiberglass bull perched on the sign makes this land-
AMERICAN mark easy to find. Del's has been serving Route 66 travelers since 1956 with American and Mexican food. Eggs, pancakes, and bacon fill the breakfast menu, and the spicy chiles rellenos and hand-cut steaks keep customers returning. This is good, reliable food and one of the only places open until relatively late. Windows all around make for great nighttime neon viewing. ✉ 1202 E. Tucumcari Blvd. (Rte. 66) ☎ 575/461–1740.

¢ ✕ **Rubee's Diner.** From breakfast to dinner, what you'll get at this friendly,
AMERICAN bustling little joint is a good square meal. Huevos rancheros in the morning come with fresh green lettuce, tomatoes, and some of the tastiest panfried potatoes around. Eggs are cooked exactly the way you ask. The red chile is rich—loaded with beef—and not spicy. Burritos, burgers, and a basic BLT are also available. They close at 7 pm weekdays, and at 4 pm on Saturday. ✉ 605 W. Tucumcari Blvd. (Rte. 66) ☎ 575/461–1463 ⊟ No credit cards ☼ Closed Sun.

¢ ▥ **Blue Swallow Motel.** Here it is: the retro motor court of your dreams.
Fodor's Choice Built in 1939, the glowing neon, the tidy grounds, the spotlessly clean
★ rooms furnished with vintage and antique furniture, and the abundant charm of Bill and Terri, the proprietors, all come together in one neat, feel-good package. The Blue Swallow is a landmark and a genuine pleasure for an overnight. The rooms are not the supersize, supermodern ones you get at the chains down the road, but that just isn't what this place is all about. Arrive before sunset if you can and take a seat at a table on the front lawn; the views of the Western sky exploding with color are not to be missed. There is a feeling of camaraderie among the guests here—many of whom are diligently following Route 66 in its entirety—that lends a real sweetness to an already unique experience. **Pros:** one of the best-preserved motels on all of Route 66; pet-friendly

rooms available; free breakfast offered at nearby Pow-Wow Restaurant. **Cons:** no pool or hot tub; closed in winter. ✉ *815 E. Rte. 66* ☎ *575/461–9849 or 866/461–9489* ⊕ *www.blueswallowmotel.com* ⏳ *12 rooms* ⚒ *In-room: a/c, Wi-Fi. In-hotel: Wi-Fi hotspot, some pets allowed* ▭ *AE, D, MC, V.* ☽ *Closed Dec.–Feb.*

HEADING TO HIGH COUNTRY

From the hub city of Roswell, U.S. 70 shoots out of the flatlands west toward mountain peaks. The route's slow climb in elevation is apparent beginning near the lush valley of San Patricio. Here, in an area known as the Hondo Valley, the shrubs and scattered forest dotting the otherwise naked hillsides provided inspiration for many of the late artist Peter Hurd's stunning landscapes.

Onward and upward, the pines thicken and grow taller. The Rio Ruidoso (Spanish for "River of Noisy Water") dances alongside the highway, as the air grows cooler and fragrant. It's easy to imagine this majestic land as it was when outlaws, Native Americans, merchants, ranchers, and lawmen battled each other for control of the frontier; you can contemplate the stillness by taking a solitary horseback ride or hike on a wilderness trail, or by lake fishing on reservation land controlled by the Mescalero Apaches. Near the town of Ruidoso, there are more modern diversions, like skiing, shopping, horse racing, and casinos.

LINCOLN

12 mi east of Capitan on U.S. 380; 47 mi west of Roswell on U.S. 70/380 to Hondo, then 10 mi northwest on U.S. 380 to Lincoln.

It may not be as well-known as Tombstone, Arizona, or Deadwood, South Dakota, but Lincoln ranks right up there with the toughest of the tough old towns of the Old West. Mellowing with age, the notorious one-street town has become a National Historic Landmark and a state monument. A single ticket ($5) still grants entry to all attractions (you can purchase the ticket at Historic Lincoln Center, Tunstall Store Museum, or Lincoln County Courthouse Museum).

The violent, gang-style Lincoln County War consumed this region between 1878 and 1881, as two factions, the Tunstall-McSween and the Murphy-Dolan groups, clashed over lucrative government contracts to provide food for the U.S. Army at Fort Stanton and area Native American reservations. The local conflict made national news, and President Hayes ordered Lew Wallace, governor of New Mexico, to settle the conflict. One of the more infamous figures to emerge from the bloodshed was a short, slight, sallow young man with buckteeth, startling blue eyes, and curly reddish-brown hair called Billy the Kid.

He is said to have killed 21 men (probably an exaggeration), including Lincoln County's sheriff William Brady—for whose murder he was convicted in 1881 and sentenced to hang. Billy managed to elude the gallows. On April 28, 1881, though manacled and shackled, he made a daring escape from the old Lincoln County Courthouse, gunning down two men and receiving cheers from townspeople who supported his group, the Tunstall-McSweens. Three months later a posse led by Sheriff Pat Garrett tracked down Billy at a home in Fort Sumner, surprised him in the dark, and finished him off with two clean shots. One of the West's most notorious gunmen, and ultimately one of its best-known folk legends, was dead at age 21.

GETTING HERE

Getting to Lincoln is part of any sightseeing adventure, as it's a very scenic drive. Take U.S. 380, heading east out of Carrizozo for 32 mi, or heading west 56 mi from Roswell. It's an easy day trip from Ruidoso, via NM 48 or back on U.S. 70 to U.S. 380.

VISITOR INFORMATION

The **Historic Lincoln Center**, on the eastern end of town, serves as an information center for the Lincoln State Monument, which encompasses the buildings listed below. There's a 12-minute video about Lincoln and exhibits devoted to Billy the Kid, the Lincoln County War, cowboys, Apaches, and Buffalo Soldiers, African-American cavalry troops who earned a sterling reputation as fierce protectors of Western frontiers. The center's guides and attendants dress in period costumes and lead a walking tour through town on the hour, vividly describing each building's role as a setting in the Lincoln County War. ⊠ *Main St. (U.S. 380); far eastern end of Lincoln, on south side of road* ☎ *575/653–4025* 🖃 *$5 pass grants access to all historic buildings* ☉ *Daily 8:30–4:30.*

Lincoln State Monument (⊠ *U.S. 380* ⌂ *Box 36, 88338* ☎ *575/653–4372*).

EXPLORING

Dr. Wood's House was once occupied by a country doctor specializing in treatments for chest ailments. The doctor's house is filled with pre-1920s furnishings along with books, instruments, and pharmaceutical supplies from his era. ⊠ *Main St. (U.S. 380); north side of highway, midway between Historic Lincoln Center and Tunstall Store Museum* ☎ *No phone* ☉ *Daily 8:30–4:30.*

When church services, weddings, funerals, and other regularly scheduled functions are not taking place here, Lincoln's historic **Iglesia de San Juan Bautista**, originally built in 1887, can be viewed free. The tiny church was built and restored entirely from local materials. Roof beams and other wood elements including *latillas* (small branches laid on top of larger, rounded wood beams known as vigas) were dragged by oxcart from the nearby Capitan Mountains. ⊠ *Main St. (U.S. 380); south side of highway between Montaño Store and Lincoln County Courthouse Museum* ☎ *575/257–7067* 🖃 *Free* ☉ *Daily 8:30–4:30.*

⟳ The **Lincoln County Courthouse Museum** is the building from which Billy the Kid made his famous escape. You can walk in the room where Billy was imprisoned and view a hole in the wall that just might have been caused by the gun he fired during his escape. Display cases contain historical documents, including one of Billy's handwritten, eloquent letters to Governor Lew Wallace, defending his reputation. The Lincoln State Monument office is here. ⊠ *Main St. (U.S. 380); far west side of town, south side of highway* ☎ *575/653–4372* ☉ *Daily 8:30–4:30.*

José Montaño ran a saloon and boardinghouse within his **Montaño Store** for more than 30 years after the Civil War. Governor Lew Wallace stayed here when trying to arrange a meeting with Billy the Kid. Today, displayed writings in both English and Spanish describe the history of the site. ⊠ *Main St. (U.S. 380); east end of town, south side of road* ☎ *No phone* ☼ *Daily 8:30–4:30.*

Lincoln was first settled by Spanish settlers in the 1840s. The short, round **Torreon** fortress served as protection from Apache raids in those days; it came in handy during the Lincoln County War, too.

☽ Nothing has changed much at the **Tunstall Store Museum** since the days of the Old West. When the state of New Mexico purchased the store in 1957, boxes of stock dating from the late 19th and early 20th centuries were discovered here, still unused. The clothes, hardware, butter churns, kerosene lamps, and other items are displayed in the store's original cases. ⊠ *Main St. (U.S. 380); about midway through town on north side of road* ☎ *575/653–4049* ☼ *Daily 8:30–4:30.*

WHERE TO EAT AND STAY

$$$ ✕ **Tinnie Silver Dollar.** Just 2 mi east of the U.S. 70 turnoff to Ruidoso
AMERICAN is the little town of Tinnie and this real find of a restaurant. The food at the Silver Dollar is more than worth the drive (it's owned by the well-run local Cattle Baron chain), and if you're in need of a place to stay, they have two well-appointed guest suites. Aside from enjoying a really fine meal of traditional favorites like filet mignon, rack of lamb, lobster tail, or chicken piccata, you can relax knowing that you're supporting a business with a mission: the Silver Dollar's profits go to support the Second Chance Boys' Ranch, an on-site program geared to helping neglected boys between the ages of 10 and 16 regain self-esteem and learn the skills they need to make good life choices. The Sunday champagne brunch is a favorite that draws folks from miles around. Ask about the haunted mirror and the building's ghost. ⊠ *U.S. 70* ☎ *575/653–4425* ⊕ *www.tinniesilverdollar.com* ☼ *No lunch (except for Sun. brunch)* ▭ *AE, D, MC, V.*

$ ⛫ **Ellis Store Country Inn.** In 1850 this bed-and-breakfast was a modest two-room adobe in a territory where settlers and Mescaleros clashed; during the Lincoln County War, Billy the Kid was known to frequent the place. These days, rooms in the main house are decorated with antiques. Behind the main house is the Mill House, which has four guest rooms and a large common room and is ideal for families. Casa Nueva has two suites with reproduction antiques and a country-French feeling. Owner Jinny Vigil cooks six-course gourmet meals in the evening, which are served in a wood-paneled dining room called Isaac's Table. The breakfasts could stir even the most avid sleeper, and the lush, well-manicured garden is becoming increasingly popular for June weddings. Reservations for dinner are a must, and the public can have breakfast here, too, but only if you make reservations. Note that you must advise management if you're traveling with children. **Pros:** beautiful inn; excellent food. **Cons:** the four Mill House rooms share two bathrooms. ⊠ *U.S. 380, mile marker 98* ⛫ *Box 15, 88338* ☎ *575/653–4609 or 800/653–6460* ⊕ *www.ellisstore.com* ⇆ *8 rooms, 4 with bath* ⚒ *In-room: no a/c, no phone, no TV. In-hotel: restaurant* ▭ *AE, D, DC, MC, V* ⦿*BP.*

$
♨
Fodor's Choice
★

Wortley Hotel. It's easy to imagine this hotel as it was during the days of the Lincoln County War. Rebuilt after a fire in 1935, the original inn was where Deputy U.S. Marshal Bob Ollinger ate his last meal at noontime on April 28, 1881. After hearing gunfire from the courthouse down the street, he ran outside—only to meet up with one of Billy the Kid's bullets during the outlaw's famous escape. These days, there isn't nearly so much action here, but there's plenty of charm—and you can soak it in while sitting in a rocker on the wooden porch or throwing a game of horseshoes. A major renovation has brought this property back to life, and the antique furnishings in the rooms are a nice touch. Guests are treated to a full breakfast, and can order dinner from the lunch menu—there aren't any dinner restaurants in town. In the **Wortley Dining Room** (¢), open Wednesday through Sunday, 8 am–3 pm, you'll find delicious basics cooked up with good cheer. Vic, one of the owners and also the chef, cooks everything from amazing breakfasts—basics like eggs and bacon or Mexican classics like huevos rancheros or *migas*—to lunches of superfresh Cobb salads, enchiladas, grilled chicken, and tasty burgers. He will also prepare any of the lunch-menu items for dinner on request, if you're an overnight guest. **Pros:** friendly, easygoing owners; good food; a great rest. **Cons:** somewhat irregular hours based on occupancy; call ahead. ⊠ *U.S. 380* ☎ *575/653–4300* ⊕ *www.wortleyhotel.com* ➾ *5 rooms* ♨ *In-room: no a/c, no phone, no TV. In-hotel: restaurant* ⊟ *D, MC, V* ☺ *Closed early Dec.–mid-Mar.*

SAN PATRICIO

14 mi south of Lincoln, 45 mi west of Roswell on U.S. 70/380.

Ranchers, farmers, artists, and others who appreciate the lush, green loveliness of the Hondo Valley live in San Patricio and the nearby villages of Tinnie and Hondo. The Rio Ruidoso flows into the Rio Hondo here, providing a watery boon to farmers and wildlife alike. During the harvest, fresh cider and produce are sold at roadside stands.

GETTING HERE

If you blink, you'll miss the tiny village of San Patricio as you cruise along U.S. 70 on your way to or from Ruidoso.

EXPLORING

★ The late artist Peter Hurd lived in the Hondo Valley on the Sentinel Ranch, which is still owned by his son, Michael Hurd, whose paintings are also displayed in the gallery. The **Hurd–La Rinconada Gallery** displays Peter's landscapes and portraits. The artist is famous for Western scenes but gained some notice when a portrait he painted of Lyndon B. Johnson displeased the president, who refused to hang it in the White House. Also on display are the works of Hurd's late wife, Henriette Wyeth (Andrew Wyeth's sister). Michael is an amiable host who has established an international reputation with a series of paintings he calls "The Road West," his vision of the lonely desert scenery surrounding his home. Michael's sister Carole Hurd Rogers and her husband, Peter Rogers, also an artist, live near the ranch as well. Paintings by Jamie Wyeth, father Andrew Wyeth, and grandfather N. C. Wyeth round out the impressive collection at the gallery. Signed reproductions and some original paintings are for sale. ✉ *U.S. 70, mile marker 281* ☎ *575/653–4331 or 800/658–6912* ⊕ *www.wyethartists.com* ☉ *Mon.–Sat. 9–5.*

WHERE TO STAY

$$$ ▥ **Hurd Ranch Guest Homes.** Modern and Western furnishings and paintings, sculpture, and Native American artifacts decorate the adobe casitas on the Sentinel Ranch. Peter Hurd made them available to friends and to customers who needed accommodations while he painted their portraits. The rooms have washing machines and dryers, fully equipped kitchens, and fireplaces. The newest one is named after actress Helen Hayes, who was a family friend and frequent visitor. Facilities also are available for weddings and conferences. **Pros:** beautifully furnished casitas; rural, rustic and peaceful. **Cons:** no refunds on reservations made within 30 days of stay; nothing but nature around for miles. ✉ *Off U.S. 70, turn south toward San Patricio at mile marker 281, 20 mi east of Ruidoso* ✉ *Box 100, 88348* ☎ *575/653–4331 or 800/658–6912* ⊕ *www.wyethartists.com* ⬎ *5 casitas, 1 suite* ⚘ *In-room: a/c, kitchen, refrigerator. In-hotel: laundry facilities* ▭ *AE, D, MC, V.*

RUIDOSO

20 mi west of San Patricio on U.S. 70.

A year-round mountain resort town on the eastern slopes of the pine-covered Sacramento Mountains, Ruidoso retains a certain rustic charm. Shops, antiques stores, bars, and restaurants line its main street, and in winter, skiers flock to nearby Ski Apache. In summer, Ruidoso is a paradise for outdoors lovers and Texans seeking respite from the blazing heat of lower elevations.

The general quality of lodging and dining options in town is very good, and service is friendly and laid-back, as are most patrons. Cuisine tends toward basic American and Americanized Mexican, but a handful of restaurants serve fresher and more updated variations on this theme.

GETTING HERE

Whichever direction you're coming from, east or west, Ruidoso is easy to find—and a real pleasure after leaving the heat from the valleys below. From 13 mi north of Alamogordo, in Tularosa, you'll turn east and head up U.S. 70 for 33 mi. From Roswell, head west on U.S. 70/380 for 70 mi, just past the even smaller village of Ruidoso Downs. You then head north NM 48, also called Sudderth Drive, dropping you immediately into Ruidoso.

VISITOR INFORMATION

Ruidoso Valley Chamber & Visitor Center (✉ *720 Sudderth Dr.* ☎ *575/257–7395* ⊕ *www.ruidoso.net*).

EXPLORING

Fodor's Choice ★ ☽ **Hubbard Museum of the American West.** The museum houses the **Anne C. Stradling Collection** of more than 10,000 artworks and objects related to the horse—paintings, drawings, and bronzes by master artists; saddles from Mexico, China, and the Pony Express; carriages and wagons; a horse-drawn grain thresher; and clothing worn by Native Americans and cowboys. The **Racehorse Hall of Fame** celebrates accomplished horses and jockeys and screens rare and contemporary video footage. Activities at the children's interactive center include pony rides, horse demonstrations, and puzzles. In front of the museum is a dramatic bronze sculpture by Dave McGary of eight galloping horses—*Free Spirits at Noisy Water*. Aside from being beautiful, the monument represents a minor feat of engineering, since of the eight horses only nine hooves actually touch the ground. An indoor children's exhibit offers kids the chance to climb and touch an adobe home, a tepee, a wagon, as well as lots of other hands-on activities. ⊠ *U.S. 70, Ruidoso Downs* ☎ *575/378–4142* ⊡ *$6* ۞ *Daily 9–5.*

Fodor's Choice
★
ᖷ
Lincoln County Cowboy Symposium. This legendary gathering of cowboy poets, musicians, chuckwagon cooks, artists, craftspeople, and—of course—cowboys takes place the second weekend of October at Ruidoso Downs racetrack. The three-day event includes the Chuckwagon Competition, in which participants cook Old West–style food in full regalia. Horsemanship skills, blacksmithing, and all sorts of activities for kids are part of this fun weekend. Dances on Friday and Saturday night are a big hit with people of all ages. ⊠ *1461 U.S. 70, Ruidoso Downs* ☎ *575/378–4431* ⊕ *www.cowboysymposium.org* ⊡ *$20 per day.*

The **Mescalero Apache Indian Reservation,** bordering Ruidoso to the west, is inhabited by more than 4,500 Mescalero Apaches, most of whom work for the tribal government or for the tribally owned **Inn of the Mountain Gods** (⇨ *Where to Stay, below*), one of the state's most elegant resorts and a major destination for visitors from all over the country and Mexico. Also on the reservation are a general store, a trading post, and a museum where a 12-minute video about life on the reservation is screened. Regular talks are also given on the history and culture of the Mescalero Apaches. There are campsites here (with hookups at Silver and Eagle lakes only) and picnic areas. The July 4th weekend dances, which include a rodeo, powwow, and the lovely dances of young women going through puberty rites, are open to the public. *Tribal Office:* ⊠ *106 Central Mescalero Ave., off U.S. 70, Mescalero* ☎ *575/671–4494* ⊕ *www.mescaleroapache.com* ⊡ *Free* ۞ *Reservation and tribal museum weekdays 8–4:30.*

Ruidoso Downs is so close to Ruidoso you won't realize it's a separate township, but Ruidoso Downs Racetrack and museums are the area's huge draws. The summer horse-racing season keeps the 9,800 or so permanent residents entertained after the snow and ski bunnies disappear.

Ruidoso Downs Racetrack & Casino, the self-proclaimed home of the world's richest quarter-horse race, has a fabulous mountain vista as the setting for cheering the ponies. On Labor Day the track is the site of the All-American Quarter Horse Futurity, with a total purse of as much as $2.5 million. Twenty percent of revenues from the **Billy the Kid Casino,** which has some 300 slot machines, funds the races. Casino gambling allowed at horse-racing tracks is credited with reviving the sport in New Mexico by attracting quality horses and competition. The casino is decorated with murals suggesting nearby historic Lincoln, where Billy the Kid once hung out. The facility offers year-round, full-card simulcasting from the nation's largest tracks. ⊠ *1461 U.S. 70W,*

Ruidoso Downs ☎ *575/378–4431* ⊕ *www.raceruidoso.com* ⊠ *Racetrack open seating is free, reserved seating $5 and up; Turf Club $10, higher on special weekends* ☉ *Racing late May–early Sept., Thurs.–Sun. and Mon. holidays, post time 1* PM. *Casino Sat.–Thurs. 11–11, Fri. noon–midnight.*

NEED A BREAK?

Sacred Grounds Coffee & Tea House (⊠ *2825 Sudderth* ☎ *575/257–2273*) is a locally owned place with great organic coffee, an impressive variety of exotic teas, plus homemade pastries, muffins, and cookies, delicious hot breakfast cereal from Bob's Red Mill, fluffy quiches (try the green-chile-chicken), and tasty sandwiches. The space is cozy, but the patio out front is a great spot to enjoy the mountain air. Enjoy free Wi-Fi while you rejuvenate.

WHERE TO EAT

$
SOUTHERN

✕ **Can't Stop Smokin'.** The lines often stretching out the door of this log cabin building are a testament to the tasty, tender "New Mexico–style" barbecue for which this down-home joint is known. Beef, pork, turkey, and chicken are given deluxe smokehouse treatment and then slathered with in-house secret sauces. Sides—like Elsie's garlic potatoes, mustard potato salad, and Southern-style biscuits—come with the plates served by the gregarious, friendly staff. Meals are served to-go only, but there's a big, covered side porch and another open one out front to eat on. The pies are the only disappointment here. ⊠ *418 Mechem Dr.* ☎ *575/630–0000* ⊕ *www.cantstopsmokin.com* ⊟ *AE, MC, V* ☉ *Closed Tues.*

¢
AMERICAN

✕ **Lincoln County Grill.** This little cabinlike place on a hill is known for quick service and good inexpensive food. Step up to the counter to order hearty Texas chili, old-fashioned hamburgers, or the local favorite green-chile chicken-fried steak. At breakfast you can grab eggs served with fluffy, homemade biscuits. New Mexican food, like huevos rancheros, and enchiladas, are also on the menu. Vinyl-covered tables are decorated with old coffee-, tea-, and tobacco-tin images. This is a great stop for families in a hurry and on a budget. ⊠ *2717 Sudderth Dr.* ☎ *575/257–7669* ⊕ *www.lcgrill.com* ⊟ *AE, MC, V.*

¢
AMERICAN

✕ **River's Edge.** Custom-made wraps and a delicious variety of home-made soups are served at this friendly spot known mostly for lunch or early dinner (they close at 6). If you get overwhelmed by the checklist of wrap ingredients, the counter staff can happily advise you on some tasty combos. There's shady outdoor seating—a treat in summer. ⊠ *2404 Sudderth Dr.* ☎ *575/630–5394* ⊟ *MC, V* ☉ *Closed Wed.*

¢
AMERICAN
Fodor's Choice
★

✕ **Village Buttery.** A long-time local favorite for lunch (they're only open from 10:30 until 2:30), the Buttery serves savory soups, creative sandwiches, fluffy quiches, and delectable desserts. Soups, like the tomato basil or the chunky cream of broccoli, are main-course worthy—add a fresh salad and a slice of buttermilk pie, and you're good to go. If you can find a table, eat on the patio in warm weather. ⊠ *2107 Sudderth Dr.* ☎ *575/257–9251* ⊕ *www.thevillagebuttery.com* ⊟ *AE, MC, V* ☉ *Closed Sun.*

7

WHERE TO STAY

$$ ▦ **Black Bear Lodge.** Tucked into the secluded tall pines of the Upper
Fodor's Choice Canyon, each of this adults-only inn's four spacious rooms has its own
★ Jacuzzi, wood-panel ceiling, and fireplace. Owner Carol Olson, who
re-created the property from a 1930s-era restaurant, has created a great
room that has all the coziness of a family room. Privacy is emphasized
above communal gatherings here, and you're on your own for break-
fast (although breakfast items, as well as homemade cookies and other
snacks, are stocked in the common-area refrigerator). The front porch
is a wonderful place to sit and watch dozens of hummingbirds frolic
during the spring and summer. **Pros:** restful and romantic. **Cons:** no
children allowed (a pro for some). ⊠ *428 Main St.* ☎ *575/257–1459
or 877/257–1459* ⊕ *www.blackbearruidoso.com* ⇥ *4 rooms* ⟐ *In-
room: a/c, no phone, DVD, Wi-Fi. In-hotel: Wi-Fi hotspot* ⊟ *AE, D,
MC, V* ⦿⎮ *CP.*

$$$ ▦ **Inn of the Mountain Gods.** There is nothing run-of-the-mill about this
Fodor's Choice beautifully designed hotel and resort. The luxurious rooms and com-
★ mon areas are decorated with contemporary Southwestern flourishes
and nods to the inn's Mescalero Apache ownership. Stunning bronze
crown dancer sculptures are found at the entrance to the resort, which
includes a 38,000-square-foot casino with 1,000 slot machines. The
views here are stunning; many windows overlook a serene lake and
(in winter) the nearby snow-crusted mountain peak of Sierra Blanca.
Big-game hunts, a championship golf course, guided fishing trips, wedding facilities, excellent food; it's all here. This resort is more Aspen
in feel than southeastern New Mexico—with all the graciousness and
none of the pretense. **Pros:** luxury and a great staff. **Cons:** lingering
smell of cigarette smoke in the public areas; if you don't like the casino
scene, even at the high end, this is probably not the place for you.
⊠ *287 Carrizo Canyon Rd.* ☎ *575/464–7777 or 800/545–9011* ⊕ *www.
innofthemountaingods.com* ⇥ *273 rooms* ⟐ *In-rooms: a/c, Wi-Fi. In-
hotel: 2 restaurants, bars, golf course, pool, bicycles, Wi-Fi hotspot*
⊟ *AE, D, DC, MC, V.*

$$$ ▦ **The Lodge at Sierra Blanca.** This comfortable hotel is next door to a
★ top-rated New Mexico golf course (the Links at Sierra Blanca) and
to the Ruidoso Convention Center. A dramatic rock fireplace looms
majestically over the lobby; the indoor pool and hot tub are enclosed
within a two-story atrium. A complimentary full breakfast (with eggs
made to order) is served in a dining area that has views onto the 9th
hole and surrounding mountains. Most rooms have views of meadows,
pine trees, or the golf course; be sure to request a room with a view.
Soft-yellow interiors with wood furnishings complete the feel of cozy
luxury. King rooms have private balconies, fireplaces, in-room whirl-
pool tubs, and sitting rooms with kitchenettes. Guests get discounts
on greens fees. ⊠ *107 Sierra Blanca Dr.* ☎ *575/258–5500 or 866/211–
7727* ⊕ *www.thelodgeatsierrablanca.com* ⇥ *117 rooms* ⟐ *In-room: a/c,
kitchen (some), refrigerator, Wi-Fi. In-hotel: bar, golf course, tennis
courts, pool, gym, laundry facilities, Wi-Fi hotspot, some pets allowed*
⊟ *AE, D, DC, MC, V* ⦿⎮ *BP.*

$$ ⚴ **Ruidoso Lodge Cabins.** In the heart of Ruidoso's gorgeous, tree-filled ☾ Upper Canyon, owners Judy and Kurt Wilkie oversee a placid retreat of renovated 1920s, knotty-pine abodes. The immaculate one- and two-bedroom cabins are adorned with Western and Southwestern decor. Some have whirlpool tubs, and all have fireplaces and decks with gas grills offering serene views. Porches with Adirondack chairs are great for barbecues and gatherings. The cabins are fully equipped with kitchen utensils and dishes. You can trout fish here, right along the Rio Ruidoso, but you must arrange for your own gear. Hiking trails lead off the property through the pine forest. These folks also own the romantic, adults-only **Riverside Cottages** across the river (☎ *575/257–2548 or 800/497–7402*). **Pros:** great for families; all cabins nonsmoking. **Cons:** no pets allowed. ⊠ *300 Main St.* ⊕ *Take Sudderth Dr. north from U.S. 70 through Downtown Ruidoso; continue west through Upper Canyon, where Sudderth turns into Main St.* ☎ *575/257–2510 or 800/950–2510* ⊕ *www.ruidosocabins.com* ⌁ *10 cabins* ⚲ *In-room: a/c, no phone, kitchen, refrigerator, DVD, Wi-Fi* ⊟ *D, MC, V.*

$ ⚴ **Shadow Mountain Lodge.** Designed for couples, this lodge in the Upper ★ Canyon has king suites with fireplaces and furnished kitchens in the lodge, and cabins with queen beds, two-person whirlpools, and two-sided fireplaces opening into the living room and bedroom. The front veranda views tall pines and the lush, landscaped gardens. Separate cabins all have wood paneling and ample privacy. The staff here is gracious and attentive but not intrusive. The owners have other properties for families and larger groups—ask if you've got a family or a big group to house. **Pros:** lodge is within easy walking distance of Downtown restaurants and shops. **Cons:** children are not allowed; rooms and cabins are double-occupancy only. ⊠ *107 Main Rd.* ☎ *575/257–4886 or 800/441–4331* ⊕ *www.shadowmountainlodge.com* ⌁ *19 suites, 4 cabins* ⚲ *In-room: a/c, kitchen, refrigerator, Wi-Fi. In-hotel: laundry facilities* ⊟ *AE, D, MC, V.*

NIGHTLIFE AND THE ARTS

A 514-seat venue hosting top-tier performances from jazz musicians to international ballet dancers can be found in the **Spencer Theater for the Performing Arts** (⊠ *NM 220, north of NM 48* ☎ *575/336–4800 or 888/818–7872 information, 575/336–0055 box office, 800/905–3315 ticket orders* ⊕ *www.spencertheater.com*). The white, templelike building looms majestically amid mountain vistas just north of Ruidoso and is one of the state's cultural icons. Tickets run $20 to $55, and free tours are given Tuesday and Thursday beginning at 10. Local children sometimes act in special free summer performances; outdoor summer music concerts are also offered.

SPORTS AND THE OUTDOORS

Run by the Mescalero Apaches on 12,003-foot Sierra Blanca, **Ski Apache** (⊠ *1286 Ski Run Rd.* ☎ *575/336–4356; 575/257–9001 snow report* ⊕ *www.skiapache.com*) has powder skiing for all skill levels on 55 trails and 750 acres. One of Ski Apache's distinctions is its high mountain elevation surrounded by desert. This unique climate can produce heavy snowfall (averaging more than 15 feet each winter) followed by days of pleasant, sunny weather. With the largest lift capacity in New Mexico, this huge resort can transport more than 16,500 people hourly. Ski Apache also has the state's only gondola. The season typically runs from Thanksgiving through Easter, and the snowmaking system is able to cover a third of the trails. Lift operations are open daily from 8:45 to 4; the ski area charges adults $54 for full-day lift tickets. Slightly higher fees apply for certain dates, including the week between December 26 and January 1, and special weekends in January and February. Snowboarding is allowed on all trails. Families should check out the Kiddie Korral Program for children ages four to six. Although there are no overnight accommodations at the resort, day lodges have two cafeterias, three snack bars, and outdoor grills. From Ruidoso take NM 48 for 6 mi, and turn west on NM 532 for 12 mi.

CAPITAN

22 mi north of Ruidoso on NM 48, 12 mi west of Lincoln on U.S. 380.

Capitan is famous as the birthplace and final home of Smokey Bear, the nation's symbol of wildfire prevention. The original bear concept was created in 1944, and the poster bear is still seen in public service announcements issued by the Ad Council. After a devastating 1950 forest fire in the Capitan Mountains, a bear cub was found badly burned and clinging to a tree. Named Smokey after the poster bear, he lived in the National Zoo in Washington until his death in 1976, when he was returned home for burial.

GETTING HERE

Capitan is an easy day trip from Ruidoso; get there by heading north up Sudderth Drive and through the canyon via NM 48. Or, if you're on U.S. 380, it's about equidistant (20 mi) between Carrizozo and Hondo.

VISITOR INFORMATION

Capitan Chamber of Commerce (✍ Box 441, 88316 ☎ 575/354–2273 ⊕ *www. villageofcapitan.com*).

EXPLORING

♻ Displays at the **Smokey Bear Historical Park** visitor center explain forest-fire prevention and fire ecology. A theater with informational films is offered at the 3-acre park, which also contains a picnic area. Capitan's original train depot is adjacent to the museum and gift shop. The site hosts special events for youngsters, such as an Easter egg hunt, Halloween night, and Smokey's Christmas at the Park. ⊠ *118 Smokey Bear Blvd., off NM 380* ☎ *575/354–2748* 🖼 *$2* ⊙ *Daily 9–5.*

CARRIZOZO

37 mi northwest of Capitan on U.S. 380, 58 mi north of Alamogordo on U.S. 54.

Back when railroad crews began using this site as a supply center, the community that rose up was named after *carrizo*, the reedlike grass growing in the area. The extra "-zo" appeared when the carrizo grew so thick a ranch foreman added it to the town's name for emphasis.

The ranching community incorporated in 1907 and in 1912 became the county seat of Lincoln County. About 1,000 residents live in this charming, isolated town at the junction of U.S. 54 and U.S. 380.

GETTING HERE

At the crossroads of U.S. 54 and U.S. 380, Carrizozo is easy to get to, so long as you've got your own vehicle, as there's no public transportation

VISITOR INFORMATION

Carrizozo Chamber of Commerce (✉ Box 567, 88301 ☎ 575/648–2732 ⊕ http://carrizozochamber.org).

EXPLORING

Near Carrizozo is the stark **Valley of Fires Recreation Area** operated by the Bureau of Land Management. According to Native American legend a volcanic eruption about 1,000 years ago created a valley of fire here. When the lava cooled, a dark, jagged landscape remained. A ¾-mi trail penetrates the lava-flow area, which looks like a *Star Trek* backdrop and covers 44 mi (it's 5-mi wide in some places). Crevices and bowls trapping precious water nurture ocotillo and blooming cactus, creating natural landscaping along the well-maintained trail. The visitor center has a gift shop with souvenirs and books. Caving is allowed; get permits at the visitor center. ✉ *U.S. 380, 4 mi west of Carrizozo* ☎ *575/648–2241* 💲*$3 per individual, $5 per carload* ⊙ *Information center daily 8–4.*

WHERE TO EAT AND STAY

¢ ✕ **Outpost Bar & Grill.** Rural restaurants in southern New Mexico have a

AMERICAN long-standing rivalry over who makes the best green-chile hamburgers

Fodor's Choice in the region. Many fans will tell you that the winner is right here—and

★ many will tell you this is the best one found *anywhere.* Besides cooking awesome burgers and killer homemade fries, this bar and grill has a wacky hunting-lodge decor full of animal heads, snakeskins, and painted cow skulls. The massive antique wooden bar is the centerpiece of the establishment. ✉ *415 Central Ave. S* ☎ *575/648–9994* ▬ *No credit cards.*

¢ 🏨 **Sands RV Park & Motel.** The nicely maintained rooms here have extras including refrigerators and microwaves (there's a little supermarket just a few blocks up the street), Wi-Fi, and cable TV. An RV park ($12) with extra-wide spaces, some shade trees, and full hookups and showers is also on the premises. **Pros:** a good place to overnight if you don't want to continue on to Ruidoso. **Cons:** beds are on the soft side. ✉ *1400 Central Ave.* ✉ *Box 873, Carrizozo 88301* ☎ *575/648–2989* 🛏 *12 rooms, 16 RV sites* ♿ *In-room: refrigerator, Wi-Fi. In-hotel: laundry facilities, Wi-Fi hotspot, some pets allowed* ▬ *AE, D, MC, V.*

CAMPING

¢ ⛺ **Valley of Fires Recreation Area.** This small campground sits atop an island of sandstone surrounded by lava. The facilities are comfortable and clean, but it's prohibitively hot here in summer. ✉ *U.S. 380, 4 mi west of Carrizozo* ☎ *575/648–2241* ♿ *Flush toilets, pit toilets, partial hookups (electric and water), dump station, drinking water, showers, fire grates, grills, picnic tables, electricity, public telephone, ranger station* 🛏 *20 RV sites with partial hookups, 5 tent sites.*

7

EN ROUTE

Twenty-eight miles south of Carrizozo, take CR B-30 east off U.S. 54 and in 5 mi you come to **Three Rivers Petroglyph Site,** one of the Southwest's most comprehensive and fascinating examples of prehistoric rock art. The 21,000 sunbursts, lizards, birds, handprints, plants, masks, and other symbols are thought to represent the nature-worshipping religion of the Jornada Mogollon people, who lived in this region between AD 900 and AD 1400. Symbols were pinpointed and identified through the extensive work of two members of the Archaeological Society of New Mexico's Rock Art Recording Field School. Fragrant desert creosote and mesquite can be found here, along with cacti that blossom brilliantly in early summer. A rugged trail snakes for 1 mi, and from its top you can see the Tularosa Basin to the west and the Sacramento Mountains to the east. A short trail leads to a partially excavated prehistoric village. You can camp at the site, and there are 10 covered shelters with picnic tables, barbecue grills, restrooms, and water. Two RV sites with electricity and water are available for $10 per night. ⊠ *CR B-30 east off U.S. 54* ☎ *575/525–4300* ◫ *$2 per vehicle.*

ALAMOGORDO

58 mi south of Carrizozo on U.S. 54, 46 mi southwest of Ruidoso; 68 mi northeast of Las Cruces on U.S. 70.

Defense-related activities are vital to the town of Alamogordo and to Otero County, which covers much of the Tularosa Basin desert. Look up and you might see the dark, bat-shaped outline of a Stealth fighter swooping overhead—Holloman Air Force Base is home to these high-tech fighter planes. Many residents work at White Sands Missile Range, where the nation's first atomic bomb exploded at Trinity Site on July 12, 1945. If you find U.S. 70 closed temporarily, it's due to test launches (locals have grown accustomed to this). South of Alamogordo huge military exercises involving both U.S. and foreign troops are conducted at the Fort Bliss Military Reservation along Route 54. It's not all that surprising that flying objects can be mistaken for Unidentified Flying Objects in this state.

GETTING HERE

From El Paso, take U.S. 54 north from I–10, or take U.S. 70 northeast if coming from Las Cruces. U.S. 82 west from Artesia is a direct route and crosses both expansive prairie and the lush forests of Lincoln National Forest around Cloudcroft. Greyhound provides bus service.

Contacts Greyhound (☎ *800/231–2222* ⊕ *www.greyhound.com*).

VISITOR INFORMATION

Alamogordo Chamber of Commerce (⊠ *1301 N. White Sands Blvd.* ☎ *575/437–6120 or 888/843–3441* ⊕ *www.alamogordo.com*).

EXPLORING

Tasty nuts are the crop at **Eagle Ranch Pistachio Groves and Heart of the Desert Vineyards,** where you can buy pistachios baked into cranberry biscotti, pistachio-filled chocolate candies, and the nuts themselves, as well as the wines being produced in the proprietary winery. Linger in the coffee shop or art gallery. George and Marianne Schweers own the

CLOSE UP

Exploring White Sands National Monument

BEST TIME TO GO
You'll find delightful temperatures between October and April. Daytime temps in the summer hover at close to 100 degrees, though you'll find most of the activities offered in June, July, and August.

EXPLORING
On Your Own. It's most fun to discover the dunes on foot. There are several areas to park and just head out into the sand, or you can take a walk on the 1-mi **Big Dune Trail,** which will give you a good overview of dunes. More avid hikers will love the 4¾-mi **Alkali Flat Trail,** and the 600-yard **Boardwalk** is wheelchair-accessible. Kids and the young at heart will thrill at sledding down the taller dunes. Bring your own plastic sled or purchase one at the gift shop. Don't sled over vegetation or into parking lots or roadways!

With a Ranger. Rangers lead hour-long tours daily starting at the visitor center one hour before sunset. Dusk is a busy time in the desert, with plants opening blooms and creatures scurrying about. These are fun walks to join to learn more about the flora and fauna and to take photographs.

Under the Moonlight. Once a month from May to September, you can explore the dunes under the full-moon light on a 1-1.5 mi ranger-led hike. In April and October full-moon bike rides are offered. The monument

is closed to cars for the bike rides, and as many as 200 riders can join. Reservations are essential for all moonlight events.

Under the Stars. Two special events organized by outside groups are held at the monument in September: A star party, where you can bring your own scope or gaze through high-powered telescopes brought by other participants (both pros and hobby astronomers). Unless you're a backpacker willing to pack your gear into the backcountry, this is the only time during the year that camping is allowed in the park. The second event is a balloon fiesta, where about 50 balloons show up to float placidly over the gorgeous dunes. Call for specific dates for both events (☎ 575/479–6124).

Park Facilities. There are no restaurants, overnight accommodations or camping available in the park (camping is allowed during the star party in September). The closest restaurants and accommodations are in Alamogordo, 14 miles to the east. Las Cruces is 52 miles to the west. A very basic selection of packaged sandwiches, snacks, and drinks are available at the main visitor center. It's best to pack a picnic lunch and lots of water before arriving at the monument so you can enjoy as much time as possible amidst the dunes. The **Heart of the Sands Nature Center** near the end of the dune drive has a picnic area with shaded tables and grills.

7

family farm here, which has been growing pistachios—an unusual crop for New Mexico—since 1972. The ranch has 12,000 pistachio trees and is the largest such grove in the state; a vineyard was planted in 2003 and is now producing wines—their signature wine is a crisp Pistachio Rosé, a Zinfandel–Chenin Blanc blend with a hint of pistachio essence. They offer free wine tastings daily, but not until noon on Sunday. If you have an RV and would like to camp overnight, ask for permission at the store to camp at the picnic area—there's no charge for self-contained vehicles. ✉ *7288 NM 54/70, 4 mi north of White Sands Mall* ☎ *575/434–0075 or 800/432–0999* ⊕ *www.heartofthedesert.com* ⊙ *Mon.–Sat. 8–6, Sun. 9–6. Free farm tours late May–early Sept., weekdays at 10 and 1:30; early Sept.–late May, weekdays at 1:30.*

Ⅽ The multistory structure that houses the **New Mexico Museum of Space History** gleams metallic gold when the sun hits it at certain angles. Its centerpiece is the **International Space Hall of Fame,** into which astronauts and other space-exploration celebrities are routinely inducted. A simulated red Mars landscape is among the indoor exhibits. Outside, the **Stapp Air and Space Park** displays a rocket sled from the 1950s and other space-related artifacts. The scenic **Astronaut Memorial Garden** has a view of White Sands National Monument. The **Clyde W. Tombaugh IMAX Dome Theater and Planetarium** screens films and presents planetarium and laser light shows. Weeklong annual space-shuttle camps for children take place from the first week in June through the first week in August. ✉ *At top of NM 2001; from U.S. 70 take Indian Wells Rd. to Scenic Dr.; from U.S. 54 take Florida Ave. to Scenic Dr.* ☎ *505/437–2840 or 877/333–6589* ⊕ *www.nmspacemuseum.org* ▨ *Museum $6, IMAX tickets $6 ($6.50 for evening shows)* ⊙ *International Space Hall of Fame daily 9–5. Tombaugh IMAX Dome Theater and Planetarium shows Sun.–Thurs. on the hour 11–5, Fri. and Sat. on the hour 11–6..*

Ⅽ If there's a train buff in your family, the **Toy Train Depot** in Alamogordo's Alameda Park is a must-see. Here, a narrow-gauge train rumbles along a 2½-mi track, and a depot, built in 1898, displays elaborate toy train layouts in five rooms. There are live steam engines on display, and you can hear real whistles and rumbles from nearby heavy freight trains (the attraction is only 50 yards from the Union Pacific main line). One room in the depot is an incredible re-creation of the railroad system between Alamogordo, Cloudcroft, and Ruidoso. ✉ *1991 N. White Sands Blvd., Alameda Park* ☎ *575/437–2855 or 888/207–3564* ▨ *Train $4, displays $4, combo ticket $6* ⊙ *Wed.–Sun. noon–4:30.*

Ⅽ **White Sands National Monument** encompasses 145,344 acres of the largest **Fodor'sChoice** deposit of gypsum sand in the world, where shifting sand dunes reach ★ 60 feet high. The monument, one of the few landforms recognizable from space, has displays in its **visitor center** that describe how the dunes were (and are continually) formed from gypsum crystals originating at a dry lake bed called Lake Lucero, where winds and erosion break down the crystals into fine particles of sand. A 17-minute introductory video at the visitor center is very helpful if you intend to hike among the dunes. There are also a gift shop, snack bar, and bookstore.

A 16-mi round-trip car ride takes you into this eerie wonderland of gleaming white sand. You can climb to the top of the dunes for a photograph, then tumble or surf down on a sled sold at the visitor center. As you wade barefoot in the gypsum crystals you notice the sand is not hot, and there's even moisture to be felt a few inches below the surface. Gypsum is one of the most common minerals on earth and is finer than the silica sand on beaches. A walk on the 1-mi **Big Dune Trail** will give you a good overview of the site; other options are the 4¾-mi **Alkali Flat Trail** and the 600-yard **Boardwalk**. The **Nature Center in the Dunes** museum has exhibits and other information that includes interpretive displays with depictions of animals and plant life common to the dunes, along with illustrations of how the dunes shift through time. The center usually is open during regular hours, but is staffed by volunteers (so it sometimes closes unexpectedly). Call first to make sure it's open. The picnic area has shaded tables and grills. Backpackers' campsites are available by permit, obtainable at the visitor center, but there aren't any facilities. Once a month from May to September, White Sands celebrates the full moon by remaining open until 11, allowing you to experience the dunes by lunar light. Call for information and reservations for monthly auto caravans on Saturday to **Lake Lucero**, the source of the gypsum sand deposit. Rangers lead tours daily at sunset, starting at the visitor center. ⊠ *Off U.S. 70, 15 mi southwest of Alamogordo, Holloman AFB* ☎ *575/479–6124* ⊕ *www.nps.gov/whsa* ⊠ *$3* ☉ *Late May–early Sept., daily 7 am–9 pm (visitor center daily 8–7); early Sept.–late May, daily 7–sunset (visitor center daily 8–6).*

OFF THE BEATEN PATH

White Sands Missile Range Museum & Missile Park. Here you can see outdoor displays of more than 50 rockets and missiles along with indoor exhibits honoring historic contributions of scientists including rocketry genius and inventor Wernher von Braun. The museum also contains accounts of early Native American inhabitants who occupied the surrounding Tularosa Basin. A newer display is an exhibit building with a cutout of the interior of the V-2 missile. ⊠ *White Sands Missile Range; turn east off U.S. 70, 45 mi southwest of Alamogordo or 25 mi northeast of Las Cruces, take access road 5 mi to gate and stop for visitor's pass; you must have current driver's license and insurance to enter, as well as photo identification for all passengers* ☎ *575/678–8824* ⊕ *www. wsmr-history.org* ⊠ *Free* ☉ *Museum weekdays 8–4, weekends 10–3; Missile Park daily dawn–dusk.*

WHERE TO EAT AND STAY

$$
AMERICAN
Fodor's Choice
★

✕ **Memories.** A welcome break from the chain restaurants that dominate in Alamogordo, this pleasant restaurant inside a lovely, gray Victorian turns out soups, salads, and sandwiches for lunch. Try the famous baked-potato soup and updated classic American favorites for dinner—steak, prime rib, or seafood, and excellent vegetarian lasagna are among the offers. Try the Italian cream cake or the coconut-cream pie to appreciate why Memories has such a sterling reputation for desserts. ⊠ *1223 New York Ave.* ☎ *575/437–0077* ⊟ *AE, D, MC, V* ☉ *Closed Sun.*

¢
AMERICAN

✕ **Waffle and Pancake Shoppe.** This bustling restaurant is on the short list of locals and visitors in the know for tasty, and big, breakfasts and early lunches (they close at 1). Aside from fluffy waffles and pancakes (which can come loaded with all sorts of toppings), they serve very good Mexican breakfasts and lunches—the chile verde plate for breakfast is great, as are the chicken enchiladas for lunch. Standard American fare, like eggs and bacon, and sandwiches round out the menu. A friendly greeting will almost certainly ring out the minute you walk through the door, making you feel like a long-lost friend. Steve, the owner, is the former mayor of Alamogordo. ⊠ *950 S. White Sands Blvd.* ☎ *575/437–0433* ▭ *D, MC, V* ⊗ *No dinner.*

$$ ⊡ Holiday Inn Express. Alamogordo has a number of hotels, not many of them notable. This midprice chain option is the exception. Expect friendly, professional service, immaculate grounds and hotel, and spacious, comfortable rooms. Beds are triple sheeted with plush linens and comforters, and dark-wood furniture and cool, calming beige walls make for a pleasurable stay. Continental breakfasts are generous. **Pros:** walking distance to chain restaurants. **Cons:** property starting to show its age a bit. ⊠ *100 Kerry Ave.* ☎ *575/434–9773* ⤵ *80 rooms* ⚄ *In-room: a/c, refrigerator, Wi-Fi. In-hotel: pool, gym, laundry facilities* ▭ *AE, D, DC, MC, V* ⦿| *CP.*

CAMPING

¢   ⚠ **Alamogordo Roadrunner Campground.** Motel-style amenities, such as
☺   a lounge and a recreation room, are available at this facility. There are also inviting patches of green lawn and trees where you can pitch your tent. The staff here is friendly and it's one of the more fun campgrounds/RV parks you'll find. Two 12-foot by 12-foot log cabins each have a double bed and set of bunk beds. The Wi-Fi has limited range. ⊠ *412 24th St., 1 block east of U.S. 70/54* ☎ *575/437–3003 or 877/437–3003* ⊕ *www.roadrunnercampground.com* ⚄ *Flush toilets, full hookups, guest laundry, showers, grills, picnic tables, general store, play area, swimming (pool), Wi-Fi* ⤵ *67 RV sites, 10 tent sites, 2 cabins* ▭ *MC, V.*

CLOUDCROFT

19 mi east of Alamogordo on U.S. 82.

Cloudcroft was established in 1898 when the El Paso–Northeastern Railroad crew laid out the route for the Cloud Climbing Railroad. The natural beauty and business possibilities for creating a getaway from the blistering summer heat in the valley below were obvious and plans were quickly made for a mountaintop resort. You can still see the Mexican Canyon trestle from this era as you drive NM 82 to the west of town. This incredibly steep, twisty, and scenic drive links Cloudcroft to the desert basin below and gains 4,700 feet in elevation during the steepest 16-mi stretch. Be sure to pull off the road and take a look.

One way this little mountain town promotes itself these days is with the slogan "9,000 feet above stress level," and from its perch high above the Tularosa desert valley the town lives up to the claim. Flowers and ponderosa and other greenery give the air an incredible mountain fragrance, and the boardwalks lining the main street, Burro Avenue, lend the town a kitschy Old West atmosphere that's a bit contrived, though still charming. Despite a significant influx of retirees and big-city expats over the past few years, the town has held onto its country friendliness.

There are two festivals that bookend the warm season here, and a number of others in between. Mayfest happens over Memorial Day and Aspencade is held the first weekend of October. The July Jamboree, and a Labor Day weekend fiesta are two more events held, along with street dances and the melodramas that most of the residents seem to participate in. Festivals typically include arts-and-crafts booths and all sorts of calorie-laden munchies.

Cloudcroft has the southernmost ski area in the United States, although it's a very small operation and only open during years when snow is abundant (snowfall is about 90 inches a year on average). It's a nice place for beginner skiers to get their snow legs. Contact the Chamber of Commerce for season info and ticket prices.

It is well worth getting off the boardwalks of the main village and getting into the forest to explore the countless trails and canyons, either on foot or on a mountain bike. There are trails for every level of fitness—don't miss having a hike in the clean, cool mountain air before you head back down to the heat below.

GETTING HERE

Despite its remote-seeming location, Cloudcroft is a fairly short drive up the hill from Alamagordo, via U.S. 82. From Artesia, it's 89 mi west on U. S. 82. It's a gorgeous drive from Ruidoso; 12 mi southwest on U.S. 70 then south again for 28 winding, beautiful miles on NM 244.

VISITOR INFORMATION

The **Lincoln National Forest Sacramento Ranger District headquarters** (⊠ 61 *Curlew St., off U.S. 82* ☎ *575/682–2551* ⊕ *www.fs.fed.us/r3/lincoln/ hiking.htm*) has maps showing area hiking trails—which are abundant and well worth taking the time to explore. Numerous mountain-bike trails are also open. The national forest Web site is a great resource for hiking and biking. The office is open weekdays 7:30–4:30.

Cloudcroft Chamber of Commerce (⊕ *Box 1290, 88317* ☎ *866/874–4447* ⊕ *www.cloudcroft.net*).

EXPLORING

Ⓒ The **National Solar Observatory–Sacramento Peak,** 20 mi south of Cloud-
Fodor's Choice croft on the Sunspot Highway at an elevation of 9,200 feet, is des-
★ ignated for observations of the Sun. The observatory, established in 1947, has four telescopes, including a 329-foot Vacuum Tower that resembles a pyramid. One observation point has a majestic view of White Sands and the Tularosa Basin. During the day you can inspect the telescopes on a self-guided tour and watch live, filtered television views of the Sun. Interactive displays at the visitor center allow you to, among other activities, make infrared fingerprints. The community of Sunspot, home of the observatory, is an actual working community of scientists—not a tourist attraction—so you should stay within areas designated for visitors. ⊠ *3010 Coronal Loop, off Sunspot Hwy., Sunspot* ☎ *575/434–7000* ⊕ *http://nsosp.nso.edu* ⊠ *Visitor center $3, self-guided tours free* ☉ *Visitor center daily 9–5.*

EN ROUTE Five miles south of Cloudcroft on Highway 6563, take Forest Road 64 (paved) to **Nelson Canyon Vista Trail** for a well-marked walking trail with absolutely breathtaking views of White Sands. This ¼-mi walk among the shade of tall trees is made all the more sweet if you've recently spent time down in the blazing summer heat of the Tularosa desert.

7

WHERE TO EAT AND STAY

■TIP→ Few establishments in Cloudcroft take credit cards. There are a couple of ATMs in town, but you should bring some cash.

¢   ✕ **Big Daddy's Diner.** You'll catch a whiff of Big Daddy's tasty food as
AMERICAN   you turn off U.S. 82 into Cloudcroft. There's something for everyone
Fodor's Choice   at this homey joint, where the staff seems to know darned near every-
★   one by first name. Don't expect anything fancy—just solid American
☾   favorites, and some Mexican staples, too, like enchiladas and huevos
rancheros. Though the menu leans heavily on meat, these folks happily
accommodate vegetarian requests. Big Daddy serves tasty and tender
barbecue on the weekends. It's worth trying the fried peanut butter
and jelly sandwich for breakfast for a twist on a classic. ⊠ *1705 James
Canyon (U.S. 82)* ☏ *575/682–1224* ⊕ *www.bigdaddysdinercloudcroft.
com* ⊟ *MC, V.*

$ ✕ **Western Bar & Cafe.** Locals jokingly refer to the regular morning gath-
AMERICAN   erings here as "the old men's club," where all the latest happenings in
Cloudcroft are discussed at great length, and sometimes with great
passion. Come in as you are (this place is casual personified) and get
ready for great big helpings of local favorites such as chicken-fried
steak. Don't expect pepper-encrusted ahi here: this is basic, rib-sticking
Western food served in a simple, no-frills room where the wood tables
and chairs and paneled walls may remind you of your grandparents'
living room. The bar next door is great if you require more than water
and sodas or one of the number of good microbrews, like the amus-
ingly named Arrogant Bastard Ale. ⊠ *304 Burro Ave.* ☏ *575/682–2445
restaurant, 575/682–9910 bar* ⊟ *No credit cards.*

$ ☷ **Cloudcroft Hotel and Mall.** If you'd like to be in the thick of things,
or just want to park your car and spend your time strolling around
town, this is the hotel for you. You're within walking distance of dining and nightlife, shopping, and outdoor activities. The seven spacious
rooms have ceiling fans (fine for the cooler temperatures at this altitude) and claw-foot tubs. Gallo's, a restaurant in the attached shopping
arcade, offers room service to guests. **Pros:** very friendly staff; immaculate accommodations. **Cons:** hotel is right Downtown, so there aren't
any grounds or gardens. ⊠ *306 Burro Ave.* ☏ *575/682–3414* ⊕ *www.
cloudcrofthotel.com* ⤢ *7 rooms* ☖ *In-room: kitchen (some)* ⊟ *AE, D,
MC, V* ⏍❘ *CP.*

$$ ☷ **The Lodge.** The imposing Bavarian-style architecture of The Lodge,
★   with its tower and dramatic details, has drawn all sorts of notable
characters over the years, including Judy Garland, Clark Gable, and
even the Mexican revolutionary Pancho Villa. The bar was owned
by Al Capone at one point. The outside looks like an Alpine lodge,
but the interior, with its dark-wood furnishings and plush carpeted
stairways, seems to have come right from a Gothic novel. Rooms are
furnished with antiques, fluffy comforters, and ceiling fans. Rebecca's
Restaurant ($$$) serves Continental cuisine in a beautiful room that is
full of sunlight during the day and romantically lighted with candles
at night. Rebecca is the resident ghost of a chambermaid apparently
murdered by her lumberjack lover in the 1930s in the hotel—and she's
reputedly quite playful. **Pros:** a gorgeous, historic property with lovely

rooms and wonderful service. **Cons:** it's worth asking specifically not to be placed in the Pavilion, which is subpar and very different from the main lodge. ⊠ *601 Corona Pl.* ☎ *575/682–2566 or 800/395–6343* ⊕ *www.thelodgeresort.com* ⇆ *47 rooms* ⚬ *In-room: Wi-Fi. In-hotel: restaurant, bar, golf course, pool, gym, spa, some pets allowed* ▤ *AE, D, DC, MC, V.*

$$ 🏨 **RavenWind Lodging & Spa.** Morning dew on sparkling grass and the fragrant scent of a juniper forest greet visitors awakening in sublime isolation at RavenWind (22 mi southeast of Cloudcroft). The 75-acre ranch owned by transplanted upstate New Yorkers Russ and Elaine Wright was built specifically to create a refuge where people can rest and renew themselves—or hike, mountain bike, and explore to their heart's content. You have your choice of a separate, secluded two-bedroom house (where children are welcome) or rooms in the main lodge, which has wooden porches and native rock walls. RavenWind is popular with horse owners, who can transport and then board their animals in stables ($20 daily per horse). For some real pampering, or to work out the kinks from the busy life you left behind, talk to Russ—he's a licensed therapeutic massage therapist. **Pros:** gorgeous mountain meadow setting; wonderful breakfasts. **Cons:** no kids allowed in main lodge; two-night minimum stay required. ⊠ *1234 NM 24, Weed* ☎ *575/687–3073* ⊕ *www.ravenwindranch.com* ⇆ *2 rooms, 1 2-bedroom house* ⚬ *In-room: kitchen (some), refrigerator (some), Wi-Fi. In-hotel: spa, laundry facilities* ▤ *No credit cards* ⦿⦿ *MAP.*

For cabin rental information, call the Cloudcroft Chamber of Commerce, or try **Cabins at Cloudcroft** (☎ *575/682–2396 or 800/248–7967* ⊕ *www.cloudcroftnm.com*). Rates are $75 to $170 for one- to four-bedroom cabins.

CAMPING

¢ ⛺ **Deer Spring RV Park.** You can savor the forested surroundings and shade in this sanctuary far removed from any major community. The grassy site has full hookups and pull-through parking. ⊠ *2089 Rio Penasco Rd., off NM 130, about 18 mi east of Cloudcroft, Mayhill* ☎ *575/687–3464* ⊕ *www.deerspringrvpark.com* ⇆ *60 RV sites* ⚬ *Showers, guest laundry, Wi-Fi* ▤ *No credit cards* ⊙ *Closed Nov.–Mar.*

Southwestern
New Mexico

WORD OF MOUTH

"New Mexico is the best place right now for green chiles, particularly down in the area of Hatch. You can get them mild, medium, or hot. The chile verde is usually, but not always, hotter than the chile colorado. Chiles, like most peppers, tend to get sweeter as they redden."

–MikePinTucson

Updated by
Lynne Arany

Calling southwestern New Mexico a borderland may seem a bit obvious, but it is one in the broadest possible sense. The proximity of Mexico is inescapable as you travel through the region, but so is the delightful blend of the people whose cultures have met and mingled in this area since long before there was a border. Southwestern New Mexico is a trove of diversity, from the scenery, to the people and their cultures, to the food.

Both Albuquerque and El Paso are convenient gateways, but the hub of southern New Mexico is Las Cruces (the Crosses, so named because of the number of people buried in the area due to hardship and Apache attacks). With a population of about 75,000 (and growing quickly), Las Cruces is bordered to the east by the jagged and beautiful Organ Mountains. Sunset often colors the jagged peaks a brilliant magenta, called "Las Cruces purple," and they are depicted endlessly by local painters and photographers. Nearby, Old Mesilla once served as the Confederate territorial capital of New Mexico and Arizona.

The incredible, irrigated lushness in the fertile Mesilla Valley would surprise the hard-pressed Spanish settlers who passed through the area 400 years ago. Miles of green fields and orchards track the path of the Rio Grande from north of El Paso to north of Las Cruces, with water from the huge Elephant Butte reservoir irrigating some of the country's most prolific pecan and chile pepper farms. New Mexico's largest body of water, Elephant Butte Lake, is a mecca for water sports and fishing. Nearby, you can soak in natural hot springs and enjoy laid-back, small-town New Mexico in Truth or Consequences. The Bosque del Apache National Wildlife Refuge is a resting place for millions of migrating birds each year. Whether you're a bird enthusiast or not, it is quite a treat to witness the sky fill up with enormous varieties of birds taking off or landing in the marshy area.

Outdoors enthusiasts from all over head to the Gila (pronounced *hee*-la) National Forest and Gila Wilderness areas for access to fantastic camping and hiking and natural hot springs. Old mining towns remind you of the thousands who came here on their quest for silver, copper, and other minerals once found abundantly in the ore-rich hills. Several small museums display the region's minerals, along with fine pottery created by early indigenous inhabitants. This rugged, mountainous area, with its breathtaking vistas and seemingly endless span of trees, was home at different times to two Western legends: Geronimo and Billy the Kid. The hub of the area is Silver City, one of the great small towns of the West. Here you'll find a lively art scene, numerous community festivals, and friendly locals.

TOP REASONS TO GO

Mineral soak. Immersing yourself in hot mineral water is an absolute delight, and between the healing waters in Truth or Consequences and the natural pools near the Gila Cliff Dwellings you'll have ample opportunity to soak while exploring this region.

Art and architecture walk. Silver City's historical district is the locus for the town's friendly arts community and some big-city-caliber galleries. Don't miss the restored buildings along Bullard Street and the stonework along the Big Ditch.

The Gila Wilderness. If you can spare two to three full days to explore the cliff dwellings *and* the Catwalk, it will be time well spent. In an otherwise dry region, the lushness of the Gila is amazing.

Old mining towns. Take some time to wander around Hillsboro and Kingston, Pinos Altos, Mogollon, or Chloride. The remaining buildings, from well-preserved and open for business, to crumbling piles of adobe, are reminders that the area was once full of bustling towns.

ORIENTATION AND PLANNING

GETTING ORIENTED

Whether you're coming up from El Paso or down from Albuquerque, I–25 and I–10 make it easy to hit the highlights of southwestern New Mexico. Although hilly, the area's roads aren't mountainous until you get onto NM 152 between I–25 and Silver City or up into the Gila National Forest, making most travel fairly quick. In the northern part of this region, many off-the-beaten-path treasures await via U.S. 60 heading west from Socorro.

WHAT'S WHERE

Along the Camino Real. History, rich and deep, accompanies this well-trod route, from the earliest indigenous traders who first marked it, to Spanish colonists and frontier settlers, to the space-age scientists who ply the interstate today. Find remnants of missions, pueblos, and 19th-century military forts, and spectacular avian wildlife (Bosque del Apache), delicious hot springs (Truth or Consequences), rural charm (and chile) in Hatch, and memorable wineries in Old Mesilla.

Heading west on U.S. 60. From the town of Socorro, you can follow scenic and solitary U.S. 60 all the way into Arizona. The route passes through a handful of small, quirky villages. Enjoy fabulous pie in Pie Town; gape at expansive mountains, and marvel at the giant antennae at the Very Large Array. Touring this immutable area often feels like a trip through the Old West.

Gila National Forest area. In the central part of this region, starting about 10 mi north of Silver City, lies a vast wilderness—diverse and immense. You'll want to allow lots of time to explore the area. From the famed Gila Cliff Dwellings, to abandoned mining towns, to lush canyons replete with waterfalls, plan to devote a fair amount of time here; you won't regret a moment of it.

SOUTHWESTERN NEW MEXICO PLANNER

WHEN TO GO

Mild and sunny winters are this region's major draw. From May to September, though, it's just plain hot. Really hot. And dry. The mountain areas provide a respite and are generally 10 degrees cooler during the day. Unless you're used to dry, intense heat, plan summer outdoor excursions for early morning or late afternoon. Wear sunscreen, sunglasses, and a hat in the midday sun, and don't just carry plenty of water—drink it. Temperatures drop in the evenings, so keep a light jacket or sweater on hand. Spring is cooler, but it can bring strong, dusty winds. The weather between mid-September and early November tends to be delightful and balmy, and the sunsets and moonrises at this time are fantastic. During the fall harvest this whole valley takes on the rich scent of roasting chiles.

GETTING HERE AND AROUND

AIR TRAVEL

Albuquerque International Sunport (✉ *2200 Sunport Blvd. SE, Albuquerque* ☎ *505/244–7700*) is 210 mi north of Las Cruces. **El Paso International Airport** (✉ *6701 Convair Dr., El Paso, TX* ☎ *915/780–4749*) is the main gateway to southern New Mexico. The major airlines with scheduled service are American, Continental, Delta, Frontier, Southwest, and US Airways. **Grant County Airport** ✉ *Airport Rd., 10 mi southeast of Silver City, Hurley* ☎ *575/388–4554*), near Silver City, is served by Great Lakes Airlines, with direct daily service from Albuquerque.

BUS TRAVEL

Greyhound (☎ *575/524–8518 in Las Cruces, 800/231–2222 for all other destinations* ⊕ *www.greyhound.com*) provides bus service to towns on I–10: Las Cruces, Deming, and Lordsburg (no service to Silver City). **Silver Stage Lines** (☎ *800/522–0162*) provides shuttle service to Las Cruces and Silver City from El Paso International Airport. **Las Cruces Shuttle & Taxi Service** (☎ *575/525–1784* ⊕ *www.lascrucesshuttle.com*) makes regular runs daily between El Paso International Airport and Las Cruces, Deming, and Silver City. **Roadrunner Transit** (☎ *575/541–2500*) operates public buses in Las Cruces.

CAR TRAVEL

Two major interstates travel through southwestern New Mexico, I–10 from west to east and I–25 from north to south. U.S. 70 connects Las Cruces to Alamogordo and the southeast. From Albuquerque, the drive is about two hours to Truth or Consequences, three hours to Las Cruces. Silver City can be accessed from minor highways leading off I–10 and I–25. From Las Cruces, I–10 leads south to El Paso.

The quality of the region's roadways varies widely, particularly in remote rural areas. Drive with caution on the narrow highways, which particularly in mountainous areas have no shoulders. On minor roadways, even if paved, be alert for curves, dips, and steep drop-offs. If you veer too far into unexplored territory with primitive, unpaved roads, make sure you have a vehicle with high clearance and four-wheel drive, such as an SUV.

You can rent a car from one of the national agencies at either Albuquerque International Airport or El Paso International Airport. Avis, Hertz, and Enterprise have rental locations in Las Cruces. Auto dealerships in some communities rent cars.

TRAIN TRAVEL

Amtrak (⌂ *Union Station, 700 San Francisco St., El Paso, TX* ☎ *915/545–2247 or 800/872–7245* ⊕ *www.amtrak.com*) services El Paso, Texas, and Deming, New Mexico, on the Sunset Limited, which operates between Los Angeles and New Orleans.

GUIDED TOURS AND OUTFITTERS

The Festival of the Cranes, Hatch Chile Festival, and Fort Bayard are a few of the tour destinations and events that UNM's excellent continuing-education program, **Story of New Mexico** (☎ *505/277–0077 or 505/277–0563* ⊕ *http://dce.unm.edu*), offers to the public. Trips start in Albuquerque and comprise small groups; all transportation is provided.

Leah Gray Jones, with **Wilderness Ventures** (☎ *866/7677–2008, 575/539–2800* ⊕ *www.gilawildernessventures.com*), has run guided trips on horseback through the Gila Wilderness for well over two decades; horses are always well-matched with a rider's skills, and all levels of experience are welcome.

WolfHorse Outfitters (☎ *575/534–1379* ⊕ *www.wolfhorseoutfitters.com*) is a Native American guide service offering superb, customized horseback, backpack, and hiking expeditions into the heart of Gila country. Most are led by owner Joe Saenz, who is of Warm Springs Apache ancestry, and convey an especially rich appreciation of the land and its history.

ABOUT THE RESTAURANTS

The cost of a meal in this area is extremely reasonable, although the food options are limited compared to what you'll find farther north. There are a couple of outstanding restaurants in Truth or Consequences and Silver City. Mexican food is an almost sure bet in this area, especially if you're a fan of the locally grown green chiles. You won't get far before you realize that barbecue joints and steak houses are almost as numerous as the Mexican restaurants. Las Cruces has several tasty ethnic-food restaurants in the university district; again, generally at very reasonable prices.

ABOUT THE HOTELS

Whether they're historic lodgings or chain hotels, you'll find many of the accommodations in this part of the state incorporate Spanish influences in their architecture. Haciendas, mission-style buildings with tile roofs, and courtyards with fountains and gardens are everywhere here—evidence of the style first introduced by Spanish colonists more than four centuries ago.

8

WHAT IT COSTS				
¢	$	$$	$$$	$$$$
Restaurants	under $10	$10–$15	$16–$22	$23–$30	over $30
Hotels	under $70	$70–$120	$121–$175	$176–$250	over $250

Restaurant prices are per person for a main course at dinner. Hotel prices are for two people in a standard double room in high season, excluding 10%–12% tax.

PLANNING YOUR TIME

The Rio Grande flows through the fertile Mesilla Valley, known for its plump green chile peppers and acres of thick, shaded pecan groves. Try leaving I–10 and following the green agriculture fields along NM 28, which begins just north of El Paso and ends at Old Mesilla. The shops and restaurants in Old Mesilla's historic plaza make for an easy, leisurely afternoon of wandering. The adobe buildings are virtually unchanged from the way they appeared a century ago. From Las Cruces, just north of Old Mesilla, take NM 185 north through the farm valley on the route that leads to Hatch, where you can stop for lunch or dinner to sample some of the famed chile.

You could easily spend several days (or weeks) exploring the old, but still lively, mining town of Silver City and the vast Gila National Forest, which surrounds it. New Mexico's largest lake, Elephant Butte, begins at the hot springs haven of Truth or Consequences and tracks north for miles alongside I–25. The Bosque del Apache Wildlife Refuge near Socorro provides a haven for countless species of birds. Heading west at Socorro on U.S. 60, you'll find rural villages such as Magdalena and Quemado. On the Plains of San Agustin, look for the awesome array of giant, gleaming, white radio antennae that are part of the National Radio Astronomy Observatory.

ALONG THE CAMINO REAL

What many travelers don't realize as they head south from Albuquerque on I-25 is that the typically scenic Southwestern stretch of highway they're driving is actually a deeply historic route. It's essentially the same one trod for centuries: first by early indigenous peoples making there way in and out of Mexico to trade for macaw feathers and copper bells, followed by late-16th-century Spanish colonists, who would call its full extent—from Veracruz, Mexico, to Santa Fe—*El Camino Real*, the Royal Road. Aside from a harrowing stretch, known as the Jornada del Muerto (Journey of Death), early travelers mostly kept to the meandering banks of the Rio Grande. The Rio Grande, with its life-giving flow slicing the center of New Mexico, is the reason this route became so important here, and it continued to define the region in centuries to follow.

Rich agriculturally, the cottonwood-lined valleys from Albuquerque to Las Cruces drew missions and pueblo settlements. As Apache raids escalated in the 1800s, military forts were raised along the route as well. It would take the completion of the Atchison, Topeka & Santa Fe

GREAT ITINERARY

IF YOU HAVE 5 DAYS

Head south from Albuquerque on I–25, turning west onto U.S. 60 when you hit Socorro. Pause in the old cattle-trail town of **Magdalena,** take a gander at the **Very Large Array,** and, yes, get some pie in **Pie Town,** then turn south on either NM 12 or NM 32 (they both merge into U.S. 180) to begin your journey into the **Gila National Forest and Wilderness region.** If it's a weekend, definitely detour to Mogollon, and if not, proceed directly to the **Catwalk** and enjoy a good long hike into Whitewater Canyon. Stay overnight in Glenwood, or a bit farther south at the deeply satisfying **Casitas de Gila, taking in the Aldo Leopold Vista en** route. On Day 2 you can wander the lovely Old West town of **Silver City,** which abounds with galleries and shops (also check out the Mimbres pottery display at WNMU Museum). Dine in town at one of the surprisingly sophisticated restaurants, or venture up to historic **Pinos Altos** and stay at Bear Creek Motel & Cabins.

Noting that these Gila roads are winding and slow, begin Day 3 on the **Trail of the Mountain Spirits,** driving north on NM 15 to the **Gila Cliff Dwellings.** Take a side hike to a sheltered natural hot spring if there's time, then head back south

on NM 35 past Lake Roberts, and make your way east on NM 152 across Emory Pass into Kingston. Day 4 takes you south on NM 27, past the barely-there ghost town of **Lake Valley,** then east on NM 26 into **Hatch** for a perfect green-chile-fired lunch at the Pepper Pot. You might turn south on I–25 to Las Cruces and take in **Old Mesilla** and a few stops on the **Mesilla Valley Wine Trail,** or turn north on the interstate and head right to the retro-funky town of **Truth or Consequences.** Stay at Blackstone's and soak in the mineral-rich hot springs—the curative waters are piped right into the guest rooms. On Day 5, continue north, where you can detour west after about 10 miles onto NM 52 through the 1800s mining town of **Chloride.** Or, stay on I–25 and make your way directly to **El Camino Real International Heritage Center,** and leave time for a stop at **Bosque del Apache National Wildlife Refuge,** just south of **Socorro.** And remember that you needn't stick to I–25 when you're traveling north–south through the Royal Road (El Camino Real) region: south of Truth or Consequences, rural NM 185 and 187 weave alongside it, and to the north, NM 1 and then NM 47 through Isleta Pueblo are the prettiest ways to make your way back up to Albuquerque.

8

Railroad in 1882 to bring an end to the original Camino Real trail. By then Spanish Land Grant compounds and frontier towns had become quite established, and now in the 21st century crops of chiles and pecans, onions, and grape orchards flourish in a land still occupied by many of those same little towns. Today, unhurried travelers can choose smaller byways that interlace the interstate and experience historical remnants of this centuries' old passageway.

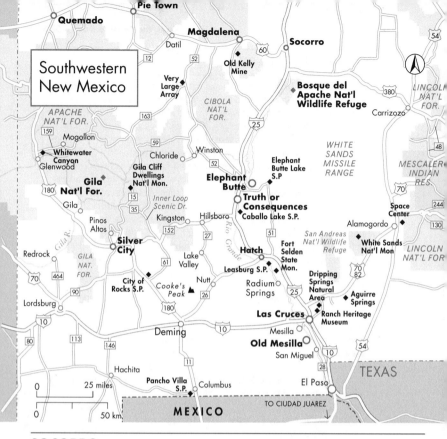

SOCORRO

78 mi south of Albuquerque; 72 mi north of Truth or Consequences.

The town of Socorro, population about 9,000, traces its roots back to the earliest Spanish expeditions into New Mexico when explorer Juan de Oñate established a permanent settlement along the Rio Grande in 1598. Native Americans provided corn for the expedition, inspiring Oñate to give the community a name that means succor, or help. The San Miguel Mission church was established in 1628, but Spanish settlement was virtually erased during the Pueblo Revolt of 1680 and did not reestablish itself until 1816. If not for this early and lengthy period of dormancy in the area, the city might have been the capital of New Mexico, with its prime location in a large, fertile valley, amid then-thriving pueblos, abundant water sources, and tremendous mineral wealth.

Socorro's business district now occupies historic buildings that surround its sleepy square, which has a park with a gazebo and a plaque commemorating the arrival of Juan de Oñate. The town's claim to fame is the highly regarded New Mexico Institute of Mining and Technology (now more commonly called New Mexico Tech) founded in 1893 as the New Mexico School of Mines—though, unfortunately, the student population doesn't translate into town vibrancy or any sort of nightlife.

TRINITY SITE

Only a monument remains at **Trinity Site,** where the world's first atomic bomb exploded, on July 16, 1945. The resulting crater has been filled in, but the test site and monument are open for public viewing and self-guided tours two days of the year. The McDonald ranch house, where the first plutonium core for the bomb was assembled, can be toured on those days. Picnic tables are available. It's wheelchair-accessible. ■TIP➔ There are no vehicle services or gas at the site, and visitors must bring their own food and water. ⊠ Off I–25, 34 mi southeast of Socorro ⊹ Exit 139 (10 mi south of Socorro), at San Antonio, and go 12 mi east on U.S. 380 and turn south onto paved road, NM 525 (there is a large sign for Trinity Site), for 5 mi until route reaches Stallion Range Center gate; visitors (everyone over age 16 must present photo ID) will be met at the gate and escorted 17 mi east to site ☎ 575/678–1134 ⊕ www.wsmr.army.mil ⊠ Free ☉ 1st Sat. of Apr. and Oct., gate open 8–2.

The institution's original specialties were chemistry and metallurgy, but along with scientific research now there are programs in medicine, engineering, and business.

GETTING HERE

Socorro is the gateway to the region if you're coming from Albuquerque—the small city is easily reached via I–25, 78 mi south of the Duke City. If you're driving to central New Mexico from Arizona via lonely but scenic U.S. 60, it's the last town you reach before coming to I–25.

Contacts **Socorro Heritage & Visitors Center** ☎ 575/835–8927 ⊠ 217 Fisher Ave. ⊕ www.socorronm.gov).

EXPLORING

More than 2,000 mineral specimens are on display at the New Mexico Bureau of Geology and Mineral Resources' **Mineralogical Museum,** among them samples from the area's ore-rich mining districts of Magdalena, Santa Rita, and Tyrone. Exhibits cull from the museum's fabulous collection of more than 15,000 items, which has been called Coronado's Treasure Chest, as it contains everything the explorer wished he'd found in New Mexico but didn't. There is an excellent fluorescent minerals display, as well as mining memorabilia and some fossils. Tours can be arranged. ⊠ *New Mexico Tech, 801 Leroy Pl.* ☎ *575/835–5140* ⊕ *http://geoinfo.nmt.edu* ⊠ *Free* ☉ *Weekdays 8–5, weekends 10–3.*

EN ROUTE

Hundreds of different types of birds, including snow geese, cranes, falcons, and eagles, can be spotted from viewing platforms and directly through your car window at the popular **Bosque del Apache National Wildlife Refuge.** Besides serving as a rest stop for migrating birds, the Bosque del Apache also shelters mule deer, turkeys, quail, and other wildlife. Photo opportunities abound on the 15-mi auto loop tour; you can also hike through arid shrub land or bike through the refuge or take a van tour. October and November are the months the cottonwoods show their colors. In winter months, the refuge echoes with the haunting cries of whooping cranes flocking for the evening. Snow geese are

8

so thick on lakes at times that shores are white with feathers washed ashore. Whether you're a bird-watcher or not, it is well worth bringing binoculars or a spotting scope to get some idea of how many varieties of birds land here (nearly 400 species have been spotted since 1940). The Festival of the Cranes (⊕ *www.friendsofthebosque.org*) in mid-November draws thousands of people. ⊠ *1001 NM 1, off I–25 San Marcial Exit 124 for northbound traffic and Exit 139 for southbound traffic, San Antonio* ☏ *575/835–1828* ⊕ *www.fws.gov/southwest/refuges/ newmex/bosque* ⌸ *$3 per vehicle* ⊘ *Refuge daily dawn–dusk; visitor center weekdays 7:30–4, weekends 8–4:30; tour road open Apr.–Sept.*

Heading south on I–25 beyond Socorro and San Antonio, there are a couple of noteworthy stops. The first one, one of the region's most compelling attractions, is **El Camino Real International Heritage Center.** The beautiful, contemporary Heritage Center opened in 2005, after many years and much effort by New Mexicans to create a monument to El Camino Real de Tierra Adentro, the Royal Road. The history of the period from 1598 through the late 1800s—when Spanish and Mexican colonists traveled the 1,500-mi route from Veracruz to Santa Fe most heavily—is the focus of the captivating exhibits here. But El Camino was also a vital trade route that linked ancient peoples from North America to Mesoamericans, and that earlier era is touched on as well. The kind of determination needed to cover this rugged ground is amazing to consider, particularly while gazing at the unbroken horizon and stark environment of the Jornada del Muerto ("Journey of the Dead Man"), the nickname for the region this part of the road passed through. Today, this international trade route lives on in the form of the near parallel I–25. There are picnic tables, but no food is available here. ✛ *30 mi south of Socorro, off I–25 Exit 115, east to NM 1 frontage road, south 1½ mi, east onto CR 1598, about 3 mi to center* ⬡ *Box 175, Socorro 87801* ☏ *575/854–3600* ⊕ *www.elcaminoreal.org* ⌸ *$5* ⊘ *Wed.–Sun. 8:30–5.*

Not far from the Camino Real Center, **Fort Craig National Historic Site** was established after the New Mexico Territory became part of the United States to prevent raids by the Apache and Navajo peoples and to secure the trade routes within the region. The growth of Socorro and what is now Truth or Consequences can be traced to the protection the fort provided between 1854 and the mid-1880s, when it was decommissioned. Battles west of the Mississippi River during the American Civil War were relatively rare, but in 1862 the Confederate army crossed the Rio Grande and headed to Valverde, north of Fort Craig, with the goal of cutting off the fort from the Union military headquarters in Santa Fe. Confederate forces first were sent into retreat but later won a few battles and made the Union forces withdraw. The rebels later occupied Santa Fe for a few months. Today, signs describe the various buildings and solitary life at the outpost, where only a couple of masonry walls and numerous foundations remain. Historic markers are very informative, however, and a well-maintained gravel trail winds among the ruins. The roads to Fort Craig, which is about 35 mi south of Socorro, can become hard to pass during rainy weather. During the closest weekend to significant dates of February 21 and 22, historical reenactors re-create the Civil War Battle of Valverde and even "capture" the nearby city of Socorro in a grand finale. ⊠ *Off I–25 San Marcial Exit 124 or Exit 115; follow signs from exit for about 10 mi* ☎ *575/835–0412* ⊕ *www. blm.gov* ⊠ *Free* ☉ *Daily dawn–dusk.*

WHERE TO EAT

¢ ✕ **La Pasadita.** Wander off the main drag into this place and you'll real-
MEXICAN ize that it's a well-kept secret among locals. The New Mexican food here is really good, and really inexpensive. Don't be put off by the lack of charm on the outside; order at the counter, sit down at a table, and wait for the friendly staff to bring you a plate of their wonderful food. The burrito plate with red chile is big and mouthwatering, and the combo plates are H-U-G-E. Don't miss what may be the very best sopaipillas in all of New Mexico—light, flaky, and soooo good with honey. ⊠ *230 Garfield St.* ☎ *575/835–3696* ⊟ *No credit cards* ☉ *No dinner. Closed weekends.*

$ ✕ **Socorro Springs Restaurant & Brewery.** This microbrewery and restau-
AMERICAN rant is right on the main drag and is almost always full of happy locals drinking good beer and eating calzones, thin-crust pizzas, homemade soups, and big, fresh salads. It's hard to go wrong here, unless you're in a hurry. "Hurry" isn't on this menu, though the service is friendly. ⊠ *1012 N. California St.* ☎ *575/838–0650* w*www.socorrosprings.com* ⊟ *D, MC, V.*

¢ ✕ **Sofia's Kitchen & Burrito Tyme.** This cheap and simple insider's favorite
AMERICAN offers drive-through, carryout, or eat-in dining. If you choose the latter, step inside the bustling mural-lined space, sit down at one of the solid wood tables. Wherever you dine, take your pick from a menu that wan-ders from basic biscuits-and-gravy to fajitas combo plates to barbecue ribs with plenty of side dishes. Leave room for cherry pie or chocolate cake for dessert. ⊠ *105 Bullock Blvd.* ☎ *575/835–0022* ⊟ *MC, V.*

WHERE TO STAY

$ ▦ **Best Western Socorro Hotel & Suites.** A favorite of groups and small conventions that otherwise might have limited options in a town this size, this older outpost of the chain offers condensed versions of some of the luxuries of larger resorts. You can expect the chain's usual quality and contemporary, modern flourishes in standard rooms; a friendly staff rounds out an easy stay. **Pros:** within walking distance of several restau-rants. **Cons:** right off the freeway; typical chain-hotel charm. ⊠ *1100 N. California St.* ☎ *575/838–0556* ⊕ *www.bestwesternnewmexico.com* ⇗ *120 rooms* ⅙ *In-room: a/c, refrigerator, Wi-Fi. In-hotel: pool, gym, laundry facilities, some pets allowed* ⊟ *AE, D, DC, MC, V* ⦿⏐*CP.*

TRUTH OR CONSEQUENCES

75 mi south of Socorro on I–25; 72 mi north of Las Cruces on I–25.

Yes, Truth or Consequences really did get its name from the game show of the same name. The show's producer, Ralph Edwards, suggested that a town adopt the name to honor the production's 10th anniversary in 1950. The community, which had been known as Hot Springs, accepted the challenge, earning national publicity for the stunt. A portion of the community rebelled, though, withdrawing from T or C (as the town is frequently called) and incorporating as Williamsburg. T or C's name is a favorite point of contention for some of the old-school residents.

Centuries ago the area's earliest inhabitants came here for relaxation and the waters' healing properties—hot water being a universally enjoyed healing method. In the 1930s bathhouses tapping into the soothing mineral waters were established near the Downtown district. This area, with street after street of neat old buildings, some covered in art deco tiling, struggles economically despite the draw of the springs—with many shops out of business or boarded up. Despite this, there is a casual, friendly vibe among the people here that leaves you rooting for the little town. There is much hope among locals that the developing Spaceport (⇨ *Exploring, below*) will bring needed revenue and business to the area.

T or C bills itself as the "most affordable spa town in America" and about a half-dozen spas (which, though charming, compared with the luxury resort spas of Santa Fe or Scottsdale, some might consider rustic) operate at prices that are quite reasonable compared to those in other parts of the Southwest. Facilities, even in the most affordable establishments, are very clean and many offer therapeutic treatments like massage, Reiki, and reflexology. There is a small group of resorts and restaurants especially notable for the style and quality they bring to a town where amenities tend toward the modest, to say the least. Their proprietors' dedication to raising the standard and visibility of the town is commendable and their establishments make T or C a more interesting, and tasty, destination.

GETTING HERE

Truth or Consequences is a good midpoint if traveling from Albuquerque south toward Las Cruces or Silver City—it's just off I–25, about a 2½-hour drive south of Albuquerque, a 1-hour drive north of Las Cruces, and a 2-hour drive east of Silver City.

Contacts Sierra County Tourism ✉ *211 Main St.* ☎ *575/894–1968 or 800/831–9487* ⊕ *www.sierracountynewmexico.info).*

EXPLORING

☻ At the distinctively homespun **Geronimo Springs Museum,** you can visit a room dedicated to Ralph Edwards' career and his very personal connection to the town that renamed itself after his quiz show, and you can view the giant skull of a woolly mammoth that was excavated in the nearby Gila National Forest. There's also a pictorial history of the dental chair, an essential display on cowboy hats and the personalities that wear them, and a pretty darn good collection of early Mimbres, Tularosa, Alma, and Hohokam pottery. Also check out the excellent bookshop with regional titles. The county visitor center is next door. ✉ *211 Main St.* ☎ *575/894–6600* ⊕ *www.geronimospringsmuseum. com* 🖂 *$5* ☾ *Mon.–Sat. 9–5, Sun. noon–4.*

Hay-Yo-Kay Hot Springs has seven naturally flowing pools, including one that, at 10 feet by 20 feet, is the largest and longest established in the hot-springs district. The standard price for the hot baths is $6 per person for a half-hour soak indoors, $11 for a half hour in an outdoor pool. Add $1.50 for a towel, and another 50¢ for a bottle of water.

Space Tourism

Spaceport America. It may be hard to imagine as you gaze into the infinite blue of New Mexico's southern sky, but someday soon those wispy contrails you see lingering from rocket engines may be the residue of vehicles carrying tourists into Earth's orbit—and beyond.

In October 2005 the White Sands Missile Range hosted the first of a series of X Prize Cup competitions, aimed at enabling private industry to become involved in (relatively) economical space travel. Some of the launch technologies that resulted have been pivotal to the development, barely five years later, of the facility that will house Virgin Galactic and make space tourism a reality (though cash flow is more likely to come from suborbital satellite launches and payload cargo). Visitor centers in both Hatch and Truth or Consequences are planned to launch as soon as Spaceport flights are operational; bus tours that will originate from those centers are part of the program. But to get on board SpaceShipTwo, it will cost you around $200,000. ⊠ *70 mi northwest of Las Cruces, 43 mi southeast of Truth or Consequences, Spaceport* ⊕ *www. spaceportamerica.com.*

Massage, Reiki, and reflexology therapists are on call for varying fees. Packages are available—for instance, a soak and a 50-minute massage cost $65. ⊠ *300 Austin Ave.* ☎ *575/894–2228* ⊕ *www.hay-yo-kay.com* ⊟ *AE, D, DC, MC, V.* ⊙ *Wed.–Sun.*

OFF THE BEATEN PATH

NM 52 leads about 40 mi west from I–25, near Truth or Consequences, to **Winston** and **Chloride,** two fascinating mining towns just east of the Gila National Forest. Prospectors searching for silver in the nearby ore-rich mountains founded the towns in the late 1800s; abandoned saloons and false-front buildings, and pioneer relics still remain. Though the communities are designated ghost towns, the moniker is belied by the 50 or so residents currently living in each place, and Chloride has several businesses in operation. The **Pioneer Store Museum** (☎ *575/743–2736* ⊕ *www.pioneerstoremuseum.com*) is an amazing time-capsule-like building in Chloride. The owners have painstakingly restored the building using the complete stock of original goods and records—the store had been boarded up in its entirety in 1923. It's a treasure trove of Western boomtown history. The proprietors are great, and the Web site is a resource for general information on the area. ⌂ *Don and Dona Edmund, HC 30, Box 134, Winston, NM 87943* ⊠ *50 mi northwest of Truth or Consequences.* ✛ *Take I-25 exit 89 (southbound), turn left on NM 181, then right onto NM 52, or exit 83 (northbound), turn left on NM 181, then left onto NM 52. 87943*

EN ROUTE

Caballo Lake State Park provides winter nesting grounds for golden and bald eagles, often sighted gliding aloft as they search for prey. Fishing and water sports are popular at the lake, and hiking trails lead through the desert areas where yucca, century plants, and numerous varieties of cacti are abundant. A great time to visit is late March or early April, when prickly pears and other succulents are in bloom. ⊠ *State park exit (Exit 59) off I-25, about 16 mi south of Truth or Consequences and 58*

8

mi north of Las Cruces ☎ *575/743–3942* ⊕ *www.emnrd.state.nm.us/ PRD/caballo.htm* ✉ *$5 per vehicle* ⊙ *Visitor center daily 7:30–4:30, open later in summer.*

WHERE TO EAT

$$ ✕ **Bella Luca.** Best bets here are the specials, which might include home-
ITALIAN   made ravioli Fra Diavolo with full-bodied, spicy sauce. But the kitchen, and the service, can be uneven, and folks who arrive from afar with high expectations from its buzz-worthy early days might be disappointed. Here in tiny T or C though, it is still a standout. Wood-fired pizzas, Pomodoro linguini (order it when tomatoes are in season), a good bruschetta, and a varied regional beer list are highlights, as are the zesty, deep-flavored fruit sorbets (blood orange, berry). There's an interesting wine list, too. The renovated building, with a gorgeous pressed-copper ceiling, makes for an appealing frontier-meets-modern vibe. ✉ *303 Jones St.* ☎ *575/894–9866* ⊕ *www.cafebellaluca.com* ☰ *AE, D, DC, MC, V* ⊙ *Closed Tues.*

¢ ✕ **Happy Belly Deli.** Tuck away the breakfast burrito in a sundried-tomato
AMERICAN   tortilla; the spinach, onion, and feta cheese omelet; the kielbasa scramble; or one of the tasty bagels, and you'll be sated for hours—there's potent coffee, too. Lunch options include soups, salads, and sandwiches. Try the hummus or grilled polenta-and-provolone sandwiches, or build your own. This is a cozy spot with a handful of tables and no pretensions, but a pleasant patio doubles the size. ✉ *313 N. Broadway* ☎ *575/894–3354* ☰ *D, MC, V* ⊙ *Closed Sun. No dinner.*

¢ ✕ **Little Sprout Market & Juice Bar.** This light-filled corner space specializes
CAFÉ   in local, organic produce and good-for-you packaged goods. Delicious breakfasts and light lunches are also featured—think salads, soups, and tasty sandwiches. And they make a mean smoothie. Eat here in one of their booths, or take your feast with you on a picnic. ✉ *400 N. Broadway* ☎ *505/894–4114* ⊙ *No dinner. Closed Sun.* ☰ *MC, V.*

$$ ✕ **Los Arcos Steak & Lobster House.** Juicy, thick steaks and seafood (from
STEAK   lobster to blackened catfish) are the draws at this old-school, white-stucco establishment with Spanish-style arches across the facade. Steaks are aged in-house and are reliably good. The Southwest decor is enhanced by a cactus garden. Homemade soups, desserts, and freshly baked bread add to the aromas and the cheery ambience. The bar is a popular hangout. ✉ *1400 N. Date St.* ☎ *575/894–6200* ☰ *AE, D, MC, V* ⊙ *No lunch.*

WHERE TO STAY

All the lodgings listed offer soaks and treatments to the public, with the exception of the Pelican Spa, which is open only to overnight guests. It's advisable to call ahead and check availability. River Bend Hot Springs offers private and shared hot pools right next to the Rio Grande, making for a scenic and relaxing soak.

$ ▦ **Blackstone Hotsprings Lodging & Baths.** Unassuming from the outside,
Fodor'sChoice   Blackstone has such a creative personality that visitors need simply turn
★   the corner into the colorful midcentury-style courtyard—which echoes
HOTEL   Blackstone's origins at a 1930s motor court—to be won over. With just the right dose of quirkiness, the very well-appointed accommodations

reveal the owners' good humor: a tasteful assortment of *Jetsons, Lucille Ball,* and *Twilight Zone* memorabilia adorn the themed rooms. Each has its own private soaking tub for unlimited indulgence in the healing waters, and a kitchenette (no stove). The lush wet room ($25 per hour)—with plants, waterfalls, a shower, and hot pool—transports you somewhere far away from this desert locale. Two huge private tubs are available for $5 per half hour. The in-house coffee is a custom blend and it's fantastic. The staff is helpful and can offer savvy tips on local dining and sightseeing. **Pros:** irresistible blend of handcrafted design and pure luxury; a truly relaxing getaway. **Cons:** no restaurant. ✉ *410 Austin St.* ☎ *575/894–0894* ⊕ *www.blackstonehotsprings.com* ⤢ *3 rooms, 4 suites* ⟐ *In-room: a/c, refrigerator, Wi-Fi. In-hotel: Wi-Fi hotspot* ▭ *AE, D, DC, MC, V.*

¢ 🏨 **Charles Motel & Spa.** The inexpensive rooms at the Charles are a
MOTEL favorite among artists and healers who espouse all sorts of interesting and unorthodox approaches to health. Various alternative therapies are practiced. Costs depend on the treatment and its length, but $5 will buy you an hour-long soak in one of the nine indoor soaking tubs fed from natural hot springs ($4 for a half hour). For $8 (and a reservation) you can soak in one of two outdoor Jacuzzis up on the roof. The huge (400-square-foot) guest rooms, many of which have kitchenettes, have so much extra space you can easily imagine settling in for months rather than days; in fact, excellent weekly rates are offered. There is a nice gift shop on the premises with locally made pottery and other goods. **Pros:** separate men's and women's spa facilities. **Cons:** furnishings are aging; mattresses are a bit soft. ✉ *601 Broadway* ☎ *800/317–4518 or 575/894–7154* ⊕ *www.charlesspa.com* ⤢ *20 rooms* ⟐ *In-room: a/c, kitchen (some), refrigerator (some). In-hotel: spa, Wi-Fi hotspot, some pets allowed* ▭ *AE, D, MC, V.*

¢ 🏨 **Pelican Spa.** Color is the name of the game at this great little hotel-
HOTEL spa oriented around a rock courtyard and tucked behind a coyote fence right Downtown. Soaking tubs in private, serene spaces are reserved for guests only. Rooms are vibrantly colored and furnished with a mixture of contemporary and retro furniture; many have separate sitting areas and kitchens. Not all rooms are located on-site, but all are within minutes of the main building. The Aqua Room ($80) has an in-room soaking tub. The property also rents about 20 rooms located elsewhere around town. **Pros:** underwent a top-down renovation recently. **Cons:** rooms and public spaces a bit cramped. ✉ *306 S. Pershing* ☎ *575/894– 0055* ⊕ *www.pelican-spa.com* ⤢ *4 rooms* ⟐ *In-room: a/c, Wi-Fi. In-hotel: some pets allowed* ▭ *D, MC, V.*

$ 🏨 **Riverbend Hot Springs Lodging & Mineral Baths.** All the pools (five pub-
Fodor'sChoice lic and three private) at Riverbend are right on the Rio Grande, with
★ sweeping views of Turtleback Mountain. With its days as a youth hostel
HOTEL well behind it, Riverbend now offers a smart balance of contemporary comfort with a touch of retro bohemian spirit. Beautiful stonework surrounds the tubs, and inspired stone mosaics line the spa's winding paths; a lovely open-slatted wooden pergola shades a fleet of chaise lounges, all facing riverside. Several styles of room are available—a few are set in cleverly camouflaged and vibrantly painted, single-wide mobile homes,

8

and all have modern furnishings. A casita and several larger suites are ideal for families or groups. Private tubs at $15 an hour are a treat and a bargain. Massage treatments are available by appointment. **Pros:** comfortable, casual ambience; staff pays serious attention to details. **Cons:** layout less than ideal if you're seeking privacy; no meals available on-site. ⊠ *100 Austin St.* ☎ *575/894–7625* ⊕ *www.riverbendhotsprings. com* ⇆ *9 rooms, 1 casita* △ *In-room: a/c, kitchen (some), refrigerators, Wi-Fi (some). In-hotel: Wi-Fi hotspot, some pets allowed* ⊟ *D, MC, V.*

$$ ▣ **Sierra Grande Lodge & Spa.** This elegant property led the way for the
Fodor's Choice small but impressive upward trend in lodging in T or C. In a compact
★ 1937 building in the heart of town, this inn feels like a secluded retreat
HOTEL because of the massive walls and boulders surrounding its mission-style exterior. The simple, tasteful rooms have hardwood floors and serene prints on the walls; some have grand jetted tubs, though their open location adjacent to the sleeping areas may not appeal to everyone. Bathrooms are well-appointed, and many have extra-large showers. Guests can soak in an outdoor or indoor kiva-style hot tub swirling with steamy water from natural, underground hot springs; massages, facials, and other holistic body therapies are available by appointment in the spa. Breakfasts are delicious and are made with mostly local ingredients. The lodge is within easy walking distance of several restaurants. **Pros:** understated elegance; wonderful staff. **Cons:** rooms are on the small side; bathers must walk through the lobby to get to the tubs; restaurant no longer in operation. ⊠ *501 McAdoo St.* ☎ *575/894–6976* ⊕ *www. sierragrandelodge.com* ⇆ *16 rooms, 1 suite* △ *In-room: a/c, Wi-Fi. In-hotel: Wi-Fi hotspot* ⊟ *AE, D, MC, V* ⧆ *CP.*

CAMPING

¢ ⚠ **Caballo Lake State Park.** Three camping areas offer views of the lake, which is within walking distance of each site. Cottonwoods and other trees shade two sites; the other has desert landscaping. The tent sites ($8) are lakeside. You can stock up on goods at a grocery store, bait shop, and gasoline station 3 mi from the park. Developed sites for RVs cost $10 to $14 ($18 with sewer). ⊠ *Take state park exit (Exit 59) off I–25, 16 mi south of Truth or Consequences* ☎ *575/743–3942* ⊕ *www.emnrd.state.nm.us/prd/caballo.htm* ⇆ *136 sites* △ *Flush toilets, full hookups, partial hookups, dump station, drinking water, showers, fire grates, fire pits, grills, picnic tables, electricity, public telephone, ranger station, play area, swimming (lake)* ⊟ *No credit cards.*

SHOPPING

Black Cat Books & Coffee (⊠ *128 N. Broadway* ☎ *575/894–7070*) beckons for a used-book browse and a superlative cup of java. **Rio Bravo Gallery Fine Art Inc.** (⊠ *110 E. Broadway Ave.* ☎ *575/894–0572* ⊕ *www. riobravofineart.net* ⊗ *Wed.– Sun. noon–5*) carries the richly saturated SX-70 Polaroids of H. Joe Waldrum, along with paintings and sculpture by contemporary local artists.

ELEPHANT BUTTE

5 mi east of Truth or Consequences on NM 51.

More than a million people each year visit **Elephant Butte Lake State Park,** whose 36,500-acre lake is New Mexico's largest. A world-class competition lake for bass fishing, it also offers catfish, pike, and crappie fishing year-round. Boaters come here in droves, and when the wind picks up so do the windsurfers. Special events include an April balloon festival and July drag-boat racing. The lake, known as Elephant Butte Reservoir, was created in 1916 by **Elephant Butte Dam,** a concrete structure 306 feet high and 1,674 feet long. The stretch of the Rio Grande below the dam is stocked with trout during colder months; these fish attract anglers as well as many species of waterfowl, including raptors. The lake level is dependent on the water conditions in the state, which fluctuate wildly, and it's worth noting that there are no trees around this lake—making the hot months a challenging time to camp. It's best to check the conditions before you plan a vacation around the lake.

The state park straddles Elephant Butte Lake and the Rio Grande east of I–25 for about 50 mi (from south of Fort Craig to just north of Truth or Consequences). To take a scenic drive from Truth or Consequences, head east on NM 51, turn north at NM 179 for about 2 mi, head southeast on NM 195, and take a loop drive of about 5 mi to Elephant Butte Dam. At the end of the dam turn north for overlooks of the lake and a view of the rocky elephant-shape island formation that inspired the name of the reservoir. To visit the **Dam Site Recreation Area** turn west on NM 177, where you'll find a terraced picnic area with striking views and tall shade trees. A private concessionaire operates a restaurant, lounge, marina, and cabins. ⊠ *3 mi north of Truth or Consequences* ☎ *575/744–5923* ⊕ *www.emnrd.state.nm.us/prd/elephant.htm* ✑ *$5 per vehicle.*

WHERE TO EAT AND STAY

¢ ✕**Hodges Corner Restaurant.** Owner Ray Hodges believes in hearty food
AMERICAN and lots of it—so if you're in the mood for a heaping plate of thick barbecued pork ribs, cube steak, or deep-fried fish, this is the place for you. Late in the day, the ultracasual dining area is usually filled with hungry anglers who've stopped to relax and chow down after a day of fishing. Come in earlier in the day to buy a bucket of home-fried chicken to take with you to the lake. ⊠ *915 NM 195* ☎ *575/744–5626* ▭ *D, MC, V.*

$ ⊞ **Dam Site Resort.** The lodgings at this resort are a fun step back in time.
RESORT The lodge was built in 1911 for the dam's administration and engineering offices. The "cabins" are quaint, neo-pueblo, stucco structures built by the Civilian Conservation Corps in the 1940s. The resort has been established as an official historic district, and the restoration of the buildings is top-notch. The lodge operates as a B&B and is furnished with many period antiques. The spacious covered porch overlooks the marina. The cabins are an experience in retro-chic, and all have views of the lake, and kitchenettes (you must furnish utensils, plates, etc.). The bar-restaurant ($), open weekends only, serves steaks, seafood, and sandwiches—and some excellent margaritas. On Saturday nights between about Easter and Labor Day, dance bands play blues or rock

8

on the outdoor patio, which also has a bar. Booking is done through the Dam Site Marina office. **Pros:** beautiful, historic property with great lake views. **Cons:** staffing is minimal (though down-home friendly); basic rooms have few amenities and no Internet. ⊕ *5 mi east of 3rd St. light in Truth or Consequences* ⊠ *77B Engle Star Rte.* ☎ *575/894–2073* ⊕ *www.thedamsite.com* ⟿ *8 rooms, 16 cabins* △ *In-room: a/c, no phone, kitchen (some), no TV. In-hotel: restaurant, bar, water sports, some pets allowed* ⊟ *AE, D, MC, V.*

$ **⊡ Elephant Butte Inn & Spa.** The mesa-top property feels like a resort
HOTEL and has panoramic views of the lake. Get a lake-view room if you can and enjoy the huge, lush lawn that seems to disappear into the water. **The Ivory Tusk Tavern & Restaurant** ($$) serves standard fare including hamburgers, and steak and seafood platters; there's a big Sunday breakfast buffet. A spa and full salon are on the premises for massage and beauty treatments, and golf packages are available for the Sierra del Rio Golf Course. **Pros:** peaceful property with nice views. **Cons:** area dining options are limited. ⊠ *401 NM 195, Box E* ☎ *575/744–5431* ⊕ *www.elephantbutteinn.com* ⟿ *45 rooms* △ *In-room: a/c, refrigerator (some), Wi-Fi. In-hotel: restaurant, bar, pool, spa, Internet terminal, some pets allowed* ⊟ *AE, D, MC, V* ⦿ *CP.*

CAMPING

¢ ⚠ **Elephant Butte State Park.** At night, campfires flicker along the beaches of the many sandy coves of Elephant Butte Lake. There are developed and primitive campsites, many of them delightfully secluded. Sites without hookups are first come, first served; sites with hookups can be reserved. There's a restaurant on-site. ⊠ *3 mi north of Truth or Consequences* ☎ *877/664–7787 reservations, 575/744–5923 information* ⊕ *www.emnrd.state.nm.us/prd/elephant.htm* △ *Flush toilets, pit toilets, partial hookups (electric and water), dump station, drinking water, showers, fire grates, fire pits, grills, picnic tables, electricity, public telephone, ranger station, play area, swimming (lake)* ⟿ *127 developed sites, several hundred primitive or partially developed tent sites* ⊟ *AE, D, MC, V.*

SPORTS AND THE OUTDOORS

The **Dam Site Recreation Area Marina** (⊠ *77B Engle Star Rte., 5 mi east of 3rd St. traffic light in Truth or Consequences* ☎ *575/894–2073*) is one of four or five marinas around the lake. This one rents pontoon boats, paddleboats, and kayaks year-round. Pontoon boats run $50 hourly; the other vessels cost $10 hourly. A $250 deposit is required for use of any boat.

HATCH

40 mi south of Truth of Consequences, 40 mi north of Las Cruces on NM 185 or I–25.

Hatch bills itself the Chile Capital of the World. And although chiles are grown elsewhere in the state—and some might argue taste just as good—Hatch is still considered *the* source for the headily aromatic, highly addictive, metabolism-firing, not always killer-hot state vegetable (it actually shares this honor with *frijoles,* aka pinto beans, and it's technically a fruit rather than a vegetable). Come here in the fall when the roasters are firing, and you'll immediately understand the allure of this otherwise rather indistinct small town. If you need additional tempting, consider Hatch's enviable location on the lovely NM 185/187, a two-lane river-valley road that parallels I–25 and makes for an enchanting scenic drive between Las Cruces and Truth or Consequences.

GETTING HERE
From Truth or Consequences, Hatch is a 40 mi drive along I–25 (the drive takes 35 minutes) or NM 187, which takes more like an hour, with its slower speeds and curving path.

EXPLORING
The famed **Hatch Chile Fest** celebrates 40 years in 2012. Show that you're not a chile rube and mingle with aficionados who know their Nu Mex 6-4s (an heirloom variety regenerated from 1960s seeds) from their Big Jims (a medium-hot chile, cultivated locally). Between tastes (don't worry, some varieties are no hotter than a standard bell pepper), check out the Chile Festival Parade, play some horseshoes, or sign up for the Chile Toss contest. ⊠ *Hatch Municipal Airport, NM 26, 1 mi west of town, Hatch* ☎ *575/267–5483* ⊕ *www.hatchchilefest.com* ✉ *$10 per vehicle* ☉ *Early Sept., usually Labor Day weekend.*

25 mi south of Hatch on I–25, 13 mi north of Las Cruces on I–25.

EN ROUTE

Fort Selden was established in 1865 to protect Mesilla Valley settlers and travelers. The flat-roofed adobe buildings at **Fort Selden State Monument** are arranged around a drill field. Several units of buffalo soldiers were stationed here. These were the acclaimed African-American cavalry troops noted for their bravery and crucial role in helping protect frontier settlers from Native American attacks and desperadoes. Native Americans thought the soldiers' hair resembled that of a buffalo and gave the regiments their name. Knowing the respect the Apaches held for the animals, the soldiers did not take offense. Buffalo soldiers were also stationed at Fort Bayard, near Silver City, and Fort Stanton, in Lincoln County, to shield miners and travelers from attacks by Apaches.

In the early 1880s Captain Arthur MacArthur was appointed post commander of Fort Selden. His young son spent several years on the post and grew up to become World War II hero General Douglas MacArthur. A permanent exhibit called "Fort Selden: An Adobe Post on the Rio Grande" depicts the roles of officers, enlisted men, and women on the American frontier during the Indian Wars. Camping facilities can be found at Leasburg State Park. ⊠ *Off I–25 at Radium Springs Exit (Exit 19), 25 mi south of Hatch* ☎ *575/526–8911* ⊕ *www.nmmonuments.org* ✉ *$3* ☉ *Wed.–Mon. 8:30–5.*

WHERE TO EAT
¢ ✗ **Pepper Pot.** The exterior isn't much, but once inside you're given the chance to sample some serious local heat. This is Hatch, after all, and if you're game, you can tuck into some tasty authentic Mexican and New Mexican fare—enchiladas, rellenos, *chilaquiles*—here, produced with chiles grown in the area. Not every dish will light your lips on fire—just ask the helpful staff for suggestions tailored to your penchant for heat. ⊠ *207 W. Hall St.* ☎ *575/267–3822* ▭ *No credit cards* ☉ *No dinner.*

MEXICAN

8

LAS CRUCES

323 mi south of Albuquerque and 40 mi south of Hatch on I–25; 45 mi northwest of El Paso on I–10.

The Mesilla Valley has been populated for centuries. The Spanish passed through the region first in 1598 and continued to use the route to reach the northern territories around Santa Fe. Though the Spanish could not maintain settlements in the region at all during the 1700s, by the early 1800s people were able to move in and create hamlets that grew to become Doña Ana and, eventually, Las Cruces.

In 1848 the Treaty of Guadalupe Hidalgo ended the Mexican-American War, but rendered uncertain the sovereignty of Las Cruces. The Mesilla Valley ended up split between two nations, with the town of Mesilla on the west of the Rio Grande belonging to Mexico and Las Cruces, on the eastern banks of the river, belonging to the United States. The Gadsden Purchase in 1853 made the whole area U.S. territory and Las Cruces began its ascent as the area's power center. The railroad, irrigation, agriculture, and local ranching drove the city's growth. Much of the new city was built in the Territorial and Victorian styles popular at the time. The College of Las Cruces was founded in 1880 and eventually became New Mexico State University.

Mention Las Cruces to someone today and their reply is likely to be about its status as one of the fastest-growing cities in the United States—second fastest in New Mexico, behind Albuquerque. With growth spurred by retirees looking for sun and mild winters, the defense and commercial business at White Sands Missile Range, the increasing strength of New Mexico State University, and its proximity to the business on the border with Mexico, this city of about 75,000 people *is* growing. Las Cruces is following the lead of many U.S. cities by pushing a major revitalization of its historic Downtown. The district and its surrounding residential neighborhoods date back more than a century, and a casual walk around will show all sorts of renovation—from simple painting and planting to the restabilization of entire buildings. Despite the revitalization, greater Las Cruces tends to be a bit sterile, as its historical district is surrounded by ever-expanding rings of strip malls and cookie-cutter subdivisions.

GETTING HERE

Las Cruces is at the crossroads of I-25 (north-south) and I-10 (east-west). Note that at the south end of town, I-25 merges into I-10—which then carries on south to El Paso and other points in south Texas. If that's confusing, not to worry, it's actually very easy to navigate around the rather gridlike town itself. Also note that it is U.S. 70—from I-25 exit 6, at the north end of town—that will get you to wonders near (Organ Mountains and Aguirre Springs) and far (White Sands and beyond).

VISITOR INFORMATION

Las Cruces Convention & Visitors Bureau (✉ *211 Water St.* ☎ *575/541–2444* ⊕ *www.mustseelc.org*).

EXPLORING

Many artists (painters, sculptors, actors, writers, metalsmiths) make their homes here not just because the surrounding area offers a perpetually inspiring palette, but also because the arts community is supportive and the town an affordable alternative to chic and expensive Santa Fe. Museums, a performing arts center, a renovated movie theater, and new shops and some cafés are draws. A farmers' market on the weekends makes for a fun way to spend a Saturday morning.

The Hispanic population in Las Cruces comprises descendants from the Spanish settlers as well as many Mexican immigrants; both influences add unique cultural elements to the community as well as some seriously spicy food. The emphasis on family is strong here, and kids are welcome just about everywhere.

Although Old Mesilla is listed separately in this chapter, it's so close to Las Cruces that you can comfortably go back and forth to eat, shop, or enjoy a night out.

Fodor's Choice **The Branigan Cultural Center,** in a striking 1935 Pueblo Revival building
★ embellished inside with murals by Tom Lea, offers compelling documentary shows with themes like the 1942–1964 Bracero Program (a Mexican guest workers initiative), or a reflection on Frida Kahlo's later years through rarely seen photographs. "Crossroads of History" is an excellent permanent display that covers 400 years of regional history. The city-run Branigan is a focal point—along with the Las Cruces Museum of Art next door—of the revitalized Downtown. ✉ *501 N. Main St., Downtown Mall* ☎ *575/541–2155* ⊕ *www.las-cruces.org/museums* 🎟 *Free* ☾ *Tues.–Sat. 9–4:30.*

Across an open courtyard from the Branigan Cultural Center, the **Las Cruces Museum of Art** shows the eclectic, contemporary works of regional artists. Subject matter ranges from the powerful oil paintings of Rigoberto A. Gonzalez depicting life in the borderlands region to prints, photos, and sculptures that provide a distinct perspective on the Organ Mountains and nearby ghost towns.

✉ *501 N. Main St., Downtown Mall* ☎ *575/541–2155* ⊕ *www.las-cruces.org/museums* 🎟 *Free* ☾ *Tues.–Sat. 9–4:30.*

☾ Inside the historic (1910) Atchison, Topeka, & Santa Fe Railway Depot, the **Las Cruces Railroad Museum** uses photos and ephemera to tell the story of early regional railroad history, and a model-train room and train table entertain kids especially. Temporary shows, such as one built around train travel advertisements from the last century, rotate throughout the year. Outside is a 1918 wooden caboose that awaits restoration. The museum is several blocks west of the Cultural Center, by way of the Alameda Historic District. ✉ *351 N. Mesilla St.* ☎ *575/647–4480* ⊕ *www.las-cruces.org/museums* 🎟 *Free* ☾ *Tues.–Sat. 9–4:30.*

☾ The handsomely designed **New Mexico Farm & Ranch Heritage Museum** documents 3,000 years of agriculture in New Mexico and the Southwest. Visit a re-creation of a 1,200-year-old Mogollon farmhouse, based on styles built by some of the first nonnomadic people to live in what is now New Mexico. Longhorn cattle, Churro sheep, and dairy cows are among the heritage breeds—descendants of animals the Spanish

8

brought from Mexico—raised at the museum. At milking times (11 and 3), you can learn about the history of dairy farming in New Mexico, or take a look in the "beef barn" where six different breeds of beef cattle are housed. A span of the historic Green Bridge, which used to span the Hondo River, has been reassembled over the arroyo on the grounds. Chuck-wagon cooking demonstrations are offered during special events. ✉ *4100 Dripping Springs Rd.* ✛ *Head east on University Ave., which becomes Dripping Springs Rd.; ranch is 1½ mi east of I-25* ☎ *575/522–4100* ⊕ *www.frhm.org* ✉ *$5* ⊙ *Mon.–Sat. 9–5, Sun. noon–5.*

At **New Mexico State University (NMSU)**, the home of the Aggies, museums have a decided focus on agriculture, although those on the arts and sciences also receive attention. The buildings themselves tend toward the uninspired, but there are still a few original structures from the 1907 campus design by Henry C. Trost. Get free one-day parking permits online *(*⊕ *www.nmsuparking.com)*; you can also pay for parking at meters. *Capsicum* matters greatly to New Mexicans, and much of the research into this invaluable agricultural product takes place at NMSU's **Chile Pepper Institute** (✉ *Gerald Thomas Hall, Knox St. at E. College Ave.* ☎ *575/646–3028* ⊕ *www.chilepepperinstitute.org* ✉ *Free* ⊙ *Weekdays 8–noon and 1–5),* where visitors can explore the Hall of Flame and the gift shop. Formal tours are available by appointment. Near the Chile Pepper Institute, the **Zuhl Geological Collection** (✉ *NMSU Alumni & Visitors Center775 E. College Ave.* ☎ *575/646–3616 or 575/646–4714* ✉ *Free* ⊙ *Weekdays 8–5)* comprises a rich abundance of petrified-wood samples (vibrant reds and yellows mark the Late Triassic pieces from the Chinle region of Arizona), fossils, minerals, and an oviraptor dinosaur nest. The **University Art Gallery** (✉ *Williams Hall, E. University Ave., just east of Solano Dr.* ☎ *575/646–2545* ✉ *Free* ⊙ *Early June–early Aug., Tues.–Sat. noon–4; early Aug.–early June, Tues.–Fri. 11–4, Sat. noon–4)* displays both historic holdings—19th-century Mexican *retablos,* for example, representing the world's largest collection of this religious art form—and contemporary ones, such as Robert Rauschenberg lithographs. The **University Museum** (✉ *Kent Hall, 1280 E. University Ave., at Solano Dr.* ☎ *575/646–5161* ✉ *Free* ⊙ *Tues.–Sat. 10–4),* housed in a grand 1930s white stucco, red-tile-roof WPA building, shows off NMSU's role in regional archaeological research. Exhibits draw on extensive holdings of Southwestern and Mesoamerican pottery, and temporary exhibits delve into both regional and international subjects, from Diné (Navajo) weavers to African art.

✉ *NMSU Alumni & Visitors Center:775 E. College Ave.* ☎ *575/646–0111 university information, 575/646–1839 parking info* ⊕ *www.nmsu.edu*

WHERE TO EAT

¢   ✕ **Caliche's Frozen Custard.** This beloved local joint—it opened as Scoopy's
AMERICAN   in the 1990s and longtime fans still call it that—offers all kinds of mix-ins (such as regional faves, salted and unsalted pecans) and toppings to embellish the luscious custard-style ice cream. Chili dogs are among the savory treats. ✉ *590 S. Valley Dr.* ☎ *575/647–5066* ✉ *131 Roadrunner Pkwy.* ☎ *575/521–1161* ⊕ *www.caliches.com* ▭ *MC, V.*

Sacred Ground

Symbols of Catholicism seem to be a hallmark of New Mexico, and visitors seek out adobe churches to photograph, and colorful religious icons and minishrines to buy as souvenirs. More intimate and poignant expressions of New Mexicans' deep religiosity are found in homemade shrines and centuries-old churches of healing.

Alongside the state's roadways are small memorials of flowers and crosses known in Spanish as *descansos*, or resting places, for those who have died in automobile and motorcycle accidents. The monuments, erected by family or friends to honor the memory of the dead, often on narrow, curving roads and steep embankments, serve as reminders to the living not to take safe passage for granted. Some of the descansos are elaborately decorated for various events and holidays throughout the year. Some historians say the custom of highway shrines was introduced to the Western Hemisphere four centuries ago by the first Spanish explorers, who experienced so many losses of life that their trails were strewn with crosses marking the fallen. Las Cruces, New Mexico, is thought to have obtained its name, "the Crosses," after one such site where Spanish explorers were slaughtered in a Native American ambush.

In modern times, those of Hispanic descent and others practicing the Southwest's shrine tradition have seen their custom thwarted elsewhere in the country. State highway departments in more densely populated regions order the roadside shrines to be removed because of the problems they present for road maintenance crews. But in New Mexico, road department officials go out of their way to honor the shrines held so sacred by the loved ones who maintain them. If the shrines need to be temporarily moved for maintenance, crews work with families to make sure the monuments are returned to their original spots.

Crosses in general are a revered symbol in this state, where they often can be seen high atop a barren hill where religious treks are made. The crosses are placed either by a community or, as in Lincoln, by a single, devout individual. New Mexico also is known for a variety of spontaneous shrines, created by those who report experiencing miracles or religious visions. One woman in Lake Arthur, near Artesia in southeastern New Mexico, saw the image of Christ in a tortilla she was cooking. She built her own shrine surrounding the tortilla, complete with flickering candles, and the faithful and curious can make pilgrimages to it.

In an awesome display of religious faith during Holy Week, thousands of people journey miles by foot to reach Chimayó in northern New Mexico. They seek the blessing and healing of the holy soil found in the town's Santuario (Sanctuary) church. The ground's sacredness dates from 1810, when a man discovered a crucifix glowing in the dirt. Though several attempts were made to relocate the cross, legend says the crucifix always reappeared where it was first found. Today the cross hangs above the altar, and the holy dirt can be taken from a sacred *pozito* (a small hole) in the floorboards of an adjoining room. Those seeking healing or giving thanks leave small photographs or tokens of their faith within an anteroom.

8

$$ ✕**De La Vega's Pecan Grill & Brewery.** Craft beers and classic comfort
AMERICAN   fare that favors locally grown ingredients are the draws at this bustling
spot with a smart layout, excellent service, and inviting outdoor din-
ing—complete with a view over the Mesilla Valley. Pecan wood is used
for grilling steak and chicken, and burgers and rib-eyes come smoth-
ered with green chile and Amber Ale–grilled onions. Try the Napa
salad, with just the right balance of candied pecans and fresh greens.
⊠ *500 S. Telshor Blvd.* ☎ *575/521–1099* ⊕ *www.pecangrill.com* ⊟ *AE,
D, MC, V.*

¢   ✕**Farley's Food & Fun Pub.** For a family evening out with no worries about
AMERICAN   the kids being loud or throwing their peanut shells on the floor, Farley's
☺   is the place. Choose from a huge menu of basic pub victuals: peel 'n' eat
shrimp, burgers and sandwiches, salads, wood-fired pizzas, all sorts of
appetizers, and, of course, beer. There are TVs everywhere, plus a few
video games and pool tables. ⊠ *3499 Foothills Rd.* ☎ *575/522–0466*
⊟ *AE, D, MC, V.*

$ ✕**International Delights.** A popular place to settle in with a laptop and
MIDDLE EASTERN   a cup of Turkish coffee or Moroccan mint tea, this open early-to-late
Downtown café pipes rhythmic Middle Eastern music among its tables
and comfortable outdoor patio. Order hummus (it's excellent), falafel, or
lamb couscous (Friday only) for reasonable prices. The attached grocery
offers an assortment of primarily packaged international foods. ⊠ *1245
El Paseo Rd.* ☎ *575/647–5956* ⊕ *www.internationaldelightscafe.com*
⊟ *AE, D, MC, V.*

¢   ✕**My Brother's Place.** *Tostadas compuestos* (a concoction of red or green
MEXICAN   chile, meat, pinto beans, and cheese in a crispy tortilla cup) and other
Southwestern dishes are served with flair at this Mexican restaurant–
cum–billiard parlor, where you can shoot some pool before or after
dining. The upstairs lounge is a pleasant watering hole decorated with
brightly colored chairs and piñatas. Margaritas and Mexican beer-by-
the-bottle—say, Negra Modelo or Tecate—are the drinks of choice.
⊠ *334 S. Main St.* ☎ *505/523–7681* ⊟ *AE, D, DC, MC, V.*

WHERE TO STAY

$ ⊡ **Hampton Inn & Suites.** This well-kept chain property is a highlight
HOTEL   among Las Cruces accommodations—extra clean, with great service, a
logical layout, and plenty of handy amenities (free Internet, a lap-style
pool, and fitness center, plus microwaves and refrigerators in rooms).
It's at the east end of town, with easy access to main arteries, but it's
tucked off the road so fairly quiet. **Pros:** big breakfast included; unob-
trusive contemporary decor; rooms have ample desks and ergonomic
seating. **Cons:** most restaurants are at least a five-minute drive away.
⊠ *2350 E. Griggs Ave.* ☎ *575/527–8777* ⊕ *www.hampton.com* ⇲ *73
rooms* ⌂ *In-room: a/c, refrigerator, Internet. In-hotel: pool, gym, laun-
dry facilities, laundry service, Internet terminal, Wi-Fi hotspot, parking
(free)* ⊟ *AE, D, MC, V* ⦿ *BP.*

$$ ⊡ **Hotel Encanto.** What looks like a multistory chain hotel from the out-
HOTEL   side—it was built as a Hilton in 1986—channels a gracious hacienda
inside. Rooms are furnished in a dark Spanish-colonial motif. The
large outdoor pool offers respite during the hot months. **Café España**
($) serves respectable Mexican food and the bar, **Azul**, offers music

(sometimes live) and dancing Thursday through Saturday nights. **Pros:** good accommodations for the price; close to attractions; friendly, professional staff. **Cons:** no overhead lighting in rooms; bathrooms small and standard. ⊠ *705 S. Telshor Blvd.* ☎ *575/522–4300 or 866/383–0443* ⊕ *www.hotelencanto.com* ⤴ *203 rooms, 7 suites* ⚲ *In-room: a/c, refrigerator, Wi-Fi. In-hotel: restaurant, bar, pool, gym, Internet terminal, Wi-Fi hotspot, parking (free), some pets allowed* ⊟ *AE, D, DC, MC, V.*

CAMPING

¢ ⛺ **Aguirre Springs.** This beautiful high-elevation spot is tucked alongside
the towering spires of the Organ Mountains, giving you an expansive
view of the Tularosa Basin. During drought conditions, fires may be
restricted or prohibited. If you're fortunate enough to be here when
the moon is full, make sure you catch the moonrise—you're not likely
to forget it. ⊠ *Off U.S. 70* ✛ *From I–25 take U.S. 70 northeast 14 mi, head south at Aguirre Springs Rd. an additional 6 mi* ☎ *575/525–4300* ⊕ *www.blm.gov* ⚲ *Pit toilets, fire grates, fire pits, grills, picnic tables* ⤴ *57 sites, 2 group sites (by reservation)* ⚑ *Reservations not accepted* ⊟ *No credit cards.*

Fodor's Choice
★

NIGHTLIFE AND THE ARTS

Head over to **El Patio,** in the plaza in Old Mesilla, for some of the area's
best live music. Established in 1934, this unassuming little adobe cantina is in the old office building of the Butterfield Stage Co. The cantina
is open seven days a week, live music happens Wednesday through
Saturday. ⊠ *2171 Calle de Parian* ☎ *575/526–9943.*

Nightly live entertainment is featured at the **Hotel Encanto** (⊠ *705 S. Telshor Blvd.* ☎ *575/522–4300* ⊕ *www.hotelencanto.com*) lounge.
New Mexico State University (⊠ *Pan American Center, University Ave.* ☎ *575/646–1420 ticket office; 575/646–4413 special events office* ⊕ *http://panam.nmsu.edu*) presents lectures, concerts, sports, and other
special events at its Pan American Center.

A rare two-story adobe theater, the **Rio Grande** ⊠ *211 N. Main St., Downtown Mall* ☎ *575/523–6403* ⊕ *www.riograndetheatre.com*) was
restored and refurbished inside and out in 2005. This 1926 vintage
movie house now functions as performing-arts space. Note the spritely
colored blue-and-green bas-relief trim on the brick-, tile-, and stucco
Italian Renaissance facade; the classically incised tin ceiling; and the
bright-red neon sign. With 422 seats—including a balcony—it's just
the right size for the film series, spoken word, and live music events it
currently hosts.

Tierra del Encanto Ballet Folklorico performs folk dances of Mexico at the
annual weekend **International Mariachi Festival** (☎ *575/525–1735* ⊕ *www. lascrucesmariachi.org*) in November.

SHOPPING

The upscale **Glenn Cutter Gallery** (⊠ *2640 El Paseo Rd.* ☎ *575/524–4300* ⊙ *Closed Sun.*) carries paintings from regional artists like Fred Chilton,
as well as fine jewelry.

8

Fodor's Choice If you're in town on a Wednesday or Saturday, don't miss the excellent
★ outdoor **Farmers Market** (✉ *North Main St., Downtown Mall* ⊕ *http://lascrucesfarmersmarket.org*), where approximately 200 vendors sell produce, handcrafted items, baked goods, and even geodes and fossils. Mingle with the locals and enjoy the scene, which peaks between 8 and 12:30. The **Picacho Street Antique District** (✉ *Between N. Valley Dr. and N. 3rd St.*), just beyond the railroad tracks on the western fringe of the Alameda Historic District, is a fun area to explore and look for treasures at, often, very reasonable prices.

SPORTS AND THE OUTDOORS

HIKING Starting from the **Aguirre Springs** campgrounds, two hiking trails, **Pine Tree Trail** (4-mi loop), which runs through beautiful ponderosa pine territory, and **Baylor Pass Trail** (6 mi one-way), afford exquisite views of the Organ Mountains "needles" and the Tularosa Basin beyond.
✉ *Off U.S. 70* ✛ *From Las Cruces take U.S. 70 northeast 14 mi and head south at Aguirre Springs Rd. an additional 6 mi* ☎ *575/525–4300* ⊕ *www.blm.gov* 🖾 *$3* ⊙ *Apr.–Oct., daily 8–7; Nov.–Mar., daily 8–5.*

At the **Dripping Springs Natural Area** within the Organ Mountains is an abandoned mountain resort built in the 1870s and converted decades later into a sanatorium for tuberculosis patients. Hike the 3-mile Dripping Springs Trail and you will pass the ruins of the now-empty facility as well as the naturally occurring dripping springs themselves. As you progress through the piñon-juniper and oak woodlands, you can potentially spot all manner of wildlife, including a few rock climbers testing their mettle on sheer rock walls jutting above you. This site is for day use only, and has 12 picnic sites; hikers need to register at the visitor center. ✉ *Dripping Springs Rd.; from Las Cruces head east 10 mi on University Ave. (it becomes Dripping Springs Rd.)* ☎ *575/522–1219* ⊕ *www.blm.gov* 🖾 *$3 per vehicle* ⊙ *Apr.–Sept., daily 8–7; Oct.–Mar., daily 8–5.*

GOLF An 18-hole course that hosts men's and women's NCAA championships, **New Mexico State University Golf Course** has a full-service bar and grill in addition to the pro shop, driving range, and practice green. Greens fees are $32 on weekends. ✉ *3000 Herb Wimberley Dr.* ☎ *575/646–3219* ⊕ *www.nmsugolf.com.*

OUTDOOR Built in 1908, Leasburg Dam retains irrigation water for Mesilla Val-
RECREATION ley farmland and recreational water for the **Leasburg Dam State Park.** Kayakers and anglers enjoy boating and fishing here, and on hot days the cool water draws dozens of swimmers. ✉ *NM 157, 13 mi north of Las Cruces, take I-25 to Exit 19* ☎ *575/524–4068* ⊕ *www.emnrd.state.nm.us/prd/leasburg.htm* 🖾 *Day use $5 per vehicle* ⊙ *Daily 7 AM–sunset.*

OLD MESILLA

2 mi southwest of Las Cruces on NM 28.

Historians disagree about the origins of Mesilla (called both Mesilla and Old Mesilla), which in Spanish means "Little Table." Some say the town occupies the exact spot that Don Juan de Oñate declared "the first pueblo of this kingdom."

Many of the sturdy adobe structures abundant in this community date back as far as 150 years and are still in use today. The thick walls of the adobes in this area not only helped keep the interiors cool and comfortable during hot days, but also helped defend against attacks by Apaches, who were none too excited about the influx of people into their territory.

Mesilla was established by a group of lifetime Mexican residents when the territory of New Mexico was acquired by the United States in 1848. Wishing to remain Mexican, they left Las Cruces, moved a few miles west across the new border of the Rio Grande, and established their village in Mexican territory. All this effort was for naught, because the Rio Grande not only changed its path in 1865, putting both Las Cruces and Mesilla east of the river, but the whole area had already been annexed by the United States in 1854. Mesilla had established itself well and was the largest station between El Paso and Los Angeles on the Butterfield Stage Line, and for a time served as the Confederate territorial capital, an area that covered Arizona and western New Mexico. In 1881 the Santa Fe Railroad extended its line into Las Cruces, bypassing Mesilla and establishing Las Cruces as the area's major hub of commerce and transportation.

Mesilla has seen celebrations, weddings, bloody political battles, and the milestone trial of Billy the Kid. A Mesilla jury convicted the Kid for the murder of Matthew Brady, the sheriff of Lincoln County. The Kid was transferred to the Lincoln County Courthouse to be hanged for the crime but briefly staved off the inevitable by escaping.

GETTING HERE

Old Mesilla is effectively a community within greater Las Cruces. It lies just a couple of miles southwest of Las Cruces, a short drive on NM 28, which is also locally signed as Avenida de Mesilla.

Contacts Mesilla Visitor's Center (✉ 2231 Avenida de Mesilla [NM 28] ☎ 575/524–3262 ⊕ www.oldmesilla.org).

EXPLORING

Touristy shops, galleries, and restaurants line the cobbled streets of Old Mesilla. With a Mexican-style plaza and gazebo where many weddings and fiestas take place, the village retains the charm of bygone days. It is well worth parking your car and strolling around the village and the surrounding neighborhoods, where many of the adobe homes are lovingly maintained.

On the north side of the plaza is the **Basilica of San Albino** (✉ 2070 Calle de Santiago, Old Mesilla Plaza ☎ 575/526–9349 ⊕ www.sanalbino. org), an impressive 1908 Romanesque brick-and-stained-glass building that is supported by the foundation of the adobe church, built in 1856, that originally stood here.

Cultural Center de Mesilla (CCM) lies a full block to the west of the Old Mesilla Plaza. The well-kept historic (1840s) adobe building houses the organizers of the renowned Border Book Festival. Fulfilling the mission of the multicultural, multilingual festival—which takes place annually in April—the Cultural Center sells both new and out-of-print

Spanish-language and multilanguage books for adults and children. It also carries a wonderful range of folk art and fine art, which is displayed beneath beautifully patinated vigas that line the ceiling. Festival-related music and spoken-word CDs, a large selection of collectible Mexican lobby cards and posters, Lucha Libre masks, Day of the Dead memorabilia, and woven goods from cooperatives in Juárez and Chiapas are also sold. Sodas and *paletas* (fruit popsicles) are available, too. Across the street, **Galería Tepín** (⊠ *2220 Calle de Parian)* is a small but noteworthy showcase of local and Mexican political and contemporary art. ⊠ *2231A Calle de Parian,* ☎ *575/523–3988* ⊕ *www. borderbookfestival.org* ⊘ *Fri. and Sat. 10–5, Sun. 11–5.*

OFF THE BEATEN PATH

Stahmann Farms. Pecan trees cover about 4,000 acres here, at the world's largest family-owned pecan orchard. You can take a shaded drive through the trees and drop by the farm's store to sample yummy pecan products, or take a tour of the farms (2:30 in winter, 10 am in summer). They also have a store on the plaza in Old Mesilla. ⊠ *22505 NM 28, 6 mi south of Old Mesilla, La Mesa* ☎ *575/525–3470 or 800/654–6887* ⊕ *www.stahmanns.com* ⊘ *Store Mon.–Sat. 10–6, Sun. 11–6.*

OFF THE BEATEN PATH

Mesilla Valley Wine Trail. Head south from Las Cruces on NM 28 and you'll find a rural countryside with pecan trees reaching overhead, and onions, chiles, and vineyards filling the fields. The first winery worth a look is the **Rio Grande Vineyard & Winery** (⊠ *5321 NM 28, at mile marker 25* ☎ *575/524–3985* ⊕ *www.riograndewinery.com),* just over 4 mi south of Old Mesilla. The comfortably appointed tasting room has a fine view of the Organ Mountains, and proprietor Gordon Steel is congenial and informed. Try the Queue Tendre white or the dry Syrah. The next stop, about 20 mi farther, is New Mexico's oldest winery—established by Franciscan monks in the 1600s—**La Viña Winery** (⊠ *4201 S. NM 28, La Union* ☎ *575/882–7632* ⊕ *www.lavinawinery. com),* run by proprietors Denise and Ken Stark. La Viña hosts a popular wine festival in October, and a Blues & Jazz Festival, usually in early May. A wide variety of wines is produced here—from a crisp Viognier, to Pinot Noir, to White Zinfandel. Finally, 28 mi down, you may not notice, but you will have crossed into Texas and the town of Canutillo, home of the newest winery in the bunch, **Zin Valle Vineyards** (⊠ *7315 S. NM 28, Canutillo, TX* ☎ *915/877–4544* ⊕ *www.zinvalle.com).* They favor sweet wines, such as Gewürztraminer made from grapes grown on-site. All Mesilla Valley Wine Trail wineries have tasting rooms, tours, and are usually closed midweek. Stop into **Chope's Bar & Café** in La Mesa for a bite to eat en route.

WHERE TO EAT

¢   ✗ **Chope's Bar & Cafe.** Pronounced *cho-pez,* it looks like a run-of-the-mill
MEXICAN   adobe building from the outside, but inside the 150-year-old former
Fodor's Choice   Benavides homestead you'll find happy locals and many turistas eat-
★   ing well-seasoned Mexican food and drinking ice-cold beer and tasty margaritas. Bikers join the convivial crowd in the bar next door; like the restaurant, it's still owned by the Benavides family. It's worth the 15-mi drive south from Old Mesilla for the local flavor. No credit cards are accepted in the bar. ⊠ *16145 S. NM 28, La Mesa* ☎ *575/233–3420 restaurant, 575/233–9976 bar* ═ *MC, V.*

$$$
CONTINENTAL
Fodor's Choice
★

✕ **Double Eagle.** Chandeliers, century-old wall tapestries, and gold-leaf ceilings set the scene at this elegant restaurant inside an 1848 mansion on Old Mesilla's plaza. Some say ghosts, including one of a young man who incurred his mother's wrath by falling in love with a servant girl, haunt the property. Continental cuisine, steaks, and flambé dishes are served, formally, in the main restaurant. The restaurant has its own aging room for its renowned steaks, and you can sample all sorts of delicious alcoholic infusions from the bar (the chile vodka makes a fantastic Bloody Mary). **Pepper's,** the adjoining Southwestern-style café, has more casual fare including chiles rellenos served with colorful tortilla chips. The Double Eagle Sunday champagne brunch is excellent and a good deal ($$; reservations are recommended). ⊠ *2355 Calle de Guadalupe* ☎ *575/523–6700* ⊕ *www.double-eagle-mesilla.com* ▤ *AE, D, DC, MC, V.*

$
MEXICAN

✕ **La Posta.** Once a way station for the Butterfield Overland Mail and Wells Fargo stagecoaches, this restaurant in an old adobe structure has hosted many celebrities through the years, including Bob Hope and Mexican revolutionary Pancho Villa. Some of the Mexican recipes here date back more than a century; among the best menu choices are *tostadas compuestos* (red or green chile, meat, and pinto beans in tortilla shells), and enchiladas with red or green chile. Exotic birds and tropical fish inhabit the lushly planted atrium. ⊠ *2410 Calle de San Albino* ☎ *575/524–3524* ⊕ *www.laposta-de-mesilla.com* ▤ *AE, D, DC, MC, V.*

$
ITALIAN

✕ **Lorenzo's de Mesilla.** Walk into this restaurant and it's easy to imagine you're in Sicily: a hand-painted mural of the Mesilla Valley decorates a wall, light floods in through windows. The warm, colorful decor, friendly service, and really good food make Lorenzo's a favorite among locals. Old Sicilian recipes are used to create the pastas, sauces, pizzas, sandwiches, and salads. An outdoor courtyard offers a relaxing spot for a leisurely lunch or dinner. ⊠ *1750 Calle de Mercado #4, Mercado center* ☎ *575/525–3170* ⊕ *www.lorenzosdemesilla.com* ▤ *AE, D, MC, V.*

THE ARTS

The Fountain Theatre (⊠ *2469 Calle de Guadalupe, ½ block south of Old Mesilla Plaza* ☎ *575/524–8287* ⊕ *www.mesillavalleyfilm.org*), which still has its original 1870s facade and 1920s vintage murals inside, was bought in 1905 by the prominent Fountain family, who began showing movies here in 1912. Aside from a 10-year hiatus in the 1930s when it was converted to accommodate talkies, it has remained in family hands, although now under the aegis of the Mesilla Valley Film Society. The oldest continuously operating theater in New Mexico presents independent films, amateur theater, and some chamber music concerts.

SHOPPING
SHOPPING NEIGHBORHOODS

High-quality Native American jewelry and crafts are sold at surprisingly good prices in the adobe shops of **Old Mesilla Plaza** if you have the patience to weed through multitudes of cheesy ceramic Native American dolls with feathered headdresses (not what the locals wore) and other various and sundry tourist tchotchkes. The al fresco **Farmers Market** offers homegrown produce such as watermelons and green chiles (in season), as well as handcrafted souvenirs and jewelry, on the plaza noon to 4 Sunday and 11 to 4 Friday year-round. In mid-afternoon on Sunday from September to early November, you can enjoy live mariachi music here, too. Outside the plaza historic district, in Mesilla's newer **Mercado** shopping area (about a mile northeast, back toward Las Cruces off Avenida de Mesilla), there are a number of interesting contemporary art galleries, a high-end kitchen shop, and restaurants.

El Platero (⊠ 2350 Calle de Principal ☎ 575/523–5561) offers touristy souvenirs, Southwestern gift items, and postcards in an 1860s-era building. The Italianate, stamped-metal storefront was added in 1890. Savor a piece of habanero fudge on the outside benches.

ART GALLERIES

The only artist co-op in the Las Cruces area, the **Mesilla Valley Fine Arts Gallery** (⊠ 2470A Calle de Guadalupe, southeast corner of Old Mesilla Plaza ☎ 575/522–2933 ☉ Mon.–Sat.) has a broad range of art by 30 juried artists.

Preston Contemporary Art Center (⊠ 1755 Avenida de Mercado, Mercado center ☎ 575/523–8713 ⊕ www.prestoncontemporaryart.com ☉ Tues.–Sat. 1–5) opened in 2008 to the delight of the arts community. Respected local architect Gerry Lundeen artfully balanced Mesilla's strict historic-compliance requirements in designing a natural-light-filled space ideal for contemporary works. Preston's international artists work in all media, from photography to sculpture, and the center's four annual exhibits have included the dramatically saturated botanical-pigment prints of Tom Millea; the ancient, yet modern ceramic vase forms of Terry Gieber; and mixed-media work, inspired by illuminated manuscripts, by Ellen Kochansky.

COOKWARE

Las Cosas (⊠ 1740 Calle de Mercado, Mercado center ☎ 575/541–9735 ⊕ www.lascosascooking.com ☉ Mon.–Sat. 10–6, Sun. noon–5), like its sister shop in Santa Fe, is a cook's nirvana, offering the latest and greatest in cookware, kitchen gadgets, and even cooking classes. The staff is helpful and very knowledgeable.

HEADING WEST ON U.S. 60

Maybe you're a traveler who prefers to stay off the beaten path, and venture to places you've never even heard of. If you're in the mood to take the slow road and encounter an authentic Western America decades removed from today's franchise operations, head west on old U.S. 60 out of Socorro and keep going—as far as the Arizona border if you like (this is also a popular "scenic route" for travelers headed from Tucson and Phoenix to Albuquerque and points north). The speed limit is mostly 65 mph, there's not a chain restaurant for 200 mi, and the stunning scenery hasn't changed much for 50 years.

This long, often lonely highway opened in 1926 as the first numbered auto route to cross the United States. Called the Ocean to Ocean Highway, U.S. 60 eventually ran from Norfolk, Virginia, to Los Angeles.

BORDERLAND

Lines drawn on a map do little to divide the inhabitants of two countries and three states (New Mexico, Texas, and the Mexican state of Chihuahua) who share a history dating back some 400 years. In the small border villages of Columbus and Las Palomas, Mexico, families live and do business on both sides of the international boundary line. Las Cruces, New Mexico, and El Paso, Texas, are both growing so quickly that they seem to be near the point of merging via housing developments. Anthony is the little town between the two, with a sweet, small-town feel and a dynamic community-minded sensibility. The borderland area also draws transplants from the eastern and western United States, who come to take advantage of the mild weather and placid way of life.

You might be surprised to find U.S. Border Patrol checkpoints on all major highways leading away from the El Paso area to destinations such as Carlsbad, Deming, Truth or Consequences, and Alamogordo. Uniformed officers will simply ask your citizenship, though trained dogs sometimes circle vehicles in searches for illegal drugs. The stops are routine, and law-abiding citizens should encounter no difficulty.

Earlier in the 20th century this stretch of it was a "hoof highway," the route of cattle drives from Springerville, Arizona, to Magdalena, New Mexico. Walk into any café along this dusty roadside and you're still likely to be greeted by a cowboy in spurs fresh from tending to ranch business.

People really ranch here, much the way they have for more than 100 years—prior to the era of homesteaders and ranchers, the Apaches ruled and weren't much inclined to allow ranching or settlements of any kind. Livestock production and timber are still the leading industries. U.S. 60 takes you through the heart of Catron County, New Mexico's largest county by area, and least populated by square mile. Notoriously politically incorrect and proud of it, this is a place where Confederate flags fly and animal trophies are considered high art.

After you've headed as far west as Quemado, you can head 7 mi south on NM 32 and find yourself at the northern gateway to the Gila National Forest, or make an interesting and scenic loop by continuing north on NM 36 to NM 117, which skirts the east side of El Malpais National Monument, eventually hooking up with I–40 east of Grants. To get to Albuquerque take I–40 east.

MAGDALENA

27 mi west of Socorro on U.S. 60.

Magdalena, population 300, enjoyed its heyday about a hundred years ago as a raucous town of miners and cowboys. It was once the biggest livestock shipping point west of Chicago. The Atchison, Topeka & Santa Fe Railway built a spur line from Socorro in 1885 to transport timber, wool, cattle, and ore. Lead, zinc, silver, copper, and gold all were mined in the area, but now there are more ghosts than miners.

The town took its name from Mary Magdalene, protector of miners, whose face is supposedly visible on the east slope of Magdalena Peak, a spot held sacred by the Native Americans of the area. To get a feel for the place, walk down to the Atchison, Topeka & Santa Fe Railway depot, now the town hall and library; **Mary's Boxcar Museum** is just outside. Across the street is the Charles Ilfeld Warehouse, where the company's motto, "wholesalers of everything," is a reminder of the great trade empire of the late 19th century.

EXPLORING

Histories of some of the notable buildings in Magdalena and a guide for a walking tour are available on ⊕ *www.magdalena-nm.com*. It's fun to have the printout of the walking tour while exploring the shops and cafés. Note: U.S. 60 is called 1st Street through the small town center; Main St. runs across it about midway.

The ghost town of **Kelly** (⊠ *Kelly Rd. off U.S. 60* ☎ *No phone*), 4 mi south of town, is reputed to be haunted, and during the Old Timers Reunion a 7K race finishes here (it begins in the village). During its boom time 3,000 people lived in the town. You cannot go into the mine, but you can get a permit to walk around and collect rocks at Tony's Rock Shop in Magdalena at 9th and Kelly (☎ *575/854–2401*).

Although there are arts festivals in spring and fall, the biggest event of the year in Magdalena is the **Magdalena Old Timers Reunion** (☎ *575/854–2261* ⊕ *www.magdalena-nm.com*), held for three days in early July. The festival, which draws about 5,000 and has the biggest parade in New Mexico after the state fair's, began quietly 30 years ago. With the end of cattle drives and the shutdown of the rail spur in the early 1970s, cowboys began returning at the same time each year to greet each other and reminisce. Over the past three decades, the reunion has grown into an event-packed weekend including both kids' and adult rodeos, Western swing dances on Friday and Saturday nights, a fiddling contest, a barbecue dinner, and an authentic chuck-wagon cook-off. The parade takes place Saturday morning, and the crowned reunion queen must be at least 60 years old. Most events are held at the Magdalena Fairgrounds, and admission is free.

WHERE TO EAT AND STAY

¢   ✕ **Bear Mountain Coffee House & Gallery.** Once the rambunctious West Bar,
CAFÉ   this vintage 1900 building has been restored, revealing formerly hid-
Fodor'sChoice   den charms, like the original plank floors. The dancehall side is now a
★   coffeehouse, which serves tempting blueberry muffins and hearty lunch fare, such as roast beef panini, accented with pepper-jack cheese and Dijon mustard. The Old Crow mirror from the former bar hangs on one wall, and bookish sorts should note the collection of rare and unusual Southwest lit for sale. Be sure to step through to the bar side, which displays local artwork (Holly Modine's cleverly formed baskets, Debra Nudson's brilliantly hued rag rugs). The rack of travel brochures and friendly service makes this a useful stop for those heading farther along U.S. 60. ⊠ *902 W. 1st St., on U.S. 60, town center* ☎ *575/854–3310*

⊕ *www.bearmountaincoffeehouse.com* ⊟ *AE, D, MC, V* ⊗ *No dinner. Closed Mon. and Tues.*

¢ ✗**Magdalena Cafe.** Hearty, delicious fare including steaks, burgers, hot
AMERICAN sandwiches, homemade pie, Mexican pineapple cake, and delicious milk
shakes are served on red-and-white checkered tablecloths here. The
place is usually busy with all sorts of characters, all of whom seem very
happy to be here. Service is a bit harried, but friendly. ⊠ *109 S. Main
St., town center* ☎ *575/854–2696* ⊟ *No credit cards* ⊗ *Closed Sun. and
often on other days; call ahead.*

¢ ▥ **Western Motel & RV Park.** To inspire dreams of riding the range, rooms
of knotty pine are set off with Western paintings and Native American artifacts, and some have Victorian-style flowered upholstery and
matching art. Locally handmade quilts and Mexican textiles decorate
the walls. The facility was a maternity hospital for the region in the
1920s. There are also 14 RV sites with full hookups ($30; weekly and
monthly rates available). **Pros:** Wi-Fi and a hot tub are nice additions.
Cons: funky, rustic decor may not appeal to all tastes. ⊠ *404 1st St.,
on U.S. 60, town center* ☎ *575/854–2417* ⊕ *www.thewesternmotel.com*
⥅ *6 rooms, 14 RV sites* ⚲ *In-room: a/c, refrigerator, Wi-Fi. In-hotel:
some pets allowed* ⊟ *AE, D, DC, MC, V.*

EN
ROUTE
With its 27 glistening-white 80-foot radio-telescope antennae arranged
in patterns (their configuration is altered every four months or so), the
Very Large Array is a startling sight when spotted along the Plains of San
Augustin. The complex's dish-shaped "ears," each weighing 230 tons,
are tuned in to the cosmos. The array is part of a series of facilities that
compose the National Radio Astronomy Observatory. The antennas,
which provided an impressive backdrop for the movie *Contact,* based
on the Carl Sagan book, form the largest, most advanced radio telescope
in the world. The telescope chronicles the birth and death of stars and
galaxies from 10 to 12 billion light-years away. Hundreds of scientists
from around the world travel to this windy, remote spot to research
black holes, colliding galaxies, and exploding stars, as well as to chart
the movements of planets. Visitors are permitted to stroll right up to
the array on a self-guided walking tour that begins at the unstaffed visitor center. Staff members emphasize that their work does *not* involve
a search for life on other planets. ⊠ *NM 52, south off U.S. 60; 23 mi
west of Magdalena* ☎ *575/835–7000* ⊕ *www.nrao.edu* ⌦ *Free* ⊗ *Daily
8:30–dusk.*

8

PIE TOWN

21 mi west of Datil on U.S. 60.

During the 1930s and '40s, it was said that the best pie in New Mexico
was served at a little café in Pie Town, a homesteading community just
west of the Continental Divide. Cowboys on cattle drives and tourists
heading to California spread stories of the legendary pies. Thanks to a
pair of prospering enterprises in town (and the annual Pie Festival), the
tradition of great pie in this part of the world is alive and well.

Pie Town's reputation can be traced to 1922 when World War I veteran
Clyde Norman came from Texas and filed a mining claim on the Hound

Pup Lode. Gold mining didn't go as well as he'd hoped, but he began selling kerosene and gasoline, as well as doughnuts he'd brought from Magdalena in his Model T. Eventually he learned to bake pies with dried apples, which were an immediate success. Spanish-American War veteran Harmon L. Craig, who made a great sourdough, arrived in 1923 or '24, and the two went into partnership. The post office granted the place the name Pie Town in 1927.

Craig bought Norman out in 1932. He ran the mercantile end while his wife, Theodora Baugh, and her two daughters took over the pie baking. Nowadays aficionados can dig in at the annual Pie Festival (⊕ *www. pietowncouncil.com*), held on the second weekend in September, with pie-eating and pie-baking contests, horned toad races, buckboard rides, and horseshoes.

WHERE TO EAT

¢   ✕ **Daily Pie Cafe.** The entry to this homey spot sports a hand-painted sign
CAFÉ   proclaiming HOME COOKING ON THE GREAT DIVIDE. And so it is. Owner-
Fodor's Choice   chef Michael Rawls enjoys his work, and locals and visitors appreciate
★   his culinary skills. First check the Daily Pie Chart—consider the signature New Mexican apple pie (piñon nuts and green chile make it special) or seasonal peach walnut crumb—before you fill up on the main course side of the menu. Daily Pie opens early in the morning and usually closes by 3. Trusty breakfast and lunch dishes (and an occasional Friday-night special) include good tomato-onion-cheese omelets and burritos packed with ham, eggs, and cheese. There's a sweet cabin for rent out back (daily or longer). ⊠ *U.S. 60, west end of town* ☎ *575/772–2700* ⊕ *www.dailypie.com* ⊟ *MC, V* ⊗ *No dinner. Closed Sun. and Mon. Hours vary seasonally, call ahead.*

¢   ✕ **Pie-O-Neer Cafe.** "Life goes on and days go by. That's why you should
CAFÉ   stop for pie." Such is the motto of one of New Mexico's memorable
Fodor's Choice   roadside stops. In this one-time trading post, owner Kathy Knapp serves
★   light meals (grilled cheese spiked with green chile, vegetarian soup, spinach quesadillas) from late morning through midafternoon, but pie is her stock in trade. She bakes at least 12 varieties daily—she's nimble with whatever's in season (fresh-picked plums are a special treat), and most days you can count on oven-fresh apple, cherry, chocolate cream, lemon meringue, and banana cream. On some Sunday afternoons folks dawdle on the porch, and there might be live music; a small art gallery completes the scene. The little log-cabin guesthouse just up the road is Pie-O-Neer-owned; ask about rates. ⊠ *U.S. 60, east end of town* ☎ *575/772–2711* ⊕ *www.pie-o-neer.com* ⊟ *AE, D, MC, V* ⊗ *Closed Tues.–Thurs. No dinner. Hours vary seasonally, call ahead.*

QUEMADO

22 mi west of Pie Town on U.S. 60.

Quemado (pronounced kay-*ma*-doh) means "burnt" in Spanish, and the town is supposedly named for a legendary Apache chief who burned his hand in a campfire. The bustling village, which contains several motels and cafés, is busiest in fall, when it is a favorite base for deer hunters.

Quemado Lake, about 20 mi south of town on NM 32 and NM 103, is a man-made fishing and hiking area where it's not unusual to spot herds of elk.

OFF THE
BEATEN
PATH

Fodor's Choice ★ **Lightning Field.** The sculptor Walter De Maria created *Lightning Field,* a work of land art composed of 400 stainless-steel poles of varying heights (the average is 20 feet, although they create a horizontal plane) arranged in a rectangular grid over 1 mi by ½ mi of flat, isolated terrain, and installed in 1977. Groups of up to six people are permitted to stay overnight from May through October—the only way you can experience the artwork—at a rustic on-site 1930s cabin. Fees include dinner and breakfast, and range from $150 (May to June, September to October) to $250 (July to August) per person; children and students pay $100. Dia Art Foundation administers *Lightning Field,* shuttling visitors from Quemado to the sculpture, which is on private land 45 minutes to the northeast. Thunder-and-lightning storms are most common from July to mid-September; book way ahead for visits during this time. If you're lucky, you'll see flashes you'll never forget (though lightning isn't required for the sculpture to be stunning in effect). ⊠ *PO Box 2993, Corrales* ☎ *505/898–3335 reservations* ⊕ *www.lightningfield.org* ⚑ *Reservations essential* ☉ *May–Oct.*

WHERE TO STAY

¢ ⛺ **Largo Motel & Café.** New construction is rare for the area, and this
MOTEL 2008-built single-story stucco motel with a metal roof has rooms that are simple and comfortable and are just right to wash off the trail dust and get a good night's rest. The Largo has the best café in town ($), a busy little spot known for homemade corn tortillas and biscuits, gravy, and chicken-fried steak, and excellent red-and-green chile on Mexican food dishes. The Navajo tacos are famous. They serve "a real full plate," too. Above the spacious booths are mounted trophies (the owner is a hunting guide). **Pros:** motel is clean and new; staff is friendly and easygoing. **Cons:** nothing fancy here, just your basic roadside stop; no tubs in bathrooms, just showers. ⊠ *U.S. 60 on west side of town* ☎ *575/773–4686* ⤳ *20 rooms* ⚒ *In-room: a/c, Wi-Fi. In-hotel: restaurant* ⊜ *MC, V.*

CAMPING

¢ ⛺ **Quemado Lake Campgrounds.** In the northern reaches of the Gila National Forest, six campgrounds surround Quemado Lake and provide convenient access to hiking trails or lake fishing for stocked rainbow trout. ⊠ *NM 32 and NM 103, 20 mi south of Quemado* ☎ *575/773–4678* ⊕ *www.publiclands.org* ⚒ *Pit toilets, partial hookups (electric and water), dump station, drinking water, fire grates, fire pits, grills, picnic tables* ⤳ *Unlimited primitive sites, 60 developed sites, 16 RV sites* ⊜ *No credit cards.*

GILA NATIONAL FOREST AREA

The cliff dwellings, ghost towns, and sprawling ranches scattered among hundreds of miles of desert, forest, and jagged canyons in the Gila (pronounced *hee-*la) are the legacy of the hearty souls who have inhabited this remote area over the centuries. The early cliff dwellers mysteriously disappeared sometime after the year 1000, leaving behind the ruins and relics of a culture replaced half a millennium later by Spanish explorers, roving bands of Apaches, and occasional trappers. In the 1800s Apache leaders including Cochise, Geronimo, and Victorio waged war against the encroaching Mexican and American settlers, and for a time the sheer ruggedness of the mountains provided refuge for them. Any hope for the Apaches retaining freedom in the area vanished when prospectors discovered the area was rich with minerals in the late 1800s. The mining boom began and the area was flooded with settlers. Scenic drives lead to several ghost towns from this era, including the old gold-mining settlement of Mogollon. ■ TIP➔ **Many of the roadways through the Gila are twisting and narrow—it will take you longer than the mileage alone would suggest to get to your destination. Also keep in mind that elevations range up to 10,000 feet—weather conditions vary widely, even in summer.**

SILVER CITY

235 mi southwest of Albuquerque on I–25 to NM 152; 115 mi northwest of Las Cruces, west on I–10 and northwest on U.S. 180; 152 mi south of Quemado/U.S. 60 via NM 32/12 to U.S. 180.

Silver City began as a tough and lawless mining camp in 1870, and struggled for a long time to become a more respectable—and permanent—settlement. Henry McCarty spent part of his boyhood here, perhaps learning some of the ruthlessness that led to his later infamy under his nickname—Billy the Kid. Other mining towns in the area sparked briefly and then died, but Silver City eventually flourished and became the area's most populated city. Today, even though it has 10,500 residents, Silver City retains a sense of remote wildness—largely due to the nearby Gila National Forest and vast Gila Wilderness.

GETTING HERE

Most travelers come to Silver City either from Las Cruces via U.S. 180, which turns into Silver Heights Boulevard within the city limits and intersects Hudson Street; or from Albuquerque via I–25 south, then either turning west onto U.S. 60, and south along the western extent of the Gila National Forest via NM32/12 and U.S. 180, or, exiting I-25 onto NM 152 (part of the Geronimo Trail Scenic Byway). If you're headed here from southern Arizona on I–10, you'll want to turn north on NM 90 at Lordsburg. ■ TIP➔ **NM 152 is a spectacular (and very slow) ride, but seasonal snow and ice can make for treacherous driving.** If the weather has become dicey, continue on I-25 south to Hatch, then proceed west on NM 26 to U.S. 180. Call ahead for road conditions.

Contacts Silver City/Grant County Chamber of Commerce (✉ *201 N. Hudson St.* ☎ *575/538–3785 or 800/548–9378* ⊕ *www.silvercity.org*).

EXPLORING

Since the area's copper ore is now close to depleted and the huge mine nearby all but officially closed, the town's traditional population of miners is being replaced by artists, outdoors enthusiasts, and retirees

FESTIVALS AND EVENTS

In April or May the **Celebration of Spring** happens Downtown in the Big Ditch Park, with crafts booths, activities, and lots of frolicking in the balmy weather. This fiesta marks the opening of the city's farmers' market at Bullard and 6th Street. The **Silver City Blues Festival,** which runs for three days in late May in Gough Park (Downtown), has become an international draw, but still has the spirit of a block party where young and old dance on the grass under beautiful, starry skies. September brings the **Gila River Festival** (⊕ *www.gilaconservation.org* ☏ *575/538–8078*), which celebrates the 650-mile river and the wilderness it runs through, with renowned speakers and events (films, hikes, photography workshops) on themes from biodiversity to conservation and habitat. October brings the **Taste of Silver City** where, for the price of a ticket, you can walk around Downtown sampling food and treats from many participating establishments. The calendar of events and activities at ⊕ *www.silvercity.org* gives comprehensive information, or you can call the **Silver City Main Street Project** (☏ *575/534–1700*) for Downtown events.

The **Tour de Gila** annual high-altitude ride (usually in late April or early May) brings out serious competitive cyclists (Taylor Phinney triumphed here over Lance Armstrong in 2010). The 540-km men's course is a five-day event; the women's course is slightly shorter. (⊕ *www.tourofthegila.com*)

looking for a more bohemian community than, say, Las Cruces. Thanks to efforts of preservationists, though, Silver City's origins are evident in the many distinctive houses and storefronts of the Downtown area, making it ideal for exploring by foot (pick up a self-guided walking tour map and guide at the Silver City Museum shop). The characterless strip-style development of the surrounding town belies the charm of the compact, walkable historic Downtown.

A stroll through the historic Downtown district will take you by many of the town's dozen or so art galleries, several tasty cafés, and antiques stores. Silver City's arts scene couldn't be more different from the one in Santa Fe. A local artist once said, "Silver City is where art is for *the* people, not *some* people."

The unusual mansard-roof Italianate-style Henry B. Ailman House, built in 1881, serves as headquarters for the **Silver City Museum,** whose main gallery mural of the mining and ranching community circa 1882 provides a good overview of the area's colorful history. Displays include pottery and other relics from the area's ancient (and now extinct) Mimbres and Mogollon cultures, as well as a nice lot of items from the heyday of the mining era. From the museum's tower you can catch a grand view of the eclectic architecture around town. Self-guided walking tours, with maps, are sold in the museum's store, which carries Southwest-themed books and gifts as well. The museum also has a local-history research library. ⊠ *312 W. Broadway* ⊕ *www.silvercitymuseum. org* ☏ *575/538–5921* 💲 *$3 suggested donation* ⊙ *Weekdays 9–4:30, weekends 10–4.*

OFF THE
BEATEN
PATH

El Chino Mine. The wrenching 1954 movie *Salt of the Earth* chronicled the Empire Zinc Mine strike that took place less than 1 mi away, in Hanover, and while that mine is long gone, the ups and downs of the El Chino Mine reveal a similar and compelling story about economy, race, and politics in Grant County. Now owned by Freeport-McMoRan Copper & Gold, the vast, open-pit mine—commonly referred to as the Santa Rita Mine, for the little village that was founded here in 1803, and was literally swallowed as the pit expanded in the mid-20th century—is 1,500-feet-deep and 1½ mi across. It cuts back or ceases operation when the price of copper falls too low. Copper mining in the region dates back centuries, and began in tunnels that were labored over first by indigenous populations, then by the Spanish and Mexicans. The observation point offers interpretative signage; monthly bus tours (reservations essential) provide a fascinating in-depth perspective. ⊠ *NM 152, 15 mi east of Silver City, just west of mile marker 6,Hanover* ☎ *575/537–3327 (Bayard City Hall) tours* 🖳 *Observation point free; tours $5* ⊘ *Observation point May–Oct., daily 8–dusk; Nov.–Apr., daily 8–5. Tours 2nd Tues. of each month at 10 am.*

Established in 1866, **Fort Bayard** was built by the U.S. Army when it became clear that conflict between homeland Apaches and early Anglo and Spanish settlers would not easily abate. Company B of the 125th U.S. Colored Infantry was first in command, and hundreds of African-American enlisted men, or buffalo soldiers, made their mark here. A huge Fort Bayard Days celebration takes place annually, on the third weekend of September, and visitors can watch re-enactors and learn about this national historic landmark's later life as a groundbreaking tuberculosis research facility; bimonthly tours (reservations essential) are offered. ⊠ *U.S. 180, 10 mi east of Silver City, Bayard* ☎ *575/388–4477 or 575/956–3294* ⊕ *www.fortbayard.org* 🖳 *Donations accepted* ⊘ *Tours July–Sept., 2nd and 4th Sat. at 9:30 am; rest of year varies, call ahead.*

NEED A
BREAK?

Alotta Gelato. Made on-site, the gelato here is creamy and delicious. Flavors change regularly; espresso, chocolate hazelnut, and a very unordinary vanilla are regulars, as are sorbets like raspberry and mango. It's open late if you need a nighttime snack. ⊠ *619 N. Bullard St.* ☎ *575/534–4995.*

The **Western New Mexico University Museum (WNMU)** contains the world's largest permanent display of distinctive black-on-white Mimbres pottery (is especially notable for its crisply painted animal forms). The Mimbres collection—which the museum bought for a remarkable $1,000 from the family of the man who procured most of the pieces by illicit pot hunting—fills the main floor of this 1917 Trost & Trost building that once housed WNMU's science classes and gym. Town history exhibits are displayed downstairs, including a period classroom and the original gym floor. Set on a hill on the west end of town, WNMU's campus offers a nice view of the surrounding mountains and the valley below; the museum's topmost floor is window-lined, and visitors can enjoy the broader view from that vantage point, as well as historic photos and other university memorabilia. Mimbres designs are reproduced on mugs and more in the gift shop. ⊠ *Fleming Hall, 1000 W. College*

Ave., on campus at west end of 10th St. ☎ *575/538–6386* ⊕ *www. wnmu.edu* ☜ *Donations accepted* ☉ *Weekdays 9–4:30, weekends 10–4.*

OFF THE BEATEN PATH

☾ **Shakespeare Ghost Town.** If you're heading southwest from Silver City (or west toward Arizona from Las Cruces), this is a fun stop. Portions of this settlement in the heart of a working ranch just outside the sleepy town of Lordsburg have been preserved as they were in the town's heyday as a gold and silver mining town in the late 1800s. Founded in 1856, the ghost town has been designated a National Historic Site, and original structures such as homes, saloons, and stables still stand. Living-history reenactments are staged four times a year—usually the fourth weekend of April, June, August, and October. You'll find no snack shops or other tourist amenities in Shakespeare, as owner Janaloo Hill (who grew up on the ranch, and died in May 2005) vowed not to compromise the authenticity of this genuine piece of the Old West. Shakespeare is about 50 mi from Silver City via NM 90 through Lordsburg. ⊠ *2½ mi southwest of Lordsburg, south of I–10 at Exit 22 Lordsburg* ☎ *575/542–9034* ⊕ *www.shakespeareghostown.com* ☜ *$4 regular tours, $5 reenactment events* ☉ *Tours Mar.–Dec., call for tour times and dates.*

OFF THE BEATEN PATH

☾ **City of Rocks State Park.** One look at the spires here and you'll figure out how the area came by its name. The unusual rock formations were spewed from an ancient volcano and have been eroded over the centuries by wind and rain into the marvelous shapes there today—some more than 40 feet tall. You've got to walk through the city to fully appreciate the place—and it's a great, easy adventure to have with kids (make sure you wear tennis shoes or hiking shoes). The park has a visitor center, and a large developed campground ($10 to $14) with 10 RV sites with water and electric hookups, 42 camping sites, picnic tables, grills, flush toilets, and showers. This is a great spot to camp, with sites nestled amongst the huge rocks. An on-site observatory regularly hosts star parties. ⊠ *NM 61; from Silver City, follow U.S. 180 southeast for 26 mi; then NM 61 northeast for 4 mi, Faywood* ☎ *575/536–2800* ⊕ *www.emnrd.state.nm.us/prd/cityrocks.htm* ☜ *Day use $5 per vehicle* ☉ *Visitor center daily 10–4; grounds daily 7 am–9 pm.*

8

WHERE TO EAT

$$

ECLECTIC

Fodor's Choice

★

✕ **1zero6.** Chef and proprietor Jake Politte creates dishes to rival any big-city restaurant. His menu changes constantly, based on what's available and what he feels like cooking. Asia and the Pacific Rim are clearly passions, and Politte manages to mix flavors of Italy or Mexico with Malaysian ones as if they were long-lost cousins. He uses only fresh, hand-selected ingredients, makes all his own sauces (no bottled pastes here), and his attention to detail is clear from your first bite. Giant prawns in a rich but delicate red curry on a bed of fresh spinach next to perfectly savory rice, and Khmer Krom spiced roasted pork with mild lemongrass, curried rice noodles, and fresh wok-fried vegetables are only two of the creations to emerge from his kitchen. The menu usually consists of two appetizers, three entrées, and one perfectly paired dessert. The dining room has a half-dozen tables and a big canvas theater sign from Jakarta on one wall. It's an airy, comfortable room where

SCENIC DRIVE: GERONIMO TRAIL

Geronimo Trail Scenic Byway. One of the most visually dramatic ways to reach Silver City is via NM 152, which forms the southern prong of the backward-C-shaped Geronimo Trail Scenic Byway (the northern prong is NM 52, leading into Winston and Chloride, ⇨ *discussed above in Truth or Consequences*). As you're heading south down I–25 from Albuquerque and Truth or Consequences, take exit 63, and follow NM 152 west. It's about an 80-mi drive to Silver City, and you should allow two to four hours, depending on how much you stop to look around—and weather conditions.

This twisting byway provides an exciting link to the Wild West. The remote drive (there are no gas stations) follows part of the route taken by the Kingston Lake Valley Stage Line, which operated when this region was terrorized by Apache leaders like Geronimo and outlaw bands led by the likes of Butch Cassidy. Heading west on NM 152, after about 25 mi you'll come to the mining-era boomtown, **Hillsboro,** where gold was discovered as well as silver (about $6 million worth of the two ores was extracted). The town, slowly coming back to life with the artists and retirees who've moved in, has a small museum, some shops, restaurants, and galleries. The Hillsboro Apple Festival draws visitors from all over the state on Labor Day weekend. Street vendors sell apples and apple pies, chiles, antiques, and arts and crafts.

From Hillsboro, you might consider a brief detour south down NM 27, known as the Lake Valley Back Country Byway. A landmark, west of NM 27, is Cooke's Peak, where

the first wagon road through the Southwest to California was opened in 1846. Not much is going on these days in the old silver mining town of **Lake Valley**—the last residents departed in the mid-1990s—but it once was home to 4,000 people. The mine produced 2.5 million ounces of pure silver and gave up one nugget weighing several hundred pounds. Visit the schoolhouse (which later served as a saloon), walk around the chapel, the railroad depot, and some of the few remaining old homes.

Back on NM 152, continue 10 mi west to reach another vintage mining town, Kingston, home to the **Per-cha Bank Museum** (✉ *119 Main St., Kingston* ☎ *575/895–5032* ✉ *Donations accepted* ⊙ *By appointment only*) is just a skip away from the Black Range Lodge and is well worth a visit. It was built in 1885 to handle the enormous wealth that so suddenly, and so briefly, transformed this town when a massive silver lode was discovered. All that remains intact of that era is the building itself, which is beautifully preserved, with the original vault and teller windows still in place. Photos of the town during its heyday in the late 1880s are fascinating. From Kingston, it's another 50 mi to Silver City on NM 152, which joins U.S. 180 just east of town.

the food is the star—and how. ✉ *106 N. Texas St.* ☎ *575/313–4418*
⊕ *http://1zero6-jake.blogspot.com* ▭ *MC, V* ⊙ *Closed Mon.–Thurs.*
No lunch.

$$ ✕**The Curious Kumquat.** The little café inside this international grocery
ECLECTIC is a delightful find. Salads and sandwiches are fresh and tasty and any-
thing but run-of-the-mill; prix-fixe dinners are locally sourced and cre-
ative, in the vein of pork belly with hibiscus-pickled onions or *papas
rellenos* with plum *picadilla*; the Attack of the Killer Tomato Basil
Bisque is fantastic. Outdoor seating under big, shady trees in the sum-
mer is great, or grab lunch to go before heading into the Gila. Lighter
tapas are served Thursday through Saturday evenings. ✉ *111 E. College
Ave.* ☎ *575/534–0337* ⊕ *http://curiouskumquat.com* ▭ *AE, D, MC, V*
⊙ *Closed Sun. No dinner Mon. and Tues.*

$$ ✕**Diane's Restaurant.** Fresh flowers grace the wooden tables and light
AMERICAN streams through the large windows at this cheerful bakery and eatery.
Chef-owner Diane Barrett's menu includes Hatch-green-chile Benedict, "Grandma's" spaghetti, steaks, and a deftly prepared lemon-
caper chicken. The sandwiches are all made with wonderfully tasty
house-baked bread; if you're in the mood for something sweet, don't
hesitate—this chef really shines when it comes to desserts. Bottled
microbrews and well-chosen wines are available. There's a popular Sunday champagne brunch. ✉ *510 N. Bullard St.* ☎ *575/538–8722* w*www.
dianesrestaurant.com* ▭ *AE, D, MC, V* ⊙ *Closed Mon. No dinner Sun.*

$ ✕**Jalisco's.** The Mesa family serves up hunger-busting traditional Mexi-
MEXICAN can food here, all based on old family recipes. Enchiladas and chiles
rellenos (ask for the green chile on the rellenos—strangely, they charge
extra for it, but it's worth it) satisfy big appetites in the cheerful dining
rooms decorated with art from local artists and packed with families.
✉ *103 S. Bullard St.* ☎ *575/388–2060* ▭ *D, MC, V* ⊙ *Closed Sun.*

¢ ✕**Javalina Coffee House.** Although the food menu is scant at this local
CAFÉ java spot, the coffees are good and the space comfortable for spread-
ing out and sipping. There's free Wi-Fi throughout as well as computer
rentals. ✉ *200 N. Bullard St.* ☎ *575/388–1350* ▭ *D, MC, V.*

WHERE TO STAY

$$ ⊡ **Bear Mountain Lodge.** Once owned and operated by the Nature Con-
HOTEL servancy, this serene 1928 haven was restored in 2010, and reopened
to great acclaim in the hands of new owners, Linda Brewer and John
Rohovec, who continue to offer luxury accommodations for bird-
watchers and nature lovers. You have direct access to 178 acres of Gila
National Forest land, where you can spot bird species such as the Gila
woodpecker, vermilion flycatcher, and red-faced warbler. Four second-
story rooms in the main lodge have views of mountains and forestland.
Two downstairs lodge rooms have outdoor access to a covered porch.
Four guest rooms are available in Myra's Retreat, a separate building
named for the former owner, and a great space for a larger family or
group. A two-bedroom guesthouse known as the Wren's Nest has an
exposed wood ceiling. Throughout the lodge, hardwood floors and
locally handcrafted furniture—all made from reclaimed wood—add to
the rustic elegance. The rooms and grounds now have a contemporary
touch as well, with the bright addition of sculptures and wall art from

the owners' Blue Dome Gallery, which is also onsite. Naturalist- and horseback-guided trips are available for a fee. Box lunches and dinner are available for additional charge and by arrangement. The Café, featuring local foods and an irresistible menu (roasted vegetable strata, chile-laden pot roast hash, fresh apple cider, Mexican chocolate-chip cookies, and homemade ice cream), is open to the public for Sat. and Sun. brunch. **Pros:** quiet, distinctive hideaway. **Cons:** a 10- to 15-minute drive to Silver City dining and shopping. ⊠ *2251 Cottage San Rd.; 4 mi north of Silver City via Alabama St., which becomes Cottage San Rd.* ☎ *575/538–2538 or 877/620–2327* ⊕ *www.bearmountainlodge. com* ⤳ *12 rooms, 3 houses* ⬧ *In-room: no TV, Wi-Fi. In-hotel: microwave, refrigerator, no kids under 10, some pets allowed* ☰ *AE, D, MC, V* ⚭ *BP.*

☾   ▦ **Black Range Lodge Bed & Breakfast.** It's not quite enough to describe

$ this lodge as "historic." Yes, this getaway in the old mining ghost town

BED & BREAKFAST   of Kingston, along the Geronimo Trail Scenic Byway (NM 152), has sturdy log-beam ceilings, massive stone walls, an interesting history, and an informal, rustic atmosphere that makes it nice for families, but the charm here owes a lot to the care and tending, and presence, of the gently charismatic proprietor. The "town" of Kingston—a bustling boomtown established around the turn of the 20th century and with a current population of about 30—and the surrounding area are fun to explore and fantastic by mountain bike, but keep in mind that Silver City is a full hour's drive west. Guests have access to Percha Creek and miles of hiking trails. The rooms on the north side of the main lodge have views of the mountains, and the south rooms look into the lovely greenhouse. One-bedroom suites have cozy, vine-wrapped balconies in addition to sitting areas. Breakfasts are healthy and hearty, and the kitchen is open for you to cook in if you bring your own food. There is a studio apartment, a six-bedroom house, and a beautiful one-bedroom luxury guesthouse built with the latest eco-friendly straw-bale construction techniques available as well. **Pros:** great for a group retreat or family reunion. **Cons:** no restaurants for miles; Silver City is about an hour away. ⊠ *119 Main St. (NM 152), Kingston* ⬧ *Star Rte. 2, Box 119, Kingston 88042* ☎ *575/895–5652 or 800/676–5622* ⊕ *www. blackrangelodge.com* ⤳ *Lodge, 7 rooms, 4 suites; 2 guesthouses, one with 6-bedrooms, one with 1 bedroom; 1 studio apt.* ⬧ *In-room: no a/c, no TV, no phone, kitchen (some), refrigerator (some), Wi-Fi. In-hotel: Wi-Fi hotspot, some pets allowed* ☰ *MC, V* ⚭ *BP.*

$ ▦ **Econo Lodge Silver City.** This motel on a mesa overlooking Silver City has comfortable rooms with worktables and contemporary decor. It is quiet and clean, and part of the reliable Choice Hotels chain. You'll find extra touches here ordinarily associated with higher-end lodging, such as microwaves, refrigerators, indoor pool, a hot tub, and a gym. **Pros:** breakfast spread is ample and a great value. **Cons:** service is uneven; about 1 mi from Downtown. ⊠ *1120 U.S. 180 E* ☎ *575/534– 1111 or 800/553–2666* ⊕ *www.econolodgesilvercity.com* ⤳ *62 rooms* ⬧ *In-room: refrigerator, Wi-Fi. In-hotel: pool, gym, laundry facilities, Internet terminal, Wi-Fi hotspot, some pets allowed* ☰ *AE, D, DC, MC, V* ⚭ *CP.*

$ ⚏ **Gila House Hotel & Gallery 400.** This century-old adobe, decorated with traditional Southwest furnishings and fabrics, is both an inn and art gallery—contemporary paintings hang in the public areas. The property is light-filled and appealing, and the rooms themselves are pleasantly eclectic in style and comfortable. The Continental breakfast is store-bought, but the fruit's fresh and the coffee strong. **Pros:** quiet; good location Downtown. **Cons:** rooms can be a little stuffy. ⊠ *400 N. Arizona St.* ☎ *575/313–7015* ⊕ *www.gilahouse.com* ⤴ *3 rooms* ⟡ *In-room: a/c, refrigerator, Wi-Fi. In-hotel: Internet terminal, Wi-Fi hotspot, some pets allowed* ⊟ *MC, V* ⃝ *CP.*

$$ ⚏ **Inn on Broadway.** Located on a quiet street in Downtown Silver City,
BED & BREAKFAST this popular B&B occupies a beautifully renovated Queen Anne–style home built in 1883. Well-appointed rooms are light and spacious and vary from somewhat lacy to contemporary in decor, and a fabulous front porch makes for an enjoyable stay. One room has a whirlpool bath; another has a lovely marble fireplace. **Pros:** big front porch; peaceful gardens; excellent home-cooked breakfasts. **Cons:** period decor, while not overdone, may not be everyone's cuppa. ⊠ *411 W. Broadway* ☎ *575/388–5485 or 866/207–7075* ⊕ *www.innonbroadwayweb. com* ⤴ *4 rooms* ⟡ *In-room: a/c, DVD (some), Wi-Fi.* ⊟ *AE, D, MC, V* ⃝ *BP.*

¢ ⚏ **Palace Hotel.** This grand two-story building was built in 1882 as a
HOTEL bank, but it was reinvented as a hotel in 1900. News accounts at the time touted the Palace as a first-class lodging with the intimacy of a small European hotel. The New Mexico Historical Preservation Office helped to restore and reopen the hotel in 1990, keeping much of the historical detail intact. Some rooms have Western-style furnishings, others have neo-Victorian decor such as ruffled pillow coverings and bed skirts. The upstairs garden room is a peaceful spot for playing board games or reading. **Pros:** located Downtown; steeped in history. **Cons:** no air-conditioning, which is okay most of the time at this elevation, but it can get downright hot. ⊠ *106 W. Broadway* ☎ *575/388–1811* ⊕ *www.silvercitypalacehotel.com* ⤴ *12 rooms, 7 suites* ⟡ *In-room: no a/c, refrigerators (some), Wi-Fi* ⊟ *AE, D, MC, V* ⃝ *CP.*

SHOPPING

Shops, galleries, cafés, parks, and all sorts of building renovation make walking Silver City's Downtown district a super way to explore this great little town. Yankie Street has a compact little arts district and a couple of restaurants that make it easy to while away the hours.

Seedboat Gallery (⊠ *214 W. Yankie St.* ☎ *575/534–1136* ⊕ *www. seedboatgallery.com*) is housed in a wonderfully renovated old building that was once a feed and seed store, and before that a Chinese apothecary, this gallery shows fine arts, folk art, sculpture and jewelry—all with an evident aesthetic cohesion. The proprietors, Nan and Marcia, are keen on hosting community events in the courtyard—ask them what's on the schedule.

Vendors at the **Silver City Trading Co.'s Antique Mall** (⊠ *205 W. Broadway* ☎ *505/388–8989*) stock antiques, collectibles, and various and sundry treasures and trinkets. There are some real finds in this filled-to-the-rafters space, for a lot less than you'll see in many areas. Take some time to look in the nooks and crannies.

Fodor's Choice
★ For folks drawn to the unique warmth and hand-crafted look of decorative tiles, **Syzygy Tileworks** (✉ *106 N. Bullard St.* ☎ *575/388–5472* ⊕ *www.syzygytile.com*) is a must-stop. The owners of Syzygy create their own art tiles inspired by the famed Moravian tile works in Doylestown, Pennsylvania; the results are a refreshing complement to traditional Southwestern styles.

Fodor's Choice
★ Hosana Eilert, the proprietor of **Wild West Weaving** (✉ *211D Texas St.* ☎ *575/313–1032* ⊕ *www.wildwestweaving.com*) learned her craft in Chimayó, with the masters of the Rio Grande weaving style, the Trujillos of Centinela Traditional Arts. Eilert's skills are comparable but her special sense of color and design are hers alone. She uses mostly natural dyes and handspun wool for her work, which may be used either as tapestry or rug. Her small, inviting shop on a Downtown side street also carries a well-edited line of local contemporary artisans' work: Susan Porter/Dancing Threads scarves and shawls, Rita Sherwood's found-art altars, Trina Kaiser's beaded jewelry, and woven goods from La Cooperativa de la Frontera de Palomas y Columbus.

GILA NATIONAL FOREST

8 mi northeast of Silver City via NM 15 to Pinos Altos range and Gila Cliff Dwellings portion of Gila National Forest; 60 mi northwest of Silver City via U.S. 180 to western portions of forest; 6 mi southwest of U.S. 60 at Quemado via NM 32 to northern forest areas. The eastern edge of forest can be accessed via NM 152, the Geronimo Trail Scenic Byway, which spans about 80 mi between Silver City and I–25 near Caballo Lake (which is between Truth of Consequences and Las Cruces).

The Gila, as it's called, covers 3.3 million acres—that's 65 mi by 100 mi—and was the first land in the nation to be set aside as a protected "wilderness" by the U.S. Forest Service back in 1924. The area is vast and continues to feel like a great, relatively undiscovered treasure. You are unlikely to come across any crowds, even in peak summer months. Whether you're backpacking or doing day hikes, you have 1,500 mi of incredibly diverse trails to explore. Open camping is permitted throughout the forest, although there are 18 developed campgrounds (all with toilets and seven with potable water). The Gila is an outdoors-lover's paradise: with seemingly endless trails to explore on mountain bikes, white-water rafting (the season usually starts in April), and fishing in rivers, lakes (three of them), and streams. Thirty percent of the forest is closed to vehicular traffic entirely, but the rest is open for touring.

The **Trail of the Mountain Spirits Scenic Byway** (also referred to as the **Inner Loop Scenic Drive**) snakes through 75 mi of some of the most gorgeous and scenic forest in the wilderness. The roads are paved but the sharp, narrow, and steep turns make it inadvisable for large RVs. From Silver City, take NM 15 north to Gila Cliff Dwellings National Monument. From the monument backtrack on NM 15 to NM 35 heading southeast to NM 152, which leads west back to Silver City. ■TIP→ Remember: these forest roads are slow—double your travel time estimates. And don't pass up an opportunity to fill-up your tank—gas stations beyond Silver City can be scarce.

GILA NATIONAL FOREST AND WILDERNESS RANGER DISTRICTS

All area Forest Service offices are open 8 am to 4:30 pm, Monday through Friday, and can provide maps, trail information, and travel conditions. (⊕ *fs.usda.gov/gila*)

Silver City Ranger District (⊠ *3005 E. Camino del Bosque, Silver City* ☎ *575/388–8201*)

Wilderness Ranger District (⊠ *NM 35, 11 mi north of NM 152* ☎ *575/536–2250*)

Fodor's Choice ★

At **Gila Cliff Dwellings National Monument** the mystery of the Mogollon (*muh*-gee-yohn) people's short-lived occupation of the deeply recessed caves high above the canyon floor may never be resolved. But the finely detailed stone dwellings they left behind stand in silent testimony to the challenges as well as the beauty of the surrounding Gila Wilderness. Built and inhabited for a span of barely two generations, from 1280 to the early1300s AD, its 42 rooms are tucked into six natural caves that are reached via a rugged one-mile loop trail that ascends 180 feet from the trail head. Constructed from the same pale volcanic stone as the cliffs themselves, the rooms are all but camouflaged until you are about .4 mi along the trail. You can contemplate, from a rare close-up vantage point, the keyhole doorways that punctuate the dwelling walls and gaze out upon a ponderosa pine- and cottonwood-forested terrain that looks much like the one the Mogollon people inhabited seven centuries ago. The wealth of pottery, yucca sandals, tools, and other artifacts buried here were picked clean by the late 1800s—dispersed to private collectors. But the visitor center has a small museum with books and other materials about the wilderness, its trails, and the Mogollon. It's a 2-mi drive from the visitor center to the Dwellings trail head (and other nearby trails); there are interesting pictographs to be seen on the wheelchair-accessible **Trail to the Past.**

◼**TIP→** Allow a good 2 hours from Silver City to the Cliff Dwellings via NM 15 or via NM 35; though longer in mileage, the NM 35 route is an easier ride. If you can spare the time, spend the night at one of the mountain inns close to the dwellings to maximize your time in the park.

⊠ *Off NM 15, 44 mi north of Silver City* ☎ *575/536–9461 or 575/536–9344* ⊕ *www.nps.gov/gicl* ⤳ *$3* ⊗ *Monument late May–early Sept., daily 8–6; early Sept.–late May, daily 9–4. Visitor center late May–early Sept., daily 8–5; early Sept.–late May, daily 8–4:30.*

U.S. 180 leads northwest about 50 mi from Silver City to Glenwood and **Whitewater Canyon—the gateway to the western reaches of the Gila.** A primary destination here is the splendid **Catwalk National Recreation Trail** (⊠ *Catwalk Rd. [NM 174]; turn east from U.S. 180 and proceed 5 mi*), a 250-foot-long metal walkway drilled into the sides of the massive rock cliffs of the breathtaking Whitewater Canyon—which is only 20 feet wide in places. This is one of the most verdant, beautiful canyons in the state, with the creek and tumbling waterfalls surrounded by gorgeous rocks and shade trees. The Catwalk, first installed as an access route for water lines critical to local gold- and silver-mining operations in the late 1800s, was rebuilt in 1935 for recreation purposes. A number of famous outlaws, including Butch Cassidy and the Wild Bunch, have used the canyon as a hideout because of its remote, and almost inaccessible, location. You need to be in reasonably good physical condition to scramble up some stone stairways, but the 2.2-mi round-trip trail is well-maintained and worth the effort; there is a nice alternate route that is wheelchair accessible. Bring your bathing suit so you can enjoy standing under the waterfalls and splashing in the creek. Admission is $3. Several miles north of the Catwalk on U.S. 180 is the **Glenwood State Trout Hatchery** (*Catwalk Rd. [NM 174]; turn east from U.S. 180 and proceed 1/4 mi* ☎ *575/539–2461*). There are picnic tables and a fishing pond with Rocky Mountain bighorn sheep grazing nearby. (just before the very little town of Alma, where you can get some snacks at the **Alma Grill** or Trading Post), and turn east onto NM 159. Your rewarding destination, about 45 minutes in, on a sometimes one-lane dirt road, is **Mogollon** (muh-gee-yohn). The gold-mining town, established in the 1880s, was a ghost town for many years but has been revived in the last few decades by a dozen or so residents who live there year-round. A small museum, an art gallery and a gift shop, and a café operate on the weekends. Book a stay at the Silver Creek Inn and you can spend the weekend exploring this interesting relic of the American West, as well as the breathtaking, and huge, Gila National Forest bordering it.

WHERE TO EAT AND STAY

Along the western reaches of the Gila, your best bets for dining and lodging are in the towns of Gila, Glenwood, Alma, Mogollon, and Reserve—all on (or just off) U.S. 180/NM 12. If you're venturing up to the Cliff Dwellings, consider spots in Pinos Altos or Gila Hot Springs, both along NM 15.

$$ ✕ **Buckhorn Saloon & Opera House.** Come here to see 1860s Western decor
STEAK and stay for the food—including some of the best steak and seafood
Fodor'sChoice in the region. The bar is a friendly place to gather for a drink, and has
★ live folk-flavored music Wednesday through Saturday; the dining rooms are cozy, the tablecloths white, and the walls replete with photos from the last 140 years of the area's history. The property also includes the Opera House, where melodramas are performed (on Friday and Saturday at 8). ⊠ *32 Main St., off NM 15, 7 mi north of Silver City, Pinos Altos* ☎ *575/538–9911* ⊕ *www.buckhornsaloonandoperahouse.com* ⚑ *Reservations essential* ☰ *MC, V* ☽ *Closed Sun. No lunch.*

$ ✕ **Carmen's.** Here's a great little place to stop on NM 12 in the north-
AMERICAN western reaches of the Gila National Forest. Not just because of the spicy enchiladas and chicken-fried steak, but because once you leave the hamlet of Reserve, New Mexico (population about 300), dinner options are scarce— Quemado is about 55 mi to the north. Alma and Glenwood are about 40 mi south. ⊠ *Main St., on NM 12, at NM 435, 40 mi north of GlenwoodReserve* ☎ *575/533–6990* ☰ *MC, V.*

$$ ⊡ **Bear Creek Motel & Cabins.** Gold panning, hiking, and fishing are
Fodor'sChoice among the popular activities at this Pinos Altos mountain getaway. A
★ ponderosa pine forest surrounds the silvered wood-and-stone, two-story
CABINS cabins, half of which have kitchens with cookware, and fireplaces. Rus-
☾ tic hand-hewn railings adorn the Adirondack-chair bedecked porches,

which have you sitting in the treetops—eye-level with all manner of birds and other wildlife. **Pros:** just 7 mi north of Silver City, but appealingly remote; en route to Gila Cliff Dwellings. **Cons:** dining choices nearby are limited. ⊠ *88 Main St. (NM 15), 7 mi north of Silver City, Pinos Altos Pinos Altos* ☎ *575/388–4501 or 888/388–4515* ⊕ *www.bearcreekcabins.com* ⤳ *15 cabins* ⚲ *In-room: no a/c, kitchen (some), refrigerator (some), Internet, Wi-Fi, DVD. In-hotel: some pets allowed* ⊟ *AE, D, DC, MC, V.*

$$
Fodor'sChoice
★
VILLAS

⚌ **Casitas de Gila.** On the western edge of the Gila Wilderness are five private casitas ("little houses" in Spanish) overlooking Bear Creek, nestled on 260 gorgeous acres. The night skies are brilliant, with countless stars twinkling, and the swath of the Milky Way glowing brightly. Each casita has its own spotting telescope or high-powered binoculars. Watching the stars from the shared hot tub is not to be missed. Guests have access to the organic herb garden (in season), which is super for those wanting to use the casitas' well-equipped kitchens and barbecue grills. Custom-crafted Southwestern-style furnishings, kiva fireplaces, radiant-heated floors, and generously appointed baths make for a perfect year-round getaway. The gracious and well-informed hosts offer star parties and tips on hiking and local geology; there are 9 mi of trails right on the property. There's also a very well-curated art gallery on-site. **Pros:** peace and quiet; mountain vistas and the brightest stars you've ever seen. **Cons:** be prepared for a remote getaway—it's a winding, slow (with some gravel) road for the last 4 mi, and the town of Gila doesn't offer much. ⊠ *50 Casita Flats Rd., off Hooker Loop, 30 mi northwest of Silver City, Gila* ☎ *575/535–4455 or 877/923–4827* ⊕ *www.casitasdegila.com* ⤳ *4 1-bedroom casitas, 1 2-bedroom casita* ⚲ *In-room: a/c, kitchen, refrigerator, no TV, Wi-Fi* ⊟ *AE, DC, MC, V* ⦿l *CP.*

$$
Fodor'sChoice
★
INN

⚌ **Silver Creek Inn.** Just getting to this property in the ghost town of Mogollon in the western region of the Gila is something of a thrill; the scenic and twisty mountain road that leads here has some heart-stopping, steep drop-offs along the way. Once you've arrived, settle into a room at the one-time J. P. Holland General Store, one of the original, two-story adobe structures in this old mining town, which is now all but abandoned (population about 15). The large, ochre-colored 1885 inn building has been refurbished beautifully, and further tweaks and finesses are an ongoing project for the committed innkeepers. Each of the four rooms has a private bath, and a delicious full breakfast is included in the room rate (rate is dropped $20 per person if you opt for the simpler Continental breakfast). Head here if you're looking for a relaxing getaway in an out-of-the-ordinary locale. The inn is open seasonally and is for adults 21 and over only. Walk-in arrangements are often possible, although advance reservations are recommended. **Pros:** a fantastic place to explore a ghost town and the western Gila Wilderness; an optional all-meal package is available. **Cons:** bookings are for weekends only (Friday and Saturday night), and the town itself is only open on weekends; isolated, with no Internet. ⊠ *Off NM 159; from Glenwood take U.S. 180 about 4 mi north, turn east onto NM 159 and travel about 9 mi of steep, sometimes rough, roadway, Mogollon* ☎ *866/276–4882* ⊕ *www.silvercreekinn.com* ⤳ *4 rooms* ⚲ *In-room: no*

8

a/c, no phone, no TV. In-hotel: no kids under 21 ◎ *Closed Nov.–Mar.* ⊟ *AE, D, MC, V* ❘◎❘ *BP.*

¢

MOTEL

⊡ **Whitewater Motel & Glenwood Rock Shop.** Here on the western rim of the Gila is a cozy haven of rustic Americana. The motel opened for business in 1948 and the original, hand-carved white-oak furniture is still in every room. Rooms are simple, comfortable, and immaculate. There's a long balcony off the back of all the rooms that looks out to the huge grassy yard where, when the water's high enough, you can hear the burble of Whitewater Creek beyond. Relaxing at the tables on the grass and listening to it rushing by is a real treat. The proprietor, Marianne, is also the postmistress (the post office is in the motel parking lot)—so if she doesn't pick up the phone, leave a message and be assured she'll call you back. There are two large family rooms that sleep five, for $67 a night. **Pros:** easy, economical location for Catwalk and Mogollon-area hikers; Wi-Fi available inside *and* outside the nearby library. **Cons:** no Internet; no phones. ⊠ *U.S. 180, in the center of town, west side of the street, Glenwood* ☏ *575/539–2581* ⌕ *6 rooms* ⚲ *In-room: a/c, no phone. In-hotel: some pets allowed.* ⊟ *AE, D, MC, V.*

$

INN

⊡ **The Wilderness Lodge & Hot Springs.** This basic retreat in the heart of the Gila Wilderness is a handy base if you want plenty of time to explore the Gila Cliff Dwellings, 4 mi north. An added bonus are two relaxing hot-springs pools. The lodge was built from a century-old former schoolhouse that was hauled here from Hurley and not very formally re-pieced together, making the place feel somewhat haphazard in its layout and construction, but comfortable nevertheless. The covered front porch is a great place to sit and enjoy coffee with the birds and trees. The stars at night are brilliant. Bring groceries—full, shared, kitchen facilities are available to make dinner. **Pros:** surrounded by mountains and rivers, this is truly secluded. **Cons:** no restaurants or shops nearby; shared bathrooms (except for suite). ⊠ *Off NM 15 at Gila Hot Springs, 14 mi north of NM 15 at NM 35 (40 mi north of Silver City), Gila Hot Springs* ☏ *575/536–9749* ⊕ *www.gilahot.com* ⌕ *5 rooms with shared bath, 1 suite* ⚲ *In-room: no a/c. In-hotel: some pets allowed* ⊟ *MC, V* ❘◎❘ *BP.*

Carlsbad Caverns National Park

WORD OF MOUTH

"Nothing can prepare you for the size and scope of the caverns. As you descend into the cave, you keep thinking that you must be near the bottom, but then you realize you're nowhere near. There are giant rooms the size of cathedrals that you keep passing through. It feels like another planet, otherwordly."

—bkluvsNola

WELCOME TO CARLSBAD CAVERNS NATIONAL PARK

TOP REASONS TO GO

★ **400,000 hungry bats:** Every night and every day, bats wing to and from the caverns in a swirling, visible tornado.

★ **Take a guided tour through the underworld:** Plummet 75 stories underground and step into enormous caves hung with stalactites and bristling with stalagmites.

★ **Living Desert Zoo and Gardens:** More preserve than zoo, this 1,500-acre park houses scores of rare species, including endangered Mexican wolves and Bolson tortoises, and now boasts a new black bear exhibit.

★ **Bird-watching at Rattlesnake Springs:** Nine-tenths of the park's 330 bird species, including roadrunners, golden eagles, and acrobatic cave swallows, visit this green desert oasis.

★ **Pecos River:** The Pecos River, a Southwest landmark, flows through the nearby town of Carlsbad. The river is always soothing, but gets festive for holiday floaters when riverside homeowners lavishly decorate their homes.

1 **Bat Flight.** Cowboy Jim White discovered the caverns after noticing that a swirling smokestack of bats appeared there each morning and evening. White is long gone, but the 300,000-member bat colony is still here, snatching up 3 tons of bugs a night. Watch them leave at dusk from the amphitheater located near the park visitor center.

2 **Carlsbad Caverns Big Room.** Travel 75 stories below the surface to visit the Big Room, where you can traipse beneath a 255-foot-tall ceiling and take in immense and eerie cave formations. Situated directly beneath the park visitor center, the room can be accessed via the quick-moving elevator or the natural cave entrance.

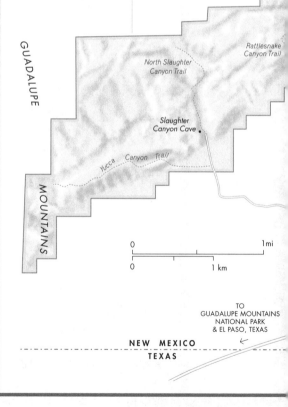

3 Living Desert Zoo and Gardens. Endangered river cooters, Bolson tortoises, and Mexican wolves all roam in the Living Desert Zoo and Gardens. You can also skip alongside roadrunners and slim wild turkeys in the park's aviary, or visit a small group of cougars. The Living Desert is located within the town of Carlsbad, New Mexico, 23 mi to the north of the park.

4 The Pecos River. Running through the town of Carlsbad, the Pecos River is a landmark of the Southwest. It skims through town and makes for excellent boating, waterskiing, and fishing. In the winter, residents gussy up dozens of riverside homes for the holiday season.

NEW MEXICO

GETTING ORIENTED

To get at the essence of Carlsbad Caverns National Park, you have to delve below the surface—literally. Most of the park's key sights are underground in a massive network of caves (there are 113 in all, although not all are open to visitors; a variety of tours leave from the visitor center). The park also has a handful of trails above ground, where you can experience the Chihuahua Desert and some magnificent geological formations.

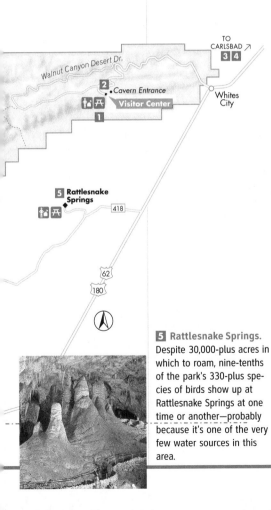

Walnut Canyon Desert Dr.

2 *Cavern Entrance*

Visitor Center

1

TO CARLSBAD ↗

3 4

Whites City

5 Rattlesnake Springs

418

62

180

5 Rattlesnake Springs. Despite 30,000-plus acres in which to roam, nine-tenths of the park's 330-plus species of birds show up at Rattlesnake Springs at one time or another—probably because it's one of the very few water sources in this area.

KEY	
	Ranger Station
	Picnic Area
	Walking/Hiking Trails

9

CARLSBAD CAVERNS NATIONAL PARK PLANNER

When to Go

While the desert above may alternately bake or freeze, the caverns remain in the mid-50s. If you're coming to see the Mexican free-tailed bat, come between spring and late fall.

Getting Here and Around

Carlsbad Caverns is 27 mi southwest of Carlsbad, New Mexico, and 35 mi north of Guadalupe Mountains National Park via U.S. 62/180. The nearest full-service airport is in El Paso, 154 mi away. The 9½-mi Walnut Canyon Desert Drive loop is one-way. It's a curvy, gravel road and is not recommended for motor homes or trailers. Be alert for wildlife crossing roadways, especially in the early morning and at night.

AVG. HIGH/LOW TEMPS.

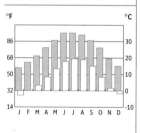

Flora and Fauna

Without a doubt, the park's most prominent and popular residents are Mexican free-tailed bats. These bats have bodies that barely span a woman's hand, yet sport wings that would cover a workingman's boot. Female bats give birth to a single pup each year, which usually weighs more than a quarter of what an adult bat does. Their tiny noses and big ears enable them to search for the many tons of bugs they consume over their lifetime. Numbering nearly a third of a million, these tiny creatures are the park's mascot.

Famous fanged flyers aside, there is much more wildlife to recommend in the park. One of New Mexico's best bird-watching areas is at Rattlesnake Springs. Summer and fall migrations give you the best chance of spotting the most varieties of the more than 330 species of birds. Lucky visitors may spot a golden eagle, a rare visitor, or get the thrill of glimpsing a brilliant, gray-and-crimson vermilion flycatcher.

Snakes generally appear in summer. ■TIP➔ **If you're out walking, be wary of different rattlesnake species, such as banded-rock and diamondbacks. If you see one, don't panic. Rangers say they are more scared of us than we are of them. Don't make any sudden moves, and slowly walk around or back away from the vipers.**

This area is also remarkable because of its location in the Chihuahua Desert, which sprouts unique plant life. There are thick stands of raspy-leaved yuccas, as well as the agave (mescal) plants that were once a food source for early Apache tribes. The leaves of this leggy plant are still roasted in sand pits by Apache elders during traditional celebrations.

In spring, thick stands of yucca plants unfold yellow flowers on their tall stalks. Blossoming cacti and desert wildflowers are one of the natural wonders of Walnut Canyon. You'll see bright red blossoms adorning ocotillo plants, and sunny yellow blooms sprouting from prickly pear cactus.

Updated by
Georgia de
Katona

On the surface, Carlsbad Caverns National Park is deceptively normal—but all bets are off once visitors set foot in the elevator, which plunges 75 stories underground. The country beneath the surface is part silky darkness, part subterranean hallucination. The snaky, illuminated walkway seems less like a trail and more like a foray across the River Styx and into the underworld. Within more than 14 football fields of subterranean space are hundreds of formations that alternately resemble cakes, soda straws, ocean waves, and the large, leering face of a mountain troll.

PARK ESSENTIALS

ACCESSIBILITY

Though the park covers a huge expanse above ground (and there are paved roads traversing the grounds), most of the parts you'll want to see are below the surface. Routes through the caverns are paved and well maintained, and portions of the paved Big Room trails in Carlsbad Caverns are accessible to wheelchairs. A map defining appropriate routes is available at the visitor center information desk. Strollers are not permitted on trails (use a baby pack instead). Individuals who may have difficulty walking should access the Big Room via elevator.

ADMISSION FEES AND PERMITS

No fee is charged for parking or to enter the aboveground portion of the park. It costs $6 to descend into Carlsbad Caverns either by elevator or through the Natural Entrance. Costs for special tours range from $7 to $20 plus general admission.

Those planning overnight hikes must obtain a free backcountry permit, and all hikers are advised to stop at the visitor center information desk for current information about trails. Trails are poorly defined, but can be followed with a topographic map. Dogs are not allowed in the park, but a kennel is available at the park visitor center.

ADMISSION HOURS

The park is open year-round, except Christmas Day. From Memorial Day weekend through Labor Day, tours are conducted from 8:30 to 5; the last entry into the cave via the Natural Entrance is at 3:30, and the last entry into the cave via the elevator is at 5. After Labor Day until Memorial Day weekend, tours are conducted from 8:30 to 3:30; the last entry into the cave via the Natural Entrance is at 2, and the last entry into the cave via the elevator is at 3:30. Carlsbad Caverns is in the mountain time zone.

9

ATMS/BANKS

There are no ATMs in the park; the nearest ones are in White's City or Carlsbad.

CELL-PHONE RECEPTION

Cell phones rarely receive decent reception in the park. Public telephones are at the visitor center.

PART CONTACT INFORMATION

Carlsbad Caverns National Park ⊠ *3225 National Parks Hwy., Carlsbad* ☎ *575/785–2232 info, 800/967–2283 reservations for special cave tours, 800/388–2733 cancellations* ⊕ *www.nps.gov/cave.*

SCENIC DRIVE

Walnut Canyon Desert Drive. This scenic drive begins ½ mi from the visitor center. It travels 9½ mi along the top of a ridge to the edge of Rattlesnake Canyon and sinks back down through upper Walnut Canyon to the main entrance road. The backcountry scenery on this one-way gravel loop is stunning; go late in the afternoon or early in the morning to enjoy the full spectrum of changing light and dancing colors. Along the way, you'll be able to see Big Hill Seep's trickling water, the tall, flowing ridges of the Guadalupe Mountains range, and maybe even some robust mule deer.

WHAT TO SEE

SCENIC STOPS

⟳ **The Big Room.** With a floor space equal to about 14 football fields, this
Fodor's Choice underground focal point of Carlsbad Caverns clues visitors in to just
★ how large the caverns really are. Its caverns are close enough to the trail to cause voices to echo, but the chamber itself is so vast voices don't echo far; the White House could fit in just one corner of the Big Room, and wouldn't come close to grazing the 255-foot ceiling. The 1-mi loop walk on a mostly level, paved trail is self-guided. An audio guide is also available from park rangers for a few dollars. Kids under 15 are admitted free of charge. ⊠ *At the visitor center* 🎫 *$6* ☉ *Late May–early Sept., daily 8–5 (last entry into the Natural Entrance is at 3:30; last entry into the elevator is at 5); early Sept.–late May, daily 8:30–3:30 (last entry into the Natural Entrance at 2; last entry into the elevator at 3:30).*

Natural Entrance. A self-guided, paved trail leads from the natural cave entrance. The route is winding and sometimes slick from water seepage above ground. A steep descent of about 750 feet takes you about a mile through the main corridor and past features such as the Bat Cave and the Boneyard. (Despite its eerie name, the formations here don't look much like femurs and fibulas; they're more like spongy bone insides.) Iceberg Rock is a 200,000-ton boulder that dropped from the cave ceiling some millennia ago. After about a mile, you'll link up underground with the 1-mi Big Room trail and return to the surface via elevator. ⊠ *At the visitor center* 🎫 *$6* ☉ *Late May–early Sept., daily 8:30–3:30; early Sept.–late May, daily 9–2.*

CARLSBAD CAVERNS IN ONE DAY

In a single day, visitors can easily view both the eerie, exotic caverns and the volcano of bats that erupts from the caverns each morning and evening. Unless you're attending the annual Bat Breakfast, when visitors have the morning meal with rangers and then view the early morning bat return, go ahead and sleep past sunrise and then stroll into the caves.

For the full experience, begin by taking the **Natural Entrance** self-guided tour, which allows visitors to trek into the cave from surface level. This tour winds past the Boneyard, with its intricate ossifications, and a 200,000-ton boulder called the Iceberg. After 1¼ mi, or about an hour, the route links up with the **Big Room loop.** If you're not in good health or are traveling with young children, you might want to skip the Natural Entrance and start with the Big Room loop trail, which begins at the foot of the elevator. This underground walk extends 1¼ mi on level, paved ground, and takes about 1½

hours to complete. If you have made reservations in advance or happen upon some openings, you also can take the additional **King's Palace** guided tour for 1 mi and an additional 1½ hours. At 83 stories deep, the palace is the lowest rung the public can visit. By this time, you will have spent four hours in the cave. Take the elevator back up to the top. If you're not yet tuckered out, consider a short hike along the sunny, self-guided ½-mi **Desert Nature Walk** by the visitor center.

To picnic by the birds, bees, and water of **Rattlesnake Springs,** take U.S. 62/180 south from White's City 5½ mi, and turn back west onto Route 418. You'll find old-growth shade trees, grass, picnic tables, and water. Many varieties of birds flit from tree to tree. Return to the Carlsbad Caverns entrance road and take the 9½-mi Walnut Canyon Desert Drive loop. Leave yourself enough time to return to the **visitor center** for the evening bat flight.

Rattlesnake Springs. Enormous cottonwood trees shade the picnic and recreation area at this cool oasis near Black River. The rare desert wetland harbors butterflies, mammals, and reptiles, as well as 90% of the park's 330 bird species. Don't let its name scare you; there may be rattlesnakes here, but not more than at any other similar site in the Southwest. Overnight camping and parking are not allowed. ⊠ *Hwy. 418 ⊹ Take U.S. 62/180 5½ mi south of White's City and turn west onto Hwy. 418 for 2½ mi.*

VISITOR CENTER

Carlsbad Caverns National Park Visitor Center. A 75-seat theater offers an engrossing film about the different types of caves, as well as an orientation video that explains cave etiquette. Some of the rules include staying on paths so you don't get lost, keeping objects and trash in your pockets and not on the ground, and not touching the formations. Besides laying down the ground rules, visitor center exhibits offer a primer on bats, geology, wildlife, and the early tribes and nomads that once lived in and passed through the Carlsbad Caverns area. Friendly rangers staff an information desk, where tickets and maps are sold. Two gift shops also are on the premises. ⊠ *7 mi west of park entrance at White's City,*

9

off U.S. 62/180 ☎ 575/785–2232 ⊙ Late May–late Aug., daily 8–7; early Sept.–late May, daily 8–5.

SPORTS AND THE OUTDOORS

BIRD-WATCHING

From warty-headed turkey vultures to svelte golden eagles, about 330 species of birds have been identified in Carlsbad Caverns National Park. Ask for a checklist at the visitor center and then start looking for greater roadrunners, red-winged blackbirds, white-throated swifts, northern flickers, and pygmy nuthatches.

Rattlesnake Springs. Offering one of the best bird habitats in New Mexico, this is a natural wetland with old-growth cottonwoods. Because southern New Mexico is in the northernmost region of the Chihuahua Desert, you're likely to see birds that can't be found anywhere else in the United States outside extreme southern Texas and Arizona. If you see a flash of crimson, you might have spotted a vermilion flycatcher. Wild turkeys also flap around this oasis. ⊠ *Hwy. 418, 2½ mi west of U.S. 62/180, 5½ mi south of White's City.*

Fodor's Choice ★

HIKING

Deep, dark, and mysterious, the Carlsbad Caverns are such a park focal point that the 30,000-plus acres of wilderness above them have gone largely undeveloped. This is great news for people who pull on their hiking boots when they're looking for solitude. What you find are rudimentary trails that crisscross the dry, textured terrain and lead up to elevations of 6,000 feet or more. These routes often take a half-day or more to travel; at least one, Guadalupe Ridge Trail, is long enough that it calls for an overnight stay. Walkers who just want a little dusty taste of desert flowers and wildlife should try the Desert Nature Walk.

Finding the older, less well-maintained trails can be difficult. Pick up a topographical map at the visitor center bookstore, and be sure to pack a lot of water. There's none out in the desert, and you'll need at least a gallon per person per day. The high elevation coupled with a potent sunshine punch can deliver a nasty sunburn, so be sure to pack SPF 30 (or higher) sunblock and a hat, even in winter. You can't bring a pet or a gun, but you do have to bring a backcountry permit if you're camping. They're free at the visitor center.

EASY

Desert Nature Walk. While waiting for the night bat-flight program, try taking the ½-mi self-guided hike. The tagged and identified flowers

---

A LONG WAY DOWN

The newest discovery in Carlsbad Caverns National Park is **Lechuguilla Cave**, the deepest limestone cave in the United States. Scientists began mapping the cave network in 1986, and though they've located more than 120 mi of caverns extending to a depth of more than 1,600 feet, much more of this area along the park's northern border remains to be investigated. Lechuguilla is not open to the public, but an exhibit describing it can be viewed at the visitor center.

and plants make this a good place to get acquainted with much of the local desert flora. The paved trail is wheelchair accessible and an easy jaunt for even the littlest ones. The payoff is great for everyone, too: a big, vivid view of the desert basin. ⊠ *Trail begins off the cavern entrance trail, 200 yards east of the visitor center.*

> **GOOD READ**
>
> ■ *Jim White's Own Story*, by early explorer Jim White, tells of this cowboy's exploits into the heart of Carlsbad Caverns, before it was developed as a national park.

Rattlesnake Canyon Overlook Trail. A ¼-mi stroll off Walnut Canyon Desert Drive offers a nice overlook of the greenery of Rattlesnake Canyon. ⊠ *Trail begins at mile marker 9 on Walnut Canyon Desert Dr.*

MODERATE

Juniper Ridge Trail. Climb up in elevation as you head north on this nearly 3-mi trail, which leads to the northern edge of the park and then turns toward Crooked Canyon. Although not the most notable trail, it's challenging enough to keep things interesting. Allow yourself half a day, and be sure to bring lots of water, especially when the temperature is high. ⊠ *Trailhead at mile marker 8.8 of Desert Loop Dr.*

Old Guano Road Trail. Meandering a little more than 3½ mi one way on mostly flat terrain, the trail dips sharply toward White's City campground, where the trail ends. Give yourself about half a day to complete the walk. Depending on the temperature, this walk can be taxing. Drink lots of water. ⊠ *Trailhead at the Bat Flight Amphitheater, near the natural cave entrance and visitor center.*

Rattlesnake Canyon Trail. Rock cairns loom over this trail, which descends from 4,570 to 3,900 feet as it winds into the canyon. Allow half a day to trek down into the canyon and make the somewhat strenuous climb out; the total trip is about 6 mi. ⊠ *Trail begins at mile marker 9 on Walnut Canyon Desert Dr.*

Fodor's Choice ★ **Yucca Canyon Trail.** Sweeping views of the Guadalupe Mountains and El Capitan give allure to this trail. Drive past Rattlesnake Springs and stop at the park boundary before reaching the Slaughter Canyon Cave parking lot. Turn west along the boundary fence line to the trailhead. The 6-mi round-trip begins at the mouth of Yucca Canyon, and climbs up to the top of the escarpment. Here you find the panoramic view. Most people turn around at this point; the hearty can continue along a poorly maintained route that follows the top of the ridge. The first part of the hike takes half a day. If you continue on, the hike takes a full day. ⊠ *Trail begins at Slaughter Canyon Cave parking lot, Hwy. 418, 10 mi west of U.S. 62/180.*

DIFFICULT

Guadalupe Ridge Trail. This long, winding ramble follows an old road all the way to the west edge of the park. Because of its length (about 12 mi), an overnight stay in the backcountry is suggested. The hike may be long, but for serious hikers the up-close-and-personal views into Rattlesnake and Slaughter canyons are more than worth it—not to

9

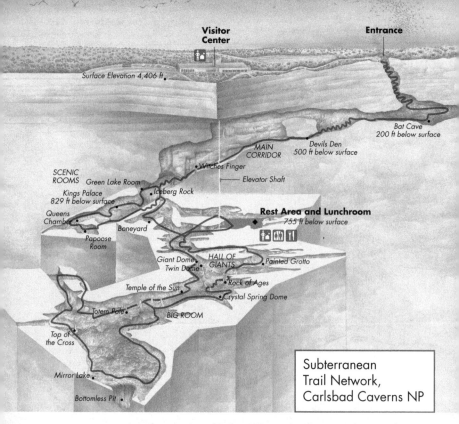

Subterranean
Trail Network,
Carlsbad Caverns NP

mention the serenity of being miles and miles away from civilization. ✉ *Trailhead 4.8 mi down Desert Loop Dr.*

North Slaughter Canyon Trail. Beginning at the Slaughter Canyon Cave parking lot, the trail traverses a heavily vegetated canyon bottom into a remote part of the park. As you begin hiking, look off to the east (to your right) to see the dun-colored ridges and wrinkles of the Elephant Back formation, the first of many dramatic limestone formations visible from the trail. The route travels 5½ mi one way, the last 3 mi steeply climbing onto a limestone ridge escarpment. Allow a full day for the round-trip. ✉ *Trail begins at Slaughter Canyon Cave parking lot, Hwy. 418, 10 mi west of U.S. 62/180.*

SPELUNKING

Carlsbad Caverns is famous for the beauty and breadth of its inky depths, as well as for the accessibility of some of its largest caves. All cave tours are ranger led, so safety is rarely an issue in the caves, no matter how remote. There are no other tour guides in the area, nor is there an equipment retailer other than the Wal-Mart located in Carlsbad, 23 mi away. Depending on the difficulty of your cave selection (Spider Cave is the hardest to navigate), you'll need at most knee pads, flashlight batteries, sturdy pants, hiking boots with ankle support, and some water.

Hall of the White Giant. Plan to squirm through some tight passages for long distances to access a very remote chamber, where you'll see towering, glistening white formations that explain the name of this feature. This strenuous, ranger-led tour lasts about four hours. Steep drop-offs might elate you—or make you queasy. Wear sturdy hiking shoes and bring four AA batteries

> **FLYING BLIND**
>
> Bats use a type of sonar system called echolocation to orient themselves and locate their insect dinners at night. About 15 species of bats live in Carlsbad Caverns, although the Mexican free-tailed is the most predominant.

and knee pads with you. Visitors must be at least six years old. Be at the Visitor Center at 12:45 on Saturday for the 1 pm tour. ⊠ *At the visitor center* ☎ *800/967–2283* ✉ *$20* ⚠ *Reservations essential* ⊙ *Tour Sat. at 1.*

King's Palace. Throughout King's Palace, you'll see leggy "soda straws" large enough for a giant to sip and multitiered curtains of stone—sometimes by the light of just a few flashlights. The mile-long walk is on a paved trail, but there's one very steep hill. This ranger-guided tour lasts about 1½ hours and gives you the chance to experience a blackout, when all lights are extinguished. While advance reservations are highly recommended, this is the one tour you might be able to sign up for on the spot. Children younger than six aren't allowed on this tour. ⊠ *At the visitor center* ☎ *800/967–2283* ✉ *$8* ⊙ *Tours late May–early Sept., daily 10, 11, 2, and 3; early Sept.–late May, daily 10 and 2.*

Lower Cave. Fifty-foot vertical ladders and a dirt path will take you into undeveloped portions of Carlsbad Caverns. It takes about half a day to negotiate this moderately strenuous side trip led by a knowledgeable ranger. Children younger than six are not allowed on this tour. ⊠ *Tours depart from the underground lunch center* ☎ *800/967–2283* ✉ *$20* ⚠ *Reservations essential* ⊙ *Tour weekdays at 1.*

★ **Slaughter Canyon Cave.** Discovered in the 1930s by a local goatherd, this cave is one of the most popular secondary sites in the park, about 23 mi southwest of the main Carlsbad Caverns and visitor center. Both the hike to the cave mouth and the tour will take about half a day, but it's worth it to view the deep cavern darkness as it's punctuated only by flashlights and, sometimes, headlamps. From the Slaughter Canyon parking area, give yourself 45 minutes to make the steep ½-mi climb up a trail leading to the mouth of the cave. Arrange to be there a quarter of an hour earlier than the appointed time. You'll find that the cave consists primarily of a single corridor, 1,140 feet long, with numerous side passages.

You can take some worthwhile pictures of this cave. Wear hiking shoes with ankle support, and carry plenty of water. You're also expected to bring your own two-D-cell flashlight. Children younger than six are not permitted. It's a great adventure if you're in shape and love caving. ⊠ *End of Hwy. 418, 10 mi west of U.S. 62/180* ☎ *800/967–2283* ✉ *$15* ⚠ *Reservations essential* ⊙ *Tours Memorial Day–Labor Day, daily at*

9

10 and 1; post–Labor Day–Dec., weekends at 10; Jan.–Memorial Day, weekends at 10 and 1.

Spider Cave. Visitors may not expect to have an adventure in a cavern system as developed and well stocked as Carlsbad Caverns, but serious cavers and energetic types have the chance to clamber up tight tunnels, stoop under overhangs, and climb up steep, rocky pitches. This backcountry cave is listed as "wild," a clue that you might need a similar nature to attempt a visit. Plan to wear your warm, but least-favorite clothes, as they'll probably get streaked with grime. You'll also need soft knee pads, 4 AA batteries, leather gloves, and water. The gloves and pads are to protect you on long, craggy clambers and the batteries are for your flashlight. It will take you half a day to complete this ranger-led tour noted for its adventure. Visitors must be at least six years old and absolutely not claustrophobic. ⊠ *Meet at visitor center* ☎ *800/967–2283* 🖅 *$20* ⚠ *Reservations essential* ☉ *Tour Sun. at 1.*

EXPEDITIONS Spelunkers who wish to explore both developed and wild caves can go on **Ranger-led Tours** (☎ *800/967–2283*). Reservations for the six different tours, which include the **Hall of the White Giant** and **Spider Cave,** known for its tight twists and grimy climbs, are required at least a day in advance. Payment is by credit card over the phone or online (or by mailing in a check, if you're making reservations 21 days or more in advance; but confirm first that space is available). Those who want to go it alone outside the more established caverns can get permits and information about 10 backcountry caves from the **Cave Resources Office** (☎ *575/785–2232*). Heed rangers' advice for these remote, undeveloped, nearly unexplored caves.

EDUCATIONAL OFFERINGS

RANGER PROGRAMS

Fodor'sChoice **Evening Bat Flight Program.** In the amphitheater at the natural cave
★ entrance (off a short trail from main parking lot) a ranger discusses the park's batty residents before the creatures begin their sundown exodus. The bats aren't on a strict schedule, so it's best to check with park staff for approximate flight times. ⊠ *Natural cave entrance, at the visitor center* 🖅 *Free* ☉ *Mid-May–mid-Oct., nightly at sundown.*

WHAT'S NEARBY

NEARBY TOWNS

On the Pecos River, with 2¾ mi of beaches and picturesque riverside pathways, **Carlsbad, New Mexico,** seems suspended between the past and the present. It's part university town, part Old West, with a robust Mexican kick. The Territorial town square, a block from the river, encircles a Pueblo-style country courthouse designed by New Mexican architect John Gaw Meem. Seven miles east of the caverns is **White's City,** grown from a tiny outpost to a small outpost. This privately owned town is

FESTIVALS AND EVENTS

MAY

Mescal Roast and Mountain Spirit Dances. This May celebration held at the Living Desert Zoo and Gardens commemorates the connection that indigenous Mescalero Apaches have long had with the Guadalupe Mountains, where mescal plants were gathered for food. Descendants of the original Mescaleros perform a blessing in their native language, and everyone gets to taste the fruit from the mescal-baking pits. ☎ 575/887–5516.

AUGUST

Bat Flight Breakfast. On the second Thursday in August, early risers gather at the cave's entrance to eat breakfast and watch tens of thousands of bats come home ($7.50, includes free entry to self-guided trails at the caverns). ☎ 575/887–6516.

DECEMBER

Christmas on the Pecos. Stellar Christmas displays decorate Carlsbad mansions along a 3-mi-plus stretch of the Pecos River. Boat tours ($17.50 Friday and Saturday, $12.50 Sunday to Thursday) run from November 26 through New Year's Eve except Christmas Eve. ☎ 575/887–6516; ⊕ www. christmasonthepecos.com.

the nearest place to Carlsbad Caverns and contains dining and lodging options, plus the essentials.

VISITOR INFORMATION

Carlsbad Chamber of Commerce (✉ 302 S. Canal St., Carlsbad ☎ 575/887–6516 ⊕ www.carlsbadchamber.com) **White's City Inc.** ✉ 17 Carlsbad Caverns Hwy., White's City ☎ 575/785–2295.

NEARBY ATTRACTIONS

9

Brantley Lake State Park. In addition to 42,000-acre Brantley Lake, this park 12 mi north of Carlsbad offers 51 developed campsites and a number of primitive camping areas, nature trails, a visitor center, and fine fishing for largemouth bass, bluegill, crappie, and walleye pike (though authorities recommend practicing catch-and-release due to the high levels of contaminants in fish caught here). You can boat here, too. ✉ CR 30 (Capitan Reef Rd.), 5 mi off U.S. 285 ☎ 575/457–2384 ⊕ www.emnrd.state.nm.us/PRD/ParksPages/Brantley.htm 🖭 $5 per vehicle ⊘ Daily dawn–dusk.

Carlsbad Museum and Arts Center. Pueblo pottery, American Indian artifacts, and early cowboy and ranch memorabilia are here, along with exhibitions of contemporary art. The real treasure, though, is the McAdoo Collection, with works by painters of the Taos Society of Artists. ✉ 418 W. Fox St., Carlsbad ☎ 575/887–0276 🖭 Free ⊘ Mon.–Sat. 10–5.

☾ **Living Desert Zoo and Gardens State Park.** The park contains impressive
★ plants and animals native to the Chihuahua Desert. The Desert Arboretum has hundreds of exotic cacti and succulents, and the Living Desert Zoo—more a reserve than a traditional zoo—is home to mountain lions, deer, elk, wolves, bison, and endangered Mexican wolves, which

are more petite than their snarly kin. Nocturnal exhibits and dioramas let you in on the area's nighttime wildlife, too. Though there are shaded rest areas, restrooms, and water fountains, in hot weather it's best to visit during the early morning or early evening, when it's cooler. ⊠ *1504 Miehls Dr., off U.S. 285 Carlsbad* ☎ *575/887–5516* ☜ *Tour $5* ☽ *Late May–early Sept., daily 8–5; early Sept.–late May, daily 8–5; last admission 1½ hrs before closing.*

Carlsbad offers a few small gift emporiums that sell candles, crafts, postcards, and Southwest silver jewelry.

WHERE TO EAT AND STAY

ABOUT THE RESTAURANTS
Choice isn't an issue inside Carlsbad Caverns National Park because there are just three dining options—the surface-level café, the underground restaurant, and the bring-it-in-yourself option. Luckily, everything is reasonably priced (especially for national park eateries).

ABOUT THE HOTELS
The only overnight option within the arid, rugged park is to make your own campsite in the backcountry, at least half a mile from any trail.

Outside the park, however, options expand. White's City, which is less than 10 mi to the east of the park, contains two no-frills motels—worth staying at only if you just cannot drive to Carlsbad or Artesia. Both are near the boardwalk that connects shopping and entertainment options. In Carlsbad there are even more choices, but many of them aren't as appealing as they once were. The hotels here are aging and not particularly well maintained, so don't expect a mint on your pillow. Still, most are clean, if less than opulent.

ABOUT THE CAMPGROUNDS
Backcountry camping is by permit only (obtained for free at the visitor center). No campfires allowed in the park, and all camping is hike-to. Commercial sites can be found in White's City and Carlsbad.

WHAT IT COSTS				
¢	$	$$	$$$	$$$$
Restaurants	under $8	$8–$12	$13–$20	$21–$30	over $30
Hotels	under $70	$70–$100	$101–$150	$151–$200	over $200
Camping	under $10	$10–$17	$18–$35	$36–$50	over $50

Restaurant prices are per person for a main course at dinner. Hotel prices are per night for two people in a standard double room in high season, excluding taxes and services charges. Camping prices are for a standard (no hookups, pit toilets, fire grates, picnic tables) campsite per night.

WHERE TO EAT

IN THE PARK

¢ ✕ **Carlsbad Caverns Trading Company.** This comfy aboveground, cafeteria-
AMERICAN style restaurant covers the basics—hamburgers, sandwiches, burritos,
and salads. ✉ *Visitor center, 7 mi west of U.S. 62/180 at the end of the
main park road* ☎ *575/785–2281* ▤ *AE, D, MC, V* ☻ *Closes at 7 pm
Memorial Day weekend–Labor Day; closes at 5 pm after Labor Day.*

¢ ✕ **Underground Lunchroom.** Grab a snack, soft drink, or club sandwich
FAST FOOD for a quick break while you're down below the surface. Service is quick,
even when there's a crowd. ✉ *Visitor center, 7 mi west of U.S. 62/180 at
the end of the main park road* ☎ *575/785–2281* ▤ *AE, D, MC, V* ☻ *No
dinner. Closes at 5 pm Memorial Day weekend–Labor Day; closes at
3:30 pm after Labor Day.*

PICNIC AREAS **Rattlesnake Springs.** Of the couple of places to picnic in the park, this is
the best by far. There are about a dozen picnic tables and grills here,
and drinking water and chemical toilets are available. ✉ *Hwy. 418, 2½
mi west of U.S. 62/180.*

OUTSIDE THE PARK

$ ✕ **Bamboo Garden Restaurant.** This well-regarded restaurant—one of few
CHINESE Asian options in southeast New Mexico— is attractively decorated and
★ has a popular buffet. ✉ *1511 N. Canal St., Carlsbad* ☎ *575/887–5145*
▤ *MC, V* ☻ *Closed Mon.*

$$ ✕ **J.J.'s Steakhouse.** In White's City, formerly the Velvet Garter, J.J's serves
AMERICAN American-style steaks, burgers, and chicken in a faux-Old West atmo-
sphere. Food quality and service is uneven, but it's a convenient place
for a meal if you don't want to drive an additional 20 mi north to
Carlsbad. There's also a full-service bar. ✉ *26 Carlsbad Caverns Hwy.,
White's City* ☎ *800/228–3767* ▤ *AE, D, MC, V* ☻ *No lunch.*

$ ✕ **Lucy's Mexicali Restaurant & Entertainment Club.** "The best margaritas
MEXICAN and hottest chile in the world" is the ambitious motto of this family-
owned Mexican food joint. All the New Mexican staples are prepared
here, plus some not-so-standard items such as chicken fajita burritos
and enchiladas served the New Mexico way—that is, flat with an egg on
top. Try the Tucson-style chimichangas and brisket *carnitas* (beef brisket
or chicken sautéed with chiles and seasonings). Low-fat and fat-free
Mexican dishes are served, and there's a full bar with 13 beers on tap.
✉ *701 S. Canal St., Carlsbad* ☎ *575/887–7714* ▤ *AE, D, DC, MC, V.*

$ ✕ **Red Chimney.** If you hanker for sweet-and-tangy barbecue, this homey,
BARBECUE log-cabin-style spot is the place for you. Sauce from an old family recipe
is slathered on chicken, pork, beef, turkey, and ham here. Fried catfish,
burgers, and delicious sourdough-topped cobbler are also served. Cold,
cold beer and wine help wash it all down. ✉ *817 N. Canal St., Carlsbad*
☎ *575/885–8744* ▤ *AE, MC, V* ☻ *Closed weekends.*

WHERE TO STAY

IN THE PARK

Backcountry camping is the only lodging option in the park (⇨ *About
the Campgrounds, above).*

OUTSIDE THE PARK

$$ ⊡ **Best Western Stevens Inn.** This friendly, family-owned hotel has under-
★ gone extensive updating and renovation in recent years. Etched glass
and carved wooden doors add a touch of elegance, and prints of western
landscapes decorate the spacious rooms while prime rib and steaks are
served in the evening at the motel's Flume Room Restaurant and Cof-
fee Shop, which opens at 5:30 am daily. **Pros:** established and comfort-
able; lots of discounts offered; airport shuttle. **Cons:** lackluster service;
noisy crowds from adjacent dance club. ⊠ *1829 S. Canal St., Carls-
bad* ☎ *575/887–2851 or 800/730–2851* ⟿ *222 rooms* ⚹ *In-room: a/c,
refrigerator, Wi-Fi. In-hotel: restaurant, bar, pool, laundry facilities,
some pets allowed* ☱ *AE, D, DC, MC, V* ⊺◉⊦ *BP.*

$$ ⊡ **Holiday Inn Express.** The area isn't renowned for its upscale accommodations, so residents and travelers were happy when this nicely
maintained hotel came on the scene in 2008. With its indoor pool and
substantial fitness center, the hotel is a reliable favorite. **Pros:** spotlessly clean; full breakfast included. **Cons:** a little farther away from
the park than some of the other hotels. ⊠ *2210 W. Pierce St., Carlsbad*
☎ *575/234–1252* ⟿ *80 rooms, 24 suites* ⚹ *In-room: Wi-Fi. In-hotel:
pool, spa, gym, Internet terminal* ☱ *AE, D, DC, MC, V* ⊺◉⊦ *BP.*

$$ ⊡ **Rodeway Inn.** This two-story motor inn just outside the Carlsbad
Caverns entrance has no-nonsense rooms with Southwestern decor.
All guests are free to use the water park, open May through Septem-
ber, which features two 150-foot waterslides. **Pros:** close to Carlsbad
National Park; water park is a boon in summer. **Cons:** cleanliness of
rooms and service are spotty. ⊠ *17 Carlsbad Caverns Hwy., look for
large registration sign on south side of road, White's City* ☎ *575/785–
2296* ⟿ *63 rooms* ⚹ *In-room: a/c, Wi-Fi. In-hotel: pool, some pets
allowed* ☱ *AE, D, DC, MC, V* ⊺◉⊦ *BP.*

CAMPING

$$–$$$ ⚞ **Carlsbad RV Park & Campground.** This full-service campground inside
the city limits has level gravel sites and an indoor swimming pool.
Camping cabins with heating and air-conditioning are available, as are
phone hookups and a meeting room. Reservations are recommended
in summer. A professional RV service center where repairs can be made
is next door. **Pros:** full-service campground; free Wi-Fi. **Cons:** sites are
close together. ⊠ *4301 National Parks Hwy., Carlsbad* ☎ *575/885–
6333 or 888/878–7275* ⊕ *www.carlsbadrvpark.com* ⟿ *102 RV sites, 41
tent sites* ⚹ *Flush toilets, full hookups, partial hookups, dump station,
drinking water, guest laundry, showers, grills, picnic tables, electricity,
public telephone, general store, play area, swimming* ☱ *MC, V.*

Travel Smart
New Mexico

GETTING HERE AND AROUND

A tour bus or car is the best way to take in the entire state. Public transportation options do exist in some metropolitan areas, but they are not very convenient for visitors. City buses and taxi service are available only in a few larger communities such as Albuquerque, Santa Fe, and Las Cruces. Don't expect to find easy transportation for rural excursions.

▌AIR TRAVEL

If you're visiting central or northern New Mexico, it's best to fly into Albuquerque, and if you're headed to the southern part of the state, El Paso may make more sense. However, El Paso is smaller and served by far fewer flights, so depending on where you're flying from it can still be easier to fly into Albuquerque than El Paso even when visiting the southern part of the state. Some visitors to Taos and northeastern New Mexico may also want to consider flying into Denver, which is an hour or two farther than Albuquerque but receives a high number of direct domestic and international flights. Santa Fe receives daily direct flights on American Eagle from both Dallas and Los Angeles. From Albuquerque airport, ground transportation is available throughout north-central New Mexico, and commuter air service is available to Farmington, Clovis, Ruidoso, Silver City, and a few other communities around the state. El Paso has ground transportation to Las Cruces. Although Albuquerque and El Paso have small, clean, and user-friendly airports, they also have relatively few direct flights compared with larger cities around the country. With a few exceptions, travelers coming from the East Coast and to a certain extent the West Coast have to connect through other airports to fly into Albuquerque and, especially, El Paso.

The least expensive airfares to New Mexico are priced for round-trip travel and must usually be purchased in advance.

Because the discount airline Southwest serves Albuquerque and El Paso, fares from these cities to airports served by Southwest are often 20% to 40% less than to other airports (whether or not you actually fly Southwest, as competing airlines often match Southwest's fares).

Flying time between Albuquerque and Los Angeles is 2 hours for direct flights (available only on Southwest Airlines and United Airlines) and 3½ to 4 when connecting through another airport; Chicago, 2 hours and 45 minutes; New York, 5½ to 6½ hours (there are no direct flights, so this factors in time for connections); Dallas, 1 hour and 45 minutes.

AIRPORTS

The major gateway to New Mexico is Albuquerque International Sunport (ABQ), which is 65 mi southwest of Santa Fe, 130 mi south of Taos, and 180 mi southeast of Farmington. Some travelers to Chama, Raton, and Taos prefer to fly into Denver (four to five hours' drive), which has far more direct flights to the rest of the country than Albuquerque—it's a scenic drive, too.

The gateway to southern New Mexico is El Paso International Airport (ELP), 50 mi southeast of Las Cruces, 160 mi southeast of Silver City, 135 mi southwest of Ruidoso, and 160 mi southwest of Carlsbad. The flight between El Paso and Albuquerque takes 50 minutes. The state's easternmost side can also be accessed via major airports in Texas, including Lubbock (170 mi east of Roswell) and Amarillo (105 mi northeast of Clovis).

▌TIP→ Long layovers don't have to be only about sitting around or shopping. These days they can be about burning off vacation calories. Check out ⊕ *www.airportgyms. com* for lists of health clubs that are in or near many U.S. airports.

Airport Information **Albuquerque International Sunport** (☎ *505/244-7700* ⊕ *www.*

cabq.gov/airport). **Denver International Airport** (☎ 303/342-2000 or 800/247-2336 ⊕ www.flydenver.com). **El Paso International Airport** (☎ 915/780-4749 ⊕ www.elpasointernationalairport.com).

MUNICIPAL AIRPORTS

Cavern City Air Terminal (CNM), Carlsbad (☎ 575/887-3060). **Clovis Municipal Airport (CVN), Carlsbad** (☎ 575/389-1056). **Four Corners Regional Airport (FMN), Farmington** (☎ 505/599-1395). **Grant County Airport (SVC), Silver City area** (☎ 575/388-4554). **Roswell Municipal Airport (ROW)** (☎ 575/624-6700). **Santa Fe Municipal Airport (SAF)** (☎ 505/955-2900). **Sierra Blanca Regional Airport (SRR), Ruidoso area** (☎ 575/336-8111).

FLIGHTS

Most major domestic airlines provide service to the state's main airport in Albuquerque; just over the border in Texas (near Las Cruces and Carlsbad), El Paso International Airport is served by American, Southwest, Delta, Continental, Frontier, New Mexico Airlines, Northwest, United, and US Airways. The state is also served by a few regional carriers. Great Lakes Airlines flies from Denver to Farmington and from Albuquerque to Silver City and Clovis (and then from Clovis on to Amarillo, Texas). Frontier Airlines flies daily from Denver to El Paso and Albuquerque. Skywest Airlines, a subsidiary of Delta, flies between Albuquerque and Salt Lake City. Santa Fe's municipal airport has daily service to and from Dallas and Los Angeles on American Eagle.

Ask the local tourist board about hotel and local transportation packages that include tickets to major museum exhibits or other special events.

GROUND TRANSPORTATION

From the terminal at Albuquerque Airport, it's 5 to 20 minutes by car to get anywhere in town. Taxis, available at clearly marked stands, charge about $10 to $25 for most trips from the airport to around Albuquerque. Sun Tran Buses stop at the sunburst signs every 30 minutes; the fare

is $1. Some hotels provide shuttle service to and from the airport. Airport Shuttle and Sunport Shuttle both cost less than $10 to most Downtown locations.

Shuttle buses between the Albuquerque International Sunport and Santa Fe take about 1 hour and 20 minutes and cost about $20 to $25 each way. Shuttle service runs from Albuquerque to Taos and nearby ski areas; the ride takes 2¾ to 3 hours and costs $40 to $50. In southern New Mexico there are daily trips between El Paso International Airport and Las Cruces (1 hour), Deming (2½ hours), and Silver City (3½ hours); the trip costs $43 to $75 each way.

There's also Greyhound bus service between Albuquerque International Sunport and many New Mexico towns and cities; times are much more limited but fares are considerably less than those charged by the shuttle services listed here.

TRANSFERS BETWEEN AIRPORTS

Around Albuquerque Airport Shuttle (☎ 505/765-1234). **ABQ Ride** (☎ 505/843-9200 ⊕ www.cabq.gov/transit). **Sunport Shuttle** (☎ 505/883-4966 or 866/505-4966 ⊕ www.sunportshuttle.com)

Between Albuquerque and Santa Fe Faust's Transportation (☎ 575/758-3410 or 888/830-3410 ⊕ www.newmexiconet.com/trans/faust/faust.html). **Sandia Shuttle Express** (☎ 505/474-5696 or 888/775-5696 ⊕ www.sandiashuttle.com).

Between Albuquerque and Taos Faust's Transportation (☎ 575/758-3410 or 888/830-3410 ⊕ www.newmexiconet.com/trans/faust/faust.html).

Between El Paso and Southern New Mexico Destinations Las Cruces Shuttle Service (☎ 575/525-1784 or 800/288-1784 ⊕ www.lascrucesshuttle.com).

▌BUS TRAVEL

Bus service on Texas, New Mexico and Oklahoma Coaches, affiliated with Greyhound Lines, is available to Alamogordo,

Albuquerque, Carlsbad, Clovis, El Paso (TX), Farmington, Gallup, Grants, Las Cruces, Las Vegas, Raton, Roswell, and several other towns and cities. Las Cruces Shuttle Service can get you from Silver City to Deming, Las Cruces, and El Paso.

Greyhound offers the **North America Discovery Pass,** which allows unlimited travel in the United States (and certain parts of Canada and Mexico) within any 7-, 15-, 30-, or 60-day period ($239 to $539, depending on length of the pass). You can also buy similar passes covering different areas (America and Canada, the West Coast of North America, the East Coast of North America, Canada exclusively), and international travelers can purchase international versions of these same passes, which offer a greater variety of travel periods and cost considerably less. Greyhound also has senior-citizen, military, children's, and student discounts, which apply to individual fares and to the Discovery Pass.

BUS INFORMATION

Greyhound/Texas, New Mexico and Oklahoma Coaches (📞 800/231–2222 ⊕ www. greyhound.com). Las Cruces Shuttle Service (📞 575/525–1784 or 800/288–1784 ⊕ www. lascrucesshuttle.com).

▌CAR TRAVEL

A car is a basic necessity in New Mexico, as even the few cities are challenging to get around strictly using public transportation. Distances are considerable, but you can make excellent time on long stretches of interstate and other four-lane highways with speed limits of up to 75 mph. If you wander off major thoroughfares, slow down. Speed limits here generally are only 55 mph, and for good reason. Many such roadways have no shoulders; on many twisting and turning mountain roads speed limits dip to 25 mph. For the most part, the scenery you'll take in while driving makes the drive a form of sightseeing in itself.

Interstate 40 runs east–west across the middle of the state. Interstate 10 cuts across the southern part of the state from the Texas border at El Paso to the Arizona line, through Las Cruces, Deming, and Lordsburg.

Interstate 25 runs north from the state line at El Paso through Albuquerque and Santa Fe, then angles northeast to the Colorado line through Raton.

U.S. highways connect all major cities and towns in the state with a good network of paved roads—many of the state's U.S. highways, including large stretches of U.S. 285 and U.S. 550, have four lanes and high speed limits. You can make nearly as good time on these roads as you can on interstates. State roads are mostly paved two-lane thoroughfares, but some are well-graded gravel. Roads on Native American lands are designated by wooden, arrow-shaped signs and you'd best adhere to the speed limit; some roads on reservation or forestland aren't paved. Even in cities, you're likely to find a few surface streets are unpaved and often bumpy and narrow—Santa Fe, for instance, has a higher percentage of dirt roads than any other state capital in the nation.

Morning and evening rush-hour traffic is light in most of New Mexico, although it can get a bit heavy in Albuquerque. Keep in mind also that from most cities in New Mexico, there are only one or two main routes to Albuquerque, so if you encounter an accident or some other delay on a major thoroughfare into Albuquerque (or even Santa Fe), you can expect significant delays. It's a big reason to leave early and give yourself extra time when attempting to drive to Albuquerque to catch a plane.

Parking is plentiful and either free or inexpensive in most New Mexico towns, even Albuquerque and Santa Fe. During busy times, however, such as summer weekends, parking in Santa Fe, Taos, Ruidoso, and parts of Albuquerque can be tougher to find.

Here are some common distances and approximate travel times between Albuquerque and several popular destinations, assuming no lengthy stops and averaging the 65 to 75 mph speed limits: Santa Fe is 65 mi and about an hour; Taos is 135 mi and about 2½ hours; Farmington is 185 mi and 3 hours; Gallup is 140 mi and 2 hours; Amarillo is 290 mi and 4 hours; Denver is 450 mi and 6 to 7 hours; Oklahoma City is 550 mi and 8 to 9 hours; Moab is 290 mi and 6 to 7 hours; Flagstaff is 320 mi and 4½ hours; Phoenix is 465 mi and 6½ to 7½ hours; Silver City is 230 mi and 3½ to 4 hours; Las Cruces is 225 mi and 3½ hours; Ruidoso is 190 mi and 3 hours; Carlsbad is 280 mi and 4½ to 5 hours; El Paso is 270 mi and 4 hours; Dallas is 650 mi and 10 to 11 hours; and San Antonio is 730 mi and 11 to 12 hours.

GASOLINE

There's a lot of high, dry, lonesome country in New Mexico—it's possible to go 50 or 60 mi in some of the less-populated areas between gas stations. ■TIP➔ For a safe trip keep your gas tank full. Self-service gas stations are the norm in New Mexico, though in some of the less-populated regions you can find stations with full service. The cost of unleaded gas at self-service stations in New Mexico is close to the U.S. average, but it's usually 15¢ to 30¢ more per gallon in Santa Fe, Taos, and certain spots off the beaten path.

RENTAL CARS

All the major car-rental agencies are represented at Albuquerque's and El Paso's airports, and you can also find a limited number of car-rental agencies in other communities throughout the state.

Rates at Albuquerque's airport begin at around $25 a day and $150 a week for an economy car with air-conditioning, automatic transmission, and unlimited mileage; although you should expect to pay more during busier times. The same car in El Paso typically goes for about the same or even a bit less, again depending on the time of year.

If you want to explore the backcountry, consider renting an SUV, which will cost you about $40 to $60 per day and $200 to $400 per week, depending on the size of the SUV and the time of year. Dollar in Albuquerque has a fleet of smaller SUVs, still good on dirt roads and with much better mileage than larger ones, and they often run extremely reasonable deals, as low as $160 a week. You can save money by renting at a nonairport location, as you then are able to avoid the hefty (roughly) 10% in extra taxes charged at airports. Check the different agencies' Web sites as there are often excellent "Web-only" car rental offers.

ROAD CONDITIONS

Arroyos (dry washes or gullies) are bridged on major roads, but lesser roads often dip down through them. These can be a hazard during the rainy season, late June to early September. Even if it looks shallow, **don't try to cross an arroyo filled with water**—it may have an axle-breaking hole in the middle. Wait a little while, and it will drain off almost as quickly as it filled. If you stall in a flooded arroyo, get out of the car and onto high ground if possible. In the backcountry, never drive (or walk) in a dry arroyo bed if the sky is dark anywhere upstream. A sudden thunderstorm 15 mi away could send a raging flash flood down a wash in a matter of minutes.

Unless they are well graded and graveled, **avoid unpaved roads in New Mexico when they are wet.** The soil contains a lot of caliche, or clay, which gets slick when mixed with water. During winter storms roads may be shut down entirely; call the State Highway Department for road conditions.

At certain times in fall, winter and spring, New Mexico winds can be vicious for large vehicles like RVs. Driving conditions can be particularly treacherous in passages through foothills or mountains where wind gusts and ice are concentrated.

New Mexico has a high incidence of drunk driving and uninsured motorists. Factor in the state's high speed limits, many winding and steep roads, and eye-popping scenery, and you can see how important it is to drive as alertly and defensively as possible. On the plus side, major traffic jams are a rarity even in cities—and recent improvements to the state's busiest intersection, the Interstate 40/Interstate 25 interchange in Albuquerque, has helped to reduce rush-hour backups there. Additionally, a major highway widening and improvement along U.S. 285/84, north of Santa Fe, has also greatly smoothed the flow and speed of traffic up toward Taos.

State Highway Department (☎ 800/432–4269 ⊕ www.nmshtd.state.nm.us).

ROADSIDE EMERGENCIES

In the event of a roadside emergency, call 911. Depending on the location, either the New Mexico State Police or the county sheriff's department will respond. Call the city or village police department if you encounter trouble within the limits of a municipality. Native American reservations have tribal police headquarters, and rangers assist travelers within U.S. Forest Service boundaries.

▌ TRAIN TRAVEL

Amtrak's Sunset Limited, from Orlando, Florida, to Los Angeles, stops in El Paso, Texas; Deming; and Lordsburg on Tuesday, Thursday, and Saturday eastbound, and Monday, Thursday, and Saturday westbound.

Amtrak's Southwest Chief, from Chicago to Los Angeles via Kansas City, stops in Raton, Las Vegas, Lamy (near Santa Fe), Albuquerque, and Gallup daily.

The state's commuter train line, the New Mexico Rail Runner Express runs from Santa Fe south through Bernalillo and into the city of Albuquerque, continuing south through Los Lunas to the suburb of Belén, covering a distance of about 100 mi. The Rail Runner offers a very inexpensive alternative to getting to and from the Albuquerque airport to Santa Fe.

Amtrak offers a **North America rail pass** that gives you unlimited travel within the United States and Canada within any 30-day period ($389 to $749), and several kinds of **USA Rail passes** (for non-U.S. residents only) offering unlimited travel for 15 to 45 days. Amtrak also has senior-citizen, children's, disability, and student discounts, as well as occasional deals that allow a second or third accompanying passenger to travel for half price or even free. The **Amtrak Vacations** program customizes entire vacations, including hotels, car rentals, and tours.

Sample one-way fares on the Sunset Limited are $100 to $200 from Los Angeles to El Paso, and $85 to $165 from San Antonio, Texas, to Deming.

Sample one-way fares on the Southwest Chief are $120 from Chicago to Lamy; $50 to $70 Denver to Las Vegas; and $65 Albuquerque to Los Angeles.

The New Mexico Rail Runner Express runs daily. Tickets cost $1 to $4 one-way, depending on the distance traveled; passes are available.

Contact Amtrak (☎ 800/872–7245 ⊕ www.amtrak.com). **New Mexico Rail Runner Express** (☎ 866/795–7245 ⊕ www.nmrailrunner.com).

ESSENTIALS

▮ ACCOMMODATIONS

With the exceptions of Santa Fe and Taos, two rather upscale tourist-driven destinations with some of the higher lodging rates in the Southwest, New Mexico has fairly low hotel prices. Albuquerque is loaded with chain hotels, and four or five new ones seem to open each year, further saturating the market and driving down prices. During busy times or certain festivals (the Balloon Fiesta in Albuquerque, some of the art markets and events in Taos and Santa Fe), it can be extremely difficult to find a hotel room, and prices can be steep. Check to make sure there's no major event planned for the time you're headed to New Mexico, and book well ahead if so. You'll find bigger big selection and some very good deals by checking the usual major travel sites, such as ⊕ *www.expedia.com.* You'll be charged a hotel tax, which varies among towns and counties, throughout New Mexico.

Most hotels and other lodgings require you to give your credit-card details before they will confirm your reservation. If you don't feel comfortable e-mailing this information, ask if you can fax it (some places even prefer faxes). However you book, get confirmation in writing and have a copy of it handy when you check in.

If you book through an online travel agent, discounter, or wholesaler, you might even want to confirm your reservation with the hotel before leaving home— just to be sure everything was processed correctly.

Be sure you understand the hotel's cancellation policy. Some places allow you to cancel without any kind of penalty— even if you prepaid to secure a discounted rate—if you cancel at least 24 hours in advance. Others require you to cancel a week in advance or penalize you the cost of one night. Small inns and bed-and-breakfasts are most likely to require

you to cancel far in advance. Most hotels allow children under a certain age to stay in their parents' room at no extra charge, but others charge for them as extra adults; find out the cutoff age for discounts.

▮**TIP**→ Assume that hotels operate on the European Plan (**EP**, no meals) unless we specify that they use the Breakfast Plan (**BP**, with full breakfast), Continental Plan (**CP**, Continental breakfast), Full American Plan (**FAP**, all meals), Modified American Plan (**MAP**, breakfast and dinner) or are **all-inclusive** (**AI**, all meals and most activities).

APARTMENT AND HOUSE RENTALS

Some parts of New Mexico are popular for short- and long-term vacation rentals, such as Santa Fe, Taos, and Ruidoso. *See the book's individual regional chapters for rental agency listings in these locations.*

BED AND BREAKFASTS

Bed-and-breakfasts in New Mexico run the gamut from rooms in locals' homes to grandly restored adobe or Victorian homes. Rates in Santa Fe and Taos can be high, but there are several properties that offer excellent value for very comparable prices; they're a little lower in Albuquerque and rival those of chain motels in the outlying areas. Good deals can be found in southern New Mexico as well.

See the book's individual chapters for names of local reservation agencies.

Reservation Services Bed & Breakfast.com (☎ 512/322–2710 or 800/462–2632 ⊕ www. bedandbreakfast.com) also sends out an online newsletter. **Bed & Breakfast Inns Online** (☎ 800/215–7365 ⊕ www.bbonline.com). **BnB Finder.com** (☎ 888/469–6663 ⊕ www. bnbfinder.com). **New Mexico Bed and Breakfast Association** (☎ 800/661–6649 ⊕ www. nmbba.org).

HOME EXCHANGES

With a direct home exchange you stay in someone else's home while they stay in yours. Some outfits also deal with vacation homes, so you're not actually staying in someone's full-time residence, just their vacant weekend place.

Exchange Clubs Home Exchange.com (☎ 800/877–8723 ⊕ www.homeexchange. com); $9.95 per month for a membership. **HomeLink International** (☎ 800/638–3841 ⊕ www.homelink.org); $119 yearly for Web access and listing in the catalog. **Intervac U.S** (☎ 800/756–4663 ⊕ www.intervac-homeexchange.com); $99.99 for membership (includes Web access and a catalog).

HOSTELS

Hostels offer bare-bones lodging at low, low prices—often in shared dorm rooms with shared baths—to people of all ages, though the primary market is young travelers, especially students. Most hostels serve breakfast; dinner and/or shared cooking facilities may also be available. In some hostels you aren't allowed to be in your room during the day, and there may be a curfew at night. Nevertheless, hostels provide a sense of community, with public rooms where travelers often gather to share stories. Many hostels are affiliated with Hostelling International (HI), an umbrella group of hostel associations with some 4,500 member properties in more than 70 countries. Other hostels are completely independent and may be nothing more than a really cheap hotel.

Membership in any HI association, open to travelers of all ages, allows you to stay in HI-affiliated hostels at member rates. One-year membership is about $28 for adults; hostels charge about $10 to $30 per night. Members have priority if the hostel is full; they're also eligible for discounts around the world, even on rail and bus travel in some countries.

Several New Mexico communities have hostels, including Albuquerque (there are two), Cloudcroft, Cuba, Oscuro (south of Carrizozo), Santa Fe, Taos, Truth or Consequences, and Tucumcari.

Information Hostelling International—USA (☎ 301/495–1240 ⊕ www.hiusa.org).

▌EATING OUT

New Mexico is justly famous for its distinctive cuisine, which utilizes ingredients and recipes common to Mexico, the Rockies, the Southwest, and the West's Native American communities. Most longtime residents like their chile sauces and salsas with some fire—in the Santa Fe, Albuquerque, and Las Cruces areas, chile is sometimes celebrated for its ability to set off smoke alarms. Most restaurants offer a choice of red or green chile with one type typically being milder than the other. If you want both kinds with your meal, when your server asks you if you'd like red or green, reply "Christmas." If you're not used to spicy foods, you may find even the average chile served with chips to be quite a lot hotter than back home—so proceed with caution (you can always request it be served on the side). Excellent barbecue and steaks also can be found throughout New Mexico, with other specialties being local game (especially elk and bison) and trout. The restaurants we list are the cream of the crop in each price category.

MEALS AND MEALTIMES

Statewide, many kitchens stop serving around 8 pm, so **don't arrive too late** if you're looking forward to a leisurely dinner.

Unless otherwise noted, the restaurants listed in this guide are open daily for lunch and dinner.

PAYING

Credit cards are widely accepted at restaurants in major towns and cities and even most smaller communities, but in the latter places, you may occasionally encounter smaller, independent restaurants that are cash only.

For guidelines on tipping, see Tipping below.

RESERVATIONS AND DRESS

Regardless of where you are, it's a good idea to make a reservation if you can. In some places (the top restaurants in Santa Fe, for example), it's expected. We only mention them specifically when reservations are essential (there's no other way you'll ever get a table) or when they are not accepted. For popular restaurants in Santa Fe, book as far ahead as you can, and reconfirm as soon as you arrive. (Large parties should always call ahead to check the reservations policy.) We mention dress only when men are required to wear a jacket or a jacket and tie—which is a rarity, indeed.

Online reservation services make it easy to book a table before you even leave home. OpenTable covers most states, including 20 major cities, and has limited listings in Canada, Mexico, the United Kingdom, and elsewhere. For American Express Card members, DinnerBroker offers 15% to 30% discounts on restaurants throughout the United States as well.

Contacts **OpenTable** (⊕ www.opentable.com). **DinnerBroker** (⊕ www.dinnerbroker.com).

WINES, BEER AND SPIRITS

Like many other states, New Mexico has some fine microbreweries; Sierra Blanca Brewing Co. and Santa Fe Brewing Co. are two of the best known. New Mexico also has a growing number of wineries, some of them producing first-rate vintages. Franciscan monks first planted their vines here before moving more successfully to northern California, and the state's winemaking industry has really taken off since the late '90s. The New Mexico Wine Growers Association (⊕ www.nmwine.com) provides extensive information on the many fine wineries around the state as well as details on several prominent wine festivals.

▌ EMERGENCIES

In an emergency dial 911.

ALBUQUERQUE

Hospitals **Presbyterian Hospital** (✉ 1100 Central Ave. SE, Downtown ☎ 505/841–1234). **University Hospital** (✉ 2211 Lomas Blvd. NE, University of New Mexico ☎ 505/272–2111).

SANTA FE

Christus St. Vincent Hospital (✉ 455 St. Michael's Dr. ☎ 505/983–3361).

TAOS

Holy Cross Hospital (✉ 1397 Weimer Rd. ☎ 505/758–8883 ⊕ www.taoshospital.org).

NORTHWEST NEW MEXICO

Rehoboth McKinley Christian Health Care Services (✉ 1901 Red Rock Dr., Gallup ☎ 505/863–7000). **San Juan Regional Health Center** (✉ 801 W. Maple St., Farmington ☎ 505/609–2000).

NORTHEAST NEW MEXICO

Alta Vista Regional Hospital (✉ 104 Legion., Las Vegas ☎ 505/426–3500).

SOUTHEAST NEW MEXICO

Carlsbad Medical Center (✉ 2430 W. Pierce, Carlsbad ☎ 575/887–4100). **Dr. Dan Trigg Memorial Hospital** (✉ 301 E. Miel de Luna, Tucumcari ☎ 575/461–7000). **Eastern New Mexico Medical Center** (✉ 405 W. Country Club Rd., Roswell ☎ 575/622–8170). **Guadalupe County Hospital** (✉ 535 Lake Dr., Santa Rosa ☎ 575/472–3417).

SOUTHWESTERN NEW MEXICO

Hospitals **Gila Regional Medical Center** (✉ 1313 E. 32nd St., Silver City ☎ 575/538–4000). **Memorial Medical Center** (✉ 2450 S. Telshor Blvd., Las Cruces ☎ 575/522–8641). **Socorro General Hospital** (✉ 1202 NM 60 W, Socorro ☎ 575/835–1140).

▌ HEALTH

High altitude can cause headaches and dizziness, so at a minimum drink at least half your body weight in ounces in water (150-pound person = 75 ounces of water) per day, and eat plenty of juicy fruit. When planning even a short day trip, especially if there's hiking or exercise involved, always pack a bottle or two of water—it's very easy to become dehydrated in New Mexico. Check with your doctor about medication to alleviate symptoms.

HOURS OF OPERATION

Although hours differ little in New Mexico from other parts of the United States, some businesses do keep shorter hours here than in more densely populated parts of the country. In particular, outside of the larger towns in New Mexico, it can be hard to find shops open past 6 pm and restaurants open past 8 or 9 in the evening. Within the state, businesses tend to keep later hours in Albuquerque, Las Cruces, and Santa Fe than in rural areas.

Most major museums and attractions are open daily or six days a week (with Monday or Tuesday being the most likely day of closing). Hours are often shorter on Saturday and especially Sunday, and a handful of museums in larger cities stay open late one night a week, usually Friday. New Mexico's less populated areas also have quite a few smaller museums—historical societies, small art galleries, highly specialized collections—that open only a few days a week, and sometimes only by appointment during slow times. It's always a good idea to call ahead if you're planning to go out of your way to visit a smaller museum.

Banks are usually open weekdays from 9 to 4:30 or a bit later and some Saturday mornings, the post office from 8 to 5 or 6 weekdays and often on Saturday mornings. Shops in urban and touristy areas, particularly in indoor and strip malls, typically open at 9 or 10 daily and stay open until anywhere from 6 pm to 9 pm on weekdays and Saturday, and until 5 or 6 on Sunday. Hours vary greatly, so call ahead when in doubt.

On major highways and in densely populated areas you can usually find at least one or two supermarkets, drugstores, and gas stations open 24 hours, and in Albuquerque, you can find a smattering of all-night fast-food restaurants, diners, and coffeehouses. Bars and discos stay open until 1 or 2 am.

MONEY

In New Mexico, Santa Fe is by far the priciest city: meals, gasoline, and motel rates are all significantly higher in the state's capital. Overall travel costs in Santa Fe, including dining and lodging, typically run 30% to 50% higher than in any other New Mexico city. Taos, too, can be a little expensive because it's such a popular tourist destination. Lodging and dining throughout much of the rest of the state are a genuine bargain. Depending on the establishment, $10 can buy you a savory dinner in Farmington, Old Mesilla, or Silver City. As the state's largest metropolitan area, Albuquerque has a full range of price choices.

CREDIT CARDS

Throughout this guide, the following abbreviations are used: **AE**, American Express; **D**, Discover; **DC**, Diners Club; **MC**, MasterCard; and **V**, Visa.

It's a good idea to inform your credit-card company before you travel, especially if you're going abroad and don't travel internationally very often. Otherwise, the credit-card company might put a hold on your card owing to unusual activity—not a good thing halfway through your trip. Record all your credit-card numbers—as well as the phone numbers to call if your cards are lost or stolen—in a safe place, so you're prepared should something go wrong. Both MasterCard and Visa have general numbers you can call (collect if you're abroad) if your card is lost, but you're better off calling the number of your issuing bank, since MasterCard and Visa usually just transfer you to your bank; your bank's number is usually printed on your card.

Reporting Lost Cards American Express
(☎ *800/992–3404 in U.S.; 336/393–1111 collect from abroad* ⊕ *www.americanexpress.*

com). **Diners Club** (☎ 800/234-6377 in U.S.; 303/799-1504 collect from abroad ⊕ www.dinersclub.com). **Discover** (☎ 800/347-2683 in U.S.; 801/902-3100 collect from abroad ⊕ www.discovercard.com). **MasterCard** (☎ 800/622-7747 in U.S.; 636/722-7111 collect from abroad ⊕ www.mastercard.com). **Visa** (☎ 800/847-2911 in U.S.; 410/581-9994 collect from abroad ⊕ www.visa.com).

▌ PACKING

Typical of the Southwest, temperatures can vary considerably from sunup to sundown. Generally, you should **pack for warm days and chilly nights** from spring through fall, but this is a huge state with a tremendous range of elevations, so the most important thing is to check local weather conditions before you leave home and pack accordingly. In April for instance, you may need to pack for nighttime lows in the 20s and daytime highs in the 60s in Taos, but daytime highs in the 80s and nighttime lows in the 50s in Las Cruces. Any time of year pack at least a few warm outfits and a jacket; in winter pack very warm clothes—coats, parkas, and whatever else your body's thermostat and your ultimate destination dictate. Remember that Taos and Santa Fe are both at about 7,000 feet elevation and winters here may be sunny, but they are cold. Sweaters and jackets are also needed in summer at higher elevations, because though days are warm, nights can dip well below 50°F. And **bring comfortable shoes**; you're likely to be doing a lot of walking.

New Mexico is one of the most informal and laid-back areas of the country, which for many is part of its appeal. Probably no more than three or four restaurants in the entire state enforce a dress code, even for dinner, though men are likely to feel more comfortable wearing a jacket in the major hotel dining rooms. If you need a rule, stick to business casual and you'll feel comfortable wherever you go.

The Western look has, of course, never lost its hold on the West, though Western-style clothes now get mixed with styles from all over the globe. You can wear your boots and big belt buckles anywhere in the state, even Albuquerque, but if you come strolling through the lobby of the Eldorado Hotel looking like Hopalong Cassidy, you'll get some funny looks.

Bring skin moisturizer; even people who rarely need this elsewhere in the country can suffer from dry and itchy skin in New Mexico. Sunscreen is a necessity. And **bring sunglasses** to protect your eyes from the glare of lakes or ski slopes, not to mention the brightness present everywhere.

▌ RESOURCES

ONLINE TRAVEL TOOLS
Check out the New Mexico Home page (⊕ www.state.nm.us) for information on state government, and for links to state agencies on doing business, working, learning, living, and visiting in the Land of Enchantment. A terrific general resource for just about every kind of recreational activity is ⊕ www.gorp.com; just click on the New Mexico link under "Destinations," and you'll be flooded with links to myriad topics, from wildlife refuges to ski trips to backpacking advice. Also excellent for information on the state's recreation pursuits is the New Mexico Outdoor Sports Guide (⊕ www.nmosg.com). Check the site of the New Mexico Film Office (⊕ www.nmfilm.com) for a list of movies shot in New Mexico as well as links to downloadable clips of upcoming made-in-New Mexico movies. A wide range of reviews and links to dining, culture, and services in Albuquerque and Santa Fe is available at ⊕ www.citysearch.com and ⊕ www.yelp.com; ⊕ www.999dine.com is a site that sells steeply discounted meal certificates to dozens of top restaurants in Albuquerque, Santa Fe, and Taos. Visit ⊕ www.farmersmarketsnm.org for information on the dozens of great farmers' markets around the state, and see ⊕ www.

nmwine.com for tours and details related to the region's burgeoning wine-making industry.

ALL ABOUT NEW MEXICO

Safety Transportation Security Administration (*TSA* ⊕ *www.tsa.gov*).

Other Resources CIA World Factbook (⊕ *www.cia.gov/library/publications/the-world-factbook*) has profiles of every country in the world. It's a good source if you need some quick facts and figures.

Timeanddate.com (⊕ *www.timeanddate.com/worldclock*) can help you figure out the correct time anywhere.

Weather.com (⊕ *www.weather.com*) is the Web site for the Weather Channel.

VISITOR INFORMATION

The New Mexico Department of Tourism can provide general information on the state, but you'll find more specific and useful information by consulting the local chambers of commerce, tourism offices, and convention and visitors bureaus in individual communities throughout the state *(listed in each town in individual chapters)*.

Contacts New Mexico Department of Tourism (☎ 505/827–7400 ⊕ *www.newmexico.org*). **Indian Pueblo Cultural Center** (☎ 505/843–3270 or 866/855–7902 ⊕ *www.indianpueblo.org*). **USDA Forest Service, Southwestern Region** (☎ 505/842–3292; 877/864–6985 for fire restrictions and closures ⊕ *www.fs.fed.us/r3*).

PASSPORTS AND VISAS
PASSPORTS

We're always surprised at how few Americans have passports—only 25% at this writing. This number is expected to grow in coming years, when it becomes impossible to reenter the United States from trips to neighboring Canada or Mexico without one. Remember this: a passport verifies both your identity and nationality—a great reason to have one.

U.S. passports are valid for 10 years. You must apply in person if you're getting a passport for the first time; if your previous passport was lost, stolen, or damaged; or if your previous passport has expired and was issued more than 15 years ago or when you were under 16. All children under 16 must appear in person to apply for or renew a passport. Both parents must accompany any child under 14 (or send a notarized statement with their permission) and provide proof of their relationship to the child.

There are 13 regional passport offices, as well as 7,000 passport acceptance facilities in post offices, public libraries, and other governmental offices. If you're renewing a passport, you can do so by mail. Forms are available at passport acceptance facilities and online.

The cost to apply for a new passport is $140 for adults, $120 for children under 16; renewals are $120 to $140. Allow six weeks for processing, both for first-time passports and renewals. For an expediting fee of $60 you can reduce this time to about two weeks. If your trip is less than two weeks away, you can get a passport even more rapidly by going to a passport office with the necessary documentation. Private expediters can get things done in as little as 48 hours, but charge hefty fees for their services.

■ TIP➔ **Before your trip, make two copies of your passport's data page (one for someone at home and another for you to carry separately). Or scan the page and e-mail it to someone at home and/or yourself.**

U.S. Passport InformationU.S. Department of State (☎ 877/487–2778 ⊕ *http://travel.state.gov/passport*).

U.S. Passport & Visa Expediters A. Briggs Passport & Visa Expediters (☎ 800/806–0581 or 202/338–0111 ⊕ *www.abriggs.com*). **American Passport Express** (☎ 800/455–5166 or ⊕ *www.americanpassport.com*). **Passport Express** (☎ 800/362–8196 ⊕ *www.passportexpress.com*). **Travel Document Systems** (☎ 800/874–5100 or 202/638–3800 ⊕ *www.traveldocs.com*). **Travel the World**

Visas (☎ 866/886–8472 or 202/223–8822 ⊕ www.world-visa.com).

▍TAXES

The standard state gross receipts tax rate is 5%, but municipalities and counties enact additional charges at varying rates. Sales tax in Santa Fe is just under 8%. If you're on a budget and plan on renting a car and/or staying in hotels, be sure to ask for the exact amount of your lodging and rental-car taxes, as they can be quite steep and can make a big dent in a tight budget.

▍TIME

New Mexico and a small portion of west Texas (including El Paso) observe Mountain Standard Time, switching over with most of the rest of the country to daylight saving time in the spring through fall. In New Mexico, you'll be two hours behind New York and one hour ahead of Arizona (except during daylight saving time, which Arizona does not observe) and California.

▍TIPPING

The customary tipping rate for taxi drivers is 15% to 20%, with a minimum of $2; bellhops are usually given $2 per bag in luxury hotels, $1 per bag elsewhere. Hotel maids should be tipped $2 per day of your stay. A doorman who hails or helps you into a cab can be tipped $1 to $2. You should also tip your hotel concierge for services rendered; the size of the tip depends on the difficulty of your request, as well as the quality of the concierge's work. For an ordinary dinner reservation or tour arrangements, $3 to $5 should do; if the concierge scores seats at a popular restaurant or show or performs unusual services (getting your laptop repaired, finding a good pet-sitter, etc.), $10 or more is appropriate.

Waiters should be tipped 15% to 20%, though at higher-end restaurants, a solid 20% is more the norm. Many restaurants add a gratuity to the bill for parties of six or more. Ask what the percentage is if the menu or bill doesn't state it. Tip $1 per drink you order at the bar, though if at an upscale establishment, those $15 martinis might warrant a $2 tip.

INDEX

PHOTO CREDITS

ABOUT OUR WRITERS

Splitting her time between New Mexico and New York these days, **Lynne Arany** enjoys the best of two places remarkable for their distinct charms and extreme diversity. Writer and updater for the Northwestern and Southwestern chapters of this Fodor's edition, author of the *Little Museums* guide to all 50 states, contributor to the *New York Times*, and a freelance travel writer and editor, Lynne has covered areas from Glasgow, Budapest, and London to the southwestern United States and Mexico. Well-practiced in the art of uncovering the less-known gems wherever she is, she finds the serendipity of the search most appealing.

Former Fodor's staff editor **Andrew Collins** lives in Portland Oregon, but resided in New Mexico for many years and still visits often (usually stuffing his carry-on bag with fresh green chiles). A long-time contributor to this guide, he's also the author of Fodor's *Gay Guide to the USA* and has written or contributed to dozens of other guidebooks. He's the expert "guide" on gay travel for About.com, and he has contributed to a variety of publications (including *Travel + Leisure, New Mexico Journey, Sunset,* FoxNews.com, Orbitz. com, and *New Mexico Magazine*).

Georgia de Katona, like many in Northern New Mexico, wears several different hats. She's been a freelance travel writer for the past nine years, after an early career as a managing editor. Travel in the United States and Latin America are her passions, though Africa is on her short list. Georgia practiced Kundalini yoga for thirteen years, and is a certified teacher who's found a niche teaching the practice to cowgirls. More recently, she's found enormous satisfaction as a medical assistant for an OB/GYN practice and has decided to pursue studies to be a Physicians Assistant. Her travel advice: The world is full of friends you've not met and foods you've not tasted. Find them!